The Essential Mary Midgley

'She has, perhaps, the sharpest perception of any living thinker of the dangerous extremism that lurks behind so much contemporary scientistic discourse.'
— **Bryan Appleyard**, *The Sunday Times*

'One of the sharpest critical pens in the West.'
— *Times Literary Supplement*

'The value of Mary's thinking is that she questions the assumptions and investigates what she calls 'philosophical plumbing' and the role of different ideas in helping map our world…Having the whole of Mary's thinking summarised in one volume is enormously valuable, enabling the reader to access the essence of her approach.'
— *The Science and Medical Network Review*

Feared and admired in equal measure, Mary Midgley has carefully yet profoundly challenged many of the scientific and moral orthodoxies of the twentieth century.

The Essential Mary Midgley is a must-have anthology of the very best of Midgley's philosophy, whose work is described by the *Financial Times* as 'common sense philosophy of the highest order.' Incorporating carefully selected excerpts from Mary Midgley's bestselling books, including *Wickedness*, *Beast and Man*, *Science and Poetry* and *The Myths We Live By*, this second edition includes some of her best work from the last twenty or so years, including *The Solitary Self*, *Are you an Illusion?* and *What Is Philosophy For?*

The Essential Mary Midgley presents a superb introduction to her work, covering the topics that she returned to frequently, such as the roots of human nature, reason and imagination, the myths of science, the importance of holism in thinking about science and the environment and the nature of the self.

Expertly edited and introduced by David Midgley, this second edition includes a new Foreword by Rachael Wiseman.

Mary Midgley (1919–2018) was one of the leading moral philosophers of her generation and has been described by *The Guardian* as 'the foremost scourge of scientific pretension in this country.' Many of her books are available in Routledge Classics, including *Beast and Man*, *Wickedness* and *The Myths We Live By*.

David Midgley is a social and environmental activist and a teacher of Buddhist philosophy and meditation. In 1996, he founded Jamyang Buddhist Centre Leeds and taught regularly at the Centre for 25 years.

The Essential
Mary Midgley

Second Edition

Edited by David Midgley,
with a new Foreword by Rachael Wiseman

Routledge
Taylor & Francis Group

LONDON AND NEW YORK

Cover image: Mary Midgley in 2010. Photograph: Sarah Lee/The Guardian

Second edition published 2026
by Routledge
4 Park Square, Milton Park, Abingdon, Oxon OX14 4RN

and by Routledge
605 Third Avenue, New York, NY 10158

Routledge is an imprint of the Taylor & Francis Group, an informa business

For Product Safety Concerns and Information please contact our EU representative
GPSR@taylorandfrancis.com. Taylor & Francis Verlag GmbH, Kaufingerstraße 24, 80331
München, Germany.

First edition published 2005 by Routledge.

British Library Cataloguing-in-Publication Data
A catalogue record for this book is available from the British Library

Library of Congress Cataloging-in-Publication Data
Names: Midgley, Mary, 1919–2018 author | Midgley, David, 1953– editor
Title: The essential Mary Midgley / edited by David Midgley;
with a new Foreword by Rachael Wiseman.
Description: Second edition. | Abingdon, Oxon; New York, NY: Routledge, 2026. |
Includes bibliographical references and index.
Identifiers: LCCN 2025034896 (print) | LCCN 2025034897 (ebook) |
ISBN 9781032961286 hardback | ISBN 9781032957821 paperback |
ISBN 9781003588160 ebook
Subjects: LCSH: Philosophy, British—20th century
Classification: LCC B1647.M471 M53 2025 (print) | LCC B1647.M471 (ebook)
LC record available at https://lccn.loc.gov/2025034896
LC ebook record available at https://lccn.loc.gov/2025034897

ISBN: 978-1-032-96128-6 (hbk)
ISBN: 978-1-032-95782-1 (pbk)
ISBN: 978-1-003-58816-0 (ebk)

DOI: 10.4324/9781003588160

Typeset in Joanna
by codeMantra

Contents

FOREWORD

'When we read the great philosophers,' Mary Midgley wrote, 'they speak to us, not as anonymous robots, but as whole people, each in their own distinctive voices. If we listen seriously to them at all, we hear a person speaking, not just a flow of ticker-tape information emitted by a knowledge-machine. ... Our response to these writings is as personal as it is to what our friends say ... That response can change our lives.'[1] Reading this collection of Mary Midgley's writing, one is struck by the aptness of this description – in this book, she lives and speaks with a voice that is as distinctive as that of any of the great philosophers who pass through its pages.

Midgley's voice is one that professional philosophers have been slow to value and attend to. Her writing is direct, full of humour and alive with metaphor and common sense. She makes doing philosophy look natural and fun. Her work lacks the outward performance of intellectual struggle and guardedness that we have come to expect from twentieth-century philosophical prose; however, it is about time philosophers recognized – as they are beginning to – the deep currents of thought that lie below the surface of Midgley's welcoming prose.

The second edition of *The Essential Mary Midgley* comes at an exciting time in Midgley scholarship. While the richness of Midgley's vision has long been recognized by scientists, environmentalists and many outside the academy (something reflected in the fact that the foreword to the first edition was written not by a philosopher but by James Lovelock), philosophers have only recently begun to give her writing proper attention. Work has been done to place her in dialogue with Philippa Foot, Elizabeth Anscombe and Iris Murdoch, and scholars have begun to explore how her moral philosophy differs from the main strands of neo-Aristotelianism with which it might naturally be compared. But there is so much more for us to do to excavate the complex metaphysics and epistemology that underpins Midgley's radically anti-Cartesian vision of the human soul. Her close travellers are Plotinus, Baruch Spinoza, David Hume, Charles Darwin, Sigmund Freud, Konrad Lorenz and Ludwig Wittgenstein; it will be enormously rewarding to think through how she brings into harmony the voices of a neo-Platonic mystic, a rationalist, an empiricist, an evolutionary scientist, a psychoanalyst, an ethologist and a philosophical anthropologist.

One key to her achievement lies in her guiding thought – a thought that is the focus of Part One of this volume: we are not just rather like animals; we are animals. For Midgley, this thought makes possible a distinctive form of investigation into the structures of human life. These structures are found 'outside' in patterns of the kind that a patient ethologist or anthropologist can identify through detailed observation. But they are also mirrored 'inside' in a web of motives that are often only obscurely understood by their subjects – as the Freudian insists. That overarching vision of the inner soul as mirroring outer reality has its source, of course, in Plotinus. To bring these patterns into view, Midgley argues, we will need to see the human animal in the context not just of human life, but of (something like) Spinozistic Nature – as one part of a whole that is itself alive.

Let me give an example of this method, and its fruits, that comes from the first extract in this collection. Midgley considers a case that might have come from any contemporary work on practical reason: *Paul is buying a house with an acre of land though he can scarcely afford it.* Midgley asks: 'What should we say he is doing?' (24). A contemporary philosopher of action might accommodate Paul's seemingly irrational action by attributing to him ignorance of the facts (he is perhaps unaware of the precarity of his finances); or she might explain away the apparent conflict by attributing to Paul a further motive that instrumentally rationalizes his risk-taking – for example, that he wants to get rich, and sees this land a speculative investment. Midgley considers another kind of explanation: Paul 'bought it to secure his privacy'; he 'hates being overlooked by strangers' (25). Now initially, this explanation might seem to characterize Paul's action as irrational – as motivated by something morbid or neurotic. Midgley remarks that Paul himself might be rather ashamed of this reason and try to hide his motive (perhaps even from himself) behind other more acceptable explanations. But, Midgley points out, 'perfectly normal people want privacy' (27). Why would this be? Midgley answers: 'Being stared at produces horror widely, not only in man, but in a great range of animal species. In most social creatures, a direct stare constitutes an open threat' (28). For Midgley, what Paul is doing can be illuminated by comparing it to superficially different patterns of behaviour observed in butterflies, in dogs and in other primates.

Midgley takes the widest possible context for Paul's action, and this enables her to locate his wish for privacy – and his willingness to act against his economic interests to get it – in the context of the 'complex set of patterns [that ethologists] discuss under the general heading of territorial instincts' (28). This wide view is the context for her highly distinctive account of practical rationality, moral psychology and ethics. *Territory* names just one set of instincts among many, each with its own complex knot of behavioural and motivational patterns: others include aggression, sex, parenting, dominance, and self-preservation. In any animal with more than one instinct, life will throw up clashes: a cat might find herself caught between her instinct to guard her territory and her instinct towards self-preservation. So too, Paul's wish for privacy might conflict with his need for community or his parental instinct not to unsettle his children by moving house. Midgley follows

Darwin in asking: what happens when a creature develops the sort of intellect that allows it not just to experience these clashes but to notice and be aware of them (see especially Chapter 4)? Unlike the cat, Paul can reflect on and be troubled by the outward incompatibility of parts of his life and the inner conflict that mirrors it. It is in the context of such a development, Midgley argues, that for practical reason moral psychology and ethics are to be situated.

Even in this thumbnail sketch, we can see something of the challenge that Midgley's vision poses to mainstream theories in the philosophy of mind, action and ethics. Her picture requires Anscombe's account of the metaphysics of human action (in Intention[2]) and of social facts (in 'Brute Facts'[3]), but now enriched and augmented by a Freudian psychology and a Darwinian science. It evokes a version of Murdoch's moral psychology but now placed within an ethological frame and a metaphysical holism that makes sense of the limits of our self-understanding. And beyond that, it points to an account of human society and politics that moves beyond the simplistic and dangerous model on which man's sole motivation is self-interest.

Donald MacKinnon, Midgley's wartime tutor, spoke of a philosopher's duty to 'interrupt.'[4] Like Midgley, he recognized that – whatever the wishes of their payrolled participants – philosophical conversations are not confined to philosophy seminars in universities. Philosophical debates about the nature of the soul, the relation between pleasure and virtue, human nature and so forth, inevitably speak to and of the real practical concerns of human life. As such, what philosophers say will, one way or another, speak to those outside the classroom. Because of this, MacKinnon warned, philosophers must be self-conscious about the conversations they are involved in. They must position themselves ready to 'interrupt' when what is being said starts to look like the sort of thing that might prove unhelpful, harmful or irrelevant, to those – such as our imagined Paul – who are grappling with the often overwhelming task of trying to live their life in a way that is broadly coherent. For MacKinnon, the mark of a great philosopher is the ability to take in the complex logical geography of a philosophical conversation and then to represent it on a map that allows others with less acute vision to see for themselves its most significant landmarks and well-worn paths. A philosopher who could do that could then 'interrupt' – she could point out routes that had not been taken and landmarks that had been ignored or given more attention than they deserved.

Midgley is that kind of philosopher. It is a great shame that for decades, philosophers did not attend to the map she has drawn and or listen seriously to the interruptions she made. For the foreseeable future, life on earth – human, dog, butterfly, whale, bison, wolf, bee, etc. – will be dominated by the environmental catastrophe that human animals have wrought. That Midgley's cartography is more relevant than ever needs hardly be stated. When a young Mary Midgley (then Scrutton) began her own philosophical journey on the eve of the Second World War, her father sent her away with a missive which might serve as her motto and our directive: 'The great thing is, to clear one's mind and REFUSE TO ACCEPT OUTWORN PRESUPPOSITIONS. Form a picture of mankind as it should be and think out the path to that state.'[5]

Rachael Wiseman May 2025

NOTES

1. Midgley, M., *Science and Poetry*, Routledge 2001, 137.
2. Anscombe, G. E. M. *Intention*, Blackwell 1957.
3. Anscombe, G. E. M. 'Brute Facts', Anscombe, G. E. M. "On Brute Facts." *Analysis*, vol. 18, no. 3, 1958, pp. 69–72.
4. MacKinnon, D., *A Study in Ethical Theory*, London: A. & C. Black London 1957, 'Introduction'.
5. Quoted in Mac Cumhaill, C. and R. Wiseman, *Metaphysical Animals: How Four Women Brought Philosophy Back to Life*, London: Chatto & Windus, 2022, p. 13.

Acknowledgements

Grateful acknowledgement is made to the following sources for permission to reproduce material in this book.

Midgley, M., *Animals and Why They Matter*, Penguin Books Ltd and The University of Georgia Press 1983.

Midgley, M., *Wisdom, Information and Wonder*, Routledge 1989.

Midgley, M., *Science as Salvation*, Routledge 1992.

Midgley, M., *Utopias, Dolphins and Computers*, Routledge 1996.

Midgley, M., *Science and Poetry*, Routledge 2001.

Midgley, M., *Wickedness*, Routledge 2001.

Midgley, M., *Beast and Man*, Routledge 2002.

Midgley, M., *Evolution as a Religion*, Routledge 2002.

Midgley, M., *Heart and Mind*, Routledge 2003.

Midgley, M., *The Myths We Live By*, Routledge 2003.

Midgley, M., *The Owl of Minerva*, Routledge 2005.

Midgley, M., *The Solitary Self*, Routledge 2010.

Midgley, M., *Are You an Illusion?*, Routledge 2014.

Midgley, M., *What Is Philosophy For?*, Bloomsbury 2018.

Preface to the Second Edition

Writing this preface in the immediate wake of the British Society for the History of Philosophy's vibrant and wide-ranging conference on 'Animals and the Environment in the History of Philosophy,' which focussed strongly on Mary Midgley's work, I am greatly heartened by the extent to which that work, until recently largely ignored by the academic philosophical establishment, now appears to be engaging the minds and hearts of a gifted generation of younger philosophers. There is far greater receptivity now to her pluralistic, inter-disciplinary and holistic approach to philosophy – to what John Cottingham aptly characterizes as humane philosophy – than was the case during the years in which she carved out her very distinctive and personal oeuvre.

This is encouraging; it suggests that, while the dangerous fantasies of scientism, against which she fought such a determined and thoroughgoing campaign for the last four decades of her life, still get more headlines than Mary Midgley's holistic approach, the latter may prove more enduring in the long run. Nor is it accidental that such an orientation coincides, among the present generation, with a deep practical concern for the perilous predicament of our ecosystem; perhaps those who have grown up from childhood with the miracles of digital technology are less impressed with these, and the scientistic outlook that goes along with a fascination for them, and more keenly aware of the damage that rampant technologies are inflicting on the more-than-human world.

When the first edition of The Essential Mary Midgley came out in her 86th year, it seemed reasonable to assume that this volume, together with her autobiography, The Owl of Minerva, published the same year, would constitute a fairly definitive summary of her life and work. As it turned out, she went on to publish three further philosophical works, culminating in the appearance of What Is Philosophy For? in the week of her 99th birthday – hence the need for a new, expanded edition.

Those three works continue the core philosophical enterprise that I identified, in the Introduction to the first edition, as the systematic critique of the conceptual outlook of scientific materialism. I am not sure that any other philosopher has carried through this task with the same sustained focus and comprehensive range, and at the same depth, as is achieved by the full body of her work; and it is more than gratifying to find that (in what measure due specifically to her influence it is of course difficult to say) that critique has now found its way into, at least, a substantial portion of the philosophical community.

It is more than gratifying because a collective awakening to the limitations and dangers of the materialist conception of reality is now a considerably more urgent desideratum than it was when she first launched that critique – we are in imminent danger of rupturing the very fabric of the global ecosystem on which all human life ineluctably depends. Though this is widely recognized, the importance of a clearly articulated philosophical critique of the forms of thought that have been at the root of this catastrophe, together with a cogent alternative approach, cannot be overstated; even if the dangers we are facing are clearly recognized, if the faulty modes of thought that have precipitated them are not transformed, we may not be able to undo the harm.

The three late works – *The Solitary Self*, *Are You an Illusion* and *What is Philosophy For?* are perhaps more explicitly directed to specific core metaphysical tenets of scientific materialism than her earlier writing. *The Solitary Self* singles out that of individualism – atomism projected onto the social sphere; *Are You an Illusion* targets physicalism – the thesis that consciousness and subjectivity can be reduced to complex physical happenings in the brain; while *What Is Philosophy For?* is mainly concerned to undermine the naïve, quasi-religious faith in the omnipotence of science that she labels Scientism.

Interestingly, the extended critique of individualism that she undertook in *The Solitary Self* begins with a thorough examination of the moral thought of a scientist who is commonly claimed as a key architect of the kind of biologically based individualist ethic that is her main target – but who, by contrast, she interprets as a direct precursor of her own, diametrically opposed position. In re-reading this work, I came to the view that perhaps Mary Midgley's single most significant philosophical influence was the moral philosophy of Charles Darwin. Her able exposition of this, comprising some 50% of the book's content, ought to go a long way towards dissociating Darwin from the unhelpful individualistic and egoistic views for which his authority has traditionally been claimed.

Though the subtitle of the book, *Darwin and the Selfish Gene*, might suggest that she is again taking up the cudgels in her celebrated debate with Richard Dawkins, in fact there is here far less direct critique of the doctrines she is concerned to debunk, and much more careful unpacking of the positive ones (deriving from the actual Darwin as opposed to the mythical ahistorical Darwin who has served as an icon for her opponents), than in the earlier, closely related, *Evolution as a Religion*. In some ways, I regret that considerations of space have prevented me from including more of this excellent volume; I have tried to include what is most essential in her presentation of Darwin's substantive views on morality and its relation to evolution, as much because of their deep influence on her own thought as because it needs to be far more widely known that Darwin had very sophisticated, and deeply humane, views on ethics that entirely contradict those, such as Huxley, Spencer, E.O. Wilson and Richard Dawkins, who claim to be his followers.

Her next book, *Are You an Illusion?*, published in 2014 at the age of 95, took up a different, most bizarre, strand of the reductionist, materialist worldview; the idea that since what is real are material entities, our belief in the existence of our own minds, in subjective experience itself, is mistaken; Descartes, apparently, was wrong to say 'I think, therefore I am' – he ought to have said, 'I am not, therefore I do not think.' Here, for those not already familiar with it, is the extraordinary quote from Francis Crick that explicitly makes this strange claim:

> 'You', your joys and sorrows, your memories and ambitions, your sense of personal identity and free will, are in fact no more than the behaviour of a vast assembly of nerve cells and their attendant molecules…
>
> … The scientific belief is that our minds – the behaviour of our brains – can be explained by the interaction of nerve cells (and other cells) and the molecules associated with them. This is to most people a really surprising concept. It does not come easily to believe that I am the detailed behavior of a set of nerve cells.
>
> (Crick, The Astonishing Hypothesis: 1994, pp. 3, 7)

This is not an isolated eccentricity; numerous other quotations, from a variety of authors, are provided to show that this plainly incoherent idea is endorsed by a substantial number of members of the scientific community. What is going on?

It might seem excessive to devote an entire book to the refutation of such an obvious fallacy. But in fact the target is well chosen; if the fundamental premise of the scientific materialist outlook is accepted – that the material universe is, as the classical scientific view of Newton and his successors held, entirely devoid of life, agency and consciousness, therefore able to be completely understood by objective, deterministic mechanical methods – then accounting for the existence, in such a world, of consciousness, minds, or subjective experience, becomes extremely difficult; we seem to be forced to the Cartesian view that minds and physical entities belong to two radically separate metaphysical realms, which are then, notoriously, difficult or impossible to weld together again.

The desperate resort of claiming that the realm of the subjective is actually non-existent, since it cannot be fitted into a materialist ontology, is certainly even less satisfactory philosophically than Descartes' gimcrack dualism, but apparently appealed more to materialistically inclined twentieth-century scientists because it eliminates awkward questions about possible interactions between mind and body. A thoroughgoing refutation of extreme physicalist 'solutions' of the mind–body problem was therefore an essential pillar of Midgley's overall critique of the materialist worldview, as much as was the positive account of human ethical nature, faithful to Darwin's actual views, presented in *The Solitary Self*.

In a sense, then, the long journey towards a more realistic, humane and coherent account of human nature that she began in *Beast and Man* had reached a conclusion. Her last book, *What Is Philosophy For?* was perhaps more a panoramic survey of the then current manifestations of scientism, and a farewell parting shot, than an exploration of new ground. Its underlying theme is the way in which over-analytical thinking – the type of thinking that is characteristic of an excessive dominance of the left cerebral hemisphere and appears prominently in both the Oxford analytic philosophical tradition and the less philosophically sophisticated scientistic writings that are her two main targets – systematically distorts our view of reality and ourselves by insisting on cutting it, and us, into isolated, separate components and overlooking the essential fact that it *is the participation of these parts in an integrated whole that actually makes them what they are*. This thoroughgoing insistence in grounding philosophical work on a holistic understanding of human nature, and of our place in the overall scheme of things, is perhaps her most distinctive and important contribution to the discipline.

There remains one more, rather different, book to be discussed; her autobiography, *The Owl of Minerva*, came out in the same year that this collection first appeared. With yet another conference on Mary Midgley and her Somerville friends in the pipeline as I write, the

20th anniversary of these two volumes seems an apt time to reflect on the impact of the life and work of these four remarkable women.

The Owl of Minerva (the title references Hegel's classic dictum: 'The Owl of Minerva flies only at dusk,' i.e., philosophy flourishes when civilization is in decline) presents many important aspects of Midgley's philosophy through a somewhat different lens, in the context of how the events and currents of thought that formed the milieu in which she came to intellectual maturity impacted the evolution of her own thought. I had not originally intended to include extracts from it in this new edition, but when I was urged to do so by Clare Mac Cumhaill, I quickly saw that there were indispensable gems there that must be considered Essential Mary Midgley.

Apart from her colourful ancestor Thomas Urquhart of Cromarty, who I acknowledge is included more for local colour and light relief than serious philosophical content, the remaining excerpts from the Owl add a great deal of valuable historical perspective, and not a little substantive analysis, to the overall presentation of her thought in this collection. Of particular interest, of course, are her extended reflections on her intellectual and personal relationship with Iris Murdoch, and to a lesser extent with the other two members of what has now become known as the Wartime Quartet, Philippa Foot and Elizabeth Anscombe. Her thoughtful and wide-ranging account of the intellectual, social and political atmosphere of the middle third of the twentieth century shines a clarifying light on the relationship of philosophy to the rest of life during that time, and how this determined and gifted group of women carved out a deeply felt and intellectually incisive challenge to the over-analytical mainstream of British (and North American) philosophy, which is only now being fully recognized as a major movement of thought.

It remains only for me to make fulsome acknowledgement of the extraordinary work of two other women philosophers, and their many collaborators, who have done so much to advance Mary Midgley's reputation, and that of the Wartime Quartet as a whole, over the past decade or more. In, I believe, 2014, Rachael Wiseman and Clare Mac Cumhaill lighted on the motif – first pointed to in the Introduction to the first edition of this book, and in *The Owl of Minerva* – of how women philosophy students at Oxford were able to flourish in the years of the Second World War, due to the absence of warring male egos dominating the scene, leading to the very creative collaboration between these four gifted thinkers.

Clearly recognizing the significance of this preciously neglected strand of twentieth-century thought, they set out to thoroughly document its sources, aims and outcomes; Mary Midgley being the only surviving member of the Quartet, they visited her regularly throughout the last four years of her life and, with her encouragement, launched the inspirational *In Parenthesis* project, aiming to bring into the spotlight the enormously important, but unduly neglected, contributions of British women philosophers in general and the Quartet in particular. It is in no small measure due to their dedicated work that this new edition can now hope to reach a wider audience, both popular and professional, than its predecessor of twenty years ago.

David Midgley May 2025

INTRODUCTION

David Midgley

Mary Midgley is a philosopher of unusually wide-ranging interests – from the nature of human wickedness to the fallacies attached to the Anthropic Principle in cosmology. The present volume is an attempt to bring together a selection of her writings that show the continuity and connectedness of these diverse themes, so as to enable the reader to gain a grasp of her thought as a whole. In this Introduction, I shall try to trace the connecting thread that leads from the initial impetus which motivated her writing through to her most recent work.

To attempt an assessment of the significance of Mary Midgley's work as a whole is at the same time to inquire into the meaning and importance of philosophy within contemporary culture and society, for one of the central features of her work throughout her career has been an abiding commitment to bringing philosophical thinking to bear directly on issues of practical concern. This commitment goes beyond an involvement in applied philosophy, in the sense of using philosophical methods to argue directly for the adoption of specific policies. It is rather a concern, not with the pursuit of abstract truth for its own sake, but with the kind of understanding which informs

DOI: 10.4324/9781003588160-1

the health and well-being of a culture or a civilization. And this might be a definition of philosophy, one that would perhaps be endorsed by some of its greatest practitioners (Socrates, Plato, Aristotle and Kant spring to mind).

At the start of this project, the publishers sent me as a model the parallel volume on David Bohm. On reflection, the connection thus made seemed to me highly appropriate; for despite working in apparently unrelated fields, both these thinkers are distinguished by their very important contributions to a crucial intellectual task of our time. This task is the restoration of the unity in our view of ourselves, and of our relationship to the natural world of which we are a part, which was dealt such a damaging blow by the rise of the conceptual outlook of scientific materialism. This worldview, with its constituent agendas of reductionism, dualism, atomism and mechanism, has dominated European thought for the last four centuries. It has now lost the rationale it had in the triumphant success of classical physics, since the new physics is quite inconsistent with the ontology and epistemology of materialism. But it continues, with immensely damaging effect, to dominate the contemporary intellectual landscape.

These damaging effects reach far beyond the confines of university departments; they distort our thinking on the crucial problems and challenges now facing humanity. Scientists like David Bohm, James Lovelock and Ilya Prigogine are now tracing the outlines of a new kind of science, able to provide insights into the complexities and subtleties of an essentially organic world which escape the relatively blunt instruments forged by Descartes, Galileo and Newton. But the seventeenth-century conception of Nature as a machine, able to be brought under control and 'fixed' by the skills of the engineer, still continues to occupy centre stage. The fantasy that bio-engineering, micro-electronics and nuclear fusion will provide solutions to the problems of ecological destruction, social disintegration and mass poverty is founded on a defective mode of thinking. The analysis of what exactly is wrong with such thinking, how it arises, and what alternative visions and concepts can help to correct it, is philosophy at its most socially relevant.

The sustained, wide-ranging and sensitive critique of the ideology of scientific materialism advanced over the past half century by Mary Midgley is perhaps the best-known aspect of her work. But there is a great deal more to her thought than the exposure of the flaws in this worldview. Her starting point and constant locus of concern is the damaging effect which this, and other one-dimensional systems of ideas, have on our moral thinking. Trained as a moral philosopher at Oxford in the 1940s, a time when the narrow and hyper-specialized tendency of Anglo-Saxon analytic philosophy was at its height, she consistently challenged philosophers, as well as physicists, biologists and psychologists, to recognize the richness and diversity of human life and the natural world, to which no monolithic reductive theoretical viewpoint can do justice.

This methodological pluralism continues and develops one of the central insights which permeates the thought of an apparently very different thinker, whose name would not normally be closely associated with Midgley's, namely the later Wittgenstein. This is his concern with the persistent tendency in our thought to distort reality by using the conceptual tools appropriate to one domain to deal with a different one. 'A picture held us captive,' says Wittgenstein. The effort to escape this bondage to compellingly simple pictures (metaphors, paradigms) requires the constant use of the philosophical imagination, and of a faculty of critical judgement independent of any preconceived theoretical position.

This is a very difficult endeavour to sustain, and one in which few of Wittgenstein's direct disciples have done anything like justice to the spirit of his inquiry. Moreover, it is notoriously difficult to see how the invaluable, but negative, corrective power of such an approach can be completed by a positive doctrine broad and systematic enough to take the place of the theories under criticism. Accordingly, despite many excellent small-scale studies which showed the virtues of clarity, precision and freedom from theoretical 'baggage' which his influence had encouraged, English-speaking philosophy after Wittgenstein suffered generally from a failure to tackle large questions, and to engage constructively with other disciplines and with matters of concern to the general public, by whom it was largely dismissed as pedantic and irrelevant.

This was especially true in moral philosophy, where the preoccupation with the intellectual virtues of clarity and precision, at the expense of others such as moral seriousness and relevance to real life, was particularly damaging. In this value-system, ethics lacked the prestige of logic, epistemology and semantics; and much work done in the field, as well as being too abstract and restricted in its terms of reference to be of much value to the non-specialist, was also of very mediocre quality.

There were, however, honourable exceptions, among them a remarkable generation of women philosophers who had the signal advantage of an Oxford philosophical training largely free of the ego-battles of their male counterparts, then away at the Front. They included Elizabeth Anscombe, Philippa Foot, Iris Murdoch and Mary Midgley, and their work was distinguished both by their deep moral seriousness and by a willingness to engage with real-world problems, going beyond the narrow limits which linguistic philosophy had set for itself. This work remained true to the spirit of Wittgenstein's quest to free philosophy from the paralysing effect of 'systems.' But until the publication, in 1978, of Midgley's *Beast and Man*, it did not show signs of giving rise to an overall intellectual structure that could take on the synthesizing and guiding role for which the discarded systems of Descartes, Kant, Hegel and the rest had been thought necessary.

THE ROOTS OF HUMAN NATURE: A NEW STARTING POINT FOR MORAL PHILOSOPHY

Beast and Man: The Roots of Human Nature marked out (and developed with great clarity and thoroughness) a new kind of approach to moral philosophy, neither restricting itself to fine-tuning our ways of discussing piecemeal and local problems nor offering a new, simplistic reductive theory treating all particular moral questions as instances of one or two universal central principles. For Midgley, there is indeed a 'central' question in moral philosophy, a 'key' to its further development – not in some final absolute sense, but as the primary location of the complex of problems which had blocked progress in the subject for the better part of a century – namely the cluster of confusions surrounding the concept of Human Nature.

It is impossible for moral philosophy to get started without a conception of Human Nature, whether this is acknowledged or not. Whatever confusions and inadequacies are embodied in the model of human nature on which a moral theory is based will be reflected in error and incoherence in its substantive conclusions. In fact, this is true, though less obviously so, for philosophy generally. This crucial issue had been addressed by Wittgenstein in his late work, especially *Philosophical Investigations* (1953). He drew attention to the importance for philosophy of giving attention to very familiar, everyday facts about the kind of beings we are – our 'forms of life,' our familiar habits of building, trading, 'asking, thanking, cursing, greeting and praying.' Observation of the context within which our concepts, and the language we use to express them, arise can help to dissolve the illusory ideal pictures of ourselves produced by metaphysical theories. If we are to understand what 'knowing,' 'perceiving,' 'consciousness,' 'certainty,' and 'meaning' are, we need to observe them, as it were, in their natural habitat – in everyday human activity.

Thus, Wittgenstein, who in his early work had carried the quest for a watertight, ultimately simple logical system to its extreme limit, ended by reversing the order of priority and giving primacy to the observations of everyday life as the 'ground floor' of our knowledge, on which the grand designs of science, mathematics and formal logic must be seen as resting (in contrast to Descartes, who had the building the other way up). In a characteristically telling metaphor, he describes the conflict between this idealising tendency of thought and the requirements of 'real-life' language:

The more narrowly we examine actual language, the sharper becomes the conflict between it and our requirement. (For the crystalline purity of logic was, of course, not the result of investigation; it was a requirement.) The conflict becomes intolerable; the requirement is now in danger of becoming empty. – We have got on to slippery ice where there is no friction and so in a certain sense the conditions are ideal, but also, just because of that, we are unable to walk. We want to walk: so we need friction. Back to the rough ground!

(Philosophical Investigations, 107)

This reassertion of the primacy of everyday knowledge and experience, of the 'natural history' of human beings as the essential basis of the understanding of mental life and mental concepts, is an immensely significant move, which has far-reaching implications over the whole field of human thought. It is one which Midgley explores with great thoroughness throughout her work. In three related ways, however, she greatly extends the scope of Wittgenstein's insight. In the first place, Wittgenstein's concern was with logic, epistemology and the philosophy of mind, traditionally seen as the central areas of philosophy (largely because of the preoccupation with deductive reasoning as the paramount feature of our mental life). Midgley applies the 'natural history' approach to ethics, where its implications are still more far-reaching, and in the process suggests a drastic re-evaluation of the significance of ethics relative to the rest of philosophy.

Second, where Wittgenstein drew his material from shrewd analysis of a few quite simple observations of everyday human activity, Midgley draws on a vast body of systematic and careful observations, scientific in the old sense of precise and methodical but not in the reductive theoretical sense. These are the findings of ethology, the systematic study of animal behaviour represented by the work of Konrad Lorenz, Niko Tinbergen, Jane Goodall, and others. Finally, by relating human nature and behaviour to its origins in the nature and behaviour of other animal species in this way, she goes significantly beyond Wittgenstein's important move of considering the human activities of interest to philosophers (perceiving, thinking, deciding, judging, etc.) in their wider context of human social life. In order to arrive at a genuinely balanced view of the latter, we need to locate it in its still more inclusive setting of the natural world as a whole. The task of helping us to gain a better awareness of our 'place in the world' was classically seen as central to the project of philosophy. In much twentieth-century philosophy, however, it was abandoned in favour of increasingly abstract and specialized theorizing, contributing to grave confusion and error within the wider culture. This, then, was the project of Beast and Man – first, to bring the concept of Human Nature back to the centre of the philosophical stage, where it belongs. Second, to show how the attempt to conceive it as radically separate from its origins in our evolutionary history has led to systematic error and confusion, with severely damaging consequences for our culture. And third, to map out an approach to philosophical questions, in ethics especially, which is consistent with this understanding of our nature, as a very particular kind of social mammal (as opposed to a Cartesian pure rational intellect in a machine body).

It is important to distinguish sharply between this approach to relating ethics and biology and that advocated by what is called 'sociobiology,' and more recent variants such as 'evolutionary psychology.' Though these approaches do have the merit of acknowledging our continuity with other species, their strongly reductionist bias distorts their analysis of the common motivational structure of humans and other animals. This makes it essentially impossible for them to do justice to the higher intellectual and ethical capacities of humans (some of which are shared by other species). Despite the claim that these approaches offer a way to bring ethics into the domain of empirical science, they are in fact highly unempirical, taking the fundamental selfishness of all human and animal motivation as an axiomatic principle. This fatally flawed assumption, held to follow from the principle of evolution by natural selection, is the essential premise of Social Darwinism – a view which, Midgley is at pains to stress, is quite contrary to Darwin's actual views and was principally the brainchild of Herbert Spencer, himself not a biologist but a social philosopher of a somewhat mystical bent.

The assumption of selfishness as the basis of motivation is not ultimately redeemed by recasting the theory in terms of 'kin selection' or 'gene selection' (following Richard Dawkins, E. O. Wilson and others), for three main reasons. First, as Midgley makes clear, the use of the everyday vocabulary of human motives – selfishness, spite and so on – in this context is necessarily misleading. Although the sociobiologist may claim that these terms are being used in a technical sense which does not imply that the individuals actually have the motives that the everyday concepts refer to, the ordinary associations of the terms cannot be effectively severed from them in this way. And in fact, both Wilson's and Dawkins's writings, like those of many of their followers, are replete with instances of sliding back from the technical to the everyday use of these terms, so that they end up with what is in effect a traditional egoistic account of human motivation, which has no actual justification in the official version of their theories.

Second, the reasoning on which the axiomatic assumption of selfishness as the evolutionary basis of motivation is founded is itself unsound. It rests on a rejection of the possibility of altruism, since, supposedly, altruistic behaviour traits would necessarily diminish the survival chances of individuals possessing them (or, in the variant accounts, their genes or kin). This presupposes that such traits as 'a disposition to sacrifice one's life if another is in danger' are separate items, which could be genetically switched on or off in isolation from the rest of life, rather than consequences of a much more general overall integrated structure of motivation which makes possible the whole interwoven fabric of social existence.

The ubiquitous atomising tendency is at work here, in the form of the assumption that – because we can refer to people's motives separately – these motives are therefore in fact separate and independent items that, like Lego pieces, can be added and taken away without affecting the rest. The whole project of genetic or evolutionary psychology, and with it that of genetically engineering people for desired personality traits, rests on this philosophical howler, criticized in detail in Beast and Man, Chapter 6, 'Altruism and Egoism.'[1] Indeed, if it were true that our psychology is constituted by such Lego-like 'units of behaviour,' each linked to a distinct gene, it would be impossible for altruistic behaviour to evolve, since social species themselves could never have come into existence.

The third reason, therefore, for rejecting the thesis that the principle of natural selection implies that all motivation must be essentially selfish is that it is inconsistent with the facts, as Kropotkin brilliantly demonstrated in his classic work, Mutual Aid: A Factor of Evolution. In response to T.H. Huxley's version of Social Darwinism, Kropotkin argued convincingly that co-operation is in fact a more important factor in evolution than competition. This work, together with its even greater (and still more unjustly neglected) successor, *Ethics: Origin and Development*, is the true intellectual precursor of Mary Midgley's efforts to integrate an account of moral life into a genuinely scientific account of human nature. Both writers, incidentally, make the point, with extensive quotations from Darwin himself, that the Social Darwinist thesis and its contemporary descendants are foreign to the spirit and substance of Darwin's own work, both in their reductionistic reliance on a priori arguments rather than empirical observation, and in their attempt to bolster an egoistic view of ethics by appeal to the principle of natural selection.

Wickedness: A Philosophical Essay continued the project of mapping out an account of human nature consistent with our evolutionary roots with an exploration of the darker side of our nature. It was written as a counterpoise to *Beast and Man*, which had striven to overcome the culturally entrenched tendency to equate animal motivation with the rejected aspects of human nature, thereby distorting our picture of both. Accordingly, the earlier book emphasized the common origin of the most valued aspects of human mental life, previously assumed to be the exclusive possession of humans. In *Wickedness*, the 'leftover business' of examining human destructiveness and evil was thoroughly explored.

The first task here was to make clear that there was a subject to be investigated. The contention that there is indeed such a thing as human wickedness comes into collision with several cherished assumptions of liberal theory. Reacting against the appalling oppression focussed around the notion of sin in traditional Christian society, there was a progressive tendency in Enlightenment and modern thought to 'deconstruct' the notions of wickedness, guilt and blame. Harmful acts came increasingly to be seen as the result of either genetic predispositions or social conditioning. Unfortunately, however, both alternatives share the drawbacks of depriving us of our concepts of freedom and responsibility, and thus fail to provide any basis for moral choice or moral development.

What is needed instead, Midgley argues, is to avoid the demonization that normally accompanies the recognition of moral defects in others – a process of alienation and denial that entirely blocks any understanding of the stigmatized individual or group, and is itself one of the most potent sources of social evil. Instead, we must seek to understand the inner processes of the wicked person, without taking from them the moral responsibility for their acts. The ensuing journey through the darker recesses of the human psyche is, to me, one of the most engrossing aspects of her work; its conclusion, in brief, is that wickedness is essentially a negative phenomenon, a failure to access some of the positive elements in our nature. Ironically, the power of the evil person often derives from what are normally morally positive qualities – the diligence and conscientiousness of an Eichmann, the courage and intelligence of Satan in Milton's Paradise Lost, the religious zeal of the protagonist in James Hogg's Confessions of a Justified Sinner. It is their lack of the complementary balancing motives of empathy, humility or self-awareness which turns these positive attributes into fuel for their destructive projects.

Having examined the 'Beast Within,' Midgley completed this phase of her work with a more practically oriented look at the 'Beast Without' in Animals and Why They Matter. This and another book published the same year, Women's Choices (co-authored with Judith Hughes), were her only book-length contributions to applied philosophy strictly so called.[2] The account of the relation between human and animal nature offered in Beast and Man clearly has dramatic implications for the range of ethical issues surrounding our dealings with other species. The neglect of these issues is one obvious effect of the assumption of a radical opposition between human and animal nature. If animals (following Plato) are the embodiment of all that is base and unworthy in our mental life, or (following Descartes) if they are actually not conscious at all, it seems to follow that it is all right to inflict on them any treatment which it suits us to inflict. The issues of animal experimentation, factory farming and other forms of institutionalized abuse of animals have of course been a major focus of moral concern with the general public for a long time. At the time the book appeared, however, it was still a grossly neglected topic in academic philosophy, and Midgley's pioneering work played a significant part in its acquiring a much more prominent place in the arena of moral philosophy. The book was also a model example of applied philosophy, combining intellectual rigour and balance with great popular clarity and force of conviction.

PHILOSOPHIZING OUT IN THE WORLD: BEYOND THE ANALYTIC STRAIT-JACKET

The genesis of the highly original approach to moral philosophy developed in Mary Midgley's early writings was a reaction to the confining intellectual climate then surrounding the subject. She began teaching again in 1965, after a break of about fifteen years during which, among other things, she had raised three children and become absorbed in the study of animal behaviour. These experiences led to a profound dissatisfaction with the image of the human being which lay in the background of the Oxford analytic tradition that still prevailed in British philosophy. Though this tradition tended to see itself as having been emancipated from the errors of the past, as a result of the revolution in philosophical method brought about by Frege and Wittgenstein, in this respect, it was still heavily under the influence of the thinking of the great philosophers of the Enlightenment – Descartes, Spinoza, Locke, Hume, Kant and the rest.

Common to all these thinkers was a view of Reason, conceived essentially as the capacity for logical deduction, as the defining characteristic of the human mental constitution, as opposed to that of animals, who possessed perception and emotion, but not Reason. (It is not irrelevant to observe that these male thinkers often held not dissimilar views about the contrast between men and women – see the extract from *Science and Salvation* in Part Three, entitled 'The Remarkable Masculine Birth of Time.') The division between Reason and Feeling has been the source of a number of problems in moral philosophy throughout its history, and is the subject of Midgley's second book, *Heart and Mind*. Traditionally, these faculties have been conceived as categorically different and mutually exclusive. Hume's classic dictum, 'Reason is the slave of the passions,' identifies reason as the faculty of pure logical deduction, completely universal and objectively certain but without relation to 'merely contingent' matters concerning the particular constitution and needs of human beings, and emotion, by contrast, as an essentially arbitrary, blind impulse, devoid of cognitive content, a 'brute fact' which arises in us and which reason can perhaps guide and correct but which is fundamentally alien to it.

In contrast, Midgley stresses the inextricable unity of these and other facets of our nature; what it is to be rational (a 'rational animal' in the Aristotelian formula) is *essentially* related to contingent truths about the structure of human motivation. Because of the kind of creatures we are, there is a wide range of important motives which are natural to us, and which frequently conflict. Rationality consists in consciously and skilfully balancing these conflicting motives so as to do justice to the full range of our emotional, physical and intellectual needs, to the demands of family, society and self, and so on. The artificial division in this process between pure logical reasoning and 'mindless' feeling which Hume's formula implies cannot be made out in practice; in a characteristic trenchant metaphor, Midgley tells us that this is like 'trying to unscrew the inside from the outside of a teapot' (*Heart and Mind*, p. 102). Hence, the principle of the 'Naturalistic Fallacy' – that it is impossible to argue validly from facts to values – which Moore, following Hume, made the cornerstone of his ethical theory, is a red herring. To the extent that the mainstream tradition of moral philosophy in Britain and the United States took Moore's principle as its starting point, there was therefore grave need of a fresh start. In *Heart and Mind* and two subsequent works, *Can't we Make Moral Judgements?* and *Wisdom, Information and Wonder*, Midgley further develops the critique of this tradition commenced in *Beast and Man*. Again, therefore, the theme is unity; the model of binary logic – the analytical method – continually causes philosophers to try to treat separately things which can only be understood as aspects of an integral whole (Heart and Mind, Reason and Feeling, Fact and Value, Mind and Body).

This separation and fragmentation is the essence of the intellectual approach known as reductionism, epitomized in the principles set out in Descartes' *Discourse on Method*; the way to understand anything is to break it down into its constituent parts, identify their individual properties, and then deduce from these the properties of the whole. The source of this reductionist bias in philosophy is of course the pervasive tendency to regard science, and in particular mathematical physics, as the model for all rational thought.

THE MYTHS OF SCIENCE: DREAMS OF OMNICOMPETENCE

The image of philosophy as the critique of the ideas which inform and guide society as a whole inevitably comes into sharp conflict with the widely held view that it is, or should be, science which performs this function. Since the Renaissance, when the position of religion as the pre-eminent source of this wisdom was first seriously challenged, the candidacy of science as successor to its vacant throne has gathered increasing momentum. A typical view, quoted by Midgley in *The Myths We Live By* (p. 14), is that of Nehru:

> It is science *alone* that can solve the problems of hunger and poverty, of insanitation and illiteracy, of superstition and deadening custom and tradition, of vast resources running to waste, of a rich country inhabited by starving people . . . The future belongs to science and to those who make friends with science.

Here science is, quite clearly, being identified with rationality generally. In this sense not only civil engineering and medicine but also social policy and administration, law, architecture and in fact the whole sphere of organized practical life are implicitly included in 'science.' The failure to distinguish clearly between this somewhat metaphorical use of the word 'science' and the narrow and specialized one referring to the domain of controlled experiments and mathematical theories is one factor contributing to the emergence of 'scientism' – the view of science as 'omnicompetent,' able to provide answers to all questions and solve all problems. Science becomes a kind of deity, able to bestow on us a miraculous salvation in which not only the large-scale evils referred to by Nehru but all forms of ignorance and suffering, even including mortality, are overcome through the application of science and technology.

One of the principal virtues of science stressed by those who advocate it in the role of primary fount of wisdom for society is objectivity. From this point of view, the principal failing of religion is that, not being in the required sense objective, the truth of its claims cannot be definitively decided by empirical tests. If religion seeks to lay down judgements about factual matters – and this has often occurred – such criticism is entirely warranted. But it oversteps the mark, and becomes dangerous, when accompanied by the failure to understand that there are other important kinds of thinking than purely factual ones. As Dobzhansky says (quoted in *Evolution as a Religion*, p. 15): 'Science and religion deal with different aspects of existence. If one dares to overschematize for the sake of clarity, one may say that these are the aspect of fact and the aspect of meaning.' If religion is at fault when it attempts to pronounce on matters of fact, science is equally so when it lays claim to authority in the domain of meaning. This is not to say that scientists are not entitled to express opinions on such matters, or even that they should not do so in the context of their scientific writings. But it should be acknowledged that in doing so they are doing theology or philosophy, not science, and that the relevant professional standards apply. The target of Midgley's criticism in two of her best-known books, *Evolution as a Religion* and *Science as Salvation*, is a recent genre of scientific, or quasi-scientific, writings in which scientists who themselves have little or no philosophical or theological training make sweeping pronouncements on philosophical matters, implicitly or explicitly appealing to the authority of science for their claims. A not unrepresentative example is the following passage from an acclaimed and widely discussed book by the cosmologists Barrow and Tipler (quoted in *Science as Salvation*, p. 22):

> [We] are cosmologists, not philosophers. This has one very important consequence which the average reader should bear in mind. Whereas many philosophers and theologians appear to possess an emotional attachment to their ideas which requires them to believe them,

scientists tend to regard their ideas differently. They are interested in formulating many logically consistent possibilities, leaving any judgement regarding their truth to observation.

As Midgley points out, the grandiose speculations which form the body of this work could not conceivably be tested by observation; furthermore, though the authors seem unaware of it, both the motivation and much of the content of their ideas relate to judgements of value and metaphysical assumptions which are not empirical matters at all. No attempt has apparently been made to relate their treatment of these questions to previous work by specialists in the relevant fields – a procedure which they would unquestionably regard as disbarring from serious consideration a comparable attempt by a philosopher to speculate at large on questions of theoretical physics.

It is important that these are not just *ad hominem* criticisms of particular authors, but rather are endemic and in fact necessary failings in the entire enterprise of constructing a supposedly scientific alternative to religion. If the concepts and methods of science are assumed to be the right ones to provide answers to the questions about the ultimate meaning and purpose of life which have traditionally been regarded as the province of religion and philosophy, and if the methods already in use in these disciplines are different ones, then it follows that the deliberations of specialists in these areas are of no significance, and the conscientious scientist should ignore them.

The source of the trouble here seems to lie in the ever-increasing tendency towards specialization in education, particularly scientific education, over the past century and a half or so. On the basis that the exponential growth of knowledge requires a progressively finer division of intellectual labour, educational policy has increasingly been based on the assumption that students of science cannot (and therefore need not!) be expected to spend time acquiring a degree of familiarity with non-scientific disciplines. The effects of this policy are very far-reaching, and are explored at length in *Wisdom, Information and Wonder*. The one which is relevant here is the tendency for such an education to make it difficult or impossible for scientists to grasp the possibility of forms of understanding different from the one in which they have been trained, leading them to assume that those engaged in other disciplines lack the capacity for 'real,' rigorous (i.e., mathematical) thought. This phenomenon is well illustrated by the preceding quotation from Barrow and Tipler, and reflected in numerous quotations from influential authors (especially E.O. Wilson, Richard Dawkins and Peter Atkins) throughout Mary Midgley's writings on these topics.

REASON AND IMAGINATION: UNDERSTANDING OUR VISIONS OF REALITY

From a philosophical standpoint, what is occurring is an example of the widespread and important problem of communication between alternative world-views. Someone who has been educated more or less exclusively in terms of a particular worldview will not normally be fully aware that this is the case, since this worldview will be transparent to them. The world *as seen through this particular lens* will appear to them to be just *the world as it objectively is in itself*. It is only by acquiring the experience of seeing the world through different lenses that this distinction comes to be understood.

History, literature, anthropology, physiology – and indeed horticulture and watercolour painting – all have their own categories and concepts, their own characteristic ways of perceiving and describing things, which enable those engaged in these studies to grasp their subject-matter in the most appropriate way. There is no one 'master science' to which all the others can be reduced, thereby rendering them unnecessary. This anti-reductionistic point is forcefully made by Midgley (in the context of discussing the problem of relating mind and body) with another striking metaphor:

> We are not looking for the relation between two places on the same map. We are trying to understand the relation between two maps of different kinds, which is a different kind of enterprise. At the beginning of an atlas, we usually find a number of maps of the world. Mine gives, for instance, world physiography (structure and seismology), world

climatology (mean annual precipitation, climatic fronts and atmospheric pressure), world vegetation, world political, world energy, world food, world air routes and a good many more. If we want to understand how this bewildering range of maps work, we do not need to pick on one of them as 'fundamental'. We do not need to find a single atomic structure belonging to that one map and reduce all the other patterns to it . . . We have to see the different maps as answering different kinds of questions, questions which arise from different angles in different contexts. But all these questions are still about a single world, a world so large that it can be rightly described in all these different ways, and many more. It is that background – not a common atomic structure – which makes it possible to hold all the maps together. The plurality that results is still perfectly rational. It does not drop us into anarchy or chaos.

The fundamentally important idea that there are *different ways of seeing the world*, which yet do not necessarily conflict with each other, is another central theme in Midgley's thought. It is related to another very important philosophical topic, namely the role of the imagination in knowledge. Imagination here does not refer to the capacity to represent to oneself things and situations which do not exist, but to the ability to form a connected vision of a range of phenomena, of the framework of relationships between them and the principles that operate in this particular domain. The target of Midgley's critique here, present as an important element in her work from the beginning but worked out in detail in *Science and Poetry* and further elaborated in *The Myths We Live By*, is another Cartesian division – that between Imagination and Reason. The reductionist tradition, following Descartes, has tended to downplay the importance of imagination, equating it with the realm of fantasy and entertainment, and to view knowledge as exclusively the product of the senses together with reason in the form of logical deduction.

Imagination, however, plays an absolutely central part in, for example, Kant's account of knowledge; it carries out the work of *synthesis* by which the individual elements of sense-perception are welded into a coherent, unified representation of an outer world. Without this unifying activity, Kant convincingly argues, we could not make any sense at all of the mass of sensations impinging on our sense organs. Hume's conception of the self as an unorganized 'bundle of perceptions,' all separate from and unrelated to each other, fails to provide a sufficient basis, not only for scientific knowledge but for any kind of coherent experience at all. This eighteenth-century empiricist account of knowledge has, however, remained influential within the philosophy of science, and still more so among scientists who are not trained philosophers, despite the widely accepted verdict that Kant's critique of Hume's atomistic model of the mind was wholly successful.

The tendency of recent philosophers to over-emphasize the analytic side of their discipline, while often overlooking the aspect of synthesis, is part of the general aspiration towards the intellectual values of science, as opposed to those of literature, which in earlier periods were regarded as equally its concern. Though she is known as a philosopher of science, Mary Midgley's background as a classical scholar, and her deep literary and historical sensibilities, have enabled her to bring another perspective to the subject. Her work serves as a reminder to the modern reader that the literary-historical mode of understanding is just as essential to philosophy as the logical-scientific one.

The underlying reason for this is that these two radically different ways of apprehending the world are of equal and universal importance in human life generally. They belong to the deepest layer of our nature as conscious creatures. Understanding someone's character, through seeing the patterns of motivation and emotional response in his or her life-story, is as vital to human survival as understanding how to make fire or grow crops, and one cannot be substituted for the other. The linear, convergent, deductive style of thinking which is central to science is perfectly adapted for finding out what makes a clock tick, but almost useless for finding out what makes a person tick. Philosophy needs both kinds, and *Science and Poetry* is Midgley's most eloquent and sustained attempt to show how they relate to one another, and how they can be combined to produce philosophy that is at once sensitive and rigorous, able to take in a vista as well as analyse the structure of a leaf.

Imagination, then, is not to be seen as an optional extra in our mental equipment, providing spare-time entertainment for the mind in the form of poetry, paintings and religious visions, but as an essential element in all our knowledge of the world, not excepting the most rigorous scientific theories. Every such theory, in fact every attempt to make sense of any aspect of the world around us, necessarily proceeds from an overall vision of the phenomena in question. Thus, Newton's investigation of optics was guided by the imaginative vision of light as a stream of minute particles; Huygens' by that of waves undulating in a fluid medium. Neither of these visions revealed the actual, fundamental nature of light as it is in itself, but both were capable of being used as tools for understanding many aspects of the phenomena, and of being refined and reworked to provide new tools yielding deeper insights and more precise predictions.

On a larger scale, all of our experience and thought is coloured by a more general set of concepts, images, metaphors and habits of thinking which go together to make up what Midgley calls a *world-picture* or a *myth*. It is important to stress here that the word 'myth,' for Midgley, in no way implies that the ideas in question are false or lacking justification. Her use of these terms is comparable to Thomas Kuhn's notion of a paradigm, in the sense of an exemplifying image or model of a set of phenomena. But the use of the word 'myth' designedly draws attention to the central role of imagination in this process, and to the wider role that myths play in the rest of human life; our concept of 'how the world fundamentally is' (*Science as Salvation*, p. 7) has, historically, derived much more from poetry and religious teaching than from science, and the world-vision of classical science itself was drawn, to a far greater extent than most scientists today probably realize, from such poetic and mystical visions.

Perhaps the most influential and powerful vision, or myth, of this kind is that of atomism, the idea that all of the immensely and seemingly irreducibly diverse range of things in Nature are in fact just different arrangements of essentially identical, indivisible and inert particles. This view was developed by Greek and Roman philosophers at a time when there was no real question of empirical evidence for it as a scientific theory, and was worked out in comprehensive detail in Lucretius' epic poem *De Rerum Natura* (Of the Nature of Things), which Midgley takes as the starting point of her exposition in *Science and Poetry*. Lucretius, then, was not primarily engaged in logical reasoning or in experimental research, but in using a literary medium to convey an imaginative vision of the nature of reality. He consciously promoted this vision as an alternative to other visions of reality associated with religious creeds, or with ethical philosophies other than his own favoured Epicurean system. So successful, however, was this worldview, when it later became the guiding vision for the enterprise of classical Newtonian physics, that many of its followers ceased to be aware that it is but one way of conceiving reality, and took it for the ultimate truth about how the world inherently is.

But the atomistic view of the world, for all its triumphant success in illuminating the workings of physical systems and the unprecedented material benefits arising from the application of this knowledge, has now ceased to serve us. It has become instead a straitjacket constricting and distorting our attempts to understand other aspects of the reality with which we need to deal. The catastrophic deficiency of the atomist worldview is its inability to encompass the essential characteristics of living entities. It views matter as essentially 'dead,' passive and inert, and the universe as consisting of nothing but matter and empty space. Locked into such a concept of reality, it is not surprising that physical scientists come out with such bizarre statements as 'Inanimate things are innately simple. That is one more step along the road to the view that animate things, being innately inanimate, are innately simple too' (Peter Atkins, quoted in *Science as Salvation*, p. 48). This is a very clear case of confusing the conceptual scheme we use to investigate reality with the reality itself. If we insist on holding fast to the atomist myth, we are approaching the job of understanding living systems with the wrong toolkit, and it will land us in deep trouble. What alternative vision, or visions, can we turn to that can serve to illuminate the realm of living things in the way that is needed?

GAIAN THINKING: PUTTING IT ALL TOGETHER

Atomism has been of inestimable value in helping us to understand those aspects of the world that can be understood without reference to the special, unique attributes of living things. For these purposes, the conception of the world as comprised of dead matter was not a hindrance. But the impact of the technologies, ways of thinking and ways of life that have grown out of this materialist conception of the world has had a cataclysmic destructive effect on the world of living things, on the planetary ecosystem. The secular culture of the modern West is in fact unusual in viewing the cosmos as basically inanimate. Is it time to reconsider the possibility that the tendency of other cultures to regard the world we live in as itself alive is more than a primitive superstition and may contain a profoundly important truth?

James Lovelock's Gaia hypothesis, formulated in the 1970s as a response to questions arising out of space research on the possibility of life on other planets, answered these questions with a profound observation; in order to continue in existence, life on Earth has to intervene actively to maintain the physical conditions which are necessary for its preservation. It does so on a colossal scale, transforming incredible quantities of energy and matter in ways that keep the environmental parameters within limits which allow the processes of life to function. As Lovelock points out, this regulating tendency is precisely the same in principle as that by which the cells and organs of individual organisms work to maintain the parameters of their internal environment within a delimited range; very much like a cell or an organism, the biosphere as a whole is involved in self-sustaining metabolic activity. In a sense, one may say that it is impossible for life to exist on a planet that is not itself alive.

The Gaia concept was initially anathematized by official science, though eagerly embraced by ecological activists and those interested in spiritual alternatives to traditional religion. To the scientists, it appeared to violate fundamental assumptions of rationality; it was rejected as imputing purpose to the biosphere, as positing a mystical, transcendent entity – Gaia – who somehow interferes with the mechanical processes of causation to bring about her own ends. But of course such a view is no more required in the case of Gaia than it is in the case of individual organisms and cells, whose self-maintaining attributes are undeniable and are held to be ultimately explicable without reference to the purposes of a transcendent being. The processes to which Lovelock draws attention are explained (in broad principle) by perfectly unmysterious relationships of dynamic equilibrium between the physical and chemical processes involved and the population dynamics of the organisms which contribute to these processes. The real problem with Gaia, one suspects, is that these scientists sensed that it threatened to provide an alternative image of 'how the world fundamentally is,' an inclusive, holistic, pluralistic and essentially organic vision in which complex interactions, connections and relationships are the prime focus of attention, and the analytic, atomistic, reductionistic way of thinking fades into the background.

As well as colliding with the metaphysical assumptions which underlie reductionistic science, Gaia Theory presents a fundamental challenge to the ethical, social, political and economic ways of thinking that have grown out of this world-view. Here the central concept which is the target of Midgley's critique is the doctrine of individualism, another core theme in her work from the outset. This is the atomistic mode of thinking projected onto the social sphere, and was, together with the doctrine of the autonomy of reason, at the centre of the Enlightenment reaction against the oppressive social order instituted by mediaeval Christianity.

The liberating effect of the change arising from placing individual life at the centre of our system of values can scarcely be overstated. Nevertheless, like all ideologies, the ideology of individual freedom has a reverse side, which when carried too far becomes as pernicious as the oppression which it was a reaction against. The alienation and fragmentation which are at the root of so many grave problems in our society today are to a great extent a consequence of an over-emphasis on individual satisfactions at the expense of communal ones. Individualism distorts social relations because it implies a view of human nature as fundamentally selfish; individualistic views of society and atomistic views of the natural world are of a piece, and the combination of the two has led to a catastrophic neglect of the dimension of wholeness, of the organic connections which make a living system (organism, society, ecosystem, etc.) able to function. In her exploration of the possibilities of Gaia Theory as an alternative vision, or myth, around which to organize our thinking on these urgent questions, Mary Midgley has provided a framework for relating the scientific insights of Lovelock *et al.* to the deep problems afflicting our culture and society. Her attempt, in her most recent work, to reintegrate our understanding of human society into our view of our terrestrial home is in a deep sense a completion of the task begun in *Beast and Man*, showing the importance, for a sound understanding of individual human nature, of relating this to its origins in the natural world.

NOTES

1. The same can be said for the strange cult of 'memetics,' which attempts to transfer this reasoning from the domain of inherited behaviour patterns, where there is at least a reasonable presumption of a physical basis which has a more or less atomic kind of structure in the form of DNA sequences, to that of culturally transmitted ideas, where there is none.

2. The latter work has, at her suggestion, been omitted from this compilation because it is out of print and somewhat tangential to the main line of her philosophical development. This is not to minimize the importance of feminist issues in her work, which I hope is brought out adequately by the inclusion of the important analysis of the role of gender in the rise of the ideology of scientific materialism at the end of Part 3.

PART 1

THE ROOTS OF HUMAN NATURE

CONCEPTUAL PROBLEMS OF AN UNUSUAL SPECIES

The overall theme of Mary Midgley's *Beast and Man* is an attempt to deepen and correct our understanding of human nature by connecting and comparing it with our understanding of the nature of other species.

In the first chapter, 'Have We a Nature?', she examines various traditional approaches to explaining human behaviour, in particular to the understanding of motive. These mostly fall into two types: those that, like Marxism and Freudian psychoanalysis, seek to explain all human behaviour in terms of one or two universal motivations (power, property, sex, etc.), and those that, like existentialism and behaviourist psychology, deny that we have any inborn or natural motives at all – our actions are entirely the product of radical free choice or of conditioning.

DOI: 10.4324/9781003588160-2

She contrasts these accounts with that of ethology, which approaches the study of human motivation on the premise that, being a mammalian species, we are likely to share the general structure of motivation found in such species. This structure comprises a number of broad ranges of motives (often misleadingly labelled 'instincts'), such as territoriality, aggression, sex, parenting, dominance, and so on, which can be made sense of in terms of the biological needs of the species.

The idea that we share a large part of our psychological nature with other species does not of course imply that there is nothing unique about human beings. But it does conflict with many traditional philosophical views which try to explain human psychology exclusively in terms of supposedly unique features – generally rationality, consciousness, and the capacity for language – thereby implying an absolute, categorical distinction between Man and Animal. The next chapter, 'Animals and the Problem of Evil,' considers the implications of this view, showing how it distorts our idea both of ourselves and of other species. Man (for this is a characteristically masculine view) is seen as essentially rational, other animals (Beasts) as essentially ruled by irrational emotions. Animals become invested with all of the negative, destructive attributes which Man wishes to disavow – we form our image of the Beast on the basis of our own shadow.

'Speech and Other Excellences,' taken from the third section of the book, entitled 'The Marks of Man,' further explores the question of human uniqueness, in particular the claims that language and rationality respectively have no counterpart in other species. Without minimizing the significance of the fact that these qualities are developed in human beings to a degree quite unprecedented elsewhere, Midgley shows their continuity with the mental capacities of other species. They are grounded in a general need on the part of social creatures to communicate with and understand the motives and intentions of other members of their community. She considers in some detail the empirical evidence that chimpanzees can in fact use a human language at a level far beyond what was previously supposed possible, reinforcing the Wittgensteinian point that the phenomenon of language can only be understood as part of a way of life involving a whole range of complex types of social interaction within a community. Much of this social structure we share, as ethological studies have shown, with other primates; this is the foundation on which the special human achievements of language and culture are built.

In this perspective, rationality is seen not as Descartes saw it, as the capacity for logical deduction, but as the art of striking a balance between the wide range of motives and considerations which bear on our choices. We have, like other social creatures, to arbitrate between our own and others' interests, to weigh the consequences of our actions, to decide on priorities and so forth. Though it might be thought that animals entirely lack the capacity to do these things, closer examination of their actual way of life shows that they not only can do so, but often could not survive if they could not. Again, this does not negate the fact that human capacities in this area vastly exceed those of other species; it does, however, provide a possible explanation of how such capacities could possibly have come into being in the first place.

SOURCES

'Have We a Nature?' and 'Animals and the Problem of Evil' – slightly abridged from Chapters. 1–2 of *Beast and Man*, Cornell University Press, 1978; 'Speech and Other Excellences' – condensed from *Beast and Man*, Chapters 10–11.

1

HAVE WE A NATURE?

UNDERSTANDING OUR MOTIVES

Every age has its pet contradictions. Thirty years ago, we used to accept Marx and Freud together, and then wonder, like the chameleon on the tartan, why life was so confusing. Today, there is similar trouble over the question whether there is, or is not, something called Human Nature. On the one hand, there has been an explosion of animal behaviour studies, and comparisons between animals and humans have become immensely popular. People use evidence from animals to decide whether man is naturally aggressive, or naturally territorial; even whether he has an aggressive or territorial instinct. Moreover, we are still much influenced by Freudian psychology, which depends on the notion of instinct.[1] On the other hand, many sociologists and psychologists still hold what may be called the Blank Paper view, that man is a creature entirely without instincts. So do Existentialist philosophers. If man has no instincts, all comparison with animals must be

DOI: 10.4324/9781003588160-3

irrelevant. (Both these simple party lines have been somewhat eroded over time, but both are still extremely influential.)

According to the Blank Paper view, man is entirely the product of his culture. He starts off infinitely plastic, and is formed completely by the society in which he grows up. There is then no end to the possible variations among cultures; what we take to be human instincts are just the deep-dug prejudices of our own society. Forming families, fearing the dark, and jumping at the sight of a spider are just results of our conditioning. Existentialism at first appears to be a very different standpoint, because the Existentialist asserts man's freedom and will not let him call himself a product of anything. But Existentialism too denies that man has a nature; if he had, his freedom would not be complete. Thus, Sartre insisted that

> there is no human nature . . . Man first of all exists, encounters himself, surges up in the world, and defines himself afterwards. If man as the Existentialist sees him is not definable, it is because to begin with he is nothing. He will not be anything until later, and then he will be what he makes himself.[2]

For Existentialism, there is only the human condition, which is what happens to man and not what he is born like. If we are afraid of the dark, it is because we choose to be cowards; if we care more for our own children than for other people's, it is because we choose to be partial. We must never talk about human nature or human instincts. This implicit moral notion is still very influential, not at all confined to those who use the metaphysic of essence and existence. So I shall sometimes speak of it, not as Existentialist, but as Libertarian – meaning that those holding it do not just (like all of us) think liberty important, but think it supremely important and believe that our having a nature would infringe it.

Philosophers have not yet made much use of informed comparison with other species as a help in the understanding of man. One reason they have not is undoubtedly the fear of fatalism. Another is the appalling way terms such as *instinct* and *human nature* have been misused in the past. A third is the absurdity of some ethological propaganda.

About the fear of fatalism I shall not say much, because it seems to me quite misplaced here. The genetic causes of human behaviour need not be seen as overwhelming any more than the social causes. Either set would be alarming if treated as predestined to prevail. But no one is committed to doing that by admitting that both sets exist. Knowing that I have a naturally bad temper does not make me lose it. On the contrary, it should help me to keep it, by forcing me to distinguish my normal peevishness from moral indignation. My freedom, therefore, does not seem to be particularly threatened by the admission, nor by any light cast on the meaning of my bad temper by comparison with animals.

As for words such as *instinct*, *drive*, and the *nature* of a species, ethologists have done a great deal of work here towards cleaning up what was certainly a messy corner of language. Much more is needed, and I shall try to do a little of it. Such words must somehow be reorganized, not just thrown away. They are necessary if we are to talk either about other species or about our own.

People may still wonder, however, why we should need, for understanding human life, concepts developed to describe animal behaviour. Perhaps I can best bring out the reason by glancing at a problem we often have when we try to understand human motivation – the shortage of suitable conceptual schemes.

Consider the case of someone (call him Paul) who buys a house with an acre of land, though he can scarcely afford it, instead of one without. How should we describe this 'scientifically'? What should we say he is doing? Plenty of economic descriptions are available. He might be meaning to grow turnips to sell or to supply his household; he might be speculating for resale, or buying as an investment or as a hedge against inflation. It is interesting that even at this stage, where all the alternatives are economic, we already need to know his motive in order to decide among them. The 'facts' of the particular transaction are not enough to classify it, or explain it, even economically, unless they include motives.[3] (Motives, of course, are not just his private states of mind, but patterns in his life, many of which are directly observable to other people.) We cannot say *what* he is doing until we know *why* he does it.

Now, what happens if the motives are not economic? Paul, it turns out, is not trying to make money out of the land at all. When asked, he says that he bought it to secure his privacy. He hates being overlooked by strangers. As his whole conduct is consistent with this, we believe him. Besides believing, however, we still need to *understand* this motive. That is, we want to see how it fits into the background of his life, and of human life generally.

Shall we accept a simple Marxist interpretation, that he is showing off his riches to establish his class status? This will not get us far. Of course, people do show off for that reason. But merely saying so does not account for the particular forms showing off takes. The ostentatious rich buy big cars, because those are what most people would like to have if they could. They do not usually display their status by burning themselves to death on piles of paper money in the streets. And it is the basic taste that we are trying to understand. Explaining motives by ostentation is always producing a box with another box inside it. We must ask next: why display *that*? This was the weakness of Thorstein Veblen's view of art as conspicuous expenditure to impress the populace. As later and more subtle Marxists have pointed out, if art is to be worth displaying, it has to have a real point in the first place.[4] Of course, a particular ostentatious person can display things he sees no point in. Whole groups within a society may do it; many Romans thus collected Greek art. But this is still parasitical. It depends on acknowledging the authority of people who do see the point, and treating them as the norm. It needs too, I think, an explicit doctrine that the thing itself actually is valuable, with reasons given. Thus, the more people explicitly praise pictures, or horses, or yachts, or abbeys to pray for one's soul, the more likely other people with no genuine taste for these things are to want them. But this wanting is a *by-product* of the praise. It is not what the praise itself is about. Ostentation, in fact, is just one of the cure-all political explanations which people produce for motives and which turn out circular. The most central case is power. The desire for power is necessarily secondary to other desires, because power is *power to do* certain things, and valuing those things has to come first. Those who really pursue power just for its own sake are neurotics, entangled in confusion by habit and destroying their own lives. Hobbes realized this:

> So that in the first place, I put for a general inclination of all mankind, a perpetual and restless desire of power after power, that ceaseth only in Death. And the cause of this is not always that a man hopes for a more intensive delight than he has already attained to; or that he cannot be content with a moderate power: but because he cannot assure the power and means to live well, which he hath present, without the acquisition of more.[5]

This puts power in its place as an insurance. But Hobbes still made it central and probably never realized how much this circular psychology limited the value of his political theory. I suspect that Marx's position was similar. Nietzsche, when he made the Will to Power a primary motive, did try to give it a more direct meaning. He thought of power as straightforward dominance over other people – indeed, more specifically still, delight in tormenting them[6] – which is certainly clearer, but happens to be false, except of psychopaths.

Now Paul certainly might be just being ostentatious, buying land he did not want, solely because he saw other rich men doing so. But if so, his case would be a parasitical one, and we should need to shift our attention, if we wanted to understand the motive, to some rich man who actually did want the stuff. This same consideration works even more strongly against another equally fashionable, and more respected, shortcut, the notion of conformity. He bought it, some say, because his society had conditioned him to value it. Now (again) some people certainly are so distractedly conventional that they will do almost anything to be like the neighbours. But their existence depends on having neighbours who are not like them, who make positive suggestions. If the neighbours too did not care what they did apart from conforming, there would be nobody to generate the standards that everybody conforms to. Society is not a subsistent Being, a creative divinity. Not everybody can always be at the receiving end of culture.

Paul, we will say, knows what he is doing, to the extent that what moves him actually is the motive he mentions, not his class or society. Indeed, both may disapprove of what he does, and he himself may even be rather puzzled by his motive, in the sense that its strength surprises him, and that it is not explicitly linked to his value system.[7] In this sense, he does not quite know what he is doing. He needs further understanding of what his motive means or amounts to. We all have motives sometimes that put us in this quandary, which is why we badly need to understand our motives better.

His motive then really is the wish for privacy. He 'hates being overlooked by strangers.'

I have picked this motive because it is one on which all the main traditional theories of motive are particularly unhelpful – a fact that may well leave Paul, if he is an educated fellow, puzzled, defensive, and even somewhat ashamed of its force. Freud does supply us with the notions of voyeurism and exhibitionism. But these are positive tastes. How will they explain anybody's dislike of being looked at? Certainly there could be an inversion here, a horror of sex. If someone has a morbid and excessive fear of being looked at, we might suspect that it is linked up with a disturbance of his sexual life, and there would be ways to check this suspicion. But perfectly normal people want privacy; indeed, everybody sometimes does so unless he is a gravely deranged exhibitionist. And since we do not need (as Freud did) to balance a contemporary concealment of sex by dragging it forcibly into every explanation, we can ask dispassionately whether there is evidence for a sexual motive of any explanatory value. This must be something more than the mere sexual aspect, which (as Freudians rightly point out) most motivation can be found to have if you really look for it. All the main strands of human motivation – affection, fear, aggression, dominance, sex, laziness – pervade our lives and have some influence in shaping all our actions. Sexual behaviour itself can obviously have its aggressive, frightened, or domineering aspect. But sexual motivation does not seem to help us in understanding the notion of privacy.

Freud's weakness here can be seen in his startlingly perverse and insensitive way of interpreting the nightmare of his patient, the

Wolf-Man.[8] As a child of five or less, this man had dreamed that, as he lay in bed, his window fell open of its own accord, and he saw six or seven white wolves standing in the walnut tree outside and staring at him intently. Freud ruled that this dream was not a dream about being stared at at all, but about staring, and that it stood for a (hypothetical) occasion when the child must have watched his parents making love. It does not matter much here that Freud's preferred view was probably wrong, since the Wolf-Man, as a Russian aristocrat, not a middle-class Viennese, would not have been sharing his parents' bedroom. What matters is Freud's overlooking the distinct and primitive horror of being stared at. The patient emphasized two things about his dream, which, he said, 'made the greatest impression on him, first, the perfect stillness and immobility of the wolves, and secondly, the strained attention with which they looked at him.'[9] Both these things Freud simply transmuted into their opposites. The stillness, he said, must be regarded as standing, contrariwise, for 'the most violent motion,' namely that of the copulating parents, and the attention had to be that of the child himself staring at them. By these principles of interpretation, anything can, quite literally, mean anything.

In citing Freud at his least helpful I do not mean to travesty him. Of course, he was often more sensible than this. But on many puzzling topics, many whole areas of life, he had really nothing helpful to say, because he was not interested in them for themselves at all, only in using them to round out a particular view of sex. And in considering many of these, parallels with other species can be helpful. Staring is one such case. It might seem a small matter, but it is part of a most important complex.[10] Being stared at produces horror widely, not only in man, but also in a great range of animal species. In most social creatures, a direct stare constitutes an open threat. Normal social approaches to those one does not know well always proceed somewhat indirectly, with various forms of greeting to show one's friendly intentions, interspersed with intervals of turning away and appearing occupied with something else. And eye contact in particular is at first limited to brief glances, often broken off and renewed. To stare steadily while you approach someone, or to stand still staring after he has seen you, is as direct a threat as can be made. Why this should be so is an interesting field for inquiry. It may well have something to do with the fact that predators naturally stare fixedly at prospective prey before jumping on it. And they are of course regarding it as an object, not as a possible friend – which is just the effect a direct stare conveys to a human being. Whatever the cause, so strong and so general is this tendency that a number of species have been able to exploit it by developing eyelike spots on their bodies, with which they frighten off their enemies. Many species of butterfly have separately developed detailed and lifelike eye-spots on their wings. Displaying these effectively frightens off predators, some of which never attack such a butterfly again. And this effect has been shown to vary according to how closely the spots actually resemble eyes.[11] Human beings, of course, deliberately produce a similar device by painting eyes on things. 'Staring eyes have a threatening effect, and spellbinding eyespots are therefore widely used as protective devices on uniforms, ships, houses and the like.'[12] Also in advertisements. But because pictures stay still, we are not so much upset by their staring. When a live human being does it, it is most unnerving. Those stared at often feel as much attacked as if they had been actually abused or hit. This is not a cultural matter. I have seen a cheerful baby, eight months old, burst into tears and remain inconsolable for some time on being stared fixedly at by strange aunts, although the aunts were only vaguely curious and absentminded. Dogs too, as is well known, can be 'stared down.' People sometimes take this as evidence that they recognize men as their superiors, but all it actually shows is that, if you exhibit hostility to someone smaller than yourself, he will dislike it and probably go away. Dogs do not stare at each other except in the challenge to a fight, when the stare appears, along with the obligatory slow, steady approach, the growl, and the bristling hair, as a natural expression of hostility. And the primates seem to avoid the direct stare strongly.

Thus, it would be little comfort, if one were overlooked by staring neighbours, to know that they were merely curious. The stare is not just a threat. It constitutes an actual intrusion.

Are we any further on with understanding what is worrying Paul? I certainly think so. If people, like other creatures, quite directly and naturally mind being stared at, this in part explains his touchiness on the subject. But what, you may wonder, about the numerous people who live at close quarters, overlooked, and do not mind it? We should notice that it is primarily *strangers* who cause alarm. People in small primitive societies know everybody around them well. So do people in stable modern neighbourhoods like villages, or indeed old-fashioned slums. They do not always like the closeness, and may move out. But at least they have had time to settle into a more or less tolerable relation with those around them, and there is likely to be some mutually accepted code about not doing irritating things like staring. Moreover, they know a great deal about each other already, so curiosity will not be so much of a problem. All the same, some privacy usually is provided. And where communities grow bigger, more of it is at once needed. Chinese and Indian cities have long been large and confusing, full of strangers.

For that reason, the houses became highly defensive – usually closed in by solid outer walls. More clothes are worn; women are locked up; manners, too, become defensive.

And everywhere, not just in our society, rich people who have made good in crowded cities move out and make space around themselves. This matter of what is called personal space is just one part of the complex set of patterns now discussed under the general heading of territorial instincts. I shall say more about it later, though not as much as I should like.[13] All I am concerned to do at the moment is to point out that there really is a range of phenomena here which needs describing, and that animal comparisons help because concepts for describing similar behaviour already exist in that area, and turn out, on the whole, quite applicable. Earlier theories of instinct ignored the matter, without actually denying it. They could leave it alone because, for one thing, nobody was trying to change people's lives radically in this respect. But so drastic have social changes been in the twentieth century that it becomes necessary to state all kinds of facts about our animal nature which used to be taken for granted – for instance, that we cannot live properly in infinite crowds or in conditions of ceaseless change.

WHAT WE CAN ASK OF OUR CONCEPTS

I am suggesting that we badly need new and more suitable concepts for describing human motivation.

The alarming truth is, of course, that it is not only animal behaviour studies that are still in the descriptive phase. Certainly, a particularly deep snowfall of virgin ignorance has till lately been observable there. People in general never knew very much about animals; they had various motives for distorting what they did know, and when in the last two centuries we in the West mainly moved into towns, we cut ourselves off from what little we might ever have discovered. (That is why the recent renaissance of this subject interests us so much.) It might seem, on the other hand, that we know plenty about that much described matter, human conduct. So we might, if we had always asked the right questions and had not been more anxious to deceive ourselves than to learn the truth. But we can always do with new questions. People like Nietzsche, Freud, and Marx, by asking new questions, have taught us much, and it is yet further questions, and a more intelligent connecting of questions, that we still need.

Merely naming an impulse as territorial may tell you quite a lot about it, just as naming it as sexual may. But you will understand much more if you have an adequate idea of how territory works generally, and still more if you know how it works in a given species, how it relates there to other motives like dominance, affection and aggression. All these general motives are groupings of particular impulses. Personal space is only one aspect of territory. But it is one that matters greatly to all advanced social creatures, including those with no fixed home. And staring is only one form of intrusion.

Freud should never be dismissed as 'unscientific' on the simple grounds that he did not make detailed predictions that could be falsified in experiment. What he was providing was concepts. His general question: 'What is the structure of human instinct?' was a perfectly sensible one. His answer was oversimple and overconfident, but his suggestions still make excellent indicators of where inquiry can start – of what, for instance, must be wrong, but points the way to what is right. He made 'good mistakes' – a most useful habit, the value of which is perhaps more familiar to philosophers than to scientists. He made possible the making of concepts.

A good concept-maker has to be a man of great general intelligence and wide interests, or he cannot make connections with other fields and is liable to produce a scheme that some other study will shatter. But he needs also, and quite as much, to be more or less soaked in, committed to, involved with, and generally crazy about his subject. A long phase of fairly omnivorous observation, of deep receptiveness and genuine wonder, is needed to appreciate the formal peculiarities of the thing one is dealing with, to see *what* about it should be laid hold on for description. That background of experience is the strength of Konrad Lorenz, Niko Tinbergen and their school. They have been animal people all their lives. Their involvement in the concrete has, as Hinde justly says, 'ensured that explanatory concepts have been chosen to suit the phenomena studied, rather than vice versa'[14] – an advantage that is rarer than it ought to be. But we still have the problem of relating the study of animal behaviour to other ways of studying man. *Homo sapiens* is an animal. (At least he is not a machine, or an angel, or a fairy or even something from Vulcan.[15]) So it would really be odd, would need a lot of accounting for, if comparative methods that make good sense over the wide range of other terrestrial species suddenly simply had no application to him at all. But *Homo sapiens* is already marked out as the property of the social sciences. And they are because of their early history to some extent committed to the view that he has no nature, or none that can be important, that his behaviour (apart from a few simple physical needs) must be understood entirely in terms of his culture.

The thing we must keep in mind here is that there is room for all methods. No one way of studying mankind has a monopoly or needs one. Innate factors can be ignored for some purposes because they are taken for granted, without therefore vanishing from the scene.

What each method has to do is to establish its usefulness. It must fill a need. It seems obvious to me that we do need to understand human motives better, both what they are and how they connect. There is a load of common-sense lore about them, some of it excellent, some confusing, some worthless. But the intellectual systems that have tried to organize it work mostly by *reducing* many motives to one or a few basic ones – sex, self-preservation, power. They tidy one province, but then they distort themselves in an effort to take over the whole. Human life simply contains more motives, even more separate groups of motives, than they allow for. We have to work out their natural relations, not hack or wrench them to fit Procrustes' bed. Comparison with other species shows possible groupings more subtle and more helpful than these fiat reductions. Certainly, this comparison itself must not be used reductively. We must not say 'university departments are really only territories.' 'Only' is an exaggeration. But with that word removed, the remark can still be useful. Similarly, a reviewer put the question: 'on Desmond Morris's own principles, should not his book *The Naked Ape* be seen as the dominance display of a rising male, eager to gain followers and compete for leadership of the troop?' Well, *among other things*, yes. And so should *Eminent Victorians, Language, Truth and Logic, Les Demoiselles d'Avignon*,[16] and half the papers in periodicals. Human contentiousness is a fact. We could never keep our heads in the babble of controversy if we did not know how to allow for it. Indeed it is just those readers least aware of the deliberately polemical, challenging element in works such as these who are most likely to be drawn in by it, to involve themselves in the amusing but irrelevant game of cops-and-robbers that the authors want to play, rather than sticking to the central questions about the value of what is being said or done.

Still, we say, these motives belong to human beings. Why should we need to look outside the human scene to understand them?

Because (as I have just suggested) our cultures limit so subtly the questions that we can ask and reinforce so strongly our natural gift for self-deception. When we ask why something that is normal in our culture is being done, official answers are always prompt. Spaniards tend not to be short of reasons for bullfighting, Romans for gladiatorial games, totalitarians for torture, Erewhonians for punishing illness. To break this circle, to make our local presuppositions stand out, fabulists have long used animals. They rely on the shock of a different context to make a familiar pattern visible at last. It often works. But of course its value depends on the power of the fabulist's own imagination, on his being able himself to take a new point of view. The device has a different kind of force when facts are used rather than fiction. When other human cultures are found acting at cross-purposes to ours or caricaturing it by pushing its vices to star-tling excess, we are impressed, and quite rightly. Here, in fact, we already accept the value of looking *away* from the familiar scene in order to understand it. Many notions first evolved for the study of primitive peoples have been found useful for the study of more com-plex ones like ourselves, who did not know they had these things because they never thought to ask, but had already half-formed puz-zles to which these notions provide the answer. (Examples are initi-ation rites and crisis rites generally, competitive giving, conspicuous expenditure.) And many half-formed suspicions about our own society have been shaken up and clarified into valuable insights by comparison with strange cultures.

What happens with patterns first spotted in animals is very similar. Someone first detects a pattern in animal behaviour – he finds, that is, a notion that unifies and makes sense of a common sequence of behav-iour, say, displacement activity, or dominance displays, or redirected aggression. He then looks at the human scene and sees something similar. So much is traditional. The further things which are needed, and which are now being vigorously developed, are a careful, thor-ough, disciplined procedure for making the original observations of animals precise and a subtler technique for comparison for checking the different sorts of variation in different species and linking them to their different sorts of causes.

The value of animal comparisons here depends on a simple point about what understanding is, which I think has come home to the public much more quickly than it has to the theorists. *Understanding is relating*; it is fitting things into a context. Nothing can be understood on its own. Had we known no other animate life-form than our own, we should have been utterly mysterious to ourselves as a species. And that would have made it immensely harder for us to understand ourselves as individuals too. Anything that puts us in context, that shows us as part of a continuum, an example of a type that varies on intelligible principles, is a great help. People welcome seeing how animals behave, either directly or on film, in just the same way in which a man who had begun to practice, say, mathematics or dancing on his own would welcome seeing others who were already doing it, though differently. There has been an arbitrary principle, laid down for a variety of reasons in European thought, that only human activities can concern us in this sort of way.[17] It is false. It comes out entertainingly when people deeply involved with owls, otters, and whatnot are interviewed for television. Towards the end of the proceedings, the animal person is asked, rather solemnly, 'And what do you think is the point of (or the justification for) spending time on these creatures?' Far from replying, 'Just what brought you here, chum – I like them. They have a life akin to mine, but different – they make me feel more at home in the world – they fill the gap between me and the dead things I have to manipulate – they help me to understand myself,' he usually answers that they are educational for children (but why? except on the grounds just mentioned) or – and this passes as a perfectly respectable reason – that nobody has succeeded in breeding them in these latitudes before. The really monstrous thing about Existentialism too is its proceeding as if the world contained only dead matter (things) on the one hand and fully rational, educated, adult human beings on the other – as if there were no other life-forms. The impression of *desertion* or *abandonment* which Existentialists have is due, I am sure, not to the removal of God, but to this contemptuous dismissal of almost the whole biosphere – plants, animals, and children. Life shrinks to a few urban rooms; no wonder it becomes absurd.

COULD PEOPLE BE BLANK PAPER?

I am sure then that the contribution of ethology is useful and that it can be fitted in without damaging anything worth keeping in the social sciences – though it certainly conflicts with the still influential Blank Paper theory. This theory, though first popularized by Locke, was brought to its extreme form by John B. Watson, the founding father of behaviourism, and was a cornerstone of the original version of that doctrine. Locke himself had meant by it merely that we are born without *knowledge*:

> Let us then suppose the mind to be, as we say, white paper, void of all characters, without any ideas; how comes it to be furnished?. . . To this I answer in one word, from EXPERIENCE; in that all our knowledge is founded.[18]

He had never doubted that we had *instincts* – that we were born adapted to act and feel in specific ways. However, Locke did supply the language for this further step, and Watson went on to take it. Man, he declared, had no instincts. This mysterious news was remarkably well publicized; there seems to be nobody who studied any sort of social science in English-speaking countries between the wars who was not taught it as gospel. Its obscurity, however, has made it increasingly a nuisance and no sort of help to inquiry. Not only do people evidently and constantly act and feel in ways to which they have never been conditioned, but the very idea that anything so complex as a human being could be totally plastic and structureless is unintelligible. Even if – which is absurd – people had no tendencies but the general ones to be docile, imitative, and mercenary, those would still have to be innate, and there would have to be a structure governing the relations among them.

Sensible psychologists have accordingly tended more and more to admit that people do have some genetically fixed tendencies. What makes this admission hard, however, is the very strong impression still prevalent that we have to *choose* between considering these tendencies and considering outside conditions, that we must be either loyal innatists or faithful environmentalists. This polarization seems much like holding that the quality of food is determined *either* by what it is like when you buy it *or* by how you cook it, but not both. Thus, Skinner, who in his early work simply ignored innate determining factors,[19] has now for some time admitted that they exist, but still doesn't want them studied, on the ground that they cannot be altered. Knowledge of them, he says,

> is of little value in an experimental analysis because such a condition cannot be manipulated after the individual has been conceived. The most that can be said is that knowledge of the genetic factor may enable us to make better use of other causes.

And again,

> since we cannot change the species of an organism, this variable [species-status] is of no importance in extending our control, but information about species-status enables us to predict characteristic behaviour, and, in turn, to make more successful use of other techniques of control.[20]

How would our inability to effect changes be received as a reason for not studying the weather, or indeed the laws of chemistry? Of course there is nothing wrong with wanting one's knowledge to be useful. But from that very angle, knowing what one *cannot* change matters as much as knowing what one can. Skinner appears to admit this so fully at the end of these two quotations that one expects him to move on to saying that psychology will have to study both. But he never does. In *Beyond Freedom and Dignity* (1971), he may still be seen apparently holding himself bound, even after recognizing the two complementary aspects, to make an agonizing, and indeed unintelligible, choice between them:

> The ethologists have emphasized contingencies of survival which would contribute these features [aggressive instincts] to the genetic endowment of the species, but the contingencies of reinforcement in the lifetime of the individual are *also* significant, since anyone who acts aggressively to harm others is likely to be reinforced in other ways – for example, by taking possession of goods. The contingencies explain the behaviour *quite apart from* any state or feeling of aggression or any initiating act by autonomous man.
>
> (pp. 185–6, my italics)

An explanation that quite patently can work only for *repetitions* of aggressive acts, and then only for those that were rewarded in the first place, is placidly extended to account for *all* such acts, including the unrepeated originals. More generally, the formula of smooth transition from 'x as well as y' to 'therefore not y' reappears constantly, as where he says:

> For 'instinct' read 'habit.' The cigarette habit is presumably something more than the behaviour said to show that a person possesses it; but the only other information we have concerns the reinforcers and the schedules of reinforcement which make a person smoke a great deal.
>
> (p. 196)

More information obviously does exist – for instance, on the one hand, about the effect of nicotine on the human organism, and on the other, about people's innate tendency to suck things. That information, however, is not supposed to concern psychologists. Again, he remarks: 'The perceiving and knowing which arise from verbal contingencies are even more obviously products of the environment . . . Abstract thinking is the product of a particular kind of environment, not of a cognitive faculty' (pp. 188–9). So why can't a psychologist's parrot talk psychology?

There is simply no need to take sides between innate and outer factors in this way. We can study both. What behaviourism, it seems, still needs is to complete its metamorphosis from a dogmatic, fighting, metaphysical creed to an impartial method of study. The strength of behaviourism is that it is a form of empiricism, that is, an assertion of the primacy of experience over dogmatic theoretical principles in forming our knowledge. So, when it finds a dogmatic theoretical principle blocking our recognition of obvious and pervasive aspects of experience, its interests lie in ditching that principle, even when it happens to be a homegrown one. This has already been done in the matter of admitting data from private experience, something that Watson ruled out on metaphysical grounds as 'the myth of consciousness.' In *Beyond Freedom and Dignity*, Skinner admits reality here admirably, speaking of 'the indisputable fact of privacy; a small part of the universe is enclosed in a human skin. It would be foolish to deny the existence of that private world' (p. 191). The question is simply, as he goes on to say, how best to describe it, what conceptual scheme to fit it into. And the same thing is true of innate tendencies.

One thing that hampers a lot of other people besides Skinner here is the tantalizing notion of a single cause. Discussions on the cause of some phenomenon – say, Truancy, Wife-beating, or the Decline of the Modern Theatre – often begin by listing a number of alternative possible causes, and go on to try to eliminate all of them but one. On this list, there is often now something called 'the genetic cause.' But as it is not adequate alone to produce the effect, it gets eliminated in an early round of the competition and is heard of no more. But *everything* that people do has its internal as well as its environmental aspect, and therefore its causes in the nature of man as well as outside him. Picking out '*the* cause' often does mean, as Skinner suggests, looking for something that we can change. But in order to see what change is going to be any use to us, the internal factor ought *always* to be investigated, because it is not isolated, but connected with a complex system that will respond in one way or another to anything that we may do. Ignoring it because we cannot alter it really would be rather like ignoring the weather, or the shape of the earth.

I am suggesting, tentatively, that there has been a quiet, but on the whole benign, change in the meaning of the word *behaviourism*. People who call themselves behaviourists now often seem to mean simply that they study behaviour. The *ism* – the defence of a creed – seems to have matured into a more modest *ology* – a name for the topic studied. Such gradual changes are benign because they allow crude positions to be made more subtle without a public outcry. But they are more benign still when they can become explicit. If one drops the general dogma that the only causal factor which can affect behaviour is more behaviour, there is really no reason why what affects it should not be inherited, why there should *not* be innate tendencies. Whether there *are* is an empirical question, not a matter of party loyalty.

Behaviourists could afford to be less defensive. Their becoming so would be a great help in the joint exploring expeditions by various disciplines which are now needed to map the disputed area. At present, social scientists tend to appear on these occasions loaded with weapons and protective clothing – technical language, unnecessary assumptions, and control experiments of doubtful relevance – while Lorenz usually turns up speaking ordinary language and using a very wide frame of reference – wearing, as it were, only binoculars, jeans and a pair of old tennis shoes, but with an excellent homemade map.[21] I try not to let my delight at this spectacle bias me. I know he is in some ways oversimple, and has made mistakes. But I still think he has a far better idea of the *kind* of problem he is up against than most of those present. He has understood that it is no use, at present, trying to make anything look final. And the view he takes of professional rigour is the right one. Rigour is *not* just a matter of ducking down inside the presuppositions of one's own subject and defending them against all comers, but of understanding them so fully that one can relate them to those needed for other inquiries. We do not just have to verify our hypotheses carefully, but also to form them intelligently. As they are bound to tie up with matters that we do not know yet, and indeed with the general structure of human thought, this requires collaboration. It cannot be properly carried out in private, between consenting colleagues who stay within the confines of a single subject.

Lorenz and his party have, however, a difficulty about method which also dogs me constantly in this book. The point of my discussion is to show how and in what cases comparison between man and other species makes sense, but I must sometimes use such comparisons in the process. I think the circle will prove virtuous, however, if it abides by the following rule: comparisons make sense only when they are put in the context of the entire character of the species concerned and of the known principles governing resemblances between species. Thus, it is invalid to compare suicide in lemmings or infanticide in hamsters *on their own* with human suicide or infanticide. But when you have looked at the relation of the act to other relevant habits and needs, when you have considered the whole nature of the species, comparison may be possible and helpful.[22]

This would not be true if the Blank Paper view that 'man has no instincts,' that there simply was no innate determining element in human behaviour, were right. But it cannot be right. It is not even clear that it can be meaningful.[23]

NOTES

1. For Freud's own discussion of this term, see his paper 'Instincts and Their Vicissitudes,' 1915, *Complete Psychological Works*, tr. and ed. J. Strachey et al. (London, 1948–74), vol. 14. For a good modern revision of Freudian views in relation to ethology, see A. Storr, *Human Aggression* (New York, 1968).
2. *Existentialism and Humanism*, tr. P. Mairet (London, 1958), p. 28.
3. The question what 'facts' are is not so simple as it might look.
4. For example, E. Fischer in *The Necessity of Art*, tr. A. Bostock (Harmondsworth, 1963).
5. *Leviathan*, Pt. 1, Chapter 11. The character of Widmerpool in A. Powell's series *The Music of Time* is a splendid study of someone who 'cannot be content with a moderate power,' having really decided, as Powell says, to 'live by the will.' The philosopher who is most reliably clear on the point that power is only a waiting room for actuality is Aristotle.
6. See, for example, *The Genealogy of Morals*, tr. W. Kaufmann, Essay 2, Section 6, end, where he makes the totally false claim that 'apes. . . in devising bizarre cruelties anticipate man and are, as it were, his prelude.' Also *Beyond Good and Evil*, Section 229. Nietzsche always regarded the fascination with power as a sign of strength, though it seems quite as plausible to say, with Hobbes, that it is a sign of weakness.
7. Such a situation can be seen in the USSR, where the demand for country houses, though ideologically incorrect, is still strong.
8. See *The Wolf-Man and Sigmund Freud*, ed. M. Gardiner (Penguin, 1973).
9. Ibid., pp. 196–8.
10. Claustrophobia and agoraphobia are other examples. They, too, seem to be primarily disorders of our spatial orientation.
11. See N. Tinbergen, *Curious Naturalists* (New York, 1968), pp. 157–71.
12. I. Eibl-Eibesfeldt, *Love and Hate*, tr. G. Strachan (London, 1971), p. 24. The very widespread fear of magical 'overlooking' by the evil eye is another example.
13. I am fairly baffled about fitting adequate examples into this book, because the explanatory power of such notions depends on following through the whole system of concepts.
14. 'Ethological Models and the Concept of Drive', *British Journal for the Philosophy of Science*, 6 (1956), 321.
15. The common use of the word *animal* which contrasts it with *man* is obscure. I have so used it for convenience sometimes, even in this book, but it must never be forgotten that we do not have a clear basis for it, as we do if we

oppose *animals* to vegetables, minerals, or machines. Drawing analogies 'between people and animals' is, on the face of it, rather like drawing them 'between foreigners and people' or 'between people and intelligent beings.'

16. For Picasso's polemical intention in this picture, and its success, see E. Gombrich, 'Psycho-Analysis and the History of Art', in his *Meditations on a Hobby Horse* (London, 1963). This whole essay is of enormous interest for my theme.

17. Just because this is our tradition, many people think of it as obvious common sense. It became the tradition, however, as a result of a deliberate and sustained campaign by Christian thinkers, using some very strange material gathered from Rationalist philosophers, to crush a natural respect for animals, and for nature generally, which they saw as superstitious. John Passmore in his book *Man's Responsibility for Nature* (London, 1971) gives a careful and fascinating account of this strange process, which explained to me many things I had always found incomprehensible.

18. Essay Concerning Human Understanding, Bk. 2.1.2.

19. The index to *The Behaviour of Organisms* (1938) has no entries under instinct, innate, inherited, genetic, or any similar term, and though the book has a section on Drive, the concept is reduced to the ideas of frequency and intensity. Yet the behaviour discussed in that book was almost entirely that of rats, so arguments against applying such notions to humans were not in any case relevant. Watson's simple and popular doctrine had deflected attention from the topic entirely. Halcyon days.

20. *Science and Human Behaviour* (New York, 1953), pp. 26 and 157.

21. This applies particularly to *King Solomon's Ring* (New York, 1952), which some people fail to recognize as a serious and seminal book, simply because it is non-technical and delightful to read. In his technical papers, Lorenz can be as hard to understand as any other scientist.

22. The thorough, painstaking background surveys with which the field observers I quote support and explain their conclusions are a necessary supplement to what I say. I refer to only a few, for the sake of simplicity, but there are now a great many good ones. About the principles for comparing species, I say a little more in Chapter 3, in the section on intelligence and instinct. For good and full discussions, see Eibl-Eibesfeldt, *Love and Hate*, Chapter 3, also Lorenz, *On Aggression* (New York, 1963), Chapters 4–6, and many astute observations in Tinbergen's *Study of Instinct* (Oxford, 1961).

23. For an admirable and moderate discussion of the matter, see *Love and Hate*, Chapter 2.

2

ANIMALS AND THE PROBLEM OF EVIL

TRADITION AND REALITY

What then is the main point that emerges from the detailed, systematic, gruelling studies of animal behaviour that have been made by trained zoologists in this century, and have been given the name of ethology?

The general point is that other animals clearly lead a much more structured, less chaotic life than people have been accustomed to think, and are therefore, in certain definite ways, much less different from men than we have supposed. (There are still plenty of differences, but it is a different difference.) Traditionally, people have congratulated themselves on being an island of order in a sea of chaos. Lorenz and company have shown that this is all eyewash. There follow various changes in our view of man, because that view has been built up on

DOI: 10.4324/9781003588160-4

a supposed contrast between man and animals which was formed by seeing animals not as they were, but as projections of our own fears and desires. We have thought of the wolf always as he appears to the shepherd at the moment of seizing a lamb from the fold. But this is like judging the shepherd by the impression he makes on the lamb at the moment when he finally decides to turn it into lamb chops. Recently, ethologists have taken the trouble to watch wolves systematically, between mealtimes, and have found them to be, by human standards, paragons of steadiness and good conduct. They pair for life, they are faithful and affectionate spouses and parents, they show great loyalty to their pack and great courage and persistence in the face of difficulties, they carefully respect one another's territories, keep their dens clean, and extremely seldom kill anything that they do not need for dinner. If they fight with another wolf, the encounter normally ends with a submission.[1] They have an inhibition about killing the suppliant and about attacking females and cubs. They have also, like all social animals, a fairly elaborate etiquette, including subtly varied ceremonies of greeting and reassurance, by which friendship is strengthened, co-operation achieved, and the wheels of social life generally oiled. Our knowledge of this behaviour is not based upon the romantic impressions of casual travellers; it rests on long and careful investigations by trained zoologists, backed up by miles of film, graphs, maps, population surveys, droppings analysis, and all the rest of the contemporary toolbag. Moreover, these surveys have often been undertaken by authorities who were initially rather hostile to the wolf and inclined to hope that it could be blamed for various troubles. Farley Mowat, doing this work in the Canadian Arctic, had his results rejected time and again because they showed that the sudden drop in the numbers of deer was not due to wolves, which had not changed their technique in a number of centuries, but to hunters, who had.[2]

Actual wolves, then, are not much like the folk-figure of the wolf, and the same is true for apes and other creatures. But *it is the folk-figure that has been popular with philosophers.* They have usually taken over the popular notion of lawless cruelty which underlies such terms as 'brutal,' 'bestial,' 'beastly,' 'animal desires,' and so on, and have used it, uncriticized, as a contrast to illuminate the nature of man. Man has been mapped by reference to a landmark that is largely mythical. Because this habit is so ancient and so deep-rooted, we had better look a little more closely at its oddity before turning to the philosophic arguments in question.

I once read a chatty journalistic book on wolves, which described in detail how wolves trapped in medieval France used to be flayed alive, with various appalling refinements. 'Perhaps this was rather cruel,' the author remarked, 'but then the wolf is itself a cruel beast.' The words sound so natural; it is quite difficult to ask oneself: do wolves in fact flay people alive? Or to take in the fact that the only animal that does this sort of thing is *Homo sapiens*. Another complaint that the author made against wolves was their treachery. They would creep up on people secretly, he said, and then attack so suddenly that their victims did not have time to defend themselves. The idea that wolves would starve if they always gave fair warning never struck him. Wolves, in fact, have traditionally been *blamed* for being carnivores, which is doubly surprising since the people who blamed them normally ate meat themselves, and were not, as the wolf is, compelled by their stomachs to do so.

The restraint apparent in wolves seems to be found in most other social carnivores, and well-armed vegetarian creatures too. Where murder is so easy, a species must have an adequate inhibition against it or perish.[3] (Of *course* this inhibition is not a morality, but it works in many ways like one.) Solitary animals and those less strongly armed do not need this defence. Lorenz gives chilling examples from roe deer and doves, in both of which species stronger members will slowly murder weaker ones if kept in captivity with them, because in a free state these creatures save themselves by running away, not by relying on the victor's inhibition. And it is clear that man is in some ways nearer to this group than to the wolf.

Man, before his tool-using days, was poorly armed. Without claws, beak, or horns, he must have found murder a tedious and exhausting business, and built-in inhibitions against it were therefore not necessary for survival. By the time he invented weapons, it was too late to alter his nature. He became a dangerous beast. War and vengeance are primitive human institutions, not late perversions; most cosmogonies postulate strife in Heaven, and bloodshed is taken for granted as much in the Book of Judges as in the *Iliad* or the Sagas. There may be non-aggressive societies, as anthropologists assure us, but they are white blackbirds and perhaps not so white as they are painted. It seems possible that man shows *more* savagery to his own kind than most other mammal species.[4] Rats (which Lorenz mentions) are certainly competitors. They, it seems, will normally try to kill any rat they meet of another tribe, but in compensation they never kill or seriously fight rats of their own tribe. Rats cannot therefore compete with Cain or Romulus, still less with Abimelech, the son of Gideon, who murdered, on one stone, *all* his brothers, to the number of three score and ten (Judges 11:5). An animal that did anything remotely similar would (surely rightly) be labelled 'dangerous.'

Current fashion brushes off the suggestion of so labelling man by ruling that such conduct is not due to nature, but to society. This misses the point. We are not now asking the small question whether a particular man, or even a particular group, picked up a practice from others or invented it. We are asking a much larger one; how did these proceedings originate for the human race as a whole? How are they psychologically possible, and indeed hard to eradicate, when many culturally induced things come and go lightly, and many others cannot be culturally induced even with the utmost effort and good will? For this inquiry, nature and culture are not opposites at all. We are naturally culture-building animals. But what we build into our cultures has to satisfy our natural pattern of motives.

It is also suggested that any excess of savagery in us over other species is merely due to our general power of carrying everything we do further, through culture and technology, than they. We build more thoroughly and better than the bee and the beaver; thus, too, we kill more thoroughly. There is certainly much in this. But the question still remains: *which* things do we choose to develop in this manner? Not every activity receives this sort of attention; for instance, only lately has the physical science necessary for medicine been developed. But the glorification of fighting is extremely widespread and ancient. Now if we compare the value of these two things for human life, this

glorification needs explaining. What culture has an epic poem cele-
brating the achievements of its great healer – or even of its engineer,
architect, or inventor? Isn't a creature with this bias rightly labelled
'dangerous'?

Yet he has always believed otherwise. Man, civilized Western man,
has always maintained that in a bloodthirsty world, he alone was
comparatively harmless. Consider the view of the African jungle given
by Victorian hunters. The hunter assumed that every creature he met
would attack him and accordingly shot it on sight. Of course, he didn't
want to eat it, but he could always stuff it (in order to triumph over his
human enemies), and anyway he assumed it was noxious; it would be
described in his memoirs as 'the great brute.' Drawings even exist of
giant pandas cast in this totally unconvincing role – and shot accordingly.[5] Yet in these days, game wardens and photographers habitually
treat lions as familiarly as big dogs. It is understood that so long as they
are well fed and not provoked, they are no more likely to attack you
than the average Alsatian. Much the same seems to hold of elephants
and other big game. These creatures have their own occupations, and,
unless seriously disturbed, are not anxious for a fight. Gorillas in particular are peace-loving beasts; George Schaller visited a tribe of them
for six months without receiving so much as a cross word or seeing
any quarrelling worth naming.[6] In this case, and no doubt in others,
Victorian man was deceived by confusing threatening behaviour with
attack. Gorillas do threaten, but the point is precisely to avoid combat. By looking sufficiently dreadful, a gorilla patriarch can drive off
intruders and defend his family without the trouble and danger of
actually fighting. The same thing seems to hold of the other simians,
and particularly of howler monkeys, whose dreadful wailing used to
freeze the white hunter's blood. Howlers have reduced combat to its
lowest and most satisfactory terms. When two groups of them compete for a territory, they both sit down and howl their loudest, and the
side that makes the most noise wins. That nervous white man, with his
heart in his mouth and his finger on his trigger, was among the most
dangerous things in the jungle. His weapon was at least as powerful as
those of the biggest animals, and while they attacked only what they

could eat or what was really annoying them, he would shoot at anything big enough to aim at. Why did he think they were more savage than he? Why has civilized Western man always thought so? I am not surprised that early man *disliked* wolves. When an animal tries to eat you, or even to eat your dinner, you cannot be expected to like it, and only a very occasional Buddhist will cooperate. But why did man feel so morally superior? Could he not see that the wolf's hunting him was exactly the same as his hunting the deer? (There are tribes that do think in this way, but it is Western thought that I am exploring.) And the superior feeling persists. As Lorenz remarks, people are inclined to disapprove of carnivores even when they eat other animals and not people, as though other animals all formed one species, and the carnivores were cannibals. 'The average man,' he says,

> does not judge the fox that kills a hare by the same standard as the hunter who shoots one for exactly the same reason, but with the severe censure that he would apply to a game-keeper who made a practice of shooting farmers and frying them for supper.[7]

This disapproval is very marked on the occasions when foxes do kill for sport or practice, destroying more hens than they can eat. You would not guess, to hear people talk at such times, that humans ever hunted foxes. In the same way, it makes a very disreputable impression when Jane Goodall reports that the chimpanzees she watched would occasionally catch and eat a baby baboon or colobus monkey, though they all lived amicably together most of the time and the children even played together.[8] But what else goes on on the traditional farm?

> Sing, dilly dilly duckling, come and be killed
> For you must be stuffed, and my customers filled.

The reason such parallels are hard to see is, I suggest, that *man has always been unwilling to admit his own ferocity*, and has tried to deflect attention from it by making animals out to be more ferocious than they are. Sometimes the animals themselves have been blamed and punished.

Such customs as the flaying of wolves were probably intended as punishments, though it is hard to separate this intention from magic. And certainly the wickedness of animals has often been used to justify our killing or otherwise interfering with them. It is a cockeyed sort of justification unless beasts are supposed capable of deliberation. We would probably do better to invoke our natural loyalty to our own species than to rely on our abstract superiority to others. Still, people do manage to think in this way. Their reasoning is certainly not always easy to follow. Ramona and Desmond Morris show, in a most interesting survey of medieval attitudes, how apes were regarded, not just as hideous, but as 'evil and ridiculous' – as failed and degraded human beings. Moreover,

> the ape's capacity for imitation gave rise to the odd notion that he deliberately copied human actions in order to convince people that he was really one of them. . . He became the prototype of the impostor, the fraud, the hypocrite and the flatterer.[9]

Once something is taken as the *prototype* of a particular quality, it is not easy to be convinced that it is not an *instance* of it. Nor do people seem to have tried hard to be clear on such points. The Morrises give interesting examples of the ritual execution of animals along with certain types of criminal, such as the medieval practice of hanging an ape and a dog on the gallows when a Jew was executed.[10] No doubt the animals executed were not exactly supposed guilty of a particular crime. But they were prominently pushed into the category of those for whom punishment was fitting; wickedness was deemed their climate. And there are not, I think, compensating instances of animals that symbolized virtue being *rewarded*. Nor do people seem to have hesitated to eat doves, lambs, nightingales, or any other creatures on account of their symbolic value.

Various philosophers have protested that I cannot be right in supposing that animals were thought of as evil. It would, they quite properly point out, be a gross confusion to mix up using something as the *symbol* of a vice with actually attributing a vice to it, and everybody knows that animals are as incapable of vice as they are of virtue. Why should I suppose that people were really as silly as this? Now because the evidence for a confusion tends to be confused, it is not always easy to clear up this kind of doubt. I was reflecting whether I was indeed wrong when a couple of things made me suspect that I was not. The first was a television documentary on sharks, which, though perfectly sensible on the whole, began, emphatically, with the words, 'These are the world's most vicious killers.' *Vicious?* (No evidence appeared in the film, incidentally, to suggest that sharks ever kill except in hunger or self-defence. The number of people they kill in the world yearly came out at twenty-six; the number of sharks people kill was not given, but was clearly vastly higher.) The second, nastier and more detailed, was a journalist's account of an expedition with a crocodile-hunter:

> 'Got him now,' he cried. He shook water from his hair and beard. 'We've got two wops [darts] in him; we can play him like a fish. Tire him out.' Finally we made the crocodile drag the skiff with him. He had no respite.
>
> 'That hook's caught right down in his gut. We'll have to be careful, or we'll kill him!'
>
> With the dawn the crocodile sought refuge in deep water. 'He's trying to stay down, now,' said Craig. 'He doesn't like this daylight business. . . Harass him like this, and he'll have to come up every half hour or so.'
>
> '*He's got the morality of a laser beam*,' said Craig as we sat there. . . '*The croc emerging from the egg will snap at anything that moves, no matter if it's a leech or a human leg*.' As he spoke he was tugging on a harpoon line, trying to *coax* the beast below to move. 'He's a *dedicated* killing machine, the killer of any fish or animal or bird.'[11]

This is ordinary, typical, present-day, vernacular speech and thinking; a great deal more like it has appeared in the public excitement over the film *Jaws*. If anyone can find a convincing meaning for it which does not involve dramatizing simple and primitive carnivores into conscious criminals just to boost human vanity, I shall be relieved and delighted. Terms like *machine* and *laser beam* ought to rule out such an idea. That they do not is an indication of the very confusion I complain of. Crocodiles, and particularly baby crocodiles, are indeed not highly advanced creatures; nor are sharks. For them, as for all carnivores, prey is simply food, not an enemy or a victim,[12] and to speak of their snapping reflex as *mechanical* would not be too misleading. But the words I have italicized leave no doubt that the hunter still manages to think of it as their conscious, deliberate choice to outrage the known rights of others. And the only possible reason for mentioning *a human leg* is a persuasion that this is something at which even a newly hatched crocodile could, if not very depraved, be expected to draw the line. Of course, this is silly. My point is that such silliness is neither rare nor unimportant. Consider again a very ordinary item from the *Guardian*, October 4, 1976. Under the headline ' "ANIMAL" MOTHER GAOLED,' the account began: 'An unmarried mother who brutally beat up her three young children was told by a judge when he sent her to prison for two years on assault and wounding charges, "You behaved like a wild animal." ' The judge could not, it should be noticed, have meant 'wild animals too occasionally do the sort of thing you have done.' He had to mean 'usually.' If wild animals usually did that, their evolution would have petered out long ago.

In case anyone feels that only the ignorant populace think like this, we might note too a passage in Wittgenstein's 'Lecture on Ethics.'[13] Wittgenstein is contrasting trivial accusations that can be laughed off with utterly serious ones where no such avoidance is possible. The serious case goes like this: 'Suppose I had told one of you a preposterous lie and he came up to me and said, "You're behaving like a beast..." '

There is nothing unusual about confusing a symbol with the thing symbolized, about projecting a fantasy. It is so common and yet so deadly a fault that we need constantly to scan our thought for it, and can probably never do so enough.[14] We are always seeing people who are unlike ourselves as threats or monsters. Our children are to us symbols of hope – so we tend to expect them to be hopeful, and to be upset if they fail to be so. At other times we may see them as threats, symbols of a world that does not need us – and then we are inclined to attribute to them hostile motives. Parents too get treated as animated symbols, whether of repression or security, rather than as individuals. And the literature of misogyny, from the Christian Fathers onward, is a prize museum of this sort of muddle. Mixing up a symbol with an attribution is, in fact, normal, in the sense in which failing to think hard is always normal. Among human beings, it is often best checked by the victim, the walking symbol himself, who can say, 'Hey, look – I am not that, but me.' But though animals can demonstrate the same point clearly to those who will take the trouble to visit them at home, we urban people do not very often do so.

There is, moreover, a special reason for manoeuvring animals into the position of instances and not only symbols of evil. We rightly connect the thought of virtue with that of our own species, because the virtues of that species are the ones that concern us. Human and humane are words of praise. Being inhuman is something terrible. It is easy from here to connect the notion of vice with other species. The use of words like brutal, bestial, beastly shows how readily we do this. And the temptation to treat the symbol as an attribution is the greater because distancing the quality protects our own self-esteem.

This way of thinking might, of course, have been balanced by favourable symbolizing, by occasions when we saw crocodiles, or still more, other animals such as lions, as embodiments of courage, patience, and other virtues. But favourable symbols too are read as attributions, and they tend to lead to venerating the beast, something that Jewish and Christian monotheism has always fiercely resisted. Monotheism does have a relatively hospitable side, a tradition in which animals can be seen as fellow-servants of God, or as aspects of his glory. But it also has a sharply exclusive and destructive side, in which the Lord tolerates no rival for our regard. In this mood, the church often and explicitly insisted that all plants and animals must be viewed merely as objects given to man as his instruments, that to have any sort of regard for them in themselves was sinful and superstitious folly. What is interesting is that many of those scientific humanists who most sternly rejected Christianity have continued this second tradition – but with man himself taking the place of the jealous God. Thus, Marx in the Grundrisse said that 'the great civilizing influence of capitalism' lay in its rejection of the 'deification of nature.' Thus, it was that 'nature becomes for the first time simply an object for mankind, purely a matter of utility.'[15]

The effect is an asymmetry about animal symbols. Favourable symbols are carefully demythologized, so that beasts shall not compete, first with God, then with man. It is not officially supposed that we ought to respect or be nice to actual lions or lambs on account of the Lamb of God or the Lion of Judah. But no similar trouble is taken in this tradition about unfavourable symbols. I do not mean that many learned persons would now say with the seventeenth-century writer Edward Topsell that 'serpents are the most ungentle and barbarous of creatures.'[16] But at the vernacular level, the kind of remark I have just mentioned about sharks and crocodiles is very common, and very similar. Moreover, the crack or fault in thought that it expresses runs through a great deal of much more ambitious thinking. The problem of how to relate man to other species remains unconsidered in a shadowy area where it naturally neighbours the problem of evil. Vapours from it float, uncriticized and hardly noticed, into arguments where they have no business. A common example is the way in which writers who want, for some reason, to praise or emphasize a particular quality in human life frequently say that it is 'what distinguishes us from the animals' without trying even casually to get the facts of the comparison right. But for the moment, I am more interested in the philosophic use of the Beast Within than in our attitude to Beasts Without.

BEASTS WITHIN

The philosopher's Beast Within is a lawless monster to whom nothing is forbidden. It is so described both by moralists like Plato, who are against it, and by moralists like Nietzsche, who are for it. Here is a typical passage from Book 9 of the *Republic*, where Plato is talking about our more unpleasant desires. These

> bestir themselves in dreams, when the gentler part of the soul slumbers, and the control of Reason is withdrawn. Then the Wild Beast

in us, full-fed with meat and drink, becomes rampant and shakes off sleep to go in quest of what will gratify its own instincts. As you know, it will cast off all shame and prudence at such moments and stick at nothing. In phantasy it will not shrink from intercourse with a mother or anyone else, man, god or brute, or from forbidden food or any deed of blood. It will go to any lengths of shamelessness and folly.[17]

Consider how odd the image is, in spite of its familiarity. Why not say, 'I have these thoughts in my off moments'? Why not at least the Other Man within? What is gained by talking about the Beast?

Here is Nietzsche, speaking of the Lion he invokes to break the chain of convention:

To create for himself freedom for new creation – for this the Lion's strength is sufficient, To create for himself freedom, and an holy Nay even to duty; therefore, my brethren, is there need of the Lion. Once it loved as holiest Thou Shalt – Now it must see illusion and tyranny even in its holiest, that it may snatch freedom even from its love – For this there is need of the Lion.[18]

But in the world, there is no such Beast. To talk of a beast is to talk of a thing with its own laws. If lions really did not draw the line at anything – if they went around mating with crocodiles, ignoring territory, eating poisonous snakes, and killing their own cubs – they would not *be* lions, nor, as a species, would they last long. This abstract Beast is a fancy on the level of the eighteenth century's idea of a Savage, noble or otherwise.

Sensible eighteenth-century people reacted to Rousseau's suggestion of taking 'savages' seriously very much in the same way that many sensible people today react to the idea of taking animals seriously. They thought it obviously outrageous, because their notion of a 'savage' was a totally unreal and standardized abstraction. They could not believe in any continuity between such mythical beings and real people – because, of course, a mythical being *is* something discontinuous with a real person. He differs in logical type.

Here are some of Dr Johnson's comments:

> A savage would as willingly have his meat sent to him in the kitchen, as eat it at the table here; as men become civilized various modes of denoting honourable preference are invented.
>
> Pity is not natural to man. Children are always cruel. Savages are always cruel. Pity is acquired and improved by the cultivation of reason.
>
> [On the question whether marriage was natural] Sir, a savage man and a savage woman meet by chance, and when the man sees another woman that pleases him better, he will leave the first.

And, in a rather fuller discussion:

> A gentleman expressed a wish to go and live three years at Otaheite, or New Zealand, in order to obtain a full acquaintance with people so totally different from all we have ever known, and be satisfied what pure nature can do for man. JOHNSON. 'What can you learn, Sir? What can savages tell, but what they have themselves seen?. . . The inhabitants of Otaheite and New Zealand are not in a state of pure nature, for it is plain they broke off from some other people. Had they grown out of the ground, you might have judged of a state of pure nature. Fanciful people talk of a mythology being amongst them, but it must be invention. They have once had religion, which has been gradually debased. And what account of their religion can you suppose to be learnt from savages?'[19]

By 'savage,' Johnson simply meant someone unfitted for society, without manners, virtues, friendly ties, skills, or sympathetic feelings, a negation of all that was admirable or interesting in people as he knew them. That this description actually applied to all primitive peoples seemed to him obvious. Yet in fact it applied to none. The last quotation shows the heart of the confusion – the idea that what is natural is to be discovered from isolation experiments, from observing creatures 'grown out of the ground' instead of by using one's intelligence to sort out the innate from the acquired elements in existing social behaviour.

Comparison with other cultures is a help because, as Eibl-Eibesfeldt puts it in *Love and Hate*:

> One may take as a starting-point that man's tendency is to vary cultur- ally whatever can be modified. In New Guinea alone several hundred dialects are spoken. This is bound up with the tendency of human beings to isolate themselves into small groups. . . But if one finds in spite of this, in certain situations, such as in greeting, or in the behaviour of the mother towards her child, the same behaviour pat- terns recur repeatedly and among the most different peoples, then it is highly probable that these are innate behaviour patterns.
>
> (p. 13)

This is quite different from expecting to find a mythical Raw or Unconditioned Man.

What anthropology did for this myth, ethology now does for the Beast myth. Kipling's Law of the Jungle is much nearer to reality than this fancy of the moralists. Beasts are neither incarnations of wick- edness, nor sets of basic needs, nor crude mechanical toys, nor idiot children. They are beasts, each with its own very complex nature. Most of them fail in most respects to conform to their mythical stereotype. This is very marked in the matter of sexual indulgence, something to which the mythical Beast is supposed to be addicted. Desmond Morris really should not have needed to point out that, among animal species, it is *Homo sapiens* that gives an exceptional amount of time and attention to his sexual life. For most species, a brief mating season and a simple instinctive pattern make of it a sea- sonal disturbance with a definite routine, comparable to Christmas shopping. It is in human life that sex plays, for good or ill, a much more serious and central part. With no other species could a Freud- ian theory ever have got off the ground. Gorillas, in particular, take so little interest in sex that they shock Robert Ardrey: he concludes that they are in their decadence.[20] Yet Tolstoy, speaking of the life of systematic sexual indulgence, called it 'the ideal of monkeys or Parisians.'[21]

If then there is no lawless beast outside man, it seems very strange to conclude that there is one inside him. It would be more natural to say that the beast within us gives us partial order; the task of conceptual thought will only be to complete it. But the opposite, *a priori*, reasoning has prevailed. If the Beast Within was capable of every iniquity, people reasoned, then beasts without probably were too. This notion made man anxious to exaggerate his difference from all other species and to ground all activities he valued in capacities unshared by the animals, whether the evidence warranted it or no. In a way this evasion does the species credit, because it reflects our horror at the things we do. Man fears his own guilt and insists on fixing it on something evidently alien and external. Beasts Within solve the problem of evil. This false solution does man credit because it shows the power of his conscience, but all the same it is a dangerous fib. The use of the Beast Within as a scapegoat for human wickedness has led to some bad confusion, not only about beasts (which might not matter) but about Man. I suspect that Man began to muddle himself at the point where he said 'The Woman beguiled me, and I did eat,' and the woman said the same about the Serpent.

Let us consider the predicament of primitive man. He is not without natural inhibitions, but his inhibitions are weak. He cannot, like the dove or the roe deer, cheerfully mince up his family in cold blood and without provocation. (If he could, he would certainly not have survived long after the invention of weapons, nor could the prolonged demanding helplessness of human infants ever have been tolerated.) He has a certain natural dislike for such activities, but it is weak and often overborne. He does horrible things and is filled with remorse afterwards. These conflicts are pre-rational; they do not fall between his reason and his primitive motives, but between two groups of those primitive motives themselves. They are not the result of thinking; more likely they are among the things that first made him think. They are not the result of social conditioning; they are part of its cause. Intelligence is evolved as a way of dealing with puzzles, an alternative to the strength that can kick its way past them or the inertness that can hide from them. And anger presents as tough a puzzle as any. The preoccupation of our early literature with bloodshed, guilt and vengeance suggests to me that these problems occupied man from a very early time. I would add that only a creature of this intermediate kind, with inhibitions that are weak *but genuine*, would ever have been likely to develop a morality. Conceptual thought formalizes and extends what instinct started.

To show that these suggestions about early man are not entirely off the mark, let us look at Bronze Age behaviour as seen in the *Iliad*. I choose the *Iliad* because historically it lies behind Plato and Plato lies behind the modern tradition I complain of. I do not make the mistake of supposing it a genuinely primitive document, applicable to Early Man as Such – but what can we do? It is one of the earliest available in a shape we can come to grips with, and the tradition is our own.

I want to go back to the question of rituals of submission – to the wolf that cannot bite its conquered enemy. Lorenz remarks, 'Homer's heroes were certainly not as soft-hearted as the wolves at Whipsnade. The poet cites numerous incidents where the suppliant is slaughtered, with or without compunction.' This is true, but the interesting thing is that the appeals were made. Counting carefully, one finds that the score is indeed gloomy; in the *Iliad*, there are six appeals and six failures. Moreover, all the suppliants are Trojans, that is, 'the other side,' and part of the point of the incidents clearly is to show Greeks in a position of power, exulting over an abject enemy. So far, so bad. But there is more to say. Achilles, refusing mercy, explains that before his friend Patroclus was killed, he used to *prefer* taking prisoners alive and selling them; it is grief and the desire for vengeance that stops him from doing so any more. In fact, most of these incidents take place just as the war reaches its climax; plainly it has had more desultory stages that Homer did not find worth singing about. There are two suppliants who offer large ransoms, and one of them nearly has his offer accepted, but his captor's brother intervenes and prevents the bargain. The *Iliad* is of course an aristocratic document, which is why little is said of the commercial spirit behind these transactions, but it is clear that that was working vigorously here in the cause of civilization. Greed and laziness were, as often, good counterpoises to violence.

Should we assume that they were the only counterpoises, that there was no direct objection to killing the helpless? I don't think we can, for this reason. The Homeric atmosphere is extremely honest and unhypocritical; nobody professes high sentiments just for looks, and nobody would believe him if he did. Yet throughout the *Iliad* runs a most ambivalent attitude to war and violence; although they are man's noblest occupation, they are terrible, piteous, lamentable, miserable, a curse and a disaster to mortals. And this too has the ring of a perfectly sincere sentiment. The God of War is constantly abused as a plague and a mischief-maker, without whom everything would go well. And in spite of the failure of supplication on the battlefield, much is said of the rights of suppliants, much of the anger of the gods against those who trample on such rights. And later Greek writings show that these suggestions were not intended or received as humbug; the rights of suppliants are an extremely serious matter with the tragedians. Nor are they enforced by social contract arguments or by prudence, but simply by insisting on the horror of the act. Even the ineffective pleas in Homer are often extremely moving; in fact, it is this very ambivalence that makes the *Iliad* a great poem, instead of a butcher's catalogue. In short, the poem speaks with two voices; it deplores what it glories in, and so somebody must take the blame.

In the *Iliad*, beasts are not needed for this role; the answer to the problem of evil is always simple; if you cannot blame the enemy, blame the gods. I think this function of gods as scapegoats has been somewhat overlooked in the history of religion; it seems very important. Where a man feels guilty and is genuinely anxious to apologize to those whom he has injured, there is much to be said for having been misled by an irresistible outside force. This pre-serves his self-respect and also his friendship for the victim. We say today, 'I just don't know what came over me,' but the Homeric Greeks did know; they could specify Zeus or Ares. All the vilest and stupidest acts in the *Iliad* result from suggestions from the gods, and anybody who really wants to apologize simply states as much. The crudest case is that of Agamemnon who, when he finally wants to withdraw from his idiotic quarrel with Achilles, apologizes by explaining that Zeus drove him mad. At this, the attentive reader will open his eyes, since the poem describes all about the beginning of that quarrel, and it was one of the few occasions when no god *did* intervene. But Agamemnon's reasoning is simple: If I did it, I must have been mad, and only Zeus could madden a king. *Quem deus vult perdere, prius dementat.*[22] No thunderbolts strike him, for the explanation is universally accepted.

It almost seems a pity that the development of religion and morality should have put an end to this convenient way of thinking. They did, however, and as the Greek notion of the gods grew steadily more dignified and noble, the problem, 'Whom can I blame for my faults?' again became pressing. I do not think it is any accident that Plato, the first Greek who consistently wrote of the gods as good, was also the first active exponent of the Beast Within. Black horses, wolves, lions, hawks, asses, and pigs recur every time he mentions the subject of evil; they provide the only terms in which he can talk about it. This is not an idle stylistic device: there is no such thing in Plato. His serious view is that evil is something alien to the soul; something Other, the debasing effect of matter seeping in through the instinctive nature. This treacherous element clearly cannot be anything properly human; it must be described in animal terms – and those of no particular animal at that, since all particular animals have their redeeming features, but a dreadful composite monster combining all the vices: in short, the Beast Within, whose only opponent is the Rational Soul. Certainly good feeling is sometimes invoked too, and given body as a Good Beast, but its goodness is supposed to consist in its obedience to Reason, not in its contributing anything itself. The white horse willingly obeys the charioteer and helps him to restrain the black;[23] it is no Balaam's Ass that hazards its own suggestions. Accordingly, the feelings named in this connection are shame, ambition, the sense of honour, *never, for instance, pity or affection, where the body might be held to make good suggestions to the soul.* Plato's map excludes such a possibility. This exclusion has been both morally and psychologically disastrous. Fear of and contempt for feeling make up an irrational prejudice built into the structure of European rationalism.[24]

ARISTOTELIAN AND KANTIAN BEASTS

Aristotle, though in general he was much more convinced of man's continuity with the physical world than Plato, makes some equally odd uses of the contrast between man and beast. In the *Nicomachean Ethics* (1.7), he asks what the true function of man is, in order to see what his happiness consists in, and concludes that that function is the life of reason *because that life only is peculiar to man.* I do not quarrel for the moment with the conclusion but with the argument. If peculiarity to man is the point, why should one not say that the function of man is technology, or the sexual goings-on noted by Desmond Morris, or even exceptional ruthlessness to one's own species? In all these respects, man seems to be unique. It must be shown *separately* that this differentia is itself the best human quality, that it is the point where humanity is excellent as well as exceptional. And it is surely possible a priori that the point on which humanity is excellent is one in which it is *not* wholly unique – that at least some aspect of it might be shared with other beings. Animals are, I think, used in this argument to point up by contrast the value of reason, to give examples of irrational conduct whose badness will seem obvious to us. But unless we start with a particular view about the importance of reason in conduct, we shall not necessarily agree. If we prefer, among humans, an impulsively generous act to a cold-blooded piece of calculation, we shall not be moved from our preference by the thought that the generous act is more like an animal's. Nor ought we to be. The claims of reason must be made good, if at all, within the boundaries of human life itself. They could be strengthened by contrasts with other species only if it were true, as sometimes seems to be suggested, that animals were, in fact, invariably wicked.

Arguments of this form have, however, flowed on unchecked. One of them is used by Kant in his early *Lectures on Ethics*, where, in the course of some rather sharp remarks about sex, he says, 'Sexuality exposes man to the danger of equality with the beasts.'[25] But how can there be such a danger? The logic of this complaint deserves attention. To be *like* the beasts is not always considered bad, since we share with them many habits, such as washing and nest-building, and the care of the young, which everybody approves of. The point might be that beasts give more time and attention to sex than people, or are more promiscuous. But even if this were true, it would not *alone* show that they were wrong to do so, or that people would be wrong to imitate them – not unless one had shown separately that animals always *were* wrong, or that people should never imitate them. This would be hard in the face of such advice as 'Go to the Ant, thou sluggard,' or 'Be ye wise as serpents and harmless as doves.' There are many activities, such as eating bananas, where the accusation 'You are behaving like an animal' could properly be met with the answer, 'But I *am* an animal.' We need to be shown – again, separately, and within the context of human life – why a particular activity is unsuitable to people. Otherwise the reference to animals here follows a form often used in popular morality when mention is made of any group considered inferior – we will call them Gonks. The argument runs:

> Some Gonkish practices are abominable
> This is a Gonkish practice
> Therefore this practice is abominable.

The only thing that could make an honest argument of this would be a real universal major premise, and in the case of animals such a premise has often been half-consciously accepted. If one assumes that *everything* animals do is evil or inferior, then the argument takes on some force. The vices of the monstrous Beast Within are being projected onto actual animals.

Kant does not really need this argument at all. The dangers that he sees in sexuality can be, and are, much better expressed in terms more central to his ethics. They are dangers of treating people as things, treating them without respect, using them as means and not as ends in themselves. These are intelligible concepts. But the notion of humanity Kant uses in developing them is an odd one, and its oddity is again brought out by his attitude to animals. He wants us to respect humanity because it is rational, not because it is conscious. We wonder about lunatics, about the old, about babies. Kant is adamant that everything in human form must be respected, but has he any business to be so? Animals give an interesting test; can we treat them as things? Or are they too ends in themselves? Kant says they are not ends in themselves because they are not rational, so we cannot have any duties to them and we may treat them simply as means to our own ends. This does not mean that we may be cruel to them. But the reason for not being cruel is that cruelty would debase our own nature. It is therefore our duty to ourselves to avoid this defilement. But why it should be a defilement we don't know. There seems to be no official reason why Kant should not say, with Spinoza, that animals, though conscious, are entirely at the disposal of man, and can be used as suits his purposes. If these purposes are otherwise impor- tant, even if they involve giving great pain to the animal, no objection could arise on Spinoza's principles, nor as far as I can see on Kant's either.[26] There would therefore seem to be no objection to enjoying giv- ing pain either. I do not just mean that the objections would be weak: I think they would be meaningless. This view seems very forced, almost as forced as Descartes' contention that animals are actually unconscious.[27] If you think cruelty wrong in general – which Kant certainly did – it seems devious to say that cruelty to animals is wrong for entirely differ- ent reasons from cruelty to people. What I have said about Plato, Aris- totle, and Kant has, I hope, shown that the use of animals as symbols of wickedness has done ethics no good, and that arguments based on it are irrelevant. But are they positively misleading? I think they are. In the first place, irrelevance itself misleads, because it distracts. Insofar as people looked for the source of evil in their animal nature, which was some- thing they could not possibly alter, they were kept occupied by a contest they could not win. They either gave their energies to trying to jump off their shadows or grew depressed at the difficulty of their position and gave up altogether. This defect is obvious in Platonism, in Stoicism and in their influence on Christianity. The trouble is that animal nature is regarded, not just as containing specific dangers, but either as evil all through or at least as totally chaotic and without any helpful principle of order. It follows that there can be no sense in trying to organize it on its own principles and no sense in studying it to see what those principles might be. Order must be imposed from outside by Reason or Grace – again a hopeless task, for why should a chaotic animal take any notice of Grace or Reason? But of course such animal nature is an unreal abstraction. Every existing animal species has its own nature, its own hierarchy of instincts – in a sense, its own virtues. In social animals, such as ourselves and the wolves, there must be natural affection and communicativeness, and, in spite of our evolutionary gaffe in inventing weapons, it is plain that we are much better fitted to live socially than to live alone or in anarchy. Nearly all our most interesting occupations are social ones. Rousseau's or Hobbes's state of nature would be fine for intelligent crocodiles, if there were any. For people, it is a baseless fantasy.

Nor does our richness in aggression disprove this.[28] It is one of Lorenz's most interesting suggestions that only creatures capable of aggression toward their own kind are capable of affection. In order to distinguish some of one's species as friends, it may be necessary at the same time to distinguish others as enemies. At the simplest level, in order to express one's love for A, it may be necessary sometimes to attack B, or at least to threaten him. Ambivalence may be ancient indeed. However that may be, he is clearly right in saying that aggression is directly bound up in most of the activities we value, and cannot simply be dropped like an old sock. It is part of our nature. But he does not mean that we cannot get along without bloodshed. For our nature is not Plato's and Nietzsche's Beast Without the Law. It is a complex, balanced affair, a structure like the Beasts Within other beasts, subject to a lot of laws, and rather more, not less, adaptable than others, because where they grew horns and prickles, we grew an intelligence, which is quite an effective adaptive mechanism. Where fighting is inconvenient, we can play chess or sue each other. Even the Beasts Within other beasts are much more adaptable here than has been believed. In particular, if they do not get what they want, they will accept something else instead. When they thirst for blood and cannot catch their enemy, they work it off by mock attacks on empty air or pieces of wood or the surrounding scenery, or by making noises, or by driving off neighbours or casual passers-by whom they do not usually hurt. This is called *redirection*.[29] Alternatively, they turn vigorously to some apparently irrelevant activity; this is called *displacement*.[30] It is very clear that without these devices most living creatures would long ago have pined away or burst from disappointment, since actually getting what one wants must be one of the world's rarest experiences. Of course, these things are possible for people, and we all practise them constantly. (The behaviour of anybody waiting impatiently for something will supply excellent examples.) But it is part of the mythical natural history of the Beast Within that it must have blood – that it will not be content to swear, break dishes, play squash or write to the newspapers instead. The limits of displacement and redirection for the human species are not clear; we have all seen that they can stretch quite wide. The 'non-aggressive' cultures cited by anthropologists provide some pretty examples. Margaret Mead's Arapesh, for instance, devote much of their lives to precautions against hostile sorcery,[31] and Ruth Benedict's Zuni Indians, while given to an apparently less sinister form of magic, openly use it as a means and a pretext for the control of aggression, which seems a rather different thing from not being aggressive in the first place.[32] ('The fundamental tabu upon their holy men during their periods of office is against any suspicion of anger.') Such ways of conducting the lightning are just the kind of thing that Lorenz wants us to study; he merely suggests that seeing them *as* displacement activities may enable us to understand them better, that ethological studies might well be useful here along with the obvious psychological and anthropological ones. But for this purpose, we must honestly recognize our own pugnacity, and modify the notion of the characteristically human that has been accepted both by common opinion and by philosophers. Neither Beasts Without nor Beasts Within are as beastly as they have been painted.

NOTES

1. Notice the word *normally* here. It has to be used or understood in describing the life of any plant or animal; there are always exceptions. Because putting it in every line is tedious, one sometimes omits it, and this must, it seems, be the reason why many people firmly believe that Lorenz said that animals

never murder others of their species, or at least that wolves never do so. This belief is a complete mistake. Lorenz describes such inhibitions as needing to be *adequate* (that is, to the purpose of preventing extinction) and says that *the most reliable* ones are found among 'the most bloodthirsty predators.' But 'the most reliable' examples of anything do not have to be infallible. And in fact he explicitly emphasizes that 'there is no absolute reliance on these inhibitions, which may occasionally fail' (*On Aggression*, p. 129) and gives examples, including infanticide in foxes (p. 119). Similarly in *King Solomon's Ring* he writes of 'the innate, instinctive, fixed inhibitions that prevent an animal from using his weapons *indiscriminately* against his own kind' (p. 196, my italics). Roe deer and solitary carnivores do use them indiscriminately; wolves and even hyenas do not.

2. *Never Cry Wolf* (Boston, 1963). See also R. Fiennes, *The Order of Wolves* (London, 1976) and L.E. Bueler's *Wild Dogs of the World* (London, 1974).

3. Again, *adequate* does not mean *total*. Since Lorenz wrote, much observation has been made of lions, a species whose inhibition is much less strong – but then, so is their sociality. For other carnivores and their customs, see Edward O. Wilson, *Sociobiology: The New Synthesis* (Cambridge, Mass., Harvard University Press, 1975) pp. 246–7. Wolves and wild dogs clearly are somewhat special. But the point here is not how widely the inhibition works in any given carnivorous species. It is that it does not work adequately in man. If it did, we should not need law or morality to restrain violence.

4. See p. 75 for the non-aggressive societies. Wilson flatly denies that man shows *more savagery*, saying 'murder is far more common and hence normal in many vertebrate species than in man . . . even when our episodic wars are averaged in' (*Sociobiology*, p. 247). How does one check such things? Certainly, since Lorenz wrote, evidence has come in that some animals are bloodier than had been supposed. No doubt this should be cheering to the human race. Beyond this, Wilson suggests that a Martian zoologist, visiting 'a randomly picked human population,' would probably see little violence. But he probably would not see much theft or sexual activity either, yet both go on. Those of us who lead protected lives do not find it easy to believe in serious wife- and child-beating, but they are evidently quite common. And how would one compute the chances of his running into a riot, a raid, or a massacre, let alone a war? These cannot just be averaged in; they are qualitatively special. The main point, however, is not to set up a contest of merit, but to make it plain that man resembles other species in having a serious problem to solve here. It is rather common now to resist this suggestion by claiming that the frequency of aggression is just an invention of the poets and historians. Were this true, it would be absolutely extraordinary: what motive, other than aggression itself, could account for such monstrous misrepresentation?

5. See *Men and Pandas* by Ramona and D. Morris (London, 1966). Giant pandas are of course wholly vegetarian, and defend themselves only if cornered.

6. See G.Schaller, *The Year of the Gorilla* (Chicago, 1964).

7. Konrad Lorenz, *King Solomon's Ring* (New York, 1952), p. 183.

8. Jane Goodall, *In the Shadow of Man* (Boston, 1971). See her index, under Predatory Behaviour.

9. Ramona and D. Morris, *Men and Apes* (London, 1966), pp. 28, 35.

10. Ibid., p. 31.

11. *Observer* colour supplement, 15 February 1976, my italics.

12. For the radical distinction between predation and aggression, see Lorenz, *On Aggression*, p. 24.

13. *Philosophical Review* 74 (1965), 3–12.

14. I. Murdoch discusses this fault well in the second and third essays in *The Sovereignty of Good* (London, 1970).

15. Quoted by Passmore, *Man's Responsibility for Nature*, p. 24, in a fascinating, if depressing, account of the process.

16. Quoted in Ramona and D. Morris, *Men and Snakes* (London, 1965), p. 41.

17. *Republic* 9. 571c, tr. Francis Cornford.

18. *Thus Spake Zarathustra*, Pt. 1, 'Discourse of the Three Metamorphoses', tr. Tille and Bozman.

19. Boswell, *Life of Johnson* (Everyman ed.), 2, 253; 1, 271; 1, 241; and 2, 34.

20. *African Genesis* (London, 1967), pp. 126–7. See also Schaller, *Year of the Gorilla*, p. 122.

21. In *The Kreutzer Sonata*. For further comparison of human sexuality with that of other primate species, see W. Wickler's book, *The Sexual Code* (London, 1969), and his article, 'Socio-Sexual Signals' in *Primate Ethology*, ed. D. Morris (London, 1967).

22. Whom God wishes to ruin, he first drives mad.

23. Plato, *Phaedrus* 254–7.

24. I shall develop this point further in Chapter 3.

25. 'Duties towards the Body in Respect of Sexual Impulse', I.Kant, *Lectures on Ethics*, tr. L. Infield (London, 1930), p. 164.

26. Kant, 'Duties towards Animals and Spirits', *Lectures on Ethics*. I shall be pursuing the very important point raised by Kant both there and in Chapter 10, pp. 218ff.

27. For Descartes, see the second section of Chapter 3.

28. Recent discussions of this topic have been sidetracked by the suggestion that the word *aggression* properly has only a political sense, that it means only official, formalized warfare. This seems quite out of accord with usage. It has been in common use throughout this century as the name of a motive, that is, of the wish or tendency to *attack* – privately or publicly, physically or emotionally, literally or metaphorically. ('He is chock-full of aggression.') That is how I use it. Wilson (*Sociobiology* pp. 22, 242, 578) suggests reserving the name *aggression* for the act ('an abridgment of the rights of another'), while calling the motive aggressiveness. This will not work because (a) without the motive, an injurious act is not a piece of aggression at all (it might be, for instance, an accident or a piece of self-defence), and (b) if the motive is there, we can still show aggression by gestures and so on, even if we do no damage. Moreover, the notion of 'rights' is quite obscure.

29. See Lorenz, *On Aggression*, index under *Redirected Activity*. Of all the ethological concepts I have come across, this seems to me the most significant politically, for it is something we usually manage not to recognize in ourselves, telling ourselves that the people on whom we work off our anger actually *are* abominable. Yet bystanders can see our self-deception plainly. Victims often cannot escape, as passing animals usually can, because human society roots them in their place. Thus, dozens of human iniquities from wife-beating to racism are caused by the passing on of offence.

30. See Tinbergen, *The Herring Gull's World* (London, 1953), Chapter 7. Displacement is also of great general interest in that, in a clear sense, it *explains* embarrassment – an essential job which I don't think has been properly done before. I suspect also that many of our activities are unsatisfying because they are really displacement activities. Overeating and much sexual activity may be examples.

31. Mead, *Sex and Temperament in Three Primitive Societies* (New York, 1935).

32. Benedict, *Patterns of Culture* (Boston, 1934), Chapter 4.

3

SPEECH AND OTHER EXCELLENCES

THE LURE OF THE SIMPLE DISTINCTION

Man has always had a good opinion of himself, and with reason. What, however, is essentially the ground of it? What finally (you may ask) does distinguish man from the animals?

Nearly everything is wrong with this question.

First – as I have been saying – unless we take man to be a machine or an angel, it should read 'distinguish man among the animals,' and animals of this planet at that, with no extraterrestrial nonsense to give us all the drawbacks of religion and none of its benefits.

Second, as the question is usually put, it asks for a single, simple, final distinction, and for one that confers praise. This results, I suppose, from the old tradition of defining things by genus and differentia; that is, by naming first the class to which each thing belongs, and

DOI: 10.4324/9781003588160-5

then the characteristic which marks it out from other members of that class. This rather hopeful scheme is supposed to enable us to find a formula stating the essence of each thing (or rather of each natural kind). And the differentia ought indeed to be in some way the thing's characteristic excellence, its central function – since that, and not just some chance quality (as in 'featherless biped'), is useful in helping us to place it sensibly, in telling us, therefore, what it is really like. The old, more or less Aristotelian, definition of man as a rational animal follows this pattern and is its best-known example.[1] Now most people today would with good reason reject this scheme as too ambitious to use outside the human scene. We cannot expect (they would agree) that things not made by man will necessarily have an essence we can grasp and a simple characteristic excellence we can see the point of. Evaluating snails from the human point of view is a fallible process and should be taken as such. We can certainly find marks that will help us to classify and understand them. But we had better not claim that by doing so we have finally expressed their true nature in a simple formula.

People are slower, however, to see that the same obstacle blocks us when we ask: What is the characteristic excellence of Man? If we mean 'what would seem distinctive about him to a nonhuman observer?' we would need first to know that observer's frame of reference, and what contrasts would strike him. If we mean 'what is the best and most important thing within human life?', the question is a real one, and we can try to answer it. But it is not about biological classification. It is a question in moral philosophy. And we do not help ourselves at all in answering it if we decide in advance that the answer ought to be a single, simple characteristic, unshared by other species, such as the differentia is meant to be. Why should a narrow morality necessarily be the right one? Why should not our excellence involve our whole nature? The Platonic exaltation of the intellect above all our other faculties is a particular moral position and must be defended as such against others; it cannot ride into acceptance on the back of a crude method of taxonomy. Oversimplicity, in fact, is what wrecks the notion of essence. Grading qualities as more and less essential – that is, more and less important to the species concerned – is not silly at all. Aristotle was doing this when he rejected two-footedness as a proper genus for man. It simply was not central enough in the life of the species; 'Bird and Man for instance are two-footed, but their two-footedness is diverse and differentiated.'[2] Birds and men, in fact, have dispensed with the support of forefeet for distinct though parallel reasons; if one mentioned those reasons, calling birds winged or flying animals and men handed or manipulative ones, one would be saying things of much greater interest. Flying and having hands are fairly essential properties, in that they make a great difference in the characteristic life of the creature. They are helpful in explaining it, where the negative 'two-footed' is not. Similarly, Lorenz criticizes Desmond Morris for

> over-emphasizing, in his book *The Naked Ape*, the beastliness of man . . . He minimizes the unique properties and faculties of man in an effectively misleading manner. The outstanding and biologically relevant property of the human species is neither its partial hairlessness nor its 'sexiness', but its capacity for conceptual thought.[3]

Lorenz's point is that conceptual thought is a *structural* property, one affecting the whole organization of the life of the species, while hairlessness and 'sexiness' in his view are minor, more local properties that affect it much less pervasively. And because each species does have its own way of life, structural properties can indeed be unique to a species. But not all of them are, and even where they are unique, that does not prove them excellent, even from the species' own point of view. Any species can have pervasive and characteristic bad habits. Conversely, what is good does not have to be unique to a species. For instance, in describing beavers, we should certainly say that their engineering capacity was one of their most outstanding features. But this does not isolate them. The elements of this capacity are present in their heritage: beavers are rodents, and gnawing, burrowing, and building industriously are a part of rodent life. And termites build, moles burrow, bees are industrious. What makes beavers special is a particular *combination and further development* of these basic faculties. Again, if we consider the extraordinarily keen and effective eyes of birds of prey, we are not forced to isolate them. We need to know that all birds have pretty good sight, which is necessary to flying, and that predators in general have to be sharper and better equipped than their prey. Or again, if the talk is of elephants, we can do justice to the miracle of the trunk without pretending that nobody else has a nose.

Structural properties, then, do not have to be exclusive or necessarily excellent. Nor do they have to be black-or-white, yes-or-no matters. And certainly no one of them is enough alone to define or explain a species. We commonly employ a cluster of them, whose arrangement as *more* or *less essential* can be altered from time to time for many reasons. And what is really characteristic is the shape of the whole cluster.

The various things that have been proposed as differentia for man – conceptual thought or reason, language, culture, self-consciousness, tool-using, productivity, laughter, a sense of the future, and all the rest – form part of such a cluster, but none of them can monopolize it or freeze it into finality. There are always more that we have not thought of mentioning yet, and among them the most obvious. What would we say about someone who had all the characteristics just mentioned, but none of the normal human affections? These, of course, are plainly very like those of many other species, so they do not get named as the differentia. But shortage of them is the commonest reason for calling people inhuman. Because of this sort of thing, it is really not possible to find a mark that distinguishes man from 'the animals' without saying *which* animals. We resemble different ones in different ways. It is also essential to remember how immensely they differ from one another. In certain central respects, all social mammals, including us, are far more like one another than any is like a snake or a codfish, or even a bee.

The logical point is simply that, in general, living creatures are quite unlike mathematical terms, whose essence really can be expressed in a simple definition. A triangle without three sides ceases to be a triangle. But a flightless bird does not cease to be a bird, nor a flying fish a fish. What is special about each creature is not a single, unique quality but a rich and complex arrangement of powers and qualities, some of which it will certainly share with its neighbours. And the more complex the species, the more true this is. To expect a single differentia is absurd. And it is not even effectively flattering to the species, since it obscures our truly characteristic richness and versatility.

People therefore need not act as if they were threatened every time something that has been supposed an exclusively human attribute is detected in other creatures. Considering the carelessness, and the real ignorance about other animals, which reigned when these criteria were set up, and also the still persisting reluctance to look at them dispassionately, we are bound to keep finding such attributes. The effect of dodging the situation by resetting the criteria each time in a way that it is hoped animals will be unable to penetrate is to separate the human differentia further and further from our central faculties. Nobody doubts that plenty of tests can be invented for aspects of language, tool use, foresight, and so on, which only man will be able to pass – though, as has already become clear, we cannot know in advance which they will be. But what reason could there possibly be for supposing that the faculties for passing those tests would be man's central and most important faculties? Is man perhaps centrally a test-passing animal? To read some of the literature, you might think so.

This notion of the human differentia has been misused in various ways. For instance, early in *The German Ideology*, Marx said:

> Men can be distinguished from animals by consciousness, by religion or anything else you like. They themselves begin to distinguish themselves from animals as soon as they begin to *produce* their means of subsistence . . . By producing their means of subsistence, men are indirectly producing their actual material life.
>
> . . . As individuals express their life, so they are. What they are, therefore, coincides with their production.[4]

In what sense do other animals *not* produce their means of subsistence?

Two interpretations of *producing* suggest themselves: one, the processing of materials rather than simply gathering them; two, the free and deliberate planning of what one does, whether it be gathering, processing, or anything else. On the first criterion, bees, beavers, and termites do at least as well as the simpler hunting-and-gathering human tribes, which shows, again, that you have to consider which animals you are distinguishing yourself from. On the second, man is indeed in a special position, but then he is so for everything he does, not just for production. Which did Marx mean? A passage from the *Paris MS* is just as ambivalent: 'Productive life is species-life . . . The whole character of a species, its generic character, is contained in its manner of vital activity, and free conscious activity is the species-characteristic of man.' This, however, gives the main emphasis not to production, but to free conscious choice. That is something found over a much wider range of activity than mere production, and certainly is a human structural characteristic, though by no means our only one. Conscious choice seems to be what Marx meant by contrasting men's 'beginning to distinguish themselves from animals' with their merely being distinguished from without to suit the special interest of some classifier. Marx, however, wanted to combine this general Kantian point with something much more specific, a concentration on man as Maker. Anthony Quinton, to whom I owe these quotations, remarks:

> This conception of human essence is Marx's materialist correction of Hegel's idealist and more or less Aristotelian notion of man as an essentially rational being. Man is, indeed, essentially rational for Marx but his reason is actualized in productive activity.[5]

This is certainly right, but I think the point must be put more widely. *Everybody* after Aristotle who proposed this sort of definition of man was arguing with Aristotle, was commenting in one way or another on the definition of man as a rational animal, and was taking previous contributions for granted. Marx did not want to deny the rationality; he wanted to give it a different twist. But to do this effectively, we need a quite different frame of argument, one where a number of different elements, all recognized as essential parts of human life, are explicitly considered together and set out in an intelligible order of priority. To do this, we have to drop the simple differentia scheme and leave any question of distinctness from other species right out of the argument. If another species were, in fact, found which did just what Marx meant by producing, it would not damage his argument about the structure of human life at all. The insistence on exclusiveness, in which so much intellectual capital has been invested, does no work whatever in the argument.[6]

DESCARTES: REASON AND LANGUAGE

The very great influence of one metaphysical scheme has, however, long made dropping the idea of the differentia impossible. This is Descartes' view of mind and body as radically divided in such a way that animals other than men cannot possibly have minds. Since this scheme places everything of value in the mind, it makes the human differentia a necessary piece of apparatus. And it has widely survived his view of the mind or soul as immortal, because it has a great appeal for mechanists.

Descartes, arriving in the course of his systematic doubt at the conclusion that he himself (since he could think) existed, asked next *what* he was. He at once rejected the suggestion, 'a rational animal' –

> What then did I formerly think I was? A man. But what is a man? Shall I say 'a rational animal'? No, in that case I should have to go on to ask what an animal is and what 'rational' is and so from a single question I should fall into several of greater difficulty.[7]

He concluded that he *himself* was simply a thinking thing, not an animal at all. His body, though attached in some way to this soul or self, was no part of it, but a distinct physical mechanism. But all the physical processes occurring in an animal belonged to the body. Animals, then, since they did not properly speaking *think*, had no souls.

Descartes therefore regarded animals as automata, operating without consciousness. They did not, he said, really *act* themselves at all; they were acted upon: 'it is nature that acts in them according to the arrangement of their organs, just as we see how a clock, composed merely of wheels and springs, can reckon the hours.'[8] For this view, he gave two reasons: their failure to talk, and the unevenness of their apparently intelligent performance. Let us take the second first.

Apparently intelligent performances by animals, said Descartes, could be shown not to proceed from real intelligence, because the same animals could at other times act stupidly. But of course the same unevenness is found in people. A horse,[9] which finds its way home cleverly, may be foolishly frightened of something that is not dangerous. A man, who sees through the false danger cleverly enough, may foolishly lose his way home. (Descartes, like others who use his model, never seems to consider what sort of a showing a human being would make if tested by members of a *more* intelligent species. Human beings are judged by their ideal performance, animals by their actual one.[10]) Relatively stupid conduct by a fairly intelligent being on an off-day is not in the least like the 'stupidity' of a machine. A car cannot even try to find its way home; a clock will not make even a bad shot at identifying danger. Stupid solutions show a consciousness of the problem.

For this and related reasons, most people today would probably not follow Descartes in thinking animals unconscious. (If they are the kind of behaviourists who think consciousness itself an obscure notion, they will do so for people as well.) Nevertheless, many still regard animals as automatic in a way in which people are not; 'they act not from knowledge but from the disposition of their organs,' as Descartes says.[11]

What does this mean?

It is not just that a causal explanation 'from the disposition of their organs' can in principle be given. This, many of us might agree, is true of people too. Where people are concerned, however, even the most rigid determinist must use other sorts of explanation as well. If we ask why a woman has suddenly rushed out of the house, the explanation may be, 'to catch her little boy; she just saw him on the ice.' This gives her *reason*; she acted 'from knowledge.' It does not compete with or deny causal explanations from her history,[12] but it must precede them; they are explanations of her rushing to save him from the ice. But now what about the action of a mother elephant who, caught with her baby in a flooded river, repeatedly saves the baby from being washed away and eventually manages to lift it with her trunk onto a ledge out of the water?[13] Again, the first explanation must be one of what she is trying to do, namely, to save it from drowning. And in doing that, how could she too not be 'acting from knowledge' – knowledge that it is in danger and would be safer on the ledge? In both cases alike, motives, and in some sense reasons must be mentioned before we can talk of cause.

To some people, this seems obvious sense; others feel that some deep principle is being betrayed. The trouble, I am sure, is in Descartes' notion of reason as a single, indivisible, yes-or-no thing without degrees; his insistence that 'brutes not only have a smaller degree of reason than men, but are wholly lacking in it,' because, as he says, 'reason is a universal tool that may serve in all kinds of circumstances'[14] – so that failing to use it shows one does not have it. But to have a universal tool is, of course, not the same thing as using it universally. And though reason can indeed in principle be used anywhere and on anything, it unluckily does not follow that everybody can in fact so use it. Someone ignorant of, or stupid at, mathematics or Russian, cannot do a particular advanced problem or piece of translation. A prejudiced or infuriated man cannot criticize his aims. A quite impractical person cannot deal intelligently with a burst pipe, nor can a fanatical flat-earther understand eclipses. And at any given time, there are problems that no human being can solve. Reason, in the sense of logic, certainly can be called a universal tool. But considered as a *faculty* – as something we are gifted with – it is not so at all. It is a set of highly varied mental capacities, practical and theoretical, which are separable and unevenly distributed among human beings, and are shaped in specific ways by their lives. This set cannot be reduced to, or derived from, the full, conscious, critical understanding of logic. That is not the differentia of men, but of logicians, and even they do not have it completely. Part of the trouble certainly is that Descartes, like Plato, saw pure, speculative reason of the logician's or mathematician's kind as lying at the core of human life – so that he was really defining man not so much by his consciousness or general intelligence as by his capacity for mathematics. But this again is a special view of what *matters* in life, of what our ambitions should be. It is not the normal meaning of reason.

In normal contexts, in fact, these speculative powers are not at all central to the notion. Someone who is plainly producing correct and even original mathematical work can still give us good grounds to wonder whether he is rational or reasonable. As I suggested earlier, these words mean much more than 'consistent.' A man who reasons consistently, but from the premise that he alone matters, is the type of unreasonableness. 'Irrational' is a rather wider term, whose main use, I think, is to say that something has gone wrong with a person's system of priorities, with his sense of what is important. It can certainly be used to refer to a mere failure in speculative reasoning – say, the groundless expectation that things will still come out right whatever we do to our environment. But I do not think we use it to classify such an erroneous attitude as a *mere* failure to get the facts right. We do this by calling it stupid. 'Irrational' makes a more general criticism, connecting that local failure with some general confusion about what is important. It suggests something wrong in the valuing system, as well as in the mere calculating power.

That suggestion I shall pursue in Chapter 4. The point here is that this sort of criticism can be made of animals as well as people. Rationality involves sanity. And a mad dog differs from a normal dog in just the same way as a mad man from a sane man. On the matter of knowing one's onions, understanding what one is about, there is not (as you might think from Descartes' remarks) a single scale reaching down from the most intelligent man to the stupidest and stopping short there, leaving all beasts equally nowhere. There are a number of scales on which both people and animals can be found variously arranged, as well as some others that are exclusive to people, and undoubtedly others peculiar to different types of animals. Of many elephants and gorillas, as well as of many unintellectual humans, we can very well say that

> He knows what's what, and that's as high As metaphysic wit can fly –[15]

a compliment that cannot be paid to every scholar. As for the use of the *word* reason, there is certainly a case for confining it to man, if we want to emphasize the importance of conscious, deliberate choice, just as there is a good case for confining the word 'language' to sets of conventional signs and not extending it, except metaphorically, to 'the language of the eyes' and other natural ways of communicating. Still, reason and sanity are often nearly synonymous. Jane Goodall, describing a chimpanzee under stress, says, 'there was a time, toward the start of this battle for dominance, when Hugo and I feared for Goliath's sanity.'[16] I think that we would probably not use the phrase 'feared for his reason' here. But the gap between the two notions in such phrases is not very large.

Altogether, in ordinary speech, 'having reason' or 'being rational' is not a yes-or-no business like having a hammer. It is much more like having insight or energy or initiative or imagination – things that can be possessed in varying degrees and also in very different forms. So we are not saying, if we concede some sort of knowledge, reason, intelligence, or purpose to the elephant, that we expect to find the next minute that it has written a Beethoven sonata or taken over the government. Nor, indeed, that it is taking legal action against the ivory trade.

People do feel a threat here: what is it? Human achievements are secure; they are unparalleled, they are all around us; there is no doubt about them. They cannot be shaken by an inquiry into their roots, elements, and origins. Yet there undoubtedly is a sense of outrage, varying from the disgust of one who finds a caterpillar in his salad to the terror of one who finds King Kong in his backyard, in people's insistence on a firm, simple differentia – a sense that is often felt to make all argument unnecessary. Might it perhaps be relevant to ask here, who is really threatening whom? On quite sober and conservative estimates, we are now moving steadily toward exterminating *all* the other most intelligent species on the planet, except possibly the dolphins – great whales, great apes, elephants, all the large predators. They meanwhile can do nothing to us except (it seems) what the Yahoos did to Gulliver – show us a mirror for what we do not much want to see. (Gulliver's horror when his clothes began to wear out and

deprive him of his differentia sums up the situation.) But, in expecting this exposure, our guilt distorts the matter. No animal is what the
Yahoos were, a mere projection of human vileness. Their species have
each their own nature, each different from and mirroring ours in a
different way. Elements of what we value will be found in all of them.

I return now to language. Descartes seems to have thought of it as a
separate capacity, parallel to that for general intelligent performance.
But perhaps it is only one area among many where intelligence can
be shown.

Language is possibly our favourite human distinguishing mark.
On the one hand, it seems an unmistakable, unsplittable single thing.
Like the clothes that mattered so much to Gulliver, you cannot miss
it. On the other hand, unlike the clothes, it is both really valuable and
intrinsic to us. It plainly calls for innate powers, which are linked to
the main structural properties of our life. Human talk involves thinking conceptually, having a sense of things absent, being capable of
abstract calculation, conscious of self, and all the rest of it. So we naturally see it as the key to our castle.

This, of course, is why the recent experiments in which chimps
have undoubtedly in some sense been taught a language have upset
people so much. The facts are briefly these.[17] Between 1966, when
she was a year old, and 1971, a chimp called Washoe was taught a
sign language called Ameslan, commonly used by the deaf-and-dumb
and consisting of hand gestures, roughly speaking one to a word. She
took to it like a duck to water. She acquired in five years a vocabulary
of about 150 Ameslan words which she could use, and another 200
which she could understand. Moreover, she uses it constantly, freely
and spontaneously in casual conversation, not just for tests or when
rewarded. Since then other chimps have also been taught the language,
with much the same degree of success. Four of them have now been
placed with Washoe in a community on an island, watched but not
interfered with. They use Ameslan constantly and spontaneously to
talk to one another. And their use of it is increasing. Moreover, they
talk to themselves, and, without having been taught to, they swear.
(The favoured swearword is the Ameslan sign for 'dirty.') One chimp,

Ally, has been deliberately exposed to both Ameslan and spoken English, and can give the Ameslan sign for an absent object when its name is spoken. This involves something linguists have called 'cross-modal transfer,' which has been supposed impossible for animals.

Earlier attempts to teach apes to talk had failed, resulting in their knowing only a few words after many years' work. This was put down to the general weakness of their intellects. But the remarkable difference between these results and the Ameslan ones suggests, offhand, that the trouble lay not so much in the intellect as in their lacking the innervations from the brain to the larynx which are necessary for speech.

This would mean that language, or the power to speak it, is actually not the unsplittable, single, unmistakable thing people had supposed. A lot of intellectual capital, however, has been invested in the idea that it is so. Defenders of the castle therefore reply that Ameslan, at least as spoken by chimps, is not really a language at all. It does not, they say, have the right structural properties, so its use does not require the rational faculties that language is normally thought to imply. Chimps may have been handed the key, but they cannot turn it. The argument here has been largely concerned with word order, and is heavily dependent on the definition of abstract terms like 'syntactical,' which were devised by linguists in the first place entirely for use in a human context and are not easy to apply in this new area. (If pressed, this kind of argument is liable to prove that a lot of human beings do not talk either.) A number of objections of this nature made in response to Washoe's early efforts have already been withdrawn by their proposers, after further study of both her performance and that of human children.[18] The inquiry goes on, and rightly; new and more detailed standards are set up for the chimps to spar with.

But we need to ask some quite different questions as well.

First, *what follows if the chimps can, in some sense, talk?* Why does it matter so much? There is something most fishy about the idea that big questions could hang on the result of these experiments *alone*. The experiments matter only if they bring to our notice an important and pervasive fact about the world. If they do so, there must be other evidence for it. The sense that these educated chimps somehow threaten the whole fabric of human superiority must mean that the notion of human superiority itself is badly confused. Neither linguistics nor human dignity can certify *a priori* that language is confined to humans. Whether it is or not is clearly an empirical question.

After discussing this question, I shall move on to one that supplements it and is equally necessary whatever comes of the experiments, namely, *if they are not talking, what are they doing?* Or, more generally, if the seemingly intelligent actions of the higher animals are never really intelligent, what are they? Notions of mechanical, imitative, or reactive explanations are usually held in the background of such discussions as if they were the obvious and simple ones. I believe they are, on the contrary, incoherent and obscure as explanations of what actually happens. They would never have been put forward except to save a received theory from disaster.

First, then, what requires *a priori* that only humans should talk? The answer is not linguistics or human dignity, but simply a piece of bad metaphysics, namely, Descartes' dualistic view that the world is divided sharply, without remainder, into lifeless objects on the one hand and human, fully rational, subjects on the other. This position cannot in any case be reconciled with evolution. For if it were true, there would have to have been a quite advanced point in animal evolution when parents who were merely unconscious objects suddenly had a child which was a fully conscious subject. And that situation makes no sense.

ON BEING ANIMAL AS WELL AS RATIONAL

I have suggested that, instead of a single distinguishing mark for man, we look rather for a knot of general structural properties, and have considered how language might form part of such a knot, instead of being an isolated miracle. This chapter will do the same for that other most venerable and impressive candidate for the position of distinguishing mark, rationality.

This discussion of rationality may strike hasty readers as perverse, because its purpose is so different from that of most treatments of the subject. They are usually concerned essentially to *celebrate* reason, and to stress what is unique about it. This celebration I wholeheartedly accept and take for granted. (It ought, I think, to be obvious by now that I am not short of respect either for reason itself or for the great Western tradition of using it.) My present purpose, however, is the distinct and supplementary one of asking how this unique thing, rationality, is possible in a being that is not just a disembodied intellect, but also and among other things some kind of animal, how it fits into such a life. Thus it will constantly be my business to look at the pattern on the other side of the carpet, at the continuity. I am asking about reason what I have been asking about language, namely, what links it to the rest of nature? What part does it play in our life? To understand this, I shall examine, through animal parallels, what conditions must have been necessary in a pre-rational creature if reasoning was to develop and what, therefore, must be retained as a setting for reason? I do this, not in the belief that reason can be 'reduced' to non-rational elements, but from the desire to make sense of our nature as a whole – to find how each of us can regard himself as one thing, not two, when part of our nature is pre-rational. I have said that it is not clear how a creature such as Plato and Descartes described could ever have evolved without celestial interference. Amputating the Cartesian Immortal Soul and leaving the rest of the compound untouched does not, as some people think, help us. The intellect is still left as an alien intruder in the world.

As for celestial interference, it obviously does not make sense in a non-religious context. But I do not think it does so in a Christian one either. Christianity is not Platonism. If God created through evolution, he surely designed it and used it properly. As I shall suggest, Bishop Butler, who was no atheist, points us toward a far more coherent view of human wholeness than Descartes. How immortality is to be conceived is certainly a difficult problem, but it is so whatever you do. Descartes' shortcut creates as many problems as it solves about *what* survives. Every religion in fact demands that far more should survive than the Intellect.

But the chief difficulty about accepting continuity between man and other species, or between the human intellect and the rest of man, now comes not from traditional religion, but from those who do amputate the soul. It stems from the deep reverence people now feel for human success, and particularly for success in science. In this area, people often do not realize how many of the difficulties raised by religion they are needlessly keeping while officially jettisoning its metaphysics. They revere what they take to be the highest human capacities, particularly the speculative intellect, so deeply that they are inclined to find natural explanations of them quite as blasphemous as religious people used to find natural explanations of the religious faculties. Reverence for humanity, which at first is a most respectable tendency, often slips across into overtly religious form. Thus, Auguste Comte instituted a regular 'worship of humanity' with rituals and a temple in Paris.[19] Thus, Nietzsche, after killing off God, came near to worshipping the future of the human race in the form of the Super-man. And H.G. Wells called one of his utopian future-fantasies *Men Like Gods*. Wells moreover endued man with so much of the divine pre-rogative that he called upon him to 'bring to trial' every other earthly organism from the rhinoceros to the tubercle bacillus, and alter it to his satisfaction or get rid of it.[20] It is much easier, it seems, to disown a particular God than to get rid of his empty seat and the paranoia that so readily surrounds it. Wells's bold and forceful imagination is very useful to us here, because he made explicit what is often covered up – that the only reason for man's having this status was supposed to be what Wells called his intelligence – by which he meant mere clev-erness, calculating power, the sort of thing that can be measured by intelligence tests. The future people in *Men Like Gods* are almost purely intellectual – they have, with a few despised exceptions, got rid of 'human weaknesses' such as loving one person better than another. (Significantly, they do not wear clothes.) Wells understood, however, that this meant that any *more* intelligent species, if one appeared, would have the same right to get rid of man. He explained this at the outset of *The War of the Worlds*, where the superintelligent Martians, who are noth-ing but enormous heads on mechanical trolleys, set out as a matter of course to annihilate the human race without examining it. They are, Wells says, merely exercising the same obvious right we ourselves have always exercised over 'the cow and the cucumber.'

Much science fiction has followed Wells in this competitive way of reasoning, which has obvious attractions for those who like the popping of ray guns and the sound of titles like *Master of a Thousand Universes*. It is, however, very obscure. What is supposed to be *that* good about cleverness? Being clever is not obviously so much more important than being kind, brave, friendly, patient, and generous that it inevitably confers an instant right of general massacre. And those qualities cannot be supposed to follow from cleverness, or be included in it; we know that the two kinds of thing can be found apart. Modern humanists cannot, of course, fall back on Plato's way of talking and say that the intellect is man's divinest faculty, his highest dignity, his link with God, the bridge by which he can approach a reality greater than himself, a mode of action superior to the grossness of physical matter, or anything remotely resembling those notions. If they are good Utilitarians (as Wells was), they should regard it only as one means among others to securing pleasure. And an impartial comparison of hedonic level between intellectuals and other types, or between simple and advanced civilizations, is not likely to suggest that it is an especially efficient one, at least not so much as to settle out of hand, and with no reference to any other qualities, the question of who is to exterminate whom. Is there actually anything more to the position that the intellect is primary than the argument which G.E. Moore noted as being relied on against the North American Indians (we are more advanced than they are because we can kill them faster than they can kill us)?[21] If not, I find the intellectualist fluff in which it is wrapped up a depressing product after the efforts of the Enlightenment.

What this way of talking relies on, of course, is the immense respect that both common sense and the philosophic tradition give to rationality. But rationality is not just cleverness. Even the word *intelligence* is often used to mean a good deal more than what Wells meant. And *rationality* always means more. It includes a definite structure of preferences, a priority system based on feeling. Now that kind of structure is not peculiar to the human race, but is also found in the higher animals. In the philosophic tradition, Reason, though not always equated with mere intellect, has usually been sharply opposed to Feeling or Desire. This has determined the attitude of most respectable philosophers to the related subjects of animals and human feelings. They have usually just dismissed animal activities from all comparison with human ones, on the general ground that, in man, decision is a formal, rational process, while animals have only feeling, which is a kind of wholly contingent slop or flow, bare matter without form, so that its analysis cannot concern philosophy. Thus, typically, even Hume, who really did want to show that feeling mattered, went to great trouble to show it simply as an undifferentiated physical force, much like gravitation, moving people in much the same sense in which gravitation moved billiard balls. *Understanding* it, for him, simply meant fitting it into a scheme of mechanics, which should be as economical and simple as possible. (Here the modern Emotivists are his successors, boiling down feeling to the straight dynamic function of being for or against something.) Hume wanted to be the Newton of psychology, an ambition that unluckily has survived him.[22] Psychology did not and does not need a Newton. It needed, and still needs, a Darwin – a careful, patient, thorough observer, who would *distinguish* the various forms of motivation, relate and compare them, and eventually work out concepts suitable for classifying and explaining them, rather than imposing in slapdash fashion an unsuitable model from an alien science.

Because I need to use the common philosophical language of *form* and *matter*, I must digress here to explain that the traditional use of these terms has been oversimple.

It will not do to analyse motivation once and for all into Thought as Form, and Feeling as blank, contingent, undifferentiated Matter. It will not do because the distinction of form and matter is never final; it is always a repeatable one. All actual matter has a form; all actual forms fit a matter. For instance, when Aristotle gave the name *hylê, wood*, to matter, he was thinking of a carpenter imposing form on wood by making it into a table. But of course, the wood before that was not just neutral stuff. It already had its own form. It was beech or pine, with a definite grain and structure. If further form was to be imposed on it, the wood would have to be chosen and prepared. (You cannot make a table out of neutral stuff, nor from a transverse slice across a freshly cut pine trunk, nor from chalk or honeycomb either.) And, to look in the other direction, the completed table along with other furniture can be treated as matter, raw material for the art of the moving man, the art historian, or the interior decorator. And so forth. So, though it is quite true that the philosopher's business is with forms, it never follows that he can disregard matter, nor that what is treated as matter for one particular inquiry will not show its formal element in another. It all depends what you are trying to do at the time.

Feeling has its forms, both in man and other species. If it had not, reason could make nothing of it, and rational decision would be impossible. The crude antithesis between feeling and reason, form and matter, is inadequate even to map the human scene – before we start trying to look for some continuity between man and other species, as we must to make evolution intelligible. If you treat morality as entirely a matter of formless feeling (as Hume did) or entirely a formal matter (as Kant did), you oversimplify disastrously. Moreover, bluntly opposing feeling and reason is inclined to lead to personifying them. Hume, who quite rightly said, 'we speak not strictly and philosophically when we talk of the combat of passion and of reason,' nonetheless fell into this trap when he added that 'reason is, and ought only to be, the slave of the passions, and can never pretend to any other office than to serve and obey them.' Making these two abstractions into Employer and Employed is no better than setting them to fight it out like a couple of drunks. 'Reason' is not the name of a character in a drama. It is a name for organizing oneself. When there is a conflict, one desire *must* be restrained to make way for the other. It is the process of *choosing which* that is rightly called reasoning. But the ill effects of the dramatization constantly appear in Romantic writing, for instance, Blake's *Marriage of Heaven and Hell*:

> Those who restrain desire, do so because theirs is weak enough to be restrained; and the restrainer or reason usurps its place and governs the unwilling.

> And being restrained, it by degrees become passive, till it is only the shadow of desire.
>
> The history of this is written in *Paradise Lost*, and the Governor or Reason is called Messiah.

Romantics like Blake gave the name Reason to desires they disapproved of – say, caution, or the force of habit, or a mere dreary negativeness – and reserved that of Desire or Passion for the ones they favoured. This has become common usage, but it is a mess. Reason and feeling are aspects of all our motives.[23] Feelings themselves have a form, and one that fits the matter. In fact, of course, it can be our duty to *feel* in one way rather than another – something for which the tradition has little room. (Criticism of 'the undeveloped heart' is moral criticism.[24]) Practical reasoning would be impossible were not some preferences 'more rational' than others. Rationality includes having the right priorities. And deep, lasting preferences linked to character traits are formally a quite different proposition from sharp, isolated impulses.

The higher animals have a structure of deep, lasting preferences too. So in showing the importance of a definite, lasting structure of feeling in human life, we show that we can rightly compare it with the parallel (though distinct) structures found in other species.

We lose nothing by this. It does not infringe on the distinctively human structural properties involved in conceptual thought and language. Acting for the common good deliberately and consciously, with a full understanding that you could do otherwise, and after explicit reflection on the alternatives, is a very different thing from doing it unthinkingly. Backing a principle that you can *state* is a very different thing from just steadily acting on it. All the same – as Kant himself recognized[25] – it is a very narrow notion of value which *confines* it to the rational and deliberate, and does not prize good feeling itself.

Let me try now to explain, however roughly, what I mean by the structure, or constitution, of human nature, so as to understand the place of the feelings within it. I want to get away from the essentially *colonial* picture (used by Blake) in which an imported governor, named Reason, imposes order on a chaotic alien tribe of Passions or Instincts. The colonial picture, which is Plato's, was handed down through the Stoics, Descartes, and Spinoza, to Kant.[26] It performed a very good service by honouring Thought. But once doubt arose about how thought could establish values, it ceased to do so. Schopenhauer, Nietzsche, and the Existentialists changed the governor's name from Reason to Will. Kant spoke of the will, but he meant by it reason in action – 'the Will is nothing but Practical Reason.'[27] But the will now stands mainly for arrogance, arbitrariness, and contempt for the natural facts.[28] Instead of being colonial, I want to look at the continuity – to use Bishop Butler's (and to some extent Aristotle's[29]) picture, to talk of what Butler called 'the whole system, as I may speak, of affections, *including rationality*, which constitute the Heart.'[30] I want to consider reason as growing out of and completing a natural balance of parts. I think we all take for granted that there is such a system, and need the idea for our practical thinking. We know that there have to be some things that are naturally more important, more central to human life, than others, and we have a good general idea which sorts of things they are, and how to compare them. We are not really in the helplessly ignorant situation philosophical discussions often suggest, where the only thing that we could safely call important is survival. Of course, important things take different forms in different ages and cultures. Of course we must, as it were, keep learning new languages. But where we know the language (as we do in our own culture) we know how to start distinguishing important things from unimportant, and thereby good from evil. Such distinguishing is very often the theme of serious novels and plays. When we are following them, we grasp the process very well. It is odd that people are struck with total ignorance when they turn to moral philosophy. Pretending that we do not have this skill is in fact a form of hypocrisy. The hypocrisy of past ages was usually classical and dogmatic; the hypocrisy of this age is romantic and sceptical. We pretend *not* to know. Instead of trying to see, we shut the curtains and revel in tragic darkness, concentrating carefully on impossible cases and taking the boring possible for granted.

NOTES

1. Aristotle himself did not give this definition, though his argument at *Ethics* 1.7 and elsewhere does suggest it. Nor (certainly) did he ever proclaim that everything should be defined in the way described. He disliked such sweeping schemes and, if asked how things should be defined, would probably have answered that 'it is the mark of an educated man to expect in each subject the sort of precision of which it is capable' (*Ethics* 1.3).

2. Aristotle, *De Partibus Animalium* 1.3.

3. *Studies in Animal and Human Behaviour*, tr. R.D. Martin (London, 1970), vol. 1, p. 14.

4. K Marx & F. Engels, *The German Ideology*, Progress Publishers, Moscow, 1968, p.6.

5. 'Has Man an Essence?' in *Nature and Conduct*, ed. R.S. Peters (London, 1975).

6. Sartre seems to be making just another move in the same game when he says that 'man as the Existentialist sees him is not definable' till he 'defines himself' (*Existentialism and Humanism*, p. 28). The notion of *defining* here seems very cloudy.

7. *Meditation 2*, in *Philosophical Writings*, tr. P.T. Geach and G.E.M. Anscombe (London, 1954), p. 67.

8. *Discourse on Method*, Pt 5, in *Philosophical Writings*, tr. P.T. Geach and G.E.M. Anscombe (London, 1954), p. 43.

9. For horses, see B. Grzimek's essay, 'On the Psychology of the Horse', in *Man and Animal*, ed. H. Friedrich (London, 1972). People concerned with trying to compare the intelligence of various species commonly agree that it differs so much in kind that it is misleading to conceive it as the same stuff, varying only in quantity.

10. 'The Hippo's feeble steps may err
    In compassing material ends,
    While the True Church need never stir
    To gather in its dividends.' (T.S. Eliot, 'The Hippopotamus').

11. *Discourse on Method*, p. 42.

12. Including 'the disposition of her organs' – hormones and so on.

13. R. Carrington, *Elephants* (London, 1958), p. 60.

14. *Discourse on Method*, p. 42.

15. S. Butler, *Hudibras*, 1.1.149.

16. *In the Shadow of Man*, p. 115.

17. Events will certainly have overtaken me before this book comes out. I can only use the information I have, which is drawn largely from Eugene Linden's sensible and perceptive little book, *Apes, Men, and Language* (New York, 1974).

18. See Linden, pp. 54 and 74.

19. I shall come back to the problems about humanism in the concluding section of this book.

20. In *A Modern Utopia* (1906), the work in which the real genius of the early Wells began to give way to 'humanist' paranoia.

21. *Principia Ethica*, p. 47.

22. See *Enquiry Concerning the Principles of Moral*s, Sections 163, 192, 227. It was in exactly the same spirit that Moore gave his book the pretentious title *Principia Ethica* and repeatedly claimed in it to be initiating a 'scientific' treatment of the subject. See, for example, p. 4 of that work.

23. 'Reason has moons, but moons not hers
    Lie mirror'd on her sea,
    Confounding her astronomers
    But O! delighting me.' (Ralph Hodgson).

24. See an admirable article by N. Dent, 'Duty and Inclination', *Mind*, 83 (1974).

25. I cannot do any justice here to the subtlety of Kant's position. Right at the outset of his argument in the *Grundlegung* he allowed that good feeling, like happiness, did have value in itself, though that value was conditional on the state of the will – that is, a bad will could negate it. About the talents, and perhaps even happiness, this makes good sense. But it is not so clear that good feeling loses all value if the will is bad – nor, indeed, quite what 'the will' is under such conditions.

26. For example, *Grundlegung*, end of Chapter 1: 'Reason, without promising anything to inclination, enjoins its commands relentlessly, and therefore, so to speak, with disregard and neglect of these seemingly equitable claims, which refuse to be suppressed by any command' (*The Moral Law: Kant's Groundwork of the Metaphysic of Morals*, tr. H. J. Paton, London: Routledge, 1997, p. 70).

27. ibid., p. 76.

28. As I. Murdoch argues in *The Sovereignty of Good*, this seems just as true of the muted, polite, Anglo-Saxon kind of Existentialism found in philosophers such as Stuart Hampshire as in the splashily coloured European variety.

29. Aristotle's position too is far too complex to be condensed here. I have called him down once or twice in this book for a kind of Greek intellectualist arrogance which he shared with Plato, but which I do not think was at all central in his thought. (It is what puts off many readers of the *Politics*.) On the positive side, however, he stands as the biologist among philosophers – indeed as the inventor of the biological attitude, which takes the world as a continuous organic whole to be studied and accepted on its own terms, not as a tiresome mass of matter tolerable only because it instantiates mathematical laws. This is beyond praise. Moreover, his method in the *Nicomachean Ethics* is exactly the one I am trying to follow here. He understands morality as the expression of natural human needs. This side of his work was largely ignored by the tradition, because biology itself was neglected. Obsession with the mathematical model, predominant in both Plato and Descartes, has left a terrible gap here.

30. Sermon 12, 'Upon the Love of our Neighbour', Section 11.

DARWIN AND THE ORIGIN OF ETHICS

There is a long tradition of ethical thought related to evolutionary theory that claims its origins in Darwin's doctrine of 'Survival of the Fittest'. Taking this slogan to mean that evolutionary theory implies that all the motivations of evolved creatures are necessarily based on self-interest—implying the impossibility of genuinely altruistic behaviour arising naturally—these thinkers, from T.H. Huxley and Herbert Spencer through to Richard Dawkins and E.O. Wilson, are led to claim either that non-self-interested behaviour is in fact impossible for humans, or that it requires us to somehow transcend the natural constitution given us by our evolutionary origins.

It is important to note that these views are remote from those actually held and expounded in some detail by Charles Darwin himself. Darwin clearly recognised that the sophisticated emotional communication of which humans are capable, in common with other social mammals, the possibilities of collaboration and mutual care that this enables, and the instinct to protect the herd or family group are among the most powerful evolutionary advantages enjoyed by this class of creatures. It is this framework of emotional relationships and complex motivational patterns that creates the foundation upon which human moralities are based.

DOI: 10.4324/9781003588160-6

The dogma that group selection—and hence altruistic behaviour—is impossible, and the related crude schemas of kin selection and gene selection invoked to explain how an illusion of altruism occurs, arise from a type of methodological reductionism that is quite foreign to Darwin's thought. It is, again, the ubiquitous atomising tendency that does violence to our picture of human nature, attempting to derive a simulacrum of real social and moral feeling from the idea of an isolated individual who enters into social relationships out of a calculating self-interest, rather than—as is actually the case—a being who is inherently and fundamentally social by nature, and who could not exist otherwise than as embedded in an encompassing network of emotional, practical, and intellectual communication with others.

With this more realistic picture of what humans are in place, Darwin, and Midgley following him, are able to give a perfectly coherent, non-paradoxical account of how morality and ethical thinking arise naturally from the interaction between the complex array of instincts of a social species with high intelligence. This intelligence is not merely a calculating ability but also the ability to communicate in sophisticated and complex ways about emotional and relational matters, as well as those that are purely intellectual.

SOURCES

'4 Pseudo-Darwinism and Social Atomism' – *The Solitary Self*, Acumen, 2010, abridged from chs. 1 & 2; 'The Natural Springs of Morality' – *The Solitary Self*, ch. 3.

4

PSEUDO-DARWINISM AND SOCIAL ATOMISM

THE MYSTERIOUS ROOTS OF ETHICS

Amid all the celebrations in the year in which I write – the year of two great Darwinian anniversaries; the 150th of the publication of his great book, the 200th of his birth – it is rather striking that so little has been heard about Darwin's idea of morality. Indeed, people reading modern neo-Darwinist writings might well suppose that he took little interest in the matter or was unwilling to discuss it. Far from this, it was central to his understanding of human life, as he made clear at the start of the third chapter of *The Descent of Man*. There, after analysing the intellectual capacities of humans, he turned to consider their active tendencies and found there something even more important. He wrote:

DOI: 10.4324/9781003588160-7

I fully subscribe to the judgment of those writers who maintain that *of all the differences between man and the lower animals, the moral sense or conscience is by far the most important*. This sense, as Mackintosh remarks, 'has a rightful supremacy over every other principle of human action'; it is summed up in that short but imperious word *ought*, so full of high significance. It is the most noble of all the attributes of man, leading him without a moment's hesitation to risk his life for a fellow creature; or after due deliberation, impelled simply by the deep feeling of right or duty, to sacrifice it in some great cause.[1]

He pointed out the difficulty that philosophers have always found in understanding the source and meaning of this compulsion. Properly hesitant about approaching so vast a question, he explained what would be his own, quite limited, angle on it:

This great question has been discussed by many writers of consummate ability; and my sole excuse for touching on it is the impossibility of here passing it over and because, as far as I know, *no-one has approached it from the point of view of natural history*.[2]

This, indeed, he does. And the remarkable thing is that he avoids the usual kinds of reduction in doing it. He does not explain morality away by pretending that it is really something else. Nor does he 'explain' it by reciting scientific facts that are not relevant to it. What he does is to put it in context: to show it as an intelligible reaction for social creatures who live, as we do, on an earth that constantly confronts them with difficulties and who have developed there in the kind of way that we have.

Understanding that natural context does, however, deeply affect the meaning of morality itself. It throws a new light on the relation between reason and feeling, something that has always been a stumbling block to moral philosophers. Unlike most modern evolutionary psychologists, who assume that we fully understand the institutions we have now and merely speculate about their evolutionary causes,

Darwin grapples with real contemporary issues about our moral constitution. This means that he can paint a picture of our social nature that is both shrewd and original, a picture that fits better both with evolutionary considerations and with actual human behaviour than those we are most familiar with today.

THE INVENTION OF DARWINISM

There are two reasons why this important discussion has been neglected. One is the very narrow, stereotypic idea of Darwin's thought that has lately prevailed. During the last half-century, people have seen him primarily as the discoverer of natural selection: the engineer who managed to bolt that final piece of mechanism into the story of evolution, thus explaining, at last, how it can plausibly have taken place. Both supporters and opponents have concentrated on this, which is indeed central to his work. But he also took much more trouble than is usually noticed to work out the *meaning* of this change: to consider just how it should affect the rest of our thinking, especially the way we think about ourselves.

On this topic, very crude ideas were at once attributed to him in his own day by people, such as Herbert Spencer, who ought to have known better. Still more surprisingly, this process has continued busily in our own time, establishing the notion of a confused reductive ideology called Darwinism that is actually quite alien to his thought. Often this doctrine is simply taken to be a vindication of savage, unbridled competition. As Steven Rose says, 'Darwinism was seen variously as justifying imperialism, racism, capitalism and patriarchy ... Today, journalists refer to board-room struggles and takeover battles for companies as "Darwinian"'.[3] And James Le Fanu, who blames not just evolutionary theory but Darwin personally for nearly all today's distresses, writes:

> The uncritical endorsement of misleading explanations can have grievous consequences. We have glimpsed in an earlier chapter some of these in the propagation of eugenic policies and the absurdities of socio-biology. But there is more, for, paradoxically, despite 150 years

of remorseless scientific progress, we are left with a surprisingly pessimistic view of humanity as the perpetrators of the terrible destructive wars of the past century and the destroyers of the planet that sustains us.[4]

It is, of course, always tempting to look for a single cause for one's troubles, but this seems to be going a bit far. In this book I want to show how misleading such talk is, not just in order to put the record straight but – more centrally – to bring the discussion of our nature back from wasteful fantasies to the central psychological topics that are of real concern to us, just as they were to Darwin. This shift is badly needed today because the travesty called *Darwinism* is now seriously influential. (About that, Le Fanu is right). The impression that we *ought* to accept crudely egoistic ideas – even if we don't like them – because they have been proved to be scientific is now quite widespread.

INDIVIDUALISM AND SOCIAL ATOMISM

Besides this twisted notion of Darwinism, another potent factor that has led to neglect of this topic is the general difficulty that an individualistic age has in understanding the function of morality at all. Today, people tend to see 'explaining morality' chiefly as a matter of discovering how beings who are each totally isolated can ever be called on to consider one another, a task that naturally proves impossible. The doctrine behind this approach is a shadowy but powerful belief in individual solitude, which may be called 'Social Atomism.' It is a combination of the deep individualism of our time – something that will occupy us throughout this book – and a prejudice about method: a general idea that it is always more scientific to consider separate components than the larger wholes to which they belong. Indeed, it is often believed that those larger wholes are actually less real. ('There is no such thing as society.')

Put together, these ideas imply that the right way to understand life, including human life, is not to look for the dominant patterns in it but to break it up into units – ultimate constituents – and find laws governing their interactions. In principle, these constituent atoms would not need to be physical ones. In fact, in the past various efforts have been made to analyse *consciousness* into mental units. Thus, Hume treated it as a series of separate impressions, and later Wilhelm Wundt, trying to analyse introspection, made a number of suggestions about possible ways of breaking it into atoms. But these enterprises proved decidedly hard, so it is no surprise that today the atomizing task is being handled in physical terms, which always suit it better.

Thus, in biology, it began to appear in the mid-twentieth century that the entity truly in charge of life was the gene, which was somehow more real than the organism it belonged to. As Brian Goodwin remarked:

> A striking paradox which has emerged from Darwin's way of approaching biological questions is that organisms, which he took to be the prime examples of living nature, have faded away to the point where they no longer exist as fundamental and irreducible units of life .... Modern biology has come to occupy an extreme position in the spectrum of the sciences, dominated by historical explanations in terms of the evolutionary adventures of genes. Physics, on the other hand, has developed explanations of different levels of reality, microcosmic and macrocosmic, in terms of theories appropriate to these levels .... It is the absence of any theory of organisms as distinctive entities in their own right, with a characteristic type of order and organization, that has resulted in their disappearance from the basic conceptual structure of modern biology. They have succumbed to the onslaught of an overwhelming molecular reductionism.[5]

The parallel with physics is indeed important, since physicists have already had to face this problem of combining explanations that work at different levels. When they lost the seventeenth-century belief in ultimate explanation by solid, separate, billiard-ball-like atoms, they gradually saw how to use the surviving parts of Newtonian physics within a wider, more flexible range of different thought patterns, each of which is helpful for its own range of problems. Being no longer bound by the crude kind of materialism that saw the physical world as made of tangible objects such as stones, they could use a much more sensitive approach to topics such as energy and, indeed, consciousness. As many people have pointed out, this change in the notion of matter calls for some rethinking of the term *materialism* itself.

Biologists, however, have not interested themselves in these problems. Instead, as Goodwin says, they have continued to look for traditional 'building blocks' – an unsuitable term that is still far too commonly used – in a way that leads them to use reductions of various kinds, extending explanatory schemes far beyond their natural scope. That range of atomistic reductions will concern us again and again in this discussion.

REDUCTIVE STRATEGIES

Reduction is always an attempt to simplify the conceptual scene. Often it springs from an impression that simplicity and clarity are always what is needed to make an explanation more scientific. But, where thought patterns have to fit a complex subject matter, this naturally does not work. The drawbacks of this slimming-down approach appear in some remarks of Lewis Wolpert's about the status of social science. Wolpert writes:

> ... The peculiarity of the social sciences is the complexity of the subject-matter.[6]

> In a sense, all science aspires to be like physics and all physics aspires to be like mathematics. In spite of recent successes, biology has a long way to go when measured against physics or chemistry. Biologists can still be full of hope ... but what hope is there for sociology acquiring a physics-like lustre?[7]

The sentence about 'aspiring' comes from Schopenhauer's remark that 'all the arts aspire to the condition of music.' It exalts purity and abstraction. But, whatever may be said of music, this ambition clearly makes no sense for science. Physics is *not* trying to be like mathematics nor like anything else. It does its own work, which is looking for general truths about the actual material world. It does not operate – or want to operate – as mathematics does, only at the level of thought; it wants real physical facts. Similarly, the other sciences, and indeed the humanities, each do their own special job of investigating particular chosen aspects of the world, so they need to use different conceptual patterns that suit those aspects.

Biology, then, is not an amateur science, struggling in an endless effort to become physics. Like history or logic, it has its own special work, which is to investigate life. And life is a quite peculiar phenomenon about which physics has absolutely nothing to say. This is why, during the past century, biologists of a reductive turn of mind have tried to play down this embarrassing topic altogether. Not only do they avoid talking about the concept of life itself (the standard dictionary of biology has no entry under the heading 'life'), but they also try their damnedest to reduce life's distinctive patterns to ones found in things that are lifeless. In fact, they still seem haunted by the wish to ground their thought safely in Newtonian physics: to show that explanation always really terminates in inert, lifeless atoms that alone can be scientifically approved and in theories describing their connections. Thus, in *The Blind Watchmaker* Dawkins explains what is distinctive about life as follows:

> What lies at the heart of every living thing is not a fire, not warm breath, not a 'spark of life'. It is information, words, instructions. If you want a metaphor, don't think of fires and sparks and breath. Think, instead, of a billion discrete, digital characters carved in tablets of crystal. If you want to understand life, don't think about vibrant, throbbing gels and oozes, think about information technology. ... It is this that I was hinting at in the previous chapter, when I referred to the queen ant as the central data bank.[8]

Similarly Atkins observes, 'Inanimate things are innately simple. That is one more step along the path to the view that animate things, being innately inanimate, are innately simple too'.[9] This style of talk is designed to conceal the spontaneous creativity that is actually central to the concept of life behind a screen of documentation, as if the calculations that describe it were the thing itself.

Of course, logical clarity of theory and the precision of mathematics are important here, as they are for every sort of enquiry. But science always oscillates between that clarity and another pole that is even more important – truth to the outside world. Anyone can become clearer by becoming more abstract, by ignoring certain ranges of facts. But when the whole world is there waiting to be understood, it is oddly perverse to ignore facts just for the sake of looking pure and 'acquiring a physics-like lustre.' And the notion of a 'hard' science as being always a more abstract one is rather odd considering the ferociously hard work involved in working out conceptual schemes for understanding complex subject matters.

These confused aspirations are remnants of seventeenth-century dualism, thought patterns that were specially devised to show matter and spirit as separate kinds of substance. The concept of life was always a serious embarrassment for that enterprise because it unmistakably brings the two things together. For that reason, people who think the glory of science depends on its sticking close to the concept of inert matter avoid the topic of life and use various sorts of reduction to show that it is not really needed.

This ambition to simplify thought for the sake of purity is central to the reductive shift from organisms to genes that we are now considering. It avoids complexity by breaking organisms into smaller units, dropping the thought patterns that were useful for understanding them as wholes. Goodwin is one of a number of biologists, some of whom we shall discuss later, who are now pointing out that biologists need to go back to this more holistic kind of understanding because it was actually very useful. As he says, this would not mean dropping the advances that come from studying genes, any more than the shift from a geocentric to a wider, Copernican view of the universe involved losing the knowledge previously gained about the earth on its own. It would merely put that knowledge in a wider, more realistic context. It is interesting that, in the case of the universe, nobody now complains that the more holistic, Copernican approach is unscientific.

It seems worth while asking, too, why the atomistic approach in biology stops at gene level. If smaller units are always more informative than larger ones, we might expect that it would be more scientific still to start from the physical particles – the quarks, and so on – of which the genes are composed, instead of taking either genes or individual human beings to be appropriate units, as is now done. However, this choice of a particular level is not exceptional. Scientific enquirers always concentrate their thinking at a particular scale because it interests them, often for reasons that have nothing to do with science. In fact, *holism* and *atomism* are not warring alternatives. They are complementary aspects of all scientific enquiry. But something particularly odd surely does occur at the point where a physical unit such as the gene begins to be thought of as directly explanatory for social and psychological patterns.

WHY WE DON'T QUITE FIT

Darwin's approach to psychological questions is quite different. He starts by mildly pointing out that *Homo sapiens* is actually a sociable species, so that individual humans can be understood only in the context of the group they belong to. Like other social animals, they are not shaped for heroic solitude but for profound cooperation with others, living interdependently in friendly association: an obvious fact that has somehow got rather lost from our recent thinking. The feelings that make all this sociability possible – our natural affections, angers, loves, fears and dependencies – are, he says, the irreplaceable springs of our action and are closely comparable with the motives that make sociability possible in other species, although of course they are not exactly the same.

The great thing that differentiates our position from theirs is, he says, simply that we have added high intelligence to that ancient repertory of feelings in a way that makes us critical about them. We have become aware of endless conflicts between motives that simply do not trouble them. A chimpanzee that has attacked a friend in a fit of temper does not apologize afterwards. The two will normally be reconciled later in the day, but the victim is usually the one who makes advances, asking to be taken back into favour. There is no sign of remorse, nor, of course, do the bystanders show disapproval. This is all very unlike the human situation. The struggle to resolve the inner conflicts that lead to these troubles is the scene of all our special human difficulties, and so of our special successes. And the development of moral thinking is a crucial tool in that struggle.

At the end of his thoughts on the matter, Darwin considers the relation between his view and the older, egocentric Hobbesian tradition. He writes:

> Philosophers of the derivative school of morals formerly assumed that the foundation of morals lay in a form of Selfishness ... [but] According to the view given above, the moral sense is fundamentally identical with the social instincts, and in the case of the lower animals it would be *absurd to speak of these instincts as having been developed from selfishness.*[10]

It may be necessary today to explain why this would be absurd; namely, because these animals are simply not clever enough to do it. They are not capable of the elaborate planning that would be needed to show good behaviour as profitable in the long run. Enlightened self-interest really does require a big cerebral cortex. He goes on:

> They have, however, certainly been developed for the good of the community ....
>
> Thus *the reproach of laying the foundation of the most noble part of our nature in the base principle of selfishness is removed*; unless indeed the satisfaction which every animal feels when it follows its proper instincts, and the dissatisfaction which it feels when prevented, be called selfish.[11]

DARWIN ON GROUP SELECTION

This is, of course, a 'group-selectionist' view. It assumes that competition can just as well arise between two communities as between two individuals, leading more cohesive societies to prevail over fractious ones. Peter Kropotkin developed this approach very interestingly in his book *Mutual Aid*. Neo-Darwinian evolutionists, however, decided that group selection was impossible and, accordingly, long ignored Darwin's espousal of it.

But, as we shall see, this disbelief in group selection has been well challenged and there is now no scientific reason to reject Darwin's view of it. After summing it up, he states his remarkable conclusion that the development of real morality – the kind that has actually been influential in the world – is not a mysterious paradox, but makes perfectly good biological sense:

> The social instincts – *the prime principle of man's moral constitution* – with the aid of active intellectual powers and the effects of habit, naturally lead to the golden rule, 'As ye would that men should do to you, do ye to them likewise'; and this lies at the foundation of morality.[12]

This striking pronouncement is not, of course, just a pious hope, but a straightforward piece of ethology: a factual comment on the life pattern of a particular species. Naturally, Darwin is not suggesting that we always, or even often, obey the golden rule, or even interpret it sensibly. He is extremely careful to point out that we don't:

> It cannot be maintained that the social instincts are ordinarily stronger in man ... than the instincts of self-preservation, hunger, lust, vengeance etc. *Why then does man regret*, even though he may endeavour to banish such regret, that he has followed the one natural impulse rather than the other? And why does he further feel that he ought to regret his conduct? ... Man in this respect differs profoundly from the lower animals.[13]

But he is saying that the social elements in our constitution still unavoidably urge us in that direction despite our other wishes, producing chronic friction. In fact, he is noting the *unavoidable centrality of inner conflict in human life* and the need that this imposes for some kind of morality to resolve it. Less intelligent animals (he says) probably don't notice the clashes and so are not troubled by the need for resolution. But if their intelligence grew they too would become aware of inner discord, would note the anomalies and would have to respond more or less as we do, although the systems they would arrive at might be very different. Accordingly, he suspects that: 'Any animal whatever, endowed with well-marked social instincts, would inevitably acquire a moral sense or conscience as soon as its intellectual powers had become as well-developed, or nearly as well-developed as in man' (71–2). In short, what makes our moral constitution possible – and indeed what makes us characteristically human – is not primarily our intellect. It is the difficulty of combining that intellect with a given set of pre-existing social feelings.

WHICH KIND OF SELF?

This account of the role of morality in our life is surely more real-istic than approaches that treat it as something external to our true nature – a set of alien rules imposed by parents or gods or rulers or by an abstract force called Reason or Society. What makes our conflicts so hard is that they are genuinely internal. Darwin surely shows here a sense of the real problems that infest human life, a sense that con-trasts sharply with the simple accounts of motivation that some of his alleged followers now give. Thus, Dawkins finds this topic quite straightforward:

> Be warned that if you wish, as I do, to build a society in which individ-uals co-operate generously and unselfishly towards a common good, you can expect little help from biological nature. Let us try to *teach* generosity and altruism because *we are born selfish*.[14]

We should note that the word *selfish* here cannot have the special, technical meaning of 'self-reproducing' that it is supposed to bear in Dawkins's discussions of 'selfish genes.' It cannot because in this pas-sage it is explicitly applied to human motives, so it must have its every-day sense as the name of a single ruling motive, one that dominates all others. Dawkins sees that this dominance may make his readers doubt whether that motive can be reformed as he proposes, so at the end of the book he explains how we can improve it. Dismissing as implausible the idea that natural outgoing motives might contribute to this, he writes:

> Even if we look on the dark side and assume that individual man is fundamentally selfish, ... our conscious foresight ... could save us from the worst selfish excesses of the blind regulators ... We can see the long-term benefits of participating in a 'conspiracy of doves', and we can sit down together to discuss ways of making the conspiracy work.[15]

All we shall need, in short, is a little enlightened self-interest.

Rather surprisingly, Dawkins seems to propose this as quite a new suggestion, a remedy, so far untried, that will clear up the problem. Actually, of course, it is a very old idea, and is in fact the solution proposed by Hobbes, whose thoughts on the topic we shall look at presently. Dawkins, however, is clearly not confident that this will be enough, for he goes on:

> We can even discuss ways of deliberately cultivating and nurturing pure, disinterested altruism – *something that has no place in nature, something that has never existed before in the whole history of the world.* We are built as gene machines and cultured as meme-machines, but we have the power to turn against our creators. We, alone on earth, can rebel against the tyranny of the selfish replicators.[16]

Thus, we find, to our great surprise, that – even though, as he has insisted for most of the book, 'we' are merely lumbering robots, passive tools in the hands of the genes – this same 'we' can yet (with a single bound) now become free to act, in effect, as supernatural beings, able to ignore the physical causes that have shaped us. The belief in the omnipotence of local physical causation that has been foundational during nine-tenths of the book suddenly dissolves at this point to allow free will and a happy ending.

FRIENDLINESS IS NATURAL

Why should such a drastic metaphysical miracle – something that 'has no place in nature, something that has never existed before in the whole history of the world' – suddenly become necessary? This emergency only arises because the author accepts such a strangely simple and extreme account of human motivation. By treating the model of individual competition as a universal explanation for all social interactions, he, like others who claim to interpret Darwin today, makes spontaneous, uncalculating sociability look impossible. Darwin's own very different views on this matter are indigestible to those who claim to be his champions, which is no doubt why they have been ignored.

On the other hand, a different public – one remote from that Dawkinsist tradition, one that is seriously interested in discussing moral issues – may well not even look at Darwin's views about them because they don't expect any enlightenment from him. And even if they do look at them they may be put off by his strong emphasis on our continuity with other social animals. Our tradition has so often relied on using crude, fantasy-laden stories about these other species – an imagery packed with villainous snakes, rats, wolves, hyenas and the rest – in order to establish its own moral status that Darwin's quiet acceptance of kinship still causes much disquiet. In fact, it is remarkable how he manages to balance a clear sense of the social capacities that make these creatures genuinely akin to us with an equal emphasis on the transformative effects of human intelligence, which make our lives so profoundly different. He makes it plain that parental affection guided by intelligence is a very different thing from parental affection without it.

Yet human parental affection still is parental affection: something bred into us because we have the good fortune to be mammals. Anyone who watches the parenting of cats, monkeys or indeed birds must see that their attitude is, in a deep sense, akin to ours. Similarly, young animals at play show affectionate regard for each other in the same way that young children do. These are obvious examples of the way in which humans are naturally linked to those around them by feelings of fellowship, just as other social creatures are. No monstrous metaphysical change is needed to explain the presence of spontaneous generosity.

Altruism, the direct wish to help others, is not a wild fantasy, not something that needs a conspiracy theory to account for it, but an everyday aspect of human motives. As Hume pointed out, a sympathetic involvement in what goes on around us is not optional; it is a basic part of our nature. We directly mind about these things: 'The interests of society are not even on their own account indifferent to us; everything which contributes to the happiness of society recommends itself to our approbation and good-will ... the very aspect of happiness pleases us'.[17]

Of course, this does not mean that we rejoice at everyone's happiness; the pleasure of those we dislike may positively annoy us. But for it to do so we do have to feel some concern about their feelings, however slight, and where we have no particular prejudice that concern does indeed naturally tend to be sympathetic. This obvious fact about empathy was, of course, ignored on principle during the Behaviourist epoch because it was deemed to be impossible.

Very interestingly, however, it has lately crept back into general acceptance owing to the discovery of mirror neurons. Now that neurologists can observe the brains of people and animals who are watching some transaction, they find that those brains do indeed echo in some degree the brain movements of those directly involved. This has allowed members of the scientifically minded public at last to accept as fact something that has certainly been a central element in their experience throughout their lives. They can now admit that we actually do perceive the anger, scorn, affection, or suffering of those around us quite as directly as we see lights or hear noises, a feat that, however surprising, is an essential part of our equipment as social animals. Is it not interesting that the twentieth century could not admit this well-known fact until it was revealed through a machine?

Of course, outgoing motives based on this kind of empathy are patchy and unreliable. All kinds of other considerations can override them and that is why conscience is needed to support them. But spontaneously helpful acts are often seen, among other social species, from meerkats to elephants, and even more often among humans because humans are – as Darwin emphasized – by nature exceptionally sociable creatures. Of course, these acts do not always involve real sacrifice, but they quite often do. For instance, news items regularly report that when a human – or even some other animal – has been in danger of drowning, not only relatives but unconnected bystanders have spontaneously plunged in to the rescue, and can sometimes die in the attempt.

Is there something fishy about calling this kind of response *disinterested*? It certainly is not a scheme planned for one's own future profit, which is what 'interested' actually means. It is indeed done to fulfil or satisfy one's own impulse, but that is true of all our actions, including completely self-destructive ones, so the point seems trivial. Bishop Butler put this neatly:

> To those who are shocked to hear virtue spoken of as disinterested, it may be allowed that it is indeed absurd to speak thus of it unless hatred, several particular instances of vice and all the common affections and aversions of mankind are acknowledged to be disinterested too.[18]

Thus, a worker who rashly insults his boss has certainly not done it to promote his own interest; he has preferred to gratify his anger.

Similarly, someone who gives money that he can ill spare to a friend in trouble has done what he wanted but not what profited him. This is also true of suicides, and indeed of anyone who consciously puts their life in danger. All these kinds of action are quite ordinary. In fact, disinterested behaviour is really not unusual at all.

NOTES

1. Darwin, C. [1871]. *The Descent of Man,* and *Selection in Relation to Sex.* Princeton, NJ: Princeton University Press, 1981, 70, first emphasis added.
2. Ibid., 71, emphasis added.
3. Rose, S. *Lifelines: Biology, Freedom, Determinism.* Harmondsworth: Penguin, 1997, 175.
4. Le Fanu, J. *Why Us? How Science Rediscovered the Mysteries of Ourselves.* London: Harper, 2009, 250.
5. Goodwin, B. *How the Leopard Changed its Spots.* London: Phoenix, 1994, 1-2.

6. Wolpert, L. *The Unnatural Nature of Science*, London: Faber, 1992, 124-5.

7. Ibid., 121.

8. Dawkins, R. *The Blind Watchmaker*. Harlow: Longman, 1986, 112.

9. Atkins, P. W. *The Creation*. San Francisco, CA: W. H. Freeman, 1987, 53.

10. Darwin, C. [1871]. *The Descent of Man,* and *Selection in Relation to Sex*. Princeton, NJ: Princeton University Press, 1981, 97-8, emphasis added.

11. Ibid., 98-9, emphasis added.

12. Ibid., 106, emphasis added.

13. Ibid., 89, emphasis added.

14. Dawkins, R. *The Selfish Gene*. London: Granada, 1976, 3, second emphasis added.

15. Ibid., 215.

16. Ibid., 215, emphasis added.

17. Hume, D. [1777]. *An Enquiry concerning the Human Understanding,* and *an Enquiry concerning the Principles of Morals*. Oxford: Clarendon Press, 1894, 178-9.

18. Butler, J. 1969. *Butler's Sermons* and *Dissertation on Virtue*. London: G. Bell & Sons.

5

THE NATURAL SPRINGS OF MORALITY

INTELLIGENCE AND REMORSE

The determined hostility of biologists to group selection is just one expression of the gulf that has opened between Darwin's own approach and the social atomism preached by those who claim to be his followers: both the 'social Darwinists' in his own day and the neo-Darwinists now. Social atomism is not really an essential part of the idea of evolution. It is essentially political: an ideology shaped by Enlightenment individualism, one that takes different forms according to the political and social pressures of the day. Its first strong expression was Hobbes's sharp reaction against religious wars, and it still echoes the simplistic rhetoric of its founder. It is not interested in relating its findings to the emotional complexity of our actual lives. And, because it comes from a political context, it is habitually polemical, dealing in extremes. I shall

DOI: 10.4324/9781003588160-8

try later to look at this very important element in our thought in its own terms and consider how we ought to use it.

But it needs to be kept separate from Darwin. He, by contrast, was trying to grasp how something as complex as actual human motivation – including moral sensibility – could possibly have evolved. He wanted to understand it ethologically, as an expression of the life-style of our species. And, unlike many people who attempt this, he did not simplify his task by reducing humans to stereotypical animals. He looked at both people and the various kinds of animals in their actual bewildering complexity. And he started his enquiry from one of the most puzzling human traits – morality – because he thought it so central.

As we have seen, in introducing this topic, he remarked that 'of all the differences between man and the lower animals, the moral sense or conscience is by far the most important.' He noted the huge, disturbing question about how words such as *ought* get their authority, recognized that it has many aspects, but proposed to look at the light cast on it from one single angle that had so far been neglected – that of natural history. This he did, sketching out a wide background of social behaviour in other animals and explaining why he thought that any sociable creature that became highly intel-ligent would be forced by its increased intelligence to develop a morality. This follows, he says, from an individual's becoming aware of inner conflict:

> *Firstly*, the social instincts lead an animal to take pleasure in the soci-ety of its fellows and to feel sympathy with them, and to perform vari-ous services for them .... *Secondly*, as soon as the mental faculties had become highly developed, *images of all past actions and motives would be incessantly passing through the brain of each individual* and that feel-ing of dissatisfaction which invariably results ... from any unsatisfied instinct, would arise, as often as it was perceived that the enduring and always present social instinct had yielded to some other instinct, at the time stronger, but neither enduring in its nature nor leaving behind it a very vivid impression.[1]

Intelligence, in fact, is not just a useful calculating tool. It is also a light that comes on within us, a new kind of self-awareness that arises whether we ask for it or not. An intelligent agent's own past acts can now haunt him, confronting him with the clash between his own motives, asking him which of the conflicting wishes he really wants to identify with.

Darwin gives an illuminating instance of the difference that intelligence could make about this. Parent swallows, he says, often desert their young to join a migrating swarm because their strong urge to brood chicks is overwhelmed by the still stronger need to migrate. If, however, they had a sharper intelligence:

> when arrived at the end of her journey, and the migratory instinct ceases to act, what an agony of remorse each bird would feel, if, from being endowed with great mental activity, she could not prevent the image continually passing before her mind of her young ones perishing in the north from cold and hunger.[2]

And something like this is indeed, as he says, a frequent human situation:

> Man, from the activity of his mental faculties, cannot avoid reflection; past impressions and images are incessantly passing through his mind with distinctness ....[3]

> At the moment of action, man will no doubt be apt to follow the stronger impulse; and though this may occasionally prompt him to the noblest deeds, it will far more commonly lead him to gratify his own desire at the expense of other men. But after their gratification, when past and weaker impressions are contrasted with the ever-enduring social instincts, retribution will surely come. Man will then feel dissatisfied with himself, and will resolve with more or less force to act differently for the future. This is conscience, for conscience looks backwards and judges past actions, inducing that kind of dissatisfaction which, if weak, we call regret, and if severe, remorse.[4]

The central peculiarity of humans is *not*, then, just their improved power of calculation. It is their wider perspective, their more comprehensive viewpoint. They have a longer view backwards and forwards in life. Their increased power of reasoning is not just a pocket calculator; it is a general intensification of inner activity. Besides recalling isolated acts, these more thoughtful beings now see the continuous course of their own conduct and can compare it with that of others. They cannot always avoid thinking about these things and – because they have become aware of the reactions of those around them – they have to see them in part from the point of view of others. That is the context in which the question of judging particular acts begins to be important.

RATIONALITY AND SANITY

Anyone used to philosophical discussions of moral issues will find it striking that Darwin sees no need to call in Reason here as an independent assessor. Unlike Kant and many other moralists, he does not treat it as an external arbiter, a power set over against the whole range of feelings, having the right to determine final choice. Quite differently, he suggests that, once the conflict is perceived, it is something in the social motives themselves that often gives them the right to prevail. And conscience – the faculty that has to decide these questions – is not a distinct professional judge inside each one of us but an aspect of the whole person who deals with the conflict: a unifying entity who had never before appeared on this stage.

What kind of authority, then, does conscience have? The affections that the impulsive act has wounded are, he says – unlike the impulse – 'ever-enduring,' chronic rather than acute. But why does ever-enduringness give them a special status? Because, as Darwin suggests, it means they are a deeper, more integral part of our nature. They are something more central to our characters than the passing impulses that often overwhelm them. It is not a mere chance that makes them keep surfacing in our lives. They are persistent because they do something crucial for us. *They are the organs that show us that we really are not alone*, the channels through which we perceive the reality of those we love. It is through them that we grasp the otherness of others. And, even though we so often ignore these messages, without that assurance, we cannot live.

Is this right? Some critics suspect that it is all too chancy, that it depends too much on our happening to be members of a particular species. Thus, Kant wrote:

> We should not dream for a moment of trying to derive the reality of this principle [duty] from the special characteristics of human nature. For duty has to be a practical, unconditioned necessity of action; it must therefore hold for all rational beings ... only because of this can it also be a law for all human wills.[5]

In this spirit we might, of course, ask: if, instead of being mammals, we were alien beings who did not have these feelings, would we then still have these duties? Kant thought that we still would, because he believed the authority of morals was independent of all feelings, arising simply from rationality – from a rational being's recognition that all other rational beings have unconditional value:

> All the objects of inclination have only a conditional value; for if there were not these inclinations and the needs grounded on them, their objects would be valueless. Inclinations themselves, as sources of needs, are so far from having an absolute value to make them desirable for their own sake that it must rather be the universal wish of every rational being to be wholly free from them.[6]

What, then, would be the situation of rational beings who just happened to have no feelings at all, or only destructive ones?

What, for instance, about Mephistopheles in Goethe's *Faust*, who declares:

> I am the spirit who always says No.
> And rightly too, for all that comes to birth
> Is fit for overthrow, as nothing worth;

> Wherefore the world were better sterilized;
> Thus all that's here as evil recognized
> Is gain to me, and downfall, ruin, sin
> The very element I prosper in.
>
> > (*Faust, Part 1*: scene iii, 73–9 translated by
> > Philip Wayne, Harmondsworth, Penguin, 1949)

This may be a consistent attitude, but is it a rational one? Or does rationality perhaps involve something more than consistency?

In common life, rationality does not mean just cognitive neatness. We are not likely to call somebody rational who reasons consistently from premises like these. The same doubt arises about single-minded fanatics even when their chosen maxim is one that we actually approve of. We may well think these people insane or sociopathic, and those conditions are not thought to be compatible with rationality.

THE VALUE OF MUTUAL DEPENDENCE

Would things be any better if these beings had no feelings at all? Kant seems to suggest – as the Stoics had done – that that would indeed be an ideal state because inclinations indicate needs, which are marks of imperfection. But, without any needs or inclinations, how could action ever start at all? Nor do we actually think that apathy – a lack of inclinations – is any sign of rationality. (Mr Spock of *Star Trek* is not really a counter-example here; he clearly has all the normal human feelings.)

What Kant and the Stoics have missed is that our need for each other – our need for all the normal intercourse of human life – is not a weakness but a strength. It is our lifeline, our essential passport to the real world. It is what points us outwards to all the riches around us, the great stores of *otherness* in which we need to live. Of course, our dependencies are dangerous, but who wants to live safely like a billiard ball or a doll that never leaves its package? Of course, the Enlightenment message about the need to be adult – to take full responsibility for our own lives – is a sound one. But to exaggerate it into a rejection of all dependence is to lose touch with the human situation altogether. If we try to do that, we lose as adults the vital, realistic sense of our entirely dependent situation that we gained as small children. We then risk ceasing to be properly human at all.

Yet the idea that all feelings, and particularly feelings of dependence, are simply weaknesses has been curiously strong in our tradition. It is related to the Greek notion that feelings are something alien and invasive, things that happen to us rather than activities. The Greek word *pathos*, latinized as *passio*, means an experience that we passively undergo. Thought, by contrast, is viewed as an activity under our control and therefore more dignified.

But our underlying acceptance of values – our love of the people and places and causes that we mind about and our commitment to them – is not something passive, not something imposed from outside. It is an active policy, a lasting decision to aim our activity in certain ways. Love and hatred are not mere opinions, they are feelings, but feelings do not just happen to us, like a stroke or a fit of sneezing. Any feelings that last longer than a mere instantaneous impulse become parts of our thought and – unless we reject them – they determine its direction.

This means that the ordinary idea of rationality is not just one of intellectual power or consistency but includes *aims*: desires and wishes that are recognizably human. And Kant, while allowing a very wide range for the possible aims of rational beings, surely took this condition for granted like the rest of us. He assumes, for instance, that these beings will value each other because consistency demands that they should do so if they value themselves. But suppose they do not value themselves, or do not do so for the right sorts of reasons? Suppose they are consumed by self-hatred, or are already considering suicide?

It is not, I suggest, just an accident that all those we think of as typical rational beings – namely human ones – have begun their lives as babies, living in a deeply affectionate and dependent relationship with those who reared them. They are shaped for life by that relation, even though, in later life, they may try to forget it and avoid acknowledging any kind of dependence. As far as we know, this background seems to be necessary to lead a creature to take others seriously enough to communicate with them at all. Doing this means seeing them as, in some sense, equals and ends in themselves.

BEES AND OTHER ALIEN SPECIES

What, however, about alien beings? Following up his suggestion about a hypothetical species that might become moral because it had become intelligent, Darwin suggests an interesting parallel:

> In the same manner as various animals have some sense of beauty, though they admire widely different objects, so they might have a sense of right and wrong, though led by it to follow different lines of conduct. If, for instance, ... men were reared under precisely the same conditions as hive-bees, there can hardly be a doubt that our unmarried females would, like the worker-bees, think it a sacred duty to kill their brothers, and mothers would strive to kill their fertile daughters, and no-one would think of interfering. Nevertheless the bee, or any other social animal, would in our supposed case gain, as it appears to me, some feeling of right and wrong, or a conscience. There would often be a struggle and ... an inward monitor would tell the animal that it would have been better to have followed the one course than the other.[7]

Obviously, however, this destructiveness would be balanced in the bee by deep loyalty and affection for its fellows, which would (again) be appropriate to the care it had received in infancy. Those feelings would have to supply the strong social motive that would activate its conscience. It is also possible, of course, that this kind of destructiveness would actually prevent bees, or bee-like creatures, from developing rationality at all. We know, after all, that human destructiveness stands in the way of human rationality and limits its scope. Darwin points out that the particular repertoire of natural feelings from which a species starts can always pose grave problems in this way to the project of harmonization. In the human case, he instances particularly the partiality of our affections, which so often blocks our attempts at justice. Yet, as he notes, this partiality is often balanced by a sense of fairness, which is also natural, one which, again, we share with other advanced social species and that has often had great influence. But for earthly creatures, as opposed to abstract minds or computers, the direct personal affection in early youth on which our partiality centres is the irreplaceable focus of all further development.

Swallows too, like most other birds, are, of course, emotionally formed by these strong bonds of affection uniting parents and young, just as mammals are. Mammals and birds share this emotional structure, even though they are not at all closely related, having in fact no common ancestry nearer than quite primitive reptiles. This is one of many interesting cases of evolutionary convergence: the development of similar features by unrelated organisms in response to situations when their needs become similar. Stephen Jay Gould drew attention to such cases in *The Panda's Thumb*. Conway Morris, however, has emphasized their significance in a much more interesting way. They show, he says, that, at many points in evolution, only one possible path of further development actually makes sense. That path will therefore be taken by all species that arrive at this juncture, despite their very different starting-points, even though alternative routes may seem to be available. Unlike Gould, who thought that in principle anything can happen in evolution, Conway Morris therefore proposes that social creatures, and eventually intelligent ones such as humans, were bound to develop.

If that is right, it suggests that the only way in which creatures could have gained high intelligence was the way in which they actually did do so – namely, in the context of strong natural affections. They might then indeed, as Darwin suggests, have developed it largely as a solution to the problems that those affections pose when they conflict, that is, to the social problems posed by living cooperatively together. Looked at from that angle, human thought and human feeling do not just happen to be housemates; they are mutually dependent elements in an organic whole.

NOTES

1. Darwin, C. [1871]. *The Descent of Man,* and *Selection in Relation to Sex.* Princeton, NJ: Princeton University Press, 1981, 72, emphasis added.
2. Ibid., 91.
3. Ibid., 89.
4. Ibid., 91.
5. Kant I. [1785]. *The Moral Law: Groundwork of the Metaphysic of Morals,* H. J. Paton (trans.) London: Routledge, 1997, 88.
6. Ibid., 90.
7. Darwin, C. [1871]. *The Descent of Man,* and *Selection in Relation to Sex.* Princeton, NJ: Princeton University Press, 1981, 72, emphasis added.

THE DARKER SIDE

These extracts continue the development of what may be called a naturalistic theory of human nature through an exploration of the nature of evil. Although generally regarded as a problem in theology, the sense of paradox and difficulty surrounding this topic does not disappear when God is removed from the equation. Again, the traditional dichotomy between libertarian and deterministic views seems to be unhelpful here; if social conditioning or genetics cause people to commit evil actions, how can they be held responsible for them? If, on the other hand, all our actions are the product of rational free choice, why does anyone choose evil, given that no one wishes to be thought of – especially by himself – as an evil person?

The general form of Midgley's answer is that wickedness arises when the vital balance between our natural motives is lost. As we saw in the preceding chapter, it is part of the function of Reason to maintain this balance; in this sense, wickedness can be interpreted as a denial of rationality, even though the evil person may be a master of logical calculation. For the most part, Midgley returns to the classical conception of evil as a negative phenomenon – an absence of some positive aspect of our nature, such as self-awareness, empathy, or impartiality, but it can also be viewed as an excess; a personality

DOI: 10.4324/9781003588160-9

dominated by excessive pride or fanatical devotion to an ideal may likewise become destructive and evil. In either case, it is an imbalance; it has causes, which may be partly social, partly genetic, and partly of other kinds, but the individual still has a choice about whether to try to correct the imbalance.

To exercise such a choice requires self-awareness; its opposite, self-deception, is therefore an integral element in the psychology of evil. We cannot, in fact, recognize an action of ours as truly morally evil without either disowning the action or fatally damaging our own personality. Consequently, the evil person must continually fabricate strategies that represent wicked acts as virtuous, or that represent wickedness itself as, in some paradoxical way, admirable.

To the extent that we all fall short of the moral standards we set for ourselves, we are all, to varying degrees, involved in self-deception; we find it necessary to disown our shadow. Stevenson's parable of Jekyll and Hyde dramatizes this, throwing into sharp relief the Faustian bargain involved in opting for a life of evil. Jekyll literally loses his soul in entering Hyde's form, for what constitutes Hyde as evil is his absence of humanity – in a sense, because he is without conscience, he is also without consciousness:

> [Jekyll] . . . thought of Hyde, for all his energy of life, as of something not only hellish but inorganic. This was the shocking thing; that the slime of the pit seemed to utter cries and voices; that what was dead and had no shape, should usurp the offices of life.

(See below, p. 104)

SOURCES

'The Problem of Natural Evil' – *Wickedness: A Philosophical Essay*, Routledge & Kegan Paul, 1984, ch. 1. 'The Elusiveness of Responsibility' – *Wickedness*, ch. 3. 'Selves and Shadows' – condensed from *Wickedness*, chs 6–7.

6

THE PROBLEM OF NATURAL EVIL

What in the midst lay but the Tower itself?
The round squat turret, blind as the fool's heart,
Built of brown stone, without a counterpart
In the whole world. The tempest's mocking elf
Points to the shipman thus the unseen shelf
He strikes on, only when the timbers start.

Robert Browning, 'Childe Roland to the Dark
Tower Came,' stanza xxx

LOOKING TOWARDS THE DARKNESS

This is an enquiry into the problem of evil, but not quite in the traditional sense, since I see it as our problem, not God's. It is often treated as the problem of why God allows evil. The enquiry then takes

DOI: 10.4324/9781003588160-10

the form of a law-court, in which Man, appearing both as judge and accuser, arraigns God and convicts him of mismanaging his responsibilities. We then get a strange drama, in which two robed and wigged figures apparently sit opposite each other exchanging accusations. But this idea seems to me unhelpful. If God is not there, the drama cannot arise. If he is there, he is surely something bigger and more mysterious than a corrupt or stupid official. Either way, we still need to worry about a different and more pressing matter, namely the *immediate* sources of evil – not physical evil, but moral evil or sin – in human affairs. To blame God for making us capable of wrongdoing is beside the point. Since we are capable of it, what we need is to understand it. We ought not to be put off from trying to do this by the fact that Christian thinkers have sometimes been over-obsessed by sin, and have given some confused accounts of it. The phenomenon itself remains very important in spite of all the mistakes that are made about it. People often do treat each other abominably. They sometimes treat themselves abominably too. They constantly cause avoidable suffering. Why does this happen?

There is at present a strong tendency for decent people, especially in the social sciences, to hold that it has no internal causes in human nature – that it is just the result of outside pressures which could be removed. Now obviously there are powerful outside causes. There are physical pains, diseases, economic shortages and dangers – everything that counts as 'natural evil.' There are also cultural factors – bad example, bad teaching, bad organization. But these cultural causes do not solve our problem because we must still ask, how did the bad customs start, how do they spread, and how do they resist counter-conditioning? Can people be merely channels? If they are channels, out of what tap do the bad customs originally flow? And if they are not mere channels, if they contribute something, what is that contribution?

The idea that we must always choose between social and individual causes for human behaviour, and cannot use both, is confused and arbitrary. In calling it arbitrary, I do not of course mean that no reasons have been given for it, but that the reasons given are not, and could not possibly be, good enough to justify so crippling a policy. Causes of different kinds do not compete. They supplement each other. Nothing has one sole cause. And in this case, the inside and outside causes of human behaviour – its individual and social aspects – supplement each other so closely that they make no sense apart. Both must always be considered. It is understandable that embattled champions of the social aspect, such as Marx and Durkheim, were exasperated by earlier neglect of it, and in correcting that bias, slipped into producing its mirror image. Nothing is easier than to acquire the faults of one's opponents. But in the hands of their successors, this habit grew into a disastrous competitive tradition, a hallowed interdisciplinary vendetta. Social scientists today are beginning to see the disadvantages of this blinkered approach. Now that it has become dominant, these snags are very serious and call for sharp attention.

However great may be the force of the external pressures on people, we still need to understand the way in which those people respond to the pressures. Infection can bring on fever, but only in creatures with a suitable circulatory system. Like fever, spite, resentment, envy, avarice, cruelty, meanness, hatred and the rest are themselves complex states, and they produce complex activities. Outside events may indeed bring them on, but, like other malfunctions, they would not develop if we were not prone to them. Simpler, non-social creatures are not capable of these responses and do not show them. Neither do some defective humans. Emotionally, we are capable of these vices, because we are capable of states opposite to them, namely the virtues, and these virtues would be unreal if they did not have an opposite alternative. The vices are the defects of our qualities. Our nature provides for both. If it did not, we should not be free.

These problems about the psychology of evil cannot be dealt with simply by denying that aggression is innate. In the first place, evil and aggression are not the same thing. Evil is much wider. A great deal of evil is caused by quiet, respectable, unaggressive motives like sloth, fear, avarice and greed. And aggression itself is by no means always bad. In the second place, and more seriously, to approach evil merely by noting its outside causes is to trivialize it. Unless we are willing to grasp imaginatively how it works in the human heart, and particularly in our own hearts, we cannot understand it. We have good reason to fear the understanding of evil, because understanding seems to involve some sort of identification. But what we do not understand at all we cannot detect or resist. We have somehow to understand, without accepting, what goes on in the hearts of the wicked. And since human hearts are not made in factories, but grow, this means taking seriously the natural emotional constitution which people are born with, as well as their social conditions. If we confine our attention to outside causes, we are led to think of wickedness as a set of peculiar behaviour-patterns belonging only to people with a distinctive history, people wearing, as it were, black hats like those which identify the villains in cowboy films. But this is fantasy.

In his book *The Anatomy of Human Destructiveness*, Erich Fromm explains his reasons for carefully analysing the motives of some prominent Nazis. Besides the interest of the wider human tendencies which they typify, he says:

> I had still another aim; that of pointing to the main fallacy which prevents people from recognizing potential Hitlers before they have shown their true faces. This fallacy lies in the belief that a thoroughly destructive and evil man must be a devil – and look his part; that he must be devoid of any positive quality; that he must bear the sign of Cain so visibly that everyone can recognize his destructiveness from afar. Such devils exist, but they are rare . . . Much more often the intensely destructive person will show a front of kindliness . . . he will speak of his ideals and good intentions. But not only this. There is hardly a man who is utterly devoid of any kindness, of any good intentions. If he were he would be on the verge of insanity, except congenital 'moral idiots'. Hence, as long as one believes that the evil man wears horns, one will not discover an evil man.[1]

In order to locate the trouble in time, we need to understand it. And to do this we have to grasp how its patterns are continuous – even though not identical – with ones which appear in our own lives and the lives of those around us. Otherwise, our notion of wickedness is unreal.

The choice of examples to avoid that difficulty is an awkward one. The objection to using the Nazis is that mention of them may give the impression that wicked people tend to be foreigners with funny accents, and moreover – since they are already defeated – are not very dangerous. Every other possible example seems, however, equally open either to this distortion or to arguments about whether what they did was really wrong. This last is less likely with the Nazis than with most other cases. I have therefore used them, but have balanced their case by others, many of them drawn from literature and therefore, I hope, more obviously universal. It is particularly necessary to put the Nazis in perspective because they are, in a way, too good an example. It is not often that an influential political movement is as meanly supplied with positive, constructive ideals as they were. We always like to think that our enemies are like this, but it cannot be guaranteed. To become too obsessed with the Nazis can therefore encourage wishful thinking. It can turn out to be yet one more way of missing their successors – who do not need to be spiritually bankrupt to this extent to be genuinely dangerous – and of inflating mere ordinary opponents to Nazi status. This indeed seems repeatedly to have happened since the Second World War when concepts like 'appeasement' have been used to approximate other and quite different cases to the Nazi one – for instance by Anthony Eden in launching the Suez expedition. In general, politically wicked movements are mixed, standing also for some good, however ill-conceived, and those opposing them have to understand that good if their opposition is not to become distorted by a mindless destructive element.

POSITIVE AND NEGATIVE

To return, then, to our problem – How can we make our notion of wickedness more realistic? To do this, we shall need, I believe, to think of wickedness not primarily as a positive, definite tendency like aggression, whose intrusion into human life needs a special explanation, but rather as negative, as a general kind of failure to live as we are capable of living. It will follow that, in order to understand it, we need primarily to understand our positive capacities. For that, we shall have to take seriously our original constitution, because only so can we understand the things which go wrong with it.

This means recognizing and investigating a whole range of wide natural motives, whose very existence recent liberal theorists have, in the name of decency, often denied – aggression, territoriality, possessiveness, competitiveness, dominance. All are wide, having good aspects as well as bad ones. All are (more or less) concerned with power. The importance of power in human motivation used to be considered a commonplace. Hobbes, Nietzsche, Adler, and others have treated it as central. This suggestion is of course wildly over-simple, but it is not just silly. All these power-related motives are important also in the lives of other social animals, and appear there in behaviour which is, on the face of it, sometimes strikingly like much human behaviour. If we accept that we evolved from very similar creatures, it is natural to take these parallels seriously – to conclude, as we certainly would in the case of any other creature we were studying, that, besides the obvious differences, there is a real underlying likeness. The physiology of our glands and nervous system, too, is close enough to that of other primates to lead to their being constantly used as experimental subjects for investigations of it. And common tradition has never hesitated to treat such dangerous motives as natural, and has often been content to call them 'animal instincts.' I shall suggest that the burden of argument lies today on those who reject this obvious and workable way of thinking, not on those who accept it.

The rejectors bring two main charges against it. Both charges are moral rather than theoretical. Both are in themselves very serious; but they really are not relevant to this issue. They are the fear of fatalism and the fear of power-worship. Fatalism seems to loom because people feel that, if we accept these motives as natural at all, we shall be committed to accepting bad conduct as inevitable, and power-worship seems to follow because what seems inevitable may command approval. But this alarming way of thinking is not necessary. There is no need to conceive a wide and complex motive like aggression on the model of a simple drain-pipe, a channel down which energy flows ineluctably to a single outcome – murder. No motive has that simple form. Aggression and fear, sex and curiosity and ambition, are all extremely versatile, containing many possibilities and contributing to many activities. And the relation of motives to value is still more subtle. We do not need to approve of everything we are capable of desiring. It probably is true in a sense that whatever people actually want has *some* value for them, that all wanted things contain a good. But there are so many such goods, and so much possibility of varying arrangements among them, that this cannot commit us to accepting anything as an overall good just because it is in some way wanted. The relation of these many goods must correspond with the relation among the needs of conscious beings, and conflicts can only be resolved in the light of a priority system amongst those needs. What we really want, if we are to understand them, is a full analysis of the complexities of human motivation.

This analysis, however, would be complicated. And many people still tend to feel that what we have here is an entirely simple issue. As they see it, the whole notion that a motive like aggression, which can produce bad conduct, might be natural is merely an unspeakable abomination, a hypothesis which must not even be considered. They often see this idea as identical with the theological doctrine of original sin, and consider that both, equally, just constitute the same bad excuse for fatalism and repression.

But this is to miss the large question. There is a real difficulty in understanding how people, including ourselves, can act as badly as they sometimes do. External causes alone do not fully explain it. And obviously external causes do not save us from fatalism. A social automaton, worked by conditioning, would be no more free than a physiological one worked by glands. What we need is not a different set of causes, but better understanding of the relation between all causes and free-will. Social and economic fatalism may look like a trouble-saver, because it may seem to make the problem of wickedness vanish, leaving only other people's inconvenient conduct, to be cured by conditioning. In this way, by attending only to outside causes, we try to cut out the idea of personal responsibility. If we blame society for every sin, we may hope that there will no longer be any sense in the question 'Whodunnit?' and so no meaning for the concept of blame either. This policy has obvious attractions, especially when we look at the appalling things which have been done in the name of punishment. Certainly the psychology of blame is a problem on its own. Resentment and vindictiveness are fearful dangers here. But when we are not just dealing with blame and punishment, but attempting to understand human conduct generally, we find that this advantage is illusory. The problem hasn't really gone away; we have only turned our backs on it. The difference between deliberate wrongdoing and mere accidental damage is crucial for a hundred purposes. People who are knocked down no doubt suffer pain whether they are knocked down on purpose or not, but the whole meaning of their suffering and the importance it has in their lives are quite different if it was done intentionally. We mind enormously whodunnit and why they dunnit, and whether the action can eventually be justified.

IS WICKEDNESS MYTHICAL?

Ought we perhaps not to mind about this? Is our moral concern somehow superstitious and outdated? Have we perhaps even – oddly enough – a moral duty to overcome it? This thought hangs in the air today as a cloud which inhibits us from examining many important questions. It may be best to look at it for a start in a rather crude form. The *Observer* for Sunday 28 February 1983 carried this report:

> **British Still Believe in Sin, Hell and the Devil**
> Most Britons still believe in the concept of sin and nearly a third believe in hell and the devil, according to the biggest survey of public opinion ever carried out in the West . . . Belief in sin is highest in Northern Ireland (91 per cent) and lowest in Denmark (29 per cent) . . . Even 15 per cent of atheists believe in sin and 4 per cent in the devil . . . Most Europeans admit that they sometimes regret having done something wrong. The Italians and Danes suffer most from such regrets, the French and Belgians least. The rich regret more than the poor . . . The rich are less likely to believe in sin than the poor.

What were these people supposed to be believing? 'Belief in sin' is not a factual belief, as beliefs in God, hell or the devil certainly are, whatever else they may involve. 'Sin' seems not to be defined in a restrictive way as an offence against God, or the minority of atheists could not have signed up for it. Belief in it can scarcely be identified with the sense of regret for having done wrong, since there might surely be people who thought that others sinned, though they did not think they did so themselves. Besides, the rich apparently do one but not the other. The word 'still' suggests that this puzzling belief is no longer fashionable. But this makes it no easier to see what the belief is actually meant to be, unless it is the simple and obvious one that some actions are wrong. Is the reporter's idea really that up-to-date people – including most Danes and even more atheists – have now withdrawn their objections to all courses of action, including boiling our friends alive just for the hell of it? This is not very plausible. What the survey itself really means cannot of course be discovered from this report. But the journalist's wording is an interesting expression of a jumble of contemporary ideas which will give us a good deal of trouble. They range from the mere observation that the *word* sin is no longer fashionable, through a set of changes in what we count as sins, to some genuine and confusing reasons for doubt and rejection of certain moral views which earlier ages could more easily be confident about. At a popular level, all that is meant is often that sexual activity has been shown not to be sinful. This does not diminish the number of sins, because, where a sexual activity is considered justified, interference with it begins to be blamed. Recognized sins against liberty therefore multiply in exact proportion as recognized sins against chastity grow scarcer.

Original sin, however, is of course a different matter. On the face of it, this phrase is contradictory. Sin must, by definition, be deliberate. And our original constitution cannot be deliberate; we did not choose it. I cannot discuss here what theologians have made of this paradox. But many of them seem to give the phrase 'original sin' a quite limited, sensible use, which has percolated into ordinary thought. They use it to indicate what might be called the raw materials of sin – natural impulses which are indeed not sinful in themselves, but which will lead to sin unless we are conscious and critical of them.[2] They are impulses which would not be present in a perfect creature – for instance, the sudden wish to attack an irritating person without delay. This kind of thing can also be described by the wider phrase of my chapter title: it is a 'natural evil.'

Now that phrase too may well seem paradoxical, particularly if we use it to describe human conduct. The phrase 'natural evil' is often used to contrast unavoidable, non-human disasters, such as plagues and earthquakes, with 'moral evil' or wickedness, which is deliberate. That is a useful distinction. But it leaves out an area between the two. *Moral evil too must surely have its 'natural history'* – a set of given ways in which it tends to occur in a given species. Not every kind of bad conduct is tempting or even psychologically possible for a given kind of being. There might – for instance – be creatures much less partial than we are, creatures entirely without our strong tendency (which appears even in very small children) to prefer some people to others. Their sins and temptations would be quite different from ours. And within the set of vices which belongs to us, some are much more powerful and dangerous than others. If this is true, it seems to be something which we need to understand. We have to look into these trends, not only for the practical purpose of controlling them, but also for the sake of our self-knowledge, our wholeness, our integrity. As Jung has pointed out, every solid object has its shadow-side.[3] The shadowy parts of the mind are an essential part of its form. To deny one's shadow is to lose solidity, to become something of a phantom. Self-deception about it may increase our confidence, but it surely threatens our wholeness.

MEPHISTOPHELES SAYS 'NO'

The notion of these natural, psychological tendencies to evil will, I think, lose some of its strangeness if we are careful to avoid thinking of them primarily as positive tendencies with positive functions, and instead try thinking of them as failures, dysfunctions. Here we stumble over an old dispute about the negativity of evil, one which has suffered, like so many disputes, from being seen as a simple choice between exclusive alternatives, when there are parts of the truth on both sides. The choice is really one between models – patterns of thought which have distinct uses, do not really conflict, but have to be employed in their own proper fields. It has, however, been treated as a matter for fighting, and in the last couple of centuries has been caught up in the general warfare declared between romantic and classical ways of thought. The older notion of evil as negative – which is implicit in much Greek thought, and in the central tradition of Christianity – was marked as classical and shared the general discrediting of classical attitudes. This whole warfare should surely now be seen as a mistaken one, a feud between two essential and complementary sides of life. But its results have been specially disastrous about wrongdoing, because this is a peculiarly difficult subject to think clearly about in any case. Only a very thin set of concepts was left us for handling it, and we are deeply confused about it – which may well account for the blank denial of its existence implied by the reported 'disbelief in sin' just mentioned. The first thing which seems needed here is to recover for use the older, recently neglected, idea of evil as negative – not because it contains the whole truth, but because it does hold an essential part of it.

Apart from its history – which we will consider in a moment – this idea is, on the face of it, natural enough. For instance, people have positive capacities for generosity and courage. They do not need extra capacities for meanness and cowardice as well. To be capable of these virtues is also to be capable of the corresponding vices, just as the possibility of physical strength carries with it that of physical weakness, and can only be understood if we think of that weakness as possible.[4] If we talk of evils natural to our species, we are of course not saying that it is as a whole just 'naturally evil,' which is an unintelligible remark. We are drawing attention to particular evils which beset it. And grasping these evils is an absolutely necessary part of grasping its special excellences. Indeed, the notion of the evils comes first. You could hardly have much idea of generosity if you did not grasp the dangers of meanness. A creature with a Paradisal constitution, immune to all temptation, would not have the vices. But it would not have or need the virtues either. Nor would it, in the ordinary sense, have free-will. Evil, in fact, is essentially the absence of good, and cannot be understood on its own. We constantly need the kind of analysis which Bishop Butler gave of selfishness – 'The thing to be lamented is, not that men have so great regard to their own good or interest in the present world, for they have not enough; but that they have so little to the good of others.'[5]

If we can use this idea, the existence of inborn tendencies to evil need not puzzle us too much. It only means that our good tendencies are not complete or infallible, that we are not faultless moral automata. But is evil negative? People resist this idea at once because they feel that it plays down the force of evil. Can a negative thing be so strong? Actually it can, and this is not a serious objection. Darkness and cold are negative, and they are strong enough. If we want to dramatize the idea, and see how a purely negative motive works out in action, we can consider the manifesto of Mephistopheles in Goethe's *Faust*. When Faust asks him who he is, he answers,

> The spirit I, that endlessly denies
> And rightly too; for all that comes to birth
> Is fit for overthrow, as nothing worth;
> Wherefore the world were better sterilized;
> Thus all that's here as Evil recognized
> Is gain to me, and downfall, ruin, sin,
> The very element I prosper in.[6]

This destruction is not a means to any positive aim. He is simply anti-life. Whatever is arising, he is against it. His element is mere refusal. Now whatever problems may arise about this diagnosis it scarcely shows evil as weak. All earthly good things are vulnerable and need a great deal of help. The power to destroy and to refuse help is not a trifling power.

NOTES

1. *The Anatomy of Human Destructiveness* by E. Fromm (London, Jonathan Cape, 1974), p. 432. Italics mine.
2. Thus for instance C.B. Moss:

   > The Church, following St Paul's teaching, has always maintained that every-body is born with a tendency to sin, a weakness of the will which, if not checked, will result in sin. This weakness was called by the Latin Fathers 'original sin' (*originale peccatum*); it is not a good name, because, strictly speaking, original sin is not sin at all, but a weakness leading to sin, just as a weak chest is not consumption.
   >
   > (*The Christian Faith* (London, SPCK, 1943), pp. 149–50)

3. See for instance his *Modern Man in Search of a Soul* (Kegan Paul, Trench, Trubner, London, 1945, translated Dell and Baynes), pp. 46–8 and 234, and *Answer to Job* (London, Routledge & Kegan Paul, 1954, translated R.F.C. Hull), pp. 133–5 and 154.
4. Aristotle's notion that the vices are essentially just excesses or defects of the tendencies which, at a right level, produce the virtues is a typical expression of this approach. No doubt it is too schematic, but it can be very useful as a starting-point for bringing this problem in focus. See the *Nicomachean Ethics*, Book II.
5. Preface to the *Sermons*, Section 40 (p. 24 of the edition of *Fifteen Sermons* published by G. Bell, London, 1969).
6. *Faust*, part 1, scene 3, translated by Philip Wayne (Harmondsworth, Penguin, 1949), p. 73.

7

THE ELUSIVENESS OF RESPONSIBILITY

How troubled men of our time are by this question of judgement (or, as is often said, by people who dare to 'sit in judgement') has emerged in the controversy over the present book . . . Thus, some American literati have professed their naive belief that temptation and coercion are really the same thing, that no-one can be asked to resist tempta-tion. (If someone puts a pistol to your heart and orders you to shoot your best friend, you must shoot him. Or, as it was argued some years ago in connection with the quiz program scandal in which a university teacher had hoaxed the public – when so much money is at stake, who could possibly resist?) The argument that we cannot judge if we were not present and involved ourselves seems to convince everyone everywhere, although it seems obvious that if it were true, neither the administration of justice nor the writing of history would ever be possible.

DOI: 10.4324/9781003588160-11

In contrast to these confusions, the reproach of self-righteousness raised against those who do judge is age-old; but that does not make it any the more valid . . . All German Jews unanimously have condemned the wave of co-ordination which passed over the German people in 1933 and from one day to the next turned the Jews into pariahs. Is it conceivable that none of them ever asked himself how many of his own group would have done just the same if only they had been allowed to? *But is their condemnation to-day any the less correct for that reason?*

Hannah Arendt, *Eichmann in Jerusalem*[1] (italics mine)

THE FEAR OF JUDGING

The uneasiness about judging which Hannah Arendt notes here makes it hard for us to approach our next question. That question is 'How does wickedness work in an individual? Granted that some things – for instance cases of gross exploitation and oppression – actually are wrong, as we have been arguing, do the exploiters and oppressors know what they are doing, or don't they?' To this query the spirit of our age replies, frowning, that the question cannot arise because there is no such thing as individual wickedness, and accordingly there are no people who can be identified as exploiters and oppressors:

About nothing does public opinion everywhere seem to be in happier agreement than that no one has the right to judge someone else. What public opinion permits us to judge and even to condemn are trends, or whole groups of people – in short, something so general that distinctions can no longer be made . . . This is currently expressed in high-flown assertions that it is 'superficial' to insist on details and to mention individuals, whereas it is the sign of sophistication to speak in generalities according to which all cats are gray and we are all equally guilty . . . 'Undoubtedly there is reason for grave accusations, but the defendant is mankind as a whole.'

(ibid. 297)

Thus, public wickedness vanishes into a social problem, as private wickedness does into mental illness. This policy excludes much more than the administration of justice and the writing of history. The knife cuts deeper. It slices off all our power of self-direction. The function of moral judgement in our inner lives is to build up a store of cases approved and disapproved for various reasons – a map by which we can orient ourselves and plot our own course when we have to make decisions. Because we each have to act as individuals, these cases must in the first place be individual ones. Moral judgements on groups and masses have to be secondary, if they can be made at all.[2] Nor can we do what the phrase 'no one has the right to judge someone else' may suggest, and build up our store entirely from verdicts on our own behaviour. Without an immensely wider range of comparisons, self-judgement could never start. When we wonder whether our own conduct is right, we need to be able to ask 'What would I think about this if somebody else did it?' We shall get no answer unless we can call on a range of comparable cases in the past when we actually have judged other people. This does not of course mean stoning them or sending them to jail, merely forming an opinion on what they have done.[3] It is an aspect of treating them with respect as responsible agents.

Equally, approval and disapproval contribute an essential element to our attitudes to all those around us – to our likes and dislikes, our fears and hopes, horror and admiration, respect and contempt for other people. To inhibit these reactions would be to treat them not as people at all, but as some kind of alien impersonal phenomena. Since it is not possible to treat *oneself* in this way, this would produce a bizarre sense of total isolation in the universe. It cannot actually be done.[4] The need to see ourselves and others as on essentially the same moral footing is in fact so deep that nobody gets anywhere near carrying out this policy. What it usually amounts to is a quite local moral campaign directed against the actual process of blaming. Moral judgement is by no means withheld; it is simply directed with exceptional ferocity against those caught blaming and punishing culprits accused of more traditional offences. This carries guidance of a negative kind for occasions when one is confronted with these offences oneself – namely 'Don't blame or punish.' That advice can sometimes be suitable and useful. But it is extremely limited. Most of life does not consist of such occasions, and most moral difficulties call for other principles, with their background of other moral judgements. Another principle which may be seen as flowing from the non-judging attitude might be 'Feel guilt for all evils; you are always involved as part of society.' This, however, seems to reduce guilt to a futile and meaningless reaction. Hannah Arendt comments that 'morally speaking, it is hardly less wrong to feel guilty without having done something specific than it is to feel free of all guilt if one is actually guilty of something.'[5] This makes sense, because guilt is a thought as well as a feeling, and when that thought is specific it has an essential function in continually reshaping our attitudes. To make it universal is to leave little more than the feeling, which can only be indulged as an end in itself.

LOSING THE INDIVIDUAL

Obviously, however, the anti-judgement campaign has a serious point, though a much more limited one than its language suggests. Apart from merely attacking *bad* moral judgements, it points to a number of confusions about the notions of judgements and responsibility. Two of them specially concern us here. In both, I think we shall find that the real objection is not to moral judgement as such. It is either to *bad*, distorted moral judgement, or to the absence of some other way of thinking – such as the social or scientific – which is needed to balance and complete it. When these other ways of thinking are absent, and moral judgement is extended on its own to do their work, things naturally go wrong. But the remedy is not to abolish moral judgement. It is to fit both together. The real trouble lies in the false antitheses which show the moral point of view as a rival to some other, when in fact they supplement each other.

The first and most familiar of these antitheses is the apparent clash between the moral point of view and that of the physical sciences, which gives us such headaches over free-will. The second one, which is our chief worry here, is related to it but not quite the same. It is the clash between the corporate point of view and the individual one. Here the trouble is not so much that the social sciences, which take the corporate point of view, assume determinism. They may not even do so. It is that, by studying large-scale events, they place themselves at a distance from which individual behaviour is simply invisible. The reasons for doing this are sound ones. For instance, the old-fashioned view of history as depending on the personal ruminations of rulers was implausible, and it is not possible to replace it by an account of the personal ruminations of everybody. The Marxist conception of history as the play of large-scale economic forces is therefore enormously useful, and there are plenty of other large-scale conceptual schemes which can supplement it.

Trouble only arises when these schemes are taken to compete with and annihilate the individual point of view – to prove it unnecessary by demonstrating that everybody is only the pawn or product of their society. This looks like a causal argument, but it cannot really be one. Causally, it would be just as true that the society was only the product of its past and present members. It is a manifesto, issued on behalf of corporate ways of thinking which are suitable for certain purposes, and designed to extend their empire over other purposes, eliminating all rivals. This imperialism is sometimes seen as a matter of metaphysics, individuals being actually 'less real' than their communities. More often today, however, it is treated as a question of method; the attack is against 'methodological individualism.' This strange language assumes that these are rival methods for a single aim – that one of them must be eliminated if the other is used, like front-wheel or back-wheel drive on a car. But the purposes and interests of different ways of thinking can be totally different. Anatomy does not eliminate physiology, nor history politics.

Large-scale thinking about societies is not an alternative to thinking directly about individuals. Both studies are necessary; each needs its own methods. And within the study of individuals, enquiry about the facts is not an alternative to practical and especially moral thinking, which works out the concepts and principles to be used in action. Moral philosophy investigates these and the conceptual schemes which underlie them and link them to the rest of our conceptual system. Thought, as applied to human life, can therefore be crudely divided like this:

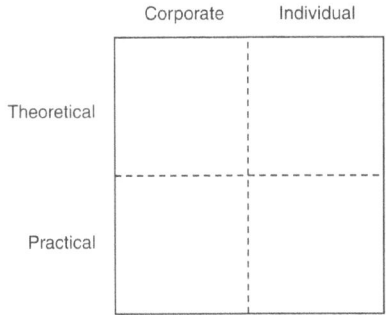

But during the last century, when an idealized picture of physical science has obsessed the imagination of the English-speaking world, and come to be taken as the only proper kind of thought, the top left-hand area has increasingly come to look like the only respectable one, because it is the only one which looks like even a bad imitation of the physical sciences. In this alarming situation, interdisciplinary tiffs which already treated neighbouring provinces as rivals and alternatives have made it fatally easy to cut along the dotted lines.

AUTONOMY VERSUS CONTINUITY

Moral philosophy, occupied chiefly with matters well down on the right, has been especially threatened. Not surprisingly, it has reacted by producing yet another false antithesis of its own. This is the violent dilemma posed between an individual's autonomy and his or her continuity with the world. Many current ways of thinking tend either to make individuals vanish into their groups, or to reduce them to their physical parts. Both these processes make it seem as if they had no real identity or control, and so to suggest that it does not matter what they do. Against these threats, defenders of autonomy have reacted sharply by painting a very different sort of individuals – purely mental entities, radically isolated, independent, self-creating and alien, perhaps hostile, to everything around them. This extreme picture appears at its clearest in existentialism, in social contract theory, and in a range of educational theories which stress self-expression to the exclusion of what a child receives from the world, though it has many other roots as well.[6]

This inflated notion of autonomy is the mirror-image of Socrates's paradox that 'nobody does wrong willingly.' Socrates eliminated the will, making moral choice seem an entirely intellectual matter. Modern autonomism leaves nothing but the will, a pure, unbiased power of choice, detached equally from the choosing subject's present characteristics and from all the objects it must choose between. In doing this it far outruns its distant ancestor Kant, more and more limited quotations from whom still appear as its warrant, and who still gets attacked for its excesses.[7] The arrogance of Sartre's remark, 'Man is nothing else but what he makes of himself'[8] is quite alien to Kant. Whatever his mistakes, Kant was always trying seriously to make sense of human life, and therefore to bring its two sides together in the end. By contrast, modern autonomism is embattled, and will have no truck with the opposition.

Both these two extreme views of human agency have a point. Each tells us something important. The nature of the self is so strange and difficult a subject that we have to deal with it by putting unbalanced insights like this together and using them to correct each other. Controversy, however, always tends to make us pit extremes against each other as rivals and force us to choose between them. On a topic so close to our lives, this is very bewildering, and the effect gets worse the subtler and more learned the disputants happen to be. Partisanship combined with great ingenuity is bound to confuse the reader who is not primarily interested in being a lawyer for either side. The large paradoxes which make good weapons of war have to be dismantled, if those of us who are not chiefly interested in fighting want to extract the much smaller nuggets of truth which they contain.

ONE-WAY SCEPTICISM

The ways of thinking by which we thus distinguish between what can and what cannot be helped, and the opinions which we build on them about actions and agents, may be rough and fallible, but they are absolutely essential for human life. Certainly, it is of the utmost importance that they should be used rightly and not wrongly. But it seems meaningless to suggest that they ought to stop being used at all. Criticisms of their current usage ought therefore surely always to be as specific, as constructive as possible. They should say in concrete terms what kind of thing is to stop and what kind of thing is to replace it. Academic controversy, however, always tends to give the advantage to the sceptic, and to put the burden of positive suggestions on his opponent. Extremely vague, destructive suggestions therefore thrive in it. At an everyday level, similar sweeping destructiveness is common. Thus, Barbara Wootton, after discussing the paradoxes which tend to arise when we try to understand and judge psychopaths, concludes that 'the psychopath may well prove to be the thin end of the wedge which will ultimately shatter the whole idea of moral responsibility.'[9] This seems to ignore the fact that all conceptual schemes run into difficulties and paradoxes when they are used for awkward and unusual cases. We can often extend them to deal with such problems; indeed, this is how we usually develop them. But we can never ensure that the same thing will not happen again with a new range of cases.

Conceptual schemes are not like electric kettles; they do not do a strictly limited job, so they have no guarantee of infallibility. Even with kettles, of course, really careless or malicious use can produce disaster, and this is still more true of conceptual schemes. What seems needed at the moment is that general denunciations of our notions of morality and responsibility, whether at a popular or a philosophical level, should carry explanations which will show, much more clearly than is done at present, where they stand on a scale of specificness which ranges from 'this kettle is no good; they must give us another under guarantee' to 'stop the world and bring me another one.' Since Nietzsche's day, what tends to happen is that the denunciation is phrased in extremely general terms, while the complaints brought to support it are quite limited, and are actually moral accusations of a familiar kind. Barbara Wootton, for instance, wants a more humane, less vindictive attitude to social offenders, but she has moral reasons for this, and clearly thinks the privileged members of society *responsible* – in a quite traditional sense – for providing it. Criticisms of this sort are attacks on particular moral misjudgements, not on moral judgement itself. Putting them in a more general, hyperbolical, Nietzschean form certainly gives them dramatic force. But the effect of this move is not what it was in Nietzsche's time. Hypocrisy is not so straightforward today. Many more people now are willing to abandon moral judgement in a quite open and simple way – to drop all attempt at concern for what is happening in the world, and treat all human action as inevitable. Hypocrisy used to be the tribute which vice paid to virtue. Today, some of the vices no longer pay it at all, and the others largely pay in a different coinage, less easily exposed by simple, hyperbolical Nietzschean methods.[10] Indeed, it may be that these methods can no longer be used for moral reform.

VICE, WEAK WILL, AND MADNESS

The last section has been intended to show that the idea of individual wickedness is not an unreal one. If that is right, we come back here to our problem about how this wickedness works, how it is psychologically and logically possible. Do exploiters and oppressors know what they are doing, or not? This question is not easy. Hasty answers to it have supplied further reasons why the use of the term 'wickedness' may seem naive. Aristotle made an interesting distinction between people of weak will, who do wrong against their real wishes and intentions, and vicious people, who do wrong contentedly and with conviction.[11] Philosophers have paid more attention to problems about the first contingent than to those about the second, which is perhaps rather surprising. Certainly, weak will is a problem, but it is one with which we are all thoroughly familiar, both from the inside and the outside. And these two views of weakness match reasonably well. We may well be uncertain what is the best way of describing the confused state in which people manage to do things which they admit to be wrong. But the description of this which we accept for our own case is also one which we can apply to other people. With vice, this is not usually so. Contentedly vicious people do not as a rule describe themselves as vicious, nor even think their actions wrong. They tend either to justify them or to reject moral questions as pointless and irrelevant. Exceptions make a curious impression. Ernst Röhm, co-founder with Hitler of the Nazi party (though later murdered by the SS), wrote in his autobiography, 'Since I am an immature and bad man, war appeals to me more than peace.'[12] To understand what he meant by this we seem to need a context – one which will show it perhaps as a real spasm of conscience, perhaps as a passing mood, but perhaps also as some kind of sarcastic joke or way of making a debating point. It cannot have the simple, literal sense that such a remark made about somebody else would have. In general, as Aristotle said, 'vice is unconscious of itself; weakness is not.'[13] There does not seem to be an inside point of view on vice. And this strengthens the suspicion that perhaps there simply is no such thing, that vice itself is fabulous. That suspicion is most often expressed today by the thought that people who commit appalling acts must necessarily be mad, that is, ill. And although the whole notion of mental illness has come under attack for other reasons, people still tend to regard it as the only possible humane response to this particular problem. A number of very interesting considerations converge to fix this habit of mind. One is, of course, the immense respect in which the medical profession is currently held, the widespread impression that the devoted work of doctors can, given time and resources, deal with every evil. Though there has been some reaction against this faith in recent years, it is still very strong, and doctors who would like to spread a more modest and realistic estimate of their powers find it hard to do so. Apart from the accidental factor that doctors here inherit the magic which is no longer attributed to priests, wish-fulfilment strongly supports this extension of the medical model. Mental disorder itself is terrifying, a vast and indistinct menace which we would be very glad to hand over to an invincible giant-killer. And in their early overconfidence in modern drugs, some psychiatrists did license the public to cast them in this role. But beyond the area of identifiable mental disorder lies another, equally appalling, which has traditionally been viewed as distinct; that of wickedness. Can it, too, be brought under the same benevolent and enlightened empire? Can we hope in this way to make obsolete the whole notion not only of punishment, but of blame, and to apply medical remedies instead?

This suggestion brings out a sharp conflict in our concepts. On the one hand, the idea that wickedness is a form of madness is very natural, because bad conduct is so readily seen as unintelligible. To say 'I simply don't understand how they could act like that' is a quite direct form of condemnation. To say 'What did you mean by it?' is to ask for justification; if no meaning can be shown which will make the act intelligible, then it will be considered wrong. On the other hand, however, madness counts as an excuse. It is assumed that so far as people are mad they cannot help what they do. Extending this medical model to cover the whole area of wickedness would therefore excuse everybody equally, flattening out the whole subtle spectrum of degrees of responsibility, and putting the genuinely unfortunate on the same footing as the sanest and most deliberate criminals. This suggestion makes little sense, if only because the sane ones will not be willing to accept any such diagnosis or treatment any more than many of the deranged, and both equally will often reject another condition which seems naturally to belong to the medical model, namely, the belief that they are suffering from a *misfortune*. Besides, most medical scientists themselves have no expectation of ever being able to extend their skills to cover this range of difficulties, and no wish to be credited with claiming such powers.

PHANTOM MORALITIES

In general, then, there are strong objections to viewing all wrongdoers as mad, as well as strong temptations to do it, and for many cases people do not find this explanation plausible. In these cases, however, another strategy often comes into play to make the offence look intelligible. This is to credit the offenders with having a complete morality of their own, which, for them, justifies their actions. This idea leads people to suppose that (for instance) the Nazis must have been original reasoners, with an independent, consistent, and well-thought-out ethical theory – a view which their careers and writings do not support at all. As Hannah Arendt points out, at the Nuremburg trials, the lack of this much-advertised commodity became painfully obvious.

> The defendants accused and betrayed each other and assured the world that they 'had always been against it' . . . Although most of them must have known that they were doomed, not a single one of them had the guts to defend the Nazi ideology.[14]

This was not just from a failure of nerve, though that in itself would be significant in a movement apparently devoted to the military virtues. It was also because there was not really much coherent ideology that could be defended. The only part of it which carried real passionate conviction was emotional and destructive; it was the hatred of the Jews. This always remained constant, but almost every other element varied according to the audience addressed and the political possibilities of the moment. The enemy might be Communism or capitalism, the elite or the rabble, France or Russia or the Weimar government, just as interest dictated at the time. It was therefore hard to say much that was positive and constructive about the aims of the regime. Germany was to expand, but why it would be a good thing that it should do so remained obscure. Hitler has been credited with ideas drawn from Nietzsche, but there seems no reason to suppose that he picked up much more than the flavour of Nietzsche's titles, such as *The Will to Power* and *Beyond Good and Evil*.[15] (Nietzsche himself, of course, violently denounced anti-Semitism, and quarrelled mortally with Wagner on the subject. This is one of many cases where he displayed strong, clear, traditional moral indignation, not at all inhibited by the kind of sceptical considerations to which many people today seem to think his kind of reasoning commits them.) Nazism at least is a good case of a moral vacuum.

THE PARADOX OF RESPONSIBLE NEGLIGENCE

To return, then, to the general problem – wickedness is not the same thing as madness, nor as a genuine eccentric morality. Both madness and honest eccentric thinking constitute *excuses*. And the notion of an excuse only works if there can be some cases which are not excusable, cases to which it does not apply. The notion of real wickedness is still assumed as a background alternative. Yet that notion is still hard to articulate.

The reason why it is so hard is, I suggest, that we do not take in what it means to say that evil is negative. We are looking for it as something positive, and that positive thing we of course fail to find. If we ask whether exploiters and oppressors know what they are doing, the right answer seems to be that they do *not* know, because they carefully avoid thinking about it – but that they could know, and therefore their deliberate avoidance is a responsible act. In the First World War, when a staff officer was eventually sent out to France to examine the battlefield, he broke down in tears at the sight of it, and exclaimed, 'Have we really been ordering men to advance through all that mud?' This is a simple case of factual ignorance, flowing from negligence. Negligence on that scale, however, is not excusable casualness. It is, as we would normally say, criminal. The general recipe for inexcusable acts is neither madness nor a bizarre morality, but a steady refusal to attend both to the consequences of one's actions and to the principles involved.

This is at least a part of what Socrates meant by his paradoxical insight that nobody does wrong willingly. (Socrates, of course, was chiefly interested in the principles rather than the consequences, but as far as the kind of ignorance involved goes the two cases seem similar.) If the wrongdoer really understood what he was doing, Socrates said, he could not possibly do it. This sounds at first like an excuse, like saying that all wrongdoers are misinformed or mad. But Socrates certainly did not mean it as an excuse. He said it as part of his attempt to get people to think more, in order to avoid wickedness. His approach to wickedness was not a remote, third-person one, directed simply to questions about the proper treatment of offenders. It was primarily a first- and second-person enquiry about how each one of us actually goes wrong. He is talking about something fully in our control, something which he takes to be the essence of sin – namely, a deliberate blindness to ideals and principles, a stalling of our moral and intellectual faculties. The balance of positive and negative elements here is complicated and will occupy us again later. But it is perhaps worth glancing here at an example drawn from Hannah Arendt's discussion of Eichmann:

> When I speak of the banality of evil, I do so only on the strictly factual level, pointing to a phenomenon which stared one in the face at the trial. Eichmann was not Iago and not Macbeth, and nothing would have been further from his mind than to determine with Richard III 'to prove a villain.' Except for an extraordinary diligence in looking out for his personal advancement, he had no motives at all. And this diligence in itself was in no way criminal; he certainly would never have murdered his superior in order to inherit his post. He *merely*, to put the matter colloquially, *never realized what he was doing*. It was precisely this lack of imagination which enabled him to sit for months on end facing a German Jew who was conducting the police interrogation, pouring out his heart to the man and explaining again and again how it was that he reached only the rank of lieutenant-colonel in the SS, and that it had not been his fault that he was not promoted. In principle he knew quite well what it was all about, and in his final statement to the court he spoke of the 'revaluation of values' prescribed by the (Nazi) government. He was not stupid. It was sheer thoughtlessness – something by no means identical with stupidity – that predisposed him to become one of the greatest criminals of that period.[16]

As she says, the administrative complexity of the modern world makes such cases increasingly common. Bureaucracy tends to look like 'the rule of nobody,' and this obscuring of individual responsibility is one thing which makes the concept of wickedness seem so hard to apply. But if we fatalistically accept that it has become impossible, we are falling for propaganda. 'The essence of totalitarian government, and perhaps the nature of every bureaucracy, is to make functionaries and mere cogs in the administrative machinery out of men, and thus to dehumanize them.'[17] It has not really changed their nature and removed their responsibility from them. It has certainly made it easier for them to do wrong, and harder to do right. But there have always been agencies that would do that, and in all ages much ingenuity has gone into building them for that very purpose.

NOTES

1. H. Arendt, *Eichmann in Jerusalem*, rev. edn (Penguin, Harmondsworth, 1963), p. 296.

2. That they cannot be made, morality being essentially a private matter, is a view which has some influence today, having been clearly expressed by R. Niebuhr in his book *Moral Man and Immoral Society* (Charles Scribner's Sons, New York, 1948). The problems he raised are real ones, but this simple solution to them has grave drawbacks. It is one of a number of ways of limiting the term *morality* to narrow spheres, which seem bound to bring it into contempt. See 'Is "Moral" a Dirty Word?' in my *Heart and Mind*.

3. We would not wish never to have any opinion, good or bad, formed about us – so 'judge not that ye be not judged' cannot forbid the forming of such opinions. The tag 'to understand all is to forgive all' cannot do so either, since forgiveness is in place only for acknowledged offences. See 'On Trying Out One's New Sword' in my *Heart and Mind*.

4. As Strawson pointed out in his admirable paper 'Freedom and Resentment' in the volume with that name.

5. *Eichmann in Jerusalem*, p. 298.

6. It is admirably discussed by John Benson in an article called 'Who is the Autonomous Man?', *Philosophy*, January (1983), vol. 58, no. 223.

7. I cannot do much to correct this here. Kant wrote the whole *Critique of Practical Reason* to explore the connection between morality and happiness, and the *Critique of Judgement* to explore that between feeling, purpose and thought. He also wrote a short preliminary book to make certain distinctions needed for this work. Significantly, he called it the *Groundwork to the Metaphysic of Morals*, not suggesting that it was his last word on the matter. (Its title in Paton's translation, *The Moral Law*, obscures this.) British philosophers, who in many other cases have now relaxed their rule of reading only one book by each philosopher, sternly adhere to it in Kant's case, and treat a few quotations from the rather dramatic opening sections of the *Groundwork* as his last words on both individuality and freedom. Both Williams and Nagel take as their chief opponent the resulting shadowy figure, who is supposed to be

Kant, but to whom they amazingly attribute 'a very simple image of rationality' (Williams, *Moral Luck*, p. 22). Kant himself spent most of his life emphasizing and studying the complexities of this concept. Unless one means to deploy his view as a whole, it is surely better to deal directly with contemporary autonomy-worship, which is our real headache today.

8. Sartre, *Existentialism and Humanism*, p. 28.

9. B. Wootton, *Social Science and Social Pathology* (London, Allen & Unwin, 1959) p. 251. Her argument, though much less subtle, seems to be essentially the same as Williams's – if an argument cannot handle every kind of case, it was a bad argument, and cannot be used anywhere. This is a quick way to empty the tool-kit in any department of thought. And did anyone ever see reason to suppose that morality was likely to be a specially simple area – one where a single way of thinking would always do the whole job? It is an enormous merit in Williams's discussion that he does justice to the complexity of life. But this makes it hard for him to draw any such simple, sweeping sceptical conclusions.

10. Notably, of course, in affectation of the Nietzschean virtues – courage and honesty.

11. *Nicomachean Ethics*, book VII.

12. Quoted by K. Heiden, *Der Fuehrer: Hitler's Rise to Power*, tr. R. Mannheim (London, Gollancz, 1944), p. 30.

13. *Nicomachean Ethics*, book VII, Chapter 8. Plato makes the same point, *Republic*, book III, 409.

14. *Eichmann in Jerusalem*, p. 175.

15. A matter checked by R.J. Hollingdale and reported in his biography *Nietzsche* (Routledge & Kegan Paul, London, 1973), p. 201.

16. *Eichmann in Jerusalem*, pp. 287.

17. *Eichmann in Jerusalem*, pp. 289.

8

SELVES AND SHADOWS

THE PROBLEM OF SELF-DECEPTION

We come back now to our original problem – the attempt to make wickedness understandable – absolved, if all has gone well, from various objections to the whole project, and equipped with some concepts which may help us. The problem, however, can still look an uncommonly awkward one. A cartoon of Edward Koren's may suggest why.[1] It shows a cheerful mechanic, tools upraised in triumph, pointing to the open bonnet of a car and telling the owner with satisfaction, 'Well, there's your problem.' Inside the car, there is nothing but a huge, prickly monster, crouched together in a sinister manner and baring its huge teeth in a knowing grin. The owner knows what's wrong now. But what is he going to do about it?

I have been suggesting that the wrong kind of approach to the problem of wickedness does make it look very much like this. Evil, considered as something positive, would indeed have to be an alien being, a demon

DOI: 10.4324/9781003588160-12

which had taken possession. The only possible kind of treatment would then be to cast it out somehow from the possessed person. (That feat is indeed often expected, not only of witch-doctors and exorcists, but also of educators, of psychiatrists and of psychoanalysts.) This casting-out will not get far unless it is somehow replanned to take account of the fact that evil traits are not just something alien. In one sense, they are simply qualities of the person who owns them, though in another they are indeed something extraneous which has attacked him. This duality is a most puzzling feature of our mental life, and a continual practical as well as theoretical problem. We try to avoid 'owning' our bad motives, not just from vanity (though that is important) but because we feel that to own or acknowledge is to accept. We dread exposure to the hidden force whose power we sense. Our official idea of ourselves has no room for it. It therefore does not seem merely humiliating and depressing (as our known faults do), but alien, inhuman and menacing to an indefinite degree. When this sense of menace gets severe, it is almost certain to get projected on to the outside world, supplying fuel for those irrational fears and hatreds which play so central a part in human destructiveness.

In what may be called contentedly wicked people – and in all of us so far as we are contentedly wicked – this process is far gone, and may involve no more conflict in the inner life than in the front shown to the world. It is the fact that no conflict is visible that makes this kind of case so opaque. But this need not force us either to assume a special alternative morality at work, or to give up the attempt at understanding altogether. Instead, we can approach this kind of case by way of the much less opaque ones where conflict is still visibly raging. Hard though this is, it seems necessary to attempt it since self-deception, in spite of its chronic obscurity, is a topic which we badly need to understand. Bishop Butler, at the end of his discussion of it, cries out suddenly:

> And, if people will be wicked, they had better of the two be so from the common vicious passions without such refinements, than from this deep and calm source of delusion, which undermines the whole principle of good, darkens that light, that *candle of the Lord within*, which is to direct our steps, and corrupts conscience, which is the guide of life.[2]

Does this mean that there are two quite separate alternatives, self-deception and vice? It seems not. Butler apparently takes 'the common vicious passions' to be something conscious and acknowledged. But the more fully conscious they are, the nearer their owners come to what Aristotle called weakness, rather than vice.[3] They suffer spasms of (say) furious or covetous action alternating with fits of repentance. People who are weak in this sense are supposed still to keep so clear an intellectual grasp of the situation that they judge their own acts impartially, as they would other people's. This seems rather strange. The disadvantages of oscillating violently in this way are obvious, and in fact if we find people who seem to do it we tend to look for an explanation in some oscillation of their physical state. Without this extra factor, it is hard to see how the oscillator's clarity of vision can really be maintained. Some self-deception seems absolutely necessary, first so that he can have some kind of a story to tell himself during his vicious fits, but also, and more deeply, because the whole process of oscillation is going to need some justification of its own, and it will be uncommonly difficult to find an honest one. The question why one is behaving alternatively like two quite different people is one that cannot fail to arise. The answer 'I just happen to be two people' has never been found to be very satisfactory. Butler's point, then, seems sound, but it is a matter of degree, not a complete dichotomy. The more chronic, continuous, and well-established is the self-deception, the deeper and more pernicious the vice. But some self-deception is probably needed if actions are to be called vicious at all.

INNER DIALOGUE AND DUALITY

I am suggesting that self-deception arises because we see motives which are in fact our own as alien to us and refuse to acknowledge them. This is not an isolated event, but is one possible outcome of a very common and pervasive inner dialogue, in which aspects of the personality appear to exchange views as if they were separate people. We are used to this interchange between alternating moods or view-points. (If we were not, we should probably find it much harder to dis-own some of them, because it would be harder to separate them from our official selves in the first place.) This inner dialogue is, I believe, the source of drama. Good plays and stories do not just show clashes between distinct individuals, externally related. They show ones which take place within us as well as outside. However black the villains, however strange the character-parts, we need to feel something within us respond to them. Drama helps inner conflict by crystallizing it. It can, of course, be used to help self-deception by externalizing villainy, but it can also help self-knowledge by showing up the participants clearly. Properly used, it always helps us to avoid that dangerous thing, an oversimple view of personal identity.

There is a great deal more to the problem of personal identity than meets the eye, or gets mentioned in current philosophical discussions. This connection with inner conflict and the problem of evil, in particular, seems to have had very little academic attention of late. It is, however, very important, on account of the existence of shadows. In this century, academic philosophy, as much as psychology, has been reluctant to pay much attention to the shadow-side of human motivation. It has not occupied itself with the agonizing question 'Can it really have been I who did that?' or with the genuine clash of reasons for answering yes or no to it. Nor has it dealt much with the still more startling division of the self into two or more embattled factions which marks the process of temptation. If we want to find a way into these problems, we had therefore better turn to those who have seriously and methodically considered them. Setting aside the religious traditions for a moment − because we are not sure how much of their conceptual equipment we shall want to accept − we are left, therefore, with works of imagination, and particularly of imaginative literature.

There is absolutely no shortage of shadows here. Resisting the urge to plunge in and round them all up, I shall deliberately start with a rather simple and schematic specimen, namely *The Strange Case of Dr Jekyll and Mr Hyde*. Critics have sometimes treated this story as a lightweight, but I think they are mistaken. Any crash course on evil must acknowledge a great debt to the Scots, and the debt to Stevenson here seems to be quite an important part of it. It is worth while, if one has not taken it very seriously, having another look.

What Stevenson brings out is the negativity of Hyde's character. Evil, in spite of its magnificent pretensions, turns out to be mostly a vacuum. That does not make it less frightening, but more so. Like darkness and cold, it destroys but it cannot replace. The thought is an old one, but we may have regarded it simply as a platitude. In the story, however, Hyde's first appearance shows it sharply:

> Street after street and all the folks asleep . . . All at once I saw two figures; one a little man who was stumping along eastwards at a good walk, and the other a girl of maybe eight or ten who was running as hard as she was able down a cross street. Well sir, the two ran into one another naturally enough at the corner; and then came the horrible part of the thing; for the man trampled calmly over the child's body and left her screaming on the ground. It sounds nothing to hear, but it was hellish to see.[4]

What makes it so is not deliberate cruelty, but callousness – the total absence of a normal human response. David Hume (a Scot of a different kind) asked, 'Would any man, who is walking along, tread as willingly on another's gouty toes, whom he has no quarrel with, as on the hard flint and pavement?'[5] Well, here is that man, and his total blindness to any feeling but his own is central to his character. As Jekyll puts it, when he is eventually driven to attempt a choice between his two lives:

> Hyde was indifferent to Jekyll, or but remembered him as the mountain bandit remembers the cavern in which he conceals himself from pursuit. Jekyll had more than a father's interest (because he shared Hyde's pleasures); Hyde had more than a son's indifference.[6]

This is why, although Hyde had

> a soul boiling with causeless hatreds, and a body that seemed not strong enough to contain the raging energies of life, [Jekyll] . . . thought of Hyde, for all his energy of life, as of something not only hellish but

inorganic. This was the shocking thing; that the slime of the pit seemed to utter cries and voices; that what was dead and had no shape, should usurp the offices of life.[7]

This fearful limitation is, of course, the reason why he cannot choose to settle for Hyde, but must continue the doomed effort to be Jekyll. He notes it again, as he draws his memoirs to a close:

> Should the throes of change take me in the act of writing this, Hyde will tear it in pieces; but if some time shall have elapsed after I have laid it by, his wonderful selfishness and circumscription to the moment will probably save it again from the action of his ape-like spite.[8]

Hyde, appalling though he is, is no princely Lucifer; he is meanly subhuman. Mention of the 'ape' here has its usual negative point. Symbolic animals stand merely for the absence of certain human powers and feelings, even though in real life animals may share these. Most animals in fact avoid trampling others underfoot, as has been noticed with annoyance when people have wanted to make horses or elephants do it. In the animal kingdom, Hyde is something special. But his specialness does not consist in a new, exciting, positive motivation. It is an emotional crippling, a partial death of his faculties.

SHADOW-SHEDDING

What has produced this crippling? It resulted in fact from a rather casual miscalculation on the part of Jekyll. (This casualness is, I think, what stops some people taking the story seriously. But the story is surely about the casualness, rather than being an expression of it.) Jekyll found, early in life, that his ambition was in conflict with his taste for dissipation, and decided to try and separate these two motives so that each could pursue its interests without hindrance from the other. He therefore accepted, and still defends to the end, the proposition that man is not truly one, but truly two. I say two, because the state of my own knowledge does not pass beyond this point . . . [but perhaps] man will be ultimately known for a mere polity of multifarious, incongruous and independent denizens.[9]

But of course he does not accept this idea seriously and literally as requiring a full separation, with an impartial distribution of chances to the multifarious denizens on a timesharing basis. He sees it simply as providing a splendid disguise, which will allow the old Jekyll his fun while protecting his reputation and his complacency. (This is where the casualness comes in.)

'I do not think I ever met Mr Hyde?' asked Utterson. 'Oh dear no sir. He never *dines* here,' replied the butler. 'Indeed, we see very little of him on this side of the house; he mostly comes and goes by the laboratory.'[10]

And again, as Jekyll puts it, 'The moment I choose, I can be rid of Mr Hyde. I give you my hand upon that.'[11] This was his whole plan for the relationship. His 'discovery' of duality therefore means merely something which others have tried out before him, namely, the hypothesis that it *doesn't matter what you do with your shadow*. Peter Schlemihl sold his shadow to the devil, never supposing that he would need it.[12] He soon found out his mistake. Dorian Gray let his picture absorb the effects of his iniquities, supposing that he could ignore it, but it got him in the end. The dismissed shadow in Hans Andersen's story came back after many years, having grown a new body, though a thin one. It was embarrassingly obsequious at first, but rapidly grew more and more domineering, and reduced its former owner to the status of its shadow. When he tried to resist, it killed him. It is well known that you can't be too careful about these things. But the project of shadow-immunity which throws most light on our present subject is another Scottish one, James Hogg's novel, *The Confessions of a Justified Sinner*.[13] This is an altogether deeper affair. The sinner, Robert Wringhim, has accepted with his whole heart the doctrine of justification by faith alone. He then becomes convinced of his own salvation, and thus believes himself to be henceforward incapable of sin. Going out to give thanks to God for this state of affairs, he is stopped by a mysterious stranger, his exact double. This person deflects him from his purpose by flattering words ('I am come to be a humble disciple of yours; to be initiated into the true way of true salvation by conversing with you, and perhaps of being assisted by your prayers').[14] Instead of joining Wringhim in thanking God, he points out to him that he is now a highly exceptional and privileged person, incapable of sin, and therefore free to commit every possible kind of action without blame. Are there not, therefore, remarkable acts to which he is called? Wringhim, who already believes most of those around him to be worthless enemies of the Lord, predestined to damnation, has no defence against the suggestion that it is his duty to kill many of them, including his own family. And this, in spite of his timidity and some other natural objections, he is finally led on to do.

The ingenious use of Calvin's doctrine thus provides Wringhim's shadow-self with a quite exceptionally wide scope for exemption from responsibility. Dorian Gray's exemption covered only his appearance. Jekyll's, even in his most prosperous days, covered only the exploits of Hyde. His own life had still to be lived normally on its previous lines. But Wringhim (or the devil who counsels him) has so arranged things that his whole active life is to be immune from judgement and from serious consequences.

Two points emerge. One, that the price of this playground is high. Freed from consequences and from judgement, action altogether loses its meaning. Wringhim is very mad indeed. Two, that what he pays this price for is, again, something utterly squalid and negative. Certainly, he is able to satisfy briefly his resentment against those who have not appreciated him, but this is hardly an aim proportioned to the tremendous metaphysical pretensions of the original scheme. His heroic acts are only a string of spiteful murders without any public or political point. The fate of all souls being in any case fixed, it is not even clear why cutting off the wicked in their prime should have the slightest value. It is a mean, unimpressive and disappointing enterprise, judged against the glittering hints dropped by the mysterious stranger, to whom Wringhim, in spite of his new-found importance and freedom, soon finds himself enslaved. Trying to get a hold on events, he asks the stranger for his name:

> 'I have no parents save one, whom I do not acknowledge', said he proudly. 'Therefore pray drop that subject, for it is a disagreeable one. I am a being of a very peculiar temper, for, though I have serv-ants and subjects more than I can number, yet, to gratify a certain whim, I have left them and retired to this city, and, for all the society which it contains, you see I have attached myself only to you. This is a secret . . . pray let it remain one, and say not another word about the matter.' It immediately struck me that this was no other than the Czar of Russia . . . I had henceforward great and mighty hopes of high preferment as a defender and avenger of the oppressed Christian church, under the influence of this great potentate.[15]

Vanity is the key to Wringhim's enslavement. And it plays a central part also in that of Jekyll, who is throughout happy to sacrifice the whole integrity of his being for the sake of his spotless reputation. Vanity comes upon him at a fatal juncture, when he has for a time renounced Hyde, and been living as himself but has finally weakened and indulged, in his own person, in a night on the tiles. Next morning

> the Regent's Park was full of winter chirrupings and sweet with spring odours. I sat in the sun on a bench, the animal within me licking the chops of memory, the spiritual side a little drowsed, promising sub-sequent penitence, but not yet moved to begin. After all, I reflected, I was like my neighbours; and then I smiled, comparing myself with other men, comparing my active good-will with the lazy cruelty of their neglect. And at the very moment of that vainglorious thought, a qualm came over me, a horrid nausea and the most deadly shuddering . . . I was once more Edward Hyde.[16]

The trouble is not, of course, that vanity is the worst of the vices. It is just that it is the one which makes admitting all the others unbearable, and so leads to the shadow-shedding project. And the reason why this project is doomed is because, as Jung sensibly points out, shadows have a function:

> Painful though it is, this [unwelcome self-knowledge] is in itself a gain — for what is inferior or even worthless belongs to me as my shadow and gives me substance and mass. How can I be substantial if I fail to cast a shadow? I must have a dark side also if I am to be whole; and inasmuch as I become conscious of my shadow I also remember that I am a human being like any other.[17]

The acknowledged shadow may be terrible enough. But it is the unacknowledged one which is the real killer.

NOTES

1. It appears on the cover of his collection of cartoons, appropriately called *Well, There's your Problem* (Harmondsworth, Penguin, 1980).
2. B. Butler, *Fifteen Sermons*, Sermon X 'Upon Self-Deceit', Section 16.
3. *Nicomachean Ethics* book VII, Chapters 1–10.
4. R.L. Stevenson, *The Strange Case of Dr Jekyll and Mr Hyde* (London, Nelson, 1956), Chapter 1, p. 6.
5. *Enquiry Concerning the Principles of Morals*, part ii, Section V, 183.
6. Stevenson, Chapter 10, p. 86.
7. Ibid., pp. 94–5, 96–7.
8. Ibid., Chapter 2, p. 25.
9. Ibid., p. 75.
10. Ibid., p. 21.
11. Ibid., p. 25.
12. These and other cases are well discussed by R. Timms in *Doubles in Literary Psychology* (Bowes and Bowes, Cambridge, 1949).
13. J. Hogg, *The Confessions of a Justified Sinner*, 1824, reprinted with an introduction by André Gide (London, Panther Books, 1970).
14. Ibid., p. 111.
15. Ibid., p. 121.
16. Stevenson, Chapter 10, p. 90.
17. C.G. Jung, *Modern Man in Search of a Soul*, p. 40.

AROUND THE SPECIES
BARRIER

In the following extracts, Midgley explores the specific ethical issues that arise in our dealings with other species. Clearly, the conclusions arrived at from a naturalistic view, such as hers, will be very different from those traditional views that regard humans and animals as categorically different. In fact, in the mainstream European philosophical tradition, the basis for according to all human beings the right to decent ('humane') treatment was held to depend on their possession of rationality. Humans lacking the full development of this capacity, such as infants and the insane, are held to participate in these rights only by a special extension of this logic; because they are in some sense potentially rational, they manage to slip inside the demarcation line.

Animals, however, for many versions of this view, fall wholly outside it; Descartes, Spinoza and Kant were all emphatic that we cannot have any moral duties towards animals. Insofar as ill-treatment of animals is disapproved of, this is on the indirect grounds that such behaviour is undignified or corrupting to the perpetrator. This kind of thinking has become internalized as a background to much contemporary debate relating to animal welfare, and is often assumed as a basis for the defence of institutionalized forms of abuse such as factory

DOI: 10.4324/9781003588160-13

farming and vivisection. As was pointed out in the last chapter, the need to reconcile oneself to actions we, at some level, know to be morally wrong leads to self-deception; this process can be seen at work in the arguments examined in the next section, 'Emotion, Emotiveness and Sentimentality'. Defenders of the abuses in question proceed, in these examples and others like them, not by answering the substantive points made by their critics, but by stigmatizing them as 'emotive', 'emotional', or 'sentimental' (in implied contrast to the 'rationality' of the defender). There follows an important analysis of the respective roles of emotion and reason in moral judgements; both are indispensable, and the argument that objections to ill-treatment of animals are 'based on emotion' is therefore spurious.

The next extract, 'Equality and Outer Darkness', compares the history of attempts to get animal rights onto the moral and political agenda with that of other similar campaigns for the rights of slaves, women and other disadvantaged groups. Most of the language used here is that of Social Contract Theory – the case for equality of rights is argued on the basis of common membership of a community; only if the implied 'contract' expressing the conditions of such membership is a fair one is it reasonable to expect the members to abide by its terms. The problem here is that the prior question of what qualifies an individual for membership of such a community is assumed to have already been answered. Thus Athenian democracy took the exclusion of slaves for granted, as Rousseau, the chief architect of Social Contract theory, took for granted the exclusion of women.

'Is a Dolphin a Person?' continues this topic with a discussion of a fascinating legal case which turned on a judge's ruling that a dolphin, because it was not human, was not a person but an item of property, and so the protection of its well-being could not excuse an otherwise illegal act, namely releasing the dolphin because the conditions of its captivity were causing it extreme suffering. Midgley presses the point at issue: what are the morally relevant characteristics that determine the applicability of the term 'person' in this sense, i.e., as a member of the moral community? Simply not being biologically human, lacking spoken language or lacking the ability to calculate, etc., are, she compellingly argues, insufficient grounds for excluding non-human animals from our moral universe.

SOURCES

'Emotion, Emotiveness and Sentimentality' – *Animals and Why They Matter*, Penguin Books, 1983, ch. 3. 'Equality and Outer Darkness' – *Animals and Why They Matter*, Ch. 6. 'Is a Dolphin a Person?' – *Utopias, Dolphins and Computers*, Routledge, 1996, ch. 9.

9

EMOTION, EMOTIVENESS AND SENTIMENTALITY

THE STIGMA OF EMOTION

What does it mean to say that scruples on behalf of animals are merely emotional, emotive, or sentimental? What else ought they to be?

Charges of this kind are a very common way of dismissing these scruples, and other scruples as well. Just what these charges mean, however, is not so clear as one might suppose. We badly need to get it clear, because the relation between emotion and reason is a very central crux of our lives. What else, besides emotion, is in general needed for a valid scruple, and how is its presence detected? 'Emotivist' theories of ethics have suggested that morality altogether is nothing but the expression of emotion, or of attitudes formed from it.[1] If this were right, the complaint that scruples about animals were only this would be vacuous. But is it vacuous? What does it mean? We had

DOI: 10.4324/9781003588160-14

better consider some examples. Here, for a start, is a piece from an article about controversy over the conditions of battery chickens (italics are mine throughout):

> The ammunition consists largely of several rounds of *emotion* followed by a quick burst of *uninformed* allegations about costs . . . For some people, the subject will always be an *emotive* one. Birds which cannot spread their wings or indulge their instincts to scratch arouse public indignation and sympathy. Yet many consumers have been quite ready to accept the benefits of factory farms.[2]

Next, with slightly more attempt at subtlety, part of a scientist's defence against criticisms of his piece of research entitled 'Development of Grooming in Mice with Amputated Forelimbs':

> X's letter appears to treat the *dual issues of rationality and sensitivity* in our dealings with nature, and as such is an *important emotional expression*. However, I am surprised at his unawareness of the importance [of the work; a defence of which follows] . . . Because of my concern for the animals' welfare, I rejected possible alternatives, including technically difficult and potentially devastating central lesions (which would have been hidden and thus might have caused less *emotional reaction* on the part of observers). The fact that the animals in this study, by all available criteria, lived a full and apparently well-adjusted life . . . suggests that *surface emotional reactions* may not be sufficient for either a rational or humane orientation to the world in which we live.[3]

Next comes a piece which is rather different, because the scruples involved are ecological rather than humane and might just as well have applied to plants:

> The trouble with wildlife conservation today is the same as when it first gained impetus as a movement in the late 50s, namely that it draws *emotive opinions* into what should be *objective discussions* . . . Conservationists ought to touch down occasionally from their flights of *euphoric*

fancy to realize that the nation must plan its land-use to best effect (including ecological assessments) and that it *cannot afford* the *luxury* of ill-used or inappropriately used acreage on any large scale. In opposing the prospect of forested uplands in Scotland, Y neglects the fact that those uplands were once forested by nature and have since been *miserably* denuded by man (and beast). Is there any landscape more *desolate and bleak* than that of the southern uplands of Scotland?[4]

Then, because it is important to understand the charge in quite general terms, I add a piece (self-explanatory, I think) on a quite different topic:

The . . . material was presented in a *needlessly biassed and sensational form*. All these things tend to reduce morale and the quality of intelligence work. I feel frankly that, in 1979, it is high time that the name of the Agency was changed. CIA, those three initials have become what we in the US refer to as a *buzz word*. It isn't a word, but they're buzz initials. You say 'CIA' and that immediately *triggers* images of the Bay of Pigs, and the demise of Allende in Chile. Why do we have to harness CIA operations? Because we don't trust our President, because we don't trust our Director? Because power corrupts? *These things sound so nice* when they're said in the old halls of academia . . .

Americans want a strong intelligence organization; they feel their Government should know what's going on in the world. On the other hand, they don't much like hearing about dirty tricks or the connivery that is involved in espionage. *They'd be delighted to have the operation run and not hear too much about it.*[5]

What charges are actually being made here? We all feel that some accusation or other is present. This impression is so strong that people often find that their most natural response is denial. We incline to say at once, 'I have absolutely no emotion in the matter,' and to say this even when it is plainly false. ('Damn you, I haven't lost my temper.') We do that, of course, in order to avoid the related but much stronger charge of being actually overcome and carried away by emotion, of being so emotional that our thought is paralysed.

Now the word *emotion* and still more *emotional* certainly can be used for such violent and incapacitating states ('Don't get emotional'). But these words are just as often, or even more often, used in a wide and more neutral sense for all sorts of feeling, strong and weak. The word *sentiment* has the same ambiguity. Our emotional life includes the whole range of our feelings, motives and sympathies. This whole range, obviously, is not something which paralyses thought or any of our other faculties. It is the power-house which keeps the whole lot going. In this wide sense there is nothing objectionable about emotion at all; quite the contrary. Accordingly, anyone accused of being emotional about injustice or oppression or war or bad science or anything else can quite properly reply, 'Of course I feel strongly about this, and with good reason. It is a serious matter. Anyone who has no feeling about it, who does not mind about it, has got something wrong with him.' Strong feeling is fully appropriate to well-grounded belief on important subjects. Its absence would be a fault. This is the element of truth in Emotivism; morality does require feeling. The Emotivist's mistake is in supposing that it requires nothing else; in trying to detach such feelings from the thoughts that properly belong to them.[6]

MORE THOUGHT NOT LESS FEELING

It might be better if we made this move of admitting appropriate feeling more often. As it is, the idea does sometimes get around that merely having strong feelings is, in itself, a fault in controversy. The real fault must lie, not in the presence of feeling, but in the absence of thought, or in the unsuitability of feeling to thought. The word *emotion* is slightly troublesome here, because we do not tend to use it much of ourselves. The verb, as commonly conjugated, seems to run: 'I am convinced – you are excited – he is getting emotional.' Our own feeling, particularly when we are sure it is suitable, does not seem to call for comment. But what matters for controversial purposes, as we all know when we think about it, is not its strength but its suitability.

Things are very similar if we turn from the question of *being emotional* (or sentimental) to that of *being emotive*. Here the charge shifts from that of wallowing in emotion oneself to that of trying to produce it in other people. Now this attempt in itself is not wrong. All argument involves trying to change feelings, because all belief involves feeling. Even a scientist or historian, if he thinks a colleague is making a mistake, can quite properly try to *rouse his suspicions* on the matter, to *make him unhappy* about the error, to *weaken his confidence* in it, to *rouse his curiosity* about an alternative suggestion and eventually to induce a *confident acceptance* of it. In itself, this is quite a proper aim. In fact, it is a service which we all owe each other in cases where we are genuinely convinced that there is a mistake. The wrongness lies in attempting such enterprises for the wrong reasons and by the wrong methods – in trying to produce the emotion itself directly, by non-rational methods, rather than to argue honestly and openly about the issues. The word *emotive* is actually itself something of a buzz-word, coined specially to label these wrong cases. What stinks, then, is not actually the attempt to alter feeling, but the absence of the only sort of context which can justify this. That context requires genuine beliefs to which those feelings would be appropriate, and willingness to argue these beliefs on their own merits. There is however another misleading idea which distorts both the charge of emotion and that of emotiveness, namely, an impression that strong feeling is in itself more objectionable than calm feeling, and that states of indifference, involving no feeling, would really be the best of all. In which state is it better that serious political debating should go on? Here again, what really matters is surely not (apart from extremes) the strength of the emotion, but its suitability. Anyone who reports a danger to people who have not yet noticed it is liable to be called emotional or emotive. If sincere, he is himself frightened, and he is quite properly trying to produce fright in others. Fright is the emotion appropriate to his beliefs; he has reason for it. Does that make him unreliable? The case is common:

> E'en such a man, so pale, so woebegone,
> Drew Priam's curtain in the dead of night
> And would have told him, half his Troy was burned—

He was emotional all right, and also apparently emotive. Was that a fault? Suppose that at this point someone else appears and reassuringly explains that it is all an idle rumour, what are we to say about him? Actually, he is a spy in the pay of the enemy, plotting to keep Priam quiet in bed till the Greeks have control of the city . . . He is not a bit emotional (why should he be? His side is winning). And towards Priam, his aims do not seem emotive. He is trying after all to produce calm, to get rid of emotion. But of course he still embodies all the objectionable part of emotiveness. He is trying to work directly on emotion for his own ends, by-passing normal thought. (Compare subliminal suggestion.) Again, what is really wrong is the attack on thought, and it would be much better to say so. This fellow is a traitor and a fraud. These perfectly adequate descriptions of what is wrong with him do not need any mention of emotiveness to complete them.

In general, then, the charge we are analysing seems to be one of introducing *inappropriate* feelings into controversy. Clearly, this does not only happen in cases involving animals. Is there any reason to suppose that it must always happen there, that all emotion is inappropriate to animals, and that, if it occurs, it is false, and is merely being indulged in for its own sake? (That indulgence would be sentimentality.) This strange view is a form of absolute dismissal. More modestly, the point may be that the particular feeling expressed at the time is inappropriate to the particular case. This often is what is meant, and in detail this charge often turns out to concern only two quite limited reasons for inappropriateness – ignorance and insincerity. In themselves, these charges are serious. Both of them, however, need suitable evidence. And both are much better made under their own names, without the red herring of reference to emotion.

EMOTION AND IGNORANCE

Let us now look at the extracts which I gave at the start of this chapter, to see typical examples of these two charges. The charge of ignorance is particularly prominent in example B. To answer his critics, the author puts forward three propositions of which he considers they have shown their ignorance. These are:

1. that his research is very important,
2. that he could have done it by methods still more objectionable, and
3. that the method which he did use did not damage the mice as much as those other methods would have done – indeed, 'by all available criteria,' it did not damage them at all.

Had the critics known these truths (he implies) they would not have made fools of themselves by getting so excited. In calling their response an 'important emotional expression,' he seems to mean that it would have been appropriate but for the above-named facts, and that this might actually have consequences for other, less admirable, research. So he is not an absolute dismisser.

It is worth looking briefly at his arguments, because they illustrate the grotesque standard of reasoning commonly found in such defences, something from which accusations about emotion often distract attention. Argument 1 is of course relevant, but is unfortunately not much use, since all researchers suppose their own work to be important, and (as those responsible for allotting grants etc. well know) nearly all of them can make a case for it which sounds at least as plausible as this one to people outside the field. To cut any ice, the pleas need to be supported by good explanations of how this crucial topic has to be explored *by these particular methods*. This involves showing a field of inquiry so structured as to have reached a bottle-neck. No attempt is made to do this. Instead, the author's vague remarks about possible alternative methods culminate in argument 2 – that there were still nastier methods which he could have used. This presumably is always true. It can therefore scarcely do him much good, especially as he rashly lets out that they were more difficult anyway. The main point of this suggestion seems to be its bearing on point 3, which is the nub of his case. Here he accuses his critics of ignorance about what does and what does not actually constitute damage to mice. It is noteworthy that he rightly treats this, not as a matter of taste, but as a factual question on which it is possible to be mistaken. Some imaginary observers might, he says, make a mistake about it, supposing his method to be nastier than a particular alternative one, merely because its effects are more obvious. Since his attackers are not actually these observers at all, but are scientists who have read his reports, this is a complete red herring. It serves, however, to evoke a picture of ignorant, superficial criticism ('surface emotional reactions') – of rustics gaping in at the dentist's window and supposing that he is assaulting his patient. The real truth (he continues), which those rustics failed to see, is that 'by all available criteria, the mice lived a full and apparently well-adjusted life.' All criteria (that is) except having forelegs . . .

This recalls a remark which used often to be made about the early films of thalidomide children. How well they manage (the commentators used to marvel), how lively they are, how active and sociable they contrive to be! Nobody, however, has ever thought that this could be made into a defence of thalidomide, or could show that deprivation of limbs did not matter.

The issue here is about what constitutes damage and welfare for a given species. It is one which can be quite important in animal cases, and it is of course true in general that people can make mistakes about it, and can suppose an animal to be ill-treated when it is not. For instance, someone who heard that a particular zoo's python had not eaten for a year might well suppose that it was being starved, or at least that its appetite was affected by illness. But he would be wrong; pythons are like that. Similarly, it might seem cruel to keep a mother rabbit apart from her babies except for one visit a day. But it would not be; she only visits them once a day in any case. And so on. Such questions (as I have pointed out) are factual ones, not matters of taste or ones calling for an existential decision. (Talk of 'fact – value distinctions' is not very helpful here.) Of course there are always border-line cases. But in general, the way to find out what is good or bad for a given species, what constitutes a normal, healthy life for it, is intelligent, informed observation. It must, however, be the full, systematic observation of a zoologist prepared to be interested in the species for its own sake, not casually for purposes of exploitation. And in these days, it ought to take advantage of the disciplined skills of ethology.[7] If somebody equipped with these skills were to come forward with such an extraordinary proposition as that mice did not really need their forelegs, he would have to bring much better evidence than the adapted behaviour of amputees. It is well known that young creatures have an amazing power of adapting to early mutilations, and that this could not prove the process to be no injury. But of course the commoner situation is that where a scientist working in another field, who merely uses the creatures and does not study them, casually throws out this sort of suggestion. He has then no more right to be listened to than he would have if he made similar suggestions about people. It is he, not his critics, who shows ignorance.

Things are rather similar with the battery hens in the first extract. The authors do not so explicitly accuse those who object to battery conditions of being ignorant about hens, but what they say scarcely makes sense unless they do want to bring that accusation. One does not say that 'for *some people* the subject will always be an emotive one' when one means that these people are those properly informed about the subject. This wording strongly suggests that the people in question are ones who just happen to have a peculiar background or emotional constitution. Again, to speak next of '*public* indignation and sympathy' suggests still more strongly that these excitable creatures are not experts, but ignorant citizens. It seems to follow that 'birds which cannot spread their wings and indulge their instincts to scratch' would arouse the misguided sympathy only of these proles, while the real experts would know better. This is the direct opposite of the truth. People unused to birds might think that all was well, because they could not distinguish deprived birds from normal ones, and do not know what is *not* going on that ought to be. Those who do understand birds know the importance of these activities so well, and have made it so clear, that it is against English law to keep any bird in conditions where it cannot perform them – except poultry, which are exempted purely for commercial reasons, not for scientific ones.

EMOTION AND INSINCERITY

The main charge brought in this extract (and also in D) is however that of insincerity. We must look at it next. Here the objector does not deny that the feeling expressed by those with scruples is appropriate, nor that their information is correct. He just denies that the feeling itself is strong or persistent enough to deserve attention. 'These scruples,' he says, 'are mere hot air. You are profiting by this institution, and will no doubt continue to do so. Your collusion disqualifies you from criticizing it.'

This point has, of course, nothing specially to do with animals. It is one that can be made on any moral question, but it is always a point about the disputers, not about the dispute. The objector simply makes a prediction about his opponents' scruple – namely, that it will continue to be outweighed by their avarice, laziness or greed. He does not ask whether it ought to be. He just asks them, how much do they really mind? The question is a proper and important one. But it is quite mad to suppose – as people seem to – that some sort of trap prevents the answer 'yes, I do mind a lot, and now let's do something about it.' People who want change are not disqualified from asking for it by their involvement in existing institutions. If they were, no change could ever be brought about. Thus, when Lord Shaftesbury began his agitation for the Factory Acts, it would have been no use for the mill-owners to resist reform by saying to the reformers, 'You are wearing clothes which we have made and will probably go on buying more, so you have no right to complain of our methods.'

When a product – whether clothes, eggs, meat, medicine or the CIA – is produced by iniquitous means, the people who consume that product are among the first who do have a right to complain about it. They are being made jointly responsible. It is their business to demand that the producer should find less objectionable ways of producing it. His business is to try to do this. Only if he has shown, carefully and convincingly, that there are no such ways, and found that his clients still insist on the product, can he shift any share of his own discredit onto them. Certainly they must in the end accept their share of the costs involved. But so must he, and the first move is with him. He cannot block criticism merely by swearing that his methods are the only possible ones, and that any reform must be at the consumers' expense. Experience has shown that people with vested interests can never be trusted on such questions. The mill-owners did not actually founder in their predicted general bankruptcy after the Factory Acts, nor did prices rise disastrously. Welfare veal, humanely produced, turns out to cost less than veal from calves crammed into crates and unable to lie down.[8] Nobody loses except the crate manufacturers and their existing customers, and they not much. It is just that nobody thought of trying it before.

To sum up this point about sincerity in general, it is quite true that 'he who wills the end wills the means also,'[9] but this never stops us willing a change of means. Those with a vested interest in the means, however, naturally tend to claim that this change is impossible, and to suggest that this fact is so well known that people demanding it cannot mean what they say. Extract D illustrates this process with an almost lyric elegance; it seems a shame to spoil the effect by comment, but a few remarks are called for. Heims's argument rests entirely on dealing with feeling instead of thought, on ignoring all conceptual links between his opponents' disgust and the undisputed facts to which it is an appropriate response. He treats the disgust merely as an unlucky natural phenomenon, caused by the 'triggering of images' (as it might be by a bad smell), and proposes a piece of psychological engineering to remove the trigger. This move is meant to isolate the feeling from its grounds. He then proclaims its isolation from all practical bearing, from any genuine will for change, thereby dismissing it, not just as a feeling, but as a trivial feeling, not meant to affect action. (This is a charge of sentimentality.) Against such feelings, arguments are out of place, so he does not argue. He simply claims that his countrymen are already as convinced as he is that his methods are the only possible ones. They are, therefore, already his collaborators, kept from admitting their convictions only by hypocrisy. The accusation of hypocrisy is often quite an effective way of silencing critics and making them feel ashamed. We should resist it. During any reform, when people are beginning to notice that something is wrong and trying to see how to alter it, some confusion and inconsistency between theory and practice is normal. It is even necessary. This is not yet hypocrisy. The kind of hypocrisy which invalidates criticism is a deliberate, chronic condition, that of somebody who has settled finally back into accepting the *status quo*. The normal confused condition is uncomfortable but transient. We can always alter practice rather than theory.

THE ISSUE OF INAPPROPRIATENESS

In giving rather short shrift to these particular writers' charges of ignorance and insincerity, I am not, of course, suggesting that reformers do not need to be well informed and honest. They do. I am just pointing out that these special limited charges – which require their own evidence – never follow from the general accusation, if it is an accusation, of being emotional. I have suggested that the real charge, which that accusation expresses rather badly, is one of introducing *inappropriate* feeling into controversy.

Now there certainly are real questions, arising all over the moral field, about what feeling actually is appropriate. How much ought we to mind about the preservation of wilderness? or about art? or about the beauty of the countryside? How important is knowledge, or freedom? Ought they always to give way to the contentment of the greater number? How, in general, are conflicts between such various values to be resolved? These are real and serious moral questions.

Accordingly, people who try to deal with them (like the author of extract C) merely in terms of the presence or absence of emotion as such, fall instructively flat on their faces. He objects to 'emotive opinions' and demands an 'objective discussion.' He then defends his own eccentric preference for spruce monoculture by the use of emotive words like 'miserably . . . desolate and bleak' and insinuates, falsely, that it will constitute a return to primitive conditions. Examined more closely, he is seen to be a lifeboat man.[10] He operates with a simple contrast between values which he sees as unreal ('euphoric fancy') and real ones – namely, those of economics, what we can afford. This notion of

reality as co-extensive with economics is the one that brought Howard
Hughes to his wretched solitary death, and which indeed more generally has given us the word 'miser' – literally, a miserable person. Money
is a useful means, but it cannot possibly be an end, let alone the only
real end of life. It is not actually particularly real; you certainly can't eat
it. A romantic obsession with it does indeed give meaning to some people's lives. But there is no sort of reason for the rest of us to accept their
short cut through the business of understanding and comparing values.

THE PLACE OF FEELING IN MORALITY

These questions about priority among values are the central business
of morality. They are not our business here and now, because we are
still concerned, in this chapter, with getting animals an admission
ticket to the moral scene at all. We are still confronting the rationalist notion that they fall outside it. On this view morality is entirely a
contract between rational beings. Feeling has no part in it and cannot
concern it. And animals concern us only through feeling.

This is a most odd and lop-sided view of morality. There are all kinds
of things wrong with it, of which trouble over animals is only a small
part, though a very illuminating one. As often happens over lopsided
notions, it has been answered by another, equally unbalanced towards
the other side. This is Emotivism, which makes morality entirely a
matter of feeling.

Nothing forces us to accept either of these over-simplifications. We
have to do justice to both feeling and thought. This means considering
them together, and as aspects of the same process. For instance, the
thought that a great danger threatens has not been completed – it is
not yet a proper thought – unless it includes some fear and some wish
for action. And fear which includes no thought at all about the nature
of the danger is incomplete fear. It is more of a physical state than a
proper feeling. Similarly, real indignation is not just an emotional state,
but one formed by and containing the thought of the special sort of
outrage which calls for it. No separate nuts and bolts are needed to
screw these two elements together.

Rationalists however, when they speak of feelings, seem to concentrate only on those emotional states whose completing thought is much less clear. These states are the target for the kind of argument we have been considering. And of course they do occur. The kind of indefinite fear just mentioned exists, though it is not common. And feelings like disgust at blood and wounds can be mere physical reactions. We can feel them at surgical procedures we entirely approve of. And it is often hard – especially for people like us who are seldom confronted with bloodshed – to be sure whether this kind of feeling has any meaning or not. If it never had, it seems that we ought always to ignore it and try to get over it. At least we would never be justified in objecting to the actions which caused it. (Thus people with a physical revulsion to cats do not think that their feeling shows that cats are wicked, or even that cat-keeping is so. It is just that they are sometimes a nuisance, like noise.) But it seems clear that, in fact, disgust at bloodshed often does have a meaning. It has played a great part in the development of more humane behaviour, because it can alert people's imagination to what they are doing, and wake their sympathies for the victims. The same thing happens with unthinking revulsions to unfairness, meanness, ingratitude, envy and the like. The revulsion itself is not significant, but it can become so in the context of fuller thought. Real scruples, and eventually moral principles, are developed out of this kind of raw material. They would not exist without it. This is the answer to our question at the outset about what *more*, besides feeling, a valid scruple requires.

It will not do, therefore, to keep the two things separate – to write, as extract B does, about 'the dual issues of rationality and sensitivity' if this means that they can be handled apart. Sensitivity requires rationality to complete it, and vice versa. There is no siding onto which emotions can be shunted so as not to impinge on thought. People sometimes try to provide such a siding by treating questions which they find it hard to think about as aesthetic. Extract C suggests this view of ecological scruples. Certainly aesthetic considerations can often be separated from moral ones; trains of reasoning may well sit on such a siding. But these trains are only waiting to come back onto the main moral line and approach the question: how much do aesthetic considerations matter when weighed against others? Questions about animals, if similarly parked on a siding marked 'Emotion,' will do the same. Feeling is not going to take us out of the moral universe. It is not possible to keep two parallel independent systems of values – one aesthetic or emotional and the other rational or moral – and prevent their ever meeting. We cannot do this because each of us has only one life to live. We must therefore sometimes settle priority questions *between* emotional or aesthetic values and values of other kinds. To compare and relate these various kinds is the central business of morality, which is itself the weigher, not an item on one of the scales.

NOTES

1. Emotivist ethics may be found briefly expounded by A.J. Ayer in Chapter 6 of his early book *Language, Truth and Logic* (London, Gollancz, 1936; Penguin Books, 1971), and in a more considered form by C.L. Stevenson in *Ethics and Language* and *Facts and Values* (New Haven, Yale University Press, 1945 and 1963). Criticisms of it are now extremely common; a good one is G.J. Warnock's in *Contemporary Moral Philosophy* (London, Macmillan, 1967), Chapter 3.

2. Article in the *Guardian*, (24 October 1979).

3. Discussion piece in *Science* 179 (18 May 1973).

4. Letter in *New Scientist*, (10 January 1980).

5. R. Heims, former head of the CIA and sometime US Ambassador in Iran, in an interview, *Observer* (9 December 1979).

6. The much more subtle relations which really do exist between morality and emotion are well discussed by Bernard Williams in his paper 'Morality and the Emotions,' in *Morality and Moral Reasoning*, ed. Casey (London, Methuen, 1971), reprinted in his *Problems of the Self* (Cambridge, Cambridge University Press, 1973).

7. An admirable exposition of methods which make it possible to approach these awkward problems soundly and objectively can be found in *Animal Suffering: The Science of Animal Welfare* by Marian Stamp Dawkins (London, Chapman & Hall, 1980). She gives special attention to discovering the actual preferences of battery chickens.

8. See an article 'Loose Housed Calves Make a Cheaper Veal,' in *The British Farmer and Stockbreeder* for 12 April 1980. At that time Quantock Veal, the biggest veal producers in the UK, turned over to the method. For a fuller account, see *Ag, the Journal for Non-Violence in Agriculture*, no. 59, June 1980. For more information on the whole topic, see *Factory Farming: A Symposium*, ed. J.R. Beilerby (London, Education Services, 1970).

9. Kant, *Groundwork of the Metaphysic of Morals* (tr. H.J. Paton under the title of *The Moral Law*, (London, Hutchinson, 1948), Chapter 2, pp. 80–1).

10. The reference is to the 'lifeboat ethic' of withholding aid from poor countries, on the grounds that the 'lifeboat' will sink if it takes on too many passengers, proposed by Garrett Hardin in 'Living on a Lifeboat' in *Bioscience*, October 1974, and more fully in *The Limits of Altruism* (Bloomington, Indiana, 1977). [Ed.]

10

EQUALITY AND OUTER DARKNESS

CAN ANIMALS BE EQUAL?

It is not till the last decade that philosophers have seriously and persistently extended the concept of equality, and that of basic natural rights, to animals. But they have done it now.

> All animals are equal . . . No matter what the nature of the being, the principle of equality requires that its suffering be counted equally with the like suffering – in so far as rough comparisons can be made – of any other being.
>
> (Peter Singer)[1]

DOI: 10.4324/9781003588160-15

And on rights,

> Within an absolute context it is difficult to see how any of us, men
> or beasts, have any rights at all; and we certainly therefore have no
> rights upon them. In less absolute terms, any principle, or prince, that
> accords rights to the weak of our own species must also accord them
> to animals.
>
> (Stephen Clark)[2]

Again –

> 'The right not to be tortured, then, is shared by all animals that suffer
> pain; it is not a distinctively human right at all', and 'Whatever ration-
> ale is provided for granting humans a right to liberty, it seems that a
> relevantly similar one is available in the case of at least some other
> species of animals'.
>
> (James Rachels)[3]

Of course not all philosophers agree, but the disagreement has so
far focused mainly on the proper use of words like *rights* and *equality* rather than on defending traditional dismissive habits of thought
and practice as a whole.[4] Moreover, the interesting term *speciesism* has
been coined to describe discrimination against non-humans, thereby
branding it as an offence against equality, parallel to racism, sexism,
ageism and the like. Isolated writers had said these things before, but
this is the first large-scale attempt to extend liberal concepts to the
borders of sentience.

Historically, this movement was made possible by the other liberation movements of the 1960s, converging with the increasing
interest in animals which we noticed earlier, an interest which has
for the first time begun to publicize the relevant facts widely. Books
and films about wildlife have told people something about the complexities of animal existence and its likenesses to human existence,
and also about the widespread threats of extinction, which are

themselves a new feature of our age, never considered in traditional thought. At the same time, books and films about such things as factory farming have been able, though with much more difficulty, to spread some information about how animals are actually treated within our civilization.[5] And again, many of the practices revealed are themselves new; tradition is dumb on how to regard them. The discrepancy revealed between ideals and practice is bound to bring into play concepts like equality and natural rights. This move, however, is not just a historical accident. Logically, these concepts demand this use as soon as it is open to them, because they have no built-in limit. They are essentially tools for widening concern, and concern, though it may attenuate with distance, is certainly possible in principle towards anything which we suppose to feel. Normally prejudice restricts it, but these concepts exist to break down prejudice, as they have repeatedly done. They are essentially destructive. Along with notions like liberty and fraternity, they work to dissolve the screens of callous habit and reveal hidden injustice. All these concepts are vague. All must be supplemented, once their work of revelation is done, by other, more detailed and discriminating ideas. But vague though they are, they are very powerful. They melt away the confused excuses given by custom, appealing from local laws and usage to the deeper standards required for change. Everybody who wants reform must sometimes use such concepts, but perhaps all those who do so are sometimes appalled at what they reveal, and find themselves retreating in alarm behind some ill-chosen bush. We must shortly glance at the record of these evasions in the case of the cluster of liberal, French-revolutionary concepts which are our present business. Repeatedly, even people who have used them well have set up crude barriers to halt them at various frontiers, notably those of race and sex – barriers which have crumbled scandalously as soon as they were examined. The dialectical road-block so far thrown up at the species-barrier is not less crude than these were, but far more so, because it has received even less attention. Anyone hoping to reinforce it will have to do the job over again from scratch.

This does not mean that there is nothing wrong with the liberal concepts themselves. They are notoriously obscure. It may well be sensible to halt them for interpretation and replacement long before they reach the species-barrier. But if one does not do this — if one puts complete confidence in notions like equality and natural rights — one lies open to Peter Singer's challenge. His opening chapter, indeed, is directed specially to egalitarians; it has the fighting title 'All Animals are Equal, or Why Supporters of Liberation for Blacks and Women Should Support Animal Liberation Too.' This does not mean, however, that conservatives on these matters can ignore the whole business. In our civilization, everyone who thinks at all has an egalitarian element in his thinking. We all need to clear up these concepts.

THE PROBLEM OF EXTENT

What, first, about equality? This is a rather abstract ideal, distinguished from most others by needing a great deal of background before it can be applied. Who is to be made equal to whom, and in what respect? Historically, the answers given have mostly concerned rather narrow groups. The ordinary citizens of a particular state — often a small one, such as Athens or Rome — demand to share certain powers of a still smaller group, such as their nobility, on the ground that they are all already equally *citizens*. The formula needed is something like 'let those who are already equal in respect x be, as is fitting, equal also in respect y.' Outsiders, such as slaves, foreigners, and women, who are currently not equal in respect x, cannot benefit from this kind of argument. It requires a limited public.

The notion of equality is a tool for rectifying injustices within a given group, not for widening that group or deciding how it ought to treat those outside it. As is often necessary for reform, it works on a limited scale. Those working for equality take a certain group (such as that of Athenian citizens) for granted, and ask in what ways the nature of that group dictates that its members should be equal. This question is well expressed by social-contract language: what are its members here for? why did they form it? what, merely by belonging to it, do they agree to do? As we shall see, answers to this vary. But this variation does not affect the main point – namely, that the binding principle of the group tends to emerge as the basis of political obligation, and is easily extended to account for *all* obligation. This is no accident, for it is a central purpose of social-contract thinking to demolish a certain set of non-contractual moral principles – namely, those which tell citizens to obey their betters regardless of their own choice and interest. It demolishes these by applying a strong reducing agent – egoism. It asks, 'Why should I obey the government?' and accepts only answers delivered in terms of self-interest. There is much to be said for this. But when the same process is applied to other sorts of moral principle, results are much less satisfactory. Problems concerning the relations of the group to those outside it, and possibilities of widening the group, as well as relations within the group itself which are not considered as part of its egoistic binding principle, become insoluble. The notion of moral agents as equal, standard units within a contractual circle which constitutes the whole of morality is a blind and limited one. Contract has its place in morality, not vice versa.

It may seem strange and paradoxical to suggest that the notion of equality has these self-defeating properties. We will look in a moment at instances which show the paradox in action. It is true, of course, that the snags are not part of the concept itself. They belong to its supporting apparatus. But since some apparatus of this kind seems needed to bring it into operation, it is very hard to avoid them. The concept itself, as I just remarked, is very abstract, and can in principle be extended to any limit. In theory, when slaves or the like are noticed, the 'equal' group can always be extended to include them. But in practice two things make this very hard. One is simply the well-known difficulty about realistic political objectives. It is hard enough already to persuade the nobility to treat all citizens as, in some particular respect, equal. If we try at the same time to include slaves in the argument, we may well destroy our chances. Reforming movements which won't set limited objectives simply fail; they are not serious. So the 'equal' group comes to be defined as, for instance, that of free citizens, and habit perpetuates this restriction even when it is no longer needed.

The other trouble, which goes deeper and will occupy us longer, comes from invoking egoism as the bond which is to keep the equal units together. The private self-interest of group members is often best served by keeping the group small. Where, therefore, pooled self-interest replaces hierarchical bonds, things may become worse, not better, for those currently excluded from the group. And if the whole of morality is in some sense reduced to egoism, the objections to this way of thinking become very hard to state.

EGOISM AND THE SOCIAL CONTRACT

All contract theorists have, of course, seen that there are difficulties about reducing morality to contract, and not all of them want to move far in this direction. The fervour with which they insist on reduction varies according to the violence of the emergency which they see before them. Hobbes, facing the bleak savagery of the seventeenth-century wars of religion, used a simple, sweeping version of contract theory, aimed at getting rid of all those numerous aspects of morality which he thought led to general destruction, and particularly self-destruction. He took the original respect in which people were equal, x, to be simply the power to kill. Everybody is strong enough to kill somebody else some time, and without a contract he may always do it. Since death is incomparably the worst possible disaster for each of us, that distressing fact alone is what makes it worth everyone's while to sign the contract, and equal protection of life is what they all gain. This self-preservatory decision is then the source of all obligation. For Hobbes, obligation simply is the fear of danger to one's life if a regulation is neglected. To make this doctrine work, the various duties and virtues have to be twisted into some very strange shapes; in particular, 'the definition of INJUSTICE is no other than the *not performance of contract.*'

But it is impossible to extract from this tiny hat that large rabbit, morality. People expect and owe to each other much more than life and the means to life – certainly more than not-killing – and also much more than justice, even if justice is given a wider and more natural definition than Hobbes gives it. Human psychology is altogether not what he hopes for. People do not live in the future to this extent. They are (as their conduct constantly shows) much less interested in just surviving than Hobbes suggested, less prudent, less clever, less farsighted, less single-minded, and much more interested in having the sort of life which they think satisfactory while they do survive.

THE IMPORTANCE OF FREEDOM

Hobbes, of course, wrote in an age of civil war, and has special reason to dwell on death. ('The Passion to be reckoned upon is Fear.'[6]) He therefore stressed above all the value of the state as a life-preserver, and described the outer darkness, the state of nature, as a state of war – a 'war of every man against every man.' Rousseau, in more peaceful times, took the life-preserving job as done and looked past it to other aims. He asked, now that we are surviving, what do we want the state to do for us? He answered that above all we want it to make us free and independent, to preserve us from every form of slavery. We want equality, not as an end in itself, but 'because liberty cannot exist without it.'[7] The degree of equality we want is therefore simply that which will make it impossible for anybody to enslave anybody, whether by violence, rank, or commercial pressure. The emphasis has now shifted from viewing everybody as equally a possible threat to viewing them as originally equal in their capacity and wish for independence. (Thus Emile is to be taught 'to live rather than to avoid death' and to live in the present.[8]) That capacity and wish for independence must be explained. Rousseau explains them by an admittedly mythical description of primitive man as originally solitary and speechless, each person being able to maintain him or herself alone, wandering separately in the woods like bears, and hardly ever meeting.[9] He found it a standing paradox and tragedy that civilization had sacrificed this primitive independence to other, less crucial advantages.

In spite of its staggering implausibility, this myth of primal solitude has a solid moral point. It means simply that people – as they are now – are potentially autonomous, capable of free choice, wanting it and needing to have a say in their own destiny. Rousseau's remark that 'man is born free' means that people are not beings like ants, shaped by and for their community and unable to exist without it, but are true individuals who can live alone, and can therefore stand aside from it and criticize it. Emile, once grown up, is directed to travel, to see many societies and put himself in a position to ask 'Which is my country?'[10] This native capacity and wish for independence is what makes it necessary that the contract shall be so framed that 'all, being born free and equal, alienate their liberty only for their own advantage.' In this way 'each, while uniting himself with all, may still obey himself alone and remain as free as before'[11] so that 'men who may be unequal in strength or intelligence become every one equal by convention and legal right.'[12] Any other kind of contract is a fraud. The contract now ceases to appear as a single area of light and safety, immediately surrounded by outer darkness. It is more like a patch of fertile country, chosen and fenced for improvement, but surrounded by a much larger expanse of very similar terrain, which shares most of the characteristics which make the enclosed land attractive. Social motivation is something far wider than political order.

THE NATURAL NEED FOR FREEDOM

Now to conceive the social contract in this way involves certain psychological views about the kind of beings who make it, that is, about human nature. *Nature* is here, as usual, a fruitfully ambiguous word, combining related views about facts and values. Why is independence so important to *Homo sapiens?* Why is it not better to live under a benevolent despotism on the lines of *Brave New World?* Rousseau's – or anyone's – reasons for rejecting this suggestion are in part factual, involving evidence about people's actual capacities and wishes, and in part moral, involving objections to certain ways of treating these: (1) People are not like ants, and (2) it would therefore be wrong to treat them as if they were. But neither these facts nor these moral judgements are derived from contract. They are the considerations which make this kind of contract necessary. Rousseau was always willing to appeal to distinct psychological and moral principles in order to explain why the contract had to take this special form.

In passing, it must be noticed at this point that bears are not ants either, nor are they cog-wheels. They, like people, are true individuals. The kind of liberty which Rousseau celebrates here is one which all the higher animals can share, and which all desire. It is outward liberty. It is not a rarefied, intellectual brand of free-will, depending on advanced thought and speech. It is a plain matter of not being imprisoned, bullied and oppressed, of having one's own way.

This outward freedom is what the self-governing devices of the contract are designed to secure. (Free-will, notoriously, cannot be produced by institutions and, if present, can survive in gaol.) Outer freedom does indeed give scope for a much wider inner freedom, which different species will use each in their own way, and for people, freedom of thought and speech will follow. But to see this, one must know the facts about the constitution of the various creatures concerned. And adaptation to liberty is a fact about the constitution of bear as well as man. This appeal to natural facts – indeed to any considerations other than the contract itself – always causes political alarm, because the beauty of contract ethics is its simplicity. The contract myth – which is never regarded as literal history – is essentially a fence against arbitrary tyranny. It exists to make authority depend on the consent of the governed. Its main use is to cut out other, more superficial and biased, supposed sources of political obligation. It appears at its best in the opening chapters of the *Contrat Social*, where Rousseau makes hay of the jumbled religious-cum-historical theories which were used in his day to shore up the remains of feudalism. Rousseau's derision was a proper answer to theorists who derived the obligation of subjects from the right of conquest, implying that conquerors were entitled to perpetual obedience from the descendants of those they enslaved, or from the supposed biblical ancestry of kings. Nothing but the general will of the governed, he said, could relevantly justify government. As a lever for dislodging unwanted rulers, this principle is excellent. But where that is no longer the problem, difficulties crowd in. Now that we are demanding something more than mere survival from the contract, we shall need a different sort of inducement to obey the general will. Is that will infallible in promoting the liberty we now want, or can it make mistakes? If it can, must not other considerations besides actual consent be relevant after all? In disputes, might not the minority be right? What, in that case, binds the non-consentors to obey their fallible government? And – still more puzzlingly – what binds those who were never consulted at all, such as foreigners? What, in particular, binds women? All these questions except the last seemed to Rousseau extremely serious. He admitted the tension between the simplicity of contract and the complexity of morality as real, and he made tremendous efforts to resolve it. He never fell back on Hobbes's simple, reductive solution of eliminating one pole – reducing morality at a stroke to enlightened self-interest, expressed in contract. He saw conflicts about political obligation as real, because he understood that human psychology was complex.

THE DIFFICULTY OF LOOKING DOWNWARDS

The last question, however, struck him as merely a joke, and a joke in bad taste. It was perfectly obvious to him that women's consent to the contract was not needed, and he resented questions about the matter which could only tend to parody his own contentions, distracting people from the serious business of reform. Before glancing at the arguments with which Rousseau and others have justified this dismissal, we have to notice here, as a gloomy general feature of revolutions, something which may be called the Paradox of One-Way Equality. Inequalities above one's own level tend to be visible: those below it to be hidden. This is not just a joke; there is a real conceptual difficulty involved. For instance, readers of *Animal Farm*, encountering the principle 'All Animals are Equal,' usually take it to mean that all animals are, in fact, equal. They are mistaken. It refers only to farm animals. In the first flush of revolution, these animals do suggest, and uncertainly agree, that rats are comrades. Attempts to act on this idea, however, peter out almost at once, and the only other outside candidates ever named are rabbits. Foxes, badgers, hedgehogs, deer, mice, voles, weasels, etc. and the whole tribe of wild birds, as well as everything smaller, are simply forgotten.[13] It is interesting, though depressing, to see the same principle at work throughout the liberation movements of the 1960s; each group of oppressed people, on sighting another, tended at once to see it as a distracting competitor, not as a friend and ally. The story is dismal. It is summed up in the reply of Stokely Carmichael, the noted Black Power leader, to black women who offered to work for his cause: 'The only place for women in the SNCC is prone.'[14] Equally and on the other hand, nineteenth-century women, struggling against odds for the right to education and interesting work, took for granted the cheap labour of uneducated female servants. (It was still common, during my own childhood before the war, for professional women to refuse on principle to do even the simplest cookery or housework, in order to protect their status. The group they identified with was defined by class as well as by sex.) It is amazingly hard even to conceive, let alone to fight for, serious widening of one's group at the same time as trying to equalize status within it. This difficulty is a real limitation on the use of the idea of equality itself and those ideas related to it. Another striking instance is the development of democracy at Athens, where, with infinite efforts, they forged and defended that *isonomia* – equality before the law – of which, as Herodotus said, 'the very name is most beautiful.'[15] This they did while their women were all incarcerated in harems and their daily labour done by slaves. The American Declaration of Independence, likewise, proclaims the proud belief that all men are created free and equal, while explicitly excluding women and implicitly (as far as some of the signatories went) non-European slaves as well. We call this kind of thing hypocrisy, and no doubt rightly. But, as we have already noticed, hypocrisy is not a simple matter. It is rather seldom the full-scale Tartuffe phenomenon of fully conscious deception. In most of us most of the time, it indicates conflict and confusion. To call hypocrisy 'the tribute which vice pays to virtue' is not just to point out that Tartuffe finds dissimulation worth his while. It is also to observe that people cannot all at once become quite good, any more than they can all at once become utterly villainous. Havering and inconsistency are a condition of most human attempts at goodness. They are often best understood by giving them the benefit of the doubt – by viewing them dynamically as real attempts, and trying to see what blocks them. (This is not a defence of inconsistency, it is a suggestion about how to deal with it.)

In the cases just mentioned, the facts so strangely ignored are visible to us today, partly in the way that paint on one's neighbour's face may be visible, because we are not inside them, and partly because others have already pointed them out. The work which used to be done by slaves is done for us by machines, invented and still produced through a good deal of industrial servitude, much of it in distant countries. Hypocrisy is not, as people seem sometimes to think, an exclusive patent of the Victorian age. Nobody sees everything. This patchiness of vision is certainly a fault, often a disastrous one, but it is a different fault from Tartuffery. When a privileged group tries to consider extensions of privilege, quite special difficulties arise about being sharp-sighted. The notion that one has already drawn a correct and final line at which such extensions must end cannot be trusted at all. It is not trustworthy over animals.

NOTES

1. *Animal Liberation* (London, Jonathan Cape, 1976), p. 9.
2. *The Moral Status of Animals* (Oxford, 1977), p. 34.
3. In 'Do Animals Have a Right to Liberty?', in *Animal Rights and Human Obligations*, ed. T. Reagan and P. Singer (Englewood Cliffs, NJ, Prentice-Hall, 1976).
4. The journal *Inquiry* devoted a whole issue to these discussions (*Inquiry* 22, 1979), and they have continued vigorously. A more recent survey may be found in *Animal Rights and Human Morality* by B.E. Rollin (New York, Prometheus Books, 1981).
5. For farm animals, a good source is still R. Harrison's *Animal Machines* (London, Stuart, 1964). Things have not changed very much. On animal experimentation, *Animals in Research* (ed. Sperlinger, John Wiley & Sons, 1980) gives an excellent survey of the facts and some good discussion. Singer's *Animal Liberation* also has good, brief, informative chapters on both topics.
6. *Leviathan*, Part I, Chapter 14.
7. *Social Contract*, Book I, Chapter 13.
8. *Emile*, Everyman edn (tr. Barbara Foxley), p. 10.

9. *Discourse on the Origin of Inequality*, Part I.

10. *Emile*, Book 5, Everyman edn, p. 437.

11. *Social Contract*, Book I, Chapters 2 and 6.

12. *Social Contract*, Book II, Chapter 1.

13. Orwell's story is, of course, so transparently a fable meant for human applica-
    tion that little attention is usually paid to its literal meaning. The opening of
    it is, however, very interesting in its direct literal sense. Orwell plainly knew a
    lot about conditions on farms, and the speech of Old Major the boar, which
    rouses the other creatures to revolt, deserves more attention than it gets. The
    ironies of the tale get an extra dimension here, which is certainly intentional.

14. See G. Greer, *The Female Eunuch* (London, Paladin, 1971), p. 301.

15. Herodotus, *History*, Book III, Chapter 80.

11

IS A DOLPHIN A PERSON?

THE UNDOUBTING JUDGE

This question came up during the trial of the two people who, in May 1977, set free two bottle-nosed dolphins used for experimental purposes by the University of Hawaii's Institute of Marine Biology. It is an interesting question for a number of reasons, and I want to use most of this discussion in interpreting it, and tracing its connection with several others which may already be of concern to us. I shall not go into details of the actual case, but shall rely on the very clear and thoughtful account which Gavin Daws gives in his paper, ' "Animal Liberation" as Crime.'[1]

Kenneth le Vasseur, the first of the two men to be tried, attempted through his counsel what is called a 'choice of evils' defence. In principle, the law allows this in cases where an act, otherwise objectionable, is necessary to avoid a greater evil. For this defence to succeed, the act

DOI: 10.4324/9781003588160-16

has to be (as far as the defendant knows) the only way of avoiding an imminent, and more serious, harm or evil to himself or to 'another.'

Le Vasseur, who had been involved in the care of the dolphins, believed that their captivity, with the conditions then prevailing in it, actually endangered their lives. His counsel,

> in his opening statement for the defence, spoke of the exceptional nature of dolphins as animals; bad and rapidly deteriorating physical conditions at the laboratory; a punishing regimen for the dolphins, involving overwork, reductions in their food rations, the total isolation they endured, deprived of the company of other dolphins, even of contact with humans in the tank, deprived of all toys which they had formerly enjoyed playing with – to the point where Puka, having refused to take part consistently in experimental sessions, developed self-destructive behaviours symptomatic of deep disturbance, and finally became lethargic – 'comatose.' Le Vasseur, seeing this, fearing that death would be the outcome, and knowing that there was no law that he could turn to, believed himself authorized, in the interests of the dolphins' well-being, to release them. The release was not a theft in that Le Vasseur did not intend to gain anything for himself. It was intended to highlight conditions in the laboratory.
>
> (Daws: 356–7)

But was a dolphin 'another'? The judge thought not. He said that 'another' would have to be another person, and he defined dolphins as property, not as persons, as a matter of law. A dolphin could not be 'another person' under the penal code. The defence tried and failed to get the judge disqualified for prejudice. It then asked leave to go to Federal Court in order to claim that Thirteenth Amendment rights in respect of involuntary servitude might be extended to dolphins. This plea the judge rejected:

> Judge Doi said, 'We get to dolphins, we get to orangutans, chimpanzees, dogs, cats. I don't know at what level you say intelligence is

insufficient to have that animal or thing, or whatever you want to call it, a human being under the penal code. I'm saying that they're not under the penal code and that's my answer.

(Daws: 365)

At this point – which determined the whole outcome of the trial – something seemed perfectly obvious to the judge about the meaning of the words 'other' and 'person.' What was it? And how obvious is it to everybody else? In the answer just given, he raises the possibility that it might be a matter of intelligence, but he rejects it. That consideration, he says, is not needed. The question is quite a simple one; no tests are called for. The word 'person' just means a human being.

WHAT ARE PERSONS?

I think that this is a very natural view, but not actually a true one, and the complications which we find when we look into the use of this interesting word are instructive. In the first place, there are several well-established and indeed venerable precedents for calling non-human beings 'persons.' One concerns the persons of the Trinity, and indeed the person-hood of God. Another is the case of 'legal persons' – corporate bodies such as cities or colleges, which count as persons for various purposes, such as suing and being sued. As Blackstone says, these 'corporations or bodies politic . . . are formed and created by human laws for the purposes of society and government'; unlike 'natural persons,' who can only be created by God. The law, then, can if it chooses create persons; it is not a mere passive recorder of their presence (as indeed Judge Doi implied in making his ruling a matter of law and not of fact). Third, what may look nearer to the dolphins, the word is used by zoologists to describe the individual members of a compound or colonial organism, such as a jellyfish or coral, each having (as the dictionary reasonably puts it) 'a more or less independent life.'[2]

There is nothing stretched or paradoxical about these uses, for the word does not in origin mean 'human being' or anything like it. It means a mask, and its basic general sense comes from the drama. The 'masks' in a play are the characters who appear in it. Thus, to quote the Oxford Dictionary again, after 'a mask,' it means 'a character or personage acted, one who plays or performs any part, a character, relation or capacity in which one acts, a being having legal rights, a juridical person.'

The last two meanings throw a sharp light on the difference between this notion and that of being human. Not all human beings need be persons. The word *persona* in Latin does not apply to slaves, though it does apply to the State as a corporate person. Slaves have, so to speak, no speaking part in the drama; they do not figure in it; they are extras.

There are some entertaining similar examples about women. Thus:

> One case, brought before the US Supreme Court in the 1890s, concerned Virginia's exclusion of a woman from the practice of the law, although the pertinent statute was worded in terms of 'persons'. The Court argued that it was indeed up to the State's Supreme Court '*to determine whether the word "person" as used (in the Statute) is confined to males*, and whether women are admitted to practise law in that Commonwealth'. The issue of whether women must be understood as included by the word 'persons' continued even into the twentieth century . . . In a Massachusetts case in 1931 . . . women were denied eligibility for jury service, although the statute stated that every 'person qualified to vote' was so eligible. The Massachusetts Supreme Court asserted: 'No intention to include women can be deduced from the omission of the word male.'[3]

FINDING THE RIGHT DRAMA

What is going on here? We shall not understand it, I think, unless we grasp how deeply drama is interwoven with our thinking, how intimately its categories shape our ideas. People who talk like this have a clear notion of the drama which they think is going on around them. They know who is supposed to count in it and who is not. Attempts to introduce fresh characters irritate them. They are inclined to dismiss these attempts sharply as obviously absurd and paradoxical. The question who is and who is not a person seems at this point a quite simple and clear-cut one. Bertie Wooster simply is not a character in *Macbeth* and that is the end of the matter.

It is my main business here to point out that this attitude is too crude. The question is actually a very complex one, much more like 'who is important?' than 'who has got two legs?' If we asked 'who is important?' we would know that we needed to ask further questions, beginning with 'important for what?' Life does not contain just one purpose or one drama, but many interwoven ones. Different characters matter in different ways. Beings figure in some dramas who are absent from others, and we all play different parts in different scripts.

Even in ordinary human life, it is fatal to ignore this. To insist on reducing all relationships to those prescribed by a single drama – such, for instance, as the Social Contract – is disastrous. Intellectuals are prone to such errors, and need to watch out for them. But when we come to harder cases, where the variation is greater – cases such as abortion, euthanasia or the treatment of other species – this sort of mistake is still more paralysing. That is why these cases are so helpful in illuminating the more central ones.

It is clear that, over women, those who limited the use of the concept 'person' felt this difficulty. They did not want to deny altogether that women were persons, since in the dramas of private life women figured prominently. Public life, however, was a different stage, whose rules and conventions excluded them (queens apart) as completely as elephants or angels. The fact that private life often impinges on public was an informal matter and could not affect this ruling. Similarly at Rome, it is clear that slaves actually played a considerable part in life. In Greek and Roman comedy, ingenious slaves, both male and female, often figure as central characters, organizing the intrigue and supplying the brains which the hero and heroine themselves unfortunately lack. This, however, was not going to get them legal rights. The boundaries of particular situations and institutions served to compartmentalize thought and to stop people raising questions about the rights and status of those who were for central purposes currently disregarded.

I think it will be helpful here to follow out a little further the accepted lines of usage for the word person. How complete is its link with the human bodily form? What, for instance, about intelligent alien beings? Could we call them persons? If not, then contact with them − which is certainly conceivable − would surely require us to coin a new word to do the quite subtle moral job which is done at present by 'person.' The idea of a person in the almost technical sense required by morality today is the one worked out by Kant.[4] It is the idea of a rational being, capable of choice and therefore endowed with dignity, worthy of respect, having rights; one that must be regarded always as an end in itself, not only as a means to the ends of others.

Because this definition deals solely with rational qualities, it makes no mention of human form or human descent, and the spirit behind it would certainly not license us to exclude intelligent aliens, any more than disembodied spirits. The moral implications of the word 'person' would therefore, on our current Kantian principles, surely still have to attach to whatever word we might coin to include aliens. C.S. Lewis, describing a planet where there are three distinct rational species, has them use the word hnau for the condition which they all share, and this term is naturally central to the morality of all of them.[5]

Now if intelligence is really so important to the issue, a certain vertigo descends when we ask 'where do we draw the line?' because intelligence is a matter of degree. Some inhabitants of our own planet, including whales and dolphins, have turned out to be a lot brighter than was once thought. Quite how bright they are is not yet really clear to us. Indeed it may never become so, because of the difference in the kind of brightness appropriate to beings with very different sorts of life. How can we deal with such a situation?

ATTENDING TO THE MIDDLE GROUND

The first thing needed is undoubtedly to get away from the single, simple, black-and-white antithesis with which Kant started, the antithesis between persons and things. Most of Kant's argument is occupied with this, and while it remains so he does not need to make finer distinctions. *Things* (he says) can properly be used as means to human ends in a way in which *people* cannot. Things have no aims of their own; they are not subjects but objects. Thing-treatment given to people is exploitation and oppression. It is an outrage, because, as Kant exclaims, 'a man is not a thing.' Masters sell slaves; rulers deceive and manipulate their subjects; employers treat their secretaries as part of the wallpaper. By dwelling on the simple, stark contrast involved here, Kant was able to make some splendid moral points which are still vital to us today, about the thorough-going respect which is due to every free and rational human being. But the harsh, bright light which he turned on these situations entirely obscured the intermediate cases. A mouse is not a thing either, before we even start to think about a dolphin.

I find it interesting that, just as the American courts could not quite bring themselves to say that women were not persons, so Kant cannot quite get around to saying what his theory certainly implies, that animals are things. He does say that they 'are not self-conscious and are there merely as a means to an end,'[6] that end being ours. But he does not actually call them things, nor does he write off their interests. In fact, he emphatically condemns cruel and mean treatment of them. But, like many other humane people who have got stuck with an inadequate moral theory, he gives ingeniously unconvincing reasons for this. He says – what has gone on being said ever since – that it is only because cruelty to animals may lead on to cruelty to humans, or degrade us, or be a sign of a bad moral character, that we have to avoid it.

This means that if we can show that, for instance, venting our ill-temper on the dog will prevent our doing it on our families, or if we can produce certificates to show that we are in general people of firm moral character, not easily degraded, we can go ahead with a clear conscience. Dog-bashing, properly managed, could count as a legitimate form of therapy, along with gardening, pottery and raffia-work. In no case would the physical materials involved be directly considered, because all equally would be only objects, not subjects. And there is nothing degrading about simply hitting objects.

In spite of the appalling cruelty which human beings show towards animals the world over, it does not seem likely that anyone regards them consistently in this light, as objects. Spasms of regard, tenderness, comradeship and even veneration, alternating with unthinking callousness, seem to make up the typical human attitude to them. And towards fellow-human-beings too, a rather similar alternation is often found. So this cannot really be an attitude confined to things. Actually even cruelty itself, when it is deliberate, seems to require that its objects should not be mere physical objects, but should be capable of minding what is done to them, of responding as separate characters in the drama. More widely, the appeal of hunting, and also of sports such as bullfighting, seems to depend on the sense of outwitting and defeating a conscious quarry or opponent, 'another,' able to be one's opposite in the game or drama. The script distinctly requires non-human characters, who can play their parts well or badly. Moby Dick is not an extra. And the degradingness of deliberate cruelty itself surely requires this other-regarding element. 'Another' is not always another human being.

INDIRECT JUSTIFICATIONS

The degradingness of cruelty is of course widely admitted, and le Vasseur's counsel used this admission as the ground of an alternative defence. He drew attention to his client's status as a state employee, which conferred authority on him to act as he did in coming to the defence of 'another,' in this case the United States, whose social values were injured by what was being done to the dolphins. This argument was rejected, on the ground that, in the eyes of the law, cruelty to animals is merely a misdemeanour, whereas theft is a felony. Accordingly the choice of evils could not properly be resolved in such a way as to make theft the less serious offence. It is interesting that this argument makes no objection to treating the United States as 'another' or 'another person' – it does not insist that a person simply means a human being – but rests instead on contending that this 'other' finds its values more seriously attacked by theft than by cruelty to dolphins.

This sort of argument is not easy to come to grips with, even in the case of an ordinary individual person, still less in that of a nation. How serious an evil is cruelty? Once it is conceded that the victim's point of view does not count, that the injury is only to the offender or somebody of which he is part, we seem to be cut off from the key considerations of the argument and forced to conduct it in a strained manner, from grounds which are not really central. Is cruelty necessarily depraving? On this approach, that seems partly to be a factual question about how easily people are depraved, and partly perhaps an aesthetic one about how far cruel acts are necessarily disgusting and repellent.

These acts seem to be assimilated now to others which are repellent without being clearly immoral, such as eating the bodies of people whom one has not killed, or watching atrocities over which one has no control. The topic becomes a neighbour of pornography rather than of abortion and euthanasia. (In the disputes about permissiveness in the 1960s, an overlap actually developed here at times, as when a London art gallery organized a happening in which some fish were to be electrocuted as part of the show, and efforts to ban this were attacked as censorious manifestations of aesthetic narrow-mindedness.)

Something seems to have gone wrong with the thinking here. The distinctive feature of actions attacked on purely aesthetic grounds should surely be that their effects are confined to those who actually perform them. No other sentient being is harmed by them. That is why they pose problems for libertarians when bystanders object to them. But cruelty does not pose this kind of problem, since the presence of 'another' who is harmed is essential to it. In our case, it is the dolphin, who does seem to be 'another.' Can we avoid thinking of it in this way? Can the central objection to cruelty really be something rather indirect, such as its being in bad taste?

MORAL CHANGE AND THE LAW

The law seems to have ruled thus here. And in doing this, the law shows itself to be in a not uncommon difficulty, one that arises when public opinion is changing. Legal standards are not altogether independent of moral standards. They flow from them and crystallize in ways designed to express certain selected moral insights. When those insights change deeply enough, the law changes. But there are often jolts and discrepancies here, because the pace of change is different. New moral perceptions require the crystals to be broken up and reformed, and this process takes time. Changes of this kind have repeatedly altered the rules surrounding the central crux which concerns us here; the stark division of the world into persons and property. Changing attitudes to slavery are a central case, to which we must come back in a minute. But it is worth noticing first that plain factual discoveries too can make a difference.

When our civilization formed the views on the species barrier which it still largely holds, all the most highly developed non-human animals were simply unknown. Legend apart, it was assumed that whales and dolphins were much like fish. The great apes were not even discovered till the eighteenth century and no real knowledge of their way of living was acquired until within the last few decades. About better-known creatures too, there was a very general ignorance and unthinking dismissal of available evidence; their sociality was not noticed or believed in. The central official intellectual tradition of our culture never expected to be forced to subtilize its crude, extreme, unshaded dichotomy between man and beast. In spite of the efforts of many concerned thinkers, from Plutarch to Montaigne and from Blake to John Stuart Mill, it did not develop other categories.

If alien beings landed tomorrow, lawyers, philosophers and social scientists would certainly have to do some very quick thinking. (I don't expect the aliens myself but they are part of the imaginative furniture of our age, and it is legitimate to use them to rouse us from our dogmatic slumbers.) Science fiction, though sometimes helpful, has far too often side-tracked the problem by making its aliens just scientists with green antennae – beings whose 'intelligence' is of a kind to be instantly accepted at the Massachusetts Institute of Technology, only of course a little greater. Since neither dolphins nor gorillas write doctoral theses, this would still let us out as far as terrestrial non-human creatures were concerned. 'Persons' and their appropriate rights could still go on being defined in terms of this sort of intelligence, and we could quietly continue to poison the pigeons in the park any time that we felt like it.

The question is, why should this kind of intelligence be so important, and determine the limits of our moral concern? It is often assumed that we can only owe duties to beings capable of speech. Why this should be thought is not altogether clear. At a simple level, Bentham surely got it right: 'The question is not *can they talk? Nor can they reason? But can they suffer?*'[7] With chimps, gorillas and dolphins, however, there is now a further problem, because people have been trying, apparently with some degree of success, to teach them certain kinds of language. This project might have taught us a great deal about just what new categories we need in our attempt to classify beings more subtly. But unluckily it has been largely obscured by furious opposition from people who still have just the two categories, and who see the whole proceeding as an illicit attempt to smuggle contraband from one to the other.

This reaction is extremely interesting. What is the threat? Articulate apes and cetaceans are scarcely likely to take over the government. What might happen, however, is that it would become much harder to exclude them from moral consideration. In particular, their use as experimental subjects might begin to look very different. Can the frontier be defended by a resolute and unbreakable refusal to admit that these animals can talk?

THE MEANING OF FELLOWSHIP

It is understandable that people have thought so, but this surely cannot really be the issue. What makes creatures our fellow-beings, entitled to basic consideration, is not intellectual capacity, but emotional fellowship. And if we ask what powers can give a higher claim, bringing some creatures nearer to the degree of consideration which is due to humans, what is most relevant seems to be sensibility, social and emotional complexity of the kind which is expressed by the forming of deep, subtle, and lasting relationships. The gift of imitating certain intellectual skills which are important to humans is no doubt an indicator of this, but it cannot be central. We already know that both apes and dolphins have this kind of social and emotional complexity.

If we ask what elements in 'persons' are central in entitling them to moral consideration, we can, I think, get some light on the point by contrasting the claim of these sensitive social creatures with that of a computer of the present generation, programmed in a manner which entitles it, by current controversial usage, to be called 'intelligent' and certainly able to perform calculations impossible to human beings. That computer does not trouble our sleep with any moral claims, and would not do so however much more 'intelligent' it became, unless it eventually seemed to be conscious, sensitive and endowed with emotions.

If it did seem so, we should have the Frankenstein problem in an acute form. (The extraordinary eagerness with which Frankenstein drove his researches to this disastrous point is something which contemporary monster-makers might like to ponder.) But those who at present emphasize the intelligence of computers do not see any reason to want to call them persons, nor to allow for them as members of the moral community. Speech alone, then, would scarcely do this job for the apes. What is at issue is the already glaring fact, which speech would make it finally impossible to deny, that they mind what happens to them – that they are highly sensitive social beings.

These considerations are not, I think, ones confined to cranks or extremists. They seem fairly widespread today, and probably occur at times to all of us, however uncertain we may be what to do about them. If so, and if the law really allows them no possible weight, then we seem to have reached the situation where the law will have to be changed, because it shocks morality. There is an obvious precedent, to which the dolphin-liberators tried to appeal:

> When the dolphins were taken from the tanks, a message was left behind identifying the releasers as the 'Undersea Railroad', a reference to the Underground Railroad, the Abolitionists' slave-freeing network of pre-Civil War days. Along the Underground Railroad in the 1850s, it

sometimes happened that juries refused to convict people charged with smuggling slaves to freedom. That was the kind of vindication le Vasseur and Sipman were looking for . . . They did not consider themselves to be criminals. In fact they took the view that, if there was a crime, it was the crime of keeping dolphins – intelligent, highly aware creatures with no criminal record of their own – in solitary confinement, in small, concrete tanks, made to do repetitious experiments, for life.

(Daws: 362)

If we go back to the alien beings for a moment and consider whether even the most intelligent of them would have the right to keep any visiting human beings, however stupid, in these conditions, even those of us least partial to astronauts may begin to see the point which le Vasseur and Sipman were making. It surely cannot be dismissed merely by entrenching the law round the definition of the word 'person.' We need new thinking, new concepts, and new words, not (of course) just about animals but also about our whole relation to the non-human world. We are not less capable of providing these than people were in the 1850s, so we should get on with it.

NOTES

1. G. Daws, '"Animal Liberation" as Crime' in H.B. Miller and W.H. Williams (eds), *Ethics and Animals* (Totowa, NJ, Humana Press, 1983).
2. It is also interesting that 'personal identity' is commonly held to belong to continuity of consciousness rather than of bodily form, in stories where the two diverge. Science fiction strongly supports this view, which was first mooted by J. Locke, *Essay Concerning Human Understanding*, bk 2, Chapter 27, Section 15.
3. S.M. Okin, *Women in Western Political Thought* (Princeton, NJ, 1979), p. 251.
4. See I. Kant, *Foundations of the Metaphysic of Morals*, tr. L.W. Beck (Indianapolis, Bobbs-Merrill, 1959), Section 428–32, p. 46. In the UK, a more available translation is that called *The Moral Law*, tr. H.J. Paton (London, Hutchinson, 1948), pp. 90–2.
5. C.S. Lewis, *Out of the Silent Planet* (London, John Lane, 1938).
6. I. Kant, 'Duties towards Animals and Spirits' in his *Lectures on Ethics*, tr. Louis Infield (London, Methuen, 1930), p. 239.
7. J. Bentham, *Introduction to the Principles of Morals and Legislation*, Chapter 17.

PART 2

PHILOSOPHIZING OUT IN THE WORLD

The metaphor of 'Philosophical Plumbing,' elaborated in the piece which follows under that title, has become something of a Mary Midgley trademark. She uses this image to underline the importance she attaches to the practical role of philosophy in relation to society at large. Though philosophy does have abstract and technical aspects, which may seem very remote from matters of general concern, it is essential that it does not lose sight of its roots in the conceptual problems which arise in the rest of life. Concepts are not to be found ready-made and final in some ideal logical space; they are tools devised for particular jobs in particular circumstances. When circumstances change, or we need to do other jobs, we may run into unexpected problems. It is there that the work of the philosopher begins.

Much of Midgley's early work stemmed from a desire to bring philosophy, which under the influence of the analytic movement had become somewhat detached and isolated, back into the world in this

DOI: 10.4324/9781003588160-17

way. *Wisdom, Information and Wonder*, while not one of her best-known books, is of central importance in that it represents her only full-scale engagement with the main themes of the analytic tradition, the original soil out of which her work grew. The background to these issues is discussed in the next extract, from the opening part of the book. The increasing trend towards specialization, almost universal in twentieth-century academic life, resulted, in the case of philosophy, in the withdrawal of engagement from issues of general concern just noted.

The next extract, 'The Withdrawal of Moral Philosophy,' looks in more detail at the abdication of analytic philosophers, following G.E. Moore, from the responsibility of delivering any substantive moral conclusions as a result of their work. Moore's Intuitionist version of ethics was succeeded by Emotivism, Prescriptivism, and various other forms of 'meta-ethics,' which shared the view that any attempt to use moral reasoning to arrive at a substantive conclusion was vitiated by the 'Naturalistic Fallacy' – it is impossible to argue validly from facts to values.

Such sterile, formalist views are typical of what happens when conceptual analysis is carried on in isolation from the concrete situations and problems from which philosophical questions arise in the first place. Wittgenstein, in his later work, recognized the self-extinguishing nature of such insular, over-abstract analytic thinking, and painstakingly showed how an ideal conception of language and thought, unrelated to their actual roots in human life, leads to a characteristic kind of philosophical illusion. But in fact the crucial insight here was due to Moore himself, who in his Defence of Common Sense showed powerfully that the attempt to locate the foundations of our knowledge in abstruse logical and metaphysical reasoning is a fundamental mistake. Our most secure knowledge is of the straightforward kind represented by such propositions as 'Today is Wednesday,' 'I am over six feet tall,' and 'It's raining.'

Moore and Wittgenstein thus pointed the way out of the prison which analytic philosophy, under the spell of Descartes, had made for itself. The attempt to produce an impregnable justification of all our theoretical and moral beliefs by means of irrefutable logical analysis is doomed to failure. Philosophy must emerge from its self-imposed solitude and return to the world with which, ultimately, it has to deal – the world of flesh-and-blood human beings, with concrete moral and conceptual problems which need sorting out.

This tendency to try to substitute a formal, linear, deductive structure for the rich but messy complexities of our actual lives appears in perhaps its most crude and extreme form in physicalist reductionism, the doctrine that our subjective experience – consciousness itself – is wholly explainable by, and in fact consists in nothing but, the motions of molecules and electrical forces within out brains. Some form of this doctrine has been widely espoused, for the past century or so, by philosophers, and still more widely by scientists and in popular discourse; its ancestry goes back to the Greek atomists, the Charvakas of ancient India and others, especially Thomas Hobbes.

This view, and the bizarre conclusion that appears to follow from it, that consciousness, subjective experience, is non-existent, though it was resisted by most twentieth-century physicalist philosophers, has recently been enthusiastically embraced by many scientists, and is the main target of Midgley's penultimate book, *Are You an Illusion*; this critique was followed up, as part of a more general deconstruction of the constellation of ideas that go under the heading of Scientism, in her final oeuvre, *What Is Philosophy For?* Rejecting the dichotomous framing of the 'Mind-Body Problem' stemming from Descartes' strict ontological separation of these two aspects of our nature, she articulates an understanding of the relationship between the subjective and objective aspects of our experience which removes the temptation to consider these as competing and incompatible candidates for ontological primacy. Neither excludes the other, nor can one be 'reduced to' or explained away in terms of the other; rather, they are different modes of understanding of that experience, different lenses through which to see it, both indispensable in their own terms.

The next extract, the introductory chapter of *Heart and Mind*, continues the theme of providing a rounded, integrated account of our mental life with some suggestions towards a more rounded and integrated account of the psyche than that which – by and large – the analytic tradition had inherited from Enlightenment thought. The division of the psyche into separate 'Faculties' – Reason, Emotion, Volition, etc. – results in a fragmented picture of the Self, and an artificial account of mental function. In particular, Midgley stresses the inappropriateness of trying to pull apart the elements of feeling and thought (Heart and Mind) as they appear in our moral thinking. Our conception of ourselves, of our motives and plans and those of others, and of the world in which we are acting, are seamlessly interwoven with our feelings and desires. As she says in the Foreword to the book, the central theme of the essays collected in it (comprising most of her early papers together with some broadcast talks) is 'the unity of that very complex creature, a human being, and the need to respect that unity in our view of morals.'

The final extract in this section, 'On Trying Out One's New Sword on a Chance Wayfarer,' originally a BBC broadcast, is an incisive critique of the idea of cultural relativism in morals. This is the view that it is impossible to criticize the moral attitudes prevailing in other cultures, because any judgement we make is from the standpoint of those of our own culture; there is no neutral standpoint from which such a judgement can be made. As a corrective to narrow-minded and dogmatic attachment to a particular code of morality, this has a point, but if raised to the status of an absolute principle, it becomes incoherent. Morality could not have the significance it has if the principles underlying it were local and relative in this way. The details of how they are expressed may vary between cultures, and this may well invalidate judgements made on the basis of inadequate study and appreciation of the structure and beliefs of another culture. But unless these details related to universal values such as justice, integrity, compassion, or others of the same order, they could not be the values of a human culture at all. As Midgley says, 'Morally as well as physically, there is only one world, and we all have to live in it.'

SOURCES

'Philosophical Plumbing' – abridged from *Utopias, Dolphins and Computers*, Routledge, 1996, Chapter. 1. 'Wisdom and Contemplation' – condensed from Chapters 1–2 of *Wisdom, Information and Wonder*, Routledge, 1989. 'The Withdrawal of Moral Philosophy' – condensed from *Wisdom, Information and Wonder*, Chapters 14–16. 'Escaping from Solitude' – condensed from *Wisdom, Information and Wonder*, Chapters 22–3. 'Sciencephobia and Its Sources' – condensed from *Are You an Illusion?*, Routledge, 2014, Chapter 3. 'What Is Materialism' – condensed from *What is Philosophy For?*, Bloomsbury, 2018, Chapters 20–21. 'The Human Heart and Other Organs' – condensed from *Heart and Mind*, Methuen, 1981, Chapter 1. 'On Trying Out One's New Sword on a Chance Wayfarer' – *Heart and Mind*, Chapter 5.

12

PHILOSOPHICAL PLUMBING

WATER AND THOUGHT

Is philosophy like plumbing? I have made this comparison a number of times, wanting to stress that philosophizing is not just grand and elegant and difficult, but it is also needed. It isn't optional. The idea caused mild surprise, and has sometimes been thought rather undignified. The question of dignity is a very interesting one, to which we will come back at the end of this chapter. But first, I would like to work the comparison out a bit more fully.

Plumbing and philosophy are both activities that arise because elaborate cultures like ours have, beneath their surface, a fairly complex system which is usually unnoticed, but which sometimes goes wrong. In both cases, this can have serious consequences. Each system supplies vital needs for those who live above it. Each is hard to repair when it does go wrong, because neither of them was ever consciously planned

DOI: 10.4324/9781003588160-18

as a whole. There have been many ambitious attempts to reshape both of them. But, for both, existing complications are usually too widespread to allow a completely new start.

Neither system ever had a single designer who knew exactly what needs it would have to meet. Instead, both have grown imperceptibly over the centuries in the sort of way that organisms grow, and are constantly being altered piecemeal to suit changing demands as the ways of life above them have branched out. Both are therefore now very intricate. When trouble arises, specialized skill is needed if there is to be any hope of locating it and putting it right.

Here, however, we run into the first striking difference between the two cases. About plumbing, everybody accepts this need for trained specialists. About philosophy, many people – especially British people – not only doubt the need, they are often sceptical about whether the underlying system even exists at all. It is much more deeply hidden. When the concepts we are living by work badly, they don't usually drip audibly through the ceiling or swamp the kitchen floor. They just quietly distort and obstruct our thinking.

We often don't consciously notice this obscure malfunction, any more than we consciously notice the discomfort of an unvarying bad smell or of a cold that creeps on gradually. We may indeed complain that life is going badly – that our actions and relationships are not turning out as we intend. But it can be very hard to see why this is happening, or what to do about it. We find it much easier to look for the source of trouble outside ourselves than within. Notoriously, it is hard to see faults in our own motivation, in the structure of our feelings. But it is in some ways even harder – even less natural – to turn our attention to what might be wrong in the structure of our thought. Attention naturally flows outwards to faults in the world around us. Bending thought round to look critically at itself is quite hard. That is why, in any culture, philosophy is a relatively late development.

When things do go badly, however, we have to do this. We must then somehow readjust our underlying concepts; we must shift the set of assumptions that we were brought up with. We must restate those existing assumptions – which are normally muddled and inarticulate – so as to find the source of trouble. And this new statement must somehow be put in a usable form, a form which makes the necessary changes look possible.

QUARRELS BETWEEN PHILOSOPHY AND POETRY?

The need to readjust our concepts is the need that philosophy exists to satisfy. It is *not* just a need felt by highly educated people. It is a need that can spoil the lives even of people with little interest in thinking, and its pressure can be vaguely felt by anyone who tries to think at all. As that pressure becomes fiercer, people who are determined to think particularly hard do sometimes manage to devise a remedy for this obscure discomfort, and this is how philosophy first got started. Time and again in the past, when conceptual schemes have begun to work badly, someone has contrived to suggest a change that shifts the blockage, allowing thought to flow where it is needed.

Once this has happened, the bystanders tend to heave deep sighs and say, 'Aha – of course, I knew that all along. Why didn't I happen to say it before?' (Sometimes indeed they think that they have done so . . .) These new suggestions usually come in part from sages who are not full-time philosophers, notably from poetry and other arts. Shelley was right to say that poets are among the unacknowledged legislators of mankind. They can show us the new vision. But to work the new ideas out fully is still a different kind of work. Whoever does it, it is always philosophical business. It needs, not just a new vision, but also the thorough, disciplined articulation of its details and consequences.

Much of this work is boring, and it can sometimes prove astonishingly long and difficult, but it is indispensable. Any powerful new idea calls for a great deal of change, and the more useful that idea is going to be, the more need there is to work out these changes fully. For doing this, it really is very helpful to be acquainted with other visions and other sets of changes, to have some background training in the way that past conceptual developments have worked. Of course there have been some self-educated philosophers who didn't have the advantage of this background – Tom Paine was one – but the work is much harder for them.

Great philosophers, then, need a combination of gifts that is rare. They must be lawyers as well as poets. They must have both the new vision that points the way we are to go and the logical doggedness that sorts out just what is, and what is not, involved in going there. It is this difficult balancing act that has gained them a respect which is different from the respect due to either kind of work on its own. It accounts for the peculiar prestige which philosophy still has, even among people who are extremely vague about what it is or why they might need it.

Keeping these two functions together is hard. Where philosophy is salaried and professionalized, the lawyer-like skills are almost bound to predominate, because you can examine people to test their logical competence and industry, but you can't test their creativity. These skills are then no longer being used to clarify any specially important new vision. Philosophy becomes scholastic, a specialized concern for skilled plumbers doing fine plumbing, and sometimes doing it on their own in laboratories. This happened in the late Middle Ages; it seems to have happened in China, and it has happened to Anglo-American philosophy during much of this century.

THE VISION THING

This self-contained, scholastic philosophy remains an impressive feat, something which may be well worth doing for its own sake. It is quite right that there should be deeply specialized thought, like some mathematics (for example) that most of us cannot penetrate at all. But if philosophers treat this esoteric area as their central business, they leave a most dangerous gap in the intellectual scene. This work cannot, of course, stop the other aspect, the visionary aspect of philosophy, from being needed, nor that need from being supplied. The hungry sheep who don't get that creative vision look up and are not fed. They tend to wander round looking for new visions until they find some elsewhere. Thus, a good deal of visionary philosophizing has been imported lately from Europe and from the East, from the social sciences, from evangelists, from literary criticism and from science fiction, as well as from past philosophers. But it doesn't necessarily bring with it the disciplined, detailed thinking that is needed to apply it to life.

The living water flows in, but it is not channelled to where it is needed. It seeps around, often forming floods, and it finally settles in pools where chance dictates, because the local philosophic practitioners won't attend to it. In fact, the presence of these alien streams often merely exasperates them. They suspect that the public has no business to ask for visions at all, and that unlicensed merchants have certainly no business to supply them.

So we get a new version of the old 'quarrel between philosophy and poetry' that Plato worried about in the *Republic*, a demarcation dispute embittered by modern professional territorialism and academic specialization. Philosophers are tempted to imitate other academic specialists by defensively narrowing their subject. They follow the specialized scientists, who claim that nothing counts as 'science' except the negative results of control-experiments performed inside laboratories, and the specialized historians, who insist that only value-free, non-interpreted bits of information can count as history. Ignoring the philosophic howlers that are so obvious in these claims, these philosophers in their turn also rule that only technical, purely formal work, published in learned journals and directed at their colleagues, can count as 'philosophy.'

Do they still do this? Much less so, I think, than they did a little time back. In the last few decades, many people have indeed noticed the absurdity of over-specialization, the emptiness of the heavily defended academic fortress. But unfortunately, these absurdities are built into hiring-and-firing and promotion procedures that will take a long time to change, even when the need for change is widely understood. Meanwhile, it needs to be loudly and often said that this contracting of territories, this defensive demarcation-disputing among professionals, is not just misguided. It is pernicious and thoroughly unprofessional. Learning is not a private playground for the learned. It is something that belongs to, and affects, all of us. Because we are a culture that values knowledge and understanding so highly, the part of every study that can be widely understood – the general, interpretative part, the ideology – always does seep out in the end and concern us all. The conceptual schemes used in every study are not private ponds; they are streams that are fed from our everyday thinking, are altered by the learned, and eventually flow back into it, influencing our lives.

This is not true only of philosophy. In history, for instance, ideas about the nature of social causation, about the importance or unimportance of individual acts or of economic and social factors, are constantly changing. Historians can't actually be neutral about these things, because they have to pick out what they think worth investigating. Selection always shows bias, and must have its eventual influence. All that specialist scholars gain by refusing to attend to this bit of philosophy is ignorance about their own thinking, ignorance of their own commitment and of the responsibility it carries. The same thing is true of science. One has only to think of the part that concepts like 'relativity' or 'evolution' have played in our everyday thought during the twentieth century to see this. But of course, philosophy is the key case, because it is the study whose peculiar business it is to concentrate on the gaps between all the others, and to understand the relations between them. Conceptual schemes as such are philosophy's concern, and these schemes do constantly go wrong. Conceptual confusion is deadly, and a great deal of it afflicts our everyday life. It needs to be seen to, and if the professional philosophers don't look at it, there is no one else whose role it is to do so.

THE SELF-HELP OPTION

Ought we each to be able to do this on our own, on a do-it-yourself basis? This attractive idea probably lies at the heart of British anti-intellectualism. We do sometimes manage this private philosophizing, and there is, of course, a great deal to be said for trying. But it is extremely hard to get started. Indeed, as I mentioned, often we find it hard to imagine that anything definite is wrong with our concepts at all. This is the crucial paradox. Why are we not more aware of our conceptual needs? The difficulty is that (as I have mentioned), once this kind of work is done, conceptual issues drop out of sight and are forgotten. That is why people have the idea that philosophy has never solved any problems. Systems of ideas which are working smoothly become more or less invisible. (This, of course, is what provoked my original comparison with plumbing, another service for which we are seldom as grateful as we might be.) Until they explode, we assume that the ideas we are using are the only ideas that have ever been possible. We think either that everybody uses these ideas or that, if there are people who don't, they are simply unenlightened, 'primitive,' misinformed, misguided, wicked, or extremely stupid.

DIGNITY AND DEPENDENCE

Is the approach I have been suggesting undignified? The reason why it can seem so is not, I think, just that it is too familiar and domestic, but that it postulates *needs*. It treats philosophy, like food and shelter, as something that we must have because we are in real trouble without it. We are perhaps more used to the thought that philosophy is splendid but gratuitous, and that it is splendid because it is gratuitous – something grand and exalted (like diamonds) which is not useful, but ought to be pursued all the same. On this view, intelligent people philosophize because they can see a special kind of supreme value in doing so, and perhaps everybody is capable of seeing this. But this taste is seen as something a bit removed from the rest of life, and independent of it. It is felt that our regard for philosophy ought to be a disinterested one, that there is something mean about dependence.

There really is a point in both these ways of talking, and it is not easy to balance them properly. The idea of disinterested detachment is indeed important. Pure knowledge, pure understanding, certainly is an end in itself, an aim which it is absurd to describe as 'useless.' But this talk of disinterested detachment can be misleading, both in the case of knowledge and in that of art, because it can easily sound as if we were describing a luxury, a hobby, an extra. When Socrates said that the unexamined life is unliveable to man, I don't think he meant just that our species happens to have a peculiar taste for understanding, an unaccountable and noble impulse to philosophize.

That is the way people often do interpret this kind of claim, and it's particularly often brought forward as a reason for doing science. But Socrates was surely saying something much stronger. He was saying that there are limits to living in a mess. He was pointing out that we do live in a constant, and constantly increasing, conceptual mess, and that we need to do something about it. He knew that the presence of this mess, this chronic confusion, is something we don't much want to think about because it indicates the thoroughly undignified fact that we are inherently confused beings. We exist in continual conflict because our natural impulses don't form a clear, coherent system. And the cultures by which we try to make sense of those impulses often work very badly. So – said Socrates – unless we acknowledge the resulting shameful confusions and do something to sort them out, none of our projects, whether grand or mundane, is likely to come to much. This means that we have to look at the confusions where the problems are actually arising, in real life. The kind of philosophy that tries to do this is now called Applied Philosophy. This suggests to some people that it is a mere by-product of the pure kind – a secondary spin-off from nobler, more abstract processes going on in ivory towers. But that is not the way in which European philosophy has so far developed.

Socrates started it by diving straight into the moral, political, religious, and scientific problems arising in his day. He moved on towards abstraction, not for its own sake, but because it was needed in order to clear up the deeper confusions underlying these primary messes. The same is true of Kant's preoccupation with freedom, which shaped his whole metaphysic. Good metaphysics has always been directed by considerations which are practical as well as theoretical, substantial as well as formal. Metaphysicians who claim to be free from these considerations certainly haven't really got shot of them. They are merely unaware of their own motivations, which is no gain at all.

WHAT SHOULD WE DO?

Granted, then, that the confusions are there, is abstract philosophical speculation really a helpful remedy? Are the plumbers any use? Obviously this kind of speculation can't work alone; all sorts of other human functions and faculties are needed too. But once you have got an articulate culture, the explicit, verbal statement of the problems does seem to be needed.

Socrates lived, as we do, in a society that was highly articulate and self-conscious, indeed, strongly hooked on words. It may well be that other cultures, less committed to talk, find different routes to salvation, that they pursue a less word-bound form of wisdom. But wisdom itself matters everywhere, and everybody must start from where they are. I think it might well pay us to be less interested in what philosophy can do for our dignity, and more aware of the shocking malfunctions for which it is an essential remedy.

13

WISDOM AND CONTEMPLATION

It was indeed, said Er, a sight worth seeing, how the souls severally chose their lives.

Plato, *Republic*, book 10, 620

MOON-MONSTERS AND FREE PEOPLE

In H.G. Wells's novel *The First Men in the Moon*, the human explorer finds that the native lunar creatures vary greatly among themselves in shape, size, gifts, character, and appearance. Though they all belong to a single ant-like species, each one has been modified to fit its place in life exactly. In each, some single organ is enlarged at the expense of all the others.

'Machine hands' indeed some of them are in actual nature – it is no figure of speech, the single tentacle of the mooncalf-herd is profoundly

DOI: 10.4324/9781003588160-19

modified for clawing, lifting, guiding, the rest of them no more than necessary subordinate appendages to these more important parts. The making of these various sorts of operative must be a very curious and interesting process. Quite recently I came upon a number of young Selenites confined in jars from which only the forelimbs protruded, who were being compressed to become machine minders of a special sort. The extended 'hand' in this highly developed system of technical education is stimulated by irritants and nourished by injection, while the rest of the body is starved . . . It is quite unreasonable, I know, but such glimpses of the educational methods of these beings affect me disagreeably. I hope, however, that may pass off, and I may be able to see more of this aspect of their wonderful social order. That wretched-looking hand-tentacle sticking out of its jar seemed to have a sort of limp appeal for lost possibilities; it haunts me still, although of course it is really in the end *a far more humane proceeding than our earthly method of leaving children to grow into human beings and then making machines of them.*

(Emphasis mine)

The problem that Wells so sharply outlined in those last words is still with us. All human advance needs specialization, yet this specialization conflicts with individuality. Both trends are necessary. In every growing civilization, the various types of work, and the ways of life that go with them, grow ever more elaborate and diverge further and further from each other. Indeed, this constant forking is part of what we mean if we say that a civilization is growing at all, that it is not stagnant. But it forces the people involved to pursue increasingly different ideals. And there is one essential human ideal – the ideal of wholeness and balance of faculties – from which they are all constantly being driven further and further away. The question is simply, how can we best guard against the dangers this brings?

THE FRAGMENTATION OF KNOWLEDGE

The best-known and most obviously sinister of these dangers is indeed the condition of the 'machine hands' – people who get stuck with arduous, boring, and undervalued work, work that nobody wants to do. But this danger does not stand alone. Others as pernicious are linked to it and block our efforts to deal with the whole tangle. In particular, there is a danger at the other end of the spectrum which needs attention. It lies in the condition of people whose work is officially very highly valued indeed. It is the effect of specialization on those who pursue knowledge. To be alarmed at this effect is not to cast doubts on the value of pursuing knowledge for its own sake. Accepting that ideal entirely, we can still ask, 'In what sense is a thing known if five hundred people each know one constituent of it and nobody knows the whole?' Or again: what if this truth has a thousand constituents and half of them are not now known to anyone, but only stored in libraries? What if all of them exist only in libraries? Is it enough that somebody knows how to look them up if they should ever be needed? Indeed, is it enough that this person has access to a system which will look them up? Does the enquirer even have to understand the questions which these truths would answer? (Knowing what the questions are is a very important element in real knowledge.) What is needed if something is to count as being known at all?

This question has long been an important one, but recent developments in the sheer quantity of academic output have made it even more pressing. It is now claimed – and claimed by some as a triumph of progress – that human knowledge is doubling itself exponentially every seven years, a process held to have begun in the late 1960s.[1] The grounds given for this are that the number of scientific papers published in the world is increasing at this rate. Does anybody suppose that the reading-time available has increased so as to allow all this stuff to be read and digested? All academic departments are now bombarded with floods of incoming articles, only a tiny proportion of which could they possibly read, even if they did nothing else – whereas in fact they must find time to do their own work as well. The main effect of this flood of paper (apart from exhausting the world's forests) must therefore be to pile up articles which, once they are published, nobody reads at all.

Those who welcome this expansion say that this difficulty will be met by increasing the number of scientists so that the supply of readers will be large enough to keep up with the flood. But, even if this could be done, the trouble is not only that these scientists too, in their turn, will also write papers. It is the one just mentioned – that, if the knowledge provided is split up among too many recipients, it no longer constitutes knowledge at all. The strange policy at present favoured for our universities, of exalting research over teaching, simply means that this unusable store will be increased still faster, while the process of educating people to think about the knowledge they have will be starved and downgraded. Since the current plan also separates research institutions from teaching ones, it entails starving the researchers too of the essential stimulus that teaching so notoriously gives. Much the quickest way to find out that you do not understand something properly is to try to explain it to somebody else, and this has traditionally been the way in which difficult knowledge has been kept alive, working, and fertile – as much in the physical sciences as elsewhere.[2]

LIVING OR DEAD?

Einstein was much concerned about this problem. He wrote, 'Knowledge exists in two forms – lifeless, stored in books, and alive, in the consciousness of men. The second form of existence is after all the essential one; the first, indispensable as it may be, occupies only an inferior position.'[3] Was Einstein right? If he was wrong, then we can stop worrying about this question and about many others as well. The libraries need then never be visited again except to fetch bits of useful information, as one goes to a shop to fetch butter, and all research not reasonably likely to be useful could be dropped. This conclusion is not a welcome one, but the other alternative is disturbing too. If Einstein was right, then our knowledge ought surely to be something alive in our consciousness. It should be working there, which means it must work as part of us. The memory-man at the fair cannot be our ideal model, however infallible his recall may be. Merely holding information as an inert piece of property, or handing it on like a dead fish to students, cannot be enough.

Academics are often aware of this problem. But they tend to speak of it resignedly as something quite insoluble. They often believe that the mere recent increase in the amount of knowledge inevitably involves its continual subdivision into smaller and smaller fractions distributed among more and more holders. 'The days of the Renaissance polymath are past,' they say; 'greater riches now demand a less unified kind of safekeeping.'

If this gloomy conclusion were true, it would mean that we have moved into the condition of misers whose wealth has become so cumbrous that they must lock it away for safety and cannot actually use or enjoy it at all. (Perhaps indeed a miser may be defined as some-one who has no idea what to do with any given resource except to store it.) As we shall see, the right use of knowledge is simply not compatible with this indefinitely continued subdivision. It involves understanding, which means treating knowledge as a whole. Without that wider outlook, the whole ideal of knowledge as it has always been understood evaporates.

But of course the wider outlook has not become impossible. What it requires is not that every scholar should master all the details of all subjects. That feat would have been impossible already in Renaissance times. What is needed is that all should have in their minds a general background map of the whole range of knowledge as a context for their own speciality, and should integrate this wider vision with their practical and emotional attitude to life. They should be able to place their own small area on the map of the world, and to move outside it freely when they need to. This is not even necessarily a particularly time-consuming business. It is a matter of a different general attitude much more than of detailed indoctrination.

At an academic level, things could be dramatically improved if the first and last sections of papers, where the reasons for raising the ques-tion and the consequences of answering it are discussed, got much more attention, and the quality of reasoning shown in them was given far more weight than the mere number of papers published – a num-ber which, considered as a measure of merit, is of little more value than the number of the writer's hairs. More widely, however, much of the change could be achieved in childhood simply by attending to the questions which children spontaneously ask, and to a range of other wide questions which link these spontaneous questions together. Once this is done, it saves a great deal of time in detailed teaching. Details make much better sense when they have a context, and what makes sense is far easier to remember. For the point is not just that different specialities need to be related to each other. It is that they all need to be related to everyday thinking, and made responsible to it. They must even acknowledge their own emotional aspect – which is invariably present – and relate that to everyday feeling. All this is of course disturbing, since remoteness from everyday thought and feeling, or even actual contempt for them, is often one of the first things that higher education seems to teach people. The reasons why I think this apparently awkward suggestion has to be made, and the ways in which it can finally come to seem less outrageous, will I hope emerge in the course of this enquiry.

KNOWLEDGE AT WORK

> A thing, then, that every soul pursues as the end of all her actions, dimly divining its existence, but perplexed and unable to grasp its nature with the same clearness and assurance as in dealing with other things, and so missing whatever value those other things might have – a thing of such supreme importance is not a matter about which those chosen Guardians of the whole future of our commonwealth can be left in the dark.
>
> (Plato, *Republic*, book 6, 505)

In our thinking today, what does that 'live working' of knowledge that Einstein mentioned involve? On this point, we shall need to pay special attention to the views of scientists, simply because the idea of 'science' is now much the most influential model held up for intellectual enquiry in general. This idea of science is not actually at all a clear one. It groups together a wide range of physical sciences, which vary greatly among themselves in their nature, methods, and functions, not to mention an uneasy annexe for the 'social sciences,' which are visibly rather different again. All the same, as an ideal, the notion of 'science' as a single model, giving laws to all other kinds of organized thought, is today a predominant one. And it is for 'science' as so conceived that the kind of specialization we have been discussing is above all accepted and defended. Yet in this area the notion of pure knowledge as a self-justifying end in itself is also strongly proclaimed and honoured. So it becomes important for us to understand just what kind of an end contemporary scientists take knowledge to be. How do they view it?

Current scientists disagree remarkably about this from those past philosophers – such as Plato, Aristotle, and Spinoza – who called forth and established that special respect for knowledge which is such a marked characteristic of our culture. Those philosophers thought that the aim was contemplation itself – the aim not merely of all discovery but of life itself. For them, knowledge was simply an aspect of wisdom. It was part of an understanding of life as a whole, out of which a sense of what really mattered in it would become possible. Knowledge indeed had the same goal as love; contemplation was the highest human happiness. Thus, Aristotle, at the end of a book devoted to the question of what the final goal of human effort is, concludes that it must be an activity of 'the best thing in us.' (Like Einstein, he said explicitly that it could not be a mere state; it had to be an active working.) He goes on:

> Whether it be reason or something else which is thought to be our natural ruler and guide, and to take thought of things noble and divine – whether it be itself also divine or only the most divine element in us – the activity of this in accordance with its proper virtue will be happiness . . . The pursuit of this is thought to offer pleasures marvellous for their purity and their enduringness, and it is to be expected that those who know will pass their time more pleasantly than those who enquire.[4]

And again:

> (Thought) is *active* when it *possesses* its object. Therefore the possession rather than the receptivity is the divine element which thought seems to contain, and the act of contemplation is what is most pleasant and best.[5]

Here the idea of possession is explicitly made an active one, distinct from mere storing, and consisting in the interaction between the mind and what it contemplates. Similarly Plato, while he praises the intellectual life as central for human existence, insists that certain aspects of that life stand out as furnishing the point for the rest. Not everything is equally worth knowing, and there are some central, architectonic forms of knowledge without which others would have no value. Knowledge about what goodness means must be the centre, because it is what shows the point of all other knowledge, indeed of all other activity. At a minimal level, without touching on the religious awe that was crucial for Plato, this means that our sense of value-contrasts is needed for the very possibility of our perceiving anything else. The polarity of good and bad is an essential dimension of our world, the condition of our knowing it at all. The value of understanding the difference between good and bad cannot therefore be reduced to, and equated with, the value of any other particular thing, not even of knowledge. It has a different kind of place in the world and in our thinking. This is what makes Plato compare goodness to the sun, which is the source both of life itself and of the light which makes it possible for us to gain knowledge of life:

> This, then, which gives to the objects of knowledge their truth and to him who knows them his power of knowing, is the Form or essential nature of Goodness. It is the cause of knowledge and truth; and so, while you may think of it as an object of knowledge, you will do well to regard it as something beyond truth and knowledge, and, precious as both are, of still higher worth.[6]

Plato therefore sees all other studies as simply parts of the contemplation of goodness and stages towards its greater fullness:

> This is the right way of approaching and being initiated into the mysteries of love, to begin with examples of beauty in this world, and using them as steps to ascend continually with that absolute beauty as one's aim, from one instance of physical beauty to two and from two to all,

then from physical beauty to moral beauty, and from moral beauty to the beauty of knowledge, until from knowledge of various kinds one arrives at the supreme knowledge whose sole object is that absolute beauty, and knows at last what absolute beauty is.[7]

Thus Plato, and it was from this base that he and Aristotle launched the whole enterprise of organized European scholarship, and convinced the world of its importance. By contrast, present-day scientists tend to say little about contemplation, and also to exalt discovery over knowledge. Their typical view is probably the one expressed by the sociobiologist Edward O. Wilson when he writes:

> Newly discovered truths, and not truth in some abstract sense alone, are the ultimate goal and yardstick of the scientific culture. Scientists do not discover in order to know; they know in order to discover. Humanists are the shamans of the intellectual tribe, wise men who interpret knowledge and transmit the folklore, rituals and sacred texts. Scientists are the scouts and hunters. No one rewards a scientist for what he knows. Nobel prizes and other trophies are bestowed for the new facts and theories he brings home to the tribe.[8]

During the last century, many humanists too have become as eager as the scientists to disown even the quest for wisdom, let alone the responsibility for possessing and using it. Thus, the great historian F. W. Maitland said that he never dealt in opinions, only in materials for the forming of opinions. Similarly, English-speaking moral philosophers spent the middle years of this century emphasizing the logical gap between facts and values, and insisting that it was none of their professional business either to make moral judgements themselves or to help other people to make them. Academic literary critics, too, have been moving steadily further and further away from their traditional function. They no longer want to be thought of as ready to help readers in using great literature to deepen and enlarge their vision of the world, a vision meant to be actively used and lived by. Instead, these critics are more and more occupied with highbrow technical battles between various theories of criticism – theories which are not even meant to concern anybody but other scholars.

There is a real change here. The point is no longer just that some parts of these studies are difficult and technical, understandable only by those who specially study them. That has always been true, and it does not matter. What matters is the belief that professionals should be concerned only with these parts. On this view, it is the mark of an untrained amateur to discuss – especially in public – any aspect of one's enquiry which could naturally interest what are significantly called 'lay people.' Knowledge is increasingly divorced from wisdom.

IS WISDOM FORGOTTEN?

We should note here, before going any further, the possibility that something much larger and more serious is wrong with this narrowed use of the intellect than has so far been mentioned. In an admirable book called *From Knowledge to Wisdom*, Nicholas Maxwell has argued that the radical, wasteful misdirection of our whole academic effort is actually a central cause of the sorrows and dangers of our age. Of course (he remarks) there are other things which one might naturally name as the main source of our troubles. One could, for instance, reasonably pick on 'the inertia of our institutions, which renders them, and us, incapable of responding to the crisis.' But, he adds,

The intellectual/institutional inertia of the academic enterprise is, in a major way, responsible for the general inertia of institutions . . . Granted that enquiry has as its basic aim to help enhance the quality of human life, it is actually profoundly and damagingly *irrational, unrigorous*, for enquiry to give intellectual priority to the task of improving knowledge . . . Problems of knowledge and understanding need to be tackled as rationally subordinate to intellectually more fundamental problems of living . . . The fundamental intellectual task of a kind of enquiry that is devoted, in a genuinely rational and rigorous way, to helping us improve the quality of human life, must be to create and make available a rich store of vividly imagined and severely criticized possible actions, so that our capacity to act intelligently and humanely in reality is thereby enhanced.[9]

The point is related to the one that Marx expressed so disastrously badly when he said that what is necessary is not to understand the world, but to change it. Marx's remark misses two vital points: first, that proper understanding is a condition of proper change, not an alternative to it, and, second, that what needs doing in the world is as often concerned with preserving it as with changing it. All the same, so far as Marx meant that what is necessary is not just to talk about the world, or to be informed about it, but to act rightly in it – 'acting' being taken to include inner as well as outer action – he was surely right. Thinking out how to live is a more basic and urgent use of the human intellect than the discovery of any fact whatsoever, and the considerations it reveals ought to guide us in our search for knowledge, as they ought in every other project we pursue. In arguing this point – which Kant would have found congenial – Maxwell proposes that we should replace the notion of aiming at knowledge by that of aiming at wisdom. I think this is basically the right proposal. I suspect, however, that there is, in a sense, even more wrong with the current notion of aiming at knowledge than Maxwell has noticed. Even on its own terms, this notion does not make sense. It presupposes a notion of knowledge that is unrealistic and self-defeating. It is not – what I think Maxwell sometimes suggests – a wrong but genuine option, it is no sort of option at all.

I think we need to develop gradually the notion of wisdom which this approach involves, and to grasp better its proper relation to knowledge. These are not easy problems. Perhaps the essential point for the moment is that 'knowledge' is not the name of a distinct, modern, and enlightened ideal which has superseded wisdom as the goal of all our efforts. Knowledge can indeed be an ideal, an end in itself, not merely a means to other ends. But it has then to be seen as one among other human ends, as having its own place in our priority system as a whole. If this is not done, knowledge itself is insulted, and the search for it is distorted. Moreover, I think Maxwell is surely right in saying that this distortion, because it wastes our intellectual powers, has played a serious part in distorting our lives.

NOTES

1. For the quite special absurdity of this mindless accumulation in non-scientific subjects, see S. Gollini's article 'Research in the Humanities', *Times Literary Supplement*, 3 April 1987.
2. A point strongly stressed by Sir George Porter in a protest against the policy in his Anniversary Presidential Address to the Royal Society, supplement to *Royal Society News* 4 (6) (1987).
3. A. Einstein, *Ideas and Opinions* (London, Souvenir Press, 1954), p. 80.
4. Aristotle, *Nicomachean Ethics*, book 10, 1177ab.
5. Aristotle, *Metaphysics*, book 13, 1072b.
6. Plato, *Republic*, book 6, 508.
7. Plato, *Symposium*, 212b.
8. E.O. Wilson, *Biophilia* (Cambridge, MA, Harvard University Press, 1984), p. 58.
9. N. Maxwell, *From Knowledge to Wisdom: A Revolution in the Aims and Methods of Science* (Oxford, Basil Blackwell, 1984), p. 2.

14

THE WITHDRAWAL OF MORAL PHILOSOPHY

Bones And murder?

George And murder too, yes.

Bones He thinks there's nothing *wrong* with killing people?

George Well, put like that of course . . . But, *philosophically*, he doesn't think it's actually, inherently, wrong in itself, no.

Bones *[amazed]*. What sort of philosophy is that?

George Mainstream, I'd call it. Orthodox mainstream . . . In the circumstances I was lucky to get the Chair of Moral Philosophy. Only the Chair of Divinity lies further below the salt.

Tom Stoppard, *Jumpers*

THE IDEA OF THE MODERN

G.E. Moore's first book, Principia Ethica, which came out in 1903, changed the face of English-speaking moral philosophy for more than

DOI: 10.4324/9781003588160-20

half a century, extending the surface revolution we have already noticed to ethics, and justifying the total retreat of the learned from this central area of everyday human thought. The personality of its author was very important here. In this book, the young Moore emerged at once as a prophet, already displaying his extraordinary personal force, though he scarcely yet showed his real greatness. This greatness was expressed later, when Moore supplied the central and deepest new insight for linguistic philosophy, an insight concerned with the dependence of all intellectual systems on common sense, with its vehicle common language. Moore then began to explore a deep sense in which common thought and language have to be primary, because they flow from and express the way in which people actually live, while intellectual systems, however important and however influential, grow like branches out of this living thought. The systems therefore cannot simply displace or ignore it, as Russell tended to assume they could; they cannot treat it as a mere vulgar error. They have to find their place somewhere within it, as the parts of the city that Wittgenstein later described all find their place within that city and go to make it a whole. Though this basic respect for common sense had often been hinted at earlier in the British empiricist tradition – notably by Reid, Locke, and Butler – it had never before been fully developed. Nor is it at all easy to develop it without falling into a slick relativism, a readiness to exalt as 'common sense' whatever ideas happen temporarily to prevail. All the same, Moore in articles such as 'The defence of common sense' and Wittgenstein in all his later work did make progress towards that development. I take this progress to have been the real achievement of the linguistic or analytic movement.

Principia Ethica, however, contained very little of this spirit. It did indeed, in some sense, exalt ordinary thought on moral matters, or at least what Moore took to be ordinary thought. But it did so by treating it as something which was not really thought at all but pure intuition, unrelated to the main system of other existing ideas. Moore declared that all the reasoning used to support moral judgements was empty because it was vitiated by a 'naturalistic fallacy.' The whole mass of argument by which ordinary people – as well as philosophers – normally test and compare these judgements was useless. Thus the book painted in strong colours the irrationalist, anti-cognitive picture of morals that Russell later reproduced at the end of his *History*.

It is of great interest that this message was so eagerly welcomed. One thing this shows is that the times were ripe for it. Both within and without the academic field, many people were exhausted by the confusion of existing moral arguments and were ready for a shortcut. But in order to enforce this particular shortcut so effectively, something more was needed. Much of the book's force was due to its philosophical style, which was exceedingly prophetic. With the enviable confidence of youth, Moore dismissed virtually all earlier moral philosophers as simply incompetent. He explained that – barring a partial exception for Sidgwick – these people had been mere bunglers, incapable of seeing a vast fallacy – a fallacy so gross and central that it made their whole work, not just inadequate, but quite useless as argument. Before 1903, therefore, there had in effect been no relevant argument about ethics at all:

> The offering of irrelevant evidence generally indicates that the philosopher who offers it has had before his mind, not the question which he professes to answer, but some entirely different one. Ethical discussion, hitherto, has perhaps consisted chiefly in reasoning of this totally irrelevant kind.[1]
>
> [The naturalistic fallacy] is to be met with in almost every book on ethics . . . It is a very simple fallacy indeed. In general, ethical philosophers have attempted to define good, without recognizing what such an attempt must mean . . . We are, therefore, justified in concluding that the attempt to define good is chiefly due to want of clearness as to the possible nature of definition.[2]

Words like 'almost,' 'perhaps,' and 'chiefly,' which might seem to soften these bizarre claims actually do not, because they are promises that are never kept. It should have been very important to Moore to examine any exceptions there might be to his ukase, even partial ones, but he never did. These qualifications therefore are just a stylistic trick, fully deserving Bernard Williams's remark, 'Moore's philosophy is marked by an affectation of modest caution, which clogged his prose with qualifications but rarely restrained him from wild error.'[3]

At this time of day, naturally, there would be no point in criticizing Moore himself for this, but the response of his successors is still important. Moral philosophers did not in fact give up teaching traditional ethics, as one might have thought they ought to if they believed Moore. Yet, as we noticed earlier in discussing prophets, they gave to Moore's own teaching on the subject an awe-struck reverence very different from his own parricidal attitude. It is not surprising that readers enjoyed his sweeping approach, but what made them take it so seriously? One might have expected *Principia Ethica* to be treated as philosophers treated Ayer's *Language, Truth and Logic* – as a clever squib from a promising young man who would have something useful to say one day. Why – far from this – did it take people so long to see the weaknesses in the idea of a single, all-pervading 'naturalistic fallacy' or 'gap between facts and values' and the total transformation of ethics which was supposed to follow from exposing it?

What made this possible was, I think, the power of two linked ideas that were very influential at the time and still are so today – the ideas of modernness (or modernity) and of professionalism. The notion of modernness painted a single, benign change as taking place throughout all aspects of civilization. In this change (as Mr Slope put it in *Barchester Towers*) the rubbish of past ages was everywhere being carted away, and there was no difficulty at all in identifying that rubbish. The slums to be cleared were already marked, and they were known to cover most of the main areas of existing thought. There was therefore nothing surprising about finding that all one's predecessors had been mistaken. A uniformly dark past was giving way to a uniformly bright present and future.

The trouble with this idea has always been, not just that it lumps together a huge rag-bag of quite different changes, but that it cannot cope with continuing change at all. The single revolution can have no successors. There is no indication at all of what is supposed to happen after it – for instance, twenty, forty, or eighty years later; for instance, today. In all areas of life where the word 'modern' was used like this as a sufficient, self-explanatory ideal, and above all in the arts, this idea has made endless trouble, leaving its pious proponents to flounder strangely now in talk about 'post-modernism' and similar strange entities. But, in its day, the concept was strong and liberating, and Moore's title appeals to a deep faith in it, which his public shared. In his time, Newton's *Principia* was still seen as founding modern science once for all – a science differing from all its predecessors as day from night, a definitive science which would never need to be altered for the future. That is the claim which the title *Principia Ethica* – equally with the title *Principia Mathematica* chosen by Russell and Whitehead – is meant to echo. No rumours about relativity or quantum mechanics had yet disturbed the peace. The perspective was Pope's:

> Nature and Nature's laws lay hid in night:
> God said, *Let Newton be!* and all was light.

Later, of course, as J.C. Squire sadly added,

> It did not last: the Devil howling 'Ho!
> Let Einstein be!' restored the status quo.[4]

But, in the opening years of the century, *Principia* still meant permanence. The modern was the final.

FACTS AND VALUES

> In this life we want nothing but Facts, sir, nothing but Facts.
> (Mr Gradgrind in Chapter 1 of *Hard Times*)

The part of *Principia Ethica* that reached the public and shaped people's lives was the last chapter, on 'The Ideal,' which contained a bold, impassioned, and unconventional exaltation of certain aesthetic and personal values over everything else in life – an exaltation every bit as dogmatic and as unexplained as Monod's later exaltation of scientific ones. The rest of *Principia Ethica* – the part which furnished the ground-rules for later professionalism – did not concern itself at all with arguing for the value-judgement that exalted those ideals, which Moore took to be already accepted and obvious, but with proving the impossibility of using any arguments to support any value-judgements whatever, and these were the chapters in which he damned the earlier moral philosophers. His attack showed – besides its great savagery – two other very odd unexplained features. First, it concentrated exclusively on logical rather than moral considerations. Moore did not say that his predecessors' views were bad because they would lead people to live badly, but that they were bad because they were confused, and were so, moreover, always with the same confusion, namely, the naturalistic fallacy. At this time of day, that name must still stand because it is not worthwhile inventing another. But certainly, as Bernard Williams remarks, since, so far as the thing can be identified at all, it is neither naturalistic nor a fallacy, 'it is hard to think of any other phrase in the history of philosophy that is such a spectacular misnomer.'[5]

Moore's wholesaleness was surely the core both of his error and of his appeal. His system, had it worked, would have been splendidly simple and economical, and we can see why it seemed to work. The half-truth from which he started was the tempting observation that all difficult moral arguments run into a dark patch somewhere. The error lay in concluding that there is therefore a *single*, incurably dark patch into which they all run, so that all that can be done is to placard its irremovable darkness. Moore's own terminology of failure to define 'good' was so strange, so remote from the language of his various victims, that it was easy for a writer of his buoyant, confident cast to carry his readers over the huge differences between the varying views he attacked, and to feel satisfied that they all fitted the same Procrustean bed. His successors, however, noticed its shakiness uneasily and substituted the idea of a logical gap between facts and values (or emotions, or attitudes) or between description and prescription. In each case, the appearance of uniformity was kept up by remaining very abstract. In each, the notion of the gap could be made plausible because, in moral as in other thinking, it is natural, when we reach a difficult point, to describe the previous, secure, accepted part of our thinking as representing 'the facts.' And it can be very important to distinguish this relatively secure area from the questionable one where choices have now to be made. Thus, 'separating questions of fact from questions about value' can be a perfectly reasonable procedure. The mistake lies in supposing that no conceptual link can ever be found between them, in exalting a temporary separation, made for the sake of argument, into a permanent, impenetrable logical barrier.

Facts are data – material which, for purposes of a particular enquiry, does not need to be reconsidered. They are never completely 'raw data,' 'brute facts,'[6] because anything that we can think about at all has already been *shaped* by our concepts. And the data of any serious moral problem always incorporate quite complex pre-existing value-judgements and conceptual schemes. When, therefore, we reach these gaps or dark patches in our thinking, what we do is to work on the surrounding concepts, and to bring in others where necessary until (ideally) we construct a path across this particular dark area. The history of thought shows plainly how this has repeatedly been done. And although this work is very hard – though it is often done badly and is in a sense never finished – yet all the same, particular puzzles can be solved so completely that they are forgotten, and later generations see the solution simply as part of 'the facts.' The word fact, in its normal usage, is indeed not properly opposed to value, but to something more like conjecture or opinion, as Geoffrey Warnock reasonably points out:

> I believe that we all have, and should not let ourselves be bullied out of, the conviction that at least some questions as to what is good or bad for people, what is harmful or beneficial, are not in any serious sense matters of opinion. That it is a bad thing to be tortured or starved, humiliated or hurt, is not an opinion; it is a fact. That it is better for people to be loved and attended to, rather than hated or neglected, is again a plain fact, not a matter of opinion.[7]

YOUR FACTS AND MY FACTS

Interestingly, too, even 'facts' in the narrower sense in which they are not supposed to incorporate values tend to change their appearance where there are changes of value. We do not find it easy to see facts in a *way* which fails to fit our value-judgements. Thus, as European thought came to accept that slavery was wrong, its bad consequences came to be accepted as facts. But those who opposed this process took themselves to be equally factual. Thus Boswell:

> I will resolutely say that [Dr Johnson's] unfavourable notion of it [the slave trade] was owing to prejudice and imperfect or false information . . . To abolish a status which in all ages God has sanctioned and man has continued, would not only be robbery to an innumerable class of our fellow-subjects, but it would be extreme cruelty to the African Savages, a portion of whom it saves from massacre, or intolerable bondage in their own country, and introduces into a much happier state of life; especially now when their passage to the West Indies and their treatment there is humanely regulated. To abolish this trade would be to 'shut the gates of mercy on mankind'.[8]

Again, it is worthwhile to notice this angle on certain well known words of Russell's. They are not brought in here to belittle him. Everybody is inclined to say foolish things on this kind of topic, and the fact that Russell never minded making a fool of himself is on the whole a valuable trait in his character; it gave him the excellent habit of readily acknowledging his mistakes. But the point is to show what a strange and misleading effect, right across the spectrum of life, can flow from the notion of 'facts' as things totally detached from feelings and the will:

> I went out bicycling one afternoon, and suddenly, as I was riding along a country road, I realized that I no longer loved Alys. I had had no idea until this moment that my love was even lessening. The problem presented by this discovery was very grave.[9]

He treats it from then on as something irremediable – exactly as someone might discover that they have a flat tyre, although they had no idea till that moment that its pressure was even lessening, and can then be presented with its flatness as a simple datum, beyond their power to alter. It is extraordinarily transparent bad faith to treat one's own most complex and central motives like this. Certainly, we can make sudden discoveries about those motives, but, when we do, they cannot be simple and final. They call for investigation and rethinking of the whole surrounding territory. And a great deal of this thinking will not be an attempt to discover any more facts, but a reflection on what one now wants to think and to feel, leading to questions about what one is now prepared to do, and to struggles to do it. It seems to me that Russell would not have described this experience in that way, nor begun to think of it in that way, without the unrealistic notion of simple, value-free facts that was built into his philosophy.

This mention of how the facts sometimes seem to vary with the values does not tip us into helpless scepticism. It simply calls attention to the unity of the moral enterprise, to the web of conceptual links between all its various facets. The process of change could, of course, be described just as well the other way round, in the form in which it often appeared to those who underwent it, as a recognition of the facts which entailed a rejection of slavery. What was happening was a single complex process with three conceptually linked aspects – a changing view of the facts, a change of feeling, and a change in action, arising out of a changed sense of what action could be decently contemplated. It has been a real misfortune, not just for philosophy but for our civilization itself, that philosophers in the tradition we are discussing have tended to concentrate entirely on separating these factors and putting them in competition with each other, rather than on investigating the relations between them. In an age when the world itself changes so fast, it is vital to attend to this relation and to notice where it goes wrong. This is certainly difficult. But that is not a reason for saving ourselves the trouble by ruling that it cannot be done.[10]

NARROWING THE BOUNDS

Moore himself believed, with all the massive force of his pile-driving personality, that readers who avoided the irrelevancies induced by this *single fallacy* would find themselves left with the scheme of values displayed in his last chapter. Throughout, he recurred to visual metaphors; only look in the right direction and you cannot fail to see the colours before you. Alien approaches always seemed to him to be due to an unaccountable failure to look, a failure caused by an inner confusion which he was disturbed to find all around him. As Leonard Woolf says:

> When Moore said 'I *simply* don't understand *what* he means', the emphasis on the 'simply' and the 'what' and the shake of his head over each word gave one a glimpse of the passionate distress which muddled thinking aroused in him.[11]

Keynes, similarly, has recorded the devastating effect Moore used to produce simply by saying, '*Do* you *really* think *that?*'[12] To those around him, Moore seemed quite simply to be gazing at a clearly revealed truth.

But this was not the situation for his academic successors. They did not necessarily see the moral scene in the least as Moore saw it. They had each their own view of morality, views which – as the world grew more and more confused from the time of the First World War – became increasingly various. The link between the two parts of the book was a loose one, depending largely on Moore's own character. What the academic successors chiefly saw in the book was something quite different, namely a way of keeping moral philosophy clear of confusing moral conflicts in the real world altogether. If the faults in bad ethics were always logical faults, then what was needed to combat them was simply training in the relevant areas of logic. And, if those logical faults were always due to just one newly discovered fallacy, then a full understanding of that fallacy could be the sole theme of professional training. This saved moral philosophers from the quite new danger that they might have to hand over their papers to the logic department and find themselves out of work altogether.

Of course, I do not want to suggest that tribal and professional considerations of this kind were the only thing that led Moore's successors to accept the idea of the naturalistic fallacy. They were also moved by real and important moral considerations about the faults of existing doctrines, especially of utilitarianism, which we will look at shortly. But these were really moral objections – as they had a perfect right to be – and it was unfortunately central to Moore's method to treat them as purely formal ones. This greatly distorted the attack, concentrating it officially always on logical incompetence rather than on vice, folly, or danger. If this purely formal approach were really the only one open to philosophers – if they were always interested only in logical correctness – then they need not concern themselves at all about the moral implications of what was being argued. They should be perfectly satisfied with consistent iniquity. And indeed it began to be assumed that moral philosophers ought to be neutral in this way about substantial moral questions.

THE PROJECT OF MORAL NEUTRALITY

In the opening passage of his book *Ethics and Language*, C.L. Stevenson sounded the trumpet for this crusade:

> One would not expect a book on scientific method to do the work of science itself, and *one must not expect to find here any conclusions about what conduct is right or wrong.* The purpose of an analytical study, whether of science or ethics, is always indirect. It hopes to send *others* to their tasks with clearer heads and less wasteful habits of investigation . . . It does not require the analyst, as such, to participate in the enquiry that he analyses. In ethics, any direct participation of this kind might have its *dangers. It might deprive the analysis of its detachment, and distort a relatively neutral study into a plea for some special code of morals* . . . The present volume has the limited task of sharpening the tools which *others* employ.
>
> (Emphases mine)[13]

Thus, moral philosophy could be done just as well by someone who did not take the slightest interest in actual moral problems as by someone concerned about them – indeed, perhaps better, since the temptation to partiality would be less. Officially, this move to neutrality is itself just a formal one, undertaken purely in the interests of clear thinking. But the reasons Stevenson gave for making it were moral reasons, reasons concerned with the dangers of taking sides. These are dangers of unfairness and oppressiveness, dangers of interfering with the reader's freedom of choice by undue influence. Now fairness and freedom are of course in themselves perfectly good moral values, but why, out of all the values that could be named, are these ones alone suddenly getting this preferential treatment? What makes Stevenson so partial to fairness and freedom? Why are unfairness and oppression not getting equal time and equal favour? More seriously, in cases where this particular kind of fairness and freedom conflict with other values – as they very often can – in what scales ought they to be weighed? The world is full of value-conflicts of this kind; they have always been the starting-point of moral philosophy. Emotivist ethics had only one way of dealing with them, namely, pleading professional exemption from the conflict. The most that Stevenson offered for these difficulties was a kind of therapy for the participants – an offer to make them clearer about what it was that they were trying to do. The philosopher himself was to remain neutral; in his professional capacity, he did not have moral problems. He remained a detached analyst, whose training evidently had not included any sessions on the couch. In considering how likely this is to be the slightest use, it is worth noticing the parallel that Stevenson draws with the case of science. His idea of the philosophic supervisor who 'sends others to their work with clearer heads,' without himself bothering to study the subject they are working on, has proved less than satisfactory there.

This third-person approach is so strange that it may puzzle us how it can have remained for several decades, not just accepted, but treated as the core of moral philosophy. Considerations about professional status do seem to me to throw some light on this, because in general impartiality is indeed something often required of professionals – only you do have to get the right kind of impartiality. Doctors are supposed to devote themselves impartially to curing even their most odious patients, but they are still supposed to be on the side of health against disease. Barristers have to be ready to defend even abominable clients, but they still ought to be on the side of the law. I think that philosophers like Stevenson felt a kind of parallel in their situation to these initial demands for impartiality, and did not see how it could have any limits. Taking sides on moral questions seemed to them amateurish, something which, if they did it at all, they should only do in their spare time. From this angle, earlier moral philosophers – who certainly had taken sides strongly on such questions and supported their opinions by argument – appeared to be indeed the helpless amateurs that Moore had called them. They were convicted of being – as I remember hearing them called – 'pre-Copernican.'

I think that the anti-naturalist campaign sprang partly from the wish to assert the freedom of individual moral agents to make their own value-judgements boldly and honestly. This is the stance that Stevenson seems to be endorsing, and it seems to have been motivated too by another unacknowledged but substantial moral aim, namely, a distaste for the whole idea of blame and punishment. Moore's approach to morality was one that laid little stress on punishment and weakened the notion of blame almost to vanishing-point.

THE FLIGHT FROM BLAME

> And they all with one consent began to make excuse.
>
> (St Luke's Gospel, 14.18)

Moore, of course, was not the pioneer here; the work had been begun by the classical utilitarians. John Stuart Mill and Jeremy Bentham had already turned their critical searchlight on confused and sinister ancient notions of punishment with tremendous effect. They had begun, too, to undermine the notion of blame by treating it as a mere secondary appendage of punishment. Thus Mill:

> We do not call anything wrong, unless we mean to imply that a person ought to be punished in some way or another for doing it; if not by

law, by the opinion of his fellow-creatures; if not by opinion, by the reproaches of his own conscience.[14]

Thus the reproaches both of others and of one's own conscience began to be viewed primarily as a part of the punishment – as deterrents to further wrongdoing, rather than as judgements which might or might not actually be justified by the evidence. Moore carried this idea still further. Although elsewhere he attacked Mill sharply, in this matter and in many others he remained extremely close to the utilitarian thought in which he had been brought up. In the main part of his book, he was quite as extreme a consequentialist in morals as Mill or Bentham. (There are some isolated remarks on punishment in the last chapter which seem to tell a different story, but they are at odds with the official doctrine of the book.[15]) He thought it obvious that actions were valueless in themselves and that only the states they produced could have value. He therefore followed the utilitarians in reducing all terms concerned with duties to a purely causal meaning, and he phrased that reduction even more strongly than Mill had. Thus, he says, 'The assertion, "I am morally bound to perform this action" is *identical with* the assertion, "This action will produce the greatest possible amount of good for the universe" ' (emphasis mine).[16] For Moore, as for Mill and Bentham, words like 'duty,' 'right,' and 'wrong' are essentially predictive terms, simply noting the good or bad consequences to be expected. And Moore goes on to give an equally reductive account of general principles, writing, 'An ethical law has the character, not of a scientific law, but of a scientific prediction.'[17]

This approach implies an extraordinarily detached, purely descriptive attitude, possible only for remote spectators – perhaps for astronauts, able to watch what is happening on a distant planet but quite shut off from influencing it. Moore's definitions leave out the whole practical element in this moral language – the leverage, the deontic force, that gives such words their main meaning. In the same spirit, he goes on to emphasize how uncertain these predictions are. Things may easily not go as we expect, and in that case, we shall simply turn out to have done wrong instead of right. Good intentions are of little account.[18] Morality is simply a device for producing, on average, rather better results than we would get without it. This has an implication which is important, though Moore does not mention it. If it is true, then blame, in its existing sense, can no longer be attached to doing wrong. That conceptual link must be finally broken.

THE FLIGHT FROM THOUGHT

What this did for the philosophers was to supply them with a reason for retreating from the business of moral judgement, which was seen as essentially one of allotting blame. (Praise seems to have been strangely forgotten.) Moore's position seemed to offer a welcome way out to humane people who were attracted in general by the reforming programme of utilitarianism, but who were still put off it by its emphasis on punishment, and who thought its theory of value vulgarly reductive. That Moore's own theory of value was just as reductive escaped notice, partly, no doubt, because its values were themselves less crude, partly too, no doubt, because it came at the end of his book. What was professionally noticed was the technique Moore provided for resisting the arguments used, both by utilitarians and by other philosophers, to establish their respective value-theories. The idea of a 'naturalistic fallacy' served, in fact, as an all-purpose blunderbuss for shooting down every kind of argument (apart from simple causal argument) which anyone might bring in support of any moral position. Since Moore himself used it against metaphysical ethics, its firing-range was evidently not restricted to targets which could, even in his wide sense, be called 'naturalistic.' In fact its animus was not so much anti-naturalistic as anti-thought, opposed to moral reasoning as such.

In the hands of trained intellectuals, anti-intellectual weapons like this have an odd effect. They supply a very easy way of putting other people down, and in particular they bear hardly on students. Coming up to university to study moral philosophy, these innocent individuals often expected, indeed hoped, to employ their minds on moral problems. Anti-naturalism required them, in effect, to stop thinking on these topics. It attacked equally all the available kinds of moral thinking, without supplying any new alternative to them. And its destructive zeal was particularly strongly directed against a theory which, for large-scale political purposes, was still one of the most frequent, reputable and natural sources of reforming arguments – namely, utilitarianism.[19]

Among philosophers today, this way of arguing is largely discredited because of its formal confusions. But the more we now discredit it, the more pressing I think it now becomes to understand how it came to command so much respect. We may ourselves be subject to influences no more cogent or relevant. In our age, the revulsion against 'making moral judgements' has a powerful hold both on theory and on practice. It runs right across the intellectual spectrum from B.F. Skinner[20] to Bernard Williams[21] – a distance which might otherwise seem hard to measure. The words 'judgmental' and 'moralistic,' widely used as terms of abuse, testify to the strong link that has been forged in our century between the idea of moral judgement and the idea, not just of blame, but of unjustified blame. The precept 'judge not, that ye be not judged' has been inflated and given an absurdly wide meaning. The sense of awe which we quite properly attach to a very strong, final kind of judging – a kind which can perhaps belong only to God – has been strangely extended to cover also the weak and limited sense that is used in phrases like 'moral judgement.' The precept accordingly gets some such meaning as 'form no opinions, lest opinions be formed about you.' But this makes no sense because we do not even want people to form no opinions about us. We need the natural, sincere reactions of those around us if we are to locate ourselves morally or socially at all. They give us our bearings in the world. No child ever grows up without constantly experiencing both disapproval and approval, and the serious possibility that both will continue is essential for our lives. Sometimes we need to accept disapproval and to learn from it, sometimes to soften it by friendliness and argument, sometimes to persist in spite of it. But, if we did not know that it was there or understand its grounds, we could not begin to do any of these things.

So unfamiliar is this idea today that even readers who are inclined to accept it so far may want to stop it at the point of agreeing that we may each need to accept blame for ourselves, but still to deny that we can ever properly blame others. The internal difficulties of this idea are perhaps obvious; it is like a world where everybody gives presents but nobody will receive them. But, besides this, blame – the expression of disapproval – has an essential function in the interpretation of many important acts, both private and public. The question is often who is responsible – that is, who did something? Attempts to dissolve this question altogether have some odd consequences, as the following news item illustrates:

> Suicide has been officially abolished in the Irish Republic. A decision by the High Court in Dublin last April means that verdicts of suicide must not be brought in by coroners . . . The law has always prevented coroners from apportioning blame; verdicts on road accident victims, for example, could not say who was to blame . . . The High Court ruled that this prohibition extended to suicide, coroners could not blame victims for their own deaths either . . . All verdicts are now open and record merely the medical causes of death. Dr Bofin said, 'What concerns me more than the suicide problem is that we cannot bring in verdicts of accidental death either . . . We cannot exonerate anybody.' Some coroners and juries are thought to be reluctant to bring in suicide verdicts for humanitarian reasons, not wishing to upset relatives.[22]

As the unfortunate coroner quoted points out, half the point of such enquiries is to exonerate the people who did not do these things, or who could not help doing them, and to clear them from confusions which link them with those who did. The whole idea of excusing people on special grounds ceases to work if all grounds and all ways of acting are made equal. Since the wish to admit legitimate excuses is often what leads people to attack the practice of blame in the first place, this is a very serious nuisance.

THE NEED TO DISCRIMINATE

Where do we stand on all this today? The proposal to abolish blame wholesale is certainly still with us, though it is starting to be damaged by protests from the unfortunate officials – not just coroners but probation officers, social workers, and many more who are expected to put it into practice. If we are inclined to shrug off these protests by simply blaming the protesters themselves, the central difficulty again emerges that we are still making use of blame. Everybody who accepts this proposal makes some tacit exceptions to it. Typically, as is sensible enough, we still blame the powerful – rulers, officials, politicians, and the like. We also blame ourselves, and we blame those who blame others. This is not getting rid of the practice. The difficulty in doing so is not just a chance inconsistency in our thinking, for which we ourselves could be blamed. Praise and blame are unavoidable forms of moral light and shadow. Without them, the world would appear as a uniform grey. Depression sometimes does confront people with such a world, when they have ceased to care about anything that happens around them. But this can scarcely be seen as an ideal.

Thus, the idea of a blame-free world seems not to make sense, and the onus of making sense of it rests on those who apparently demand it. Unless that is done, our aim must surely be (as Aristotle might have put it[23]) to blame the right people, in the right way, for the right things, on the right occasions, neither more nor less than is suitable. And, as philosophers, it is our business to explore the conceptual difficulties in understanding this task and also the psychological difficulties in carrying it out. It is because this work is so hard and so important that unrealistic proposals for ceasing to judge altogether are so misplaced. Of course monstrous excesses are committed under the pretext of blame. They are also committed under a huge variety of other pretexts, for instance that of love. But it makes no sense to blame the practice of blame itself for all these excesses.

The trouble is not that the abolishers lack moral concern. It is that this concern is so selective, concentrated wholly on one particular field of iniquity among the many which press on us. All other vices – greed, envy, pride, sloth, cowardice, destructiveness, meanness, dishonesty, even the main jungles of cruelty and injustice themselves – seem to be forgotten in the obsession with one particular area where these last two vices are indulged under the pretext of blame. As things are now, the practice of blame provides us with a rough taxonomy and ranking system for distinguishing and relating these and the many other vices which are a most important feature of our lives. The idea of abolishing it seems to depend on the value-judgement that the practice itself is a worse evil than the vices it exists to indict. That judgement, if squarely made, would itself be a contribution to this taxonomy, and it would take a lot of defending.

Is such a judgement actually made? It is not often explicitly stated, and the idea of it may seem a trifle fantastic. But it is often implied by the general shape of discussions, by the selection of problems, and by the kind of moral indignation that writers express. All this adds up to a tone and approach which are often baffling to readers until they pick up the clue of the judgement just mentioned.

THE IMPOSSIBILITY OF EVASION

All ages have their peculiar moral obsessions. It is my impression that, today, a self-righteous preoccupation with putting down self-righteousness holds that position, serving as a displacement activity, especially among intellectuals, to deflect us from the serious and increasingly difficult large questions about how we ought to live. It is not actually meant to affect practice, and, when it does do so, it leads to confusion. Outside the libraries, meanwhile, non-intellectuals, and all of us a good deal of the time, can still go on using ordinary, self-righteous disapproval of the more picturesque vices around us to fulfil this displacement function.

'Anti-naturalist' moral philosophy arose, I suggest, mainly out of this defensive attitude, and has owed much of its appeal to it. Though it has had certain incidental uses and virtues, the general effect of this kind of philosophy has been destructive. It is primarily a way of not doing something which not only needs doing but needs doing by philosophers – namely, taking up the intellectual floorboards and doing some hard plumbing on the intellectual schemes which are expressed in choice and action. Unsatisfactory though the results of this will always be, the work is essential. The sense of professional modesty which made moral philosophers bow discreetly out of it has been as misplaced as it would be for someone who knows a bit about plumbing to stand back modestly when the pipes burst, or for someone who can speak a little Spanish to be silent in a frantic misunderstanding on a train because he cannot speak pure Castilian. Might we make things worse? Sure, we might in everything we do. But the emergency exists already, and at least we have one part of the equipment needed to understand it – namely, some acquaintance with the quirks of conceptual schemes, and some experience of their past working in parallel cases.

We cannot stop people thinking. Moral philosophy will be done in any case, well or badly, under that name or another, as people under strain try to adapt their concepts to changing circumstances. Somebody is going to make suggestions for new ways of treating problems. People who do that are not in any way committed – as seems so strangely to be thought – to claiming that they are the Pope, to issuing orders and behaving like a dominant parent. Instead, they are offering help in a cooperative enterprise which everybody feels to be necessary. They are joining in the attempt to answer questions that already arise. The current demand for medical ethics, and its growing extension to legal and other professional problems, shows how widely the need is felt. We will discuss possible responses to it in the next chapter. It does not always work well, but it must be done somehow. Moore, when he became a mature and admirable philosopher, engaged in the defence of common sense. As is well known, that does not mean accepting everything that people now say and think at its face value, but sorting out its surface confusions to reach the gold that underlies it. This process often involves rejecting theories and methods currently approved by scholars, because they do not fit our real needs. It is vital that we should not hesitate to do this when it is necessary.

It will be noticed that in this discussion I have flatly refused to accept Moore's claim that his move was a purely formal one, and have suggested instead what seems to me a much more plausible moral reason for it. Whether this particular suggestion (about the distrust of blame) is accepted or not, I want to be quite clear that there is always reason to reject purely formal explanations of any move of anything like this size – not only in moral philosophy, but also in the central areas of metaphysics, for instance over things like free will and causal necessity, personal identity and the relation between mind and body. Large formal changes on these matters are never just adjustments to the mechanics of reasoning. They are changes in the way we see and handle the world. They are suggestions about how it would be better to do this. Our attempt to find better and worse ways of regarding the world and of acting in it is not – as Russell thought – an irrelevant interference with our efforts to discover the truth about it. It is the whole enterprise within which those efforts are a part. We build within our moral and metaphysical assumptions. We can develop these assumptions by confronting them with all kinds of new experiences, and also by checking them against each other. But, in doing this, we do not have to make the moral ones always give place to the ones concerned with theoretical truth. For instance, if we have a strong preference for a particular way of life, it is perfectly in order for us to look for reasons to justify that bias, and to try to convert others to it, provided that we show honestly that that is what we are doing. This is the way in which Plato, Aristotle, and others have given reasons for exalting the life of the intellect, linking them to particular analyses of what a human being is and what kind of a thing the world is, and others – Nietzsche, for example – have given reasons for not doing so, linking them to different analyses. In choosing between world-views of this kind we are not forced to confine ourselves to looking for factual evidence. We can properly bring to this work all kinds of elements in our existing world-views. Dorothy Emmet has illuminatingly likened the moral scene to 'a prism emitting light of many different colours which are not at war with each other, but are all needed to complete the sum.'[24] What constitutes bias is not acceptance of one's own existing scheme of values, because that scheme is always relevant. It is refusal to look at anyone else's.

NOTES

1. G.E. Moore, *Principia Ethica* (Cambridge, Cambridge University Press, 1903), preface, p. ix.
2. Ibid., pp. 14–15.
3. B. Williams, *Ethics and the Limits of Philosophy* (London, Fontana Masterguides, 1985), p. 16.
4. Both these couplets are apparently isolated epigrams, and I have followed *The Oxford Dictionary of Quotations* in attributing the second to J.C. Squire.
5. B. Williams, *Ethics and the Limits of Philosophy* (London, Fontana Masterguides, 1985), p. 121. The logical weaknesses of the whole 'naturalistic fallacy' approach and the best ways to avoid them are discussed with beautiful clarity in J. Kovesi's shrewd little book, *Moral Notions* (London, Routledge & Kegan Paul, 1967).
6. See G.E.M. Anscombe, 'Brute Facts', *Analysis* 19 (1958).
7. G. Warnock, *Contemporary Moral Philosophy* (London, Macmillan Papermac, 1967), p. 60.
8. J. Boswell, *Life of Johnson* (London, Dent & Dutton, 1906, Everyman Edition), vol. 2, p. 148.
9. B. Russell, Autobiography (London, Allen & Unwin, 1967), vol. 1, p. 147.
10. On facts and values in general, see my *Beast and Man* (Hassocks, Harvester Press, 1979), Chapter 9, and 'On the Absence of a Gap between Facts and Values', *Proceedings of the Aristotelian Society* 54 (suppl.) (1980).
11. L. Woolf, *Sowing* (London, Hogarth Press, 1961), pp. 135–6.
12. M. Keynes, *Two Memoirs* (London, Rupert Hart-Davies, 1949), p. 85.
13. C.L. Stevenson, *Ethics and Language* (New Haven, Yale University Press, 1944).
14. J.S. Mill, *Utilitarianism* (London, Dent & Dutton, 1910, Everyman Edition), Chapter 5, p. 45.
15. G.E. Moore, *Principia Ethica* (Cambridge, Cambridge University Press, 1903), pp. 214–16, 221.
16. Ibid., p. 147.
17. Ibid., p. 155.
18. Ibid., pp. 174–6, 182.
19. The peculiarly ill-judged attacks on Mill are in Moore, *Principia Ethica*, Chapter 3, pp. 64–72, 77, and 102. They are interspersed with some shrewd and admirable general criticisms of hedonism. Because Moore had a real sympathy with hedonism, these criticisms, along with the last chapter, are to my mind the best parts of the book.
20. It is a prime theme of Skinner's manifesto, *Beyond Freedom and Dignity* (London, Cape, 1972).

21. See B. Williams, *Ethics and the Limits of Philosophy* (London, Fontana Master-guides, 1985), pp. 177, 194. I have discussed Williams's views on the relation between the idea of blame and that of morality in my original article 'The Flight from Blame', *Philosophy* 62 (241) (1987), Section 9, but have omitted this section in the present version.

22. Report in the *Guardian*, some time in early November 1985.

23. This indeed is what he does in his admirable investigation of excuses. See Aristotle, *Nicomachean Ethics*, Book 3, Chapters 1–5.

24. D. Emmet, *The Moral Prism* (London, Macmillan, 1979).

15

ESCAPING FROM SOLITUDE

Is this mine own countree?

Coleridge, The Ancient Mariner

MOORE ON COMMON SENSE

In a number of his articles, Moore set about amputating the unnecessary, isolating shell, in which Descartes had enclosed the self, with great zest and some success. But he always became entangled before the end with pieces of it that he had not fully managed to throw away. Probably his most successful onslaught is the one in 'The Defence of Common Sense.'[1]

Here he starts by putting it to his readers that both he and they know with certainty a long list of truisms, for instance, that their own bodies exist and have long existed on the earth, that this earth has itself long existed, along with many other bodies on it, and that some of these bodies are human and belong to other, equally conscious beings who have and have had experiences of their own. What follows from

DOI: 10.4324/9781003588160-21

all this? Moore's manner might suggest at first that he merely expects to stun his readers into admitting their belief in these truisms by a burst of honesty, in the style that might have been used by Dr Johnson. But this is not all. Moore does indeed mean to shift the mood of the argument in this direction by his contagious honesty and courage, to show up the element of chronic humbug in scepticism, but he knows that an argument is needed as well. He understands that people may rightly hold on to strange and paradoxical conclusions which they have reached by reasoning, since some strange and paradoxical conclusions are indeed true. (For instance, the world really is round and there really are people on the other side of it.) It is still necessary, however, that these conclusions should make sense. Moore, therefore, goes on to ask what anyone who claims to doubt these truisms means by their doubt. As he points out, it is hard to see what a doubt can mean if it is impossible to express it except in terms which imply that it has already been settled:

> No philosopher has ever been able to hold such views consistently. One way in which they have betrayed this inconsistency, is by alluding to the existence of other philosophers. Another way is by alluding to the existence of the human race, and in particular by using 'we' in the sense in which I have already constantly used it, in which any philosopher who asserts that 'we' do so and so, e.g. that 'we sometimes believe propositions that are not true', is asserting not only that he himself has done the thing in question, but that very many other human beings, who have had bodies and lived on the earth, have done the same.[2]
>
> (Emphasis Moore's)

As he goes on to point out, this fact is particularly glaring when these philosophers discuss 'common-sense beliefs' which they want to reject.

When such a philosopher says, 'No human being has ever known of the existence of other human beings,' he is saying, 'There have been many other human beings besides myself, and none of them (including myself) has ever known of the existence of other human beings.' If he says, 'These beliefs are beliefs of common-sense, but they are not matters of knowledge,' he is saying 'There have been many other human beings, besides myself, who have shared these beliefs, but neither I nor any of the rest has ever known them to be true.'[3]

In short, this argument, like all other arguments, is necessarily conducted in the language of a many-personed world. And this has not happened just by chance, through an oversight which greater care might rectify, but because there is not and could not be any other sort of language. The whole point of language is to make possible communication between distinct people, just as the point of a bridge is to join two distinct banks. By opening our mouths to speak at all, we concede Moore's truisms. Even if we merely say inwardly, 'I think, therefore I am,' we have in effect also said, 'I speak; therefore you are too – all of you, including the whole multitude of you that has been needed to invent language.'

How conclusive is Moore's argument? Here, as with other answers to sceptical contentions, a strangely unreal approach is often taken, by which 'the sceptic' is treated with awe as a mythical, essentially impregnable, wily being who is determined to keep up the game for ever and who always has one more shot in his locker. If he is resolute enough (people say), if he is really hard-nosed, he will refuse to admit the relevance of the fact that he uses language, and then where will you be? Or perhaps he will retreat into a more ingenious kind of solipsism, or offer to go away and invent a private, non-interlocutory language.[4] Anyway, who can be sure that he has not got some sort of further trick up his sleeve? The extraordinary thing about this line is that it treats the argument as if it were a game played between contending parties with conflicting aims and interests, instead of what, as we have earlier noticed, it always ought to be – a genuine attempt by each single person to think out the issue. Moore's point is not just a blow intended to knock down an opponent. It is a genuine question to each of us, namely: If you doubt the existence of other minds, what do you mean by this doubt? What do you think is true instead? Since the very language in which you express this doubt implies a thoroughgoing, confident belief in the existence of those minds, what further question do you actually want to put? Moore is rightly shifting the question from 'Are you sure that you know this?' to 'What do you mean by this?'

THE MEANING OF MEANINGLESSNESS

Questions can only make sense in a context where they can arise, and this must be a context containing clear alternatives. It makes perfectly good sense for me to doubt whether I have locked the door, or added up my bill correctly, because I know what I think might have happened if I have not. But what is the alternative to the existence of the whole physical world, or of all other minds? Dreams will not supply it, for they exist only within the world and by reflecting parts of it. The only other faint attempt that has been made to supply one is Descartes's idea of the Great Deceiver who imposes it all, and this, besides being demented, fails to work, because the Deceiver himself evidently is some kind of other mind. This incredibly general kind of doubt is not just unreasonable, it is unreal; it does not make sense. This point is important because many people have attacked Cartesian doubt on the weaker ground that it is merely unreasonable in the sense of uncalled-for, unhelpful, or imprudent. Locke, for instance, wrote that

> We shall not have much reason to complain of the narrowness of our minds, if we will but employ them about what may be of use to us; for of that they are very capable . . . It will be no excuse for an idle and untoward servant, who would not attend his business by candlelight, to complain that he had not broad sunlight. The candle that is set up in us shines bright enough for all our purposes . . . If we will disbelieve everything because we cannot certainly know all things, we shall do much-what as wisely as he who would not use his legs, but sit still and perish, because he had not wings to fly.[5]

This way of talking concedes the existence of broad sunlight, or of wings that can fly, and only claims that as a matter of brute fact they happen not to be available to us. It is not obvious why, if that were all, ambitious thinkers who are keen to fly or to reach the sunlight need be deterred from trying to gain these advantages. And indeed the fact that, since Locke wrote, human beings *have* in a peculiar and limited sense learnt to fly shows the uncertain limits of such ambitions. But suppose the ambition had been to produce a round square, or dark light, or a true falsehood, or even a perpetual-motion machine? Or again, suppose somebody asks for subscriptions in order to found a society of solipsists, and does so on the ground that solipsism is true? Proposers of these schemes would need something more than a mere general claim that supposedly impossible things sometimes turn out to be possible after all. They would need to show a clear, specific sense in which these words could have meaning, a sense which would also carry a specification of what was wanted and the reasons for wanting it. As it happens, I do possess a round square – namely, a little steel cylinder, measuring one inch each way. If this was all that was needed, it could easily be supplied. Similarly, there could be all manner of poetic ways in which one might describe something as dark light or a true falsehood, and the inventors of perpetual-motion machines can beaver on at redefining their aim, as well as at actually fulfilling it. Correspondingly, what is needed in the case of Moore's truisms is a clear sense in which they can be denied. It is not enough merely to pronounce the words of denial, any more than it is enough to pronounce the words 'round square.' It is necessary also to make sense of them, to show how they could be applied. And because the truisms are so sweeping, this involves a great range of concepts. It calls on us to show how the denial can fit into the general landscape of our thought, and what changes would be needed to accommodate it there. In particular, its effect on the notion that we have of ourselves, a notion which is the centre of this inner landscape, must be properly filled in and made plausible.

That is the burden that lies on anyone who wants to propound and defend the Cartesian picture, once questions begin to be asked about it. The burden is, of course, one of explanation rather than of proof. In principle, it is perfectly possible, once the question is put, to show that some particular image or way of thinking does have a point, and so to justify its use. But this justification will only hold for the kind of use that has actually been pointed out; it will not be an all-purpose licence. This is the situation about many popular images that have been far too widely used; for instance, the notion of inevitable progress, whether in biological evolution or in human history, the notion of competition in economics, and the machine analogy in psychology. The Cartesian picture of a solitary knower isolated in his cabin is, on the face of things, very likely to form one of this group, simply because it is so extravagant – it goes so far beyond what its inventor's purposes required. Those purposes centred on some special doubts about the relation between the various sciences, and about the kind of thinking that could best be used in them. There was no special intention of constructing a general model for the human condition, still less of proving that that condition was one of incurable solitude. If anybody now wants to use it for this purpose, they have to give their own explanation of what their reasons are, which would be quite different from those that relate it to the quest for knowledge. Individualistic moral systems, such as Existentialism and Social Darwinism, which do make that emphasis, cannot properly draw support from Cartesian views about the nature of knowledge, even though, historically speaking, they have certainly grown out of those views. And as far as the quest for knowledge itself goes, the Cartesian model has visibly reached the limits of its use and begun to be a real hindrance.

CLEARING UP THE CONCEPT OF KNOWLEDGE

That is the moral that emerges from Moore's 'Defence of Common Sense.' As I mentioned, it does not emerge quite clearly. This is largely because, in that article, Moore still used the notion of *knowledge* in the traditional way, without paying any special attention to its meaning. He did not explicitly centre his discussion on the nature of the knowing or doubting subject, but simply claimed that he and others *know* these truisms. Since this kind of claim had long been understood as a claim by an imprisoned astronaut to have somehow smuggled in information about something outside his cell, it was not clear why Moore seemed to think that he had overcome the difficulty of this. And he made this confusion worse both by worrying at considerable length about the position of sense-data, which he ought to have been jettisoning, and by the wording of his claim that he and others had 'frequently known' the truisms. This sounds as if knowing were a special kind of process or performance, like a gaolbreak, whose nature was already well understood, and he was reporting that the prisoners did actually go through it successfully at times – perhaps twice a year? The traditional sceptic then naturally asks for the process to be demonstrated, and for its success to be proved, perhaps by producing external objects gathered during the gaolbreak by methods distinct from ordinary experience. And of course this cannot be done.

But the real enquiry is quite different. As Wittgenstein puts it, 'We are asking ourselves: What do we do with a statement "I know …"? For it is not a question of mental processes or mental states.'[6] People who say 'I know' or 'She knows' are not making a report about some special state or performance by themselves or someone else, as they would be by saying 'I'm hot' or 'She's slipping.' They are making claims, as much as they would by saying something like 'The bridge is safe now,' or 'I can show you the way.' These are not primarily remarks about the speaker, but something much more like offers to take responsibility. Any questions that arise about them will most naturally be questions directly about the outside objects involved – for instance about the bridge, or the particular route to be taken. Accordingly, the question often raised by Descartes and others, 'How do you know that you know?', has perhaps as little sense as 'How do you know that you offer?' or 'How do you know that you thank?' The meaning of the word 'know,' like that of other words, is its use. This word is not the name of a peculiar mental state or process because, like very many other words, it is not a name at all. Its work is not the work of referring or corresponding to some set object, but of helping people to distinguish between the more reliable and the less reliable parts of the world around them. In doing this, speakers offer their own guarantees, which are of course understood, like all other human guarantees, to be fallible. Though it is our business as citizens and language-users to offer these guarantees carefully and responsibly, and therefore only to offer them when we do have reason to feel certain, it is not our business to be omniscient. The appearance of permanent, lifelong confidence which seems to attach to some uses of words like 'know' is a superficial one, and does not even attach to all their uses. As Wittgenstein remarks, 'One always forgets the expression, "I thought I knew."'[7] The context of human life supplies the normal background for this claim, as it does for all others. And the perfectly sensible quest for better evidence and more careful reasoning in the sciences does not in the least require that we should step outside that context and become gods.

THE STATUS OF TRUISMS

This is a central case where to treat of meaning widely as use, rather than narrowly as reference or correspondence, saves us from a whole mass of unnecessary confusion. There is no reason to expect a word like 'know' to be the name of a peculiar kind of process, nor to suppose that this word can be given an unrealistic sense which interferes with its previous function, merely to meet the demands of a theory. But until this general point about the way in which words have meaning has been grasped, Moore's truisms are puzzling. What is supposed to be their status? Can Moore be saying that there really is a particular set of propositions – perhaps even a particular number of them, say a hundred? – which are infallibly known, by contrast to all others, which cannot be so known? If so, there would be a real difficulty about the fact that they seem at times to change. For instance, people used once to think it a truism that the world was flat, and that it was impossible for people to go to the moon, and that events could be genuinely simultaneous with one another. Accordingly, slapdash relativism, emphasizing such cases, sometimes seems to destroy Moore's point. Yet open-minded readers still feel its force. There really does seem to be something dishonest and confused about pretending to doubt things which in fact we do not see how to doubt. And it surely is not honest to evade this difficulty by pretending to treat seriously a position like full-scale solipsism, or belief in Descartes's Great Deceiver, when we know very well that, if anyone actually defended these positions, we would rush them round to get psychiatric help as quickly as possible. All this is disturbing because the appeal of the sceptical stance has always centred on its apparent honesty. Moore, however, seems to be showing it here as dishonest, and indeed, when we think about it, this alarming fact is seen to have a wider application. As suggested earlier, in the actual world, rampant humbug quite as often takes the form of pretending not to know things that one does know as of pretending to know things one does not know, and is equally discreditable in both forms. The sceptic as folk-hero is no sort of reliable guide. So what are we to do?

Shaking the kaleidoscope slightly, Wittgenstein gives the matter a much more hopeful twist. The point, he says, is not that these particular propositions have a special intrinsic quality, making them alone permanently and absolutely certain. It is that, for every individual and every society, some set of propositions at any time must occupy this base position. That set provides the background against which other things are questioned; it forms the underlying world-picture. Its various elements are not themselves in principle incapable of being questioned. But they cannot be questioned unless some other set gains a special force and solidity, and supplies a ground adequate to make questions arise about them. He gives the useful analogy of a river-bed:

95. The propositions describing this world-picture might be part of a kind of mythology. And their role is like that of rules of a game; and the game can be learnt purely practically, without learning any explicit rules.

96. It might be imagined that some propositions, of the form of empirical propositions, were hardened and functioned as channels for such empirical propositions as were not hardened but fluid; and that this relation altered with time, in that fluid propositions hardened, and hard ones became fluid.

97. The mythology may change back into a state of flux, the river-bed of thoughts may shift. But I distinguish between the movement of

waters on the river-bed and the shift of the bed itself, though there is not a sharp division of the one from the other.

98. But if someone were to say, 'So logic too is an empirical science' he would be wrong. Yet this is right; the same proposition may get treated at one time as something to test by experience, and at another as a rule of testing.

99. And the bank of that river consists partly of hard rock, subject to no alteration or only to an imperceptible one, partly of sand, which now in one place now in another gets washed away, or deposited.[8]

How well does this image do its work? It is designed to do justice to both of two conflicting demands, the first of which has in recent times been stressed out of all proportion to the second. The first is the need to remember that we might be wrong. The second is the need to be honest about the extent to which we actually believe that we are, on some central points, right, and to register our claim that we are so. In stressing the first more than the second, theorists have always had some special purpose. They have concentrated their scepticism either on particular beliefs which they really doubted, or on a social need for tolerance, or else, more generally, on attacking the disproportionate confidence now placed in 'science' by comparison with other forms of knowledge. In order to do these things, however, they have inevitably always still been taking for granted an immense range of other propositions which they had no reason to doubt, and have also been strongly affirming certain truths, in which they insist that it is necessary to believe. But nothing at all can be strongly affirmed unless a whole mass of truisms is taken for granted as a background for it. For instance, it is not possible to stress the variety of cultures and the need to take seriously the beliefs of unfamiliar ones, without taking every one of Moore's truisms for granted, because, unless they were all true, those other cultures could never even have existed. If we did not commit ourselves to a great mass of such beliefs – and commit ourselves in the sense of positively endorsing them, not just being willing to gamble – we could not think or act at all. The peculiar way of talking that seems to treat all beliefs as equally valid in their own cultures is an artificial, anthropological approach; it is essentially a way of talking about *other people*. The world, however, does not consist only of other people. Each of us is somewhere inside it, not a superhuman anthropologist observing it from outside. For each of us, the question of just where we stand in that world is a crucial one.

The need to bring these two half-truths together effectively seems to me a central one both for our thought and our life today. Wittgenstein's river-bed image is designed to help us there, and it surely does so. More sharply and simply, Neurath made a similar point when he suggested that a sensible person at sea in a leaky boat will be willing to sit on some unexamined parts of that boat whilst repairing the others. A purist who, by contrast, refused to start any repair work until all the timbers beneath him had been guaranteed sound would become a martyr to principles whose value is a trifle obscure.

PHILOSOPHIZING OUT IN THE WORLD

What is the use of studying philosophy if all that it does for you is to enable you to talk with some plausibility about some abstruse questions of logic etc., and if it does not improve your thinking about the important questions of everyday life?

(Wittgenstein, letter to Norman Malcolm)[9]

Philosophy seems, then, to have been paroled from the ivory tower. How can we best use it once it is loose? How shall we avoid the various kinds of trouble that led to its being locked up in the first place?

This seems to be part of the wider question, how are we to apply our thinking to reality? How can we close the gap which constantly tends to open between theory and practice, between our minds and the world? Human intelligence is not automatically self-directing. One of the most striking things about it is how unevenly it gets applied. In every culture, intense loving attention to certain chosen problems contrasts with a startling neglect of others, some of which are far more pressing, not only for justice, or for happiness, but for mere survival. Large, obvious, central questions can be entirely ignored.

This is natural, because they are very frightening. To move towards them when we have not been thinking about them before is especially hard. Our thought therefore tends strongly to stay in its established tracks, and also to shift those tracks themselves gradually and imperceptibly away from these problems. All human patterns of thought contain defence mechanisms designed to do this, mechanisms which very much need our attention. They are not necessarily illicit. We do have to have some defence against the vastness and alarmingness of the surrounding world, some sunscreen against its glare. But we also need to have some inkling how we are providing that defence, some awareness, however dim, of the part our own motivations play in the matter.

In this enquiry, we have been watching a number of these defence mechanisms at work. As citizens, the one that most of us chiefly rely on is sheer inattention, but we usually supplement this by some quarrelsomeness. Our tribal loyalties enable us, in the first place, to distract ourselves from large issues by feuding over small ones, and in the second, if that fails, to blame our opponents for what goes wrong in the world, to use what energy we do give to these matters partly in feuding against these opponents, and to feel excused for our inaction by regarding them as all-powerful. When we turn from this general background to ask about the special forms that these defences take for intellectuals, we find, naturally enough, that this same method is widely used there too. An obsession with controversy continually distorts our approach to our enquiries. It has a tendency to split us up into ever smaller groups with less and less understanding of each other's projects. This is not, as is often supposed, a necessary effect of enquiry itself, nor an advantage to it. It is a pathological by-product of our attitude to it. I want to say a word more in ending, because I think the matter is extraordinarily neglected.

Our tribal loyalties serve to oversimplify our dilemmas. Most of the time they work to keep us fairly near to where we started. But, if we start to disagree with members of our existing tribe, the easiest way to deal with the painful stress of opposition is to sign up for a ready-made opposing group. This ensures that our intellect never has more than two alternatives to consider, and that it usually knows in advance which of them to reject. However bad both these alternatives may be, we find it fearfully hard to reject both of them and apply our minds directly to the problem. Even very highly trained intelligence can be dominated in this way by tribal feeling, and the training can be used merely to obscure the process. If we do not become much more aware than we now are of these restricting forces, we become their helpless victims, and our thought does not engage with the world at all.

INTELLIGENCE IS NOT ENOUGH

As I have insisted throughout, this attention to motive and context is not a distraction from the real work of philosophy, but an essential part of it. The meaning of words depends on how they are used and intended.[10] We cannot split off feeling from intellect and look for our salvation from intellect alone, though that policy of division is of course often recommended today. Many people, for instance, suggest that what is wrong with the human race is simply a shortage of intelligence, a shortage which can perhaps be cured by raising IQ through genetic engineering. This is an odd suggestion. Never mind the technical and scientific problems of IQ-raising, it is clear that we don't use a tenth of the intelligence we have got already. If we had more, we would certainly squander it in the same ways as we do now. Very high intelligence can be seen running to waste all round us, both inside and outside our institutions. Outside them, it runs to waste in suicide and depression, in quarrelling, alcoholism, neurosis, and organized crime, in various ways of killing time without much enjoyment, and most recently down special sinks designed for it, called computer games. Inside the institutions, it lavishes itself on intrigues and obsessions of the most various kinds, on internal feuds and deceptions, and on finding ways to block measures introduced by other people.

These remarks are not intended as just one more denunciation of mankind, but simply as a reminder. We know already that these things are true. My present point is just that they make clear that it is sense we lack, rather than intellectual power. And, when we are wondering how to apply intellectual power to the world, some of this sense is what we chiefly need. That does not mean that we don't need philosophy. In finding and formulating the rules that underlie sense, the inarticulate patterns by which it works, in noting their clashes and inadequacies and looking for ways of dealing with them, we are bound to be doing philosophy whether we recognize it or not. Philosophy is the formalization of an ancient art which used to be called the search for wisdom, but we have got too prissy to use such words today.

TRAPS AND ENTANGLEMENTS

Many things, however, make it hard for philosophers today to take this wider view. Disputatiousness itself, as active inside the ivory tower as outside it, and indeed so habitual a part of academic life that it may seem strange to complain of it, generates many obstacles. One of these is the mere disinterested love of paradoxes, the tendency to keep them as pets for their own sake, and because they are a fertile source of arguments. Philosophers addicted to this may react to something like the euthanasia problem with delight, by simply adding half a dozen new twists to make it still more insoluble. They may indeed not see that anything else could possibly be called for; the idea of actually helping to find a solution to it may seem to them downright unprofessional. There is also the technique of taking a small slice out of the side of the problem and providing it with an entirely negative solution. This habit flows from a convention which already does a lot of harm inside the ivory tower itself, namely the rule that, in prestige, the negative always wins. Scholars who reject something are always one up on scholars who accept it, and it pays to raise very small issues, because this makes it easier to avoid accidentally appearing to have accepted something after all.

Notice, for example, the well-known article called 'Euthanasia: some fallacies,' in which Dr Hammer attacked the arguments used by Professor Tongs. Tongs had rashly cited an example involving mercy-killing in the course of a paper attacking somebody else about something quite different. In the approved style, Hammer began his attack with a disclaimer, stressing that neither he nor Tongs was saying anything about the wider issue of euthanasia itself; his intention was simply to find fault with Tongs's reasoning. This he did for thirty pages, without, so far as he could see, committing himself to saying anything at all about the actual problem. Here, however, he proved mistaken, as Mr Shovel pointed out in an article of equal length called 'Euthanasia: a reply to Hammer.' Shovel showed that some of Hammer's own arguments were invalid, unless they had the support of certain substantial views about euthanasia, for which of course he had produced no argument. (It is worth just noting that nobody, from the Angel Gabriel downwards, has ever produced an article about which this kind of criticism could not be made.) However, in the general shortage of helpful material about life and death, these articles are regularly placed on the reading lists of first-year students. They also get, for stimulus on this subject, Professor Poker's famous article 'Is murder wrong?' The populace, says Poker, seems to think that it is, but it is not altogether easy to find out what are their grounds for doing so. Are people perhaps afraid of getting murdered themselves? Are they, in their muddled way, attempting to increase the general happiness? Are they perhaps moved by some confused notion about rationality? Poker has no trouble in setting up these various straw men in indefensible forms. His language is neatly adapted to stun his simple-minded readers into feeling that they must somehow either manage to accept one – and only one – of these bad arguments, or withdraw their objections to murder. They become very confused. But the one thing that emerges clearly for their immediate purpose is that, during the rest of their university course, it will be much safer to agree with Poker, and to learn to adopt his methods, than to expose themselves by asking what he means or by trying to defend their principles against him.

Am I being unfair to Poker? Is he perhaps a valuable Socratic gadfly? He might be. This is an open question. We can look at what is going on and see how well he has suited his particular kind of sting to the horse before him, and how the total symbiosis is working out. But we are not forced to assume that all stinging is valuable, merely because

Socrates had a sting. That sting had Socrates, and Poker's hasn't. And Socrates did not set examinations.

In these brief suggestions I have been trying to locate some of the central difficulties that arise when, starting from a contemporary academic position, we try to apply philosophical thought again to those problems in the world where it is most needed. I have suggested that what chiefly wastes our efforts here is not lack of intelligence or even of application, but the distorting effect of bad intellectual habits which have a strong emotional basis. I have concentrated on just one of these, the addiction to dispute. Though this has of course some admirable uses, it can serve too easily as a defence mechanism, an alternative to direct work on the central problems rather than a tool for it. Perhaps indeed it serves as displacement behaviour, irrelevant but intense activity relieving the strain of unresolved conflicts. Other psychological dangers of related kinds will certainly arise, which is one reason why I have been insisting throughout that the motives for philosophizing are not irrelevant to its substance, but are something that should have active and constant attention. What we cannot do, however, is to erect a negative defence against all these dangers – to prevent all sophisticated thinkers from attending to all important questions. This has been thoroughly tried in this century, and it does not emerge as a sane option. If thinking is our professional concern, then wisdom and wonder are our business; information-storage, though often useful, is just an incidental convenience. So we will do better to pursue wisdom and wonder, however haltingly and weakly, than to rival Wells's moon-monsters with the contents of our computer-assisted memory-banks. That, too, is how the story of The Crock of Gold ended:

> And they took the Philosopher from his prison, even the Intellect of Man they took from the hands of the doctors and lawyers, from the sly priests, from the professors whose mouths are gorged with sawdust, and the merchants who sell blades of grass, the awful people of the Fomor and then they returned again, dancing and singing, to the country of the gods.

NOTES

1. G.E. Moore, 'The defence of common sense', in his *Philosophical Papers* (London, Allen & Unwin, 1959), p. 32.
2. Ibid., pp. 40–1.
3. Ibid., pp. 42–3.
4. That the idea of such a private language is incoherent is a central point of Wittgenstein's *Philosophical Investigations*, tr. G.E.M. Anscombe (Oxford, Basil Blackwell, 1963).
5. J. Locke, *Essay Concerning Human Understanding*, book 1, Chapter 1, Section 5.
6. L. Wittgenstein, *On Certainty*, tr. D. Paul and E. Anscombe (Oxford, Basil Blackwell, 1974), para. 230.
7. Ibid., para. 12.
8. Ibid., paras. 95–9.
9. N. Malcolm, *Ludwig Wittgenstein: A Memoir* (London, Oxford University Press, 1958), p. 39.
10. This was the point that always occupied R.G. Collingwood; see for instance his *Autobiography* (Oxford, Oxford University Press, 19 Press, 1939), Chapters 5 and 6, and the opening sections of his *An Essay on Metaphysics* (Oxford, Clarendon Press, 1940).

16

SCIENCEPHOBIA AND ITS SOURCES

ARE YOU NOTHING?

What is it that frightens people today so much about Science? How can such a useful study – one that gives us many of the facts on which we build our lives – sometimes strike ordinary people as an alien and destructive force?

This is not just due to traditional clashes between science and religion. Those clashes have often yielded to further thought, and anyway religion itself – at least in the United Kingdom – is less central to our lives than it once was. What remains now, and is far more disturbing, is a certain anti-human attitude that seems to be associated with Science: a claim that Science has disproved beliefs that we need for ordinary life; that it shows up our ordinary attitudes as worthless because they are unscientific.

A striking part of that claim is this doctrine that our inner selves, as we experience them, don't really exist at all. The question is now not

DOI: 10.4324/9781003588160-22

just 'Do you believe in God?', but – what is surely more alarming – 'Do you believe in yourself?' This idea has been floating around for some time and has had some very distinguished supporters. Besides some philosophers, whose views don't often reach the general public, Francis Crick (Mr DNA himself) told us sternly twenty years ago in his book *The Astonishing Hypothesis* that: ' "You," your joys and your sorrows, your memories and your ambitions, your sense of personal identity and free will, are *in fact* no more than the behaviour of a vast assembly of nerve cells and their attendant molecules'.[1]

What does this mean? An unsophisticated reader might naturally hear it as a straightforward insult. And in fact the cyberbullies who currently torment children apparently like to say exactly this: 'You are nothing.' Another possibility, which we will have to consider later, is that it really means 'Don't let talk about these personal matters interfere with your work; they are irrelevant to your professional business.' The suggestion here is that the truth at which science aims is an isolated one, separated from all the affairs of everyday life: an abstract Truth, unpolluted by vulgar details. What Crick and his followers actually mean by it is not at once clear, but officially it seems to be something quite close to this second possibility, namely, that our consciousness is not real because the only real things in the world are those revealed by the physical sciences. He does not discuss evidence for this, and it certainly looks like a wild philosophical speculation, but he assures us that it has somehow been scientifically established:

> The *scientific belief* is that our minds – the behavior of our brains – can be *explained* by the interaction of nerve cells (and other cells) and the molecules associated with them. This is to most people a really surprising concept. It does not come easily to believe *that I am the detailed behaviour of a set of nerve cells.*[2]

Similarly, the neuroscientist Susan Greenfield, looking at an exposed brain in an operating theatre, reflected that, 'This was all there was to Sarah, or indeed to any of us . . . We are but sludgy brains',[3] and the eminent neurophysiologist Colin Blakemore writes:

The human brain is a machine which *alone accounts for all our actions*, our most private thoughts, our beliefs . . . *All our actions are products of the activity of our brains*. It makes no sense (in scientific terms) to distinguish sharply between acts that result from conscious attention and those that result from our reflexes or damage to the brain.[4]

Thus, if we want to understand why (for instance) Napoleon decided to invade Egypt or Russia, what we need is *not* – as we might think – some knowledge of the political background and of Napoleon's state of mind, but simply facts about the state of his brain, which alone can account for his action. Nor can any question even be raised about how far he was responsible for these invasions.

ON BEING A NECESSARY ILLUSION

This is not a very intelligible story. It has, however, become amazingly widely accepted today among respectable scientists, as can be seen from a Special Issue run by the prestigious magazine *New Scientist* on 23 February 2013. Here, half-a-dozen authors who clearly feel no need to justify their strange positions assure us that, although the 'intuitive sense of self is an effortless and fundamental human experience,' it is still 'nothing more than an *elaborate illusion*... Some thinkers even go so far as claiming that there is *no such thing as the self*' (p.33, emphases mine). 'You are being *tricked* into thinking that you live in the present' (p.37); ..., 'your self can even be *tricked* into hovering in mid-air outside the body' (p.40). (So apparently it is real enough to be really tricked; is that not odd?) And again – 'Much of what we take for granted about our inner lives, from visual perception to memories, is little more than an elaborate *construct of the mind* (sic). The self is just another part of this illusion' (p.37). (Here, remarkably, the Mind makes things still harder by appearing as both deceiver and deceived).

If we are to understand this surprising piece of news, we surely need to know what it means. It should be made clear right away that this is not the Buddhist doctrine of no-self. That doctrine starts with the same destructive step of rejecting the substantial, immortal self of tradition, but it does so in order to deploy a quite different, richer and more subtle world-view, one which calls for a distinctive life, dedicated to consideration for others and understanding of the ultimate mysteries – one in which we would identify primarily with a much larger whole. The kind of exclusive materialism which we are now considering makes absolutely no such constructive suggestion. It does not even explain whether accepting our non-existence is supposed to make us change our lives at all. At first, it seems that it may well do so:

> Many of our core beliefs about ourselves do not withstand scrutiny. This presents a tremendous challenge for our everyday view of ourselves, as it suggests that in a very fundamental way we are not real. Instead, our self is comparable to an illusion - but without anybody there that experiences the illusion.[5]

But later all this turns out not to matter in the least. The same writer goes on to say – 'Yet we may have no choice but to endorse these mistaken beliefs... *The self is not only a useful illusion, it may be a necessary one*'.[6] So apparently things should go on just as they are.

SOME QUERIES

These are surely very odd claims. In the first place, we naturally ask just who it is that is being thus deluded? Illusions don't float about in midair; somebody has to entertain them. This was one thing that Descartes got right. As he pointed out you can't be mistaken if you aren't there in the first place. 'Deceive me who may,' cried Descartes in his *Second Meditation*, 'he cannot bring it about that I who am deceived do not exist.' And that still seems to hold.

Then again, scientists are not supposed to tell lies, so what is meant by saying that we must accept a falsehood here because it is useful and necessary? Normally, talk of 'useful illusions' refers to false beliefs which we want *other people* to hold, beliefs such as the public's conviction that its rulers are acting responsibly. But here we are being asked to accept lies ourselves while still knowing them to be lies. How would that work?

That question has a wider application because this way of saving oneself the trouble of answering unwelcome opinions by claiming that they are just tricks played on us by evolution is at present increasingly widespread. As we shall see, it is now standardly used about Free Will and very often too about religion. We shall have to come back to it later.

It is puzzling too, that this illusory self has now acquired an author – an active deceiver – as is clearly implied by words like 'tricked' and 'elaborate.' Wasn't the whole point of this move to get rid of active agents?

And again, what does Susan Greenfield mean by saying, 'this was all there was to Sarah?' If we ask, 'who is this Sarah?' will the answer be, 'well of course, like everybody else, she is just a standard mass of brain-cells and molecules – though I believe her hippocampus does have an interesting twist round towards the right'? Or might our informant add, 'Oh yes and I believe her surname was Palin or something like that'? Or perhaps not.

And then again, how is this selficide supposed to relate to the current emphasis among biologists on selfishness as an evolutionary force, or indeed to the general individualistic flavour that pervades today's political thinking?

It also seems remarkable that Crick and his followers are quite satisfied with the reality of brain cells. Why do they not pursue their reductive course right down to quarks or electrons, or whatever may be the currently favoured physical terminus? In view of this hesitation, we can reasonably ask, what is the actual aim of this reductive journey?

NOTES

1. Crick, F. The Astonishing Hypothesis: The Scientific Search For The Soul. New York: Touchstone, 1994, 3, emphasis added.
2. Ibid., 7, emphasis added.
3. Greenfield, S. *Brain Story: Unlocking Our Inner World of Emotions, Memories, Ideas* and *Desires.* London: BBC Books, 2000, 12.
4. Blakemore, C. The Mind Machine. London: BBC Books, 1999, 270, emphasis added.
5. Westerhoff, J. "What Are You?" New Scientist 2905 (23 February 2013), 37.
6. Ibid., 37.

17

WHAT IS MATERIALISM? (AND BY THE WAY, WHAT IS MATTER?)

ALARMING AMBIGUITIES

That sober volume, *The Oxford English Dictionary*, which never gives variations just for the fun of it, offers us two widely different meanings for 'materialism.' On the one hand, it says that this means 'the opinion that nothing exists except matter and its movements and modifications'; on the other, that it means 'devotion to material needs or desires, to the neglect of spiritual matters.'

If we wonder how the word managed to combine an abstract, rather technical, ontological meaning like this with an everyday one which – as the quotations show – carries a load of disapproval, we need only look, as we have done before in these cases, at the symbolism that our indefatigable imaginations have built around it. 'Material Needs' suggests to us primarily food and sex, and the less creditable

DOI: 10.4324/9781003588160-23

worldly interests such as riches – while 'spiritual' suggests something more uplifting, therefore good.

But it is not clear how these two moral categories can be linked with the metaphysical division of the world into matter and spirit. Indeed, this connection is remarkably crude. Plenty of unquestionably bad things, such as hatred and revenge, are spiritual rather than material; plenty of material needs, such as our love for each other, which leads us to touch and embrace our loved ones, are good. Thus, this commonplace symbolism does not give us a reliable moral compass.

That is probably one reason why philosophers have recently begun to avoid the ambiguous word 'materialism' altogether, and now speak of 'physicalism' instead. This word, as the OED kindly explains, was invented by the logical positivists of the Vienna Circle as a name for the view that 'reality is all reducible to certain kinds of physical entities' or, as Carnap puts it, all science can be expressed in the language of physics.

This change plainly struck theorists as simply a neat way to wall off serious ontology from crude, everyday moralizing about human conduct. But moving from everyday speech to technical language always has its price, and in this case the price is high. If 'physical entities' mean only ones that can be described in the language of physics, then everyday life simply contains hardly any physical entities at all. Physics never speaks of loaves and apples, pens and paper, men and women, bricks and mortar. It always speaks, far more abstractly, of solids and liquids, protons and electrons, vacuums and black holes.

The philosophers of the Vienna Circle were not actually trying to redescribe the physical world more accurately, and certainly not to describe it more fully. What they chiefly aimed to do was to remodel language in a more enlightened way so as to get rid of human agents and – more particularly – to get rid of souls. This topic concerned them specially because they were campaigning atheists. Their definition was above all an anti-religious campaign. It was meant as part of a much wider drive on behalf of the Enlightenment, something that clearly had plenty of point in early-twentieth-century Vienna, which was then still the church-centred capital of the Holy Roman Empire.

In this context, it is interesting to notice some more recent changes. According to Google's Ngram database, the word 'soul' 'experienced a steady decline in usage across the twentieth century, [but] this trajectory surprisingly reversed in the mid-1980s, to such an extent that as of the most recent data available, it was more common in English than the word "brain".'[1]

This recent reversal and the current wider use of the word have clearly arisen from the world of music, but they are by no means confined to it. As Eric Austin Lee and Samuel Kimbriel say in the introduction to their lively book *The Resounding Soul: Reflections on the Metaphysics and Vivacity of the Human Person*:

> There remains something perplexing about the human need to express certain aspects of lived experience with reference to a 'dead hypothesis'. Why is the word soul so damn useful?... In historical terms, the idea of humans as 'ensouled' arose not as some bloodless hypothesis but from within a powerful set of practices concerned with fostering human potentiality and vitality. To understand this point is also to understand why, despite protestations to the contrary from certain academic circles, the soul is still very near at hand.[2]

Thus, William Desmond, describing Dusty Springfield's singing, writes:

> It is not the self of the singer that communicates the spread of the thrill – it is soul . . . The voice raises the banal to the exalted, making more of the less, transforming, ensouling . . . This is a song of . . . astonishment before the being of the beloved . . . Even in an age of science and technology, these ways of speaking persist. People will not forfeit their souls easily.[3]

In fact, as Austin Lee and Kimbriel remark:

> There is something curious about the frequency with which the term 'soul' is now used in English in reference not to human beings but to inanimate objects. There is soul food and soulless fast food, soul

music and soulful music, and apparently, according to a friend, even my old Raleigh three-speed bike has 'got soul'.⁴

Similarly, I have seen an advertisement for 'Soul Style India Pale Ale.' We may be tempted to dismiss this whole orgy of soul-talk as meaningless, but I don't think we can do that, partly because its sheer volume surely shows that it means something, and partly because the clear use of words like 'soulless' shows us exactly what that something is. This is talk about activity, vivacity, vitality, zing, and it connects them with the experience of the human subject, returning that subject to the centre of the stage, refusing to accept the reductive, disinfecting campaign of scientistic puritans such as the Vienna Circle.

THE AWKWARD PERSISTENCE OF HUMANS

Yet, more than a century after that circle's depersonalising efforts, this last ambition is evidently still seen as very important. Thus, Stephen Pinker, called on to discuss artificial intelligence, raises his flag against human agents at once like this:

> Thomas Hobbes's pithy equation of reasoning as 'nothing but reckoning' is one of the great ideas in human history. The notion that rationality can be accomplished by the physical process of calculation was vindicated in the twentieth century by Alan Turing's thesis that simple machines can implement any computable function . . . This is a great idea for two reasons. First, it completes a naturalistic understanding of the universe, exorcising occult souls, spirits and ghosts in the machine. Second, it opens the door to artificial intelligence – to machines that think . . . A human-made information processor could, in principle, duplicate and exceed the powers of the human mind.⁵

But here things have evidently begun to go wrong. It is quite true that Hobbes said that all reasoning is only reckoning⁶ – indeed, in one of his wilder fits of reductivism he went beyond that and said that it is all only *addition* and *subtraction*. He intended this highly implausible ruling to prove that any talk not reducible to these mathematical terms is talk such as 'Accidents of Bread in Cheese, or Immaterial Substance,'[7] and has no meaning.

But however laudable that aim might be, Hobbes's general remarks about reasoning can't be defended. The term 'reasoning' obviously covers a vast range of activities from pondering, brooding, speculating, comparing, contemplating, defining, enquiring, meditating, wondering, arguing and doubting to proposing, suggesting and so forth – activities without which none of the secure rational conclusions that are being sought could ever be reached.

In fact, Pinker's claims make plain how obscure the meaning of the Vienna Circle's supposedly clear term 'physicalism' actually is, and indeed beyond that, they raise serious questions about the whole meaning of reduction. What does it mean to say that reality is all reducible to certain kinds of physical entities? No doubt a rabbit, if boiled down, will be found to consist of certain kinds of physical entities. But that does not prove that, before the boiling, it was not alive or was not a real rabbit, and certainly not that rabbits are an illusion. The chemicals that the boiling process reveals are not in any way more real than the original whole animal. Indeed – unless we go back to Plato's conception of the superior reality of the Forms? – the whole idea of different degrees of reality makes little sense.

INTELLIGIBILITY AND REALITY

Is the chemical and physical story perhaps more intelligible, more explanatory than the biological one? If it seems so, surely this only means that it can be fitted into a neater, simpler, more abstract conceptual scheme than an ordinary biological explanation – a scheme nearer to that North Pole of abstraction, pure mathematics. This process is often called 'explaining' and the word is used as if it meant 'explaining completely.' Thus, as we have seen earlier, Crick tells us that 'the scientific belief is that our minds – the behaviour of our brains – can be explained by the interaction of nerve cells (and other cells) and the molecules associated with them.'[8] He takes this to mean that this process is a complete account of its nature; nothing more need be said. Apparently, things not mentioned in this story are unreal, so our minds can be dismissed as illusions.

But why on earth should this follow? To *explain* something is simply to answer whatever questions arise about it, and normally there are many kinds of such questions. There is nothing to stop minds, or rabbits, being understood in more than one way – fitted into more than one conceptual scheme, and still remaining as real, and as complex, as they were in the first place. In fact, explanation usually asks for a wider background, within which both ways of thinking make sense.

SOUL PHOBIA

The philosophical scientists of the Vienna Circle were, as I say, not trying to redescribe the physical world more accurately, and certainly not trying to describe it more fully. Nor indeed were they trying to redefine reality itself. They were merely trying to 'reduce' everyday speech to abstract technical terms – terms less tainted with unwelcome social ideas from everyday existence, such as consciousness and indeed life itself. Carnap's claim that all science can be expressed in the language of physics implied that the proper scientific description of (say) an apple would be a phrase translated first into chemical terms, and from them into still more abstract physical ones. But obviously attempts at this reduction would fail to convey the necessary background concepts of trees and fruit, of ripening and being eaten, without which apples cannot be explained at all. It would not succeed in describing them and most likely could not effectively describe anything.

Physics, in fact, has – like its parent, dualism – no appropriate way of describing living things, indeed, no notion of life itself. That is why the word 'biology' and the sciences it describes have been invented, and it is why the Vienna Circle's plan of describing reality solely in the language of physics is not really practical at all. That plan is part of a vast, unworkable project of disinfection – a flight from everyday life – to which Pinker points when he writes that his little piece of Hobbesian reduction 'completes a naturalistic understanding of the universe, exorcising occult souls, spirits and ghosts in the machine.' The belief that this understanding has actually been completed, and is now a secure part of science, is part of the 'modern' reductivist creed that we are discussing, the creed that so many people today urge us to believe in. Marilynne Robinson, in her shrewdly titled book *Absence of Mind*, astutely calls it 'the myth of the threshold.' As she says, in what we call modern times, this conditioning has been part of our upbringing:

> I was educated to believe that a threshold had indeed been crossed in the collective intellectual experience, that we had entered a realm called 'modern thought' and we must naturalize ourselves to it . . . [The details of this crucial event were not made clear and were not thought to matter]. What we had learned from Darwin, Marx, Freud and others were insights into reality so deep as to be ahistorical . . .
>
> The schools of thought that support the modernist consensus are profoundly incompatible with one another, so incompatible that they cannot collectively be taken to support one grand conclusion. . . [And yet there is still a] core assumption that remains unchallenged and unquestioned. . . [It] is that the experience and testimony of the individual mind is to be explained away, excluded from consideration . . . The great new truth into which modernity has delivered us is generally assumed to be that the given world is the creature of accident . . . Once it was asserted and is now taken to have been proved that the God of traditional Western religion does not exist . . . An emptiness is thought to have entered human experience with the recognition that an understanding of the physical world can develop and accelerate through disciplines of reasoning for which God is not a given.[9]

Pinker's casual, super-confident reference to this orthodoxy is typical of our times except that he attributes it to a philosopher rather than a scientist. The creed is usually taken to be essentially scientific, established by some technical discovery or other – probably by the discovery that the earth is not the centre of the solar system, though this is not always distinguished from the discovery that the earth is not flat.

Thus, this contemporary orthodoxy is well known to date back at least to the sixteenth century, and it can only be called 'modern' by contrast to that century's best-known predecessor, the 'Middle Ages.'

As Robinson says, however, this creed has also been linked with many later sages – Darwin, Marx, Freud, and whatever other notables are viewed at any time as able to explode an old-fashioned, supposedly religious approach. Its main function, however, is not to get rid of God but to support materialism by eliminating human subjects. As Pinker says, it exorcises 'occult souls, spirits and ghosts in the machine,' in order to make room for abstract science.

CONSTRUCTING THE VACUUM

Thus, instead of getting rid of dualism, as was intended, the 'modern' outlook keeps to a strange, one-legged variety of it which simply establishes physical science as the champion of old-fashioned Matter against old-fashioned Spirit. What this destroys is not superstition but the idea of the individual thinker. It aims to undermine the observers' and theorists' own minds, their confidence in their own judgement, in themselves as able to judge. As we have seen, it leads to Crick's vacuum, where minds are held to have vanished altogether.

This sweepingness can, of course, look good on the title page. But it has increasingly awkward consequences when – as is bound to happen – reasoners need to take notice of their own impressions, their opinions, their convictions, their doubts, their range of consciousness, their relations with others, their experiences and their inner life. Serious physicalists must then claim that these items – which they are actually using – don't exist. ('I myself,' says Crick, 'like many scientists, believe that the soul is imaginary and that what we call our minds is simply a way of talking about the functions of our brains' (Crick, *The Astonishing Hypothesis*, p.3, note). So who is this 'I myself'?) Whether we call them illusory, like Crick, or simply refuse to talk about them at all on the grounds that they are vulgar everyday matters, we are no longer supposed to mention these things, which have been excluded from the province of science. But since we are all vulgar, everyday people, needing to talk about vulgar, everyday things all the time, even when we are doing science, this is very inconvenient. As Merleau-Ponty explains:

> I cannot conceive myself as nothing but a bit of the world, a mere object of biological, psychological or sociological investigation. I cannot shut myself up within the realm of science. All my knowledge of the world, even my scientific knowledge, is gained from my own particular point of view, or from some experience of the world, without which the symbols of science would be meaningless. The whole universe of science is built upon the world as directly experienced, and if we want to subject science itself to rigorous scrutiny and arrive at a precise assessment of its meaning and scope, we must begin by reawakening the basic experience of the world, of which science is the second-order expression.
>
> (*Phenomenology of Perception*, trans. Colin Smith, Routledge, 2002, Preface, p.ix)

The area where this need is most striking is, of course, experience itself, which, in spite of being subjective, often needs to be described, and notoriously contains, as Merleau-Ponty says, the whole mass of solid empirical evidence on which science itself depends. Thus, the case for the existence of rabbits all rests eventually on accepting particular people's reports of having personally seen, heard, touched, or tasted particular rabbits – reports which inevitably contain terms quite alien to the language of physics. Because of this, Pinker's 'naturalistic understanding of the universe' can only be called 'naturalistic' if '*nature*' – the real universe – is understood, for this purpose, as simply consisting of the abstract world that physics describes.

Only what is mentioned by physics is then real, and the physicist can safely say, in the words of the old rhyme:

> I'm the Master of this College,
> What I don't know isn't knowledge.[10]

NOTES

1. E. Austin Lee and S. Kimbriel, *The Resounding Soul: Reflections on the Metaphysics and Vivacity of the Human Person* (Eugene, OR, Cascade Books, 2015), p. 3.
2. Ibid., p. 3.
3. Ibid., p. 354.
4. Ibid., p. 3.
5. S. Pinker, 'Thinking does not involve subjugating', in *What do you Think about Machines that Think* (Edge, 2015), Harper Perennial. Available online: https://www.edge.org/response-detail/26243.
6. Leviathan, Chapter 1, Section 5.
7. Ibid.
8. F. Crick, *The Astonishing Hypothesis* (New York, Touchstone, 1994), p. 7
9. M. Robinson, *Absence of Mind: The Dispelling of Inwardness from the Modern Myth of the Self* (New Have, CT: Yale University Press, 2010).
10. Anon, *The Masque of Balliol* (1881).

18

THE HUMAN HEART AND OTHER ORGANS*

THE FUNCTION OF THE HEART

If we talk of hearts today, we usually do it only in two rather restricted contexts; the romantic or the medical. A heart is either the focus of a love affair, or the seat of a disease. These two matters seem widely separated, not connected except externally and by chance. But a much wider use of the word is possible, and deserves examination. When Lady Macbeth, sleepwalking, moans because she cannot clean the smell of blood off her hands, her watchful Doctor says:

---

* Since this chapter was written as an Introduction linking the themes of the separate papers collected as Heart and Mind, it is replete with references to these. Rather than edit out these references, have disrupted the flow and sense of the chapter, I have retained them and refer the reader together which would to the original book for clarification. [Ed.]

DOI: 10.4324/9781003588160-24

What a sigh is there! The heart is sore charged.

And her waiting-woman replies:

> I would not have such a heart in my bosom for all the dignity of the
> whole body.
>
> (Macbeth, Act V, scene i)

These people are talking in a perfectly natural way, but one which
has become a trifle awkward for us now, partly through sentimental
misuse of words like 'heart,' partly because of certain changes in the
pattern of our thoughts. What they are speaking of is the *core* or centre
of someone's being, the essential person, himself as he is in himself
and (primarily) to himself. By comparison, both the romantic and the
medical aspects of his life are partial and dependent. On the one hand,
love affairs do not depend only on certain special feelings, but on the
whole character. On the other hand, someone who has to have a heart
operation needs a surgeon whose heart is in his work, a stout-hearted
one, who in unexpected difficulties will take heart rather than lose
it, one whose heart will not easily sink or fail him. A medical student
who, at heart, has never really cared for his work, would never become
this kind of surgeon whatever his brains. The surgeon too, on his side,
needs a stout-hearted patient, not a faint-hearted one – a patient who
will put his heart into the business of recovery.

In this wide and still natural way of speaking, the hearts of both
doctor and patient form an essential part of the business. Of course
one of them may be *heartless* in a narrower sense – callous, selfish,
unsympathetic. But to be that, to have any distinct character, he still
needs this structured core to his being. It is where his priorities are
formed. It is the organized set of central feelings by which he is habitually moved. Hearts may be narrow and hard, cold and flinty, but they
are still a crucial element in people's activities.

How then does this centre relate to the mind or brain? Here too
we can choose between a wider and a narrower use. We certainly can
contrast the mind or brain sharply with the heart, as I did just now

in speaking of the medical student. He may have a first-class mind – meaning that he always passes exams well – without any necessary consequences about his heart or character. But that is not the only way to think of the matter, nor the most natural one. When Macbeth says:

> O full of scorpions is my mind, dear wife

this is not at all the same thing as complaining about bugs in a computer program. And again:

> *Macbeth*. Canst thou not minister to a mind diseased,
> Pluck from the memory a rooted sorrow,
> Raze out the written troubles of the brain,
> And with some sweet oblivious antidote
> Cleanse the stuff'd bosom of that perilous stuff
> Which weighs upon the heart?

> DOCTOR. Therein the patient must minister to himself.
> MACBETH. Throw physic to the dogs, I'll none of it.
>
> (Act V, scene iii)

The mind which is diseased is not the intellect, it is something quite close to what we still call the heart. The heart is the centre of concern, the mind is the centre of purpose or attention, and these cannot be dissociated. This does not prevent the mind from being the seat of thought, because thought in general is not just information-handling or abstract calculation, such as computers do, but is the process of developing and articulating our perceptions and feelings. This is still true even if we confine the term to serious, 'directed' thought, ignoring more casual musings:

> But men at whiles are sober,
> And think, by fits and starts,
> And if they think, they fasten
> Their hands upon their hearts.
>
> (A. E. Housman, *Last Poems*, x)

Thought is not primarily the sort of thing which is tested in exams. It is the whole organized business of living – seen from the inside.

All this matters because many things on the current intellectual scene tend to make us disconnect feeling from thought, by narrowing our notions of both, and so to make human life as a whole unintelligible. We are inclined to use words like 'heart' and 'feeling' to describe just a few selected sentiments which are somewhat detached from the practical business of living – notably romantic, compassionate and tender sentiments – as if non-romantic actions did not involve any feeling. But this cannot be right. Mean or vindictive action flows from and implies mean and vindictive feeling, and does so just as much when it is considered as when it is impulsive. In general, too, ordinary prudent action flows from prudent feeling, though this is something to which we are so well accustomed that we take it for granted. It may seem like pure habit – until a sudden threat startles us into consciousness of the motive.

We are in fact so constituted that we cannot act at all if feeling really fails. When it does fail, as in cases of extreme apathy and depression, people stop acting; they can die in consequence. We do not live essentially by calculation, interrupted occasionally by an alien force called feeling. Our thought (including calculation) is the more or less coherent form into which our perceptions and feelings constantly organize themselves. And the compromise between various, conflicting, strong, and constant feelings expresses itself in our heart or character.

Of course I am not denying that there can be discrepancies and conflicts between thought and feeling, or between feeling and action. There can. (They provide some of our most serious problems, which is why we have quite a good vocabulary for talking about them.) But they have to be exceptional. In general, feelings, to be effective, must take shape as thoughts, and thoughts, to be effective, must be powered by suitable feelings. Speculative thought is no exception; it depends on the powerful feelings of interest and curiosity. When we speak of a thought as conflicting with a feeling, both thoughts and feelings are really present on both sides; the distinction is just one of emphasis.

For instance, if a normally prudent housewife, overcome (as we say) by an impulse, blows everything on a wild investment, at least two thoughts and also two feelings are involved. Her habitual, steady desire for security was borne down by the detailed, but misleading, calculations which her intellect so vigorously produced. She did not operate with her normal degree of organization, but she still operated as one person, not two. Disentangling the intellectual from the emotional aspects of this whole is performing a piece of abstraction, one which needs enormously more care than theorizers usually give it.

THE DIVORCE BETWEEN FEELING AND REASON

Why, now, does all this matter? The unity of the human personality, which I am stressing, seems obvious. As I have said, however, it badly needs to be plugged today because of a whole web of theoretical habits which tend to obscure it and make it inexpressible. In this book, my main business will be with the strands of this web spun by British moral philosophy, which from the eighteenth century on has occupied itself with a dispute about whether morality is a matter of reason or feeling, ignoring the obvious fact that it is both. Its question has been, in Hume's words,

> concerning the general foundation of Morals; whether they be derived from Reason, or from Sentiment; whether we attain the knowledge of them by a chain of argument and induction, or by an immediate feeling and finer internal sense.
>
> (Enquiry Concerning the Principles of Morals, Section I)

This dilemma is false. The metaphor of *foundation* is disastrous; a building can only sit on one foundation, so it looks as if we have to make a drastic choice. But we don't. Morality, like every other aspect of human activity, has both its emotional and its intellectual side, and the connection between them can't be just an external one, like that between stones brought together for a building. It is an organic one, like that between the shape and size of an insect.

This barren dispute sprang up in the first place as part of a wider controversy, which was only less barren because it was more quickly recognized as being merely a question of emphasis – the dispute between rationalism and empiricism in the theory of knowledge. Does knowledge – people asked – depend on reasoning or on experience? Very plainly the answer must be – yes, on both, but in different ways, and the next move must be to go on and investigate these different sorts of dependence.

Since Kant's day, this has been fairly well understood as far as theoretical knowledge is concerned. In moral philosophy, however, empiricists have been a lot slower to see that they could not treat the issue as a football match which, by vigorous cheering, they might one day hope to win. Hume's question only makes sense if it is treated as one about emphasis. It must be dealt with by accepting both elements as inseparable, and going on to a patient analysis of the parts they play in the whole.

THE DIVORCE BETWEEN NATURE AND WILL

I begin then, deliberately, with a rather simple paper, 'Freedom and Heredity,' dealing with the most troublesome and clamorous current form of this old dispute between feeling and reason – namely, the war at present proclaimed as arising between human nature and the free human will. We are called upon to choose between these concepts, to decide whether we are free beings, or members of the species *Homo sapiens*, with an inherited mental and emotional constitution. But are tomatoes fruit or vegetables? Does a house need shape or size? The two things imply each other. A being which had no natural constitution could not be free; the word freedom would make no sense applied to it. Such a creature would have nothing which it needed to be free to do. And the natural constitution which man actually has is no obstacle to his making free choices, since in fact it is so formed that it commits him to choosing. There is no football match to be won here. There are two imperfectly understood half-truths, both of which in practice we recognize, and which we must somehow fit together. This is certainly hard, because our ideas of freedom and of nature have been developed in different contexts and are not shaped to fit each other. As has long been recognized, very careful logical plumbing is needed to understand free will, and people who want to do it will always have to think hard. But the present controversy does not only flow from this general, long-standing difficulty about free will and causal necessity. It arises because the notion of the will has been fantastically narrowed and isolated, since Nietzsche, in a melodramatic attempt to expand human freedom into omnipotence.

For Kant, the will meant practical reason. It was a name for the whole person, considered as a responsible chooser. Nietzsche, distrusting thought, exalted it as simply the courage to pursue one's own desires. The existentialists, seeing that desires are part of nature, and anxious to free the individual from entrapment in anything natural, separated it off from desire as well, and exalted it still further as the seat of pure choice. But choice in this isolation becomes so pure as to be quite meaningless. And although existentialist jargon is no longer specially fashionable, this is still the only way of thinking open to those who want to divorce the essential self from human nature. That self becomes a mere vacuous abstract force without direction.

What is missing is the background map of the *whole* self, within which both the natural desires and the shaping will which develops to organize them can find a context. As I remarked when discussing hearts, certain areas within this whole are brightly lit by current thought and intellectually familiar, but the brighter this light is, the darker and more mysterious we find the gaps between. A sharp beam is focused on the body as the object of medical science. This, however, makes it even harder to peer into the surrounding gloom, even at those neighbouring areas of the mind which (as Macbeth saw) must often be understood for the treatment of disease itself. Elsewhere a different and weaker light (probably pink) vaguely illuminates the feelings, or certain selected feelings. But this is not supposed to be a very complex or important area. And elsewhere again, there looms in the darkness, uncertainly lit in green from yet another direction, a further item called the will. How are these bits and pieces to be connected? The human being who is the object of various sciences seems to bear no relation to the one who feels, or to the subject making decisions, yet he must operate as a whole. We cannot choose between these items; we need a map which contains them all. Of course, the roots of these difficulties are not new. People's understanding of themselves has always been fragmentary. Probably it always must be so, probably it would always be subject to the paradoxes which Pope noticed in the *Essay on Man*:

> – Placed on this isthmus of a middle state,
> A being darkly wise and rudely great,
> With too much knowledge for the Sceptic side,
> With too much weakness for the Stoic's pride,
> He hangs between, in doubt to act or rest,
> In doubt to deem himself a god or beast,
> In doubt his mind or body to prefer,
> Born but to die, and reasoning but to err. . .
> Created half to rise, and half to fall,
> Great lord of all things, yet a prey to all,
> Sole judge of truth, in endless error hurled,
> The glory, jest and riddle of the world:
>
> (*Essay on Man*, Epistle 2, 3–18)

What is new in this century, however, is the contribution of academic specialization to the splitting process. Mind and body, scepticism and stoicism, god and beast, are now topics belonging to different disciplines. Each is supposed to be discussed in its own appropriate terms, and any area so far neglected is suspect; since there is no proper way of discussing it, it tends to look like unsuitable ground for academic consideration altogether. Within each discipline, there is a further tendency to keep narrowing the territory; to be suspicious of outlying areas and concentrate only on things which can be made to look perfectly clear and complete. In any given subject, this leads to feuds between rival factions, each claiming to have the right centre. The only remedy for this fragmentation is to stand back and take a wider view of the key concepts as parts of a whole.

I begin with the most awkward and mysterious case, the will. Those who consider our nature as something mean, limited and mechanical are of course reluctant to allow it any part in the honourable function of creativity. They follow Nietzsche in crediting the unassisted will with the creation both of moral values and of art. But when did mere will-power, decisiveness and determination ever make an artist, or indeed a real moral reformer? Talents are gifts. It is not a deprivation, or an infringement of freedom, that each of us must live as the person he is, with the brain and central nervous system that he has, instead of shopping around for one that would suit him better. (What him?) Not even God can invent himself from scratch.

The fear of determinism arises largely from people's habit of treating all causes as enemies rather than friends, deprivations rather than gifts. Gifts are *enabling* causes; it is hard to see how we would manage without them. Actually, this non-religious rejection of physical causes in the name of freedom requires a far narrower, more bloodless and ascetic view of the self than does any religion. For Christianity, the true self is indeed the soul, but the body is a necessary and suitable expression for it; the resurrection of the body will ensure that whole people, not just ghosts, inhabit Heaven. For Buddhism too, the soul must find a body to fit it. But those who want to say that heredity does not shape a human personality at all seem to take that personality as something sexless and abstract, a mere standard will which happens to have got shut up in a particular body. What are our talents then?

Accordingly, I suggest that we must treat Creation and Originality, not as supernatural interventions, but as aspects of our whole imaginative capacity, and therefore of our whole nature. There is no danger in admitting their genetic sources. We need not isolate them as pure products of the parthenogenetic will. In the next paper, 'G. E. Moore on the Ideal,' I discuss an equally mysterious, and related, attempt to isolate the power of moral judgement from the rest of our nature.

NATURALISM AND REDUCTIVISM

The insistence on narrowing the notion of morality sprang from fear that, if it were more widely conceived, it would become contaminated, that autonomy would be sacrificed. To understand why the philosophers swung their small searchlight over the moral scene like this, refusing to spread its beam, we have to grasp the danger which they were trying to avoid. They called it naturalism.

It was the danger of distorting and degrading morality by resting it on the wrong sort of arguments, and particularly on arguments taken from the natural sciences. The clearest case of this distortion is one Moore gave – crude 'evolutionary ethics' or Social Darwinism.[1] You are an ethical naturalist if you say that 'good' simply means 'evolved,' so that more evolved societies – i.e. more civilized ones – are necessarily better than less evolved ones. Or again, if you say that the fittest – that is, the most successful – individuals ought always to prevail because evolution demands it, and 'ought' means something like 'is called for by evolution.'

These examples are striking; anyone can see that there is something wrong with them. But actually so many things are wrong with them that they are not very useful; they do not help us to isolate the fault we are after. Evolutionary ethics is an outstanding conceptual pigs' break-fast, a classic showpiece of non-thought. Every term in these con-tentions needs defining, and any reasonable definition of the terms will wreck the conclusions. To condemn this sort of ostentatiously muddled thinking is not to condemn all argument from the natural sciences, or from the concept of nature: it is to condemn bad argu-ment. Consider now a clearer case; the defence of Moore's own posi-tion about the value of contemplating art and beauty. Is it *naturalism* if I argue (for instance, in a dispute about education) that attention to art is very important, and support this view by reference to the facts about the various capacities of children, and about what experience shows us of how people and societies develop without art? Or if I give a sim-ilar account of the importance of play? These are facts about human needs, facts which really might have been different. (It does not seem to be necessary that any intelligent being would need art, beauty or play in exactly this way.) Experience is required for the understanding of such needs, and that understanding is necessary if we are to build a priority system. It is an understanding, not just of odd impulses, but of our nature as a whole. If 'naturalism' means arguing in this way, it is absolutely necessary for ethics. The real danger to the autonomy of morals, in fact, is not naturalism, but crude reductivism, and the characteristic vice of reductivism is not its reference to nature, but its exclusiveness, its nothing-buttery. A crude reductivist claims, for instance, that, 'after all, a person is *really* nothing but £5 worth of chemicals.' This sounds hard-headed; besides the chemicals, what else is there? But in fact if we deliver £5 worth of chemicals – or even £6 worth – to an employer, after promising that we will get another person for him by Monday morning, he will detect a difference and is likely to be dissatisfied. He will be so too if we deliver a corpse.

This is not necessarily because he demands an extra entity, such as an immortal soul. It is because the word 'person' necessarily means a certain very highly organized, active item, and raw materials are not what it refers to at all. The whole is more than the sum of the parts, and there is nothing superstitious about this. In the same way, anyone who said that, after all, 'good' meant nothing but 'pleasant' or 'evolved' would be grossly distorting language. But of course this does not stop him showing some less direct relation between the concepts if he will take the trouble to make it plausible. It certainly cannot show that the notion of goodness is conceptually isolated from all relations to other ideas. Permanent conceptual quarantine is impossible and autonomy does not require it. It is reductivism that wrecks many attempts to find a 'scientific basis (or foundation) for morality.'

What is a *basis* or *foundation*? The words evidently do not mean here what Hume chiefly meant by them – namely, the essential element in morality itself. They mean something more like an explanation or justification (Hume had this meaning in mind as well, as he shows when he asks how we know moral truths, but it is a different question).

A model which naturally occurs to us here is that of the Foundations of Mathematics. These are the logical principles which mathematics must take for granted – the set of assumptions which are necessary if mathematical reasoning is to be valid. Is there a similar set for moral reasoning? Now there do seem to be some forms of thinking which it needs to use. These may centre (as Hare suggested) round the idea of universalizing, of regarding oneself as just one among others, so that each should do as he would be done by. They may also include the larger cluster of notions within which Kant first put forward this suggestion – ideas like responsibility, freedom, rationality, respect for persons, and treating others as ends in themselves. Without these ways of thinking, we may say, there could be no morality. But it does not follow that they alone would be enough to constitute it. Our reason for adopting this way of thinking is certainly not just an intellectual one.[2] As far as mere intellect goes, either calculating egoism or identification with the whole species would do just as well. To think in terms of distinct individuals capable of mattering to each other, and so think morally, we need our emotional constitution too. Intelligent psychopaths who lack normal emotions are amoral; they do not arrive at a moral position by pure reasoning.

Our emotional constitution is not revealed by logic. It is a very large and general empirical fact – something which might in principle have been otherwise. The attempt to reduce morality to its minimal logic is itself reductive; it is one more piece of illicit nothing-buttery. Mathematics actually is in the surprising position of having no empirical part, of being essentially a branch of logic. Morality is not. It, like most other realms of thought, involves empirical considerations as well. These determine the detailed forms of thought it needs. In speaking of such a creature as man, it makes no sense to isolate the rational will. I am suggesting that exclusive concentration on the will is itself a form of reductivism. This may seem surprising, since 'reductivism' is a name usually given to campaigns proceeding from the opposite direction. But the central fault – the arbitrary contraction of scope – is the same in both cases. To put this point in context, I deal next with the more familiar forms of reduction.

In ethics, these come in two main kinds – psychological and physical. Psychological reduction flourishes most today in the form which Moore already concentrated on, namely hedonism, the reduction of good to pleasure – whether private pleasure, as Freud believed, or, as Bentham thought, the pleasure of the greater number. Physical reduction, on the other hand, deals in the entities of biology and, through them, of physics. Thus, when an honest man insists on revealing an awkward truth in the teeth of bribes and threats, the psychological reductivist explains that (in spite of all appearances) this man is really only maximizing pleasure – either his own or other people's. The physical reductivist, however, retorts that *he* – the truthteller – is not really doing anything. What is really happening is just activity in his glands, brain and nerves, or even (still more bizarrely) in his genes.

The trouble with these high-sounding views is simply their obscurity, and particularly the obscure use of the word *really*. Do these two views compete? Or can both be true? Does either eliminate the ordinary descriptions of the event? What do they actually claim? The psychological version looks at first like a simple accusation of humbug. But humbug is only possible where the real thing sometimes occurs to imitate, and the case we consider should clearly be the real one. As for the physical version, that version must apply to both. Real humbug and real heroism are for it equally to be described as – after all *really* – only activity in the cells. But this seems idle. The social and moral descriptions (humbug and heroism) which we started with still apply, and are still needed, they make an essential distinction. The physical one which we add does a different job; it is perfectly compatible with them, but it cannot replace them. What special honour is being claimed for it?

To make sense of the reduction, we must drop the metaphysical word 'really' and treat both suggestions as claims about explanatory power. The idea then is not that we were mistaken about what happened, but that it is best explained in a certain way. But to say *best* here lands us again in the same trouble about competition. Is there (why should there be?) any single explanation which is for all purposes the best one? To explain something is to remove a particular doubt or misunderstanding. And there is no limit to the number of doubts and misunderstandings that can arise.

Normally, when we say that a particular explanation is the right or real one, and supplants others, we are taking for granted a definite question which it was meant to answer. We share with our hearers an unspoken assumption about the job for which explanation is needed. This gives it no licence to monopolize the whole subject indefinitely.

In the case of truthfulness, it is obscure how physical explanation could be helpful at all. Hedonism is much more obviously relevant. We may raise the question why truthfulness is so important, and hedonism is directly designed to answer such questions. As it happens, however, it is rather bad at answering this particular one. And even in more favourable cases, it usually seems to provide only part of the truth. Psychological reductions usually start from genuine and useful insights, but distort them by wild claims to exclusive status.

INSIDE AND OUTSIDE

I have discussed the evils of Reductivism at some length, partly because they are really important, partly to make it clear that I do see what philosophers were objecting to in their somewhat obsessive resistance to Naturalism. Undoubtedly, however, they over-reacted, giving so wide a sense to 'naturalism' in the name of autonomy that they were left with an impossibly narrow territory for moral thinking.

'The Objection to Systematic Humbug' discusses one form of this narrowing, namely the sharp line which some moral philosophers have drawn between motive and action. They insist that the business of morality is really only with outside action – or alternatively, that it is really only with motive.

This is a fine example of the kind of reductive mistake which has found itself a special jargon today by misusing the word *about*. Is architecture really about people? or about the principles of safe construction? Is morality about acts, or about motives? The falsity of these dilemmas is obvious and the usage stinks. In moral philosophy, the effect is to separate the judgements passed on acts and motives entirely, and therefore to dislocate the inner and outer aspects of life. Recently the preference has been given to the outer, on grounds rooted in metaphysical behaviourism – the view that nothing except outwards action is fully real, so that questions about feeling and motive must be secondary. A person, on this view, is (after all) nothing but his behaviour patterns. Here psychological questions about the self become entangled with the ontological ones already touched on; questions about 'what there is' or rather about what it means to say that various kinds of things *are*. There is a tradition, going back to Plato, of treating mind and matter as rival candidates for complete reality – of considering one *less real* than the other. Extreme practitioners deny the reality of one or the other entirely. Here idealists (like Berkeley and Leibniz) are balanced by materialists (like Hobbes and Marx). Descartes thought both contenders equally real, but so different that there was no intelligible relation between them.

All these positions are very mysterious. The trouble is that, once you begin to think of mind and matter as distinct things, rather than as aspects of a single world, it becomes remarkably hard to bring them into any intelligible relation. And – to return to my present theme – this difficulty reflects and aggravates that of relating the various parts of the self.

Behaviourism therefore is an important element on the scene, and its story is an interesting one. It was originally invented, and still officially serves, simply as a guiding principle of method in psychology. Reacting against psychologists who relied heavily on introspection, J. B. Watson and his followers proclaimed early in the twentieth century a programme in psychology which would ignore data from consciousness and deal only with outward behaviour. This policy declaration need not have carried condemnation of other kinds; after all, there could in principle be as many legitimate ways of doing psychology as there are of doing geography. But in fact it was put forward, especially in its early stages, with a good deal of crusading zeal, involving, not just a distrust of other methods, but a metaphysical conviction that their data must be invalid, since inner consciousness was indescribable, unknowable, and perhaps actually unreal. Behaviourism is thus the mirror opposite of subjectivism. Subjectivism, in its various forms, doubts the reality of the outside world and accepts as certain only the deliverances of consciousness. Behaviourism reverses this process. The piquant thing about this antithesis is that both extremes are often favoured by rather similar people and for similar reasons. Both parties want to be tough-minded, economical and realistic; both are suspicious of religion and the subtler aspects of traditional morality.

But which metaphysic to choose? Here is another of those numbing dilemmas which I have been describing. Without a proper connecting background, there can be no choice. One must simply toss up. In the social sciences, the choice often makes itself very simply on occupational grounds. A sociologist can hardly be a subjectivist; a subjectivist would hardly have taken to sociology in the first place. Philosophers, however, have more positive reasons for moving towards behaviourism. They have tried subjectivism, and, as may happen with an unreliable brand of car, many of them still bear the scars. Modern philosophy starts from Descartes' 'I think, therefore I am,' which is deliberately chosen as the most subjective position possible. Descartes himself of course did not mean to stay locked up in the self. He meant to prove the reality of the external world in such a way as to make it safe for the physics of Galileo, and so, finally, for common sense too. But this has turned out a desperate project.

Repeatedly, Descartes' systematic doubt has led its users away from their goal. Hume pursued its sceptical branch, which stresses the isolation of the single self, to a terminus in total paralysis and confusion.[3] At that end lies solipsism, the view that there actually is nothing except one's own consciousness – and anyone who can make sense of that is welcome to it. (If he were right he would, of course, be by definition in a very different situation from the rest of us . . .) Along the idealist branch, which allows many selves, Hegel built on a grandiose extension – the Absolute – a superself containing all the others. But this causes serious alarm by its metaphysical top-heaviness. British empiricism, always wedded to economy, cannot join the Hegelian orgy; it must take something nearer to Hume's path.

But British empiricism is polygamous. It is also wedded to science and to common sense, and it cannot finally accept a notion of the world which is too mean for their purposes. Economy is an important ideal to it, but it is not committed to the life of a starving miser. Bertrand Russell was the last great empiricist who tried hard and systematically to give a credible account of the world from the subjective starting-point. He still asked; granted only my consciousness with its sense-data, what else need exist? His various attempted

310 THE ESSENTIAL MARY MIDGLEY

answers depict a series of bizarre universes, each stranger than the last, presenting no foothold either to common sense or to any science except certain selected aspects of physics. (In particular, *The Analysis of Matter* really deserves the attention of science-fiction addicts.) Now, outraging common sense never worried Russell. He was content, indeed pleased, to suppose it unable to penetrate the real world. But science was another matter. Unlike Hume, Russell had no interest in scepticism as such. He lived in a scientific age and took science very seriously. His failure there marks the end of an empiricist epoch. It is perverse and unrealistic to form a metaphysical notion of the world which is too limited for the purposes of one's actual thinking. Metaphysical notions exist to be *used*. The scepticism which started as honourable unpretentiousness begins in such circumstances to look very much like humbug.

In emergencies like this, the kaleidoscope of thought must be shaken and a new starting-point found. G.E. Moore, in his 'Defence of Common Sense' gave the right shake,[4] and Wittgenstein made use of it to call attention to a new pattern. Philosophers began to look at language. This has given rise to a certain amount of groaning from those who accuse them of preferring to think about words rather than about reality. Whatever their incidental vices, however, the reason for the move is a quite different and completely sound one.

Language is public. If you talk, you cannot possibly be the first of your kind. I makes sense only by contrast with *you, he, she, it,* and *they.* A solipsist could not say I.[5] If Descartes had thought about this, he would not have assumed that he must start his enquiry, like a doomed escapologist, from the awkward position of being locked up inside his own consciousness, with no accomplice to release him. If we did start there, escape really would be impossible. But we don't.

Those of us who are lucky enough to begin life at all to the extent of being able to talk, begin it in a shared world. Our inner lives, like other people's, occur within that world, as parts of it. From the start, a great deal of communication flows in and out of our various minds unnoticed and without difficulty; we take it for granted. Of course elsewhere the stream can be blocked, and in bad cases, people really can be trapped inside their private towers or cellars. Naturally, we attend to such blocks more than to the satisfactory background flow, on the sound general principle of neglecting what is all right. But to do this is to recognize blocks as a special, if common, misfortune, not as the normal condition of life.

The subjectivist philosophical approach, from which so much was hoped, has infiltrated literature and coloured our imaginations in a hundred ways which I cannot go into here. My present business is just to point out that, on its own ground as a tool of thought, it has terrible faults, and has certainly come to the limit of its usefulness. About the relation of mind and body in particular, it has produced vast problems which it can do nothing to solve.

That question, then, must be somehow restated. We must pose it in a way which avoids the suggestion of a race where two contenders – mind and body – compete for a prize, namely, the status of reality. In any decent sense of *real*, both are quite real. And 'reduction' of one to the other will not help. We are not making some sort of quasi-physical enquiry about what material the world is really made of – mind or matter, earth or fire, rock, or gas. That kind of thing must be left to physics. Instead, we are talking about the relation between two real aspects of everybody's life, the inner and the outer – our consciousness, and the outer world of which we are conscious, which includes human bodies.

Economy does not call on us to get rid of either. Since our problem concerns their relation, to sink one of them will not solve it. Subjectivism, which offers to melt down the outer world into a relatively insubstantial mirage, does not make sense for beings like us who can successfully reach out to that world's other inhabitants by language. Behaviourism, which offers to ignore the inner experience, also splits on the rock of language, because speech is essentially a transaction between two conscious beings. We do not speak simply to our hearer's behaviour patterns. Proper speech is only possible where we regard the hearer as having a state of mind which we address – as receiving and interpreting what we say. (This is why it is so exasperating to find that one has been talking to a telephone answering machine.)

The kind of being that can talk cannot possibly be just a mind or just a body. Neither can he be a mere loose combination of these, considered as two separate items. The mind is not in the body as a pilot is in a ship, but much more as the inside of a teapot is inside the outside. The fit need not be perfect – there are places where the contours diverge quite a lot. But they are still parts of a whole, and in general both can only be understood together, by grasping the nature of that whole. We are not compelled to say 'a man is really his body.' He is the whole, of which mind and body are equally just aspects, much more like temper or size or intelligence than they are like teeth or toes. Unquestionably, this is a far better way to think of human beings as they are in this world, and I do not think that problems about how they may have to be envisaged in the next world ought to be allowed to interfere with it. If there is a next world (a point on which I have no views), it will naturally call for quite different ways of thinking. But in this world, we must deal with a person as a whole.

This, as I take it, is the first message for ontologists of Wittgenstein's *Philosophical Investigations*. And it is perhaps the central reason why, if Wittgenstein had not existed, someone else would have had to attend to language. The second is the better-known point that *metaphysical* language must be examined. It really is not clear what we mean by calling such very general things real or unreal; translations must be given. These two moves together release us from the subjectivist prison and give us back the world. Many philosophers, however, view such largesse with suspicion and continue to look the gift horse in the mouth. They see subjectivism and behaviourism as the only possible alternatives, so that releasing us from one of them must bind us to the other. The outer world, it seems, may now be real, provided only that *we* are not present to inhabit it. *We* must be reduced to our outward actions: any inner accompaniment that is conceded must be unreal and ghostly. This discreet and sophisticated form of behaviourism appears in the ethical view which I discuss in 'The Objection to Systematic Humbug.' According to it, morality is entirely concerned with outward acts, and has nothing to say about thoughts and feelings except indirectly as causes of action. I argue that this gives us a quite distorted view of morality. And in 'Is "Moral" a Dirty Word?' I go on to point out that this distorted view is indeed sometimes found in normal speech – but only when we use the word 'moral' and its derivatives as terms of abuse.

Morality, which is confined to outward behaviour already, has a bad name, and with reason.

NOTES

1. *Principia Ethica* (Cambridge, 1948) pp. 45–54, and my *Beast and Man,* pp. 155–8.
2. See *Beast and Man*, Chapter 11, 'On Being Animal as Well as Rational'. The position I deploy there, and in the present section, is in some ways parallel to that – or those – which Lawrence Kohlberg develops in his lively and stimulating article 'From Is To Ought; How to Commit the Naturalistic Fallacy and Get Away With It', in T. Mischel (ed.) *Cognitive Development and Epistemology* (New York, Academic Press, 1971). Kohlberg's objections to relativism, behaviourism and anti-naturalism are not unlike mine, though the strategy by which he resists them is different. I have not found it possible to discuss his views without complicating my argument unduly, but I am glad to see them.
3. *Treatise of Human Nature*, Book 1, part IV, Section vii. Compare his confident and optimistic tone in the Introduction to the same book. A more moderate sceptical position appears in the later *Enquiry concerning the Human Understanding*, Section xii.
4. *Philosophical Papers* (London, Allen & Unwin, 1959).
5. See *Beast and Man*, p. 357, note.

19

ON TRYING OUT ONE'S NEW SWORD ON A CHANCE WAYFARER

All of us are, more or less, in trouble today about trying to understand cultures strange to us. We hear constantly of alien customs. We see changes in our lifetime which would have astonished our parents. I want to discuss here one very short way of dealing with this difficulty, a drastic way which many people now theoretically favour. It consists in simply denying that we can ever understand any culture except our own well enough to make judgements about it. Those who recommend this hold that the world is sharply divided into separate societies, sealed units, each with its own system of thought. They feel that the respect and tolerance due from one system to another forbids us ever to take up a critical position to any other culture. Moral judgement, they suggest, is a kind of coinage valid only in its country of origin.

DOI: 10.4324/9781003588160-25

I shall call this position 'moral isolationism.' I shall suggest that it is certainly not forced upon us, and indeed that it makes no sense at all. People usually take it up because they think it is a respectful attitude to other cultures. In fact, however, it is not respectful. Nobody can respect what is entirely unintelligible to them. To respect someone, we have to know enough about him to make a *favourable* judgement, however general and tentative. And we do understand people in other cultures to this extent. Otherwise a great mass of our most valuable thinking would be paralysed.

To show this, I shall take a remote example, because we shall probably find it easier to think calmly about it than we should with a contemporary one, such as female circumcision in Africa or the Chinese Cultural Revolution. The principles involved will still be the same. My example is this. There is, it seems, a verb in classical Japanese which means 'to try out one's new sword on a chance wayfarer.' (The word is *tsuji-giri*, literally 'crossroads-cut.') A Samurai sword had to be tried out because, if it was to work properly, it had to slice through someone at a single blow, from the shoulder to the opposite flank. Otherwise, the warrior bungled his stroke. This could injure his honour, offend his ancestors, and even let down his emperor. So tests were needed, and wayfarers had to be expended. Any wayfarer would do – provided, of course, that he was not another Samurai. Scientists will recognize a familiar problem about the rights of experimental subjects.

Now when we hear of a custom like this, we may well reflect that we simply do not understand it; and therefore are not qualified to criticize it at all, because we are not members of that culture. But we are not members of any other culture either, except our own. So we extend the principle to cover all extraneous cultures, and we seem therefore to be moral isolationists. But this is, as we shall see, an impossible position. Let us ask what it would involve.

We must ask first: Does the isolating barrier work both ways? Are people in other cultures equally unable to criticize us? This question struck me sharply when I read a remark in the *Guardian* by an anthropologist about a South American Indian who had been taken into a Brazilian town for an operation, which saved his life. When he came back to his village, he made several highly critical remarks about the white Brazilians' way of life. They may very well have been justified. But the interesting point was that the anthropologist called these remarks 'a damning indictment of Western civilization.' Now the Indian had been in that town about two weeks. Was he in a position to deliver a damning indictment? Would we ourselves be qualified to deliver such an indictment on the Samurai, provided we could spend two weeks in ancient Japan? What do we really think about this? My own impression is that we believe that outsiders can, in principle, deliver perfectly good indictments – only, it usually takes more than two weeks to make them damning. Understanding has degrees. It is not a slapdash yes-or-no matter. Intelligent outsiders can progress in it, and in some ways will be at an advantage over the locals. But if this is so, it must clearly apply to ourselves as much as anybody else.

Our next question is this: Does the isolating barrier between cultures block praise as well as blame? If I want to say that the Samurai culture has many virtues, or to praise the South American Indians, am I prevented from doing *that* by my outside status? Now, we certainly do need to praise other societies in this way. But it is hardly possible that we could praise them effectively if we could not, in principle, criticize them. Our praise would be worthless if it rested on no definite grounds, if it did not flow from some understanding. Certainly we may need to praise things which we do not *fully* understand. We say 'there's something very good here, but I can't quite make out what it is yet.' This happens when we want to learn from strangers. And we can learn from strangers. But to do this, we have to distinguish between those strangers who are worth learning from and those who are not. Can we then judge which is which? This brings us to our third question: What is involved in judging? Now plainly there is no question here of sitting on a bench in a red robe and sentencing people. Judging simply means forming an opinion, and expressing it if it is called for. Is there anything wrong about this? Naturally, we ought to avoid forming – and expressing – *crude* opinions, like that of a simple-minded missionary, who might dismiss the whole Samurai culture as entirely bad, because non-Christian. But this is a different objection. The trouble with crude opinions is that they are crude, whoever forms them, not that they are formed by the wrong people.

Anthropologists, after all, are outsiders quite as much as missionaries. Moral isolationism forbids us to form *any* opinions on these matters. Its ground for doing so is that we don't understand them. But there is much that we don't understand in our own culture too. This brings us to our last question: If we can't judge other cultures, can we really judge our own? Our efforts to do so will be much damaged if we are really deprived of our opinions about other societies, because these provide the range of comparison, the spectrum of alternatives against which we set what we want to understand. We would have to stop using the mirror which anthropology so helpfully holds up to us.

In short, moral isolationism would lay down a general ban on moral reasoning. Essentially, this is the programme of immoralism, and it carries a distressing logical difficulty. Immoralists like Nietzsche are actually just a rather specialized sect of moralists. They can no more afford to put moralizing out of business than smugglers can afford to abolish customs regulations. The power of moral judgement is, in fact, not a luxury, not a perverse indulgence of the self-righteous. It is a necessity. When we judge something to be bad or good, better or worse than something else, we are taking it as an example to aim at or avoid. Without opinions of this sort, we would have no framework of comparison for our own policy, no chance of profiting by other people's insights or mistakes. In this vacuum, we could form no judgements on our own actions.

Now it would be odd if *Homo sapiens* had really got himself into a position as bad as this – a position where his main evolutionary asset, his brain, was so little use to him. None of us is going to accept this sceptical diagnosis. We cannot do so, because our involvement in moral isolationism does not flow from apathy, but from a rather acute concern about human hypocrisy and other forms of wickedness. But we polarize that concern around a few selected moral truths. We are rightly angry with those who despise, oppress or steamroll other cultures. We think that doing these things is actually *wrong*. But this is itself a moral judgement. We could not condemn oppression and insolence if we thought that all our condemnations were just a trivial local quirk of our own culture. We could still less do it if we tried to stop judging altogether.

Real moral scepticism, in fact, could lead only to inaction, to our losing all interest in moral questions, most of all in those which concern other societies. When we discuss these things, it becomes instantly clear how far we are from doing this. Suppose, for instance, that I criticize the bisecting Samurai, that I say his behaviour is brutal. What will usually happen next is that someone will protest, will say that I have no right to make criticisms like that of another culture. But it is most unlikely that he will use this move to end the discussion of the subject. Instead, he will justify the Samurai. He will try to fill in the background, to make me understand the custom, by explaining the exalted ideals of discipline and devotion which produced it. He will probably talk of the lower value which the ancient Japanese placed on individual life generally. He may well suggest that this is a healthier attitude than our own obsession with security. He may add, too, that the wayfarers did not seriously mind being bisected, that in principle they accepted the whole arrangement. Now an objector who talks like this is implying that it *is* possible to understand alien customs. That is just what he is trying to make me do. And he implies, too, that if I do succeed in understanding them, I shall do something better than giving up judging them. He expects me to change my present judgement to a truer one – namely, one that is favourable. And the standards I must use to do this cannot just be Samurai standards. They have to be ones current in my own culture. Ideals like discipline and devotion will not move anybody unless he himself accepts them. As it happens, neither discipline nor devotion is very popular in the West at present. Anyone who appeals to them may well have to do some more arguing to make *them* acceptable, before he can use them to explain the Samurai. But if he does succeed here, he will have persuaded us, not just that there was something to be said for them in ancient Japan, but that there would be here as well.

Isolating barriers simply cannot arise here. If we accept something as a serious moral truth about one culture, we can't refuse to apply it – in however different an outward form – to other cultures as well, wherever circumstance admits it. If we refuse to do this, we just are not taking the other culture seriously. This becomes clear if we look at the last argument used by my objector – that of justification by consent of the victim. It is suggested that sudden bisection is quite in order, *provided* that it takes place between consenting adults. I cannot now discuss how conclusive this justification is. What I am pointing out is simply that it can only work if we believe that *consent* can make such a transaction respectable – and this is a thoroughly modern and Western idea. It would probably never occur to a Samurai: if it did, it would surprise him very much. It is *our* standard. In applying it, too, we are likely to make another typically Western demand. We shall ask for good factual evidence that the wayfarers actually do have this rather surprising taste – that they are really willing to be bisected. In applying Western standards in this way, we are not being confused or irrelevant. We are asking the questions which arise from *where we stand*, questions which we can see the sense of. We do this because asking questions which you can't see the sense of is humbug. Certainly, we can extend our questioning by imaginative effort. We can come to understand other societies better. By doing so, we may make their questions our own, or we may see that they are really forms of the questions which we are asking already. This is not impossible. It is just very hard work. The obstacles which often prevent it are simply those of ordinary ignorance, laziness and prejudice. If there were really an isolating barrier, of course, our own culture could never have been formed. It is no sealed box, but a fertile jungle of different influences – Greek, Jewish, Roman, Norse, Celtic, and so forth, into which further influences are still pouring – American, Indian, Japanese, Jamaican, you name it. The moral isolationist's picture of separate, unmixable cultures is quite unreal. People who talk about British history usually stress the value of this fertilizing mix, no doubt rightly. But this is not just an odd fact about Britain. Except for the very smallest and most remote, all cultures are formed out of many streams. All have the problem of digesting and assimilating things which, at the start, they do not understand. All have the choice of learning something from this challenge, or, alternatively, of refusing to learn, and fighting it mindlessly instead.

This universal predicament has been obscured by the fact that anthropologists used to concentrate largely on very small and remote cultures, which did not seem to have this problem. These tiny societies, which had often forgotten their own history, made neat, self-contained subjects for study.

No doubt it was valuable to emphasize their remoteness, their extreme strangeness, their independence of our cultural tradition. This emphasis was, I think, the root of moral isolationism. But, as the tribal studies themselves showed, even there the anthropologists were able to interpret what they saw and make judgements – often favourable – about the tribesmen. And the tribesmen, too, were quite equal to making judgements about the anthropologists – and about the tourists and Coca-Cola salesmen who followed them. Both sets of judgements, no doubt, were somewhat hasty, both have been refined in the light of further experience. A similar transaction between us and the Samurai might take even longer. But that is no reason at all for deeming it impossible. Morally as well as physically, there is only one world, and we all have to live in it.

PART 3

THE MYTHS OF SCIENCE

A central theme of the preceding sections has been the critique of the idea of Reason, understood as the capacity for logic and mathematics, as the essential defining characteristic of humanity. The enormous importance of this idea in recent thought derives to a large extent, of course, from the spectacular success of mathematically based science since the time of Descartes and Galileo. This success has unfortunately led to a widespread feeling that there are no limits to what Science can do; that the standards of rigour, precision and certainty which have been attained in some parts of physics can be extended to all branches of thought by the handy expedient of 'reducing' these other disciplines to physics.

Such reductionist and imperialist ambitions on behalf of science are potentially very dangerous; they encourage a one-sided development of technical knowledge and material progress at the expense of spiritual insight and cultural development. In particular, in two of her books, Mary Midgley investigated an interesting phenomenon – the

DOI: 10.4324/9781003588160-26

way in which the officially secular (and often anti-religious) culture of science can become an alternative religion in its own right. Visions of salvation, immortality, omniscience, and omnipotence every bit as extravagant as anything in the field of religion are found with surprising frequency in the writings of some scientists, who often deride philosophy and theology as empty speculation. The first of these books, *Evolution as a Religion*, grew out of the controversies surrounding evolution into which she had become drawn as a result of writing *Beast and Man*; the second, *Science as Salvation*, followed the trail into still more bizarre speculations arising out of theoretical physics, especially cosmology.

The next extract, 'Salvation and the Academics,' looks at the general nature of this phenomenon, showing that the presence of religious elements in recent scientific thinking is more frequent, and more significant, than might be supposed. The desire to find a single, impregnable structure of thought capable of answering all questions, both factual and spiritual, has not disappeared with the demise of mediaeval theocracy, but has been transferred from actual religion to a science-based substitute for it.

The three following chapters, from Evolution as a Religion, examine various aspects of quasi-religious ideas based on evolutionary theory. Notoriously, Darwin's evolutionary theory was seen as competing for a piece of intellectual territory formerly claimed by religion – the origin and destiny of Man. Although Darwin consistently refrained from engaging in metaphysical or transcendental speculations about its implications, others, both at the time and more recently, have emphatically not done so. Evolutionary theory has been the vehicle for a wide range of extravagant ideas claiming to illuminate the meaning of life, the destiny and purpose of the human race, and sometimes to provide a 'universal acid' capable of explaining everything. Two main variants on evolution-based visions of our destiny are common.

First there are those based on the idea of evolution as a linear upward progression of which Man represents the highest development to date (echoing the strand in Christian thought to the effect that the world exists for the sake of Man). This progress is assumed to be destined to continue towards the ultimate goal of a super-human being. Invariably, the 'direction' of evolution (a notion foreign to Darwin's original theory) in this story is that of increasing intellectual powers – specifically, of course, the ability to do science. In this scenario, the ultimate aim, not only of science, or even of all human activity, but of the universe itself, is to produce a 'Theory of Everything.' Our descendants (perhaps not organic beings at all but some mysterious kind of computers) would be able to be aware of an infinite quantity of information, and thereby to 'know the mind of God.'

Opposed to this Panglossian fantasy is the pessimistic vision of 'Nature Red in Tooth and Claw.' The chief lesson of evolution, according to this view, is that life is ineluctably governed by a law of ruthless selfishness. Genuine altruism, and even co-operation that is not based on hard-nosed calculation of advantage, are supposed to be impossible; hence attempts to base ethics on such values as these are misguided and should be abandoned. Though this may not appear to be a religious idea, Midgley shows that it has significant analogues in many religious cults; as she says, 'the drama to which this picture contributes is certainly spiritually ambitious enough to constitute a faith and in some sense a religion.'

The next extract, 'Biotechnology and the Yuk Factor,' addresses another form of scientific hubris in the sphere of biology. Objections to various aspects of 'bio-engineering' based on a sense that it is intrinsically wrong to tamper with the basic structure of life are seen, by those committed to the technologies in question, either as irrational religious prejudice or as an unthinking emotional reaction – the 'Yuk Factor.' The logic of commercial cost-benefit calculations, or of supposedly scientific risk-assessment, cannot do justice to the important moral insights contained in such visceral reactions. Though they cannot necessarily be cashed in such directly pragmatic terms, Midgley ably shows us how these insights can be cogently articulated into a compelling case for extreme caution in this field. The notion that we can rearrange gene sequences to produce life-forms with any characteristics we choose, and thereby produce a genetically engineered Utopia, is a good example of atomistic, reductionist thinking leading to false theology. Our simplistic conceptual schemes mislead us into believing we have the key to the Universe, and can safely play at God.

The final piece in this section, 'The Remarkable Masculine Birth of Time,' examines some of the psychological origins of this way of thinking. As she convincingly shows – anticipating a major study of the subject by Margaret Wertheim[1] – the seventeenth-century vision of a mathematically based, reductive science, through which Man would be able to conquer and control Nature, is deeply connected with patriarchal and misogynistic elements in the male psyche. Imagery of violent conquest, and of torture and rape, are routinely used in describing the scientist's quest for domination over Nature. Alongside these are frequent denunciations of the shortcomings of women – the extraordinary resistance to women scientists, often persisting into the late twentieth century, is documented in detail in Wertheim's book. As Midgley remarks elsewhere, the strident objections in some scientific quarters to James Lovelock's use of religious imagery in his Gaia theory may have more to do with the sex of the deity than with opposition to religious thinking as such.

SOURCES

'Salvation and the Academics' – abridged from *Science as Salvation: A Modern Myth and its Meaning*, Routledge, 1992, Chapter 1. 'Evolutionary Dramas' – *Evolution as a Religion: Strange Hopes and Strange Fears*, Methuen, 1985; 'The Irresistible Escalator' – abridged from *Evolution as a Religion*, Chapters 4–6; 'The Service of Self and the Service of Kali' – abridged from *Evolution as a Religion*, Chapters 14–15. 'Biotechnology and the Yuk Factor' – *The Myths We Live By*, Routledge, 2003. 'The Remarkable Masculine Birth of Time' – abridged from *Science as Salvation*, Chapters 7–8.

1. *Margaret Wertheim, Pythagoras' Trousers: God, Physics and the Gender Wars*, Fourth Estate, 1995.

20

SALVATION AND THE ACADEMICS

SALVATION IS NO LONGER OFFICIAL

The idea that we can reach salvation through science is ancient and powerful. It is by no means nonsense, but it lies at present in a good deal of confusion. Its many strands – some helpful, some not – greatly need sorting. In the seventeenth century, when modern science first arose, it was an entirely natural thought. The great thinkers of that time took it for granted as central to their endeavour. Nature was God's creation, and to study it was simply one of the many ways to celebrate his glory. That celebration was understood to be the proper destiny of the soul, the meaning of human life.

Since that time, things have changed greatly. For a number of reasons, God has been pushed into the background. The conceptual maps that he once dominated go on, however, being used as if they did not

DOI: 10.4324/9781003588160-27

need much revision. This makes trouble on many issues, and notions about the special saving power of science are among them.

Does this language of salvation seem alarmingly strong? I use it because I want to stress how deeply these matters affect all of us, not only scientists and not only intellectuals. Any system of thought playing the huge part that science now plays in our lives must also shape our guiding myths and colour our imaginations profoundly. It is not just a useful tool. It is also a pattern that we follow at a deep level in trying to meet our imaginative needs.

This book is therefore not just about our attitudes to science but about those imaginative needs. It is about myth-making, not just as a private vice, but as a vital human function. The way we use science for this function is, however, today not an acknowledged academic topic.

Officially speaking, academic studies don't now offer salvation at all. Their journals certainly don't expect to be used by people desperately seeking for the meaning of life, and such people could usually not read them anyway. As in the Tower of Babel, each discipline speaks only in its own tongue. There is no interdisciplinary language for discussing the relations of studies to one another, nor to the world around them. Least of all is there any such language for considering the general meaning for us of each study, the part that it plays in life.

Obviously, this increasing technicality in the sciences has served very important functions. What makes it troublesome today is that it leaves unserved the general need for understanding, and whatever spiritual needs lie behind it. The promise of satisfying those spiritual needs has played a great part in establishing the special glory of the abstraction 'science' in our culture, and in forging the idea that we are a scientifically minded people. It has built up a strong emotive and romantic conception of 'science' as a spiritual power – a most ambitious estimate of what this abstraction is and can do.

Recent worries about the dangers that may flow from technology have not really changed this way of thinking. These dangers are still mostly attributed to misuse of science rather than to science itself. There has indeed long been an explicit anti-science strain in our culture, with impressive ancestors such as Blake, and it has gained some strength lately. But it is still a descant – the main anthem is still one of praise. And until the last few decades, many acute and polymathic scientists were happy to explain why this high estimate of their occupation was justified.

FROM TOO MUCH TO TOO LITTLE

They are far less willing to do that now. Many scientists, if they are asked what – beyond its obvious usefulness – is the function of science, will either evade the question, make vague euphoric noises, or give answers that seem almost pathologically modest, parsimonious, and negative. They claim that they are merely humble standard operatives in an immense, impersonal falsification factory, busied solely in examining an endless succession of detailed hypotheses about the physical world and in proving most of them to be false, by a single, prefabricated 'scientific method.' In slightly less stern and more realistic moods, they may mention a conceptual background out of which these suggestions arise. But unless they have had some historical training, these scientists are most unlikely to suggest that this background could have anything to do with the rest of human thought, still less with the rest of life. The isolation of 'science' from other topics is widely held to be necessary for its purity.

There has been a remarkable move from claiming far too much to claiming far too little. C.H. Waddington, in his book *The Scientific Attitude* (1941), noted what had already begun to happen.

> Responsible scientists, looking at their colleagues, saw the obvious fact that most specialists were quite unfitted to play an important part in the evolution of general culture; but, far from acknowledging that this was a sign of science's failure, they accepted it almost with glee as an excuse which let them out of the necessity of thinking about wider issues.[1]

In fairness, we should notice that many specialists in the humanities do this too, and with even less excuse. But the special hopes that the age places on science make its withdrawal a particularly serious matter. Nobody today supposes that the distinction of our epoch depends on its being a historical, or a literary, or a philosophical one. But they do suppose that about its being scientific.

It is easy to see how the specialists' rather frantic modesty arose. It was a reaction against excess. Philosophers of science invented it as a way of disqualifying the Marxist and Freudian sages who claimed the prestige of science for their vast metaphysical systems. In particular, in Britain, the last great generation of Marxist polymaths – Needham, Bernal, Haldane, and the rest – were most alarming to less well-educated scientists. They were charismatic, popular and learned writers, using the authority of science skilfully to back their political views. Thus, Bernal argued that communism was simply the logical conclusion of the whole scientific endeavour:

> Already we have in the practice of science the prototype for all common human action . . . The methods by which this task is attempted, however imperfectly they are realized, are the methods by which humanity is most likely to secure its own future. In its endeavour, science is communism.[2]

Now people like Bernal could certainly have been answered. But answering them was not specialized scientific work; it involved wider thinking. More orthodox scientists who wanted to avoid this saw that it would be easier to outlaw these unfairly well-educated sages instead by narrowing the idea of 'science,' so as to shut their kind of speculation out of it by definition.

They therefore contracted science and pulled up the drawbridge. A disturbance followed when it was noticed that they had accidentally left the whole of evolutionary theory outside in the unscientific badlands as well. But special arrangements were made to pull it in without compromising the principle. That principle was to minimize the business of 'science' – to define it as narrowly as possible, confining its prestige to detailed, provable, specialized work.

THE EXALTATION OF NOT BEING WRONG

Was this wise? People choosing this policy were assuming that the prestige, the value of science, centres on never making a mistake – on precision, specialization, and infallible correctness. But is that its real point? Science surely has a more positive value, both for the world at large and for scientists themselves when they are not making this kind of defence. The glory of science is not that it never makes mistakes, which is plainly false anyway. It is much more a matter of dealing with supremely interesting topics – matters that can seriously affect the way we see human life.

For instance, the conception of order in the universe is a crucial background to our thought, and just how that order is conceived – just what kind of causal necessity we picture – affects the whole arrangement of our concepts. Again, the way in which we think of the relation between our own species and all other living things is an essential element in shaping our inner maps. So is the notion that we have of 'life' – of the meaning of the difference between what is living and what is not.

The idea that science really matters, that it has a key place in shaping the rest of thought, still prevails, and is far more than just a conviction of its indirect usefulness through technology. When Karl Popper – often inclined to minimalism – made in 1972 the startling claim that science is 'perhaps the most powerful tool for biological adaptation which has ever emerged in the course of organic evolution,'[3] he was plainly thinking of it as something immensely larger than the accumulation of unconnected, detailed, negative facts. He was indeed claiming for it a status considerably higher than the one Waddington had outlined for his own much wider conception of science thirty years earlier. Waddington said:

> Science *by itself* is able to provide mankind with a way of life which is, firstly, self-consistent and harmonious, and, secondly, free for the exercise of that objective reason on which our material progress depends.

So far as I can see, *the scientific attitude of mind is the only one which is, at the present day, adequate in both these respects.* There are many other worthy ideals which might supplement it, but I cannot see that any of them could take its place as the basis of a progressing and rich society.[4]

(Emphases mine)

This exalted status obviously could not be claimed for a mere batch of stored facts, however large. Stored facts are like stored tools or stored musical instruments, valueless unless you know how to use them, how to connect them with other things, how to understand them. It is surely the interpretative scheme, not the stored data waiting to be interpreted, that we have in mind when we make large claims like this for the value of science.

THE HIGH HOPES

Clearly, many people still think science quite as important as Popper and Waddington did. Putting it crudely, many people have long looked, and still do look, to science for an important aspect of their salvation, and these are by no means only people who themselves know much science. If the public had not to some extent shared this hope, it would scarcely have spent even as much money as it has on pure research. Many scientists themselves, too, would probably not have chosen it as the occupation of their lives if they had not agreed with them. There are many branches of science, perhaps particularly in theoretical physics, which students choose because of a vision of how the world fundamentally is, a vision in which they have faith and which they want to follow out in detail.

In spite of today's official modesty, large claims revealing this kind of faith still constantly appear in books that officially do nothing to back them. There has, indeed, recently been an exuberant expansion of claims to moral and intellectual territory which earlier pioneers of modern science sternly disowned.

In particular, there are today what seem to be renewed offers of an explanation in terms of purpose – something which physical science has officially forsworn since the time of Galileo. Thus, Richard

Dawkins joyfully proclaims that, since we now have modern biology, 'we no longer have to resort to superstition when faced with the *deep problems; Is there a meaning to life? What are we for? What is man?*'[5] (emphasis mine). Dawkins offers science as able to deal with all that, and as the only alternative to superstition in doing so. Similarly, Stephen Hawking speaks of his cosmological enquiry as a response to an ancient, timeless human longing:

> Ever since the dawn of civilization, people . . . have craved an understanding of the underlying order in the world. Today we still yearn to know *why we are here* and where we came from. Humanity's deepest desire for knowledge is justification enough for our continuing quest. And our goal is nothing less than a complete description of the universe we live in.[6]

A complete description? Is there such a thing? Since there is, in principle, no limit to the questions that might need answering, it is not a clear idea, but does it even point in the right direction? Would a complete description, of the kind that could be approached through science, be the kind of answer expected by the question 'why are we here?' Hawking writes that when a satisfactory cosmological theory has emerged,

> we shall all – philosophers, scientists and just ordinary people – be able to take part in the discussion of the question *why it is that we and the universe exist*. If we find the answer to that, it would be the ultimate triumph of human reason – for then we would know *the mind of God*.[7]
>
> (Emphases mine)

In what sense could modern cosmology be pointing towards that? Does it seem plausible that this ancient, universal human longing was always a desire for the kind of scientific theory that Hawking and his colleagues now hope to forge? This would be strange, since before the last few hundred years, nobody anywhere ever dreamt of looking for that kind of theory. Even today very few people in the world have heard of it.

The ancient desire was surely a quite different one. It was a desire for kinds of explanation that are both much wider and more immediate. The wish to know 'why we are here' unmistakably asks a question about the point and purpose of existence. The word is 'why,' not 'how.' The ancient question is not about the remote physical causes that may have made that existence possible – it is a purpose-question; it is teleological. The phrase, 'the mind of God,' too, could scarcely cover a mere account of causes. It cannot avoid referring to purpose.

Incidentally, the word God, which suddenly appears at several points in Hawking's argument, badly needs explaining. It is notoriously a most obscure and ambiguous word, yet it gets no discussion and does not figure in either the index or the glossary to *A Brief History of Time*. It is treated as unproblematic. Hawking doesn't, in fact, seem to have heard that many people – anthropologists, historians of thought, philosophers, theologians – have already done a lot of useful work on such matters, have detected many of the more obvious bugs in the program, and could have saved him some unnecessary confusion.

QUESTIONS ABOUT TELEOLOGY

This is not just a cheap jibe at Hawking. The point is central to our theme. Teleology – reasoning from purpose – is, I believe, a much more pervasive, much less dispensable element in human thought than has usually been noticed. I will suggest that it is doubtful, in fact, whether our imaginations can work at all without it. General attacks on it have often indeed exposed misuses of it – pieces of bad and ill-controlled teleology. But the idea of dropping it altogether may not be much more practical than that of stopping breathing. Purpose-centred thinking is woven into all our serious attempts to understand anything, and above all into those of science.

HOW MUCH DOES MEANING MEAN?

The idea that we need to think teleologically is not fashionable today, and may be dismissed as extravagant. I will suggest that that dismissal grows less plausible once you notice the extravagance and implausibility of the views that are supposed to displace it – the bugs now infesting the idea of radically mindless matter. The suspicious reader can perhaps put off worrying about my suggestions for curing these infestations until we have had a good look at them.

It may be best, too, to repeat that there is no need at the moment for that alarmed reader to reach for the anti-God button. This attribution of meaning to orderly phenomena is something extremely modest, mild, and general. It is nothing as bold and specific as an Argument from Design to an intelligent, humanoid creator. It is simply the assigning of orderly things by our minds to a different mental category from the 'buzzing, blooming confusion' that wallows behind them, the disorderly background of undigested experience.

The point is just that this category of the intelligible necessarily counts as akin to mind, because the order we detect in it is of the kind our minds acknowledge. It is quite true that the religions have grown out of this unifying, ordering vision. But then, so have the sciences. The kinship between these two ways of thinking is far closer than has been recognized. The idea that being scientific simply means being irreligious is a particularly naive one. It has caused a lot of confusion and will get us nowhere.[8]

Anyone who doubts this might like to try the experiment of finding more suitable, antiseptic words to replace the religious language used in a certain famous exchange between Einstein and Bohr. Disturbed by the implication of real disorder in Bohr's interpretation of quantum mechanics, Einstein said, 'God does not play dice.' Bohr replied, 'Einstein, stop telling God what to do.'[9] Because Bohr is held to have won this debate and his views are still widely accepted, this conversation is now widely quoted in discussions of the topic. But those quoting it seldom offer a carefully secular paraphrase to show just what he had established, nor do they explain why this language struck these great men as so well fitted for their purpose.

The close dependence of all scientific explanation on mental concepts has become still clearer lately in the widespread use of terms like *communication* and *information* to describe all sorts of non-conscious interactions. Why are these metaphors proving so helpful, so enormously convenient that some people do not notice they are metaphors at all? Such people innocently suppose that to say 'DNA contains the necessary information' is to say something as straightforward as that it contains the necessary carbon and hydrogen.

More perceptive writers guard themselves against animism by explaining that DNA does not literally think or talk. But they still do not often ask themselves *why* it should be so helpful – indeed so essential – to go on as if it did. Exactly what parts of the comparison are useful? Why is it so necessary? How should we speak if we were not allowed to use it? The use of such categories is, I believe, a necessary condition of the way our minds work on such subjects. We understand today that it is a bad idea to exterminate the natural fauna of the human gut. But trying to exterminate the natural fauna and flora of the human imagination is perhaps no more sensible. We have a choice of what myths, what visions we will use to help us understand the physical world. We do not have a choice of understanding it without using any myths or visions at all. Again, we have a real choice between becoming aware of these myths and ignoring them. If we ignore them, we travel blindly inside myths and visions which are largely provided by other people. This makes it much harder to know where we are going.

Acknowledging matter as somehow akin to and penetrated by mind is not adding a new, extravagant assumption to our existing thought-system. It is becoming aware of something we are doing already. The humbug of pretending that we could carry on intellectual life in an intrinsically unintelligible world is akin to the humbug of pretending that we could live without depending on other people. Just as we wildly claim to stand only on our own feet, without any help from others, so we wildly claim that we would be quite capable of 'imposing order' on an intrinsically disordered universe. In both cases, we take for granted an external support without which we could not live, and pride ourselves on managing so cleverly without it. There is nothing parsimonious about this kind of conceit.

WHY DOES SCIENCE WORK?

Behind these questions lies a vast issue about mind and matter, which this book cannot of course resolve. I am trying here only to get past a few bad supposed solutions to it, which at present block thought on a really interesting topic. As may be plain, this topic is essentially the one which caused Einstein often to remark that the really surprising thing about science is that it works at all. Puzzlement does not arise out of some eccentric and optional religious enquiry, but out of the simple observation that the laws of thought turn out to be the laws of things. As C.S. Lewis put it:

> We find that matter always obeys the same laws which our logic obeys . . . No one can suppose that this can be due to a happy coincidence. A great many people think that it is due to the fact that Nature produces the mind. But on the assumption that Nature is herself mindless, this provides no explanation. To be the result of a series of mindless events is one thing; to be a kind of plan or true account of the laws according to which these mindless events happen is quite another . . . It is as if cabbages, in addition to resulting from the laws of botany, also gave lectures in that subject . . . We must seek the real explanation elsewhere.
>
> I want to put this other explanation in the broadest possible terms and am anxious that you should not imagine I am trying to prove anything more, or more definite, than I really am . . . *Unless all that we take to be knowledge is an illusion, we must hold that in thinking we are not reading rationality into an irrational universe, but responding to a rationality with which the universe has always been saturated.*[10]
>
> (Emphasis mine)

As he notes, this might lead to many sorts of philosophical positions, not necessarily theistic ones. To find our way, I shall simply try to do something crude which is often helpful in such cases – namely, to point out some very bad ideas that are currently accepted. By seeing what not to think, we can often move towards the parts of the map which will help us. Besides, the appeal of certain mistakes often lights up aspects of the problem which we would otherwise miss.

LISTENING TO THE IMAGINATION

In considering all this, I believe that we must attend seriously to myths, metaphors, images, and the other half-conscious apparatus of thought surrounding the official doctrines. I shall point out strange compensatory fantasies found in the work of various scientific writers – some of whom have been, in theory, austerely bent on disinfecting the world of traditional teleology – noting how they often seem to end up with a far cruder, less rational teleological doctrine than those they were attacking. Throw purpose out through the door, and it seems to creep in up the drains and through the central heating.

Scientific reviewers, when discussing writings of this kind, often treat the myths as a side issue. Concentrating on what is acceptable as science, they expect the rest to fade away harmlessly into the general culture. But it does not necessarily do this. It can hang around like a fog, changing the atmosphere of thought and influencing ideas quite strongly. It tends to be the part of a book that people remember. In particular, it can be expected to have a strong effect on students.

Attending to the workings of the scientific imagination is not a soft option, and it is not mere gossip. This material has a far closer, more organic connection with our official thinking than may appear. It is not just a harmless, licensed amusement. It plays a part in shaping the world-pictures that determine our standards of thought – the standards by which we judge what is possible and plausible.

THE REINFLATION OF PHYSICS

Recent attempts to make traditional materialism consistent have often resulted in making it romantic, superstitious, and irrationalistic. There have also been lately, as already mentioned, a number of attempts by cosmologists to expand materialism by recolonizing, as an official part of their subject, territories formerly ruled illicit, in particular, by relegitimizing teleology.

Since the Big Bang became widely accepted, the urge to find some sort of purposive story for the cosmos has become almost irresistible. (If, as now seems possible, theorists dissolve the Big Bang again, it will be interesting to see what becomes of this trend.) This attempt to think about cosmic purpose would surely be legitimate if it were approached realistically, with some recognition of our own ignorance and the scale of the task. It should start from some serious enquiry about the tools, aims and capacities involved. It would mean investigating first the legitimate and illegitimate workings of the human imagination, the way in which we organize our own purposes, and our moral relation to the biosphere we live in.

To do this, however, it would have to start modestly by examining that given human centre, by looking into our own thoughts and the affairs with which we are familiar. There would be no assurance at all of directly detecting by science the grand history of the whole. That, however, is what is at present projected. Vast and gratifying conclusions about cosmic matters are drawn directly from very slender theoretical arguments, arguments that are often scarcely scrutinized because they peep out only briefly, like very early mammals, from a protective thicket of equations.

NOTES

1. C.H. Waddington, *The Scientific Attitude* (West Drayton, Penguin, 1941), p. 81.
2. J.D. Bernal, *The Social Function of Science* (London, Routledge & Kegan Paul, 1939), concluding paragraph.
3. K.R. Popper, *Objective Knowledge* (Oxford, Clarendon Press, 1972), p. 237. *The Scientific Attitude*, p. 170.
4. C.H. Waddington, *The Scientific Attitude* (West Drayton, Penguin, 1941), p. 170.
5. R. Dawkins, *The Selfish Gene* (London, Granada, Paladin, 1978), p. 1.
6. S.W. Hawking, *A Brief History of Time* (London, Bantam Press, 1988), p. 13.
7. Ibid., p. 175.
8. See a most illuminating discussion in G. Richards, *On Psychological Language* (London, Routledge, 1989), Chapter 1.
9. For this whole dispute, see the opening sections of *Quantum Theory and Measurement*, ed. J.A. Wheeler and W.H. Zurek (Princeton, Princeton University Press, 1983).
10. C.S. Lewis, *Christian Reflections* (Glasgow, Collins, Fount, 1967), p. 89.

21

EVOLUTIONARY DRAMAS

There is grandeur in this view of life.

Charles Darwin

SCIENCE AND SYMBOLISM

The theory of evolution is not just an inert piece of theoretical science. It is, and cannot help being, also a powerful folk-tale about human origins. Any such narrative must have symbolic force. We are probably the first culture not to make that its main function. Most stories about human origins must have been devised purely with a view to symbolic and poetic fittingness. Suggestions about how we were made and where we come from are bound to engage our imagination, to shape our views of what we now are, and so to affect our lives. Scientists, when they find themselves caught up in these webs of symbolism, sometimes complain, calling for a sanitary cordon to keep them away

DOI: 10.4324/9781003588160-28

from science. But this seems to be both psychologically and logically impossible.

Our theoretical curiosity simply is not detached in this way from the rest of our life. Nor do scientists themselves always want it to be so. Some of the symbolic webs are ones which they approve of, and promote as part of the ideal of science itself. For instance, Jacques Monod, as an atheistical biochemist, does not just rejoice at getting rid of the theistic drama. He at once replaces it by another drama, just as vivid, emotive, and relevant to life, in which Sartrian man appears as the lonely hero challenging an alien and meaningless universe:

> It is perfectly true that science attacks values. Not directly, since science is no judge of them and must ignore them; but it subverts every one of the mythical or philosophical ontogenies upon which the animist tradition, from the Australian aborigines to the dialectical materialists, has based morality, values, duties, rights, prohibitions. If he accepts this message in its full significance, man must at last wake out of his millenary dream and discover his total solitude, his fundamental isolation. He must realize that, like a gypsy, he lives on the boundary of an alien world; a world that is deaf to his music, and as indifferent to his hopes as it is to his sufferings or his crimes.[1]

But 'discovering his total solitude' is just adopting one imaginative stance among many possible ones. Other good scientists, very differently, have used the continuity of our species with the rest of the physical world to reprove human arrogance and to call for practical recognition of kinship with other creatures. Many, like Darwin and the great geneticist Theodosius Dobzhansky, have held that an attitude of awe and veneration for the wonders of the physical world is an essential condition for studying them properly. Others have talked in a more predatory way about the joys of the chase and the triumph of catching facts. Both motives, and many others, are evidently so habitual in science that they are only not mentioned because they are taken for granted.

It seems often to be assumed that they are therefore irrelevant, that Science itself is something so pure and impersonal that it ought to be thought of in complete abstraction from all the motives that might lead people to practise it. This, unfortunately, cannot work because of the importance of world-pictures. Facts are not gathered in a vacuum, but to fill gaps in a world-picture which already exists. And the shape of this world-picture – determining the matters allowed for in it, the principles of selection, the possible range of emphases – depends deeply on the motives for forming it in the first place. Imagination, which guides thought, is directed by our attitudes. For instance, predatory and competitive motives tend to produce a picture dominated by competition and predation – one in which these elements do not only play their part, as they did for Darwin, but are arbitrarily and dogmatically isolated as sole rulers. Thus, in a familiar distortion which will concern us repeatedly, the sociobiologist M.T. Ghiselin flatly declares:

> The evolution of society fits the Darwinian paradigm in its most individualistic form. The economy of nature is competitive from beginning to end. Understand that economy, and how it works, and the underlying reasons for social phenomena are manifest. They are the means by which one organism gains some advantage to the detriment of another. No hint of genuine charity ameliorates our vision of society, once sentimentalism has been laid aside. What passes for co-operation turns out to be a mixture of opportunism and exploitation.
>
> The impulses that lead one animal to sacrifice himself for another turn out to have their ultimate rationale in gaining advantage over a third, and acts for the good of one 'society' turn out to be performed for the detriment of the rest. Where it is in his own interest, every organism may reasonably be expected to aid his fellows. Where he has no alternative, he submits to the yoke of servitude. Yet, given a full chance to act in his own interest, nothing but expediency will restrain him from brutalizing, from maiming, from murdering – his brother, his mate, his parent, or his child. Scratch an 'altruist' and watch a 'hypocrite' bleed.[2]

As we shall see, this claim is essentially pure fantasy, not only unsupported by the empirical facts which are supposed to be its grounds, but actually contrary to them, such as they are. Is this a quite exceptional aberration? Some will suspect that it must be, not only because the world-picture involved is a bad one, but because scientists ought to be so impartial that they either do not have anything so unprofessional as a world-picture at all, or, if they have one, do not let it affect their work. But this is a mistaken ideal. An enquirer with no such general map would only be an obsessive – someone who had a special motive for collecting facts indiscriminately. He would not be a person without an attitude, or without special motives, but one with motives so odd as to inhibit the kind of organizing activity which normally shapes people's ideas into some sort of coherent whole. Merely to pile up information indiscriminately is an idiot's task.

Good scientists do not approximate to that ideal at all. They tend to have a very strong guiding imaginative system. Their world-picture is usually a positive and distinctive one, with its own special drama. They do not scrupulously avoid conveying any sense of dark and light, of what matters and what does not, of what is to be aimed at and what avoided at all costs. They use the lights and shadows to reveal the landscape. Like those who argue usefully on any other subject, they do their best work not by being neutral but by having strong preferences, being aware of them, criticizing them carefully, expressing them plainly and then leaving their readers to decide how far to share them.

Symbolism, then, is not just a nuisance to be got rid of. It is essential. Facts will never appear to us as brute and meaningless; they will always organize themselves into some sort of story, some drama. These dramas can indeed be dangerous. They can distort our theories, and they have distorted the theory of evolution perhaps more than any other. The only way in which we can control this kind of distortion is, I believe, to bring the dramas themselves out into the open, to give them our full attention, understand them better and see what part, if any, each of them ought to play both in theory and in life. It is no use merely to swipe at them from time to time, like troublesome insects, while officially attending only to the theoretical questions. This will not make them go away, because they are a serious feature of life.

DARWIN'S BALANCE

The drama that attends a theory need not, then, be mere melodrama. When sensationalism is present, it is either irrelevant or – if it really belongs to a theory – shows that that theory is bad. The drama that goes with a good theory is simply the expressive aspect of the theory itself. In order of time, it is often conceived in advance of much of the supporting evidence. But when further facts accumulate, it ought to respond to them by refining and subtilizing its cruder outlines. This process usually makes it less extreme and one-sided, and so moves it away from the gratuitous sensationalism which marks melodrama. That does not make it less stirring or less important for life; it can make it more so. This imaginative and emotional deepening is part of the growth of a theory, not just a chance ornament. When the young Darwin immersed himself in the arguments about cosmic purpose in Paley's theological textbook *The Evidences of Christianity*, and repeatedly read *Paradise Lost* on exploring trips from the *Beagle*,[3] he was neither wasting his time nor distorting his scientific project. He was seriously working his way through a range of life-positions which lay on the route to the one he could finally use.

The result of this long preliminary pilgrimage was to make his own picture unusually balanced and inclusive. To keep it so is, however, terribly hard. He himself made clear that he felt this difficulty deeply, and was constantly dissatisfied with his efforts, constantly changing his books to do justice to some neglected angle. The vastness of the truth and the one-sidedness of formulae always haunted him.

This haunting by no means reduced his work to an undramatic neutrality. Instead, the tension of opposites makes the drama which he shows us comprehensive and Shakespearian, so that it includes every mood. Gillian Beer has lately pointed out how rich his style is in fertile metaphors and models, which he continually uses to supplement and correct each other.[4] Centrally, he will not lose hold of either of the two emotional responses which belong most naturally to evolutionary speculation – on the one hand, optimistic, joyful wonder at the profusion of nature, and on the other, pessimistic, sombre alarm at its wasteful cruelty. Since he cannot qualify every sentence, selective quotation often makes him seem enslaved to one or other of these attitudes. And others who have made real efforts to come to terms with the conflict have been misrepresented in the same sort of way.

No malice is needed for this distortion. Even given goodwill, the difficulty is immense. What is needed is not just a set of rules for handling factual disputes, of the kind which is recognized as part of scientific training. Since this vast issue involves our whole view of our place in the world, discussion of it calls out and reflects the whole shape of the character. The way in which we treat it inevitably reveals our weaknesses and prejudices. Dozens of awkward truths about ourselves are relevant to this subject; our avoidance of any of them projects a distortion onto the screen of our theory. Obviously we shall never escape their influence. What is needed is the kind of effort which Darwin made to become aware of them, to separate them from the more narrowly factual issues, and to watch out for their dangers. Am I exaggerating these dangers? Some physical scientists are likely to feel that the kind of thing I have been describing does indeed happen in other disciplines, notably in the humanities, but does not normally happen in their own, and cannot really have mattered to Darwin. I only wish that they were right.

The destructive message of this book is a somewhat dismal one. It concerns the sort of trouble which arises when, with writers less careful than Darwin, the dramas take over. About evolution, theory itself has again and again been distorted by biases flowing from oversimple, unbalanced world-pictures. The trouble does not, of course, lie in mere wish-fulfilment of the obvious kind which paints the world as we should like it to be. It involves being obsessed with a picture so colourful and striking that it numbs thought about the evidence required to support it. Standards of proof then fall headlong.

Half the trouble of course takes place out of sight, in the mere choice of problems, in taking some things for granted and being quite unpersuadable about others, in unconsciously placing the burden of proof on one's opponents, and sometimes in pure tribal feeling which confines one's attention to the fellow-specialists who already share one's premises. Of course, it is true that the resulting mistakes are usually not as bad as the exaggerated forms in which they are reflected by outsiders, and also that they are 'not part of science.' Mistakes never are. But since what is needed in order to correct them is not to avoid all world-pictures altogether, but to form better ones, this whole process is a matter for real scientific concern.

FALSE LIGHTS

There are two distortions in particular which will mainly concern us here, and they had better be indicated, however crudely, right away. Neither is new; both have often been denounced. But both persist, not just in the minds of outsiders ignorant of evolutionary theory, but also in those of many scientists who develop and expound it. The first is the better known and the more obviously pernicious. It is the 'Social Darwinist' idea, expressed by Ghiselin, that life has been scientifically proved to be essentially competitive, in some sense which exposes all social feeling as somehow mere humbug and illusion. The phrase 'survival of the fittest' has been used, ever since Herbert Spencer first coined it, to describe an individualistic law showing such things as cooperation, love, and altruism to be unreal, a law which (somewhat mysteriously) both demands and predicts that they should always give way to self-interest.

This has often been exposed as nonsense. Since many very successful species of social animals, including our own, have evolved these traits, have survived by them and continue to live by them, their unreality cannot be the message of evolutionary theory. But because of its strong dramatic force, as well as various political uses, this notion persists through repeated attempts to correct it, and often twists up the ideas even of those who think they are helping to get rid of it. It is especially troublesome in the American sociobiology debate, where its wide publicity makes it, just now, the most prominent hotbed of noisy errors about evolution.

The second main distortion may be called Panglossism, or the Escalator Fallacy. It is the idea that evolution is a steady, linear upward movement, a single inexorable process of improvement, leading (as a disciple of Herbert Spencer's put it) 'from gas to genius'[5] and beyond into some superhuman spiritual stratosphere. This idea, first put forward by Jean-Baptiste Lamarck at the beginning of the nineteenth century,[6] convinced Spencer instantly and completely.

It did not convince Darwin at all. He thought it vacuous, pointed out the obscurity of the metaphor 'higher,' and relied on no such paid-up cosmic insurance policy to bail out the human race. He developed his own view of selection on the humbler model of a bush – a rich radiation of varying forms, in which human qualities cannot, any more than any others, determine a general direction for the whole.

Here too, however, what he rejected has been kept by many people as a central feature of the idea of evolution and seen as a key part of 'Darwinism.' Still unsupported by argument, it too continues to produce some extremely strange theorizing, and in its less obvious way also to do a great deal of damage. These two kinds of drama are, in fact, the shapes into which the two main strands of feeling about evolution naturally develop, if they are not held in balance and forced to correct each other. They are the hypertrophied forms of cosmic pessimism and cosmic optimism, respectively. Since both these moods are common, theory-builders often oscillate between them rather casually and produce views which owe something to both. Unluckily, this is not the same thing as the synthesis which Darwin attempted. It can merely give us the worst of both worlds.

NOTES

1. J. Monod, *Chance and Necessity*, tr. A. Wainhouse (London, Fontana, 1974), p. 160.
2. M.T. Ghiselin, *The Economy of Nature and the Evolution of Sex* (Berkeley University of California Press, 1974), p. 247.
3. For both these influences see G. Beer's excellent discussions in *Darwin's Plots: Evolutionary Narrative in Darwin, George Eliot and Nineteenth Century Fiction* (London, Routledge & Kegan Paul, 1984), especially pp. 30–40 and 83–8.
4. ibid.

5. Quoted by J. Moore, *The Post-Darwinian Controversies; A Study of the Protestant Struggle to Come to Terms with Darwin in Great Britain and America 1870–1900* (Cambridge, Cambridge University Press, 1979), p. 167, from Edward Clodd.

6. In his Philosophie Zoologique (1809) and Histoire Naturelle des Animaux sans Vertèbres (1815–22).

22

THE IRRESISTIBLE ESCALATOR

When the unclean spirit is gone out of a man, he walketh through dry places, seeking rest, and findeth none. Then he saith; I will return into my house from whence I came out; and when he is come, he findeth it empty, swept and garnished. Then goeth he and taketh with himself seven other spirits more wicked than himself, and they enter in and dwell there. And the last state of that man is worse than the first.

Gospel according to St Matthew 12: 43–5

THE KALEIDOSCOPE RESHAKEN

Evolution, then, is the creation myth of our age. By telling us our origins, it shapes our views of what we are. It influences not just our thought but our feelings and actions too, in a way which goes far beyond its official function as a biological theory. To call it a myth does not of course mean that it is a false story. It means that it has great symbolic power, which is independent of its truth.

DOI: 10.4324/9781003588160-29

How far the word 'religion' is appropriate to it will of course depend on the sense we finally give to that very elastic word. In any case, however, it seems worthwhile to notice the remarkable variety of elements which it covers, and their present strange behaviour. While traditional Christianity held those elements together in an apparently changeless and inevitable grouping, we did not notice how diverse they were. But now that the violent changes of modern life have shaken them apart, they are drifting about and cropping up in unexpected places. Ambiguity of the same fruitful but dangerous kind affects the names of other complex human concerns – names such as *morality, politics, art, sport* and indeed *science*. This ambiguity is dangerous when we do not properly understand it, when we treat these complex conceptual groupings as if they were plain, single ideas. Confusion gets worse when displaced elements migrate from one main grouping to another. And today, a surprising number of the elements which used to belong to traditional religion have regrouped themselves under the heading of science, mainly around the concept of evolution.

The first thing I want to do here is to draw attention to this phenomenon, an alarming one, surely, above all for those who hold that getting rid of religion is itself a prime aim of science. If the fungicide shares the vices of the fungus, something seems to have gone wrong. But the phenomenon is of wider interest than this to all of us. Why does it happen? Why is this kind of cosmic mythology so strong and so persistent?

The simplest explanation, no doubt, would be mere force of habit, the still-surviving toxic effect of Christian conditioning. But that is not a plausible story today. The days of really confident Christian education are simply too far behind us, and the leading myth-bearers are themselves too rebellious, too critical, too consciously and resolutely anti-Christian. If they are indeed the mental prisoners of their opponent, in an age when fashion is on their side and so much change is so easily accepted, there has to be a special reason for it. The power of these ideas still remains to be accounted for. This indeed is often somewhat uneasily recognized, but the explanations given for it tend to be crude and hasty. The matter is too important for this. We need very badly to understand the influences involved.

In trying to understand them, we shall, I believe, do best if we detach ourselves as far as possible from the old Voltairean notion of a ding-dong battle between science and religion. Enquiring more calmly, we shall, I think, find that there is not one all-embracing reason why religious elements persist, but many distinct though related ones. Religion, like other complex human concerns, seems to be built up out of a wide set of natural tendencies which can be variously combined, so that it itself varies enormously in character according to the way in which we relate them. The same is true of science and also of art. Attempts to eliminate any such main grouping merely scatter its component tendencies in their crudest form to join other colonies. (Puritan attempts to get rid of art have shown this very plainly.) If we want to attack the evils infesting any special grouping, we need to look at it carefully to see just what its actual elements are at the time, and how far they necessarily go together.

Classical Greek, for instance, had no word for 'religion' at all, and certainly arranged what we think of as its elements differently from how we do. Chinese, it seems, not only has no word for 'religion' but none for 'God' either, which causes difficulties for missionaries. It would be very short-sighted to suppose that this state of affairs flowed from an absence of what we call religion, and more enlightening to suggest that it meant a greater pervasiveness of it, whereby it was taken for granted all over the texture of life. The stark division of life into sacred and profane often posited in the west has not been attempted in China. Religion is less of a detached, specialized matter.

Whatever the merits and demerits of this, it is probably important for us, and especially for those of us who distrust religion, not to suppose that current western definitions of it are necessarily the last word. This is specially important in connection with those definitions devised in the nineteenth-century positivist tradition to show religion as a childhood stage in the development of the human race, something which the west was rapidly outgrowing, though primitive peoples still unfortunately remained bogged down in it. More honest anthropology and history have made this tendentious, patronizing stance impossible today. We need a far more open mind. Perhaps indeed the concept of religion may be asked to look again at the Delphic inscription, 'know thyself.' But if so, the concept of science must certainly be asked to accompany it.

PIE IN THE FUTURE: PROPHECIES AND PROMISES

We had better start by glancing at a few typical cases of the phenomenon in question: occasions when science appears to be stealing its supposed opponent's clothes. In this chapter, I shall concentrate on prophecies, because they provide a specially clear example. It is a standard charge against religion that it panders to wish-fulfilment, consoling people for their present miseries by promising wonders in the future, thus dishonestly gaining support by dogmatic and unwarranted predictions. With this charge in mind, let us look at the concluding passage of an otherwise sober, serious and reputable book on the chemical origins of life on earth. The writer, a molecular biologist, having discussed evolution and described it, tendentiously but unemotionally, as a steady increase in intelligence, turns his attention to the future. Mankind, he says, is likely to throw up a new, distinct, and more intelligent type, which will then become 'reproductively isolated.' He then goes on (and I have not cheated by removing any words like 'possibly' or 'perhaps'):

> He [man] will splinter into types of humans with differing mental faculties that will lead to diversification and separate species. From among these types, a new species, Omega man, will emerge either alone, in union with others, or with mechanical amplification to transcend to new dimensions of time and space beyond our comprehension – as much beyond our imagination as our world was to the emerging eucaryotes . . . If evolution is to proceed through the line of man to a next higher form, there must exist within man's nature the making of Omega man . . . Omega man's comprehension and participation in the dimensions of the supernatural is what man yearns for himself,

but cannot have. It is reasonable to assume that man's intellect is not the ultimate, but merely represents a stage intermediate between the primates and Omega man. What comprehension and powers over Nature Omega man will command can only be suggested by man's image of the supernatural.[1]

Do any doubts arise? Just one. There may be a problem about timing. Major steps in evolution have been occurring at steadily decreasing intervals, and the next one may be due shortly. It must be the one the writer is waiting for. He adds: 'On such a shortened curve, conceivably Omega man could succeed man in fewer than 10,000 years.' Ordinary evolution, however, is too slow to allow of this startling development. So what is to be done? The reply comes briskly.

How then can Omega man arise in so short a time? The answer is unavoidable.
Man will make him.

This is apparently a reference to genetic engineering, something specially important to those whose faith leans heavily on the dramatic idea of infallible, escalator-type evolution. They demand from that idea, not just an inspiring account of the past, but also hope for continued progress in the future. But the human race cannot be confidently expected to evolve further in a literal, biological sense. Human social arrangements, even in simple cultures, block normal natural selection. And the more elaborate they get, the more they do so. Nineteenth-century Social Darwinists attacked this problem with a meat-axe, calling for deliberate eugenic selection and harsh commercial competition, so that the race could go back to being properly weeded and could continue to progress. As we now know, however, these schemes were not just odious but futile. The scale was wrong. Commercial competition has no tendency to affect reproduction. And as for 'positive eugenics,' it is not possible to identify desirable genes nor to force people to breed for them. Even if it were, their spread would still be absurdly slow.

The natural conclusion is that such schemes should be dropped, that the human race must take itself as it is, with its well-known vast powers of cultural adaptation, and make the best of its existing capacities. But this thought is unbearable to those whose faith in life is pinned to the steady, continuing, upwards escalator of biological evolution. 'If evolution is to proceed through the line of man to a next higher form,' as Day puts it, there simply has to be another way. That wish, rather than the amazingly thin argument he produces about recurrent evolutionary steps, is evidently the ground of his confidence. This confidence itself is of course not new. In the 1930s, the geneticist H. J. Muller made a very similar prediction:

> And so we foresee the history of life divided into three main phases. In the long preparatory phase it was the helpless creature of its environment, and natural selection gradually ground it into a human shape.
>
> In the second – our own short transitional phase – it reaches out at the immediate environment, shaking, shaping and grinding to suit the form, the requirements, the wishes, and the whims of man. And in the long third phase, it will reach down into the secret places of its own nature, and by aid of its ever-growing intelligence and co-operation, shape itself into an increasingly sublime creation – a being beside which the mythical divinities of the past will seem more and more ridiculous, and which setting its own marvellous inner powers against the brute Goliath of the suns and planets, challenges them to contest.[2]

THE ILLICIT ESCALATOR

This pattern, it should be noticed, is quite incompatible with regular Darwinian scientific theory. The idea of a vast escalator, proceeding steadily upwards from lifeless matter through plants and animals to man, and inevitably on to higher things, was coined by Lamarck and given currency by Herbert Spencer under his chosen name, 'evolution.' Darwin utterly distrusted the idea, which seemed to him a baseless piece of theorizing, and avoided the name. As far as he could see, he said, 'no innate tendency to progressive development exists . . . It is curious how seldom writers define what they mean by progressive development.'[3] His theory of natural selection gives no ground for it and does not require it. As has been pointed out,[4] it arranges species in a radiating bush rather than on a ladder, accounting for all kinds of development, and also for some cases of unchangingness and of 'regression,' equally as limited responses to particular environments. The notion of a ladder is of course derived from the older one of the stationary stair, the scala naturae, which combined some sensible ideas about increasing complexity with some far less sensible ones about hierarchy and government. No ladders are needed for classification. Linear development, or orthogenesis, is an idle fifth wheel to the coach.

Darwin saw no reason to posit any law guaranteeing the continuation of any of the changes he noted, or to pick out any one of them, such as increase in intelligence, as the core of the whole proceeding. Spencer, by contrast, instantly saw a complicated law of increasing heterogeneity: to him, 'brief inspection made it manifest that the law held in the inorganic world, as in the organic and the superorganic.'[5] Accordingly, as one of his followers pointed out with pride, 'the Theory of Evolution dealing with the universe as a whole, from gas to genius, was formulated some months before the publication of the Darwin–Wallace paper' (a priority claim which Darwin never wanted to dispute).[6]

From that time to this, Spencer's bold, colourful and flattering picture of evolution has constantly prevailed over the more sober, difficult one of Darwin, not only in the public mind, but also surprisingly often in the minds of scientists who had reason to know its limitations. That distinguished physicist J.D. Bernal shaped it in a way which bears some relation to Day's in a remarkable Marxist Utopia published in 1929. Pointing out that things might get a trifle dull and unchallenging in the future, when the state had withered away after the triumph of the proletariat, Bernal predicted that only the dimmer minds would be content with this placid paradise. Accordingly, 'the aristocracy of scientific intelligence' would give rise to new developments and create a world run increasingly by scientific experts. Scientific institutions would gradually become the government and thus achieve 'a further stage of the Marxian hierarchy of domination.' The end result would be that scientists 'would emerge as a new species and leave humanity behind.'[7]

THE PROBLEM OF DIRECTION

To light up the difficulties further, it will be worthwhile taking a further look at Jonathan Glover's tantalizingly titled book, *What Sort of People Should There Be?*[8]

Glover's discussion is interesting because his tone and official intention are so different from the naïve, evangelistic Utopianism we have just been seeing. But at root I think he is just as machine-struck, just as carried away on a wave of undiagnosed faith in technology as such. On the surface, he is highly moderate and reasonable. He quotes Muller's prophecies with suitable contempt, commenting that 'the case for genetic engineering is not helped by adopting the tones of a mad scientist in a horror film.' His declared aim is not to transform the human race according to a blueprint but to increase its freedom by allowing it certain valuable kinds of development which would otherwise be closed to it. He notes the difficulty of deciding who is to be in charge and warns us of the twin dangers of totalitarian, state-organized transformation and of anarchic, unbalanced changes produced by free enterprise in the 'genetic supermarket' so amazingly proposed by Robert Nozick.

He does not, however, seem to notice the idiocy of this proposal. Nozick, while rejecting a genetically engineered Utopia on the grounds mentioned earlier, advises such a market 'meeting the individual specifications (within certain moral limits) of prospective parents'[9] as a means to securing a wide and varied spread of future types, and also as an expression of the parents' freedom. There being no point on which parents are so reliably conventional as their hopes for their children, what this would presumably bring about would be a society solidly manufactured for the demands of the previous age, and a gene pool needing to be altered radically in each generation by a set of people incapable of taking any other direction. All this supposing: (1) that it could work; (2) that the poisoning of parent–child relations which would follow on such open manipulation did not destroy family life altogether; and (3) that the choices offered were not in any case totally determined within a very narrow range by the scientists running the market.

Glover, however, accepts the scheme at Nozick's valuation and notes no danger but anarchy. All along, he gives the impression that the changes he expects from a moderate form of this scheme would be merely of the same order as those produced by new information technology or forms of transport. Yet, immediately after the passage just quoted, he writes:

> But behind the rhetoric is a serious point. If we decide on a positive program to change our nature, *this will be a central moment in our history*, and the transformation might be beneficial to a degree we can scarcely now imagine.[10]

And his main message certainly is that though we must act cautiously, we must on no account let this unique opportunity slip. Why should this particular technology be expected to make a change which would count as a central moment in the history of the human race?

In answer, something must I think be said bluntly and generally for a start about the misleading effect of propaganda claims made on behalf of any line in learning or technology which has recently had some striking successes. Claimants here do not have to be dishonest, or more than usually obsessed by the need for research money, to be led on to exaggerate. There is a dazzlement, an unavoidable confusion of vision, which makes realistic foresight temporarily impossible. Molecular biology or biochemistry (if we may use the more convenient name) has been in this situation since the discovery of DNA. The world has seemed to be its oyster. It is neither accident nor some sinister prejudice on my part which accounts for the high proportion of quotations from biochemists in this book.

Resounding discoveries have combined with a sense of a commanding position on the frontiers of the physical and biological sciences to generate among these scientists a euphoric sense of cognitive omnipotence, of possessing methods which have been finally tested as correct and will be universally applicable. To many of them, their position appears to be that of missionaries from the physical sciences, spreading physical methods once for all over the hitherto recalcitrant realms of the life sciences, and thus over all remaining intellectual areas of the slightest interest. The great physicist David Bohm comments:

> Molecular biologists have discovered that in the growth and reproduction of cells, certain laws that can be given a mechanical form of description are satisfied (especially those having to do with DNA, RNA, the synthesis of proteins). From this, most of them have gone on to the conclusion that ultimately all aspects and sides of life will be explained in mechanical terms. But on what basis can this be said? . . . It should be recalled that at the end of the nineteenth century, physicists widely believed that classical physics gave the general outlines of a complete mechanical explanation of the universe. Since then, relativity and quantum mechanics have overturned such notions altogether . . . Classical physics was swept aside and overturned . . . Is it not likely that modern molecular biology will sooner or later undergo a similar fate? . . .
>
> The notion that present lines of thinking will continue to be validated indefinitely by experiment is just another article of faith, similar to that of the nineteenth-century physicists . . . Is there not a kind of 'hubris' that seems rather often to penetrate the very fabric of scientific thought, and to capture the minds of scientists, whenever any particular scientific theory has been successful for some period of time? This takes the form of a fervently held belief that what has been discovered will continue to work indefinitely, ultimately to cover the whole of reality.[11]

Physicists, in fact, have abandoned the simple-minded mechanistic thinking which is the basis of biochemical superconfidence, and biochemists are liable to find themselves in the position of missionaries returning to Rome to find that a new pope has reversed the doctrines they were preaching. And though it is in a sense an accident that this has happened so soon, that superconfidence could not have endured long in any case. It is in the nature of science that such bold projections into the future always have to be modified.

PLACING THE NEED

So much, then, for the mere degree of euphoric confidence which is radiated, the general certainty of being able to make useful changes. Besides this, if we are to speak of a central moment in human history, we would need another component, the sense of a special need, correctly located, which that technology and no other can satisfy. Much more is needed here than the mere general belief, on which most of us would probably agree, that there is a terrible lot wrong with human nature. (Those who do not believe that there is such a thing as human nature at all will not be interested in genetic engineering to alter it in any case.) Any diagnosis which would show this technology to be relevant would have to fix what is wrong convincingly in a quality, or set of qualities, with a distinct genetic basis which could be changed, and say what changes were called for. Without that diagnosis, there is nothing momentous.

I find it remarkable that Glover's book does not deal at all in arguments about the nature of this need. Many of the changes he discusses are seen as relatively minor additions to the amenities and achievements of life: the production of musical prodigies, cleverer physicists or especially 'imaginative and creative' people. Others deal with alterations which seem equally slight (at least in Glover's view) but are distinguished by needing some sort of science-fiction device to bring them about, for instance, the power to see directly into each other's thoughts at all times, or to switch off an unwelcome desire by some mechanical device. Here the writer is chiefly occupied with persuading us not to be too prejudiced against these (as he thinks) promising devices. But this overlooks the more obvious question: why these particular changes should be picked on. He claims that the first would make us more considerate and the second more autonomous. Neither story convinces me, but even if they did, it is hardly plausible that they would make all the difference needed for the salvation of the human race.

In general, the guiding aim which Glover sets up is increased variety to enrich human freedom, rather in the spirit of Nozick and of John Stuart Mill's *Essay on Liberty*. Mill said:

> As it is useful that while mankind is imperfect there should be different opinions, so it is that there should be different experiments of living; that free scope should be given to varieties of character, short of injury to others . . . Human nature is not a machine to be built after a model, and set to do exactly the work prescribed for it, but a tree, which requires to grow and develop itself on all sides.[12]

Why, however, do we need genetic engineering to supply this many-sidedness, when we already have (as Mill pointed out) a bewilderingly wide range of options genetically provided, most of which we have never even glanced at owing to the narrowness and repressiveness of our cultures? In order to have reason to call in the engineers here, we would need reason to believe that human nature had failed us. Mill's whole book on Liberty is a celebration of human nature, a declaration of faith that it will not fail us. Glover's is the exact opposite, and the difference is crucial.

To make Glover's remedies relevant, we would have to be convinced by good evidence that what holds back human achievement at present is lack of natural variety, that is, lack of talent. This seems a strange view, which would need a great deal of support. On the face of things, enormous potential for variety is already present, as is shown by the differences between people in different cultures, and the main thing that blocks our achievements is not lack of talent, which is running to waste all round us, but bad social arrangements and neurotic confusion in individuals. To commission more varied talents in that situation seems like pouring more good materials into a factory already choked by confusion and maladministration.

Even if it might be nice to have more musical prodigies, then, this sort of thing does not seem enough to constitute a central moment in human history. Nor does it at all answer the intriguing question of Glover's title, 'what sort of people should there be?' On this point, he simply accepts existing notions. The questions about conflicting values, which would seem primary if we are really discussing future directions for our society, do not get raised at all.

NOTES

1. From W. Day, *Genesis on Planet Earth: The Search for Life's Beginning* (East Lansing, Mich., House of Talos, 1979), pp. 390–2.
2. H.J. Muller, *Out of the Night* (New York, 1935). Quoted by J. Glover in *What Sort of People Should There Be?* (Harmondsworth, Penguin, 1984), p. 32.
3. From F. Darwin and A.C. Seward (eds.), *More Letters of Charles Darwin* (London, John Murray, 1903), pp. 338–49.
4. For a good statement of this point, see S.J. Gould, *Ever Since Darwin* (Harmondsworth, Penguin, 1980), Chapter 2.
5. D. Duncan (ed.), *The Life and Letters of Herbert Spencer* (London, Williams, & Norgate, 1908), p. 555.
6. E. Clodd. See A.C. Armstrong, Transitional Eras in Thought, with Special Reference to the Present Age (New York, Macmillan, 1904), p. 48.
7. J.D. Bernal, *The World, The Flesh and the Devil* (London, Cape, 1929), pp. 68–73. Quoted by B. Easlea, *Science and Sexual Oppression* (London, Routledge & Kegan Paul, 1983), pp. 19–21.
8. J. Glover, *What Sort of People Should There Be?* (Harmondsworth, Penguin, 1984).
9. *Anarchy, State and Utopia* (Oxford, Blackwell, 1980), p. 315n.
10. Glover, *What Sort of People Should There Be?*, pp. 32–3.
11. 'On the subjectivity and objectivity of knowledge', in J. Lewis (ed.), *Beyond Chance and Necessity* (London, Garnstone Press, 1974), pp. 127–8.
12. J.S. Mill, *Essay on Liberty*, Chapter 3 (London, Dent, Everyman edn, 1972), pp. 115 and 117.

23

THE SERVICE OF SELF AND THE SERVICE OF KALI

Though Nature, red in tooth and claw
With ravin, shrieked against his creed. . .
Are God and Nature then at strife
That Nature lends such evil dreams?
So careful of the type she seems,
So careless of the single life;
'So careful of the type?' but no
From scarped cliff and quarried stone
She cries, 'A thousand types are gone;
I care for nothing; all shall go.'

Alfred Lord Tennyson, In Memoriam, LV–LVI

DOI: 10.4324/9781003588160-30

NATURE'S REDNESS AND THE ABUSE OF COMMON SPEECH

We move on now from strange beliefs based on optimistic distortions of evolutionary theory to ones based on pessimistic distortions, from Lamarck's escalator to nature red in tooth and claw. Are we then still in realms which ought to be called religious at all? Certainly this is a gloomy and alarming cult. But it is still one celebrated with powerful incantations, such as Tennyson's and that of M.T. Ghiselin (quoted on p. 340 and to be looked at again shortly). As we have already seen, even the cosmic escalator, when set against a sufficiently vast and disheartening backdrop, can give a deeply gloomy impression. Yet the drama to which this picture contributes is certainly spiritually ambitious enough to constitute a faith and in some sense a religion.

We need to notice here the general place of gloomy elements in religions. Most of the Greek and Roman deities were sometimes deeply destructive, and some – Hecate, Nemesis, Pluto – dealt with death as their main function. Still more interesting is the Hindu trinity of Brahma, Vishnu, and Siva – Creator, Preserver, and Destroyer. Siva, and still more his wife Kali, stand for death. And death is indeed a most necessary balance to the rich fertility that flows from the first two members. In the context of the whole, these deities supply a grave and becoming element. When, however, they are worshipped on their own, some very odd activity and even odder motivation tend to be involved. Thugs serve the goddess by ritual murder of strangers. Still more remarkably, ecstatic devotees perish by throwing themselves under the car of Jagarnath.

That exaltation of pure destruction seems to me to be the main inspiration of Ghiselin's hymn to egoism and of other passages like it. This is a paradoxical suggestion, since in theory these passages celebrate an all-conquering urge to self-preservation. The emphasis in them, however, is never on the delights of the life which is to be preserved. It is all on an uncompromising determination to ditch all competitors. The mood celebrated is one of total destructive callousness. Tennyson and Ghiselin differ, however, about who owns this mood.

For Tennyson, it is still the figure of personified nature. Since God is still present, this shows us a kind of Huxleyan cosmic war in which another mood is still contending against this one. Ghiselin, by contrast, makes the mood entirely universal and uses no personification. He attributes it directly to all organisms.

Since most organisms are plants, which do not have motives, this seems strange. But in any case, sociobiologists say plainly that they are not actually talking about motives at all. When they use words which are the ordinary names of motives, they officially do so with a quite different and technical meaning. This equivocation makes possible a chronic, pervasive play upon words. A colourful, familiar psychological myth is conveyed through the everyday meanings, and from time to time endorsed in unmistakable terms by the author – as it is here – without needing any actual discussion or support, because officially nothing but a theory in population genetics is on sale.

Trouble centres on the word selfish. For sociobiologists, this word is officially not the name of a motive at all, but a term used to describe a complicated, highly abstract and unfamiliar causal property – the tendency to maximize one's own gene representation in future generations. This is much like using the word cruelty to describe all behaviour which will cause suffering to anyone else in any future generation, or the word sloth to describe all that which will fail to affect them. Why such a word should ever have been chosen, if no reference to real selfishness was meant, is hard to imagine. Similar senses, however, are also given to the equally unsuitable motive-words, 'spite' and 'altruism.'

Now clumsy and ill-chosen scientific terms do not do much harm where their use is segregated from ordinary discourse. But this is not such a field. And there is in any case one kind of situation where they cannot be harmless, namely where their everyday sense also applies, and gives a common, familiar meaning with important consequences. The dangers of this situation are of course multiplied when a wide audience is being addressed. And it happens that the claim to detect ordinary, literal selfishness as an underlying motive, vitiating claims to other and better motives, is just such an everyday move.

Its consequences are necessarily important, because it is so often used to justify retaliation.

The fact that 'selfishness' in its ordinary sense is not just the name of a motive but of a fault naturally makes things much worse. To widen the imputation of selfishness is to alter people's view of the human race. This widening had of course already been deliberately undertaken by various thinkers who have developed theories of psychological egoism, and had been given a special political function by Hobbes and his followers in social-contract theory. People in society were then held not to have any motive in their interactions other than self-interest. If this bizarre story had been true, the notion of selfishness could never have arisen. Had regard for others really been impossible, there could have been no word for failing to have it. And it needs to be stressed that the word 'selfish' in its normal use is essentially a negative word. It means a shortage of this normal regard for others. Calling somebody selfish simply does not mean that they are prudent or successfully self-preserving. It merely says that they are exceptional – and faulty – in having too little care for anybody else.

Accordingly, egoist writers cannot properly use the term 'selfish' at all. Their theory excludes it. This is so obvious that usually they do not make this mistake. There is, however, a temptation to cheat by retaining it, because this makes possible the use of egoism to justify retributive bloody-mindedness based on a low opinion of our fellow-men. Egoist cheats enquire why we should be expected to bother about the rest of the human race, which has been proved guilty of the sin of selfishness? They warn anyone who is still rash enough to be unselfish that they are out on a limb and should quickly fall in line with the already universal tendency.

VARIOUS STRUGGLES FOR VARIOUS EXISTENCES

The absurdity of this talk has of course often been pointed out, and no one has any excuse for again attempting today to foist it on a long-suffering public. Historical chance, however, has favoured it by entangling it twice with apparently reputable scientific views. The first time this happened was in economics, when the early political economists conceived the idea that enlightened self-interest was the best path to promoting the interests of all, and called for commercial free enterprise unshackled by any restraints imposed to protect its victims. The second time was over evolution.

This happened quite independently of Darwin. Tennyson published In Memoriam in 1850. Malthus had published his Essay on Population in 1798. The Origin of Species did not come out till 1859. Many others besides Darwin could see the drama implicit in the idea of a struggle for existence, and could project it loosely from the field of chaotic human life in a disturbed and rapidly changing society on to the vast, vague background of organic life generally. Where Darwin's invaluable special insight came in was in also grasping the differences between these fields. This released his imagination to work realistically in the biological one, and to work out in detail the way in which natural selection could be seen as a constructive force. Most other theorists oscillated in an uncontrolled way between the two fields, assuming what suited them about biology to make the points they wanted to make about society at the time.

Here again, of course, the dominant figure was Herbert Spencer, who had no hesitation at all about this proceeding. With only the most casual acquaintance with biology he promoted his notion of the 'survival of the fittest' as a social ideal. This had enormous effect, above all in the United States, where he outsold every other philosopher in his day. Two examples of the kind of thing which resulted must suffice; we are all too familiar with it still. Both come from direct disciples of Spencer's in America:

> The millionaires are a product of natural selection, acting on the whole body of men to pick out those who can meet the requirement of certain work to be done . . . It is because they are thus selected that wealth – both their own and that entrusted to them – aggregates under their hands . . . They may fairly be regarded as the naturally selected agents of society for certain work. They get high wages and live in luxury, but the bargain is a good one for society. There is the intensest

competition for their place and occupation. This assures us that all who are competent for this function will be employed in it, so that the cost of it will be reduced to the lowest terms.[1]

And again, with a sharp illumination of the fatalistic aspect, Richard Hofstadter in his admirable analysis of Social Darwinism observes how:

> acceptance of the Spencerian philosophy brought about a paralysis of the will to reform . . . Youmans [Spencer's chief American spokesman] in Henry George's presence denounced with great fervour the political corruption of New York and the selfishness of the rich in ignoring or promoting it when they found it profitable to do so. 'What do you propose to do about it?' George asked. Youmans replied 'Nothing! You and I can do nothing at all. It's all a matter of evolution. Perhaps in four or five thousand years evolution may have carried men beyond this state of things.'[2]

For one example from Europe, we can look at *Hitler's Table-Talk*:

> If we did not respect the law of nature, imposing our will by the right of the stronger, a day would come when the wild animals would again devour us – then the insects would eat the wild animals, and finally nothing would exist except the microbes . . . By means of the struggle the elites are continually renewed. The law of selection justifies this incessant struggle by allowing the survival of the fittest. Christianity is a rebellion against natural law, a protest against nature.[3]

Darwin himself set his face steadily against this kind of thing, which appalled him, and he went to considerable trouble in *The Descent of Man* to point out the deep general difference between the kind of qualities which could make it possible for a social group to survive over many generations,[4] and those that might keep a single individual afloat for his lifetime. Recent attempts to convict him too of 'Social Darwinism' do not refute this; they only show that (as is obvious) he was a man of his age; that there were limits to his criticisms of accepted ideas and institutions. This is true of all of us. But the particular mistake of treating all animal life as a matter of individual cut-throat competition was one which it was out of the question for Darwin to make, because he was a serious, full-time naturalist. He knew a great deal about the life of (for instance) birds, about parental care, warning cries, and loyalty to the family and flock. 'The social instincts' were a central interest of his. In his mind they were always present in proper balance against the waste and cruelty of natural life.

HUXLEY AND THE EXAGGERATION OF CONFLICT

T.H. Huxley, too, spoke out extremely strongly against the Spencerist mystique. Indeed, he did so more often than Darwin, because in his day it had grown even more influential and was beginning to be an alarming force in politics. But Huxley's approach was significantly different just because he was not a naturalist. (His first ambition in life had been to be an engineer, and his one field trip on the Rattlesnake never really altered this angle.) To him, it was convincing enough that brutal competition ruled unchallenged over all other life-forms, provided that the human race was excepted. Human virtues, for Huxley, were a sudden 'ethical process' undertaken in reverse of the entire remainder of the 'cosmic process,' that is, of laws governing everything else in the universe.

This view leaves as quite legitimate a Hitlerian description of evolution, and only objects to the inclusion of man within it. Huxley's attempt to stop at this point has been very widely imitated, but it is surely an almost impossible enterprise. If it had really been true that no organism stood in any relation to any other except a competitive one – if mutual destruction had been the only kind of interaction – the idea that a single species could suddenly engage in something else would indeed have been an extraordinary one. Alfred Russell Wallace's idea that an immortal soul had been suddenly implanted would be the least that would be needed to account for such a reversal, and even this seems quite inadequate for the job.[5]

It is necessary to abandon this dramatic picture for something much more realistic. In fact, nature is green long before she is red, and must be green on a very large scale indeed to provide a context for redness. Organisms co-operate, profiting by each other's presence. As Darwin already pointed out in *The Origin of Species*, the 'struggle for existence' can often be described just as well as a mutual dependence.[6] And harmless coexistence as parts of the same ecosphere is also a very common relation.

The astonishment with which Europeans tend still to see films of creatures of different kinds quietly grazing together, with carnivores resting placidly at no great distance, testifies to the unreality of our drama. This relation, too, is certainly more positive than the ignorant among us might suppose. A grazing animal which is kept in a field with another of a different species may not seem to pay it any attention, but if one is removed, the other will be much upset, and will pine. (It would be hard to say more of many coexisting pairs of human beings.) Among social creatures, positive gregariousness, a liking for each other's company, is the steady, unnoticed background for the conflicts. For less social creatures and for plants, the ability to live among others with a steady, mild exchange of benefits is usually a necessity. Ghiselin's story that all this co-operation is really only a carefully thought-out means to individual survival is just a gratuitous animistic fancy. It would be quite as sensible to say that the individuals are only there for the sake of the collectivity, which has subtly deluded them into supposing that they exist only for themselves.

SOCIOBIOLOGICAL SENSE AND NONSENSE

The extraordinary thing about sociobiology is that, officially and properly speaking, it arises from the recognition of this sociality in advanced creatures and is simply a set of theories to account for it. Although its rhetoric treats that sociality as a myth, its theoretical task is to admit it as a fact and to make evolutionary sense of it.

In essence, it is simply a study of the conditions under which social tendencies can be inherited in the process of natural selection. It arose from an insight of the great geneticist J.B.S. Haldane's about how capacities for altruistic behaviour could be passed on in evolution. If the Spencerist view of natural selection as plain, cut-throat, individual competition had been correct, this would simply have been impossible. Biologists had long realized this, but could not see what happened instead. What Haldane grasped was that tendencies leading to self-sacrifice *could* be transmitted provided that they were helpful to those who shared one's genes. This is 'kin-selection.' Willingness to die in defence of children or other relatives may destroy the first individual who has it, but if enough descendants who share that tendency are left, genes conducive to it survive and may possibly spread to the whole community. The question just is, how many descendants are enough?

The story goes that Haldane, having thought of this in a pub, promptly seized an old envelope and became immersed in calculations. He finally emerged, declaring, 'I am willing to die for four uncles or eight cousins,' that being the number who are needed to replace one's own genes in the tribal gene-pool. This is the sort of calculation which has been the prime business of sociobiologists ever since, and as Wilson puts it, the 'central theoretical problem' of the discipline is still 'how can altruism, which by definition reduces personal fitness, possibly evolve by natural selection?'[7] The calculations have now become very sophisticated, and often give surprising and interesting results.

It is worth noticing, however, even in this initial casual story, how easily a confusion arises which has caused trouble ever since. Haldane spoke as if the answer to his genetic calculations could *decide* whether he would – or perhaps should? – die for his relatives. Of course all such strong, direct interpretations are wild and illicit. All that can reasonably be concluded from such evidence must remain very general and statistical, claiming merely that, where innate traits are transmitted without benefiting their owner, they must on average have benefited close kin in rough proportion to their closeness. The defence of children, in fact, does not stand alone. It is merely the strongest and simplest case.

WHO OR WHAT IS SELFISH?

Once this is realized, the puzzle about how altruistic traits can have developed ought to vanish; it has been solved. It continues, however, to worry sociobiologists and to present itself as somehow disturbing and anomalous. The 'problem of altruism' keeps recurring. To solve it, a model is developed whereby each organism is really aiming at its own advantage, but finds it not in this life but in 'inclusive fitness,' that is in having many descendants. In some way, this is held to remove the anomaly, to show that nothing was really done for the sake of others after all. Alternatively, organisms themselves are seen as being genuinely altruistic, but being so only as the dupes of their genes, which appear as the real agents, egoists behind the scenes organizing the performance. Thus, Richard Dawkins in *The Selfish Gene*:

> The argument of this book is that we, and all other animals, are machines created by our genes. Like successful Chicago gangsters, our genes have survived, in some cases for millions of years, in a highly competitive world. This entitles us to expect certain qualities in our genes. I shall argue that a predominant quality to be expected in a successful gene is ruthless selfishness . . . If you wish . . . to build a society in which individuals co-operate generously towards a common good, you can expect little help from biological nature. Let us try to teach generosity and altruism, because we are born selfish.[8]

And E.O. Wilson:

> The individual organism is only the vehicle (of genes), part of an elaborate device to preserve and spread them with the least possible biochemical perturbation . . . The organism is only DNA's way of making more DNA.[9]

Dawkins's remarks here show with beautiful clarity the full series of moves needed to complete this confusion. First, there is the old-fashioned 'beanbag' genetics, similar to that used by Monod, which supposed genes themselves to be isolated items tossed around in a randomizer, rather than the closely linked and regularly interworking components which they are now known to be. (Geneticists tend to despise sociobiology, and with some reason.) Then there is the animistic move – which Monod would have sharply rejected – of personifying the gene and describing this supposed competition in highly emotive terms as a deliberate project. Then comes the point where the quickness of the hand most needs to deceive the eye – the transfer of 'selfishness' from genes to organisms – 'we are born selfish.'

Finally, there is the quite explicit drawing of a social moral – an extraordinary move if the behaviour of genes had really been the only thing under discussion – to the effect that human nature is totally iniquitous and unregenerate, and any salvation for it can only come from some outside source. Since, in this highly anti-theistic context, no outside source is imaginable, this can only be the Huxleyan position in its most forbidding and discouraging form. It can only amount to a counsel of despair: the resigned, fatalistic acceptance of iniquity as inevitable, which is the usual moral of Spencerist theorizing. This is strongly supported by Dawkins's habitual rhetoric in elevating the gene from its real position as a humble piece of goo within cells to a malign and all-powerful agent:

> It does not grow senile; it is no more likely to die when it is a million years old than when it is only a hundred. It leaps from body to body down the generations, manipulating body after body in its own way and for its own ends, abandoning a succession of mortal bodies before they sink in senility and death. The genes are the immortals.[10]

This impression, of course, depends on treating the type as a single entity and forgetting that each particular gene dies in the cell it belongs to. It would be no more and no less true to say that humanity did this, being represented successively by different individuals but transcending and outlasting them all. Again, the causal importance of genes is constantly exaggerated by a meaningless downgrading of other kinds of causes:

> By dictating the way survival machines and their nervous systems are built, genes exert ultimate power over behaviour . . . Genes are the primary policy-makers; brains are the executives . . . The logical conclusion to this trend (towards increasing intelligence) not yet reached in any species, would be for the genes to give the survival machine a single overall policy instruction – 'do whatever you think best to keep us alive'.[11]

If that were the situation, what could possibly be the sense of trying to defeat the genes by trying (for the first time in human history, as Dawkins explains) to start up some genuine altruistic behaviour – a move which must necessarily be just one more wily device on their part to secure their own survival?

We should notice that 'ultimate power' is a meaningless phrase; science recognizes no causes which are not themselves subject to other causes, and the process of heredity has any number of other kinds of cause as well as genetic ones. But if there were indeed a being with 'ultimate power,' it would presumably be one against which we were totally impotent. Though this idea has no place in science, it is extremely suggestive to the religious sensibilities. Worship, as we have already seen, is not only something carried out in Gothic buildings by people singing *Hymns Ancient and Modern*. It has many other forms and can be entirely informal. It is certainly the mood most strongly suggested by Dawkins's discussions of the gene.

THE DIFFICULTY OF NOT TALKING ABOUT MOTIVES

Sociobiological thinking, then, seems to conduct, side by side with its perfectly respectable attempt to account for the inherited co-operative tendencies of plants and animals, a very different and far less respectable myth-making activity. This commits it *either* (if individual selfishness is meant) to supporting a psychological egoism which is inconsistent with the very recognition that these tendencies exist, or (if gene-selfishness is preferred) to a story which is quite meaningless unless it is taken literally as a fatalistic acceptance of a non-human entity, endowed with such power over us that its purposes determine all our acts, and against which it is therefore senseless to strive. And if both ideas are combined, both drawbacks are available together.

Can this really be the situation? Officially, as has been pointed out, sociobiologists cannot be proposing psychological egoism, because they are not supposed to be talking about motives at all. But since they are claiming that what they call selfishness is indeed the root cause of most, if not all behaviour, what they say continually has this meaning. When readers understand it this way, the writers usually express surprise at such perverse misinterpretation of a harmless technical term. But they do it themselves all the time. In each sociobiological writer, an everyday Mr Hyde proceeds on his Hobbesian debunking psychoanalytic path, entirely regardless of scientific Dr Jekyll, who has just outlawed it. There is constant and explicit mention of motives, often even of conscious motives, as critics have repeatedly pointed out. Yet again, I give a few entirely typical examples. In *On Human Nature*, which appeared in 1978, after the matter had been well aired in controversy, Edward O. Wilson writes that nearly all altruism is of the 'soft-core' kind, which means that it is

> ultimately selfish. The 'altruist' expects reciprocation from society for himself or his closest relatives. *His good behaviour is calculating, often in a wholly conscious way* . . .... The capacity for soft-core altruism can be expected to have evolved primarily by selection of individuals and to be deeply influenced by the vagaries of cultural evolution. *Its psychological vehicles are lying, pretense and deceit, including self-deceit, because the actor is most convincing who believes that his performance is real.*
>
> (My italics)[12]

This kind of story is continually stated, as it is here, explicitly as an account of motivation, an account which is meant to conflict with other possible accounts of it and prove them to be mistakes or lies. If these stories had really been only about evolutionary function, that clash could not arise.

As for the rare 'hard-core altruism' or genuine self-sacrifice, that, Wilson goes on to explain, is certainly no better. 'Pure, hard-core altruism based on kin-selection is the enemy of civilization.'[13] It is not (he explains) really an unusual case of genuine charity, but a mere mindless death-wish. That, again, makes it a motive, and Wilson's calling it 'irrational' can only mean that the only possible rational motive is self-interest. This can be nothing but crude, Hobbesian psychological egoism, altered only by the bizarre substitution of gene-maximization for self-preservation as the individual's aim.

Sociobiology is a false light because it is 'reductive' in the sense of ruling out other enquiries, of imposing its own chosen model as the only norm. But, far more serious than this negative drawback, it is also, like many such reductive disciplines, engaged on its own monstrous enterprise of illicit inflation. To balance the austere renunciation of religious ideas and of a normal view of human standing in the biosphere, which Wilson and Dawkins denounce, they offer us a mystique of power, vicarious indeed but evidently, from the fervent tone which celebrates it, nonetheless exciting for that.

NOTES

1. W. Sumner, *The Challenge of Facts* (1887), p. 67.
2. R. Hofstadter, *Social Darwinism in American Thought* (New York, Braziller, 1959), p. 47.
3. H. Trevor-Roper (ed.), *Hitler's Table-Talk* (London, Weidenfeld & Nicolson, 1963).
4. C. Darwin, *The Descent of Man* (reprinted, Princeton, NJ, Princeton University Press, 1981).
5. A view which first appeared in his *Natural Selection and Tropical Nature: Essays on Descriptive and Theoretical Biology* (London, Macmillan, 1891) and increasingly pervaded his later work. Wallace had been converted from his earlier Darwinian position by spiritualism. See J.R. Moore, *The Post-Darwinian*

Controversies: A Study of the Protestant Struggle to Come to Terms with Darwin in Great Britain and America 1870–1900 (Cambridge, Cambridge University Press, 1979) pp. 184–7.

6. See its third chapter, especially the opening few pages.

7. E.O. Wilson, *Sociobiology: The New Synthesis* (Cambridge, MA, Harvard University Press, 1975), p. 3.

8. R. Dawkins, *The Selfish Gene* (London, Oxford University Press, 1976), pp. 2–3.

9. E.O. Wilson, *Sociobiology: The New Synthesis* (Cambridge, MA, Harvard University Press, 1975), p. 3.

10. Dawkins, *The Selfish Gene*, p. 36.

11. Ibid., p. 64.

12. E.O. Wilson, *On Human Nature* (Cambridge, MA, Harvard University Press, 1978), pp. 155–6.

13. Wilson, *Sociobiology*, p. 157.

24

BIOTECHNOLOGY AND THE YUK FACTOR

THE BIFURCATION OF MORALS

We have been noticing that human beings are not loosely composed of two separate items. There is no perforation down the middle that reads 'Tear here to detach body from mind.' Nor, as is also sometimes suggested, do they consist of only one of these items, the other having been thrown away. In observing this, we have noticed, too, the absence of another suggested perforation in these beings, one which would be marked 'Tear here to detach reason from feeling.' In real life, we tend not to find that reason and feeling are separate items. They are interdependent aspects of a person, divisible only for thought. But attempts to separate these factors and set them at war have been extremely common. It is worthwhile to see how they are working now on some current issues that concern many of us. We might ask,

DOI: 10.4324/9781003588160-31

then, what kinds of moral objections are there to interventions such as xenotransplantation, genetic engineering, and bioengineering generally? In answering such questions, ethicists often like to divide moral arguments firmly into two sets, ones that point to dangerous consequences and ones that say the act itself is intrinsically wrong. But unless the two angles are brought together again at some point, this division can split the subject disastrously.

It is often hard to consider probable consequences on their own, since we really do not know what they are likely to be. On the other hand, trying to consider intrinsic objections on their own, apart from consequences, seems unrealistic. We feel that these direct objections must be irrational because the only rational way to judge things is, as utilitarians suggest, by weighing their consequences. People are inclined to dismiss intrinsic objections as emotional, subjective, something that can't really be justified or argued about at all. But, as just noticed, the probable consequences themselves often are not clear enough to make reasoned conclusions possible either. So both lines of enquiry fail.

It is not very helpful to see debates in this way as flat conflicts between thought and feeling because, usually, both are engaged on both sides. In the case of bioengineering, I think this approach has been specially unfortunate. People often have the impression that reason quite simply favours the new developments, although feeling is against them. This stereotyping paralyses them because they cannot see how to arbitrate between these very different litigants.

In fact, however, debate hardly ever really is between these two. Feelings always incorporate thoughts – often ones that are not yet fully articulated – and reasons are always found in response to particular sorts of feelings. On both sides, we need to look for the hidden partners. We have to articulate the ideas behind emotional objections and to note the emotional element in claims that are supposed to be purely rational. The best way to do this is often to start by taking the intrinsic objections more seriously. If we look below the surface of feeling, we may find thoughts that show how the two aspects are connected.

In the case of biotechnology, such thoughts do indeed emerge. What is really worrying the objectors is not, I think, the detail of any particular proposal. It is the hype, the scale of the proposed project, the weight of the economic forces now backing it, and the sweeping change of attitude that is being demanded. Biotechnology on the scale that many people are now demanding it does not appear to be compatible with our existing concepts of nature and species – concepts that are part of our current science as well as of everyday thought. A new ideology is being proposed that would remodel those concepts to fit the new technologies, envisaging species as unreal and nature as infinitely malleable. Hard experience may, of course, cut these vast aspirations down to size anyway. The hopes offered may be disappointed, as happened with earlier technological miracles such as nuclear power. But whether they are or not, we need to be critical of attempts like this to remodel our whole idea of nature on the pattern of one particular, currently favoured technology. We know that seventeenth-century mechanists were mistaken in supposing the world to be made of clockwork, and a twentieth-century repetition of their overconfidence does not seem likely to work out any better. So questions about biotechnology raise wide issues, not just about the relation of thought to feeling and of acts to consequences but also about where our world pictures come from and what needs to happen when we change them.

GETTING WHAT WE ASK FOR

To begin, however, with the question of acts and consequences: it is interesting to note that some consequences are not just a matter of chance. Acts that are wrong in themselves can be expected to have bad effects of a particular kind that is not just accidental. Their badness follows from what is wrong in the act itself, so that there is a rational, conceptual link between them and their results. These consequences are a sign of what was wrong with the act in the first place.

I shall suggest later that this kind of connection between act and consequence does indeed help us to make sense of the objections raised to bio-engineering. But we should notice first that this kind of reasoning isn't something new and sinister. It is commonplace in other realms of morals. For instance, it is no accident that habitual and systematic lying, or habitual and systematic injustice, have bad effects in human life. These habits can be expected to destroy mutual trust and respect, not accidentally, but because accepting those consequences is part of the act. Acts of lying or injustice are themselves expressions of disrespect and untrustworthiness, so they unavoidably call for more of the same.

Similarly, institutions such as torture, or slavery, or any gross subjection of one class to another, have moral consequences that are not accidental. We can expect those consequences to follow, not because of a contingent causal link (like expecting that a tornado may kill someone) but because they are effects that anyone who acts in this way invites and is committed to accepting. Slavery asks for resentment, bitterness, and corruption, attitudes that cannot fail to produce the sorts of acts that express them. In a most intelligible phrase, those who institute slavery *get what they are asking for*. Hubris calls for nemesis, and in one form or another it's going to get it, not as a punishment from outside but as the completion of a pattern already started.

This language of 'getting what you asked for' seems to me important. It has been heard on all sides and from all kinds of people in Britain lately about 'mad cow disease.' That disease apparently arose because, in order to save expense, sheep's brains, along with other animal waste, were used as an ingredient in cattle feed. This device seems to have transferred a disease of sheep to great numbers of cattle, who had to be slaughtered. The disease then spread to humans who had eaten the beef, giving an indefinite and still increasing number of people a new and disastrous form of an illness known as Creutzfeldt-Jakob disease.

People who say that this kind of consequence might have been expected are not, of course, saying that there is a particular causal law to the effect that 'feeding animal waste to herbivores always gives them an illness that can ravage the meat industry and then destroy humans.' Nor are they saying that 'wickedness is always punished.'

Their thought is less simple and has both a moral and a causal aspect. It runs, I think, something like this:

> You can't expect to go on forever exploiting living creatures if you don't pay some attention to their natural needs. You ought not to be trying to do that in the first place. Neglecting the species-nature of cows is wrong in itself. It is a gross insult to the life of the animals. So it should be no surprise that this insult upsets their health, with unpredictable further consequences. These consequences are not, then, an accident. They flow directly from the moral obtuseness that goes with greed.

THE ROLE OF FEELING IN MORALS

I have not said anything yet about how far this way of objecting is justified. I am merely explaining it. Later on, I want to look more closely at some of the ideas involved in it, especially at the key concepts of 'species' and 'nature.' But just now I want simply to spell out its reasoning, pointing out that it is not just a formless emotional cry. These people are not, as is sometimes suggested, merely expressing an inarticulate disgust at the unfamiliar by exclaiming 'yuk.' Their further conversation shows that they are saying something intelligible, something that needs to be answered. To state the point briefly, they are objecting to attacks on the concept of species. And I think there is good reason for that objection.

This point needs to be made because direct, intrinsic objections to bioengineering often are seen as being beneath the level of the real argument. They are described as 'the yuk factor.' They may still be treated with respect for political reasons, because they are known to be influential. And they may also be tolerated because of a general belief that all ethics is irrational anyway – a notion that feeling is always separate from reason – so that their wildness is not particularly surprising. Often, too, these objections are expressed in religious language, and many people now seem to think that religious language cannot be understood by outsiders. Religious thought is conceived as being so isolated from the rest of our reasoning as scarcely to count as thought at all, so this, too, can make them seem undiscussable. (For that reason,

I shall avoid religious language in this discussion, trying to keep it entirely in secular terms.) Thus, current forms of relativism and subjectivism can generate a mindless approach to morals, a sort of weary tolerance of sensible and foolish scruples alike. I think we can do better than this. We can try to understand them. In the first place, I am suggesting generally that the 'yuk factor,' this sense of disgust and outrage, is in itself by no means a sign of irrationality. Feeling is an essential part of our moral life, though of course not the whole of it. Heart and mind are not enemies or alternative tools. They are complementary aspects of a single process. Whenever we seriously judge something to be wrong, strong feeling necessarily accompanies the judgement. Someone who does not have such feelings – someone who has merely a theoretical interest in morals, who doesn't feel any indignation or disgust and outrage about things like slavery and torture – has missed the point of morality altogether.

UNNATURAL?

Of course, we know that these feelings are not an infallible guide. Of course we need to supplement them by thought, analysing their meaning and articulating them in a way that gives us coherent and usable standards. Unanalysed feelings sometimes turn out to be misplaced. Disgust can spring from chance associations or unfamiliarity or mere physical revulsion, such as a horror of cats. We always have to look below the surface. We must spell out the message of our emotions and see what they are trying to tell us. And we have actually quite a good, flexible vocabulary for doing this, for articulating their meaning and seeing how much it matters.

For instance, if somebody says that agriculture or contraception or keeping animals as pets is unnatural, others can understand what objection they are making even if they disagree. A reasonable argument can follow, weighing pros against cons. It is true that agriculture was indeed the first move in shifting human life away from the approximate balance with its surroundings that seems to have marked a life spent in hunting and gathering. And contraception is indeed a considerable interference with a central area of human social and emotional life.

These are real objections that can be spelled out, made clearer, and set against other considerations. All parties can then consider the balance and ask what matters most, which is where the thinking comes in. Gradually, given time and good will, agreement is often arrived at. This has happened about countless issues in the past, often resulting in the whole issue being forgotten. The work may be hard, but in principle these are matters that can be decided in rational terms – not ones that must be left to a brute clash of inarticulate feelings, even though they arose from feelings in the first place.

Nor is the notion of something's being wrong because it is *unnatural* an empty one. Suppose that someone suggests that it is unnatural to bring up children impersonally without individual bonds to carers, as Plato proposed, and as modern theorists like Shulamith Firestone and the behaviourist J.B. Watson have also demanded. Or, that it is unnatural to prevent children from playing or to keep them in solitude. Most of us are likely to agree with this objection, to accept its language, and to feel outrage if these things are seriously proposed.

Of course, the notion of *human nature* has often been distorted and misused. Yet it is clear that we need it and rely on it on such occasions. The same is true of the notion of *human rights*, in spite of many obscurities. That too is supposed to follow simply from membership in our species. These rights are not cancelled by culture, as they would be if we were simply moulded by our society and had no original nature. They are rights that are supposed to guarantee the kind of life that all specimens of *Homo sapiens* need: a kind different from what might suit intelligent kangaroos or limpets or pure disembodied minds. That is why people complain that human beings who are badly treated have been 'treated like animals.' It is taken for granted that we know what a distinctively human nature demands.

This point is often hard to remember today simply because the notion of human nature has so often been misused for political purposes by people wanting to resist reform. The whole idea has been well pummelled during the Enlightenment. But that doesn't mean we can do without it. Of course, this notion, like many other important ones, is many-sided, wobbly, and often obscure. It is so because our nature is complex and makes conflicting demands, between which we have to arbitrate. But we cannot dispense with the idea. It is a standard we must use whenever we want to assess and criticize our institutions. We need some conception of the human nature that we think they ought to fit as a criterion for judging them. We are always developing and updating that notion, but we never try to do without it. We need it for understanding both our own moral reactions and other people's, rather than merely fighting about them. Accordingly, when people who are worried about new technologies complain that they are unnatural, we should try to understand what they are objecting to. We might find something serious.

A notable example of this in our tradition occurred when people began to be sensitive about cruelty, which they really had not been before. In the sixteenth century, a few bold people, such as Montaigne, began to express disgust and outrage about judicial torture and the use of cruel punishments, and also about the abuse of animals. They said that these customs, which had largely been taken for granted as perfectly normal and justified before, were *monstrous*, *unnatural*, and *inhuman*. Because of the strength of their indignant feeling, other people listened and gradually began to agree with them. The notion of what is *human* took a surprising turn to include this kind of response to suffering.

This meant that, during the Enlightenment, the 'humane' movement gathered strength, articulated its objections, and became a real political force. People began to think seriously that it was a bad thing to inflict suffering when they didn't need to. They no longer felt that they ought to repress their sympathetic feelings as unmanly. Attention to that range of sympathetic feelings stirred up reasoning that altered our worldview. It called for different ideas about the entire status of humanity and of the natural world that we inhabit, ideas that are still being developed and are still very important to us today.

HOW SOLID ARE SPECIES?

Let us turn, then, from this general discussion to listen for a moment to the people who now express their disgust about bio-engineering and ask what these objectors are thinking, rather than merely what they are feeling. There are, after all, quite a lot of them, many of them thoughtful people, who have strong views about it. As Jean Bethke Elshtain put it in an article on cloning:

> This is an extraordinarily unsettling development . . . It was anything but amusing to overhear the speculation that cloning might be made available to parents about to lose a child, or having lost a child to an accident, in order that they might reproduce and replace that lost child. This image borders on obscenity . . . The usual nostrums are no use here. I have in mind the standard cliché that, once again, our ethical thinking hasn't caught up with technological 'advance'. This is a flawed way to reflect on cloning and so much else. The problem is not that we must somehow catch up our ethics to our technology. The problem is that technology is rapidly gutting our ethics. And it is *our* ethics. Ethical reflection belongs to all of us – all those agitated radio callers – and it is the fears and apprehensions of ordinary citizens that should be paid close and respectful attention.[1]

This is surely a reasonable demand, whether we are eventually going to agree with their objections or not. And their thought is not, I think, particularly obscure. It centres on the concept of the *monstrous*. Bio-engineering, at least in some forms, is seen as monstrous or unnatural, in a sense that means a great deal more than just unusual or unfamiliar. This sense is very interesting and needs to be examined.

The natural element that is seen as threatened here focuses on the concept of a species. Our tradition has so far held that this concept should be taken pretty seriously, that the boundaries of a species should be respected. One obvious example of this is the objection generally held to sexual intercourse with other animals. At a popular level, too, this conviction is reflected in the symbolism of our myths. Traditional mixed monsters – minotaurs, chimeras, lamias, gorgons – stand for a deep and threatening disorder, something not just confusing but dreadful and invasive. Although benign monsters such as Pegasus and archangels are occasionally found, in general the symbolism of mixing species is deeply uncanny and threatening. Even less mixed monsters, such as giants and three-headed dogs, are so framed as to violate the principles of construction that normally make life possible for their species. They too are usually seen as alien and destructive forces. Science too has up till now supported this tradition by taking species seriously and in general still does so today. Of course, scientific ideas about it have changed in one very important respect. We now know that species are not permanent, timeless essences – that they have been formed and can change and decay – and also that a few species hybridize and mingle at their borders.

All the same, on the whole biologists still see species as profoundly shaped by the niches that they occupy. Fertile hybrids are known to be rare and usually unsuccessful. Current biology tends to stress rather strongly the extent to which each species is adapted to fit its niche and must keep its parts exactly suited to each other if it is to survive. Biologists are now much given to studying *evolutionary functions*: to asking why creatures have just this or that set of characteristics and explaining how this set is needed to fit them for their own peculiar way of life.

On the whole, then, today's evolutionary biology tells us that however much we might want to have a world filled with novelties and monsters, chimeras and winged horses and three-headed dogs, we can't, because in the real environment these would not be viable life forms. We can make mice with human ears on their backs in the laboratory, but they could not survive in the wild. Similarly, the lion–tiger hybrids that can sometimes be bred in zoos could not make a living in the habitat of either parent species. Their muddled mix of inherited traits unfits them for either parent's lifestyle. In fact, it seems that actually very few evolutionary niches are available at any given time, and that these are normally far apart, accommodating only the rather widely varied creatures that now occupy them. Most of the range of apparent possibilities between is not habitable. That is why there have been so many extinctions; threatened species could not usually find somewhere else to go. Any change that is not directly demanded by altered outside circumstances is likely to be lethal. Evolution, in fact, knows what it is about when it puts together the repertoire of characteristics that marks a species.

TAKING CHARGE OF NATURE

Lately, however, some distinguished champions of bio-engineering have started to tell a different story, claiming that this whole idea of firm divisions among species is out of date. Not only (they say) can some characteristics be moved about among species, but there is no reason in principle why all characteristics should not be so moved. Species are not serious entities at all, merely fluid stages on a path along which organisms can always be shifted and transformed into one another. This transformability is called algeny, a name modelled on alchemy, but this time (it is claimed) not a mistake but a genuine advance. (The name has not been devised as a joke by outside critics. It comes from Joshua Lederberg, a Nobel laureate biologist and past president of Rockefeller University who is a powerful champion of bioengineering.[2])

Algenists propose, then, that just as the alchemists thought of all chemical substances as merely stages on an unbroken continuum, so biologists should see living species as stages on a continuum along which, in principle, they can always be moved and exchange their properties. As in alchemy, this process has a direction, the word 'alchemy' itself being apparently derived from an Arabic word for 'perfection.' For the alchemists, all metals were in the process of becoming gold. Alchemists saw themselves as midwives accelerating this natural process of improvement. And, notoriously, this was for them not just a commercial enterprise but also a mystical and religious one. When Meister Eckhart wrote that 'copper is restless until it becomes gold'[3] he was speaking figuratively of the soul's struggle for salvation, a way of thinking that still impressed Newton.

In the same way today, the mystics of the genetic revolution see themselves as experts engaged in completing nature's work and especially in the business of ultimately perfecting humanity. As Robert Sinsheimer puts it,

> The old dreams of the cultural perfection of man were always sharply constrained by his inherited imperfections and limitations
>   . . . The horizons of the new eugenics are in principle boundless – for we should have the potential to create new genes and new qualities

yet undreamed of . . . Indeed this concept marks a turning-point in the whole evolution of life. For the first time in all time, a living creature understands its origin and can undertake to design its future. Even in the ancient myths man was constrained by essence. He could not rise above his nature to chart his destiny. Today we can envision that chance – and its dark companion of awesome choice and responsibility.[4]

More recently, Gregory Stock has carried this banner further in a widely sold book called *Redesigning Humans: Choosing Our Children's Genes.*[5] In his first chapter, which is called 'The Last Human,' he remarks that 'we are on the cusp of profound biological change, poised to transcend our current form and character on a journey to destinations of new imagination.' This journey, as he later explains, has become possible because the technological powers we have hitherto used so effectively to remake our world are now potent and precise enough for us to turn them on ourselves . . .

> With our biological research we are taking control of evolution and beginning to direct it . . . Ray Kurzweil, the inventor of the Kurzweil reading machine, the Kurzweil music synthesizer and other high-tech products, . . . [predicts that] 'We will enhance our brains gradually through direct connexion with machine intelligence until the essence of our thinking has fully migrated to the far more capable and reliable new machinery' . . . By 2029, computer technology will have progressed to the point where 'direct neural pathways have been perfected for high-bandwidth connection to the human brain'
>   . . . As Hans Moravec . . . points out in *Mind Children* . . . once we build human-equivalent computers, they will figure out how to build superhuman ones . . . One day we will manipulate the genes of our children in sophisticated ways, using advanced germinal choice technologies . . . The desire and the perceived need are clear.[6]

This last point is important to Stock because he realizes that not all his readers will at once agree that they feel this irresistible desire.

He meets that difficulty with two alternative strategies which are both familiar legacies from the Marxist Utopian tradition. Part of the time, he assures us that we probably do want these changes even if we aren't aware of it yet. But it doesn't much matter if some of us don't want them, because everybody else does, so these things will happen anyway. The rest of the time, he concedes that perhaps we don't quite want them yet, but urges us to get over this weakness by nerving ourselves to follow our spiritual destiny – not because we know what it is but, on the contrary, just because we don't. Ironically, embracing the challenges and goals of these transformative technologies is an act of extraordinary faith. It embodies an acceptance of a human fate written both in our underlying nature and in the biology that constitutes us. We cannot know where self-directed evolution will take us, nor hope to control the process for very long . . .

> In offering ourselves as vessels for potential transformation into we know not what, we are submitting to the shaping hand of a process that dwarfs us individually . . . From a spiritual perspective, the project of humanity's self-evolution is the ultimate embodiment of our science and ourselves as a cosmic instrument in our ongoing emergence . . . We know all too well our limitations, our ineptitudes and weaknesses. No wonder the idea that we would attempt to fashion not only our future world but our future selves terrifies many people . . . We would be flying forward with no idea where we are going and no safety-net to catch us . . . If, instead of blinding ourselves with Utopian images we admit that we don't know where we are headed, maybe we will work harder to ensure that the process itself serves us, and in the end that is what we must count on.[7]

This vision would, of course, look more impressive if it was really *ourselves* that we were offering up as vessels to this mysterious process rather than our unfortunate descendants. But in that case, we should, of course, probably be even less willing to sign up for it. The pronoun *we* operates very oddly in these contexts.

Stock also quotes, though a little less confidently, from the 1992 manifesto of a sect called The Extropians, so named because they don't believe in entropy. It is a letter to Mother Nature:

> Mother Nature, truly we are grateful for what you have made us. No doubt you did the best you could. However, with all due respect, we must say that you have in many ways done a poor job with the human constitution. You have made us vulnerable to disease and damage. You compel us to age and die – just as we're beginning to attain wisdom. And, you forgot to give us the operating manual for ourselves! . . . What you have made is glorious, yet deeply flawed . . . We have decided that it is time to amend the human constitution . . . We do not do this lightly, carelessly or disrespectfully, but cautiously, intelligently and in pursuit of excellence . . . Over the coming decades we will pursue a series of changes to our own constitution . . . We will no longer tolerate the tyranny of aging and death . . . We will expand our perceptual range . . . improve on our neural organization and capacity . . . reshape our motivational patterns and emotional responses . . . take charge over our genetic programming and achieve mastery over our biological and neurological processes.[8]

If we 'reshape our motivational patterns and emotional responses,' presumably making them different, how do we know that we shall then want to go on with these projects that we have started? Where is this confidence in I-know-not-whattery supposed to come from? Faith is certainly in great demand in these quarters, and it is not in short supply. Similarly, species transformations are confidently seen as being quite straightforward. Thus, Thomas Eisner writes,

> As a consequence of recent advances in genetic engineering, [a biological species] must be viewed as . . . a depository of genes that are potentially transferable. A species is not merely a hard-bound volume of the library of nature. It is also a loose-leaf book, whose individual pages, the genes, might be available for selective transfer and modification of other species.[9]

NOTES

1. J.B. Elshtain, 'To Clone Or Not To Clone', *in Clones and Clones, Facts and Fantasies about Human Cloning*, ed. M.K. Nussbaum and C.R. Sunstein (New York, W. W. Norton, 1998), p. 184.

2. J. Lederberg, 'Experimental Genetics and Human Evolution', *Bulletin of the Atomic Scientists*, October 1996, p. 6.

3. T. Burckhardt, *Alchemy, Science of the Cosmos, Science of the Soul*, tr. W. Stoddart (London, Stuart and Watkins, 1967), p. 25.

4. R. Sinsheimer, 'The Prospect of Designed Genetic Change', *Engineering and Science* (April 1969), pp. 8–13, emphases mine.

5. G. Stock, *Redesigning Humans* (London, Profile Books, 2002).

6. Ibid., pp. 1, 13, 20–1, 124–5.

7. Ibid., pp. 173, emphasis mine.

8. Ibid., p. 158.

9. 'Chemical Ecology and Genetic Engineering: The Prospects for Plant Protection and the Need for Plant Habitat Conservation', *Symposium on Tropical Biology and Agriculture* (St Louis, Mo., Monsanto Company, 15 July 1985).

25

THE SUPERNATURAL ENGINEER

IMAGES OF ALIENATION

What does this idea of separable leaves amount to? Scientifically, of course, the idea doesn't work. This language reflects an unusable view of genetics, so-called 'bean-bag genetics' of the crudest kind: one gene, one characteristic. From the metaphorical angle too, the implications of these pictures are not encouraging. The idea of improving books by splicing in bits of other books is not seductive because in books, as in organisms, ignoring the context usually produces nonsense. Nor is the parallel with the chemical elements, which is more seriously meant, any more hopeful. Of course, it is true that atomic scientists did, up to a point, confirm the alchemists' suspicion that it was possible to break the boundaries between elements. They broke them at Los Alamos and Hiroshima and on a number of other occasions since, for instance at Chernobyl. But these events did not generate any general recipe for breaking them safely and successfully. Nor did researchers

DOI: 10.4324/9781003588160-32

discover that the elements evince any general progress toward ultimate perfection, either in gold or in Homo sapiens.

Another more powerful image, however, lurks behind this one. It is the image constantly suggested by the word 'engineering': the simple analogy with machines. Cogs and sprockets can in principle be moved from one machine to another since they are themselves fairly simple artefacts, and the working of these machines is more or less fully understood by their designers. Those who use this analogy seem to be claiming that we have a similar understanding of the plants and animals into which we might put new components. But we did not design those plants and animals. This is perhaps a rather important difference. The really strange and disturbing thing about all these images is the alienation of the human operator from the system he works on. He appears outside the system. He is an autonomous critic, independent of the forces that shape everything around him, a fastidious reader in a position to reshape books to suit his own taste, a detached engineer redesigning a car to his own satisfaction. Even when the book or car in question is a human body – perhaps his own – this designer stands outside it, a superior being who does not share its nature. Readers can always get another book if they don't like the first one, and car-owners are not much surprised at having to get another car.

What sort of being, then, is this operator supposed to be? He (it surely is a he) can only be a Cartesian disembodied soul, a ghost working on the machine. He 'lives in his body' only in the sense in which a yachtsman might live in his boat. Like so much of the science fiction that has influenced them, these images are irremediably dualist, implying a quite unreal separation between ourselves and the physical world we live in. Today we are supposed to have escaped from Descartes' dualistic prison, but some of us don't even want to try to.[1]

NEW TECHNOLOGIES, NEW WORLDVIEWS

How seriously ought we to take these algenic manifestos? Need we really worry about their strange metaphors?

Of course, not all bio-engineers sign up for this bizarre ideology, or want to. They may well not speak or write in these terms. All the same, it surely does seem that they are often acting in those terms, whether consciously or not. The scale on which the whole work is going forward, the colossal confidence expressed in it, the way in which it distracts attention from other possible enterprises, the rate at which money flows into it rather than in other directions, all seem to imply a belief that its possibilities are unparalleled – potentially infinite. It is taken for granted that this is the best way to solve our problems. It is expected, quite generally, that social questions will have this kind of biochemical solution.

This is surely what appals the objectors. What they are essentially rejecting is not any particular single project. It is this huge uncriticized impetus, this indiscriminate, infectious corporate overconfidence, this obsessive one-way channelling of energy, fired by a single vision. The speed and scale involved are crucial. Single projects, introduced slowly, tentatively, and critically, would not necessarily disrupt our whole idea of nature. We have got used to many such changes in human history. But it always takes time to learn to live with them, to get a realistic idea of their pros and cons, to fit new things into our lives without wasteful misdirection. It is already taking us a long time to do that with existing inventions such as contraception and rapid transport.

Anyone who doesn't think this kind of delay is necessary – anyone who wants people to rush with aplomb into this mass investment of mind and resources – does have to be calling for a drastically changed view of nature as a whole, a view that claims that our power and knowledge are such that we can rationally expect to alter everything. To feel this kind of confidence, we would need to stop seeing the natural world as a colossally complex system with its own laws, a system that we, as a tiny part of it, must somehow try to fit into. We would need, instead, to see it simply as a consignment of inert raw material laid out for our use.

To say that this change is *unnatural* is not just to say that it is unfamiliar. It is unnatural in the quite plain sense that it calls on us to alter radically our whole conception of nature. Our culture has of course already moved a long way in the direction of making that shift, from Bacon's trumpet calls in the seventeenth century to Henry Ford's in the twentieth. Of late, however, environmental alarms have sharply slowed that triumphalist movement, making us try to be more realistic about our own vulnerability and dependence. The ideology of algeny is clearly a step backward from that painful struggle toward realism.

In fact, our culture is at present trying to ride two horses here. It is poised uneasily between two views of nature. The confident, contemptuous Baconian view already pervades many of our institutions, notably in intensive farming, where the feeding arrangements that produced mad cow disease are nothing exceptional. Market forces see to it that short-termism and institutionalized callousness already rule the way in which we rear animals for food. Seeing this, proponents of bioengineering sometimes ask why we should object to moving further in this direction. Doesn't consistency demand that we extend the conquest that we have begun and mechanize our lives completely?

Consistency, however, is notoriously not always a virtue, as the public is uneasily aware. The fact that you have cut off somebody's arm is not always a reason why you have to cut off their leg as well. It is one thing to have drifted into having faulty institutions that one doesn't yet see how to change. Deliberately adopting an ideology that entirely obscures what is bad about them is quite another.

That ideology is what really disturbs me, and I think it is what disturbs the public. This proposed new way of looking at nature is not scientific. It is not something that biology has shown to be necessary. Far from that, it is scientifically muddled. It rests on bad genetics and dubious evolutionary biology. Though it uses science, it is not itself a piece of science but a powerful myth expressing a determination to put ourselves in a relation of control to the non-human world around us, to be in the driving seat at all costs rather than attending to that world and trying to understand how it works. It is a myth that repeats, in a grotesquely simple sense, Marx's rather rash suggestion that the important thing is not to understand the world but to change it. Its imagery is a Brocken spectre, a huge shadow projected onto a cloudy background by the shape of a few recent technological achievements.

The debate then is not between Feeling, in the blue corner, objecting to the new developments, and Reason in the red corner, defending them. Rhetoric such as that of Stock and Sinsheimer and Eisner is not addressed to Reason. It is itself an exuberant power fantasy, very much like the songs sung in the 1950s during the brief period of belief in an atomic free lunch, and also like those in the early days of artificial intelligence. The euphoria is the same. It is, of course, also partly motivated by the same hope of attracting grant money, just as the earlier alchemists needed to persuade powerful patrons that they were going to produce real, coinable gold. But besides these practical considerations, in each case there is also a sincere excitement, a devout faith, a real sense of contacting something superhuman. The magician becomes intoxicated with the thought that he is at last getting his hands on a power that lies near the heart of life. This kind of exaltation has a significant history. In our culture, it arose first in the seventeenth century, when theorists became fascinated by the burgeoning marvels of clockwork automata. This was the point at which technology began to shape the imagery by which people depicted their world and so to *dictate their metaphysic* – a process that continues and that has profound effects. On each occasion, prophets have gone far beyond the reasonable expectation of useful devices from the new form of work. Each time, they have used this new form to reshape their whole vision of the world, and of themselves, on the pattern of what was going on in their workshops.

In the case of clockwork, Descartes, Newton, and the eighteenth-century mechanists managed to shape a powerful vision that displayed the whole material world as one vast clock, claiming that the right way to understand any part of it was simply to find its 'mechanism,' that is, the part of the machine that drove it. The cogs of this machinery were supposed to work always by direct physical impact. That imagery was so strong that, when physicists themselves began to move away from it at the end of the nineteenth century, their attempt raised deep distress in the profession. Einstein and many others felt that rationality itself was threatened. And a general belief in this kind of clockwork undoubtedly remains today, in spite of the shift to electronic machinery. We still talk of 'mechanisms,' and we are still not really happy about action at a distance, as in gravitation. And we are still using this language when we talk of 'bio-engineering.' But for the last century, we have not been in a position to suppose, as Laplace did, that clockwork is literally the universal structure of the world.

THE RELEVANCE OF 'GOD'

The difficulties of the physicists' shift from strict mechanism show up as a problem that cannot help recurring. How can people who see the world as a reflection of their current favourite technology handle the change from one technology to another? The status of a world-view that revolves around a particular technology must vary with that technology's practical success and failure. Yet worldviews are expected to be permanent, to express timeless truths. Finality is expected when they are supposed to be religious and no less so when they are supposed to be scientific.

The mechanistic picture was both religious and scientific. From the religious angle, it did not, in its original form, mark any sharp break from earlier views, since God was still the designer. The stars were still busy, as they were in Addison's hymn,

> For ever singing as they shine
> 'The hand that made us is divine'[2]

This ambiguity was what enabled the pattern to catch on so widely, allowing the general public to accept Pope's celebration of it:

> Nature and Nature's laws lay hid in night:
> God said 'Let Newton be' and all was light.[3]

On the clockwork model, the world thus became amazingly intelligible. God, however, gradually withdrew from the scene, leaving a rather unsettling imaginative vacuum. The imagery of machinery survived. But where there is no designer, the whole idea of mechanism begins to grow incoherent. Natural selection is supposed to fill the gap, but it is a thin idea, not very satisfying to the imagination.

That is how the gap that hopeful biotechnicians now elect themselves to fill arose. They see that mechanistic thinking calls for a designer, and they feel well qualified to volunteer for that vacant position. Their confidence about this stands out clearly from the words I have emphasized in Sinsheimer's proposal that 'the horizons of the new eugenics are in principle boundless – for we should have the potential to create new genes and new qualities yet undreamed of . . . For the first time in all time *a living creature* understands its origin and can undertake to design its future.'[4] Which living creature? It cannot be human beings in general; they wouldn't know how to do it. It has to be the elite, the biotechnologists who are the only people able to make these changes. So it emerges that members of the public who complain that biotechnological projects involve *playing God* have in fact understood this claim correctly. That phrase, which defenders of the projects dismiss as mere mumbo jumbo, is actually a quite exact term for the sort of claim to omniscience and omnipotence on these matters that is being put forward.

The God-shaped hole in question has, of course, been causing trouble for some time. After the triumphal Newtonian spring, physics got increasingly complicated, to the point where J.C. Squire revised Pope's epitaph, complaining that

> It could not last; the Devil howling 'Ho!
> Let Einstein be!' restored the status quo.[5]

ATOMS, COMPUTERS, AND GENES

At this point, a new world picture ought to have emerged, a picture drawn, this time, not from technology but from science itself. But, as Squire said, the public found these new physical theories so obscure that nobody managed to express them in a convenient image. The idea of 'relativity' only generated a social myth, a vague cultural relativism about human affairs. Not till after the Second World War did three new, much more colourful images emerge in rapid succession. They all reached the general public, and they were all reflections of new technologies. They are the ones that occupy us today.

First, at the physical level, the idea of the atom was dramatized by bombs and by the promise of atomic power, so that the world seemed to consist essentially of atoms. Second, in human social life, computers emerged, and it was promptly explained that everything was really information. And third, on the biological scene, genetic determinism appeared, declaring that (among living things at least) everything was really genes and we were only the vehicles of our genes, but that (rather surprisingly) we nevertheless had the power to control them.

It has proved quite hard to relate these three different world-pictures, all of them reductive, but requiring different reductions. In theory, of course, they should not conflict. As far as they are scientific, they should, properly speaking, all find their modest places within the wider field of science. But world-pictures like this are not primarily science. The science that is supposed to justify them is quite a small part of their content. They are actually metaphysical sketches, ambitious maps of how all reality is supposed to work, guiding visions, systems of direction for the rest of our ideas. And because these visions draw their strength from particular technologies in the outside world, belief in them fluctuates with the success of their parent technology and particularly with its disasters.

The news of Three Mile Island and Chernobyl took much of the steam out of the atomic myth. Though we still know atoms are important, we do not turn to them today for salvation. Bioengineering has not yet had a similar disaster; if it does, the consequence will surely be the same. As for artificial intelligence, hard experience has cut back many of the claims that were made in its early days. But computers are still becoming more and more central in our lives and the metaphysical notion that 'everything is really information' gains strength with the acceptance of them. Thus, today nobody is surprised to read in a book written by two (otherwise respectable) cosmologists the following strange jumble of metaphysical claims:

> An intelligent being – or more generally, any living creature – is fundamentally *a type of computer* . . . A human being is *a program* designed to

run on a particular hardware called a human body . . . A living human being is *a representation of a definite program*.[6]

Thus in a way that is surely very remarkable, our technology and our economics combine to shape our worldview. As Jeremy Rifkin reasonably points out:

> Every new economic and social revolution in history has been accompanied by a new explanation of the creation of life and the workings of nature. The new concept of nature is always the most important strand of the matrix that makes up any new social order. *In each instance, the new cosmology serves to justify the rightness and inevitability of the new way human beings are organizing their world by suggesting that nature itself is organized along similar lines* . . . Our concepts of nature are utterly, unabashedly, almost embarrassingly anthropocentric . . . The laws of nature are being re-written to conform with our latest manipulation of the natural world . . . The new ideas about nature provide the legitimizing framework of the Biotech Century . . . Algeny . . . is humanity's attempt to give metaphysical meaning to its emerging technological relationship with nature.[7]

POSSESSED BY A TECHNOLOGY

Of course, technology is an important part of our life. Of course, each new technology does teach us something about the world around us – often something very important. We can rightly draw from these lessons models to help us understand wider phenomena, so far as those models are actually useful.

The trouble only comes in with the obsession with a particular model that drives out other necessary ways of thinking. The objectors are saying that the luminous fascination of bio-engineering is making us constantly look for biochemical solutions to complex problems that are not biochemical at all but social, political, psychological and moral. For instance, much of the demand for liver transplants is due to alcohol. But it is a lot harder to think what to do about alcohol than it is to call for research on transplants. Similarly, infertility is largely caused by late marriage and sexually transmitted diseases. But changing the customs that surround these things calls for quite different and much less straightforward kinds of thinking. Again, food shortages throughout the world are caused much more by faulty systems of distribution than by low crop yields, and – in the opinion of most experienced aid agencies – the promotion of patented transgenic crops in poor countries is calculated to increase the faults in those distribution systems, not to cure them.

I touch on these examples briefly and crudely here, merely to show that objectors who are moved by strong emotion are not necessarily being merely irrational and negative. My aim throughout has been to point out the solid thoughts that may be found underlying this particular emotion and to suggest that – here as in other issues of policy – we had better take such thoughts seriously. Strong feeling no more invalidates these contemporary protests than the equally strong feeling that accompanied early protests against slavery and torture invalidated those campaigns. In all such cases, we need to understand what the excitement is about, not simply to dismiss it. And here, if we look into what is causing the alarm, we shall find that this is not a mere local or passing issue. These remarkable proposals flow from a long-standing, unrealistic attitude to the earth, of which we are often unaware.

NOTES

1. K. Devlin, *Goodbye Descartes* (New York, John Wiley, 1997); G. Ryle, *The Concept of Mind* (London, Hutchinson, 1951), Chapter 1.
2. J. Addison, 'Ode', *Spectator*, no. 465.
3. A. Pope, 'Epitaph Intended for Sir Isaac Newton'.
4. R. Sinsheimer, 'The Prospect of Designed Genetic Change', *Engineering and Science*, April 1969, pp. 8–13.
5. Or perhaps, as some authorities claim, Hilaire Belloc.
6. J.H. Barrow and F.W. Tipler, *The Anthropic Cosmological Principle* (Oxford, Oxford University Press, 1986), p. 659, emphases mine.
7. J. Rifkin, *The Biotech Century* (London, Gollancz, 1998), pp. 197–8, emphases mine.

26

THE REMARKABLE MASCULINE
BIRTH OF TIME

PUTTING NATURE IN HER PLACE

Was Aristotle right to encourage wonder, awe, and reverence towards the physical world? It is one of the points that the founders of modern science held against him. Thus Descartes wrote, 'Know that by nature I do not mean some goddess or some sort of imaginary power. I employ this word to signify matter itself.'[1] Similarly, Robert Boyle, in his *Enquiry into the Vulgarly Received Notion of Nature*, complained that

> men are taught and wont to attribute stupendous unaccountable effects to sympathy, antipathy, *fuga vacui*, substantial forms, and especially to a certain being. . . which they call Nature; for this is represented as a kind of goddess, whose power may be little less than boundless.[2]

DOI: 10.4324/9781003588160-33

Accordingly, Boyle complained, 'the veneration wherewith men are imbued for what they call nature, has been a discouraging impediment to the empire of man over the inferior creatures of God.'[3]

This was an important element in the new notion then being forged of what it was to be scientific. With a similar disapproval of wonder, Descartes earlier expressed the hope 'that those who have understood all that has been said in this treatise will, in future, see nothing whose cause they cannot easily understand, nor anything that gives them any reason to marvel.'[4] Wonder itself was to cease. Explanations were to become so clear that there was to be no more mystery. Not only would everything on earth now be understood, it would also be demythologized, disenchanted, depersonified, and seen, in the bleakest of daylight, as not specially impressive after all. Matter, fully debunked, was from now on to be recognized as what the New Philosophy declared it to be – mere inert, passive, mindless stuff, devoid of spontaneity, of all interesting properties such as sympathy and antipathy, and above all destitute of any creative power. All pleasing forms that might seem to belong to matter were to be credited, not to it, but directly to God the Creator.

God, seen as fully active and fully intellectual, was the beneficiary now credited with these powers, reft from Nature. Having intelligence as well as creative power, God could do directly – either at the moment of creation or through later miracles – all that had been previously thought to need special adaptations in matter itself. And that is what the men who founded the Royal Society (by and large) took him to do.

It is surely extraordinary that nineteenth- and twentieth-century thinkers have supposed that they could take over this attitude to matter unaltered, while eliminating the omnipotent Creator who gave sense to it, as well as the immortal soul which took its status from him. The metaphor of matter as machinery still continues to run around like a chicken with its head off, though the Designer who gave a sense to it has been removed.

Peter Atkins, echoing Monod, rejoices that 'the Creator had absolutely no job to do' and 'can be allowed to evaporate and disappear from the scene.'[5] To make sure of that, it would be necessary both to understand much better what is involved in the idea of creation and to abolish the impoverished seventeenth-century ideas about mind and matter with a thoroughness that Atkins does not begin to conceive of. Before starting to raise any questions about a creating God, we need to make room for the creative powers of matter, to recognize once more the complexity of nature. The pre-adaptations that made life a possible option must, after all, still be lodged somewhere.

NATURE AND HER TORMENTORS

What went wrong? It may be easier to see that if we notice the way in which the pioneers of mechanism went about reshaping the concept of Nature. Very properly, they wanted to try the experiment of depersonalizing it. With that in view, the first step they surely needed to take was to stop using the feminine pronoun, or indeed any personal pronoun for 'Nature' altogether. But this was not done. We come here to one more of the strange compensatory myths, dreams, or dramas that are my theme. The literature of early modern science is a mine of highly coloured passages that describe Nature, by no means as a neutral object, but as a seductive but troublesome female, to be unrelentingly pursued, sought out, fought against, chased into her inmost sanctuaries, prevented from escaping, persistently courted, wooed, hated, vexed, tormented, unveiled, unrobed, and 'put to the question' (i.e. interrogated under torture), forced to confess 'all that lay in her most intimate recesses,' her 'beautiful bosom' must be laid bare, she must be held down and finally 'pierced' and 'vanquished' (words which constantly recur).

Now this odd talk does not come just from a few exceptionally uninhibited writers. It has not been invented by modern feminists. It is the common, constant idiom of the age. Since historians began to notice it, they have been able to collect it up easily in handfuls for every discussion. I can't spend time on doing that here, but I will just give briefly a few well-known examples from Francis Bacon, who was something of a trailblazer in the matter.

Bacon dismissed the Aristotelians as people who had stood impotent before Nature, destined 'never to lay hold of her and capture her.' Aristotle (said Bacon), being a mere contemplative, had 'left Nature herself untouched and inviolate.' By contrast, Bacon called upon the 'true sons of knowledge' to 'penetrate further' and to 'overcome Nature in action,' so that 'passing by the outer courts of nature, which many have trodden, we may find a way at length into her inner chambers.' Mankind 'would then be able, not just to exert a gentle guidance over Nature's course,' but to 'conquer and subdue nature to shake her to her foundations' and to 'discover the secrets still locked in Nature's bosom.' Men (Bacon added) ought to make peace among themselves so as to turn 'with united forces against the Nature of Things, to storm and occupy her castles and strongholds.' By these means scientists would bring about the 'truly masculine birth of time' by which they would subdue 'Nature with all her children, to bind her to your service and make her your slave.'[6]

Just to show that this way of talking did not die with the crude manners of the seventeenth century, here are a couple of later echoes from Adam Sedgwick, that immensely respectable clerical professor of geology at Cambridge who was so disturbed by Darwin's theories. Sedgwick, describing true scientific method, explained how, after laws have been carefully formulated, investigators must always 'again put nature to the torture and wring new secrets from her.'[7] And, shifting to the military end of the spectrum, Sedgwick also described Newton as having 'stormed the sky with mathematical artillery.'[8]

SCIENTISTS EMBATTLED

What, then, was all this destructiveness directed against? It is evident that, at this point, there did develop a sense of real alarm and disgust − a resolve to *écraser l'infâme* − directed against earlier views which were seen, not just as mistaken, but as odious because religiously wrong − as pagan and superstitious.

The campaign waged by members of the Royal Society, and by seventeenth-century mechanists generally, was not, as their atheistical successors often suppose, a campaign against religion as such. It was primarily a campaign against the *wrong* religion – against what seemed like nature-worship, against a religion centring on the earth, and apparently acknowledging a mysterious pagan goddess rather than an intellectual god. All the great scientific pioneers claimed to be campaigning on behalf of Christianity. And with most of them, this was not just a political move – as again people now tend to think – but a matter of real conviction.

Nor was the fight only against Aristotelian thinking. Aristotelianism was indeed the traditional orthodoxy that all scientific reformers wanted to change. But the contest was three-cornered, and the most bitter hostility was between two parties of reformers – between the mechanists, represented by Descartes, and the exponents of what was called 'natural magic.' This was a belief in an all-pervading system of occult forces, of mysterious sympathies and antipathies, the sort of thing that we do indeed now tend to think of as superstitious.

It was, however, by no means just a hole-and-corner affair used by sorcerers. It was a sophisticated system expounded by scientists some of whom were not in any ordinary sense magicians at all, but were quite as learned, quite as experimental, and often quite as successful, as the mechanists. The contest was not a simple one between light and darkness.

Thus, Galileo in his *Dialogue* wrote with great respect of William Gilbert's book *De Magnete* (1600), accepting Gilbert's findings about magnets, though he differed from him about how to interpret them. Gilbert had attacked Aristotle for dividing the cosmos into a divine realm in the heavens and an inferior one on the earth, because this view dishonoured the earth. The earth, wrote Gilbert, is not to be 'condemned and driven into exile and cast out of all the fair order of the glorious universe, as being brute and soulless.' 'As for us,' he continues, 'we deem the whole world animate and all globes, all stars, and this glorious earth too, we hold to be from the beginning by their own destinate souls governed.'[9]

Gilbert and Galileo thus both wanted to bring attitudes to the earth and heavens together again. But Galileo saw this as best achieved by withdrawing superstitious reverence from the heavens while exalting the earth. 'We shall prove the earth to be a wandering body surpassing the moon in splendour, and not the sink of all dull refuse of the universe.'[10] Gilbert, by contrast, proposed to do it by extending reverence to earth as well as heaven, by looking for explanations of its behaviour in its own creative properties, and by the very significant image of the earth as mother. Gilbert wrote that all material things have 'a propensity. . . towards a common source, towards the mother where they were begotten.'[11]

In some contexts, these ideas proved surprisingly useful for science. For instance, Gilbert argued that tides are produced by the attraction of the moon, working through sympathy. Johannes Kepler, accepting this idea, added that this was only part of a general system of attraction which explains all 'heaviness (or gravity).' Heaviness, said Kepler, is simply a 'mutual corporeal disposition between related bodies towards union or conjunction. . . so that it is much rather the case that the earth attracts a stone than that the stone seeks the earth.' Kepler suggested that the moon's attraction is what produces the tides, and he added, 'If the earth should cease to attract its oceans, the waters in all its seas would fly up and flow round the body of the moon.'[12] Kepler built this idea into his refinement of the Copernican system, by which he produced tables of the planetary motions which were some fifty to a hundred times more accurate than existing tables.

To us, who are used to Newton, all this seems reasonable enough, and Kepler may sound like a typical pioneer of modern science. But this is where our foundation myths are so misleading. At the time, the mechanistic scientists who fill the rest of our pantheon rejected Kepler's view fiercely as superstitious. In particular, Galileo, who might have been expected to welcome Kepler's support for the Copernican system, simply ignored it. The trouble was that, in the mechanists' view, 'attraction' was no real explanation at all. It was just an unintelligible, vacuous name for an 'occult force.'

To mechanists, no explanation counted as intelligible unless it worked on the familiar model of push-pull, like the parts of the cog-driven machines with which they were familiar. Now it is hopelessly difficult to explain in this kind of way the well-known fact that things fall, or indeed how things stick together in the first place – how the hard particles, whose motion leads them only to bang against each other, sometimes form solid stones rather than heaps of dust. Attraction was suggested here too, but it was still viewed as a vacuous superstition.

The mechanistic systems most widely favoured, such as Descartes's theory of vortices, had no explanation for either of these things that looked even faintly plausible. In spite of this, not only was Kepler laughed out of court, but the same objection still told very strongly later against Newton. His theory of gravitation was resisted as empty and irrational well into the eighteenth century. As late as 1747, three most distinguished French scientists – Euler, Clairaut, and d'Alembert – claimed to have disproved Newton's theory of gravitation, and it was some time before the resulting controversy was settled in his favour.

EXPLANATION AND RATIONALITY

All this lights up in a most interesting way the question of *what counts as an explanation*. Familiarity is always demanded here. The mechanists thought it more rational to stick with patent non-explanations – with stories that did not pretend to explain at all – rather than to use an explanation that was fertile but unfamiliar in form. They thought, moreover, that rationality demanded complete simplicity; there must be only one explanatory system. They should therefore leave what was effectively a blank round awkward facts such as the phenomenon of falling bodies, until they could explain it by a story of the only right and familiar form.

Their faith that this better story would follow is impressive. Descartes laid it down as a demand of reason that the post-dated cheques would, in the end, always be honoured. It was certain that all temporarily puzzling items – such as magnets, tides and falling bodies – have 'no qualities so occult nor effects of sympathy and antipathy so marvellous or strange,' that their properties cannot be explained in terms of the '*size, shape, situation and motion of different particles of matter.*'[13] (emphasis mine).

(The differences among these 'different particles' themselves would, of course, only be differences of size and shape; all matter was otherwise homogeneous, inert and without qualities.) Again, 'There are no amazing and marvellous sympathies and antipathies, in fact *there exists nothing in the whole of nature which cannot be explained in terms of purely corporeal causes devoid of mind and thought.*'[14] (emphasis mine).

It is interesting to see how Descartes's double negative here conceals the huge confidence of his claim. To say 'there is nothing that cannot be so explained,' sounds quite sceptical and parsimonious. To say, 'I and my colleagues can and eventually will explain everything in these limited terms,' would sound much bolder. But they come to the same thing. The claim is that, in the end, Nature will be forced to speak the whole truth in this one language. If it seems to be saying something in some other language meanwhile, it should not be listened to.

This ruling went for gravitational attraction, and it also went for the even tougher case of living creatures. No special creative properties of matter – no *biological* properties – were to be allowed for the forming of these. Descartes declared them to be automata, mechanisms working by arrangements of inner cogs and pistons which were not even very complex. The physicist's chronic lack of interest in biology has seldom been so plainly expressed.

'Since' (wrote Descartes) '*so little is necessary to make an animal*, it is certainly not surprising that so many animals, so many worms and insects, are formed spontaneously under our very eyes in all kinds of putrefying matter'[15] (emphasis mine). These animals had of course no souls and were no more conscious than the rest of the physical world. The size, shape, situation and motion of particles would easily explain them. Or, as Peter Atkins put it in the quite recent formulation that I quoted earlier, 'Inanimate things are innately simple. That is one more step along the path to the view that animate things, being innately inanimate, are innately simple too.'[16]

The striking thing about claims like these is surely the high proportion of faith to evidence. The force supporting this faith is not any observation of facts. It is a special, very narrow, picture of what scientific rationality demands, a picture which allows only a small set of premisses. It is assumed that all explanations will be of one type, that they must all be expressed in a single language.

This assumption did of course bear good fruit where mathematics was taken to be that language, by making it possible to discover general formal structures underlying matter. But one successful set of explanations never rules out the scope for others. It is not possible that mathematics itself should do all the explaining that we need. In order to apply mathematics to the real world at all, we have to use other conceptual schemes first so as to select the items that are to be measured or counted. Just as mathematical expressions are only a small, specialized part of the ordinary language we speak, so mathematical explanations are evidently only one small part of the range of concepts by which we explain and understand things.

What seventeenth-century rationalists like Descartes hoped to do was to build round mathematics a single system of concepts continuous with it, which would be uniform, and able to give a unified explanation of the physical world. It was a magnificent idea, and nobody could know whether it would work till it had been tried. But its champions did not just try it; they declared for a fact that the world was such as to make it work. What was the basis of this faith? Brian Easlea comments:

> The mechanical philosophy certainly presents a breathtaking conception of matter and the cosmos! To say the least, its truth does not stare the natural philosopher in the face. Why, then, was it so widely subscribed to? It was one thing to reject a powerful, creative 'mother earth'; it was quite another to declare nature to consist only of inert, uninteresting matter and nothing more!. . . On the credit side, it was at least a transparently clear philosophy: *matter became, perhaps for the first time and undoubtedly for the last time, conceptually graspable by natural philosophers.* Nevertheless, despite the undoubted advantages of conceptual clarity, the proponents of the mechanical philosophy experienced the utmost difficulty in satisfactorily accounting for such ubiquitous phenomena as cohesion and the falling of heavy bodies perpendicularly to the earth's surface, not to mention the nature of the

mind's interaction with matter, how spontaneous generation occurs and how embryos are formed.

(Emphasis mine)

Easlea goes on to make – what is surely called for – a suggestion about what the extra, non-scientific motives might be that caused this very unsatisfactory piece of science to gain such authority:

> What the mechanical philosophy amounted to was, it seems, a radical 'de-mothering' of nature and the earth in preparation for, and legitimation of, the technological appropriation of the natural world that the mechanical philosophers hoped they and their successors would undertake.[17]

That is to say, the success of this approach was not due – as we were brought up to believe – solely and directly to its scientific correctness. Much of its science did turn out brilliantly successful and, on present views, correct. But the success was quite uneven. Other parts of it were, on present views, simply wrong, and were felt even at the time to be inadequate, though they sprang directly from motives which were conceived as scientific. Some problems – notably that of the connection between soul and body – were admitted to be so awkward for the mechanistic approach that they could only be solved by assuming a perpetual miracle. The need for this miracle was then welcomed as proof of the existence of God, who was needed to perform it.

If we ask how this kind of explanation by miracle differs from the assumption of occult forces, the answer plainly cannot be that it is intellectually clearer. It must be that the religious doctrines involved are sounder. And for some of these awkward problems – such as gravitation – other, non-mechanistic scientific schools had better explanations available.

THE TEMPER OF THE AGE

Of course the solid scientific achievements did play a great part in ensuring the success of the mechanistic approach. But they were supported by something much deeper and less clearly recognized – by a temper, a mood, a drama that filled a felt need at the time, and has long continued to fill it.

Mention of this does not need to tip us into an unbridled relativism. You don't need to be a full-time Marxist to see the economic attraction of a free licence to exploit nature for the age that was beginning to feel the stirrings of the Industrial Revolution and of colonial expansion. You don't need to be a full-time Jungian to see that the symbolism of Mother Earth is a strong one, which can seem threatening to people who are struggling to establish their own independent identity. The unacknowledged Anima can take some very alarming forms, and this alarm can generate bitter and destructive resentment. The denied female element within the male character was clearly giving trouble. But so, surely, were actual women in the world.

For I think you don't – finally – need to be a full-time feminist to conclude something more. When a school of thought, officially dedicated to clear, literal, unemotive speech, regularly uses a lurid language of sexual pursuit, torture and rape to describe the interaction between scientists and the natural world, trouble is also surfacing about the relations between actual men and women. At such a point, an entry in the index under the heading 'gender insecurity' doesn't seem excessive.[18] The mention of feminism in these discussions tends to produce a charge of irrelevance – why talk about that? But it is not irrelevant to correct a long-standing bias. Virism really has been chronic, and has produced some surprisingly irrational distortions. It has not been just a promotion of men's interests over women's but an obsession with a distorted ideal of maleness, an ideal which can in fact damage men's lives as well as women's.

When modern science was being formed, some consciousness of trouble about this sex-linked ideal was already arising. As we are all told at school, the Renaissance was the age of dawning individualism. It was the time when ancient hierarchies began to break up, when kings had their heads cut off and wars of religion subverted societies. It was a time of great insecurity, in which the promise of order which science offered was welcomed for other reasons besides intellectual ones. It was also, however, the age when print diffused learning far more widely than ever before, so that people heard of conditions other than their own, and became less willing to accept subjection. Already in the seventeenth century, some women (especially in France) were beginning to get a little of that learning, and beginning also to become a nuisance by asking for more. We must surely notice that this ingredient too went into the pot if we want to account fully for the strange stew that came out of it.

In any case, what begins to emerge is that the debunking of matter, the desacralizing of the earth, did strike a chord in many people that made it plausibly appear as their salvation. The particular danger that they were struggling to be free of seemed like subservience to an irrational queen or mother. That is why they welcomed – in Bacon's extraordinary phrase – the prospect of a 'masculine birth of time.' That was why the spokesmen of the Royal Society repeatedly declared that it existed to promote 'a truly masculine philosophy.' (What could that possibly mean?) That was why there was such an outbreak of bizarre sexual metaphors in writings about science, an outbreak which (I repeat) is quite real and not an invention of modern feminists. And that is surely also why the simple, clockwork machine model, in spite of its startling faults, kept so much prestige and has remained popular for so long, even when it has proved unusable in many areas, notably in particle physics.

THE TRIUMPH OF FAITH

That, too, was surely why confidence in science as such was so euphoric; why post-dated cheques for the future were so willingly accepted. Descartes's complacency is not exceptional here. From his time on, it has repeatedly been firmly claimed, both that particular scientific programmes will soon produce complete explanations and that science as a whole is about to do so. Indeed, the belief that it will is, again, a part of what has been held to be a scientific attitude.

Over the particular programmes, these claims have again and again proved delusive. They usually turn out to be merely the effect of the over-confidence that comes over hard-working people when some success does at last reward them. About science as a whole, many distinguished sages have pointed out that these claims are bound to collapse. All answers raise more questions; all explanations are provisional and incomplete. Yet the claims go on. Lord Kelvin's declaration towards the end of the nineteenth century that physics was virtually complete was only one of them. Much more recently, Peter Atkins (1981) went on record as follows:

> When we have dealt with the values of the fundamental constants by seeing that they are unavoidably so, and have dismissed them as irrelevant, *we shall have arrived at complete understanding*. Fundamental science can then rest. *We are almost there. Complete knowledge is just within our grasp. Comprehension is moving across the face of the earth, like a sunrise.*[19]

> (Emphases mine)

Similarly Stephen Hawking seems to hope that a complete cosmological theory can be produced which will make possible 'the ultimate triumph of human reason,' namely that 'we would know the mind of God.'[20]

It is worthwhile to remember this kind of remark when we come across the frequently held opinion that hard-headed incredulity is a central part of the scientific character. For scientists, as for anybody else, incredulity is bound to be selective. The wholesale commitment of seventeenth-century physicists to their models was – like that of Darwin, mentioned earlier – for their time an invaluable means of getting the best out of those models. But that is no reason for taking literally the claims that expressed it. Claims like these are chiefly interesting as proofs of what I have called a faith. They have, I think, very little to do with their official subject-matter or with any real question about the content and prospects of science itself. The commitment is always to the drama. What then is that drama?

THE CONFRONTATION

It presented itself to the seventeenth century as a conflict between light and darkness, but also between male and female as alternative possible creative principles. The female principle, Nature, as conceived in the doctrine of natural magic, was life-giving, fertile, bountiful, and generous, but also dark in the sense of mysterious and vast. Because mystery may always conceal danger, she might well be dark also in the sense of sinister and threatening. By contrast the masculine principle, the divine Creator, supplied order for that life, but produced light as well – light which is essential for life as well as for understanding.

Could not these two elements have been seen as coexisting and co-operating? Was it necessary to choose between them? In earlier times, it had seemed more or less possible to combine them, though the attempt to do so often produced serious tension. But in the seventeenth century, most disturbingly, it somehow became much harder to bridge this gap. The male and female principles increasingly appeared as alternatives, indeed as opponents.

The reason for this alarming breach looked different from different angles. From an intellectual angle it appeared, quite respectably, as simply a wider curiosity, an intenser thirst for knowledge. Reason (it seemed) had raised its standards. It was no longer content with a limited understanding of the physical world. It demanded to penetrate everywhere. For this purpose, the light must drive back all the darkness; there must be no more mysteries left. From the religious angle, the project again seemed straightforward and honourable; it was simply a matter of doing due service to God the Creator by making clear that he was responsible for everything of value in his Creation.

Why, however, should either of these harmless projects have called for violent gender-imagery, or indeed for gender-imagery at all? The answer, unfortunately, seems to be that this kind of symbolism has far deeper roots than may appear. It is not a casual weed but a structural feature of the social landscape. Even writers who notice its distorting effect often flounder instructively in their efforts to correct it.

Thus, Robert Hooke likened matter to the 'Female or Mother Principle' which was (he explained)

> abstractly considered without Life or Motion, without form, and void, and dark, a *power in itself wholly unactive*, until it be, as it were, impregnated by the second Principle, which may represent the Pater, and may be called *Paternus, Spiritus*, or hylarchic Spirit.[21]

This way of thinking about male and female was of course not new. As already mentioned, it, with its accompanying physiological fairy-tales, goes back at least to Aristotle, and had been accepted throughout the Middle Ages. But we surely have a right to ask why the bold, revolutionary iconoclasts of the seventeenth century could not throw out this piece of intellectual garbage along with so much else. And we are forced, I think, to give the obvious answer. From the psychological angle, male domination had always been insecure and uneasy. In an age of political revolt and increasing individualism, that domination felt less secure than ever. It was no longer enough for the rational male principle to be seen as the source of all order. He must now be altogether omnipotent.

NOTES

1. Descartes, *Le Monde*, in F. Alquie (ed.), *Oeuvres philosophiques de Descartes* (Paris, Gamier Frères, 1973), vol. 1, p. 349. Quoted by B. Easlea, *Science and Sexual Oppression* (London, Weidenfeld & Nicolson, 1981), p. 72.
2. *The Works of the Honourable Robert Boyle*, ed. T. Birch (London, 1722), vol. 5, p. 532. Quoted by B. Easlea, *Witch-Hunting, Magic and the New Philosophy: An Introduction to the Debates of the Scientific Revolution* (Brighton, Harvester Press, 1980), p. 138.
3. Works, vol. 5, p. 165. Easlea, *Witch-Hunting*, p. 139.
4. *Descartes on Method, Optics, Geometry and Meteorology*, tr. P.J. Olscamp (Indianapolis, Bobbs-Merrill, 1965), p. 361. Easlea, *Witch-Hunting*, p. 117.
5. P. Atkins, *The Creation* (Oxford and San Francisco, W.H. Freeman, 1987), p. 17.
6. B. Farrington, *The Philosophy of Francis Bacon* (Liverpool, Liverpool University Press, 1970), pp. 93, 92, 96, 92, 62.
7. A. Sedgwick, 'Vestiges of the natural history of creation', *Edinburgh Review* 82 (1845), p. 16. Quoted by Easlea, *Science and Sexual Oppression*, p. 103.

8. Sedgwick, 'Vestiges', p. 23.

9. W. Gilbert, *De Magnete* (New York, Dover Publications, 1968), p. 309. Quoted by Easlea, *Witch-Hunting*, p. 91.

10. Quoted in R. Dugas and P. Costabel, 'The Birth of a New Science, Mechanics', in R. Taton (ed.), *The Beginning of Modern Science* (London, Thames & Hudson, 1964), p. 265.

11. *New Philosophy of our Sublunary World*, quoted in P. Duhem, *The Aim and Structure of Physical Theory*, tr. P.P. Wiener (1914, London, Athenaeum, 1962), p. 230.

12. Kepler, 'Astronomia Nova', tr. K.R. Hall, in *Nature and Nature's Laws*, ed. M. Boas (New York, Harper, 1970), p. 73.

13. Descartes, *The Principles of Philosophy*, part 4, para. 187.

14. Descartes, *The Principles of Philosophy*, in F. Alquie (ed.), *Oeuvres philosophiques de Descartes* (Paris, Gamier Freres, 1973), p. 502, note.

15. Descartes, *Primae Cogitationes circa Generationem Animalium* (1701) quoted in J. Roger, *Les Sciences de la vie dans la pensée française die XVIIIme siecle* (Paris, Armand Cohn, 1963), p. 146.

16. P. Atkins, *The Creation* (Oxford and San Francisco, W.H. Freeman, 1987), p. 53.

17. B. Easlea, *Science and Sexual Oppression* (London, Weidenfield & Nicolson, 1981), p. 73.

18. See Easlea, Science and Sexual Oppression, index.

19. The Creation, p. 127.

20. S.W. Hawking, *A Brief History of Time* (London, Bantam Press, 1988), concluding passage.

21. R. Hooke, 'A discourse on the nature of comets' (1682), in R. Walker (ed.), *The Posthumous Works of Robert Hooke* (London, 1705), pp. 171–2. See Easlea, *Science and Sexual Oppression*, p. 85.

PART 4

REASON AND IMAGINATION

The imperialistic visions of science examined in the last section result from a one-sided view of the nature of human understanding, which regards scientific knowledge as the product of Reason alone, unaware of the vital role played by Imagination. Scientists like Peter Atkins (see quote at the beginning of the next chapter) regard literature and philosophy as at best no more than diversions from the real work of understanding the world, which is the business of science alone. Though his may be an extreme view, it is an expression of a much more widespread tendency to regard non-scientific disciplines as 'second-best,' and as merely a provisional, inexact substitute for a future, properly scientific approach to their subject-matter. Other disciplines are merely 'on hold' until they can be 'reduced' to 'hard science.'

As we shall see in the following extracts, however, science cannot actually get started at all until other kinds of thinking have laid the conceptual foundations on which it stands. Without an initial vision of 'how the world fundamentally is,' there is no principle which a scientist can use to decide where and how to begin his investigation.

DOI: 10.4324/9781003588160-34

Historically, probably the single most important source of the vision of reality which lay behind the great scientific revolution of the seventeenth century, and has dominated scientific thinking ever since, was an epic poem written by the Roman philosopher Lucretius.

This vision, originally due to the Greek philosopher Democritus, was that of atomism – everything in the world is composed of minute, indestructible particles (atoms), whose movements, collisions, and combinations underlie the limitless variety of appearances. Its originators had no possibility of empirically confirming their theory, and in fact no interest in doing so – it was put forward for philosophical and religious reasons. And it was assumed, still without proof, by the great pioneers of physical science in the seventeenth, eighteenth and nineteenth centuries.

The atomistic worldview is essentially a materialist one; atoms are what is ultimately real, and they exist as solid, material objects, independent of our minds and having no mental qualities of their own. Everything we observe is to be explained in terms of their motions, according to deterministic causal laws. The external world is therefore essentially impersonal and devoid of moral purpose or meaning. But, as Werner Heisenberg observes in the passage quoted on p. 441, 'Atomic physics has [now] turned from the materialistic trend it had in the nineteenth century.' The vision of modern physics, Heisenberg affirms, is much closer to that of Democritus' contemporary Heraclitus, who saw the world as a perpetual flux, or fire. Energy, not matter, is the basic category, and what is real is not unchangeable atoms but rather change itself. Reality consists not of things but of process.

Not all scientists and commentators on science have caught up with this change, however. The metaphysical assumptions of materialism, reductionism, and determinism which go together with the atomistic vision are still widely taken to be axiomatic, and this leads to numerous problems, especially in relation to attempts to understand life and consciousness. Some of the problems arising from mechanistic attempts to understand life are discussed in Part Five; the most severe problems, however, are those stemming from the attempt to give a coherent account of consciousness within a materialistic world-view.

As Descartes emphasized, the fact that we ourselves are conscious is self-evident and not open to doubt. But if we look through the lens of the worldview of atomistic materialism, this obvious truth appears profoundly puzzling. Where in this picture can we find room for the phenomenon of consciousness? What mysterious motions and combinations of microscopic particles of matter could give rise to this property? As Midgley's discussion makes clear, this is the wrong way to look at the problem. Consciousness, as she says, 'is not just one more phenomenon; it is the scene of all phenomena, the place where appearances appear.' Subjectivity itself cannot be found in the objective world, but this does not mean it is any less real than the items in that world.

Descartes' attempt to deal with this radical difference of kind between consciousness and the material entities which physical science sets out to explain failed because it was at once too radical and not radical enough. By designating mind and matter as different basic substances, he separated them from one another in a way that made it impossible to fit them together again properly; but by placing them both in the category of substance he inevitably made it seem that mind was after all in some way physical, perhaps a very subtle kind of gas or the like. Subsequent attempts to 'solve the mind–body problem' generally suffered from the same difficulty; if consciousness is thought of as a substance in the way that matter is a substance, it becomes impossible to see how the same universe can contain both kinds of stuff. We end up with either materialism or idealism, either denying the reality of one or of the other; both alternatives of course do violence to our common-sense intuition, which informs us that we are conscious, and that what we are conscious of (among other things) is material objects (including our own body).

The last of these extracts considers recent attempts to tackle the problem, most of which to some degree fall foul of the difficulty just alluded to. The 'problem of consciousness,' as it is currently most often formulated, is taken to be the problem of extending the explanatory reach of science so as to be able to include an explanation of consciousness. Framing the problem in this way has an awkward tendency to dictate answers that locate consciousness in the objective world, and it is this move that is actually the source of the perplexity which surrounds the topic. As Midgley says, we need to take on board the insight that these are 'two standpoints, not two stuffs.' Objectivity and subjectivity are equal and indispensable partners in the act of knowing; if we insist on trying to include the knowing subject itself on the objective side along with what appears to it, we are bound to end up in confusion.

SOURCES

'The Sources of Thought' – abridged from Chapters 1–2 of *Science and Poetry*, Routledge, 2000; 'Atomistic Visions: The Quest for Permanence' – *Science and Poetry*, Chapter. 5; 'Putting Our Selves Together Again' – abridged from *Science and Poetry*, Chapters 7–8; 'A Plague on Both Their Houses' – *Science and Poetry*, Chapter 13.

27

THE SOURCES OF THOUGHT

IS ART A LUXURY?

Is there any connection between poetry and science? Academic specialization usually divides these topics today so sharply that it is hard to relate them on a single map. But there is one very simple map which does claim to relate them, a map which is worth looking at because it has quite an influence on our thinking. It is the map which the distinguished chemist Peter Atkins draws in the course of arguing that science is omnicompetent, that is, able to supply all our intellectual needs. He notes that some people may think we need other forms of thought such as poetry and philosophy as well as science because science cannot deal with the spirit. They are mistaken, he says. These forms add nothing serious to science:

> Although poets may aspire to understanding, their talents are more akin to entertaining self-deception. They may be able to emphasize

DOI: 10.4324/9781003588160-35

delights in the world, but they are deluded if they and their admirers believe that their identification of the delights and their use of poignant language are enough for comprehension. Philosophers too, I am afraid, have contributed to the understanding of the universe little more than poets . . . They have not contributed much that is novel until after novelty has been discovered by scientists . . . While poetry titillates and theology obfuscates, science liberates.

(From 'The Limitless Power of Science', in *Nature's Imagination*, ed. John Cornwell, Oxford University Press, 1995, p. 123)

Though this view is not usually declared with quite such outspokenness and tribal belligerence, it is actually not a rare one. A lot of people today accept it, or at least can't see good reason why they should not accept it, even if they don't like it. They have a suspicion, welcome or otherwise, that the arts are mere luxuries and science is the only intellectual necessity. It seems to them that science supplies all the facts out of which we build (so to speak) the house of our beliefs. Only after this house is built can we – if we like – sit down inside it, turn on the CD player, and listen to some Mozart or read some poetry.

As we shall see, however, this is not how we actually live our lives, still less how we ought to try to live them. Attempts to impose this pattern have distorted the intellectual scene of late from a number of angles. For instance, the idea that science is a separate domain, irrelevant to the arts, has often produced a strange kind of apartheid in the teaching of literature, a convention whereby important and powerful writings get ignored if their subject-matter concerns science, or even the physical world. Thus, criticism of Conrad's sea-stories tends to treat the storms and other natural disasters in them merely as scenery for the human dramas involved, rather than as a central part of their subject-matter. But if Conrad had simply wanted to study human behaviour, he could have stayed in Poland. Similarly, H.G. Wells and the whole vigorous science-fiction tradition derived from him were long cold-shouldered out of the literary syllabus and have not yet fully reached it – even though writers like Conrad and Henry James admired Wells deeply and saw the force of his vision. Until quite lately, even

Frankenstein was ignored. Potent ideas expressed in these writings have thus not been properly faced and criticized in the teaching of literature. These ideas are, of course, often ones about how the science by which we study the physical world relates to the rest of life, which is an extremely important topic. They include a wide range of matters that can help us in trying to understand and face the environmental crisis.

All this means that intending students face a rather bewildering choice. On the one hand, they are offered a narrow, somewhat inward-looking approach to literature. On the other hand, they face a kind of science teaching which never mentions the social attitudes and background assumptions that influence scientific thought – indeed, one that often views any mention of these topics as vulgar and dangerous. Thus, they may study either the outer *or* the inner aspect of human life, but must on no account bring the two together.

In fact, despite the efforts of many reformers, Descartes still rules. Mind and body are still held apart. Their division tends to produce a population of one-eyed specialists on both sides, specialists who are mystified by their respective opposite numbers and easily drift into futile warfare. It is surely worthwhile to take a much harder look at the misleading imaginative picture of the intellectual life which is the source of this habit.

LUCRETIUS AND THE VISION OF ATOMISM

This divisive picture is really very odd, one which does not fit the actual history of thought at all. Rereading Atkins' words lately, I began to think about his remark that poets and philosophers 'have not contributed much that is novel [to the understanding of the universe] until after novelty has been discovered by scientists.' What struck me then was the influence that a single great philosophic poem – Lucretius' *On the Nature of the Universe* – *De Rerum Natura* – has actually played in the formation of modern Western thought, and especially of Western science.

That poem was the main channel through which the atomic theory of matter reached Renaissance Europe. It was forcibly stated there, all ready to be taken up by the founders of modern physics. Of course it was the Greek atomist philosophers who had invented the theory, and no doubt their work would have reached later thinkers in some form even without Lucretius' poem. But the force and fervour of the poem gave atomism a head start. It rammed the atomists' imaginative vision right home to the hearts of Renaissance readers as well as to their minds. That vision included not just the atomic theory itself but also the startling moral conclusions which Epicurus had already drawn from it. In this way, it forged a much wider strand in Enlightenment thinking. For Lucretius did not see atomism primarily as a solution to scientific problems. Following Epicurus, he saw it as something much more central to human life. For him, it was a moral crusade – the only way to free mankind from a crushing load of superstition by showing that natural causation was independent of the gods. Human beings, he said, are so ceaselessly tormented by anxiety about natural events that they exhaust themselves in precautions against them that are useless and sometimes horrible, such as human sacrifice:

> They make propitiatory sacrifices, slaughter black cattle and despatch offerings to the Departed Spirits . . . As children in blank darkness tremble and start at everything, so we in broad daylight are oppressed at times by fears as baseless as those horrors which children imagine coming upon them in the dark. This dread and darkness of the mind cannot be dispelled by the sunbeams, the shining shafts of day, but only by an understanding of the outward form and inner workings of nature . . . How many crimes has religion led people to commit.
>
> (*De Rerum Natura*, trans. R.E. Latham, London, Penguin, 1951, book 2, lines 50–62, book 1, line 101)

Thus, it was Lucretius who launched the notion of science as primarily a benign kind of weedkiller designed to get rid of religion, and launched it in great rolling passionate hexameters which gave it a force it would never have had if it had been expressed in unemotive prose. His work is visibly the source of the anti-religious rhetoric that is still used by later imperialistic champions of science such as Bertrand Russell and Atkins himself.

WHY VISIONS MATTER

This is not just a debating point for the deplorable war of the two cultures. The story of the influence that Greek atomistic philosophers had, by way of a Roman poet, on the founding of modern science is not a meaningless historical accident. It is a prime example of the way in which our major ideas are generated, namely, through the imagination. New ideas are new imaginative visions, not just in the sense that they involve particular new images (such as Kekule's image of the serpent eating its tail) but in the sense that they involve changes in our larger world-pictures, in the general way in which we conceive life. These changes are so general and so vast that they affect the whole shape of our thinking. That is why something as important as science could not possibly be an isolated, self-generating thought-form arising on its own in the way that Atkins suggests. To picture it as isolated in this way – as a solitary example of rational thinking, standing out alone against a background of formless emotion – is to lose sight of its organic connection with the rest of our life. And that organic connection is just what makes it important.

Changes in world-pictures are not a trivial matter. The mediaeval world-picture was static and God-centred. It called on people to admire the physical cosmos as God's creation, but it viewed that cosmos as something permanently settled on principles that might well not be open to human understanding. By contrast, the atomists showed a physical universe in perpetual flux, a mass of atoms continually whirling around through an infinite space and occasionally combining, by pure chance, to form worlds such as our own. This insistence on the ultimate power of pure chance, which is still such an important principle in today's neo-Darwinist thinking, was thus already central to this early atomist vision.

In principle, this new universe was physically comprehensible because we could learn something about the atomic movements and could thus understand better what was happening to us. But it was not morally comprehensible. It had no meaning. According to Lucretius, the attempt to comprehend the world morally had always been mistaken and was the central source of human misery. In their mistaken belief that they could reach such an understanding, anxious and confused people had taken refuge from their ignorance in superstition:

> in handing over everything to the gods and making everything dependent on their whim . . . Poor humanity! to saddle the gods with such responsibilities and throw in a vindictive temper! . . . This is not piety, this oft-repeated show of bowing a veiled head before a stone, this bustling to every altar, this deluging of altars with the blood of beasts . . . *True piety lies rather in the power to contemplate the universe with a quiet mind.*
> (Book V, lines 1185 and 1194–1203; emphasis mine)

This reference to the possibility of *true piety* is interesting and we must come back to it. But his main point is a simple one. Instead of this anxious pursuit of bogus social explanations for natural events – instead of these wild speculations about irresponsible gods, people should become calmer and look for physical explanations which, though much slighter, would be reliable so far as they went, and would thus quench their anxiety.

That dynamic and chilling yet ordered world-picture made physical speculation seem possible and indeed necessary. At the Renaissance, moreover, it came together with another picture which had not been available before – namely that of the world as a machine. The invention of real complex machines such as clocks gave the human imagination an immensely powerful piece of new material. Machine-imagery changes the worldview profoundly because machines are by definition under human control. They can in a sense be fully understood because they can be taken to pieces. And if the world is essentially a machine, then it can be taken to pieces too and reassembled more satisfactorily. It was the fusion of these two imaginative visions that made modern science look possible. And it had to look possible before anybody could actually start doing it.

This dependence of detailed thought on entirely non-detailed visions is a central theme of this book. The originating visions are, of course, necessarily vague. When the Greek atomists spoke of the various kinds of atoms as having their own specific movements, they had not the remotest idea of what these movements might be or how anybody could trace them. Though it was central to their position that the movements themselves were fixed, definite and invariable, they could not, in the nature of the case, possibly supply examples. They had to convey their point through the necessarily vague medium of imagery. What they were supplying was much more like a Turner sketch than it was like a photograph, and it was not in the least like an engineer's diagram.

At this imaginative stage, then, they were putting forward a theory *about* exactness – they were envisaging an ideal of exactness comparable with that which we now think of as typical of science. But they had not got anything like an exact theory. At this stage, this kind of vagueness is not a vice, any more than it is a vice in a map of the world that it does not show the details of the small areas within it. It is natural and proper that our detailed thinking arises from imaginative roots. But it is important that we should recognize the nature of these roots – that we should not confuse the ideal of exactness with the actual achievement of it. Impressive and influential theories like this one do not originally gain their influence by telling us exact facts about the world. It is usually a long time before they can provide any such facts. Actual precision comes much later, if at all. But theories are not half-established facts either. They are *ways of looking at the facts* – pairs of spectacles through which to see the world differently. What makes theories persuasive in the first place is some other quality in their vision, something in them which answers to a wider need. There is always an imaginative appeal involved as well as an intellectual thirst for understanding. Theories always answer a number of different needs, needs which those who are moved by them are not aware of. As they are used and developed, this plurality of power-sources begins to become visible and can result in serious conflicts.

THE MEANING OF DETERMINISM

For example, the determinism which the atomists introduced – the belief in a completely fixed physical order – obviously did not originally owe its appeal to being established as an empirical fact. It is an assumption that goes infinitely beyond any possible evidence, one that is made for the sake of its useful consequences. The way in which it seemed to guarantee the regularity of nature was highly convenient for science. But of course that convenience could not show it to be true. Determinism was not and could not be a conclusion about the world proved by scientific methods. It was an assumption made in order to make the scientific enterprise look, not just plausible so far, but infinitely hopeful. In the modern age, however, that infinite hope became more or less compulsory. When twentieth-century physicists began to question this dogmatic determinism, it became obvious that scientists did not view it merely as a dispensable tool but as a matter of faith, a central plank of scientific orthodoxy. Einstein, when he objected to the reasonings of quantum mechanics by insisting that God does not play dice, was talking metaphysics, not physics. Karl Popper, commenting on this, remarks: 'Physical determinism, we might say in retrospect, was *a daydream of omniscience* which seemed to become more real with every advance of physics until it became an apparently inescapable nightmare' (In 'Of Clouds and Clocks' in his book *Objective Knowledge* (Oxford, Oxford University Press, 1972), p. 222; emphasis mine).

Popper suggests that determinism was really welcomed as much for its flattering view of ourselves as for its soothing account of the world – as much because it declared *us* infinitely capable of knowledge as because it claimed that the world itself was ordered and knowable. While both claims are unprovable, it was (he says) the first claim – our own potential omniscience – rather than the second which was really attracting theorists. It still does.

This bias towards establishing and glorifying our own status is still more obvious over mechanism – the further development of determinism which relies on machine imagery, thus producing the delightful impression that in principle we can copy or rejig all natural objects at will as well as understand them. Thus Julien de la Mettrie, meeting objections to mechanism based on the complexity of natural beings, replied that, with a bit more trouble, machines can imitate every kind of complexity:

If more instruments, more cogwheels, and more springs are required to register the movements of the planets than to denote the hours: if Vaucanson had to employ more art to produce his flautist than to produce his duck, if he had employed still more energy he might have produced a being with the power of speech

. . . The human body is a clock, but an immense one and constructed with so much artifice and skill that if the wheel which turns the second-hand should stop, then the minute-hand would still turn and continue on its way.

(*The Man-Machine*, ed. M. Solovine, p. 129)

MAGIC, CONTEMPLATION, AND RELIGION

Now, what am I not saying? I am not saying that the atomic theory would never have emerged in science if it had not had these particular philosophical and poetic roots in Greece and Rome. I am saying that, if the theory had had different roots, it would not have brought with it this particular world-picture, this myth, this drama, this way of accommodating science in the range of human activities, this notion of what it is to have a scientific attitude. (It would no doubt have brought a different one.) In particular, there seems no reason to think that the mere advance of science itself would necessarily have brought with it the Epicureans' undiscriminating, wholesale hostility to everything called religion – their notion that the value of science lay primarily in its power to make people happier by displacing religion from human life.

That idea surely is peculiar because the notion of religion that it involves is such a narrow one. It is absurd to talk as if religion consisted entirely of mindless anxiety, bad cosmology, and human sacrifice. Of course, the anxious, insatiable business of propitiatory rituals which Lucretius describes does play a large part among the vast range of human proceedings which we call religious. But it plays a large part in the rest of social life too. And in religion, it clearly belongs in a special department of that range, namely the department sometimes called magic – but magic in the crude sense of a technology aimed at manipulating the gods. Among the great religions, Buddhism rejects this kind of magic entirely and in Judaism there were strong protests against it as early as the Psalms. It was never incorporated into Christian or Islamic doctrine. The idea of bribing or bullying a deity to change your destiny is foreign to the spirit of these religions. Of course it has often crept into religious practice and often become prominent there – for instance in crude petitionary prayer and the sale of indulgences – because anxiety is such a powerful human motive. But when magic has crept in this way, reforming movements have repeatedly been formed within these religions to get rid of it and to point out that this is not what they are really about.

Pagan religions too of course contained far more admirable things than the kind of low-grade magic that Lucretius deplores. His own tradition included Aeschylus' tremendous dramas about the nature of justice, Pindar's wonderful hymns to Apollo, Plato's myths, the Eleusinian mysteries, and plenty more. And indeed, Lucretius himself furnishes an example of the splendid things that paganism could contain in the great opening passage of his poem *On the Nature of Things*. This is a straightforward hymn to Venus – an invocation of her as the spirit of life, the generous maternal force in nature which fills living things with delight and makes possible the whole admirable world around us. Here is devotion to a force and an ideal which is clearly seen as spiritual as well as physical – devotion of a kind which polytheists often express very nobly towards their deities, because, for them, those deities stand for the central forces at work in their life. When Lucretius mentions the Earth, too, he repeatedly has trouble in restraining himself from openly venerating it as our divine Mother in a way that recalls the current embarrassment of some scientists in handling the concept of Gaia – a point to which we will return in Chapter 26.*

But beyond this he shows an intense reverence too for the vast atomic system that he portrays – a system that he sees as essentially ordered and universal although in another way it is chaotic. And it is just this reverence that he wants, above all, to arouse in his readers. He

---

*   Reference is to Ch. 26 of *Science and Poetry* [Ed.]

hopes that it will take the place of the useless anxiety that now drives them to make their futile sacrifices, that it will cure them of fearing death and also of entertaining idle ambitions, since it will show that earthly success is hollow, trifling, and transient in the perspective of this impersonal but splendid universe.

This is undoubtedly a noble vision. But it does seem to be rather a narrow one. In some ways, the Epicurean ideal is quite close to the Buddhist concept of enlightenment through non-attachment, but it is much more purely negative and asocial. There is no element of Buddhist compassion here, no suggestion of delaying one's own enlightenment to promote the salvation of other sentient beings. Epicureanism offers us a private salvation if we will only respond rationally to the physical universe. But we may want to ask, can the thought of that physical universe alone be expected to produce this degree of philosophic detachment? Can such calm acceptance be expected to follow simply from the findings of physical science?

Our culture now contains many scientists deeply convinced of the atomic structure of matter. They know far more about it than Epicurus ever dreamed of. But it is not clear that this acceptance frees them from the fear of death or even tends to cure them of ambition. It doesn't necessarily make them view Nobel Prizes with lofty contempt as mere earthly trifles. If we want to get a wider perspective within which earthly success really does appear insignificant, we will probably need to turn to sages who express a more positive, constructive and generous spiritual vision. Weedkiller alone does not seem to be enough to produce a garden.

THE NEED FOR INTERPRETATION

This emotional estrangement of human life from the cosmos is, of course, only one possible way of reading the Epicurean message. And it is important to concede the part that Lucretius got right. The exaltation of science does indeed have a philosophic point. The modern scientific vision of the vast universe does have enormous grandeur. Contemplation of it certainly can enlarge our mental horizons, distract us from mean preoccupations, raise our aspirations, remind us of wider possibilities. This is a real benefit, for which we should be grateful. The trouble about it is that, once we have this new vision, there are many different interpretations that we can put on it, many different dramas that arise, and many directions in which it can lead us. It is quite hard to distinguish among those directions and to map them in a way that lets us navigate reasonably among them.

For an obvious instance, we can respond in many different ways to the miracles of modern physics. Some people see in those miracles only the possibility of more and better weaponry. That is why a high proportion of the world's trained physicists are now engaged on military research. Beyond this, there is a wider circle of people to whom these miracles chiefly mean just an increase in power, without any special idea about how that power had best be used. Out of this fascination with new power, there arises our current huge expansion of technology, much of it useful, much not, and the sheer size of it (as we now see) dangerously wasteful of resources. It is hard for us to break out of this circle of increasing needs because our age is remarkably preoccupied with the vision of continually improving means rather than saving ourselves trouble by reflecting on ends. This is the opposite bias from the fatalistic quietism of the Epicureans, who refused to think about means at all. It is not clear that ours is any more sensible than theirs. But, at a casual glance, it is just as natural a response to the grand vision of the physical world presented by modern science.

The difficulty is to make that glance more than casual, to criticize properly the various visions constantly arising in us. We need to compare those visions, to articulate them more clearly, to be aware of changes in them, to think them through so as to see what they commit us to. This is not itself scientific business, though of course scientists need to engage in it. It is necessarily philosophic business (whoever does it) because it involves analysing concepts and attending to the wider structures in which those concepts get their meaning. It starts with the fuller articulation of imaginative visions and moves on later to all kinds of more detailed thought, including scientific thought.

That is why all science grows out of philosophical thinking – out of the criticism of imaginative visions – why it takes that criticism for granted and always continues to need it. It is why the vision of an omni-competent science – a free-standing, autonomous skill with a monopoly of rationality that does all our thinking for us – is not workable. That idea, which Atkins now somewhat desperately revives, was vigorously promoted by positivistic thinkers from Comte's time on, but it does not really make much sense. All science includes philosophic assumptions that can be questioned, and those assumptions don't stop being influential just because they have been forgotten. They lie under the floorboards of all intellectual schemes. Like the plumbing, they are really quite complicated, they often conflict, and they can only be ignored so long as we don't happen to notice those conflicts.

When the conflicts get so bad that we do notice them, we need to call in a philosophic plumber – not necessarily a paid philosopher, but someone who knows how the philosophical angle matters. Rationality needs this kind of attention to the conflicts between our various assumptions because rationality itself is something much larger than mere exactness. Rationality is an ideal – one which we perceive somewhat cloudily in a vision, but towards which we can certainly move – an ideal of a just and realistic balance among our various assumptions and ideals.

THE COGNITIVE ROLE OF POETRY

What, then, about poetry and the arts generally? They too play a central part in our intellectual life because they supply the language in which our imaginative visions are most immediately articulated, the medium through which we usually get our first impression of them. Shelley said that poets are the unacknowledged legislators of the world.[1] This is strong language, but his point may really be needed in an age when literature sometimes seems to have sublimated itself into a haze of texts bombinating above us in a metaphysical stratosphere, and at other times to be viewed simply as a set of rather primitive political documents which must be reproved for failing to reach the most recently invented moral standards. ('Shakespeare was a racist' . . .)

What Shelley meant was, of course, that poets – including, of course, imaginative prose writers – are prophets, not in the sense of foretelling things, but of generating forceful visions. They express, not just feelings, but crucial ideas in a direct, concentrated form that precedes and makes possible their later articulation by the intellect and their influence on our actions. These visions are not something trivial. They are of the first importance in our lives, both when the ideas are good, and, of course, even more so when they are bad. Influential bad ideas need to be understood and resisted so that we can grasp what is wrong with them and replace them by better ones. Thus, Primo Levi, describing his early education in fascist Italy, explains how he and his friends took to chemistry largely out of disgust at the ideas presented to them by other studies, simply to get away from

> the stench of Fascist truths which tainted the sky . . . The chemistry and physics on which we fed, besides being nourishments vital in themselves, were the antidote to Fascism . . . they were clear and distinct and verifiable at every step, and not a tissue of lies and emptiness like the radio and the newspapers.
>
> (*The Periodic Table*, trans. Raymond Rosenthal,
> London, Sphere Books, 1986, p. 42)

This was a reasonable enough way of escape for students when things had gone so far. But earlier, when Fascism had not yet established itself, it needed to be resisted by people who did attend to its ideas. Fascism established itself in Italy largely by means of bad poetry that sold bad visions – by romanticizing hatred and violence, by flattering the vanity of voters and distorting historical truths. Poets, such as Gabriele d'Annunzio, played a notable part in that campaign. The intellectuals who resisted it never made the mistake of dismissing that contribution as trivial.

Writers – bad and good – who have this kind of effect do not, of course, usually do their legislating by literally spelling out theories, as

Lucretius did. They do it by showing forcefully (as novelists and dramatists can) how the new ideas would work in real life. Shakespeare does this all the time, though many of his insights are by now so built in to our thinking that we scarcely notice them. Pope and Blake, Tennyson, Nietzsche, and Eliot each powerfully shaped the spirit of their respective ages. And as for the ideal of detachment from worldly affairs which the Epicureans offered, it has taken many forms and suggested many different life styles, which have been displayed imaginatively. Plato presented one of these life styles dramatically in his portrait of Socrates. Nietzsche presented quite another in his *Zarathustra*. Plenty more patterns are available, ranging from the totally ascetic and solitary to the altruistic, patterns which would lead to very different lives. In *War and Peace*, Pierre attempts this kind of detachment and the difficulties he runs into cast a sharp light on its problems. Since we often have to make choices among paths of this kind, literature continually plays a vital part in life by stirring our imaginations and making us more aware of what particular choices can involve. If it is taught in a way which plays down or even suppresses this practical effect, something vital is lost. And we may begin to wonder why, on these conditions, it is important to study literature at all.

It is worth noticing, too, that in this way philosophy itself is a branch of literature. Any major kind of philosophizing always presents some distinctive ideal for life as well as for thought because life and thought are not really separate at all. The great philosophers of our tradition have usually displayed their ideals quite explicitly, as have those of other traditions, and if contemporary academic philosophers suppose that they are not doing this, they are mistaken. Academic narrowness is a way of life as much as any other. It is quite as easily conveyed by a style of writing, and even more easily by a style of teaching.

NOTE

1. P.B. Shelley, *The Defence of Poetry* (1820, published 1840). In *Political Tracts of Wordsworth, Coleridge and Shelley*, ed. R.J. White (Cambridge, Cambridge University Press, 1953), concluding sentence.

28

ATOMISTIC VISIONS
The Quest for Permanence

NO NEED FOR OMNICOMPETENCE

We have seen that science is not and does not need to be 'omnicompetent.' It is not an independent, solitary intellectual citadel, the only scene of rational thought, nor is it a central government under which both poetry and philosophy are minor agencies. The idea of it as thus mysteriously set apart above the rest of life is, however, an important element in our current beliefs. Modern specialization tends to cut off the physical sciences from the rest of our thinking. What we 'lay people' (as we are significantly called) mostly notice about the sciences is simply their power. Technology impresses us so deeply that we are not much surprised by the claim that scientific methods ought to be extended to cover the rest of our thought. That positivistic claim – first made by Auguste Comte and repeated by many sages since – underlies

DOI: 10.4324/9781003588160-36

many desperate attempts today in other studies, especially in the social sciences, to make themselves, in some sense, ever more 'scientific.'

This mysterious segregation of science can, however, just as easily lead to alienation and fear. Both the dangers of technology and the ideological distortions of scientistic thinking lead people to declare war on science itself. Thus, we oscillate between idealizing science and dreading it. Both these attitudes are equally wrong. Both deal in unreal abstractions. The sciences (which are many) are not cut off in this way from the rest of our thought but are continuous with it. They don't compose one solid, distinct, autonomous intellectual citadel. The many scientific ways of thinking all grow out of common thought, draw on its imagery and share its motivations. Scientists do indeed aim at objective truth about the world and, like the rest of us, they sometimes achieve it. Water really is made of hydrogen and oxygen and the liver really does secrete bile. But scientists have to select for their investigation patterns which fit patterns in the world they are going to investigate. And the reasons for that selection are by no means always obvious.

I am not suggesting, as some sociologists of science have done, that scientists just make up their results by framing experiments to prove what they already want to believe. Extreme social constructionism is not at all a convincing story. But it surely is striking how deeply scientific thinking is pervaded by patterns drawn from everyday thought and, in particular, how strong an effect the imagery chosen has on what is conceived at a given time as being scientific. To grasp this, let us look more carefully at the meaning and influence of the atomic model.

THE MEANING OF ATOMISM

As we have seen, the pioneers of modern science drew that model from the Greek atomist philosophers and more directly from the passionate Epicurean version of it given by Lucretius. They accepted it, not just as a scientific hypothesis but as part of a strong and distinctive ideology. They saw it as a symbolic pattern suggesting meanings affecting much wider areas of life. Morally, for instance, atomism seemed to point the way, not only away from religion but also away from communal thinking and towards social atomism – that is, towards individualism. And for scientific knowledge itself, atomism seemed to promise a most reassuring kind of simplicity and finality – a guarantee that the world would prove intelligible in the end in relatively simple terms, once we had split it up into its ultimate elements. In fact, *understanding the world* seemed to be essentially a matter of simplifying it so as to locate those ultimate units. The word *reductivism* is now used to stand for the belief that this kind of reduction is indeed the only, or at least far the best, way of reaching such an understanding. Both these promises – the social reliance on individualism and the intellectual confidence in final simplicity – were central elements in Enlightenment thinking. Both have been very useful to us and are still prominent in our thought today. But we are now reaching areas where they can no longer help us. On the physical side, scientists no longer think in terms of hard, separate, unchangeable atoms at all but of particles that are essentially interconnected. And, on the social side, attempts to treat people as disconnected social atoms have repeatedly turned out very badly. Yet we still find it very hard to reshape both these thought-patterns. Like a lot of other ideas which we owe to the Enlightenment, they have come to be accepted as necessary parts of rationality. Efforts to change them tend to look like attacks on reason itself. If we want to rethink them as we now need to, I think it will help to glance back and see what made them so appealing in the first place. Readers allergic to metaphysics, or to the history of thought, can probably skip this chapter.

ORIGINS: THE FEAR OF TRANSIENCE

Atomism arose in Greece out of a determined – but ultimately doomed – attempt to find something in the world which was truly fixed and immutable. Attempting to achieve this, Parmenides proposed that this ultimate unchangeable substance must be something entirely hidden, a mysterious whole lying behind changing appearances. The plurality and change that we see around us cannot (he said) be real because they seem to involve a void or nothingness between the changing items, and nothingness is not real. Change and plurality are therefore only illusions and all the things which we actually experience must be unreal. For, as Heraclitus had pointed out, these everyday things are indeed many and are in constant flux, changing as constantly as if they were made of fire. You can never get into the same river twice . . .

Putting the insights of Heraclitus and Parmenides together, it seemed (then) that the whole world around us was indeed unreal. 'Reality' must be a mysterious eternal something lying behind it, a realm which was altogether hidden from us. But this situation struck many people as implausible. Democritus and Leucippus therefore did everybody a service by introducing the idea of atoms. They suggested that the changing world consists of innumerable tiny units which genuinely are changeless – ultimately real in just the way Parmenides demanded – but which really do cause the changes which we see. They called these units *atoms*, which simply means indivisible objects.

An infinite crowd of these atoms, then, swirls around randomly through infinite space and infinite time, colliding and combining now and then by chance to form temporary universes, of which there are many besides our own. There is no purpose anywhere in this process and the gods, who have been formed by it just as much as humans have, do not try to control it. Nor do they interfere in human life. They simply live serenely on their own in the space between the universes. As for mind, it is real enough, but it too consists of atoms – very fine, spherical atoms which can move freely through the coarser particles of matter. At death, this mind-stuff dissolves away into its component atoms just like the rest of the body and is lost in the vast cosmic chaos.

We have already seen some of the moral and social consequences of this impressive vision – its usefulness in resisting superstition and also its thinness as a total philosophy for life. Let us look more closely now at its consequences for science and for our notion of what it is to be scientific. Obviously some of these are good. The sheer vastness of the perspective – the sense of infinite space and time surrounding us – is most impressive. And the central insight that visible processes can sometimes be explained by finding smaller, invisible processes going on inside them is, of course, immensely fertile for the sciences. Yet there is an unbalance in the scheme which is bound to lead to trouble. It concentrates so strongly on the atoms themselves that it has nothing much to say about how they are related.

We naturally ask what forces are making the atoms move. But on this point, the atomists were parsimonious to the point of meanness. They thought that nearly all the movement was caused by collisions between the falling atoms. They did not ask what kind of gravity made them fall in the first place. They did add the idea of a *clinamen* or bend – a kind of native, original tendency in the atoms to move slant-wise. But that seems only to have been a defence against the objection that otherwise they might fall in parallel like rain and never meet at all. No reason was given for the slant, and since the atoms have no working parts, it is hard to see how there could be any such reason. The atoms collided and sometimes got hooked together, but they never truly interacted. Nor, of course, was the slanting motion of any actual use in explaining in any detail why they behaved as they did, still less how they came to be moving in the first place. But more lethally still, even impact itself had not really been explained. The real reason why things such as billiard balls bounce off each other is that the particles at their surface have electrical charges which repel one another. But these Greek-type atoms were not supposed to exercise any force at all. Repulsion was no more available to them than attraction was. They were supposed to be totally inert.

One way or another, then, change had not really been explained at all.

TROUBLE WITH TIME

This difficulty is due to a fact about the original model which has caused lasting trouble – namely, that it is essentially static rather than dynamic. The Greek atomists' notion was that the mere shape and size of the atoms would explain their workings fully without reference to any forces at work or to the kind of whole within which they were working. Their pattern was still that of Parmenides, a timeless pattern requiring an inert whole incapable either of change or relation. The atomists had not got rid of this pattern, they had merely repeated it indefinitely on a smaller scale. Their atoms are tiny Parmenidean universes.

Later developments in physics have not, of course, borne out this insight at all. Since Faraday's time, particle physics has steadily moved away from this static model. Forces and fields are now the main players in the game and mass is interchangeable with energy. Particles are defined in terms of their capacities for action, which naturally vary with the contexts in which they are placed. There is genuine interaction between them. But this scientific development was delayed for a long time by the imaginative grip of the static model – by the belief that impact was indeed the only possible source of movement, the only force that reason could recognize. In particular, as we have seen, the notion of gravitation was long thought to be irrational because it involved action at a distance, not caused by any collision. Underlying these difficulties, there was a deep and lasting reluctance to admit that change itself could be real at all. Werner Heisenberg, in his profound little book *Physics and Philosophy*,[1] remarks on how far modern physics has now moved away from this Parmenidean obsession with the static. As he says,

> Modern physics is in some ways extremely near to the doctrines of Heraclitus. If we replace the word 'fire' by the word 'energy' we can almost repeat his statements word for word from our modern point of view. Energy is in fact the substance from which all elementary particles, all atoms and therefore all things are made, and energy is that which moves. Energy is a substance, since its total amount does not change . . . Energy may be called the fundamental cause for all change in the world...
>
> In the philosophy of Democritus the atoms are eternal and indestructible units of matter, they can never be transformed into each other. *With regard to this question modern physics takes a definite stand against the materialism of Democritus and for Plato and the Pythagoreans.* The elementary particles are certainly not eternal: they can actually be transformed into each other.

(pp. 51 and 59)

As Heisenberg explains, after these collisions, the resulting fragments again become elementary particles on their own – protons, neutrons, electrons, mesons – making up their lost mass from their kinetic energy. So if anything can be defined as 'the primary substance of the world,' it has to be energy itself. As he puts it: 'The modern interpretation of events has very little resemblance to genuine materialistic philosophy: in fact, one may say that atomic physics has turned science away from the materialistic trend it had during the nineteenth century' (p. 47). Since Heisenberg's time, physicists have begun to say that this primary substance may turn out to be, not exactly energy but some form of space itself. This, however, is not going to be much comfort for materialism.

REALITY AND INTELLIGIBILITY

What *materialism* means here, we will consider in a moment. The first thing to notice is that this shift calls for a deep change in our traditional notion of reality, a change which we have certainly not fully made yet. We are free now from the metaphysics which seemed to go with the old physics, from the notion that only the unchanging is real. We don't any longer need to posit static units as the terminus to explanation, treating all explanations as provisional until they reach it.

Change, in fact, is *not* unreal, it is a fundamental aspect of reality. Parmenides thought that changeable, interacting things were unreal because he thought change could not be understood. But this idea flows from a special notion of what it means to *understand* something. Certainly there are some forms of understanding which abstract from time and change, notably in mathematics. And this timelessness does give these explanations a specially satisfying kind of completeness. But for other problems, such as when we want to understand fire or explosions, time and change are part of the subject-matter. And there are other situations again, notably ones involving living organisms, where whole sets of interconnected changes are going on at the same time.

Yet we do gain some understanding of these matters. Thermodynamics and climatology and biology are not just a string of lies and delusions. Their explanations are in a way less complete, less final than those of mathematics, but this is because, being less abstract, they do so much more work. Their greater concreteness allows them to apply more directly to the actual world around us and that world is what we need to explain. That world is (we must insist) not an illusion. It is not a flimsy shell covering a true reality. It is the explanandum. It is the standard from which our notions of reality are drawn. No less a physicist than Richard Feynman celebrates this fact:

> A poet once said, 'The whole universe is in a glass of wine' . . . There are the things of physics, the twisting liquid which evaporates according to the wind and weather, the reflections in the glass, and our imagination adds the atoms. The glass is a distillation of the earth's rocks, and in its composition we see the secrets of the universe's age, and the evolution of stars. What strange array of chemicals are in the wine? How did they come to be? . . . There in the wine is found the great generalisation: all life is fermentation . . . How vivid is the claret, pressing its existence into the consciousness that watches it! If our small minds, for some convenience, divide this glass of wine, this universe, into parts – physics, biology, geology, astronomy, psychology and so forth – remember that nature does not know it! So let us put it all back together, remembering ultimately what it is for. Let it give us one more final pleasure: drink it, and forget it all!
>
> (Richard Feynman, *The Feynman Lectures on Physics*, Reading, Mass., Addison-Wesley Publishing Co., 1963, chapter 3, para. 7)

We need to disentangle the physics here from the metaphysics. The physical question *what stuff (if any) things are made of* is quite distinct from the much more mysterious question of *what reality (if any) lies behind the whole world of experience* – a world of which physics itself is only a part. The ontological question about a presumed reality behind appearance implies a sweeping distrust of *all* experience – including the observations made by scientists. And that distrust needs some special kind of justification.

In the passages just cited, Heisenberg is not just doing physics. He is not just telling us that modern science finds Heraclitus' conceptual scheme more convenient than that of Democritus. He is also pointing out how biased and misleading Democritus' scheme is metaphysically, how it can distort our notion of reality, leading to the notion that mind or consciousness itself is in some sense *not* real. The trouble is not just that Democritus' proposal of fitting mind into the atomic scheme by supplying it with smooth round atoms turned out not to work because there were no such atoms. Even if there had been those atoms, they still would not have furnished a usable way of thinking about mind or consciousness. To do that, we have to have a language for the subjective. We have to take seriously what happens at the first-person point of view. And there is no way of doing this inside the atomic scheme, which is irredeemably an external, third-person one.

This is why atomistic thinking led people to metaphysical materialism, to the rather mysterious idea that *only matter is real*. The Greek atomists were the first people who seriously made this striking claim, the first real materialists. Their Ionian predecessors such as Thales had taken it for granted that life and spirit were included as properties of their primal substance – water, air, or fire. Instead, the atomists seriously tried to show how life and consciousness could emerge from a world consisting only of static, inert atoms and the void.

This attempt failed resoundingly, and its failure is enormously instructive once we understand it. We are, I think, only now beginning to get it in focus. As Heisenberg says, during the nineteenth century, materialism became hugely popular and, in spite of the efforts of modern physicists, on the whole it remains so today. It became an ideology, a creed expressed in a whole stream of devout pronouncements such as that of Karl Vogt that 'The brain secretes thought as the liver secretes bile.'[2] But what do we mean by *reality* if we deny that our own experiences are a part of it? The point can't just be that experience is misleading or unreliable; it has to be that it doesn't happen at all. A brain that has been thinking doesn't deposit any tangible, measurable residue of thought in the experimenter's petri dish. Perhaps, then, conscious thought is just an illusion which should vanish from the equation entirely?

Metaphysical behaviourists such as Watson did sometimes try to take up this startling position, but they never managed to make much sense of it. Modern exponents of materialism usually take the more modest line that experience does happen but that it doesn't matter much, that it is somehow *less real*, more superficial than physical processes.

Accounts of events involving consciousness are, then, legitimate at their own level, but they are not complete or fundamental. They are only provisional. In order to be made fully intelligible, they must be reduced, by way of the biological and chemical accounts, down to the ground floor of physics, which is the only fundamental level, the terminus that alone provides true understanding. (This gravitational metaphor is itself extremely powerful and will need our attention.)

EXPLANATIONS

In this form, the materialistic creed doesn't necessarily mention the notion of *reality*, so it is less obviously metaphysical. It appears in more modern guise as a view about explanation and what can make it complete. But of course no explanation ever *is* complete, and, in so far as we do demand completeness, contributions from physics don't necessarily help it. When we ask someone to complete an explanation, what we normally want is something visibly relevant. For instance, if an explanation of a historical phenomenon such as anti-Semitism seems to have gaps in it, we ask for material that will fill them. But that material will primarily be historical or psychological because that is what our questions are about. There is no obvious reason why physical details about neurones in the brains of anti-Semites could ever be relevant to the problem. As Richard Feynman explains:

> In order for physics to be useful to other sciences in a theoretical way, other than in the invention of instruments, the science in question must supply to the physicist a description of the object in the physicist's language. They can say 'why does a frog jump?' and the physicist cannot answer. If they tell him what a frog is, that there are so many molecules, there is a nerve here, etc., that is different. If they will tell

us, more or less, what the earth and the stars are like, then we can figure it out. In order for a physical theory to be any use, we must know where the atoms are located. In order to understand the chemistry, we must know exactly what atoms are present, for otherwise we cannot analyse it.

(The Feynman Lectures on Physics, Reading, Mass., Addison-Wesley Publishing Co., chapter 3, para. 7)

This gap makes a great difference to what we mean by calling an explanation *fundamental*. If we say that a certain explanation has indeed managed to be a fundamental one, it won't be because it involves physics. It will be because it answers the central historical and psychological questions that it set out to answer. Some physicalist philosophers believe that in the future, when we know enough about brains, we shall discover quite new kinds of physical explanation which will displace all these existing forms of thought on the matter and will show that they were just superficial 'folk-psychology.' But this is simply a confusion about the kinds of work that different kinds of explanation do. Examining the physical and neurological causes at work in anti-Semitic brains would do nothing at all to explain the ideas involved, any more than examining the brains of mathematicians can explain the mathematics that they are working on. Nobody has yet suggested studying mathematics in this way, and it is no more plausible to propose relying on it for explaining the rest of conduct.

POLITICAL USES OF THE MATERIALISTIC VISION

Metaphysical materialism got into European thought in the first place as a weapon used, first by the early atomists and then by political campaigners such as Hobbes, against the dominance of religion. In modern times, the prime motivation behind it was horror and indignation at the religious wars and persecutions of the sixteenth and seventeenth centuries, and its main target was the notion of the soul as a distinct entity capable of surviving death. As we have seen, this social and political motivation was quite close to that of the ancient atomists, who were also moved by outrage at disastrous religious practices.

This motivation was a suitable one for forging a weapon in campaigns against the churches. But it was much less able to provide a balanced foundation for the whole of science, let alone for a general understanding of life. For that wider understanding, change and interaction needed to be seen as intelligible in their own terms and *the first-person aspect of life had to be taken seriously as well as the objective one.* Descartes notoriously saw this last problem and made a magnificent attempt to deal with it by making mind or consciousness the starting-point for his systematic doubt. He did succeed in getting subjectivity finally onto the philosophers' agenda, but for a long time, they were puzzled about what to do with it. Descartes still described mind ontologically, not as a first-person aspect or point of view but as a substance, something parallel to physical matter but separate from it and not intelligibly connected with it.

This kind of dualism had the fatal effect of making mind look to many scientists like an extra kind of stuff, not like one aspect (among many) of the real world but like a rival substance competing with matter for the narrow throne of reality. This vision inclined scientifically minded people to sign up for an ideology called materialism, meaning by that not just allegiance to matter but in some sense disbelief in mind. The idea of the two as rivals for the status of reality persisted. Mind was seen as an awkward non-material entity which ought perhaps to be removed with Occam's Razor, one which was certainly too exotic meanwhile to deserve serious scientific attention. And alarm about it went particularly deep in the social sciences, which were becoming increasingly sensitive about their scientific status.

This is why, through much of the twentieth century, scientists, both social and physical, in English-speaking countries were extraordinarily careful to avoid any mention of subjectivity and particularly of consciousness. In psychology, where this avoidance was fiercely enforced, it was, as we have seen, usually not treated as a metaphysic but as a matter of methodological convenience, since outside behaviour could be observed while inner states could not. But such a choice of method is never likely to be separate from metaphysics. Selection of subject-matter depends on what one thinks important, and judgements about importance are part of one's general vision of the world.

As we have seen, both the method and the metaphysics flow from background presuppositions of which we are often unconscious, presuppositions that are part of our picture of life as a whole. This element in behaviourism became obvious because, before long, strict behaviourist methods were found not to be at all convenient for psychology and had to be abandoned. The attempt to study behaviour without considering the motives behind it could not work because it is not really possible to observe and describe behaviour at all (apart from the very simplest actions) without grasping the motives that it expresses. And since we are social animals, we actually know a great deal about those motives.

It was not convenience, then, that had recommended this method in the first place. The attraction was quite a different one – namely, that it *looked scientific* if one defined scientific method in devoutly materialist terms, in a manner derived from the old atomistic vision, as a method that dispensed with the concept of mind. During the last thirty years, however, notions of mind and consciousness have rather suddenly escaped from the taboo that so long suppressed them. It has been really interesting to watch how they have now become matters of lively debate among a wide variety of academics. Much of what goes on in the now vigorous *Journal of Consciousness Studies* is metaphysics though it is often supposed only to be science. The main point of the enterprise must surely be to forge a new vision that can heal the Cartesian rift between mind and body, showing them, not as warring rivals but as complementary aspects of a larger whole. Physicists like Heisenberg saw the need for that long ago, and we need now to get on with this difficult business.

NOTES

1.   London, Penguin Books, 1989.
2.   In his *Physiological Epistles* (1847). Quoted by J. Passmore in *A Hundred Years of Philosophy* (Harmondsworth, Penguin, 1968), p. 36.

29

PUTTING OUR SELVES TOGETHER AGAIN

THE SIZE OF THE PROBLEM

In our time, something called 'the problem of consciousness' is beginning to worry scholars in a number of disciplines, including those in which, until lately, that word was not supposed to be heard at all. Territorial disputes are even breaking out over whether this new problem is the property of scientists or philosophers.[1] There are in fact many problems involved, not just one. But the most interesting of them are more or less bound to have both scientific and philosophical aspects, so that specialists will have to try and cooperate over them, hard though that may be. And, in what looks like the central and most difficult puzzle of all, both these aspects are surely present.

That central puzzle is not about 'how consciousness evolved,' nor is it about 'how we would know it was there if we didn't happen to be

DOI: 10.4324/9781003588160-37

aware of it already,' though both those questions have raised a lot of dust. The central worry is: "How can we rationally speak of our inner experience at all? How can we regard our inner world – the world of our everyday experience – as somehow forming part of the larger, public world which is now described in terms that seem to leave no room for it? On what map can both these areas be shown and intelligibly related?"

This is a genuinely difficult issue, not a false alarm. It will not yield simply to familiar methods and a good injection of research money. But it is not desperate either. We can think about it if we are willing to stand back, to look at things from farther off and to admit the size of the question. Current panic about consciousness arises largely from trying to treat it as if it were a much smaller issue than it is.

The analogy that I would like to suggest here comes from geography. We are not looking for the relation between two places on the same map. We are trying to understand the relation between two maps of different kinds, which is a different sort of enterprise. At the beginning of an atlas, we usually find a number of maps of the world. Mine gives, for instance: world physiography (structure and seismology), world climatology (mean annual precipitation, climatic fronts and atmospheric pressure), world vegetation, world political, world energy, world food, world air routes and a good many more. If we want to understand how this bewildering range of maps works, we do not need to pick on one of them as 'fundamental.' We do not need to find a single atomic structure belonging to that one map and reduce all the other patterns to it. We do not, in fact, have to do once more the atomizing work that has already been done by physics. Nor will that work help us here.

What we do need is something different. We have to relate all these patterns in a way which shows why all these various maps are needed, why they are not just contradicting one another, and why they do not just represent different alternative worlds. To grasp this, we always draw back to consider a wider whole. We look at the general context of thought and life within which the different pictures arise. We have to see the different maps as answering different kinds of questions,

questions which arise from different angles in different contexts. But all these questions are still about a single world, a world so large that it can be rightly described in all these different ways and many more. It is that background – not a common atomic structure – which makes it possible to hold all the maps together. The plurality that results is still perfectly rational. It does not drop us into anarchy or chaos.

When we are using the atlas, we can make these connections quite easily so long as we remember this wider context, because the same coastlines appear on all of them. This helps us to relate the various pictures to the world they represent. If, however, we forgot that context and tried to examine a smaller area on its own, we would be in trouble. Someone (for instance) who decides to investigate a particular square of Central Africa or Australia by cutting out and magnifying the parts of all these maps that showed that area, would find that the lines on many of these squares would not seem to bear any meaningful relation to one another at all. The political map, especially, might just show a single straight line running right across the whole area – perhaps pink on one side, blue on the other – something quite extraordinary which no other map ever shows. (There are no straight lines in nature.) And the airline map might be rather similar, but showing a different line. At this point, enquirers might give up. They might say that the maps disagreed so badly that there could only be one of them that was correct and fundamental – only one map which really showed the world at all – namely, the one that they had backed in the first place. And this seems to be very much the way in which many people are now trying to investigate the problem of consciousness.

In considering that problem, our project (as I have suggested) is not to relate two things which already appear on the same conceptual map. It's about how to relate two maps that answer questions arising from different angles. Consciousness is not just one object, nor one state or function of objects, among others in the world. It is not (as people often suggest) a function roughly parallel to digestion or perspiration. It is the condition of a subject, someone for whom all those objects are objects. The questions it raises are therefore primarily about the nature of a person as a whole, a person who is both subject and object.

When (then) we ask how consciousness can be a feature of the world, we are asking how we ourselves – as subjects – can be both items in the world and aware of it as a whole? This is not a factual question. It is a question about how to find convenient ways of thought, about how we can best think about an item that has this double position. How does that awareness fit – conceptually – both into the world and into the rest of our complex nature? Science itself has so far depended on and nurtured realism in the sense of a belief that the world is actually there. The problem now is, how to be realist about subjects – which are, it should be stressed, themselves natural phenomena, not some kind of invented spooks. Consciousness, then, is not just one more phenomenon. It is the scene of all phenomena, the place where appearances appear. It is the viewpoint from which all objects are seen as objects. The first set of questions that arise about it are questions about ourselves. These questions have to come before more strictly scientific questions about its place in the outer world, such as how it evolved. And it is important that this consciousness which we must look at contains a whole mass of more dynamic items besides simple appearances. It contains complex patterns such as emotions, efforts, conflicts, desires – aspects of our active participation in what goes on around us. If we once start to sort these things out, we shall probably have to think carefully about agency and free will as well as perception. And (if one may mention it) about time too.

PRIOR TABOOS AND THEIR DECAY

All this is very hard to deal with today. Current scientific concepts are not adapted to focusing on subjectivity. Indeed, many of them have been carefully adapted to exclude it, much like cameras with a colour filter. People have not, of course, actually supposed up to now that they were unconscious. The fathers of modern science took their consciousness for granted, since they were using it to practise science. Even the Behaviourists, who did try to deny this awkward factor, still tacitly presupposed it. Although they were officially epiphenomenalists who believed that their thoughts could not affect their behaviour, they still assumed that it was worth their own while to go on thinking and reading about scientific subjects, as if their thoughts might really have an influence on the world. They assumed that conscious beings were there to receive and understand their words. They assumed, too, that they had useful colleagues – that testimony from other conscious beings was a sound source of scientific knowledge. And so forth.

This background community of conscious subjects has, in fact, to be presupposed if any form of connected thought is to be possible at all. Until very lately, however, these subjects were not seen as something that science itself could study. They had been shut out of its domain, with good reason, during the Renaissance. Galileo and Descartes saw how badly the study of objects had been distorted by people who treated these objects as subjects, people who credited things like stones with human purpose and striving. So they ruled that physical science must be *objective*. And this quickly came to mean, not just that scientists must be fair, but that they should treat everything they studied only as a passive, insentient object.

We know that this abstraction made possible three centuries of tremendous scientific advance about physical objects. Today, however, this advance has itself led to a point where consciousness has again to be considered. Enquiries are running against the limits of this narrowed focus. In many areas, the advantages of ignoring ourselves have run out. This has happened most notoriously in quantum mechanics, where physicists have begun to use the idea of an observer quite freely as a causal factor in the events they study. Whether or not this is the best way to interpret quantum phenomena, that development is bound to make people ask what sort of an entity an observer is, since Occam's Razor has so far failed to get rid of it. This disturbance, however, is only one symptom of a growing pressure on the supposedly subject-proof barrier, a pressure that is due to real growth in all the studies that lie close to it.

The pressure is naturally strongest in the social sciences, especially in psychology. As a direct consequence of the success of physical science, the social sciences were initially designed to imitate its methods as far as possible. Sometimes this has worked well, but not always.

Social investigators who have tried to confine themselves to the methods used by their physical colleagues have repeatedly run into trouble at certain points because they found that they simply couldn't make progress without considering their subjects *as subjects* – their people as people. At these points, not even the most objective observer could dismiss the subjects' own point of view as irrelevant. It had to be acknowledged that people were in some ways different from stones.

Yet for a long time it seemed that the behaviourist project was the only possible way in which psychology could make good its status as a science. Its ideology was thus so fervently launched and so fiercely policed that its principles prevailed for the best part of a century, long outlasting the detailed work that was supposed to support them. During that time, it was as much as a social scientist's career was worth to be caught taking what B.F. Skinner so oddly called 'an anthropomorphic view of man.'[2] The methodological argument that underlay this view ran much like this:

> Only what science studies is real, Science cannot study consciousness, So: Consciousness is not real.

And, though the conclusion has officially been abandoned, both these premises are still widely accepted. Hence much of our present difficulty. The church of academic orthodoxy now officially lets its members see these problems. But if we want to see them clearly, we are going to need a more suitable set of concepts. The terms which served seventeenth-century thinkers for dismissing conscious subjects from scientific attention are not likely to be the best ones for bringing them back into focus now.

THE RETURN OF THE FIRST PERSON

We need other ways of thinking. We have to stop thinking of consciousness as a peculiar, isolated feature of certain objects – as just one particular state or function of certain organisms – and start to think of it rather as a whole point of view, equal in size and importance to the objective point of view as a whole. And we shall not get far with this if we start our investigation by worrying about whether we can recognize consciousness in other people – about the so-called 'problem of other minds.'

To suppose that we have a problem about the existence of other minds is to be in trouble already because it is to have started in the wrong place – Descartes' wrong place. If we once sit down in that place, we shall never get rid of the problem. (Bertrand Russell, who was wedded to this starting-point, never did get rid of it.) This approach conceives of minds – or consciousnesses – unrealistically as self-contained, isolated both from each other and from the world around them. It is terminally solipsistic. To avoid this unreal isolation, we had better attend in the first place to the examples that are most familiar to us, namely, our own experience and its relation with that of others familiar to us. Consciousness is not something rare and exotic found only in experimental subjects or in scientific observers. Nor does it only show us a few special phenomena such as colours and dreams and hallucinations. It is not primarily an observation-station. It is the crowded scene of our daily lives. And the main dramas going on in it do not concern just observation or perception but quite complex, dynamic currents of feeling and efforts to act. If we mean to do justice to this complexity, we have to take seriously the rich, well-organized language which we use about it every day. That language does not just express an amateur 'folk-psychology.' It is the indispensable working skeleton of all our thought – including, of course, our thought about science.

THE STARTING-POINT: SELVES IN SOLITARY CONFINEMENT

Perhaps this will become clearer if we look back again at the unreality of the traditional scheme, which is now making this problem so hard. That scheme was, of course, Descartes' sharp division of mind from body. In order to make the natural world safe for physics, Descartes pushed consciousness right out of it into a separate spiritual world, treating each soul or mind as a spiritual substance, made of a stuff alien to other earthly items.[3] Today, we cannot possibly put this extra entity, this disembodied mind, back into the natural world, though Descartes' dualistic followers still try to. (The suspicion that we may have to restore it may account for some of the alarm that now surrounds this topic.) The trouble is not just that physics leaves no room for this kind of entity, but that thinking creatures could not possibly be isolated entities of this kind. Thought involves communication. Cartesian egos, isolated inside their separate shells of alien matter, could never even have discovered each other's existence. *What thinks has to be the whole person, living in a public world.*

The 'problem of other minds' arises from positing this solipsistic self, which we might call Descartes' diamond. It is a hard, impenetrable but very precious isolated sentient substance which sits at its console in its windowless tower communicating with other, similarly secluded diamonds by signals run up between towers and relayed to these beings by a perpetual miracle. Real people, by contrast, are embodied beings living in a public world.

Descartes' reason for introducing this awkward kind of soul was his need to compromise between three conflicting kinds of demand – the position of traditional Christianity, the need to segregate physics from other studies, and the demands of everyday language. The diamond never fitted any of these systems at all well and as time has gone on the misfit has grown steadily worse. It was always an unstable notion. When it was taken seriously, it has usually tended to expand into absolute idealism – the idea that spiritual diamond-stuff was actually the stuff of the whole universe, a stuff that underlay physical matter as well as souls. Hence the mentalist tradition that runs through Leibniz, Berkeley, Hume and Hegel to modern phenomenalism.

Today, by contrast, many educated people, and in particular many scientists, assume that the opposite metaphysic – materialism – has simply conquered this whole trend and now reigns unchallenged. But it seems increasingly clear that one extreme view is no more workable than the other. Materialism and idealism are equally the products of dualism. That is why the unstable notion of an isolated self has not gone away. The ghost still haunts the machine because the machine has not changed thoroughly enough to do without it.

THE IMPORTANCE OF BABIES

At this point, we might do well to remember that this is a species whose members, as babies, communicate with other people long before they try to handle inanimate objects. They also learn other people's names before they learn their own names. And they learn to talk about other people's mental states long before they become introspective enough to discuss their own. From birth, they are equipped – just as other young social animals are – with the right capacities for expressive behaviour, and with the power to interpret that behaviour in others. These capacities are not imitated from others later. Babies born blind smile, and non-blind babies can at once interpret smiles. Deaf babies cry. And so forth.[4] This innate repertoire makes it possible for human babies, just like other primate babies, to start communicating as soon as they begin to be aware of the world at all and long before they take any other sort of action.

That is how human infants manage to take in, quite directly, the mass of facts about other people's attitudes which will be the foundation of all their social knowledge and which will – among other important things – also make it possible for them to learn to talk. They do not need inference to do this. In fact, in our species, any social inference there may be is primarily directed inwards, from our knowledge of others to ourselves, rather than outwards by analogy from ourselves to them. We gradually learn to apply to ourselves the words which we already use to describe other people's moods and characters.

We can, indeed, then have a problem of self-knowledge – a 'problem of one's own mind.' We are often amazingly ignorant about our own condition and our own motives. This ignorance can become important later in life and when we are more mature it is our business to deal with it. But there is no original problem of other people's minds. For us humans at least (whatever may happen elsewhere in the universe), the whole use of language depends on, and arises out of, the deep, innate, unshiftable sense that each of us is only one among others who experience the world in roughly the same sort of way that we do ourselves. This sense is constitutive of our thinking, not a dispensable part of its content. Autistic people, who apparently lack that sense, tend to have great difficulty in using language at all.

DO WE NEED PROOF THAT WE ARE NOT ALONE?

Do we need some sort of proof for very general assumptions such as the assumption that we live in this public world? If so, one might ask, for a start, whether it is this assumption that needs proof or its opposite? If someone decides to assume that he does indeed live alone and has invented the companions that he has so far believed to surround him, would that assumption be less in need of defence than assuming a shared world or more so? Would it somehow be more economical?

We certainly do not know enough about the initial conditions to say which of these situations would be abstractly the more probable in an imaginary world. But in considering the world that we do know we are better off. The way to test such assumptions is to ask which of them makes more sense in the context of that world. The only kind of proof that they can have consists in showing that they are necessary in order to make thought and language possible. We can see this well over two familiar assumptions:

1. That nature is regular or lawful – that unobserved facts will go on being like the observed ones so that the future will be more or less like the past, and:
2. That in general we can trust our faculties – that our senses, memory and reasoning powers are not misleading us radically all the time.

Of course, sceptics are right to say that propositions like these are too wide to be checked in experience. No check could conceivably be adequate. They sometimes conclude that it is irrational to accept these assumptions. Indeed, they sometimes hint that if we were less lazy, we would not believe them. Thus, Hume, rejecting the reality of causation, concluded that 'if we believe that fire warms, or water refreshes, it is only because it costs us too much pains to think otherwise.'[5]

But this sets an unreal standard of rationality. The objection to dropping these basic assumptions is not just that thought becomes hard without them but that it stops altogether. Hume makes it sound as if we could go on on this path if we tried, just as we could, with an effort, dismiss a particular belief which we found to be prejudiced and unfounded. That kind of limited dismissal, however, leaves the whole background of our ordinary beliefs still standing. It still leaves us a world. By contrast, the notion of dismissing that whole background – of losing the basic conditions that make any experience reliable at all – produces a total conceptual vacuum in which the dismissal itself would lose all meaning along with everything else. There is no conceivable point to which thought would then move. Attempts at disbelief of this kind would not just run into emotional difficulties due to laziness. They would hit a logical block, like attempts to square the circle.

Rationality cannot require this. It demands that we should accept the conditions which are evidently necessary for reasoning, not that we should reject them in a desperate attempt to get an irrelevant sort of proof. Indeed the word proof itself simply means 'test,' and different kinds of tests are needed for propositions that do different kinds of work.

How does this general point about what is rational and what is not – what needs empirical proof and what does not – bear on our present argument? The fact that each of us is not alone in the world – that we live among others sufficiently like us to communicate with us – is one more of these basic conditions which are needed to make human thought possible at all. It is unlucky that Descartes failed to see this when he shaped his systematic doubt and thus came to forge the unreal, solipsistic conception of the mind that we have been discussing.

Descartes' oversight is remarkable in view of the stress he laid on the fact that thought needs language. For language is clearly a corporate, social phenomenon. Anyone who is in a position to say a sentence such as, 'I think, therefore I am' has to be heir to a rich and widely shared linguistic tradition and must therefore be a member of a widespread company of similar beings. More generally still, all intelligent animals are social animals. Their thought is always a set of tools forged by a whole community. But for people in particular, the elaboration of these tools – the richness of a language that has required much time and trouble to evolve – makes the idea of a solipsistic life empty and inconceivable.

NOTES

1. See for instance J. Gray's somewhat indignant assertion of a territorial claim for science against philosophy in the *Journal of Consciousness Studies* 2 (1) (1995), p. 8.
2. This is a main theme of his last book *Beyond Freedom and Dignity* (Harmondsworth, Penguin, 1973).
3. The systematic doubt by which he reached this conclusion is beautifully set out in brief in his *Discourse on Method*, parts 4 and 5 and more fully in his *Meditations*.
4. See I. Eibl-Eibesfeldt, *Love and Hate* (Methuen, London, 1971), pp. 11–13 and 208–16.
5. D. Hume, *Treatise of Human Nature*, book 1, part 4, Section vii.

30

A PLAGUE ON BOTH THEIR HOUSES

THE VISION OF MATTER

To summarize crudely, on the idealist side, it seemed that matter must be shown as simply a form of mind, a mere logical construction out of sense-data (Leibniz, Berkeley, Hume, Hegel, Ayer). On the materialist side, it seemed equally clear that mind was only a form of matter, that 'the brain secretes thought just as the liver secretes bile'[1] (Hobbes, Laplace, La Mettrie, Marx, Skinner). T.H. Huxley managed to embrace both kinds of reduction at once, but this was an unusual achievement.[2]

Unfortunately, despite some serious attempts at subtlety in both armies, this ontological warfare was too crude a practice to sort out the difficulty. Neither alternative can really be made to work. Both, indeed, have their strengths and both have had their epochs of success. Anyone who has not yet felt the force of the idealist position need only

DOI: 10.4324/9781003588160-38

read Hume and Berkeley to discover that it is quite as easy to start dissolving away matter as it is to start abolishing mind. But after the first few moves, both enterprises run into grave difficulties. Recently, materialism has certainly claimed the field. Many people today still think it is a meaningful, reasonable doctrine. To the contrary, I want to say flatly that it is no better than its opponent and probably worse – since a world without subjects is even less conceivable than a world without objects. And if one gets rid of one alternative, one must equally get rid of the other. The whole ontological quarrel is mistaken.

The current credulity about materialism is understandable because — quite apart from the attractions of the traditional warfare against God – the way in which the dispute has lately been thought of makes it seem unavoidable. For some time, the debate has looked like one taking place within the physical sciences themselves. The combatants have tended to stay close to Descartes' idea that the two rival elements were different substances. Unless one takes the intense logical care that Aristotle used, this simply sounds like two kinds of physical stuff. Disputants – especially on the materialist side – have therefore had the impression that they were asking something close to the pre-Socratic question 'what physical stuff is the world made of?'.

Mind then naturally evaporates because it looks like a kind of gas, a gas which is certainly not recognized by modern chemistry or physics. Nor do things get better if, instead of a substance, mind is treated as a force closely comparable to physical forces. Again, there is simply no room for such an extra force on the physical table or anywhere near it. This is just the mistake which the nineteenth-century vitalists made when they tried to insert a quasi-physical force or entity called 'life' as a factor on a par with those already considered by physics and biology, instead of pointing out that the extreme complexity of living things called for quite different forms of explanation.

CONCIOUSNESS AS AN HONORARY PHYSICAL ENTITY

The current wish to take consciousness seriously has, however, led people to hope that they can legitimate it by finding it a place on the borders of physical science, without repeating the vitalists' mistake of trying to locate such an item inside it. Thus, Gregg Rosenberg suggests that 'the irreducible character of experience implies that *fundamental natural laws* are governing it, laws on the same level as those governing properties such as mass, motion and gravity.'[3] This is a variant of David Chalmers' suggestion that we should avoid reductionism by taking 'experience itself as *a fundamental feature of the world, alongside mass, charge and space-time*' (both emphases mine). Chalmers remarks with satisfaction that, if his view is right,

> then in some ways a theory of consciousness will have more in common with a theory in physics than a theory in biology. Biological theories involve no principles that are fundamental in this way, so *biological theory has a certain complexity and messiness about it*: but theories in physics, insofar as they deal with fundamental principles, aspire to simplicity and elegance. The fundamental laws of nature are part of the basic furniture of the world, and *physical theories are telling us that this basic furniture is remarkably simple.* If a theory of consciousness also involves fundamental principles, then we should expect the same.
>
> (David Chalmers, 'Facing up to the Problem of Consciousness',
> Journal of Consciousness Studies, vol. 2, no. 3, 1995;
> emphases mine)

Physics-envy could hardly be more touchingly expressed. Life, however, is essentially messy. The trouble about this kind of proposal is an extremely interesting one. Rosenberg wants to insert his new laws 'on the same level' as those of physics. This is evidently because he thinks physics is the ground floor, the bottom line, the slot for the ultimate and most important classificatory concepts, the only place for categories. So does Chalmers. And both rightly think that 'experience' has that kind of importance because it is a category-concept, a concept too bulky to be accommodated in a mere annexe on the edge of neuroscience. They therefore want to insert it as a physical category among the largest and gravest kinds of concept that they can think of.

But this place cannot be found by annexing it to physics, any more than to neurobiology. Physics is an immensely specialized science. Its basic concepts are most carefully abstracted, neatly shaped to fit together and to do a quite peculiar conceptual job. They cannot accommodate an honorary member of a different kind. The meaning that concepts like 'mass' have in physics bears little relation to their everyday meaning. Trying to add a rich, unreconstructed, everyday concept such as consciousness to this family is like trying to add a playing card to a game of chess – or perhaps more like trying to put down a real queen or knight on the chessboard. These new items are of a different logical type. They need a different type of context. They do not belong in this game at all. They can't be 'on the same level.' The category difference is too great.

Anyone who thinks that physics could conveniently build on this kind of annexe should notice that, if it did, plenty of other concepts would have as good a claim to occupy it as consciousness does. What, for instance, about *substance, necessity, truth, knowledge, objectivity, meaning, communication, reality* and *appearance, reason* and *feeling, active* and *passive, right* and *wrong, good* and *evil*? What indeed about *life*, which has only been excluded because people today don't want to look at it? All these are basic categories of our thought. If physics were enlarged to accommodate all of them, it would become continuous with the philosophy of science and, through this, with the central areas of metaphysics. This might not have worried some of its greatest proponents, from Galileo to Einstein. Perhaps indeed it needs this kind of outward connection. But such a move would run quite contrary to the Popperian limitation of the scope of science, which most scientists seem to accept today.

The physical 'level,' then, is not the meeting-place of all thought, not a set to which all really important concepts have to belong. There is no need to expect that other crucial areas of thought will turn out to be governed by universal 'natural laws' comparable with those used in physics or directly relatable to them. The quest for such quasi-physical laws governing history and the social sciences, a quest which was eagerly carried on by theorists such as Herbert Spencer, Toynbee, Spengler and Marx, has turned out disastrously misleading. And it has done so largely because it was guided by blind imitation of physics rather than by attention to the needs of its subject-matter.

However, the phrase 'fundamental natural laws' is, in current usage, firmly stuck to the laws of physics. This expresses a convention which equates *nature* with the abstractions studied by physics. Rosenberg wants to unstick this phrase slightly and to widen its scope somewhat by revising the idea of nature to take in consciousness. This widening project is surely right as far as it goes. But it has to operate on a far bolder and more drastic scale. Explaining the whole of nature is not a linear process directed downwards towards a single set of explanatory concepts. Thought is not a neat pile of bricks in which each is supported only by the one beneath it. Thought is not governed by this kind of gravitation: its connections go in all directions. The gravitational habit of explanation, now called 'foundationalism,' is, as has lately become clear, quite inadequate.

THE VANISHING SUBJECT

Chalmers' and Rosenberg's suggestions seem, then, to be one more example of the kind of mistake which has been dogging attempts to find a place for mind somewhere among the stony fields of matter ever since metaphysical materialism became the dominant fashion in the mid-nineteenth century. People have been credulous about materialism because at a deep level, they still assumed that – in however sophisticated a sense – we had to look for a single fundamental stuff, a substrate which would provide a universal form of explanation. In spite of advances in physics, which ought to have undermined this pattern, the image of matter as the *hyle* or wood out of which things like tables are made persisted, and explanation in these terms inevitably made mind look like some kind of illusion. As we have seen, when the brain has finished secreting thought, its product has no weight, nor has the brain itself necessarily got any lighter. And again, there is no gap in the physical forces working on the brain which might leave room for mind as an extra force. Perhaps, then, consciousness was, as J. B. Watson sometimes put it, simply a myth?

This is the exciting terminus to which the behaviourist psychologists triumphantly drove their train at the end of the nineteenth century. Life there proved, however, so strange and puzzling that nearly all the passengers (including Watson himself) quickly moved back from it and began travelling round the various neighbouring stations on this same branch line, looking for compromise positions. They are still doing so today.

TWO STANDPOINTS, NOT TWO STUFFS

What is needed, however, is to avoid ever going down that branch-line in the first place. These two aspects of life are not two kinds of stuff or force. They are two points of view – inside and outside, subjective and objective, the patient's point of view on his toothache and that of the dentist who studies it. The two angles often need to be distinguished for thought. But both of them are essential and inseparable aspects of our normal experience, just as shape and size are inseparable aspects of objects. The dentist is aware of the patient's pain as a central fact in the situation he studies, and the patient, too, can to some extent think about it objectively. Indeed, dentists can become patients themselves. The only kind of item that has to exist in the world in order to accommodate these two standpoints is the whole person, the person who has these two aspects. Ontology has to accept that person as a single, unbroken existent thing.

Virtually all our thought integrates material taken from the two angles. As Thomas Nagel points out in an excellent discussion of these two viewpoints, we never normally take either position on its own. Instead, we constantly move to and fro between them, combining material from both:

> To acquire a more objective understanding of some aspect of life or the world, we step back from our initial view of it and form a new conception which has that view and its relation to the world as its object . . . The process can be repeated, yielding a still more objective conception. . . The distinction between more subjective and more

objective views is really a matter of degree, and it covers a wide spectrum . . . The standpoint of morality is more objective than that of
private life, but less objective than the standpoint of physics.[4]

Thus, we combine elements derived from the two angles in various ways that suit the different matters that we are discussing, ways
that differ widely according to the purpose of our thought at the
time – much, perhaps, as we combine visual and tactile data in our
sense-perception.

As Nagel points out, objectivity is not always a virtue, nor is it always
useful for explanation. It is only one among many ideals which we
have to aim at in thinking. In many situations, an increase in detachment can be a cognitive as well as a moral disaster. This is, of course,
most obvious in private life, which (it should be pointed out) is not a
trivial and marginal aspect of life as a whole. If we are trying to understand what is making our friends unhappy, a detached approach will at
some point not only distress them but completely block our effort to
find out what is wrong. Or if we want to understand a profound play
or novel, withdrawing our sympathy may make our attempt impossible. But, much more widely, this happens also about a wide range of
problems concerned with the motivation of other people whom we
need to know about – outsiders and enemies as well as friends. Indeed
it is true to some extent of all our attempts to grasp the kind of social
phenomena which we mentioned earlier. Some degree of empathy
or sympathy with the people involved is a vitally necessary cognitive
tool for understanding any of them. We have to enter into their aims
and intentions. This is why the kind of 'objectivity' which B.F. Skinner
aimed at in psychology – the approach which abstracts from human
subjectivity altogether, treating other people as though they were simply physical objects – is a cognitive dead-end.

THE PECULIAR STATUS OF PHYSICS

Physics, by contrast, stands, along with mathematics and logic, right
at the other end of this spectrum. It is not just an immensely abstract

enquiry but one which directs its abstraction specifically to shut out the peculiarities of personal experience. That is what makes it remote from ordinary thought. Its specialization is entirely justified by its success in doing its own particular work. But the idea of using it as a place from which to explain the situation of consciousness, which stands right at the other end of the spectrum, is surely somewhat wild. This is not to say that current attempts to alter the concepts of physics in a way which can make the existence of consciousness seem less paradoxical cannot be useful.[5] Whether or not they can work in scientific terms, they do help to undercut the crude, mechanistic idea of living organisms which at present, in many people's view, simply leaves no room for consciousness. But this is an indirect kind of facilitation. It works by altering biological concepts in a way that may allow them to mesh easily again with psychological ones. It is quite a different enterprise from fitting physics and subjective experience together directly while leaving out all the aspects of life that lie between them. A shotgun marriage with physics cannot be the right way to save the respectability of consciousness.

NOTES

1. K. Vogt, *Physiological Epistles* (1847). Quoted by J. Passmore in *A Hundred Years of Philosophy* (Harmondsworth, Penguin, 1968), p. 36.
2. See 'Thomas Henry Huxley: The War Between Science and Religion' by S. Gilley and A. Loades, *Journal of Religion* 61 (July 1981), pp. 299–301. He viewed the conflict sceptically as a demonstration of the inadequacy of all theory. He considered however that, of the two positions, Humean idealism was actually the stronger. But he expressed his materialism so vigorously that his wider argument has been forgotten and he ranks (a century before Francis Crick) as the inventor of epiphenomenalism – a sad demonstration of the dangers of stating both sides of an argument.
3. 'Rethinking Nature: A Hard Problem Within the Hard Problem' by G. Rosenberg, *Journal of Consciousness Studies* 3, no. 1 (1996), 76.
4. T. Nagel, *The View From Nowhere* (New York and Oxford, Oxford University Press, 1986) opening pages. I have discussed this passage in my book *The Ethical Primate* (London, Routledge, 1994), pp. 13 and 66.
5. See for instance 'Conscious Events as Orchestrated Space – Time Selections' by S. Hameroff and R. Penrose in *Journal of Consciousness Studies* 3, no. 1 (1996), 33–54.

PART 5

GAIAN THINKING
Putting It All Together

All of the foregoing sections have been concerned, in one way or another, with the critique of the predominant current of thought in post-Reformation European science and philosophy, which could be called the analytic-atomistic approach. The extracts which follow relate to the emergence of a radically different, more holistic approach to making sense of our world, a world of which we ourselves are an integral part – the world of Gaia, our living planet.

Mary Midgley leads into this topic from a consideration of the difficulties encountered by existing moral and political theories in tackling the problem of our moral relations with animals, and still more with ethical considerations regarding the environment. It is very hard to fit the first of these topics into the framework of Social Contract ethics, and plainly impossible for the second.

Both the worldview of mediaeval Christianity and that of mechanistic science tended to regard the Earth as a mere inert store of

DOI: 10.4324/9781003588160-39

matter, and animals as a disposable resource provided for the benefit of humans. Gaia theory – going beyond conventional ecology, which emphasizes the interdependence of different life-forms – reveals how the complex web of equilibria involving living systems actively maintains the planetary conditions necessary for the continuance of life (surface temperature, the composition of the atmosphere, the salinity and pH balance of the oceans, and much else). Our current large-scale disruption of these delicate balances threatens not only the beauty and variety of the natural environment but the whole interdependent fabric of life on Earth.

Confronting this momentous challenge requires us to go beyond the limitations of atomistic and individualistic thinking. We need to shift the focus of our attention away from an exclusive concern with the relationships between individual human beings. We now must face the deep and urgent problems concerning the relationship of those individuals to the larger whole which they, together with our non-human companions and our environment, collectively constitute.

The individualist ethic of enlightenment thought does not provide a framework for thinking about the value of this greater whole, for articulating our intuitive sense of the intrinsic value of Nature and of our responsibility to refrain from damaging or desecrating it. The sense of awe and reverence that we instinctively feel in the presence of the grandeur and beauty of the natural world, while an integral part of the ethical thinking of most cultures, does not fit easily into our own. As we saw in Part Three, the idea of reverence for Nature, of Nature as a goddess, was vigorously attacked by the makers of the scientific revolution. The resistance, which, within the scientific establishment, has met James Lovelock's use of the name of the Greek goddess of the Earth for his theory, shows that such thinking is still very entrenched in our society. But, as an increasing weight of scientific evidence seems to show, the total system of life on Earth has performed the astonishing feat of regulating all the key aspects of the terrestrial environment, for over 3 billion years, to enable us to be here now. In the light of this, Midgley asks us, what attitude other than awe and reverence would be appropriate?

I have chosen to conclude this section with the closing passage of *Beast and Man*, from the final chapter entitled 'The Unity of Life,' which I hope will serve to show the continuity between Mary Midgley's most recent interests and those that started her on her philosophical career. The fragmentation of both the physical world and the person implied by reductionist and materialist ways of thinking cuts us off from experiencing the unity of our own nature and the unity, in turn, of that nature with the greater Nature which gave birth to us – and which we do not, after all, have the right to abuse, exploit, and remake in our own image.

SOURCES

'Individualism and the Concept of Gaia,' 'Why There is Such a Thing as Society,' 'Gods and Goddesses: the Role of Wonder' – Chapters 17–19 of *Science and Poetry*, Routledge, 2000. 'The Unity of Life' – excerpt from *Beast and Man*, Chapter 13.

31

INDIVIDUALISM AND THE CONCEPT OF GAIA

WORLDS AND WORLD-PICTURES

The notion that our responsibilities do not end at national frontiers – that we owe some real duty to other humans – is not, of course, a new one in our culture. It has quite strong traditional roots, which have always warred against the narrower contractual view. The idea that we might also owe duties to the non-human world is, however, much more shocking. The contractual model of rationality excludes that idea and our tradition has taken some pains to stigmatize it as sentimental, pagan, and anti-human. And until lately, prudence did not seem to call for this kind of consideration either because the natural resources available to us were seen as literally infinite. As the Soviet historian Pokrovskiy put it in 1931:

DOI: 10.4324/9781003588160-40

It is easy to foresee that, in the future, when science and technique have attained to a perfection which we are as yet unable to visualize, nature will become soft wax in man's hands, which he will be able to cast into whatever form he chooses.

(M.N. Pokrovskiy, *A Brief History of Russia*, 10th edition, 1931, translated and quoted in I.M. Matley, 'The Marxist Approach to the Geographical Environment', *Association of American Geographers' Annals* 56, 1966, p. 101).

This kind of confidence, generated by the industrial revolution, seemed for a long time to be a mere dictate of rationality, a simple correction of the earlier awe and respect for nature which now appeared primitive and superstitious. That is why we now find it so hard to take in the evidence that there was an enormous factual mistake here. For three centuries, we had been encouraged to consider the earth simply as an inert and bottomless larder stocked for our needs. To be forced to suspect now that it is instead a living system, a system on whose continued activity we are dependent, a system which is vulnerable and capable of failing, is extremely unnerving.

Yet the damage already done undoubtedly shows that this is so. How can we adjust to this change? As I have suggested throughout this book, in conceptual emergencies like this what we have to attend to is the nature of our imaginative visions – the world-pictures by which we live. In the vision belonging to the contractual tradition, the natural world existed only as a static background. It was imagined simply as a convenient stage to accommodate the human drama. That vision radically obscured the fact that we are ourselves an organic part of this world, that we are not detached observers but living creatures continuous with all other such creatures and constantly acting upon them. It blinded us to the thought that we might be responsible for the effect of these actions. In order now to shake the grip of that powerful vision what we need, as usual, is a different one that will shift it. We need a more realistic picture of the way the earth works, a picture which will correct the delusive idea that we are either engineers who can redesign our planet or chance passengers who can detach themselves from it when they please. I think that we need, in fact, the idea of Gaia.

WHY GAIAN THINKING IS NOT A LUXURY

The idea of Gaia – of life on earth as a self-sustaining natural system – is not a gratuitous, semi-mystical fantasy. It is a useful idea, a cure for distortions that spoil our current worldview. Its most obvious use is, of course, in suggesting practical solutions to environmental problems. But, more widely, as I am suggesting, it also attacks deeper tangles which now block our thinking. We are bewildered by the thought that we might have a duty to something so clearly non-human. But we are also puzzled about how we should view ourselves. Current ways of thought still tend to trap us in the narrow, atomistic, seventeenth-century image of social life which grounds today's crude and arid individualism. A more realistic view of the earth can, I think, give us a more realistic view of ourselves as its inhabitants. Indeed, we are already moving in this direction. But we need to do it much more clear-headedly. This issue is not just psychological: it affects the whole of life. Our ideas about our place in the world pervade all our thought, along with the imagery that expresses them, constantly determining what questions we ask and what answers can seem possible. They enter into all our decision-making. Twists in those imaginative areas surely account for the curious difficulty that we still have in taking the environmental crisis quite seriously – in grasping the place that it ought to have in our scheme of priorities.

WHAT, THEN IS THE THEORY?

The current Gaian thinking that I believe can help here is a new scientific development of an old concept. The imaginative vision behind it – the idea of our planet as in some sense a single organism – is, of course, very old. Plato called the world 'a single great living creature' and this is language that people in many cultures would find natural.[1] Our own culture, however, shut out this notion for a long time from serious thought. Orthodox Christian doctrine damned it as involving pagan nature-worship. And modern scientists, for their part, were for a long time so exclusively devoted to atomistic and reductive explanations that they too rejected this reference to a wider whole. Indeed, during much of the twentieth century, the very word 'holistic' has served in some scientific circles simply as a term of abuse.

Recently, however, scientists have been becoming somewhat less wedded to this odd one-sided reductive ideology – less sure that nothing is really science except particle physics. The environmental crisis has helped this shift by making clear the huge importance of ecology, which always refers outwards from particulars to larger wholes. In that changed context, solid scientific reasons have emerged for thinking that the notion of our biosphere as a self-maintaining system – analogous in some sense to individual organisms – is not just a useful but actually a scientifically necessary one. It is not surprising that an idea should combine scientific and moral importance in this way. As we have seen, science is not just an inert store of neutral facts. Its facts are always organized according to patterns which are drawn from ordinary thinking in the first place (where else, after all, could they come from?) and which often rebound in a changed form to affect it profoundly in their turn. These strong pieces of imaginative equipment need to be understood and criticized in both their aspects. We should not slide into accepting their apparent moral implications merely because they are presented as part of science.

The two-way influence of imagery is shown impressively by the powerful machine image, which was central both to the Newtonian view of the cosmos and to the Enlightenment's notion of determinism. As Karl Popper put it, 'Physical determinism . . . was a daydream of omniscience which seemed to become more real with every advance of physics until it became an apparently inescapable nightmare.'[2] The machine-imagery had taken charge of the thought. Another striking example today is the neo-Darwinist picture – now extremely influential – of evolution as essentially a simple projection of the money market. Here the noisy rhetoric of *selfishness, spite, exploitation, manipulation, investment, insurance,* and *war-games* easily persuades people that this new form of Victorian social-atomist ideology must be true because it has the support of science. By using a different imagery and a different basic pattern, Gaian thinking tends to correct this outdated bias. It does not reject the central scientific message of neo-Darwinism about the importance of natural selection. It simply points out that it is not the whole story. Making this clear is, indeed, one of its more obvious advantages.

PLANETARY CONSIDERATIONS

I have been suggesting that this way of thinking has implications far beyond science. But the scientific case for it must be sketched first, however inadequately, so as to make clear what the term 'Gaia' actually means today. I shall summarize it here and shall then only return to it briefly at the very end of the book in considering its practical applications for immediate environmental problems. At present we shall be occupied with the idea itself and its place in our life.

The idea first arose out of considerations about the difference between the earth and its sibling planets. James Lovelock was employed by NASA in the early 1960s, designing sensitive instruments that would analyse the surfaces and atmospheres of other planets. But it seemed to him that the experiments proposed for detecting life on other planets were too closely bound to expecting particular features similar to life on earth. Was a wider strategy possible? Perhaps, he thought,

> the most certain way to detect life on planets was to analyse their atmospheres . . . life on a planet would be obliged to use the atmosphere and oceans as conveyors of raw materials and depositories for the products of its metabolism. This would change the chemical composition of the atmosphere so as to render it recognisably different from the atmosphere of a lifeless planet.
>
> (James Lovelock, *The Ages of Gaia*, Oxford, Oxford University Press, 1988, p. 5)

He therefore compared the atmospheres of Mars and Venus with that of the earth and found indeed a startling difference. By this test, Mars and Venus appeared, in a simple sense, static and dead.

> They had atmospheres close to equilibrium, like exhaust gases, and both were dominated by the generally unreactive gas carbon dioxide. [By contrast] the earth, the only planet that we know to bear life, is in a deep state of disequilibrium . . . Earth's atmosphere is like a dilute form of the energy-rich mixture that enters the intake manifold of a car before combustion: hydrocarbons and oxygen mixed . . . An awesome thought came to me. The earth's atmosphere was an extraordinary and unstable mixture of gases, yet I knew that it was constant in composition over long periods of time. Could it be that life on earth not only made the atmosphere but also regulated it – keeping it at a constant composition and at a level favourable for organisms?
>
> (Lovelock, *Gaia, The Practical Science of Planetary Medicine*, London, Gaia Books Ltd., 1991, pp. 21–2; emphasis mine)

Checking what might follow from this, Lovelock found that there is indeed a whole range of mechanisms by which the presence of life seems, from its first appearance on the earth, to have deeply influenced the atmosphere in a way that made its own continuance possible when it otherwise would not have been.

The scale on which this happens is hard to grasp. We need only consider here one simple and dramatic element in it – the carbon cycle. The carbon which living things use to form their bodies mostly comes, directly or indirectly, from carbon dioxide – the somewhat inert gas which, on the other planets, acts as a full-stop to atmospheric reactions. Life is therefore always withdrawing this gas from the atmosphere, and two statistics may convey something of the scale on which it does it. First, if you stand on the cliffs of Dover, you have beneath you *hundreds of metres of chalk* – tiny shells left by the creatures of an ancient ocean. These shells are made of calcium carbonate, using carbon that mostly came from the air via the weathering of rocks – the reaction of carbon dioxide with basaltic rock dissolved by rain.

This process of rock-weathering can itself take place without life. But when life is present – when organisms are working on the rock and the earth that surrounds it – it takes place *one thousand times faster* than it would on sterile rock.[3] Coal and oil, similarly, are storehouses of carbon withdrawn from the air. All this carbon will go back into circulation one day, but meanwhile it is locked away, leaving the breathable air that we know, air that makes possible the manifold operations of life. Similar life-driven cycles can be traced for other essential substances such as oxygen, nitrogen, sulphur and that more familiar precious thing, water. There is also the matter of warmth. During the time that life has existed on earth, the sun has become 25 per cent hotter, yet the mean temperature at the earth's surface has remained always fairly constant. Unlike Venus, which simply went on heating up till it reached temperatures far above what makes life possible, the earth gradually consumed much of the blanket of greenhouse gas – mostly carbon dioxide – which had originally warmed it. Feedback from living organisms seems to have played a crucial part in this steadying process and to have ensured, too, that it did not go too far. In this way, the atmosphere remained substantial enough to avoid the fate of Mars, whose water and gases largely streamed away very early, leaving it unprotected against the deadly cold of space. Here again, conditions on earth stabilized in a most remarkable way within the quite narrow range which made continued life possible. Lastly, there is the soil. We think of the stuff we walk on as *earth*, the natural material of our planet, and so it is. But it was not there at the start. Mars and Venus and the Moon have nothing like it. On them, there is only what is called *regolith*, naked broken stone and dust. By contrast, our soil, as Lynn Margulis points out, is a museum of past life:

> Soil is not unalive. It is a mixture of broken rock, pollen, fungal filaments, ciliate cysts, bacterial spores, nematodes and other microscopic animals and their parts. 'Nature', Aristotle observed, 'proceeds little by little from things lifeless to animal life in such a way that it is

impossible to determine the exact line of demarcation.' Independence is a
political, not a scientific term.

(Lynn Margulis and Dorion Sagan, *What is Life?*, London,
Weidenfeld, 1995, p. 26; emphasis mine)

In short, if all this is right, living things – including ourselves – and the planet
that has produced them form a continuous system and act as such. Life, then, has not
been just a casual passenger of the earth's development. It has always
been and remains a crucial agent in determining its course.

PUTTING LIFE TOGETHER

I cannot discuss the scientific details further here. Orthodox scientists,
though they were at first sceptical about it, now accept this general
approach as one which can be used and debated within science.[4] Their
disputes about these aspects of it will of course go on. But, as I have
suggested, the importance of the concept is by no means confined to
science. It concerns the general framework of our thought. It supplies
an approach which, once fully grasped, makes a profound difference,
not just to how we see the earth but to how we understand life and
ourselves. The new scientific arguments bring back into focus the traditional imaginative vision of a living earth which I mentioned at the
start – a vision which is already returning but needs to be made much
clearer – and show how much we need this vision in our social and
personal thinking.

As Lewis Thomas has pointed out, this vision has already dawned
on many of us when we first saw the pictures of earth sent back by
the astronauts:

Viewed from the distance of the moon, the astonishing thing about
the earth, catching the breath, is that it is alive. The photographs show
the dry, pounded surface of the moon in the foreground, dead as an
old bone. Aloft, floating free beneath the moist, gleaming membrane
of bright blue sky, is the rising earth, the only exuberant thing in this

part of the cosmos. If you could look long enough, you would see the swirling of the great drift of white cloud, covering and uncovering the half-hidden masses of land. If you had been looking a very long, geologic time, you could have seen the continents themselves in motion, drifting apart on their crustal plates, held aloft by the fire beneath. It has the organised, self-contained look of a live creature, full of information, marvellously skilled in handling the sun.

(Lewis Thomas, *The Lives of a Cell*, London, Futura, 1976, p. 170)

(No other planet, incidentally, has continental drift and it seems that life may well have played a part in making this possible.)

THE PREVALENCE OF INTELLECTUAL APARTHEID

We will consider later what is involved in the use of the term 'life' on this planetary scale. For the moment, it seems important to consider how such suggestions made in science affect the rest of our thought. The scientific details that now articulate this picture of the living earth give it a new kind of standing because of the special importance that science has for us today. They make us bring our official scientific beliefs together with our imaginative life. As we have seen, that rapprochement is surely welcome, but it is not easy for us. Many dualisms in recent thought have urged us to keep these matters apart. We are used to hearing of a stark war between the two cultures and of a total separation between facts and values. In our universities, the arts block and the science block tend to be well separated. But we will never make much sense of life if we do not somehow keep our various faculties on speaking terms with one another.

Much of the difficulty about grasping the concept of Gaia is not scientific but comes from this fragmented general framework of our thought. It arises – for scientists as well as for the rest of us – from these artificial fences that we have raised across the scene and centrally from Descartes' original fence between mind and body. Our moral, psychological and political ideas have all been armed against holism. They are both too specialized and too atomistic. As many people are pointing out today, that slant is giving us trouble in plenty of other places as well as over Gaia. Yet we find it very hard to change it.

ONE AQUARIUM, MANY WINDOWS

This difficulty in changing concepts is, of course, a common one. We are always in trouble when we are asked to think about the world in a new way. I have suggested that it is as if we had been looking into a vast, rather ill-lit aquarium through a single window and are suddenly told that things look different from the other side.

We cannot have a single comprehensive view of the whole aquarium – a single, all-purpose, philosophic theory of everything. Many prophets, from the seventeenth century to the nineteenth, from Leibniz to Hegel and Marx, have tried to give us such a view. But their efforts have proved misguided. The world is simply too rich for such reductive strait-jacketing. There is not – as Leibniz hoped – a single underlying quasi-mathematical language into which the views from all aspects can be translated. This does not mean that no understanding is possible. We can relate these various aspects rationally because they all occur within the framework of our lives. We can walk round and look at other windows and can discuss them with each other. But we cannot eliminate any of them. We have to combine a number of different ways of thinking – the views through several windows, historical, biological, mathematical, everyday and the rest – and somehow fit them together.

When Galileo first expressed his views about the world, not only the Pope but the scientists of his day found them largely incomprehensible. Yet those ideas, when developed by Descartes, Newton, Laplace and the rest shaped the set of windows through which the whole Enlightenment looked into the vast aquarium which is our world. That is the set through which many in our own age still want to see everything. This set is now called 'modern' by those who want to use that word more or less as a term of abuse for past errors, contrasting it with various 'post-modern' sets which may be expected to replace it. Though I don't myself find this vague time-snobbery very helpful, there is no doubt that the Cartesian vision has become quite insufficient.

THE AGE OF ALIENATION

As many people have pointed out,[5] the central trouble is the dualism of mind and body. The notion of our selves – our minds – as detached observers or colonists, separate from the physical world and therefore from each other, watching and exploiting a lifeless mechanism, has been with us since the dawn of modern science (and of the industrial revolution). Descartes taught us to think of matter essentially as our resource – a jumble of material blindly interacting. Animals and plants were machines and were provided for us to build into more machines.

It is this vision that still makes it so hard for us to take seriously the disasters that now infest our environment. Such a lifeless jumble would be no more capable of being injured than an avalanche would. Indeed, until quite lately our sages have repeatedly urged us to carry on a 'war against Nature.'[6] We did not expect the earth to be vulnerable, capable of health or sickness, wholeness or injury. But it turns out that we were wrong: the earth is now unmistakably sick. The living processes (or, as we say, 'mechanisms') that have so far kept the system working are disturbed, as is shown, for instance, by the surge of extinctions.

Descartes' worldview did, of course, produce many triumphs. But it produced them largely by dividing things – mind from body, reason from feeling, and the human race from the rest of the physical universe. It produced a huge harvest of local knowledge about many of the provinces. But it has made it very hard for people even to contemplate putting the parts together.

For a long time now, our culture has tolerated this deprivation. But it has become a serious nuisance in many areas of knowledge. The rise of systems theory and complexity theory are thriving attempts to break its restraints. Another such place is the lively debate now going on about problems of consciousness – a topic once systematically tabooed by academics, but now agreed to constitute one of their most potentially interesting areas of study.[7] This change has been an intriguing showcase for the workings of intellectual fashion, and it has interesting implications for discussions of Gaia. It is clear by now that many of us want to see our aquarium – our world, including ourselves – more as a whole, indeed, that we desperately need to do this. To do so, we must attend to aspects of it which Enlightenment dualism cannot reach, aspects which simply do not appear at our traditional window.

NOTES

1. Plato, *Timaeus*, Section 33.
2. K. Popper, 'Of Clouds and Clocks' in *Objective Knowledge: An Evolutionary Approach* (Oxford, Oxford University Press, 1972), p. 222.
3. *Gaia: The Practical Science of Planetary Medicine*, p. 111.
4. For a review of recent discussions see T.M. Lenton, 'Gaia and Natural Selection' in *Nature* 394 (30 July 1998).
5. See for instance K. Devlin in *Goodbye Descartes: The End of Logic and the Search for a New Cosmology of the Mind* (New York, John Wiley and Sons, 1997) and the entire works of Richard Rorty.
6. For examples, see J. Passmore, *Man's Responsibility for Nature* (Duckworth, London, 1974), Chapter 1.
7. This is why there is now a thriving *Journal of Consciousness Studies* – something that would have been inconceivable 20 years ago.

32

GODS AND GODDESSES
The Role of Wonder

WHY 'GAIA'?

One of these areas that has been made artificially difficult – the connection between scientific thought and the rest of life – comes out
quaintly in the sharp debate about the implications of the name Gaia
itself. That name arose when Lovelock told his friend, the novelist
William Golding, that people found it hard to grasp his idea, and
Golding promptly replied, 'Why don't you call it Gaia?', which is
the name of the Greek earth-goddess, mother of gods and men. That
name, when he used it, did indeed rouse much more interest in
the theory. Many people who had not previously understood it now
grasped it and thought it useful. Others, however, particularly in the
scientific establishment, now rejected it so violently that they refused
to attend to the details of it altogether. In our culture at present,

DOI: 10.4324/9781003588160-41

people find it somewhat surprising that an idea can be large enough to have both a scientific and a religious aspect. This is because, during the last century, our ideas of religion, of science and indeed of life have all become narrowed in a way that makes it difficult to get these topics into the same perspective. (Here our window has become a good deal narrower than it was when Galileo and Newton and Faraday used it. They never doubted that these things belonged together.[1]) To get round this difficulty, Lovelock used a different image. He launched *the medical model of Gaia* – the idea of the damaged earth as a patient for whom we humans are the only available doctor, even though (as he points out) we lack the long experience of other sick planets which a doctor attending such a case really ought to have. So he invented the name *geophysiology* to cover the skills needed by such a physician.[2]

This medical imagery at once made it much easier for scientists to accept the notion of Gaia. When the point is put in medical terms, they begin to find it plausible that the earth does indeed in some way function as an organic whole, that its climate and oceans work together with living things to maintain a normal balance, and that what gravely upsets any part of the system is liable to upset others. They can see that, for such a whole, the notion of *health* is really quite suitable. And of course they find the patient Gaia, lying in bed and politely awaiting their attention, much less threatening than that scandalous pagan goddess.

SCIENTIFIC STATUS AND THE ISSUE OF GENDER

Lovelock, accordingly, came under great pressure to calm the scientists by withdrawing the goddess and for a while, he seriously considered doing so. Eventually, however, he decided that the whole idea had to be kept together because the complexity was real. As Fred Pearce put it in an impressive article in *New Scientist*:

> Gaia as metaphor: Gaia as a catalyst for scientific enquiry: Gaia as literal truth: Gaia as Earth Goddess. Whoever she is, let's keep her.

> If science cannot find room for the grand vision, if Gaia dare not speak
> her name in *Nature*, then shame on science. To recant now would be a
> terrible thing, Jim. Don't do it.
>
> (Fred Pearce, 'Gaia, Gaia, don't go away' in
> *New Scientist*, 28 May 1994)

Lovelock didn't. He does indeed constantly emphasize the scientific
status of the concept:

> I am not thinking in an animistic way of a planet with sentience . . .
> I often describe the planetary ecosystem, Gaia, as alive because it
> behaves like a living organism to the extent that temperature and
> chemical composition are actively kept constant in the face of per-
> turbations . . . I am well aware that the term itself is metaphorical
> and that the earth is not alive in the same way as you or me or even a
> bacterium.[3]

But he still writes, with equal firmness:

> For me, Gaia is a religious as well as a scientific concept, and in both
> spheres it is manageable . . . God and Gaia, theology and science, even
> physics and biology are not separate but a single way of thought.[4]

This raises the question: is religious talk actually incompatible with science? It is interesting to note that in one prestigious area of science –
an area which is often viewed as the archetype of all science – such
talk is readily accepted. That area is theoretical physics. As Margaret
Wertheim has pointed out, most of the great physicists of the past,
from Copernicus to Clerk Maxwell, insisted that their work was primarily and essentially religious. Rather more remarkably, their modern
successors still make the same claim. As she says:

> In spite of the officially secular climate of modern science, physicists
> have continued to retain a quasi-religious attitude to their work. They
> have continued to comport themselves as a scientific priesthood, and
> to present themselves to the public in that light. To quote Einstein,

'A contemporary has said, not unjustly, that *in this materialistic age of ours the serious scientific workers are the only truly religious people*'.

(Margaret Wertheim, *Pythagoras' Trousers*, London, Fourth Estate, 1997, p. 12; emphasis mine)

Einstein himself showed how seriously he took this thought by constantly referring to God in explaining his own reasoning ('God does not play dice,' . . . 'The Lord is subtle but not malicious,' and so forth). And he explicitly said that he meant it: 'Science can only be created by those who are thoroughly imbued with the aspiration towards truth and understanding. The source of this feeling, however, springs from the sphere of religion.' (Einstein, 'Science and Religion' in *Nature*, vol. 146, no. 65, 1940, p. 605).

Later physicists might have been expected to dismiss this approach as a mere personal quirk of Einstein's, but they have not. Instead, many of them have developed it in best-selling books with titles such as *God and the New Physics*,[5] *The Mind of God*,[6] *The God Particle*,[7] *The Physics of Immortality: Modern Cosmology, God and the Resurrection of the Dead*,[8] and many more.

Is there perhaps some special reason why religious talk of this kind can count as a proper language for physics, but becomes inappropriate and scandalous when the chemical and biological concerns of Gaian thinking are in question? Or is it perhaps not so much the subject-matter as the sex of the deity that makes the scandal? Is it perhaps held to be scientifically proper to speak of a male power in the cosmos but not of a female one? There is a powerful tradition which might make this odd view look plausible. As Wertheim shows, throughout the history of physics, a strong and somewhat fantastic element of misogyny has indeed accompanied the sense of sacredness that always distinguished this study. The physical priesthood was a male one guarding a male god, and it went to great lengths to protect its secrets from intruding females.

Walter Charleton, another founding member of the Royal Society, summed up many of his colleagues' antipathy towards women when he wrote,

'you are the true Hienas that allure us with the fairness of your skins. . . You are the traitors to wisdom, the impediments to industry . . . the clogs to virtue and the goads that drive us all to Vice, Impiety and Ruin'. Henry Oldenburg, the Society's first secretary, declared that its express purpose was 'to raise a Masculine philosophy' . . . This bastion of British science did not admit a woman as a full member until 1945.[9]

This talk of 'a Masculine philosophy' echoes, of course, Francis Bacon's clarion-call for the new science to produce 'a Masculine birth of time' where men could turn their 'united forces against the nature of things, to storm and occupy her castle and strongholds.'[10]

THE VALUE OF WONDER

Of course, the personifications in thinking of this kind should not be taken literally. Yet the reverent, awe-struck attitude that lies behind those personifications is surely a suitable one both for science and for our general relation to the cosmos. Einstein was not being silly. Anyone who tries to contemplate these vast questions without any sense of reverence for their vastness simply shows ignorance of what they entail. And of course, if the system of life itself is taken to have participated in the history of evolution in the sort of way that Gaian thinking suggests, then a substantial part of this reverence is surely due to that system. If it has indeed played a crucial part in stabilizing conditions on earth through billions of years, to the point where we ourselves are now here and able to profit from them – if it has managed the remarkable feat of preserving the atmosphere and controlling the temperature, thus saving the earth from becoming a dead planet like Mars and Venus and turning it instead into the cherished blue-green sphere whose picture we all welcomed – if it has done all this for us, then the only possible response to that feat is surely wonder, awe and gratitude.

That sense of wonder and gratitude is clearly what the Greeks had in mind when they named the earth Gaia, the divine mother of gods and men. They never developed that naming into a full humanization. They never brought Gaia into the scandalous human stories that they told about other gods – stories which, in the end, made it impossible to take those gods seriously at all. But the name still expressed their awe and gratitude at being part of that great whole.

And today there is evidently more, not less, reason to feel that awe and gratitude, because we have learnt something of the scope of the achievement. The sense of life itself as active and effective throughout this vast development has become stronger, not weaker, with our understanding of our evolutionary history. This is the sense that Darwin expressed when he wrote, at the end of *The Origin of Species*, 'There is grandeur in this view of life.'

INTRINSIC VALUE AND THE SOCIAL CONTRACT

It does not seem to me to matter much whether one calls this wonder and reverence *religious* or not except to people who have declared a tribal war about the use of that word. It is of course an element that lies at the root of all religions. In the great religions with which we are familiar, it always plays its part and is subsumed within a wider whole. Reverence for the creation can there quite properly inspire and enrich the reverence that is due to its creator.

But such wonder and reverence are equally essential to beliefsystems that reject religion. All such systems involve some order of values, some pyramid of priorities which has to end somewhere. In order to make sense of our lives, we have to see some things as mattering in themselves, not merely as a means to something else. Some things have to have what the theorists call intrinsic value. Secular thought in the West has not dropped that notion. Instead, during the last century, it has simply decreed that human individuality itself is the only thing that has this status. Today, it uses words such as *sacred* and *sanctity* readily to describe human life, but becomes embarrassed if they are used for anything else. People with this approach tend to be alarmed by the direct reverence for the non-human world that was expressed by people like Wordsworth and Rousseau and to treat it as something not quite serious. Here we come back to the question that I mentioned at the outset about the possible reasons why the fate of the earth should concern us.

The early twentieth century's humanistic creed that only people have value – that non-human affairs do not matter except for their effect on people – means that there cannot be any such reason. This is the unspoken creed that leaves us – or at least leaves the professional moralists among us – so puzzled by the environmental crisis – by the thought that we might actually owe some direct duty to the biosphere.[11]

Our individualism has accustomed us to using a minimalist moral approach which gives us no clue to such matters. But that minimal approach has, of course, already got a difficulty in explaining why each of us should be concerned about any other individual besides our own self in the first place – why our value-system should ever go beyond simple egoism. As we have seen, it answers this question in terms of the social contract which is supposed to make it worth while for each of us to secure the interests of fellow citizens. The answer to the question 'Why should I bother about this?' is then always 'Because of the contract which gives you your entrance-ticket to society.'

This contract model excludes dealings with anything non-human. It works quite well for political life within a nation – for which, of course, it was originally invented. But even there it leaves out most of life. Even within our own lives, we know that we cannot think of rights and duties as optional contracts set up between essentially separate individuals. Relations between parents and children are not like this, and each of us, after all, started life as a non-contracting baby. Nor indeed are most of our personal relations. But we have not yet grasped how much worse this misfit becomes when we have to deal with the rest of the world.

Even over animals, the legalistic notion of contractual rights works badly. And when we come to such chronic non-litigants as the rain forest and the Antarctic, it fails us completely. If duties are essentially contractual, how can we possibly have duties to such entities? John Rawls raised this question rather suddenly as an afterthought at the very end of his famous book *A Theory of Justice* and could only say that it was one which lay outside his contractual theory.[12] He added that it ought to be investigated some day. But, as often in such cases, the real response has to be 'you shouldn't have started from here.' Rawls' book was the definitive statement of contract ethics and it marked the end of the era when they could pass as adequate.

GRANTING CITIZENSHIP TO WILDERNESSES

Individualism is bankrupt of suggestions for dealing with these non-human entities. Yet we now have to deal with them, and promptly. They can no longer be ignored. Clearly, too, most of us do now think of the human drama as taking place within this larger theatre, not on a private stage of its own. The Darwinian perspective on evolution places us firmly in a wider kinship than Descartes or Hobbes ever dreamed of. We know that we belong on this earth. We are not machines or alien beings or disembodied spirits but primates – animals as naturally and incurably dependent on the earthly biosphere as each one of us is dependent on human society. We know that we are members of it and that our technology already commits us to acting in it. By our pollution and our forest-clearances we are already doing so.

What element, then, does the concept of Gaia add to this dawning awareness? It is something beyond the fact of human sociability, which has already been stated, for instance by communitarians. It is not just the mutual dependence of organisms around us, which is already to some extent being brought home to us by ecology. It goes beyond thinking of these organisms as originally separate units that have somehow decided or been forced to co-operate – as basically independent entities which drive bargains for social contracts with each other ('reciprocal altruism') because they just happen to need each other in order to survive. The metaphysical idea that only individuals are real entities is still present in this picture, and it is always misleading. *Wholes and parts are equally real.*

Recent habits make it hard for us to take this in. As a lot of science fiction makes clear, we are still amazingly ready to think of our species as a mere chance visitor on this planet, as something too grand to have developed here. Of course, it is true that we are a somewhat special kind of primate, one that is particularly adaptable through culture and gifted with singular talents. But those gifts and talents still come to us *from the earth* out of which we grow and to which we shall return. The top of our tree still grows from that root as much as the lower branches. We cannot live elsewhere. Our fantasies of moving to outer space mean no more than the magic tales with which other cultures have often consoled themselves for their mortality. Even people who still expect that move in the long term are beginning to see that it cannot be expected to arrive in time to relieve our present emergency. Since the end of the Cold War, NASA finds it increasingly hard to raise funds to keep space programmes going. And environmental disasters are likely to make that process harder, not easier.

All this means that, in spite of recent influences, direct concern about destruction of the natural world is still a natural, spontaneous feeling in us and one that we no longer have any good reason to suppress. Most people, hearing about the wanton destruction of forests and oceans, find it shocking and – as has become clear in the last few decades – many of them are prepared to take a good deal of trouble to prevent it. This feeling of shock and outrage is the energy source which makes change possible. It has not, of course, been properly tapped yet. As happened over nuclear power, it takes a disaster to bring such needs home to people. Yet the feeling is there, and it is surely already becoming stronger and more vocal. It is, of course, what leads people to subscribe to organizations trying to protect the environment. Though we have been educated to detach ourselves from the physical matter of our planet as something alien to us, this detachment is still not a natural or necessary attitude to us. Since we now know that we have evolved from a whole continuum of other life-forms and are closely akin to them – a point which nobody ever explained to Descartes – it is not at all clear why we should want to separate ourselves from them in this way. On this point, of course, the findings of modern science agree much better with the attitude of those supposedly more primitive cultures where people see themselves as part of the whole spectrum of life around them than they do with the exclusive humanism of the Enlightenment. They also agree better with most of our everyday thought. The element in that thought which is now beginning to look arbitrary and unreal is its exclusive humanism.

NOTES

1. On the radical interdependence between their religious and scientific thinking see M. Wertheim, *Pythagoras' Trousers, God, Physics and the Gender Wars* (London, Fourth Estate, 1997), Chapters 5 and 6.
2. This is the topic of his book *Gaia: The Practical Science of Planetary Medicine*.
3. *Gaia: The Practical Science of Planetary Medicine*, pp. 6, 11, 31.
4. *The Ages of Gaia*, pp. 206 and 212.
5. By P. Davies (New York, Simon and Schuster, 1984).
6. By P. Davies (New York, Simon and Schuster, 1992).
7. By L. Lederman and Dick Teresi (Boston, Houghton Mifflin, 1993).
8. By F.J. Tipler (New York, Doubleday, 1994).
9. *Pythagoras' Trousers*, p. 100. For more about this amazing but highly influential sexual chauvinism see B. Easlea, *Science and Sexual Oppression* (London, Weidenfeld and Nicolson, 1981).
10. Farrington, *Philosophy of Francis Bacon*, pp. 62, 92, 93; Spedding, *Works of Francis Bacon*, vol. 4, pp. 42, 373.
11. J. Passmore laid out this problem admirably in *Man's Responsibility for Nature* (London, Duckworth, 1974) and it has continued to occupy environmental philosophers ever since.
12. J. Rawls, *A Theory of Justice* (Cambridge, Mass., Harvard University Press, 1971), p. 512, cf. p. 17. I have discussed this remarkable move in *Animals and Why They Matter* (Athens, Georgia, University of Georgia Press, 1984), pp. 49–50.

33

WHY THERE IS SUCH A THING AS SOCIETY

THE SURPRISING INEFFICIENCY OF SELFISHNESS

Indignant concern on behalf of the environment does, then, already exist. Our difficulty is that we cannot see how to fit it into our traditional morality which – both in its Christian and its secular forms – has in general been carefully tailored to fit only the human scene.

How should we deal with this conceptual emergency? I do not think that it is very helpful to proceed as some moralists have done by promoting various selected outside entities such as 'wildernesses' to the status of honorary members of human society. If we claim (for instance) that a wilderness such as the Antarctic has intrinsic value because it has independent moral status, meaning by this that we have decided to grant it the privilege of treating it like an extra fellow citizen, we shall sound rather inadequate. These larger wholes

DOI: 10.4324/9781003588160-42

are independent of us in a quite different sense from that in which extra humans – or even animals – who were candidates for citizenship might be so. Our relation to them is of a totally different kind from the one which links us to our fellow citizens.

There is, indeed, something unreal about the whole way of thinking which speaks of these places as though they were distinct individual 'wildernesses,' units which are applying separately for admission to our value-spectrum. Though we divide them for our thought, they function as parts of the whole. At present, indeed, the Arctic and the Antarctic are letting us know this because their ice, melted by global warming, is affecting the entire state of the oceans. That process is already producing floods which threaten the destruction of places such as Bangladesh and Mauritius and widespread damage elsewhere. Nearer home, it also looks liable to upset the Gulf Stream in a way that may drastically chill the climate of Europe. Without that convenient warming system, we in Britain would find ourselves ten degrees colder, sharing the climate of Labrador, which is on much the same latitude. And if that change happens it could apparently happen quite quickly. Globalization is no longer a distant option. It is here already.

This is, of course, a prudential consideration. It may suggest that rational self-interest alone will be enough to guide us here – as Hobbes supposed it always would be. And of course it is true that self-interest should indeed drive us this way. The odd thing is that it does not.[1] The human imagination does not work that way. When things go well, we simply don't believe in disasters. Long-term prudence, reaching beyond the accepted, routine precautions of everyday life, is therefore an extraordinarily feeble motive.

Prudence is supposed to deal in probabilities as well as in certainties. And the increasing probability of environmental disaster has been well-attested for at least the last thirty years. During all that while, every time that the travellers in steerage pointed out that the ship was sinking the first-class passengers have continued to reply placidly, 'Not at our end.' Only very gradually and shakily is this prospect beginning to be admitted as an influence on policy – a topic that should be allowed now and then to compete for the attention of decision-makers, alongside football and teenage sex and the Dow-Jones Index and European Monetary Union. Only gradually is it beginning to emerge that ecology is actually a more important science than economics – that the profitable exchange of goods within the ship is a less urgent matter than how to keep the whole ship above water. When the story of our age comes to be written, this perspective may surely seem surprising.

Our imaginations, however, are not necessarily ruled by our reason. We do not easily expect the unfamiliar, and major disasters are always unfamiliar. When we are trying to be prudent, our thoughts turn to well-known and immediate dangers, nervously avoiding a wider scene. That is why self-interest alone cannot be trusted to answer our question about why the earth should concern us. Of course prudence must come in, but unless other reasons are already recognized, prudence usually manages to evade the larger topic. That is why we need to think about those other reasons – about the ways in which the terrestrial whole, of which we are a part, directly concerns us, and would still do so even if we could get away with abusing it. As I am suggesting, we shall never grasp the nature of that kind of concern so long as we try to model it on the civic concern that links fellow citizens. *Duties to wholes, of which one is a part, naturally differ in form from duties to other individuals.*

OUTWARD AND INWARD-LOOKING CONCERNS

Since the Enlightenment, our culture has made huge efforts to exclude outward-looking duties from Western morality. Pronouncements such as 'there is no such thing as society' and 'the state is only a logical construction out of its members' are only recent shots in this long individualist campaign. But the natural strength of outward-looking concern can be seen from the way in which many such duties are still accepted. For instance, the idea of *duty to one's country* still persists, and it certainly does not just mean duty to obey the government. The ideas of *duty to a family, clan, locality or racial group* still have great force, even in our society where they have been deliberately played down, whenever one of these groups feels threatened by outside oppression. The current revival of nationalism among various groups all over the world, and the emphasis laid on *sisterhood* by feminists, all testify to this force. In other cultures, where no attempt has been made to undermine it, its strength is unmistakable.

Another corporate claim which can operate powerfully is the idea of a *duty to posterity*. This is not just the idea of a string of separate duties to particular future individuals. It is rather the sense of being part of a great historical stream of effort within which we live and to which we owe loyalty. That identification with the stream explains the sense in which we can − rather surprisingly − owe duties to the dead and also to a great range of anonymous future people, two things which have baffled individualistic thinkers. Even when there is no conscious talk of duty, people who work in any co-operative enterprise − school, firm, shop, orchestra, theatrical company, teenage gang, political party, football team − find it thoroughly natural to act as if they had a duty to that enclosing whole if it is in some way threatened.

And this, it seems to me, is what is now beginning to happen about the earth itself, as the threat to it begins to be grasped. When an enclosing whole which has been taken for granted is suddenly seen as really endangered, all at once its hidden claims become visible. It would be good if we could accept the overwhelming existing evidence of a terrestrial emergency without needing to be hit by a direct disaster. But whatever causes that belief to be accepted, once it becomes so there is surely little doubt about the duty it lays upon us.

STATES AND ORGANISMS

It is not surprising that our mainstream tradition has played down this corporate element in morals. Political theorists such as Hobbes, Locke and Rousseau − and their contemporaries in active politics − wanted above all to stop certain dominant groups, notably in the churches, from exploiting this loyalty for their own ends. They succeeded to an extent which would surely have astonished them if they could have foreseen it, and which Rousseau at least would have found alarming.

Between them, they managed to swing the balance of moral thinking right over to its individualistic pole.

As we have seen, they did not manage to destroy the idea of corporate duty entirely. *Fraternity* was supposed to be among the ideals of the French Revolution, though in practice it was usually thrust aside by equality and freedom. Rousseau himself did try to balance the individualism of his contract theory by introducing the idea of the general will, a corporate will in the nation distinct from the mere summing of separate decisions – something to be relied on more deeply, something which individuals should seek out and follow. This and similar hints were developed by Hegel into a fully fledged organic theory of the state, by which individuals are always incomplete entities, more or less comparable with cells in a plant or animal, needing to find their place in a wider whole for full self-realization.

Up to a point, this suggestion clearly has to be true. Most of us, if we can act freely at all, want to place ourselves within such larger groupings – families, clubs, friendships, orchestras, gangs, political movements. But it is a sort of doctrine which sounds very different according to which kind of larger group we have in mind. By bad luck, Hegel centred his theory on the nation state and in particular on his own state of Prussia, which was then (in the early nineteenth century) preparing to dominate the rest of Germany and thereby the rest of Europe. Marx, following Hegel's organic approach, also expected his precepts to be taken up in Germany and, though he envisaged a distant time when nation states would not be needed, he expected them to be the main social unit for the foreseeable future. As the eventual adoption of Marxism in Russia did not produce any sort of utopia, it is not surprising that these two unattractive examples have put people off organic theories of society, or that many of them end up saying, with Nietzsche's Zarathustra: 'The State lieth in all the languages of good and evil: whatsoever it saith, it lieth: whatsoever it hath, it hath stolen' (Friedrich Nietzsche, *Thus Spake Zarathustra*, Part 1, section 'Of the New Idol').

Thus, through most of the twentieth century, many prophets in the West preached a kind of narrow and romantic individualism, a moral outlook which simply assumes that individual freedom is the only unquestionable value. This is a doctrine held in common by J.-P. Sartre and Ayn Rand. Despite the difference of style, the European and the American forms of it share a central message – social atomism. Both conceive the individual's freedom as negative – a matter of avoiding interference. Politically, however, there is rather an important difference because of the kind of entity that counts as 'an individual' is different in the two versions.

The European version still speaks of individual people and therefore stays close to real anarchism. The American one, however, expands to include 'commercial freedom.' And commercial freedom, in its modern form, is a different thing and a very strange one. The entities which it conceives as free are no longer individuals but corporations, often very big and impersonal ones. The rhetoric of 'free trade,' in fact, does not now refer to individual freedom at all. The old romantic vision of commercial freedom which (as we shall see in a moment) Herbert Spencer presented in the 1880s – a vision of heroic individual tycoons carving out the course of evolution with their bare hands – does not fit today's conditions at all, whatever may be thought of its exactness in his own day.

There has, in fact, been an extraordinary shift here in the central tenet of individualism. The metaphysical belief in human individuals as the true atoms of social life – the only properly real and sacred kind of unit – has given way. At the moment, the focus has shifted to another kind of entity, the big corporation. But since that kind of entity, in its turn, is now beginning to look rather less than ultimate – since the Internet is threatening its supremacy by building a more diffused way of doing business, while individual speculators infest it from within and shake its control – this does not seem likely to be the end of the story. These corporations may prove to be dinosaurs, entities remembered only as we remember mediaeval guilds. What surely emerges is that the whole idea of a single favoured, exclusively real unit was mistaken in the first place. *Life goes on on various scales, each of which is real and has to be thought of in its own terms.*

SOCIALITY SURVIVES

This shift of emphasis to a kind of corporate freedom is, however, just one more indication of how – as communitarians have recently been pointing out – individualist propaganda cannot destroy the corporate element in morals. Of course we still value our personal freedom very highly. Psychologically, perhaps we value it the more because of the stress produced by overcrowding, by the sheer increase in human numbers and in social mobility during the past century. We all see far more people, especially far more strangers, in our daily lives than our ancestors did, which certainly imposes stress and social exhaustion.

Yet humans – even modern, civilized humans – are still social animals to whom, on average, the desolation of loneliness is a much worse threat than the interference of their fellows. On the positive side, too, we have talents and capacities which absolutely require generous, outgoing co-operation for their fulfilment – a point which Hegel got right. Paradoxically, there are many things which a free, solitary individualist is not free to do. He cannot be a parent, a quartet-player, a tragic actor, a teacher, a social reformer or even a revolutionary. Even Nietzsche's Zarathustra noticed this difficulty: 'A light hath dawned on me. I need companions . . . living companions which follow me because they desire to follow themselves – and to go to that place whither I wish to go' (*Thus Spake Zarathustra*, Introductory Discourse, Section 9).

In fact (as Bishop Butler pointed out against Hobbes), apart from certain narrow political contexts, human beings are not in the least like the pure, consistent, prudent egoists that social contract thinking requires. And today people are coming to see this.

Of course, it is true that we need to stop the powerful oppressing the weak, so we must have political institutions to prevent the exploitation of these corporate loyalties. That is why we need a free press to answer the propaganda of governments. And since the press itself comes under commercial pressure, that pressure, working through the labour market, through advertisements and through countless other channels, is, on the whole, much more alarming today than the power of religion. But the need to ward off these dangers cannot mean that we can do without corporate loyalties altogether. The outgoing, social side of human life vitally needs them.

NOTE

1. I have discussed this fascinating point more fully in *Beast and Man* (London, Routledge Revised Paperback Edition, 1995), Chapter 6.

34

THE UNITY OF LIFE

LIVING IN THE WHOLE WORLD

Kant thought that treating others as ends was necessary or possible only within our own species. He drew a sharp line at the species border. Man, he said, 'is certainly titular lord of nature, and, supposing that we regard nature as a teleological system, he is born to be its ultimate end.' Or again, 'The end is man. We can ask, "Why do animals exist?" But to ask, "Why does man exist?" is a meaningless question.'[1] What about that? Kant is taking nature as a pyramid, converging towards a single end. This will not do, not only because we are not sure who forms the purpose. It makes no sense to consider the enormous range of animal species as existing as a *means* to anything, let alone us. They are not going in this direction at all. The oddity of suggesting that they are emerges rather pleasingly in an essay by the economist Kenneth

DOI: 10.4324/9781003588160-43

E. Boulding.[2] He is explaining that there is no need to study animal behaviour, since we have its raison d'être, man himself, the finished product, already before us. He writes,

> 'The critical question is, how much we could learn about the jet plane from studying the wheelbarrow or even from studying the automobile – If the jet plane is man, the automobile perhaps is the mammal, the wheelbarrow the fish.'

This has to mean that all animals are devices for a single known purpose (apparently something parallel to rapid transport?), devices differing only in the degree of progress they have made toward efficiency. And now that we have Mark 12 before us, Mark 3 and Mark 7 are of interest only to industrial archaeologists.

This sort of thing leaves me speechless. A device can put another out of date only so far as they are means to the *same end*. Does Boulding think it just obvious what the aim of all human life actually is? And, having solved that question, does he think it clear how all other existing species – elephants and albatrosses, whales and tortoises and caribou – are just bungling and inadequate shots at the *same* target? Is there nothing to a giraffe except being a person manqué? And if, as Wells suggested, something more intelligent turned up, would that eliminate us without further question in favour of Mark 13? *Man is not something we have designed at all*, and innumerable things about the way he works are completely mysterious to us. Kant's question 'Why does man exist?' is not at all meaningless; it has the perfectly good sense 'How can he best live? To what way of life is he best adapted?' To deal with this, we need to understand adaptation. Evidence about it must be found in other species. And the same question, in the same sense, can be asked about them too. People obsessed with the cost-benefit analysis pattern see no alternative to their own way of thinking, even though often they, like the rest of us, have a sense of chill, of oppression, of loneliness, as human life grows steadily narrower. The dungeon encloses us, the lid of the ego presses down. Under what compulsion? Why look at things this way? In *The Sovereignty of Good*, Iris Murdoch writes,

> I am looking out of my window in an anxious and resentful state of mind, brooding perhaps on some damage done to my prestige. Then suddenly I observe a hovering kestrel. In a moment everything is altered. The brooding self with its hurt vanity has disappeared. There is nothing now but kestrel. And when I return to thinking of the other matter it seems less important.

(p. 84)

Certainly we *could* (she goes on) think of this as a measure of mental hygiene, regard the kestrel as a device for regaining balance. But there is something perverse about doing so; 'More naturally, as well as more properly, we take a self-forgetful pleasure in the sheer, alien pointless independent existence of animals, birds, stones and trees.' This has to be right, because the release itself depends on the kestrel's not being such a device. If we found that we were in Disneyland, with plastic kestrels going up at carefully randomized intervals, the entire point would be lost. What we need here is to get rid of the language of means and ends, and use instead that of part and whole. Man needs to form part of a whole much greater than himself, one in which other members excel him in innumerable ways. He is adapted to live in one. Without it, he feels imprisoned; the lid of the ego presses down on him.

The world in which the kestrel moves, the world that it sees, is, and will always be, entirely beyond us. That there are such worlds all around us is an essential feature of our world. Calling the bird's existence 'pointless' means only that it is not a device for any human end. It does not need that external point. It is in some sense – a sense that can certainly do with study – an end in itself.[3] We may throw some light on the difficulties here by looking at the same problem where it crops up at the heart of Kant's aesthetic. Kant was much occupied with the Sublime, which was the (quite convenient) eighteenth-century name for things that impress us, not by being what we already want (like the

Beautiful), but by their vastness and total disregard of our needs – in a word, by their absolute Otherness. The sea is sublime; so are mountains and deserts. So even, sometimes, are very small things, if they are exceedingly strange and unaccountable.[4]

Kant's careful analysis of this element in experience, and the seriousness with which he treats it, are admirable. It is plain that he was a man genuinely disposed to be bowled over by such things. But he finds a real difficulty in understanding this concept. *What* is actually sublime? Here the rules of his Rationalist framework hamper him. It can hardly, he says, be the actual sea and mountains, for they are just dead matter, so many tons of basalt or H_2O. How can one revere that? He sees that sheer size is often central to the experience. Yet size impresses us only by contrast to the size of our own body, which seems to him a contingent matter. So he concludes that what is sublime is not the objects themselves, but what they stand for, that is, the vastness of the human task. 'The feeling of the Sublime in nature is respect for our own vocation.'[5] In part this is right. The vast does stand for the difficult, the not-yet-attempted. But it has to be more than just a symbol. It has to matter in itself, or it cannot symbolize effectively. Powerful symbols are not just dispensable manmade boxes in which we deposit ideas for convenience, retrieving them unchanged when we need them. Kant's point is that mountains and distances constitute difficulties for us, and that difficulties teach us our weakness. But mountains are not just examples of difficulties. They are not just wastefully extended treadmills. They tell us not only that we are small, but that they are great. Indeed, the first point would have no meaning without the second. If they were merely educational devices to bring home our weakness to us, we could forget about them once we had seen the point. Or, if we decided still to use them as a reminder, we should think of them, I suppose, in a resigned sort of way, as we do regard purely educational devices, perhaps rather as we think of our alarm clocks and desk calendars. (Did the Romans regard the skeletons at their feasts in this way?)

The truth is, it is no contingent fact about us that our bodies are the size they are. We – ourselves – are not, as Descartes suggested, purely mental creatures. We are not tentatively considering possible incarnations. We – ourselves – are members of a vulnerable species, easily destroyed in an avalanche, with a place on this particular planet, and none anywhere else.[6] To such beings, there is no way in which x million gallons of H_2O (including saline impurities) does not constitute an enormous and sublime ocean, nor in which whales and albatrosses, capable of dealing with it in any state of agitation, are not sublime creatures. Stunting this response is stunting our highest faculties. For (what is less often mentioned than the vulnerability) we are receptive, imaginative beings, adapted to celebrate and rejoice in the existence, quite independent of ourselves, of the other beings on this planet. Not only does our natural sympathy reach out easily beyond the barrier of species, but we rejoice in the mere existence of plants and lifeless bodies – not regarding them just as furniture provided to stimulate our pampered imagination.

Literary criticism often does not look at things this way; it tends to an official doctrine that the physical universe matters only in so far as we can make poetry out of it. I think this is cockeyed, and that no poetry of the slightest value could be made on this supposition. The trouble is, however, a discrepancy between theory and practice on the matter, not only (as I have suggested) in Kant himself, but in great writers who have followed him. For instance, Coleridge, explaining his own dejection, his failure to respond to a splendid sunset, wrote:

> O Lady, we receive but what we give,
> And in our life alone does Nature live,
> Ours is her wedding garment, ours her shroud.[7]

But this isn't and couldn't be true, and the end of that very poem shows that he didn't believe it. As Iris Murdoch says in *The Sovereignty of Good*,

> I do not think that any of the great romantics really believed that we receive but what we give and in our life alone does nature live, although the lesser ones tended to follow Kant's lead and use nature

as an occasion for exalted self-feeling. The great romantics, including the one I have just quoted, transcended 'romanticism.'

. . . Art, and by art from now on I mean good art, not fantasy art, affords us a pure delight in the independent existence of what is excellent.

(p. 85)

Man is not adapted to live in a mirror-lined box, generating his own electric light and sending for selected images from outside when he happens to need them. Darkness and a bad smell are all that can come of that. We need the vast world, and it must be a world that does not need us; a world constantly capable of surprising us, a world we did not program, since only such a world is the proper object of wonder. Any kind of Humanism which deprives us of this, which insists on treating the universe as a mere projection screen for showing off human capacities, cripples and curtails humanity. 'Humanists' often do this, because where there is wonder they think they smell religion, and they move hastily in to crush that unclean thing.[8] But things much more unclean than traditional religion will follow the death of wonder. In truth, as I have suggested, wonder, the sense of otherness, is one of the sources of religion (not the other way around), but it is also the source of curiosity and every vigorous use of our faculties, and an essential condition of sanity. And there is less difference than some people suppose between its religious and its scientific expression. When the Lord answered Job out of the whirlwind, he only said what any true naturalist may say to himself, whether he believes in any god or not.

> Hast thou entered into the treasures of the snow? or hast thou
>   seen the treasures of the hail? . . .
> Who hath divided a watercourse for the overflowing of
>   waters . . . To cause it to rain on the earth where no man is,
>   on the wilderness, wherein there is no man,
> To satisfy the desolate and waste ground, and to cause the bud of
>   the tender herb to spring forth? . . .

> Canst thou bind the sweet influences of the Pleiades, or loose the
>   bands of Orion? . . .
> Canst thou draw out Leviathan with an hook? . . .
> Will he make a covenant with thee? Wilt thou take him as a servant
>   for ever? . . .
> He esteemeth iron as straw, and brass as rotten wood . . .
> He maketh the deep to boil like a pot, he maketh the sea like a pot
>   of ointment.
> He maketh a path to shine after him; one would think the deep to
>   be hoary,
> Upon earth there is not his like, who is made without fear.
> He beholdeth all high things; he is a king over all the children of
>   pride.[9]

That is the sort of way Charles Darwin looked at the physical universe, and, unless I am much mistaken, Aristotle too.[10] That is the sort of universe in which our nature is adapted to live, not one alien and contemptible to us, from which we must be segregated. As I understand Humanism, this is its message. Humanism cannot only mean destroying God; its chief job is to understand and save man. But man can neither be understood nor saved alone.

NOTES

1. 'Duties towards Animals and Spirits', *Lectures on Ethics*, p. 239. Clearly he was thinking of the reason for the animals' existing as provided by their usefulness to man.
2. In *Man and Aggression*, ed. A. Montagu, p. 86.
3. Philosophers often accuse Kant of confusion because he uses this phrase. If they just mean that what he is saying is not wholly clear, they are right; it is rather a difficult thing to express. But often they mean rather that it doesn't make sense in an Egoist framework – that 'ends' are, by definition, internal. But Kant is denying this. He really is trying to break out of the Egoist squirrel-cage. And common sense is surely with him.
4. I. Kant, *Critique of Judgement*, tr. J.C. Meredith, Oxford, 1911. See the whole section on The Sublime.
5. Ibid., p. 106.

6. As far as I know, the doctrine of the Resurrection of the Body means that this is the proper view in a Christian context as well as in an agnostic one.

7. 'Dejection, an Ode'.

8. *Ecrasez l'infâme*: Voltaire's remark about the political iniquities of the Roman Church. But there are other things to worry about today. John Passmore in *Man's Responsibility for Nature*, an otherwise excellent book, is constantly brought up short by the fact that what seems like a helpful reaction to ecological crime also seems like a religious one. But the great religions have combined innumerable elements, many of them essential to life. These cannot be abandoned just because of the way people have misused them in the past.

9. Job, 38 and 41.

10. See, for instance, *Ethics* 6.7, where he takes it as obvious that man is not the best thing in the world. Recent Humanism tends to be more arrogant. Thus Keynes, speaking for Moore's circle, remarks, 'We lacked reverence, as Lawrence observed and as Ludwig Wittgenstein also used to say – for everything and everyone' (*Two Memoirs*, p. 99). But contemplation without reverence is a very odd thing.

PART 6

THE LIFE OF A PHILOSOPHER
A Reflective Overview

Up to this point, the sequence of extracts in this collection have been arranged without regard to chronology; however, the diachronic aspect of Mary Midgley's thought is of great interest, particularly since she herself had a deep and abiding preoccupation with both history in general and the history of ideas in particular. The emergence of her mature philosophical thought from her earliest stirrings of interest in the subject (see below, *At School at Downe House*) was framed by the years leading up to, during, and after the Second World War, and her philosophical preoccupations were significantly shaped by that devastating war. Ethical values that had taken centuries to become established throughout European civilisation had come under imminent threat, and to someone of a philosophical disposition, it had become an urgent matter to investigate the deeper sources of the trouble. What kind of ethical thinking was needed to underpin a social and political culture that could stand firm against the diseased ideologies of

DOI: 10.4324/9781003588160-44

totalitarianism (and, one might perhaps add, also against the cruder forms of American commercial capitalism, with its intellectual under-pinning of behaviourism, utilitarianism and physicalist reductionism)?

As she notes, R.G. Collingwood, almost the last representative of that earlier generation of Oxford philosophers whose refined neo-Hegelian idealism had by then become deeply unfashionable, warned sharply against the dangers of an ahistorical, over-analytic approach to the subject; Midgley's own sensibilities, steeped in the classical tradi-tion she so deeply loved, and in the wide fields of English literature which connected her in other ways to the thought of past eras, found the preoccupation with logical and linguistic minutiae of the Oxford analytic school both arid and ethically shallow.

In the fortunate (for her) circumstances alluded to in the Introduc-tion, she found congenial allies in her quest for a more deeply humane ethical standpoint than the analytic tradition was able to furnish; Iris Murdoch, Elizabeth Anscombe, and Philippa Foot, all equipped with a secure grounding in classical thought, joined forces with her, over a period of a decade or so, in working out a way to think about moral questions without either the baggage of neo-Hegelian idealism or the sterile logic-chopping of the new analytic approach.

The following extracts cast an illuminating light, both on the intel-lectual atmosphere against which she and her comrades rebelled, and on the sources and influences that provided the material for their countervailing critique. Though the vanguard of linguistic philosophy tended to disregard the concerns and methods of the great figures of the past, Oxford itself of course remained a world centre for classi-cal scholarship, and was large enough to house a number of gifted scholars who did not subscribe to the currently fashionable 'cutting edge' of philosophic thought. Such figures as Donald MacKinnon, Isaiah Berlin, E.R. Dodds, and Gilbert Murray provided the kind of stimulus, informed by wide-ranging learning and historical sensibil-ity, that helped to balance the narrow focus of the analytic mainstream; it should not be thought, however, that Mary and the other members of the quartet were lacking in analytical rigour. Indeed, Elizabeth Ans-combe, while a fine classical scholar, had perhaps the most penetrating analytical intellect of any Oxford philosopher of the time, and certainly, I think, had the deepest understanding of the revered genius of linguistic philosophy, Ludwig Wittgenstein; Philippa Foot's lapidary moral philosophy is a model of analytic clarity and precision; while Iris and Mary, the most literary minded of the four, are not, to an impartial reader, at all lacking in the qualities of methodical argument, clarity of expression and logical rigour that are the key virtues of the analytic-linguistic approach.

However, the main current of her thought at this time led away from the questions and methods of linguistic philosophy. It is regrettable, perhaps, that the interesting ideas she began to develop in her doctoral work on Plotinus never came to fruition, partly because, having left Oxford soon after commencing work on it to teach at the newly established Reading philosophy department, and soon after that moving to Newcastle to marry Geoffrey Midgley, she lacked the time and tutorial support that she needed, and partly because, as she frankly confessed, she found Plotinus' thought extremely difficult (as indeed it is). Yiota Vassilopoulou's forthcoming study of the surviving fragments of Midgley's work on Plotinus is eagerly awaited – at least by me!

I have only been able to include a fraction here of her observations on subsequent developments in philosophy in Britain. The attacks on philosophy as a university discipline under the Thatcher government naturally affected her deeply (and her husband, who was in charge of the Newcastle department when the axe fell on it, even more so). These, and other, internal developments within the academic philosophical community, led the discipline in a direction as remote from the one she sought to take it as was the earlier Oxford analytic tradition. As one quasi-scientific philosophical fashion succeeded another (formal semantics, possible worlds theories, evolutionary psychology, 'neurophilosophy' and so forth), she continued to plough her own distinctive furrow; enjoying the signal advantage of freedom from institutional affiliations (her business card read 'Mary Midgley: Freelance Philosopher'), she travelled widely, presenting her views to a very wide range of both academic and non-academic audiences, and probably had as large an influence on public life outside academia as any of her philosophical contemporaries.

The passage I have chosen as the closing words to this new edition, recalling Boethius' classic, *The Consolations of Philosophy*, highlights the impulse that was at the core of her philosophical work throughout her long career: the right motivation for doing philosophy is not intellectual curiosity, but a deep-seated desire to improve the human condition. This attitude, like Boethius' book, may be considered by many professional philosophers to be old-fashioned and even quaint; but if she is right in thinking that it is currently making a comeback, in my view this is cause for celebration.

35

BEGINNINGS
Ancestors and Downe House School

THOMAS URQUHART AND THE UNIVERSAL LANGUAGE

I shall begin this chapter with my best-known forebear, Sir Thomas Urquhart of Cromarty. He was a man who, in the year 1660, 'died suddenly in a fit of excessive laughter, on being informed by his servant that the King was restored.' He is really a great-uncle rather than a direct ancestor. But I start the family story with him because he makes such a good contrast to the sobriety of most of the others. And that contrast shows up well the amazing variety of ways in which we use our imagination.

I have a little volume of his works in which he carefully traces 'the true pedigree and lineal Descent of the most honourable family of the Urquharts, in the house of Cromarty, from the creation of the

DOI: 10.4324/9781003588160-45

World until the year of God 1652.' He names each successive head of the house, so this list allows later generations to establish comfortably their exact relationship with Adam, and thereby with God. Rather less expectedly, too, these earlier Urquharts turn out to have made some very good marriages. At various times, members of the family took as their wives (among others scarcely less notable) Narsesia, the Queen of the Amazons; Arenopas, the daughter of Hercules; Pharaoh's daughter of Termuth (the one who looked after Moses); Panthea, the daughter of Deucalion and Pyrrha; Hypermnestra, 'the choicest of Danaus's fifty daughters'; Thymelica, the daughter of Bacchus (What? Yes, that's right . . .); Nicolia, the Queen of Sheba; Lycurgus' niece Pothina; Coriolanus' sister Aequanima; Diosa, the daughter of Alcibiades; and Tortolina, the daughter of King Arthur of Britain.

The author adds many absorbing scholarly notes in which he sharply rejects other people's alternative conjectures as 'fabulous.' Having thus traced the early history of his house, he promises that he will describe at some future time 'the illustrious families from thence descended, which are yet in esteem in the countries of Germany, Bohemia, Italy, France, Spain, England, Scotland, Ireland, and several other nations of a warmer climate, adjacent to that famous territory of Greece, the lovely mother of this most ancient and honourable Stem.' He will explain, too, how it is that the names of these noble houses have unfortunately become corrupted into forms that no longer reveal their descent from the Urquharts. He will also make it clear 'why the shire of Cromarty alone, of all the places of the isle of Britain, hath the names of its towns, villages, hamlets, dwellings, promontories, hillocks, temples, dens, groves, fountains, rivers, pools. Lakes, Stone-heaps, akers [fields] and so forth of pure and perfect Greek.'

After this pedigree, the book contains a treatise called The Jewel. This is nothing less than an offer to construct a Universal Language, a language 'wherein, whatever is uttered in other Languages hath signification in it, while it affordeth Expressions, both for Copiousness, Variety and Conciseness in all manner of Subjects, which no Language else is able to reach unto.' That proposal is, as we soon see, a cunning grant-application. Sir Thomas hopes that, by offering humankind this inestimable benefit, he can make the authorities let him out of prison to pursue his promising research programme and look after his estates. He wrote his book in the Tower, where the Commonwealth authorities had reasonably imprisoned him for several years for having fought on the King's side as an ardent royalist at the battle of Worcester.

They don't seem to have found his linguistic project persuasive and, in spite of strong family feeling, I am afraid this is understandable. The argumentative part of The Jewel turns entirely on the fact that it is inconvenient to have so many languages, all of which are imperfect. A new universal one is therefore clearly needed. Having settled that point, the book wanders off into Scottish history where it gets lost and never comes back to actually inventing the ideal new language. Sir Thomas did, however, get let out of the Tower on parole and for some years went abroad, where he was living when he was struck down by laughter on the fatal news of King Charles's restoration.

My aunt Jane, in her book on the family, describes Sir Thomas as 'imaginative,' and few of us will want to quarrel with that. But what I find fascinating is the direction of his imagination – the use to which he wants to put it. His trouble is not exactly that he finds life too boring. He is not just trying to extend experience by adding extra colour to its greyness. What he wants to do is rather to impose extra tidiness – to introduce order into the vast chaos of the past. He wants to show a network of simple connections which will finally make sense of that huge unexplored region. He keeps indignantly rejecting attractive suggestions which would not fit in with this chosen order. And the maddening disorder created by the diversity of languages inspires him to organize them all round the one that he finds to be the best organized – namely Greek.

The trouble is, of course, that his idea of simplicity involves orbiting round a particular centre – his own family and his own favourite language, a pattern that is probably not the best one he could have chosen. But the ordering motive itself is surely identical with that which moves what we may unkindly call real scholars. Like them, Urquhart is a universalizer because he shares with them a kind of obsessive perseverance. He is not just normally egocentric like the rest of us. He does not just see neighbouring parts of the world as linked in a pattern round himself. He wants to extend that pattern of order to include the whole known world.

Far greater thinkers than he have shared that wish and have often been led into trouble by it. To name just one instance of someone who is only a little greater, Herbert Spencer, when he had formed his notion of evolution on a crude idea of survival of the fittest, found to his delight that this one idea could then be used to explain everything in the cosmos, from gas to genius. 'Bearing the generalisation in mind,' he said, 'it needed only to turn from this side to that side, and from one class of facts to another, to find everywhere exemplifications.'

By contrast, Darwin showed his stature by rejecting this obsessive overconfidence. He thought such generalizations empty. He probably wouldn't have been much impressed by Sir Thomas's theories either. But the same universalizing tendency keeps cropping up in our thought. And it does so with special power when the world around us seems specially chaotic – when, as in Sir Thomas's time, we are struck by political turbulence and civil war.

The seventeenth-century wars of religion were particularly horrifying because they were not just power struggles but were also conflicts between rival world views – disputes about how the world essentially is. If we ask why that century produced the tremendous crop of rationalistic philosophers who framed the Enlightenment and made way for modern science – Descartes, Hobbes, Spinoza, Leibniz – it surely makes sense to say that, at that time of profound disorder, the need for order was peculiarly strongly felt.

I am not trying to suggest that Sir Thomas belongs with figures like these. I am just noticing something about the motives for thought, something which is common to great and small thinkers, and is, in a way, easier to see in the small ones. Sir Thomas himself is not in much danger of being considered a great thinker; indeed, he is more likely to be suspected of being entirely mythical. Even a kind reader may well think that I have invented him entirely, or have at least drawn him by crudely exaggerating some of the people in Walter Scott's novel *The Antiquary*. He and his book are, however, perfectly real and he may be found occasionally mentioned as a minor character by historians.

Indeed, I should perhaps take this opportunity of saying quite generally that I am myself an almost pathologically truthful person. I attach
great importance to the difference between fiction and fact and I hate
the kind of literature that deliberately blurs it. I don't mean that I can't
tell a lie in real life when one is absolutely necessary, but I always
reckon that one should be quite clear about whether one is doing so
or not, and there is very seldom any need to do it in books. Everything
in this book is meant to be true and so far as I can I shall make it so.

DOWNE HOUSE

I moved to Downe House School, near Newbury, when I was twelve.
When my parents suggested this change I was pleased, thinking it
would be something of an adventure. And it was. Although I was
sometimes homesick, it did give me a quite new sense of space.

Early in my days at Downe, I had the interesting experience of seeing pure sense-data, or, as they are now called, qualia. It happened like
this. I was bending over a bath, stirring the water before getting into
it, when I felt a light tap on the back of my head and the world before
me suddenly turned into an expanse of white triangles. These gradually began to move and some of them went pale blue at the edges as
the scene started to reassemble itself. What had happened was that the
ceiling had come down, owing to revelry in the bathroom above. This
ceiling was only a thin, harmless layer of plaster and it shattered on
impact all over the room, filling the bath with neat white pieces which
then gradually turned blue as they absorbed the water.

Later, when I started studying philosophy and began to hear about
sense-data (which were then philosophically respectable), I remembered this scene. Later still J. L. Austin put these unfortunate sense-data
quite out of fashion; indeed he devoted much of his career to demol-
ishing them. They were tabooed for a long time, but recently, when
consciousness itself came back into fashion, they have made a comeback
under their new name as qualia. Dan Dennett doesn't believe in them.
He is trying to repeat Austin's feats of exorcism, but I don't think he'll
succeed. Of course, it is true that items like this shouldn't be built up
into solid substances, actual independent 'things,' as sense-data were for

a time. They are appearances. But appearances are part of the world; they do actually appear. I've seen them, and I'll back them to survive.

FINDING PLATO

I had decided to read Classics rather than English – which was the first choice that occurred to me – because my English teacher, bless her, pointed out that English literature is something that you read in any case, so it is better to study something that you otherwise wouldn't. Someone also told me that, if you did Classics at Oxford, you could do philosophy as well. I knew very little about this but, as I had just found Plato, I couldn't resist trying it.

This red-letter event happened on a wet, discouraging Saturday afternoon when I was sixteen. I happened to pick off the school library shelf two battered Everyman volumes of Plato's dialogues in translation and that somehow settled the matter. I think I started with the Phaedo, which tells the story of Socrates' last day – of the conversation about life and death and the soul that he is said to have had with his friends on the day when he was about to be executed. And by the time when I was forced to run off to evening chapel I was hooked.

I was startled at how the arresting imaginative vision, vividly shown in the dramatic setting of the dialogues and in the various myths and metaphors, grew directly out of the sober reasoning and in turn contributed to reshape it. And as I went on reading Plato I found that this constantly happened. He seemed to extend thought on difficult subjects in a quite new way into the realm of the imagination. Thought and feeling did not seem to be at odds here. They were collaborating in real harmony.

As I went on reading, many haunting pictures emerged, but the one that increasingly gripped me – as it has so many other people – was the central image that dominates the Republic. Socrates there describes a remarkable scene. He says:

> Imagine an underground chamber like a cave . . . In this chamber are men who have been prisoners there since they were children, their legs

and neck so fastened that they can only look straight ahead and cannot turn their heads. Some way off, behind and higher up, a fire is burning, and behind the prisoners and above them runs a road, in front of which a curtain-wall has been built, like a screen at puppet-shows between the operators and their audience, above which they show their puppets.

I see.

Imagine further that there are men carrying all sorts of gear along behind the curtain-wall, projecting above it and including figures of men and animals . . . Some of these men, as you would expect, are talking and others are not . . . Do you think our prisoners could see anything of themselves or their fellows except the shadows thrown by the fire on the wall opposite to them? . . . If they were able to talk to each other, would they not assume that the shadows they saw were the real things?

(Book 7, section 514. Translation by Desmond Lee, Penguin 1955)

This extraordinary cinematic image is Plato's way of explaining why we have such difficulty in understanding the world around us. We are (he says) just like those prisoners in the way that we treat the disconnected shadow-shows that pass before us as if they were the whole of reality. In our efforts to make sense of them, we merely look for connections between various particular images. But this is useless when we have no grasp of their real causes.

What we need to do (he says) is to turn our backs on these shadows of puppets – to break out of our fixed places, to move away towards the mouth of the cave and to walk right out towards the world outside. There, instead of flickering phantoms in firelight, we shall finally be able to see real things by the true light of the sun. That sun was actually the source of all that we saw before, and of the light which makes all sight possible, but it is itself something immeasurably more important than any of its effects.

What does this parable mean? The message that people today can see most clearly in it is that we should not be satisfied with just perceiving the physical world but should learn to understand its inner structure, mainly through mathematics. And Plato, who was a mathematician, did indeed mean this and had deep confidence in this approach. It is the part of his thought that we now grasp most easily, and it has become central to modern science.

But for Plato himself, this was only the preparation for a much more momentous change. He was calling for a general clearing of our conceptual maps, a huge philosophic effort to see the real structure, not just of physical things but of the whole world that includes them. And this world contained subjects as well as objects. It was a world in which spiritual realities were much more important, and indeed actually much more real, than physical ones.

The prisoners do not only fail to see outside physical objects; they also fail to see themselves and each other. It is no accident that Plato mentions this incapacity before he touches on the physical aspect. Our grasp of this wider world must (he says) centre on a deeper understanding of ourselves, revealing spiritual values. This understanding does indeed require intellectual disciplines such as mathematics and logic. But it goes far beyond them to a mystical understanding of goodness itself, which (like the sun) is the source of all reality, and these insights have to start with self-knowledge. It was in order to make this understanding possible that he proposed the rigorous, highly organized way of life that is described in the Republic, a lifestyle which, to many of us, seems unduly one-sided and over-cognitive.

I have been fascinated to see how Iris Murdoch, who studied the dialogues with me at college and always remained my close friend, has stayed quite close to Plato's actual doctrines here while I have gradually left them. I have eventually come, as Aristotle did, to envisage a much more continuous world containing a much wider spectrum of values, a world so complex that we need to look at it from an indefinite number of different angles, not one that is split neatly between spirit and matter. Because it is complex, I don't think that there could ever be a single Grand Theory unifying and explaining it – a Theory of Everything – nor that there is a single basic moral solution to all human problems. Like William James, I go for pluralism. As he put it:

> Prima facie, the world is a pluralism; as we find it, its unity seems to be that of any collection; and our higher thinking consists chiefly of an effort to redeem it from that crude form. Postulating more unity than the first experiences yield, we also discover more. But absolute unity, in spite of brilliant dashes in its direction, still remains undiscovered, still remains a Grenzbegriff [an ideal limit] . . . 'Reason', as a gifted writer says, 'is but one item in the mystery . . . Not unfortunately, the universe is wild – game-flavoured as a hawk's wing . . .' This is pluralism, somewhat rhapsodically expressed. He who takes for his hypothesis the notion that it is the permanent form of the world is what I call a radical empiricist.
>
> (Preface to *The Will to Believe*, pp. viii–ix)

36

OXFORD
The Philosophical Scene

ATTENDING TO HISTORY: COLLINGWOOD

Whenever I get interested in some new person's thought, I always want to know more about their life and the conditions of their age. And when I manage to do this, I always find that it does add something important to the thought. This is not a matter of substituting irrelevant gossip and psychoanalysis for the ideas. It is a way of making the ideas themselves more intelligible by getting nearer to their full meaning. You need to see in which direction the thought is moving – what problems it arose from, what ills and errors it was intended to cure, what earlier doctrines it was contradicting and what hopes for the future lay behind it – if you want to use it and see where it needs to go next. You need the background to make sense of the story. Without that context, thoughts appear as static patterns that can't really be

DOI: 10.4324/9781003588160-46

developed. For instance, Hobbes's dramatic generalizations about the need for an all-powerful state only make real sense when one reads them against the background of the dire wars of religion raging in the sixteenth and seventeenth centuries.

By contrast, a lot of formalist analytical philosophy during the twentieth century has been carried on in a deliberately anti-historical style, in a strenuous effort to abstract the thought entirely from its context. The classic example of this is G.E. Moore's Principia Ethica, which rules loudly that the only project of any interest in ethics is the linguistic one of finding (or not finding) the definition of Good. Moore and Russell originally introduced this approach as a reaction against their predecessors' Hegelian emphasis on history. But among their followers, it quickly escalated into an aggressive orthodoxy. This never became universal, but to some extent it still persists.

This has been a general tendency across many disciplines, but it naturally produces what is now called a Whig view of history, a policy of assuming that the past has been a simple progress through a series of errors towards current beliefs which are final and perfectly satisfactory. This attitude easily arose, I think, as part of that general exaltation of 'the modern' which prevailed during the first half of the twentieth century. As far as philosophy goes, R.G. Collingwood answered it resoundingly in his Autobiography in 1939. But at that time, the fashions of the day prevented most philosophers from noticing this, so it may be worthwhile to look at his remarks now.

Collingwood noted how, when he arrived at Oxford in the early 1900s, the philosophers there had just changed their attitude sharply from that of the previous generation. In that earlier generation, the main influences had been thinkers with an idealist slant, such as T.H. Green, who were much interested in political philosophy. Their ideas had affected public opinion and public life far beyond the university. Oxford courses had been designed with that in view:

> The 'Greats' school was not meant as a training for professional scholars and philosophers; it was meant as a training for public life in the Church, at the Bar, in the Civil Service, and in Parliament. The school of

> Green sent forth into public life a stream of ex-pupils who carried with them the conviction that philosophy, and in particular the philosophy they had learnt at Oxford, was an important thing, and that their vocation was to put it into practice.
>
> (p. 17)

By contrast, (he goes on) their successors in the next generation told their pupils that philosophy was a purely theoretical study which should not be expected to affect their lives at all. 'If it interests you to study this, do so; but don't think it will be of any use to you.' Accordingly, the pupils

> whether or not they expected a philosophy that should give them, as that of Green's school had given their fathers, ideals to live for and principles to live by, . . . did not get it; and were told that no philosopher (except, of course, a bogus philosopher) would even try to give it. The inference which any pupil could draw for himself was that, for guidance in the problems of life, since one must not seek it from thinkers or from thinking, from ideals or from principles, one must look to people who were not thinkers (but fools), to processes that were not thinking (but passion), to aims that were not ideals (but caprices) and to rules that were not principles (but rules of expediency). The effect on their pupils was (how could it not have been?) to convince them that philosophy was a silly and trifling game, and to give them a lifelong contempt for the subject.
>
> (pp. 48–50)

In short, it turned out that the analytic approach to philosophy was not – as its prophets supposed – one free from ideology. Instead, it was one that called for an ideology of irrationalism. This resulted in public disillusionment, but that fact did not disturb the analytic philosophers, since, as Collingwood explains, they were happy to be considered as pure theorists:

> Unlike the school of Green, [they] did think philosophy a reserve for professional philosophers, and were loud in their contempt of

philosophical utterances by historians, natural scientists, theologians and other amateurs

. . . They were proud to have excogitated a philosophy so pure from any sordid taint of utility that they could lay their hands on their hearts and say that it was no use at all; a philosophy so scientific that no-one whose life was not a life of pure research could appreciate it, and so abstruse that only a whole-time student, and a very clever man at that, could understand it.

(pp. 17, 49–51)

Philosophically, the root of this attitude was, said Collingwood, the unrealistic doctrine that fragmented thought and knowledge into separate propositions, supposedly distinct atoms of thought, each of which was supposed to be verifiable on its own. (Though he calls this approach by the name of a now-forgotten doctrine called 'realism,' this fragmentation did indeed remain as a central feature of the logical atomism preached by Russell and the young Wittgenstein.) Against this atomism, Collingwood insisted that propositions only make sense as the answers to particular questions. To understand them, therefore, we need to grasp not only what question each one is meant to answer but also why that question arises – what is the wider background that is making people ask it? And to do this, we always need the methods of history. We cannot deal with our knowledge by atomizing it – by splitting it up into separate propositions and judging each one separately:

This doctrine, which was rendered plausible by choosing as examples of knowledge statements like 'this is a red rose', 'my hand is resting on the table' where familiarity with the mental operations involved has bred not so much contempt as oblivion, was quite incompatible with what I had learnt in my 'laboratory' of historical thought . . . You cannot find out what a man means by simply studying his spoken or written statements . . . You must also know what the question was (a question in his own mind and presumed to be in yours) to which the thing he has said or written was meant as an answer.

(pp. 26, 31)

Thought, in fact, does not break down into ultimate units at all. Like life, it comes in fair-sized, fairly complex patterns, always linked together as parts of a wider background, which we have to sort out and deal with on their merits.

This does not mean that our work is impossibly complicated. It does not mean that we cannot know anything until we know everything. Human cultures contain all sorts of convenient ways of breaking up the world into manageable handfuls and dealing with one part at a time. And we can keep continually developing these ways so that they can correct one another. In this way, quite a lot of the time, we do get things right. Attending to the background pattern of questions and answers does not tip us into a helpless relativism. But it is perfectly true that this approach does stop us hoping for a universal scientific formula underlying all thought. We cannot, as Descartes hoped, find a single path to infallible certainty. But then, luckily we do not need to.

MARXIST DREAMS

One activity which was open to both sexes was politics, and this was an absorbing interest for many of us. Most students who noticed politics at all were more or less left wing and the Labour Club, which I promptly joined, had over a thousand members. The main question then was, how far left do you want to go?

Here again Iris is a significant figure. She started to investigate Communism as soon as she reached Oxford, and quickly joined the local branch of the Party. This was, of course, not just a part-time occupation like joining another political party but a commitment to unconditional devotion, more like joining a religious order. She remained a dedicated member until just after the war when she went to work for the United Nations Relief and Reconstruction Agency which cared for refugees in various parts of Europe. There she saw with her own eyes how appallingly the invading Russians had treated local political activists, including their own supporters, whom they regarded simply as alien competitors to be eliminated.

This dose of reality was enough to disenchant Iris. She left the movement at once. In this, she contrasts favourably with a lot of Communist intellectuals such as Brecht and J. B. S. Haldane, many of whom went on supporting Stalinism until the Russian invasion of Hungary in 1956 or even longer. They postponed the shock of disillusion by believing that the stories of Russian atrocities were exaggerated, and they found it possible to do this because there had been indeed been lies on both sides. By contrast, those, like Iris, who honestly faced that shock underwent a sharp bereavement. It is not surprising that some of them reacted by joining the Roman Church.

Why was this fascination so strong? It is not possible now to convey the powerful part that Communism played at that time in all our intellectual lives. The point was that, among the manifold horrors of the age, Communism did make it seem possible that there was one force that was working steadily – however poorly and imperfectly – for good. This is an immensely powerful kind of hope, a hope whose power becomes stronger the more the surrounding horrors darken.

As the 1930s went on, many people already experienced the bitterness of disillusionment and were reacting violently against their former heroes. The point at which I, along with my parents and many other people, finally became disenchanted about this was the series of treason trials that were held in Russia in the mid-1930s. Here there were simply too many similar stories coming out to be disregarded, and their details seemed to ring true. It gradually emerged that we were indeed seeing what Arthur Koestler later described so well in Darkness at Noon – a set of paranoid rulers engaged in sacrificing their most loyal supporters in a senseless attempt to protect themselves from non-existent plots. Unmistakably, what ought to have been the seedbed of Utopia was now displaying the classic behaviour so often reported in decadent empires.

From that time, I could never support the Communist Party, and I found it increasingly hard to see how other people, such as Iris, could do so – especially, of course, after the German–Soviet pact was signed in August 1939. Yet the magnetism of Communism was still powerful with most of us, simply because of the impressiveness of the people who did accept it. It still stood for idealism. The guilty feeling that, in spite of the difficulties, we all ought somehow to be Communists played the same sort of role in our lives that thoughts of being a missionary, or joining a religious order, had played in those of earlier generations. This feeling had been intensified – at least for men – by the thought that they ought somehow to fight in the Spanish Civil War.

This sort of guilt is not very clear-sighted, and it is often mixed with motives which distort any action that is taken on it. But it is a start towards taking some sort of action, perhaps a necessary step in doing so. Our idealism needed some channel, some direction to flow in and, for many of us, neither convents nor the mission field could now provide that channel. But those Communists whom we met and heard of in the West did often seem to be moved by a genuine flame of idealism, even if the ones in Moscow had now betrayed it.

This was the moral strength of Marxism, and its loss when the doctrine was discredited has been a real disaster. People do need some direction for their hopes, some ideal that seems to be working, some vision of possible upward movement, and in a fast-changing world, it is not easy to base these visions on realistic expectation.

Fantasies about the future therefore grow like mushrooms in our undisciplined imaginations. At present, for many people, these tend to take two forms. There are hopes concerned with technical miracles such as artificial intelligence, space travel, and genetic engineering. There are also economic hopes based on a faith in market forces. (These last have of course been conceived in a direct reaction against Marxism, and they share many of its obvious drawbacks.)

Both these kinds of proposal deal in means, not in ends. They make no suggestion about what we should be trying to do, only about how cleverly we are going to do it. They aim to increase our power, not to make us use it differently. However, destruction being easier than construction, an increase in power can always do more harm than good unless real efforts are made to prevent it doing so. One obvious example of this distorting effect is the invention of explosives, from gunpowder on to nuclear bombs. Another is the series of advances that people have laboriously made – from goats to chain-saws – in converting forests to pasture, thus finally producing deserts. The Sahara and much of the Central Asian Desert seem to have been made by humans long ago in this way, and as knowledge of the earth's history widens, people are finding many similar examples. We need somehow to get it into our heads that most of our troubles do not come from lack of power but from our own abuse of it.

Have we, then, moved to a more rational and realistic view of how the world works now Marxism is gone? It has certainly been a clear gain to get rid of the idea of confidence in a violent revolution. The twentieth century's savage wars have probably been responsible for this de-romanticizing of violence. Today's currently popular ideologies therefore centre on evolution rather than revolution.

This ought to be an improvement. But, unluckily, it is still none too clear that the change has made us any more realistic. With surprising speed, a whole forest of myths has grown up about techno-based futures, viewed as coming instalments of evolution. In these the migration of our species to outer space, or its improvement by genetic engineering, or its conversion into cyborgs, or the mere accumulation of information, take the place of the Marxist revolution to produce a final Utopia. This Lamarckian vision is often loosely grafted onto Darwin's theory of evolution – with which it is quite incompatible – by devices such as Teilhard de Chardin's conception of progress towards Omega Man.

Stories like these are no better than the Marxist myth; in fact, in most ways, they are worse. They are even less realistic and – what is more serious – they completely lack any moral core. There is no aspiration in them comparable to the deep sense of indignation at political inequality and oppression that lay at the root of Marxism. Essentially they are just power fantasies.

By contrast, any serious idealism today has to centre on saving the environment – on attempting somehow to halt and reverse our ferocious destruction of the natural world. This does not mean that social justice no longer matters. Suffering passengers on the sinking ship still need to be cared for. But all schemes, such as Marxism and monetarism, which try to provide for human welfare without attending to the damage we are doing to the system we live by, are hopelessly unrealistic.

THE PHILOSOPHICAL SCENE

In the autumn of 1940, Iris and I were moved from our boring and cautious essay tutor to be taught philosophy for the rest of our time by that remarkable character Donald MacKinnon. This was an enormous stroke of luck, without which I might well have drifted away from academic philosophy altogether. MacKinnon is a kind of Oxford legend because of his eccentricity, but he was an amazingly good teacher. This was entirely a matter of his direct response in tutorials, not of his lectures or his writing. It was when he shared a question with a student that he drew on his enormous powers of intellectual digging.

The eccentricity was certainly a nuisance at first. It was of a kind that (like so many other things) has now acquired a medical name. It centred, I suppose, on what is now called Tourette's Syndrome. Like Dr Johnson, MacKinnon often made strange unpredictable movements and, in particular, strange grimaces, which often seemed to express profound anguish. A lot of the stories about him are true enough. He did wave pokers and other things about in an alarming way and apparently did try to lever the fireplace off the wall with them. He did lie on the floor or beat the wall violently. In these spasms, he often seemed to be in distress and to be asking for help, which one could not give. He was prone to long silences, sometimes not seeming to hear at all what was said to him. All this was peculiarly alarming to new pupils, even when they had been warned about it, and at first I was quite terrified. But in time one learnt the language. It became clear that no actual disasters were going to follow.

The upside of all this was that he had wide and deep philosophical interests. He attended to all the big questions and took his pupils sympathetically through very varied approaches to them, showing the point of diverse surprising positions and suggesting how they might be related. In particular, he grasped the full breadth and importance of Kant's enterprise and made the time to get us used to its various aspects. I remember one tutorial when he had given me two hours – not one – in discussing a particular Kantian topic, and he ended by saying, 'I don't think we've really got to the bottom of this.

Come back on Thursday,' which I did. It was only when I taught philosophy myself and realized how desperately short of time one is that I understood his generosity. It was the more remarkable because he had at that time a heavy teaching load because so many dons were absent at the war. He himself was unfit for military service because of asthma, though he was quite young. To show the exceptional luck that we had in having such a tutor, a word is needed about the background of Oxford philosophy at that time.

Apart from the standard teaching of classic texts such as Plato's Republic, this consisted of various slightly moth-eaten traditions, all of which equally had come under attack from the Cambridge analytical philosophers, Moore and Russell, and more recently from logical positivism. The fighting text here was A. J. Ayer's book *Language, Truth and Logic*, published in 1936. Its first chapter, titled 'The Elimination of Metaphysics,' begins with a trumpet blast:

> The traditional disputes of philosophers are, for the most part, as unwarranted as they are unfruitful . . . If there are any questions which science leaves it to philosophy to answer, a straightforward process of elimination must lead to their discovery.

> (Emphasis mine)

So Ayer listed these possible kinds of question and decreed that they were all meaningless – indeed actual nonsense. He thus proved philosophy to be unnecessary, not just by citing its failures but a priori from the very nature of language, by ruling that no sentences had any meaning except those that were verifiable, which – rather surprisingly – were all held to be only the propositions of science. The Verification Principle dictated that the meaning of a sentence consists only in its verification, and this verification was only possible through sense perception, always – again rather surprisingly – within the context of science. Any meaning that might seem to belong to other kinds of talk, especially to metaphysics or ethics, was merely an emotive effect.

It never became clear how the vast range of intelligible human speech could ever have been squeezed into the bounds of science in this way. (Ayer was not much interested in science itself and did not discuss its difficulties.) Nor indeed was it explained how books such as *Language, Truth and Logic* could themselves be considered to mean anything. Did they perhaps count as parts of science? Or were they simply emotive noises? In an ordinary sense, such books are obviously metaphysical – that is, they deal with very general questions about how the world is and how to choose among the ways in which we can and should think about it. But it never emerges how they can find a place for their own enquiries.

This same difficulty comes up, of course, about the famous earlier fanfare on which Ayer's was obviously modelled – the manifesto that concludes David Hume's An Enquiry Concerning Human Understanding:

> When we run over libraries, persuaded of these principles, what havoc must we make? If we take in our hand any volume; of divinity or school metaphysics, for instance: let us ask, Does it contain any abstract reasoning concerning quantity and number? No. Does it contain any experimental reasoning concerning matters of fact and existence? No. Commit it then to the flames; for it can contain nothing but sophistry and illusion.
>
> (Emphasis Hume's)

So what happens if, instead, we decide to take in our hand *An Enquiry Concerning Human Understanding*, or one of Hume's other philosophical works . . .? Surprisingly few of Hume's readers ever ask him this question and he certainly never answered it. Empiricists are not often seen committing their own writings to the flames, nor explaining that they are actually part of science.

Destructive doctrines like these that look completely sweeping are almost always meant as contributions to an existing feud. Their real aim is narrow and familiar. Each is a stick designed to beat a particular dog with, and people know already what that dog is. Hume, suffering greatly from the Calvinistic Scottish church, marked his real target – which was already clear to his Enlightenment readers – by his talk of 'divinity or school metaphysics.' Logical positivism too had its own clear political aim. The philosophers of the Vienna Circle used it as a handy piece of artillery against religious doctrines which they identified with the clerical-fascist regime that ruled Austria in the 1920s and 1930s. They were calling for opposition to such doctrines as a part of the socialist struggle against fascism.

Ayer's use of it, however, was looser and wider. He did often take pot shots at religious doctrines, which are always soft targets for such treatment ('That a transcendent god exists is a metaphysical asser-tion, and therefore not literally significant' – Language, Truth and Logic, p. 29). But his brand of weedkiller was packaged so as to be spread much more widely. His formula could be used at will against almost any form of thought that went beyond the direct reporting of sense-data. (This would, of course, also have included a great deal of science, but that was not usually noticed.)

In this way, a whole generation of undergraduates was excited to find that all they needed to do if they wanted to refute some incon-venient doctrine was to say loudly and firmly, 'I simply don't under-stand that' or 'But what could that possibly mean?' and the opposition would have to wither away. Not understanding things became the unanswerable one-up default position for arguers and remained so for several decades.

Indeed, that notion is still influential today. *Language, Truth and Logic* was one of the most widely read of twentieth-century philosophi-cal books published in English, reaching a large public that normally never hears about these topics. And its central destructive doctrines were reinforced in 1946 by the last section of another widely read and apparently solider book, Bertrand Russell's *History of Western Philos-ophy*. In his conclusion, Russell resoundingly endorsed the positivistic approach of recent analytic philosophy, crediting it, rather remarkably, with having invented the virtue of philosophical impartiality:

> In the welter of conflicting fanaticisms, one of the few unifying forces is scientific truthfulness, by which I mean the habit of basing our beliefs upon observations and inferences as impersonal, and as much

divested of local and temperamental bias, as is possible for human beings. To have insisted upon the introduction of this virtue into philosophy, and to have invented a powerful method by which it can be rendered fruitful, are the chief merits of the philosophical school of which I am a member. The habit of careful veracity acquired in the practice of this philosophical method can be extended to the whole sphere of human activity.

(p. 78. Emphasis mine)

So, did earlier philosophers not actually know that they ought to try to be impartial and to tell the truth? And do analytic ones always succeed in doing so?

GENDER QUERIES: THE WARTIME QUARTET

As we went to lectures and classes and philosophical meetings, something rather interesting began to emerge about gender. When we were reading Greats, not many students were taking the course at all, and there were as many women as men among them. Male undergraduates then mostly came to Oxford only for a year's course, leaving the rest to be finished after the war. Since Greats was a course for the later years, the only men taking it with us were conscientious objectors, disabled people, and a few ordinands – Benedictines and Dominicans, I think. The effect was to make it a great deal easier for a woman to be heard in discussion than it is in normal times. (I have seen enough of a number of universities, both here and in the States, in later life to have checked up fully on this comparison.) Sheer loudness of voice has a lot to do with the difficulty, but there is also a temperamental difference about confidence – about the amount of work that one thinks is needed to make one's opinion worth hearing.

I think myself that this experience has something to do with the fact that Elizabeth and I and Iris and Philippa Foot and Mary Warnock have all made our names in philosophy. Not everybody will think this was a good thing, and I am certainly not suggesting that it is worthwhile waging wars so as to make such results possible. But I do think that in normal times, a lot of good female thinking is wasted because it simply doesn't get heard. Perhaps women ought to shout louder, but of course, there is still the question whether men are going to listen.

Later on, all five of us used our voices – which for better or worse we had found in this way – to resist in different ways the bizarre irrationalist climate that had been encouraged by logical positivism. In varying ways, we all attacked what may be crudely called the boo-hurray view of ethics – more politely, the idea that facts are split off from values by a logical gap that makes it impossible to think rationally at all about moral topics. Though Richard Hare had by then modified this extreme position, treating moral judgements as recommendations rather than just emotive noises and allowing that they might form a structure, the reasons that people give for these judgements were still seen as outside criticism. 'Values' were treated as a kind of arbitrary opinions, and it was widely held – not only by analytic philosophers – that, since all people are entitled to their own opinions, argument about them made no sense.

I cannot here go into the objections that we brought against this notion. The idea of summarizing them exhausts me as much as it would probably exhaust my readers. But the point is still important because subjectivism of this kind has certainly not gone away, though some extreme ways of expressing it are no longer fashionable.

All the same, at that time, this subjectivist scepticism strongly attracted people because they thought it was necessary for freedom. Judging other individuals was seen as interfering with their liberty. As one of my students later exclaimed indignantly, 'But surely it's always wrong to make moral judgements!' It didn't occur to her that this remark is itself a moral judgement. Freedom is just one value among the many between which we have to choose, and even given the importance of freedom we often need to choose – that is, to judge – between different freedoms. Being 'judgemental' or 'moralistic' in the sense of interfering is indeed a bad thing. But we do not have any way to avoid judging, except through the grave. And if we are going to make value judgements, it seems plausible to think that we might as well do it sensibly and co-operatively rather than just by making emotive noises.

Some of the best responses to this kind of philosophical subjectivism were contained in a series of short but lethal articles which Philippa Foot published in various journals during the 1950s, deploying most useful ideas which she has lately developed further in an admirable little book called Natural Goodness (Oxford University Press, 2001). At Somerville, Philippa was a year junior to me. I took to her at once when she arrived and I saw a certain amount of her then, but we became close friends only later, when she was married and we were both living in Park Town. When she was an undergraduate Philippa seemed to me a little formidable – her standards, I felt, would be very high, could I hope to meet them? She tells me now that she had exactly the same impression about me. We were both being shy and frightened of each other. This just shows how easy it is to waste the opportunities that crop up in one's life.

WHAT IRIS SAID

So in the summer of 1942, we prepared for our final exams and also tried to make arrangements for what we would do after them. During that term, those of us who had opted for the civil service received notices of the jobs to which we had been assigned. (Were we interviewed for them? Or did the authorities just take us on our tutors' recommendations? I really don't remember.) So the letters arrived. Nancy and Christine are going to the Board of Trade. Charlotte will go to Cambridge to do research on how to artificially inseminate pigs. Myself, I am going to the Ministry of Production. (Ministry of what? Yes, there was one; we will have a look at it shortly.) But what about Iris? She is still waiting. Does the civil service not want her? 'Of course they won't have me,' she said. 'I never thought that they would, with a political record like mine.' Next day the letter arrives; they are delighted to employ her. They have a place for her at the Treasury, where she will stay for most of the war. We can forget about the future for the moment and get on with taking our exams.

This we did, with anguish mostly similar to that of Mods but less pain from the climate, since we took them in June. I had my agonizing three-hour viva and the job was done. At this point, all that we wanted was to sleep. But our tutor Isobel Henderson, bless her, wanted to celebrate our Firsts properly. As a special treat, she arranged a dinner party for us with two highly distinguished contemporary sages – the historian A.L. Rowse and the Cambridge musicologist J.B. Trend. We duly dressed up and through a long evening we listened attentively to their distinguished contemporary opinions.

Bright moonlight flooded down St Giles's as the two of us eventually stumbled home to Somerville. 'So finally,' I asked, 'what about it? Did we learn something new this evening?' 'Oh yes, I think so,' declared Iris gazing up at the enormous moon. 'I do think so . . . Trend is a good man and Rowse is a bad man.' At which exact, but grotesquely unfashionable, judgement we both fell about laughing so helplessly that the rare passers-by looked round in alarm and all the cats ran away.

Iris, however, never minded being unfashionable. It may be worthwhile to point out here that this is what makes *The Sovereignty of Good* such a good book – what makes it, still, one of the very few modern books of philosophy that people outside universities find helpful. It shares that distinction with C. S. Lewis's little book *The Abolition of Man*, which shoots with equally deadly aim at the same target. Both titles are misleading; they are both actually books about the nature of freedom. Both books effectively debunk the colourful, fantastic screen of up-to-date ideas inside which we live – a screen which, despite a lot of surface activity, has not actually changed much since those books were written. As Iris puts it, 'a smart set of concepts may be a most efficient instrument of corruption' (Sovereignty of Good, p. 33). As she explains, 'We are anxiety-ridden animals. Our minds are continually active, fabricating an anxious, self-preoccupied, often falsifying veil which partly conceals the world' (p. 84). What chiefly pierces that veil is a sharp, direct perception of things that are no part of our own being. For instance;

I am looking out of my window in an anxious and resentful state of mind, oblivious of my surroundings, brooding perhaps on some damage done

> to my prestige. Then suddenly I observe a hovering kestrel. In a moment everything is altered. There is nothing now but kestrel. And when I return to thinking of the other matter it seems less important.
>
> (p. 84)

The veil, however, is persistent and terribly hard to detect. In every age, it subtly provides new, unnoticed ways of evading reality. Detecting those new forms is a prime function of philosophy, but philosophers often find it no easier than other people. ('It is always a significant question to ask about any philosopher; what is he afraid of?', p. 72.)

During the twentieth century, intellectual fashions provided escape by claiming to isolate individuals progressively, first from God, then from their own societies ('there is no such thing as society'), and finally from the rest of nature, thus crediting them with an extraordinary, supernatural kind of independence. At each stage, the reformers were resisting genuinely oppressive claims. But at each stage, the real, practical reasons for this resistance were gradually forgotten as one theorist after another (Nietzsche, Freud, Skinner, Heidegger, Sartre, Hayek, Dawkins) dived in to contribute to the exaggerated rhetoric which, when these elements were combined, added up to an extreme and reductive individualism.

That extremism made it increasingly hard to think out any intelligent reconciliation which would bring together only the best parts of the various campaigns. So (as Iris points out) what we got instead was a strange half-thought-out jumble composed of the most dramatic parts of each doctrine because these were both the most exciting and the easiest to remember:

> The very powerful image with which we are here presented . . . is behaviourist in its connection of the meaning and being of action with the publicly observable, it is existentialist in its elimination of the substantial self and its emphasis on the solitary omnipotent will, and it is utilitarian in its assumption that morality is and can only be concerned with public acts.
>
> (p. 9)

In short, it is carefully designed to distract attention from what analytic philosophers least want to think about, which is the inner life. As she said, it is indeed always a significant question to ask about a philosopher, 'what is he afraid of?', and the chronic fear that these doctrines all show is a fear of the world within. The names of these theories may not now be familiar to all of us but, as she says, we are all familiar with the ideal figure who personifies them because he dominates the stories that we read and watch:

> He is the hero of every modern novel . . . This man is with us still, free, independent, lonely, powerful, brave, the hero of so many novels and books of moral philosophy. The raison d'être of this attractive but misleading creature is not far to seek. He is the offspring of the age of science, confidently rational and yet increasingly aware of his alienation from the material universe which his discoveries reveal.
>
> (p. 80)

Since Iris wrote, environmental dangers have made us much more uneasy about this last form of alienation. Yet the power fantasy she describes is as potent as ever. What upholds it is still 'the domination of science or rather . . . the domination of inexact ideas of science which haunt philosophers and other thinkers' (p. 27). For it is not science itself that makes this wild, fluttering escape seem necessary. The demand comes from ideologies (such as that of behaviourism) which have usurped the name of science and have grotesquely exaggerated its power.

Put very crudely, what frightens us is our superstitious belief that there exists a single, vast, infallible system called science which completely explains human existence and proves that the familiar kinds of freedom that we experience every day are illusory. To escape this threat, theorists have invented a special kind of metaphysical freedom, sending us up, like autonomous hot-air balloons, to a stratosphere beyond the reach of nature and science. Is that where we want to live? Iris comments:

> I find the image of man which I have sketched above both alien and implausible. That is; more precisely; I have simple empirical objections

(I do not think people are essentially or necessarily 'like that'), I have philosophical objections (I do not find the arguments convincing), and I have moral objections (I do not think people ought to picture themselves in this way). It is a delicate and tricky matter to keep these kinds of objections separate in one's mind.

(p. 9)

This difficulty faces anyone who tries to penetrate a contemporary myth. Intellectual and emotional aspects of the current veil are so intricately meshed that it is hard to make any special point without seeming to say something morally objectionable. Throughout the past century, the concept of freedom has been treated with an unconditional reverence which has made it seem illicit even to ask, on any particular occasion, which freedom? Freedom from what? Freedom from scruple? Freedom from friendship and the bonds of affection? Freedom from principle? Freedom from all tradition? Freedom from feeling? These are the easy privileges of psychopaths, depressives, and oafs. They are not what the prophets who exalt freedom are really aiming at. What then (Iris asks) are they proposing?

Existentialism, in both its Continental and its Anglo-Saxon versions, is an attempt to solve the problem without really facing it by attributing to the individual an empty, lonely freedom, if he wishes, to 'fly in the face of the facts'. What it pictures is indeed the fearful solitude of the individual marooned upon a tiny island in the midst of a sea of scientific facts, and morality escaping from science only by a wild leap of the will. But our situation is not like this.

(p. 27)

Under the term 'existentialism,' she includes, of course, a wide tradition stretching from Dostoevsky, Kierkegaard, and Nietzsche to Heidegger and Sartre, a tradition that is less mentioned today than it used to be simply because its cruder elements are by now accepted and taken for granted. They are also echoed in a different accent by American libertarians.

She concedes that, in facing hard dilemmas, we may indeed feel our situation to be hopelessly unintelligible and irrational. But this (she suggests) is because we concentrate arbitrarily on the moment of apparent decision, ignoring the mass of imaginative work that was done earlier, work which depends above all on deliberate and selective attention. She instances a woman who has been half-consciously despising her daughter-in-law D and who, wondering whether she is being unfair, 'reflects deliberately about D until gradually her vision of D alters' (p. 17). This woman now sees facts that she did not see before, not by deceiving herself but by using 'just and loving attention.' The imagination (that is) can itself be used to pierce and unweave the veil with which it has helped to blind us. It is not just a deluding factor or a luxury item to amuse humanists. It is itself a vital organ, a workshop where we forge our view of the world and thereby our actions.

That kind of reflective, imaginative attention – not arbitrary, sudden decision – is, of course, what chiefly marks out people who are acting relatively freely and responsibly from those who are not. Certainly we have only limited control over our attention. But not even the most bigoted and fatalistic of determinists ever actually doubts that we are able to make a vast difference by exercising the measure of control that we do have over it, and that the power to do this is a part of our natural heritage. The business of the various sciences is (as serious scientists know) to help in the understanding of such natural processes, not to deny that they take place. That kind of denial is ideology, not science.

For much of the past century, modern libertarians of various stripes have been fighting a ghost war here, not against science itself but against false scientistic prophets. A glance at The Sovereignty of Good might perhaps release them for better and more cheerful occupations.

37

ESCAPING FROM OXFORD
Plotinus, Wittgenstein, and the Consolations of Philosophy

NOT DOING THE B.PHIL.

When my mother was better in the summer of 1947, I went back in Oxford to consult with Isobel Henderson and others about finding the best way to do some work in philosophy.

There were two options, much the more obvious being to take the regular course for the B.Phil. This was a graduate degree that had lately been invented, mainly at the instance of Gilbert Ryle, as a general training for young philosophers. Ryle had, I think, understood early in the war that there would be a great expansion of universities when it ended, and he wanted to make sure that plenty of well-educated philosophical graduates were there to work in them.

DOI: 10.4324/9781003588160-47

This course gave a training that was in many ways a good and thorough one. It was examined partly by set papers and partly by dissertation, and it is much respected as a philosophical qualification. The trouble about it is simply that it necessarily reflects the philosophical slant of those running it, and in my time that slant was somewhat narrowly linguistic.

Here we again come back to Iris's question. It is indeed important to ask what any particular philosopher is afraid of. It stuck out a mile that what really frightened analytic philosophers of that time was the danger of being thought weak – vague, credulous, sentimental, superstitious or simply too wide in their sympathies. Unlike their forebears in William James's time, they were much more afraid of looking weak than they were of missing something unexpected and important. They were not at all afraid (on the other hand) of being thought too narrow. So they were happy to exclude all topics that could expose them to that central danger.

It was central to this slant that – except for Peter Strawson, who was devoted to large-scale metaphysics – analytic philosophers at that time tended to treat the metaphysical enquiries of the mighty dead with suspicion, disapproval or sometimes outright ridicule. Indeed, they often followed the logical positivist lead by using the term 'metaphysic' itself to mean something outside the range of rational thought, sometimes even actual nonsense – a most confusing usage which was unfortunately encouraged by Karl Popper.

All this bothered me because this large-scale metaphysics was just what I wanted to look at. I therefore got interested in exploring the other avenue to graduate work, which was to attempt a D.Phil. thesis – a longer affair, which could take up to seven years, concentrated on a particular topic. My first thought was that this topic might be the symbolism of the Cave and the Sun in the seventh book of the Republic. In particular, what did Plato mean when he said that the intelligible world was more real than the physical one? Can there, as the Idealists thought, be degrees of reality? What (for instance) did Bradley mean by saying that 'the more anything is spiritual, so much the more is it veritably real . . . ?' This passage in the Republic turned out, however, to have been investigated in far too much detail by too many people, and in reference to too many other controversies, to leave any room for an ill-qualified newcomer.

At this point, somebody suggested investigating the neo-Platonists, who had developed this symbolism and expounded Plato's meaning in important ways. I was advised to look at some of them, and at once I liked the look of Plotinus. I could see that he was a shrewd and serious philosopher, and that he was indeed dealing with the problems that interested me.

Plotinus accepted and developed Plato's thought that there is a far vaster and more serious reality lying behind the everyday scene around us. But he also accepted Aristotle's insight that everyday realities must be taken seriously as well. Like Spinoza, he wanted somehow to relate the world of the senses intelligibly to the world of thought, rather than just dismissing it, as Plato did, as ultimately incomprehensible. He wanted to find a wider, more inclusive perspective which could bring together both these aspects of life, showing a continuity between the physical and the spiritual.

He therefore fiercely opposed the Manichees and Gnostics who thought that the physical world was simply evil. Instead he vigorously celebrated its goodness. This world (he said) is excellent at its own level. But that level is only one part of our life, and our understanding needs to move far beyond it. This is not a move to alien territory but a move in which we exercise a deeper part of our own nature, since we are ourselves spiritual as well as physical. When we move inwards, we are coming home. We are richly composite beings whose souls already extend through all the levels of reality, and the first step to better understanding of the world around us is to explore this large world within, moving steadily towards its most 'real,' most important central areas. As one Plotinus scholar puts it, by this neo-Platonic way of thinking 'philosophy came to seek the cosmos predominantly within the soul.' That soul was correspondingly seen as hugely more complex, more interesting and more philosophically important than it had appeared before. This idea was not wholly new.

Heraclitus had already suggested that our souls – the selves within us – are vaster and far less well known to us than we tend to suppose. So deep (said Heraclitus) is the soul that you could never find its boundaries, however far you might travel . . . But Plotinus took up and developed this suggestion on a quite new scale, making it clear that this self – which reaches far beyond consciousness – is not just one more kind of object alongside those that we meet in the physical world, but really is a subject – an experiencer – a kind of item that needs a quite different metaphysical treatment. That was why, although Plotinus accepted Plato's view that mathematics and other intellectual disciplines are a necessary part of spiritual development, he was insistent that they are not the whole of it. Because we are such complex beings – because we are not just dedicated calculating machines – we need to pass far beyond such abstract formulations so as to contemplate the world directly, responding to it with the whole of our being.

Much attracted by this seductive candle I fluttered round it for a bit taking advice. Some of this came from E. R. Dodds, the professor whose lectures I had earlier attended and liked. Dodds, a most impressive man, was keen to get attention given to other parts of Greek thought besides its well-trodden highways. He had written a good book called The Greeks and the Irrational, aimed at shifting the stereotype which showed Greece as full of sober, orderly characters with a public-school education. He encouraged me to go for Plotinus and agreed to be my supervisor if I did. With his help, I outlined a research topic which was to deal with Plotinus' psychology – his doctrine of the self – and this was duly accepted by the authorities. So in the autumn of 1947, I began to work on it for the D.Phil. degree.

I should say at once that I never finished that thesis. The whole scheme was indeed impossibly ambitious. It quickly turned out that Plotinus, besides his debt to Plato, was involved in controversy with a whole raft of other philosophers from Aristotle down to his own time, which was the third century AD. Some of these philosophers I had never heard of at all; all of them needed a great deal of attention. My knowledge of Greek, though now much improved, was too faltering to deal with the variety of styles and ages that I now encountered, nor did I have enough experience of how to manage libraries.

And Dodds himself, though benevolent, was not a good supervisor because he was shy and remote. In fact, he was an example of the kind of academic who is a first-rate lecturer – perfectly at ease on a platform – but not approachable socially. He was not someone you could easily consult each time that you got lost, as I constantly did, in some tangle about secondary authorities. My own social incompetence, too, which had prevented me from coping properly with Betty Ackroyd at the Ministry of Production, stood in the way of my telling him properly about my difficulties.

So I never finished working on Plotinus. But I haven't the least doubt that I was right to start doing so. I am most grateful to my advisers – particularly to Isobel Henderson – for not pressuring me to take the B.Phil. course, which would have been so obviously the prime career option. What I actually did, besides reading Plotinus himself, which was hugely valuable, was to take part in other courses that were going on. Some of these were on other parts of Greek philosophy – on Plato's later work and on Aristotle's Metaphysics and De Anima – all of which were exactly the kind of thing that I wanted. But so were the other courses that I went to, such as H. H. Price's, on contemporary philosophy, which was mainly attended by people taking the B.Phil.

WITTGENSTEIN

Thus, I got the benefit of a wide range of discussion on a lot of topics. In particular, I now began to pick up some idea of Wittgenstein's later philosophy – of the thoughts that he later published in 1953 in his Philosophical Investigations. Several people who had studied with him at Cambridge, including Peter Geach and Yorick Smithies, were at these classes. But I think it was Elizabeth Anscombe who really made this new approach visible to me. Repeatedly and carefully, she spelt out how our thought about language has to be rooted in the complexities of real life, not imposed on it from outside as a calculus derived from axioms.

Sometime during the late 1940s, Wittgenstein himself came to Oxford to speak to the Jowett Society (the philosophical discussion club). This occasion roused fierce excitement, though we had been warned in advance that it might turn out frustrating. The room, which was not very big, was packed with eager listeners. Wittgenstein, thin, spry and neat in his green pullover, made an impression of volcanic energy, tightly controlled. According to his custom, he had refused to prepare a paper himself but had agreed to reply to a short one from somebody else. A heroic character called Oscar Wood accordingly read a brief piece on Descartes's Cogito.

Wittgenstein then began to reply. For about five minutes what he said seemed incredibly important and illuminating. But then he started to see difficulties. He hesitated and interrupted himself – 'No no, that isn't it – What should one say? You see, the real difficulty here – Oh no no, it is terrible . . .' dropping his head in his hands and then beating it, and so on. We knew that this was how he habitually went on in his regular classes, but it was distracting for hearers who weren't used to it. I quickly lost the thread and forgot the invaluable thoughts that I had picked up at the beginning. (With hindsight, it might have been best to have left at that point, but we didn't know that.)

Things went on confusingly enough all the evening. I'm sure that some points did become clear, but the only bit I now remember is a row that suddenly developed after an interruption by Professor H. A. Prichard. He was the intuitionist moral philosopher who had dominated the Oxford ethical scene for a long time before the logical positivist dawn. Not surprisingly upset by something that Wittgenstein said about ethics, he loudly denounced it. There followed a strange brief scene in which two people, neither of whom was at all used to being contradicted, sharply contradicted each other. Then Prichard left, and Wittgenstein continued his mining operation on the Cogito. At the end of the evening, he said unhappily, 'Oh dear, we have not finished this,' so somebody suggested that the discussion should go on the next afternoon. He agreed, and we all came back for it, but I never found that it got much clearer.

The extraordinary thing about Wittgenstein is that he succeeded in making crucial things clear in philosophy in spite of his fearful communication difficulties. These difficulties seem to have been more or less of the kind that is now discussed under the heading of Asperger's Syndrome, and though such classifications can be slick and misleading I think the central point does seem right. There was surely a kind of emotional remoteness that shut him off in many ways from those around him. But perhaps it was the terror induced by that very sense of remoteness that made him able to stress our social nature so powerfully. Having been very close to real solipsism, he rebounded from it with tremendous violence. Thus, he was able to break away from the conviction of individual isolation produced by the Cogito and to replant us in our proper soil as social beings.

CAREER EXPERIENCES

As for my own life, in these years I also gave tutorials to several undergraduates from Somerville and, I think, some from St Hugh's as well. This was great and I got a lot from them. As it happens, two of the Somerville ones have later become rather celebrated – Anne Warburton, who was later Principal of Lucy Cavendish College at Cambridge, and Carmen Blacker, who became a distinguished Japanese scholar and, I think, reader in Japanese at Cambridge. It was Carmen who supplied me with the best example I have ever met of the diversity of moral views. When I raised the topic of conflicting customs, 'Oh, I see,' she said. 'Like, there's a verb in classical Japanese which means to try out one's new sword on a chance wayfarer?' I used this one later, with Carmen's permission, in an article with that name which now forms part of my book Heart and Mind.

All this time, however, the question of jobs and careers naturally loomed over us. In the 1940s, that topic was less frightening than it often is because universities in Britain were expanding at unusual speed. During the two decades after the war, quite a lot of new universities were founded and the older ones were enlarged to take on more students. A serious effort was being made to admit far more people to higher education.

Moreover, the newer universities sometimes put together unconventional mixtures of courses, which might employ people trained in philosophy in unfamiliar ways. (Most of these bright schemes caved in later because of practical difficulties, but they were still around in the 1940s.)

On the other hand, there were also more graduates to fill these places than there normally would have been, because of the backlog of people returning from the war. As each new job came up, the negotiations about it were anxiously watched. One intriguing thing was to see how the salaries offered reflected the distance that an aspirant lecturer would have to move away from the hub of philosophical civilization in Oxford. When I got a job in Reading – only half an hour's journey away – I was paid £400 a year. Geoff Midgley in Newcastle – five hours away – got £550. (I still have the letter offering him the place at that commencing salary.) And when Tony Flew went to Aberdeen, he got £800. I don't know what those who actually got posts in Oxford were paid, but it looks as if it must have been rather modest.

There were, of course, no mixed colleges then in Oxford. But jobs in the women's colleges there did sometimes come up and when they did I naturally put in for them. By good fortune, however, I didn't get them. In 1948, St Anne's very sensibly chose Iris as tutor rather than me and St Hugh's with equal good sense chose Mary Warnock. Sheer luck had again saved me from a mistake that I did not have the sense to avoid. I did not see that I could not possibly have settled to work properly in the steadily narrowing circle of Oxford philosophy and the feuding that went with it. Had I remained there, I would certainly have got out of philosophy altogether.

I remember particularly a meeting of the Jowett – the philosophical discussion club – at which a disciple of J. L. Austin's read a paper on a very small point of linguistic usage. Small though it was, however, that point hardly came up at all in the subsequent discussion. As soon as the speaker had finished, his critics piled in to attack him – not on this supposedly main issue but on a crowd of even smaller linguistic points arising in the course of his argument, places where they thought his wording was mistaken. The game went on for the whole evening and obviously could have gone on forever. I went away deeply depressed.

I thought of this escape again just now, thanking Providence once more, as I read Colin McGinn's account of what he calls 'the cut and thrust of philosophical debate' encouraged by the teacher of a class that he attended when he arrived in Oxford to do the B.Phil. in 1972:

> Evans was a fierce debater, impatient and uncompromising; as I remarked, he skewered fools gladly (perhaps too gladly). The atmosphere in his class was intimidating and thrilling at the same time. As I was to learn later, this is fairly characteristic of philosophical debate. It is not the sonorous recitation of vague profundities, but a clashing of analytically honed intellects, with pulsing egos attached to them Philosophical discussion can be a kind of intellectual blood-sport, in which egos get bruised and buckled, even impaled. I have seen people white and dry-mouthed before giving a talk to a tough-minded audience, and visibly shaken afterwards. In Evans I saw someone with considerable debating skills, and I was no doubt attracted to the kind of power and respect that goes with that. Plain showing-off is also a feature of philosophical life.
>
> (p. 63. Emphases mine)

Showing-off is indeed a feature of many kinds of life and of course it is often a harmless one, but that is no reason why it should be allowed to take them over. Any situation where a lot of young men are competing to form a dominance hierarchy will produce cock-fights. But – as Plato pointed out already – these fights are not part of its essence; they are distractions from it. They interfere with philosophical work. 'Tough-minded' is much too polite a word to use for people who go to a meeting, not in order to understand what someone is saying but in order to catch him or her out by picking holes in it.

As McGinn sees it, the only possible alternative to cock-fighting would be bombast, 'the sonorous recitation of vague profundities.' But surely if any other topic were in question, nobody would suppose that the people discussing it were forced to choose between bombast and a boxing match. Philosophy is no different. It can perfectly well be discussed without aggression. No doubt people discussing it will always show off at times, but they can keep their egos under normal control.

McGinn, a strenuous and athletic character himself, clearly enjoys the competitive exercise. That is fine, but why should whole philosophy departments have to do it? Perhaps it could be set up in separate arenas – Departments of Cognitive Poker, or Institutes of One-Upmanship, so as to cultivate it wholeheartedly on its own. In any case, the practice of bullying one's students – which seems to be what McGinn is describing at the beginning of this passage – is not a sport at all; it's a vice.

CONSOLATIONS OF PHILOSOPHY

It is worthwhile to notice how far this competitive conception of philosophy has taken us from the main traditional view of its place in life. That tradition comes out illuminatingly in Romeo and Juliet, when Friar Laurence is trying to make Romeo accept the fact that he has been banished:

FRIAR LAURENCE.	Thou fond, mad man, hear me but speak a word.
ROMEO.	O, thou wilt talk again of banishment!
FRIAR LAURENCE.	I'll give thee armour to keep off that word Adversity's sweet milk, philosophy To comfort thee, though thou be banished.
ROMEO.	Yet 'banished'? Hang up philosophy Unless philosophy can make a Juliet, Displant a town, reverse a prince's doom, It helps not, it prevails not, talk no more . . .
FRIAR LAURENCE.	O then I see that madmen have no ears.
ROMEO.	How should they, when that wise men have no eyes?
FRIAR LAURENCE.	Let me dispute with thee of thy estate –
ROMEO.	Thou canst not speak of what thou dost not feel!

(Act 2, Sc.3, ll. 54–65)

When Friar Laurence asks for philosophy here it may seem that he simply means connected thought – some recognition of a background, some power of thinking beyond the moment, some element of common sense. Even this, however, is more than Romeo can face. He can't endure thought of any kind. He simply is his present feeling, a feeling which resents the very possibility of thought.

This does often happen to us. Yet it is odd because our thoughts are not really hostile strangers. As Wordsworth put it, our thoughts are actually 'the representatives of our past feelings,' reminders of what we have accepted and felt at other times. The battle is not actually between thought and feeling but between our present feelings and other feelings which have prevailed in life up till now. And the most central area of these conflicts is, of course, within ourselves, not in disputes with outsiders. Most of the time, Romeo and Friar Laurence are both parts of one person. Neither part can be thrown out. They will have to be brought together somehow.

Thus, the idea of Reason and Feeling as distinct forces battling for control of our lives is always a distorted one. Yet it has been a powerful pattern in the European tradition and, in spite of various attacks on it, it still is so today. The name of 'reason' is often given not to thought itself but to a certain set of rather bourgeois motives centring on prudence and social harmony.

These, of course, are the motives that Romeo cannot bear. He sees them as his enemies and rejects them. He sees his situation as a warfare. But seeing it like that makes it look as if there is an incurable division between our central faculties – as if thought simply cannot do business with feeling at all; 'Thou canst not speak of what thou dost not feel.' Yet we all do have to speak of what we do not feel, and to think of it too. The difficulty is how to do this properly, how to bring our warring faculties together.

AN UNUSUAL CONSOLATION

The word philosophy, however, may not be being used here in quite that straightforward way. When Shakespeare made Friar Laurence speak of it, he probably did not mean only common sense and discretion but had something more specific in mind. He was thinking of Boethius' book On the Consolation of Philosophy and his audience will at once have done the same.

That book was immensely popular and well-loved throughout the Middle Ages and the Renaissance. Endless people, including King Alfred, Chaucer, and Queen Elizabeth I, translated it into their own languages. Countless readers used it, not just as a literary text but as a prop and support for life, and found it a good one. Dante set Boethius among the twelve lights in the heaven of the Sun, calling him

> That joy who strips the world's hypocrisies
> Bare to whoever heeds his cogent phrases.

For, along with Cicero's De Amicitia, the words of Boethius had provided him with his greatest consolation after the death of Beatrice.

This, in fact, was a consolation that actually did work. It was an owl that could fly even in that profound darkness. It really was adversity's sweet milk, a fact that may have something to do with the circumstances in which Boethius wrote it. He was a distinguished Roman scholar and civil servant under the Emperor Theodoric in the sixth century AD, but he fell from power and was condemned to death. He wrote his book in prison while he was awaiting execution. Eventually, after being cruelly tortured, he was bludgeoned to death at Pavia, the place of his exile. And, since he knew the regime very well, he must have expected exactly that fate.

Yet in that prison he was able to find and to express thoughts that not only supported him but have supported many other people under such burdens. By thinking, he somehow managed to arrive at a mood that was not just courageous but also deeply friendly and benign. He genuinely comforted other people.

THE WRONG KIND OF DETACHMENT

I think this story is interesting in relation to an incident that Simon Blackburn has described in a recent book. He writes:

I was once defending the practice of philosophy on a radio programme where one of the other guests was a professional survivor of the Nazi concentration camps. He asked me, fairly aggressively, what use philosophy would have been on a death march? The answer, of course, was not much – no more than literature, art, music, mathematics, or science would be useful at such a time. But consider the ethical environment that made such events possible. Hitler said, 'How lucky it is for rulers that men cannot think'.

(Being Good, Oxford University Press, 2001, p. 2)

Of course, Blackburn is absolutely right that we need to use good thinking in order to prevent social disasters, not just in order to endure them. But the one use does not exclude the other. Over the ages, people who have actually used philosophy – rather than just talked about it – have undoubtedly made it work for both purposes. The Oxford English Dictionary is not just being careless when it gives, as the second still-current sense of the word philosophical, 'characterised by practical wisdom or philosophy, befitting or characteristic of a philosopher, wise, calm, temperate.' This is indeed one of the commonest meanings of the word.

Thus, Pythagoras, when his followers called him wise, is said to have replied that he was not wise but was indeed a lover of wisdom – *philosophos*. That was the origin of the word, and it has remained the sense in which the great thinkers of the European tradition have used it. They have not differed about this central point from great thinkers in other traditions, such as the Indian, Chinese or Tibetan. Academics who now want to change their profession into one of pure detached criticism need to find a different name to put on their doors – linguistic engineer, perhaps, or grammatical consultant or conceptual analyst?

I am happy to see that, in the past decade or two, English-speaking philosophers, even at Oxford and Cambridge, seem to be moving out of this ivory tower of pure formalism and back into the marketplace. They are badly needed there, and they will surely find that the move improves their health.

Bibliography of Works by Mary Midgley

BOOKS

1978   *Beast and Man: The Roots of Human Nature.* Cornell University Press, 1978.

1981   *Heart and Mind: The Varieties of Moral Experience.* Harvester Press, 1981.

1983   *Animals and Why They Matter: A Journey around the Species Barrier.* Penguin Books, 1983.

1983   *Women's Choices: Philosophical Problems Facing Feminism.* Weidenfeld and Nicolson, 1983.

1984   *Wickedness: A Philosophical Essay.* Routledge and Kegan Paul, 1984.

1985   *Evolution As a Religion: Strange Hopes and Stranger Fears.* Methuen, 1985.

1989   *Can't We Make Moral Judgements?* The Bristol Press, 1989.

1989   *Wisdom, Information and Wonder: What is Knowledge For?* Routledge, 1989.

1992   *Science as Salvation: A Modern Myth and its Meaning.* Routledge, 1992.

1994   *The Ethical Primate: Humans, Freedom and Morality.* Routledge, 1994.

1996   *Utopias, Dolphins and Computers: Problems of Philosophical Plumbing.* Routledge, 1996.

2001   *Science and Poetry.* Routledge, 2001.

2001   *Gaia: The Next Big Idea.* Demos, 2001.

2003   *The Myths We Live By.* Routledge, 2003.

2005   *The Owl of Minerva: A Memoir*. Routledge, 2005.
2007   *Earthy Realism: The Meaning of Gaia*. Imprint Academic, 2007.
2010   *The Solitary Self: Darwin and the Selfish Gene*. Acumen, 2010.
2014   *Are you an Illusion?* Acumen, 2014.
2018   *What Is Philosophy For?* Bloomsbury, 2018.

ARTICLES

(Published under the name Mary Scrutton)

An Intellectual Novelist, *The Listener* issue 1164 (1951), 993.
The Natural History of Contradictions, *The Listener* issue 1180 (1951), 589.
Paradoxography, *The Listener* issue 1183 (1951), 743.
The Woman's Point of View, *The Listener* issue 1204 (1952), 510.
The Emancipation of Women, *The Twentieth Century* CLII, no. 901 (1952), 217–25.
Bishop Butler: A Reply, *The Twentieth Century* CLII, no. 905 (1952), 56–62.
Bourgeois Cinderellas, *The Twentieth Century* CLV (1954), 351–63.
Newcastle: Comments on a Case-history, *The Twentieth Century* CLIX (1956), 159–68.
Addiction to Fiction, *The Twentieth Century* CLIX (1956), 567–68.
On Being Reformed, *The Listener* issue 1428 (1956), 196.
Ou Sont les Neiges de ma Tante, *The Twentieth Century* (1959), 168–79.
The Month, *The Twentieth Century* CLXV (1959), 505–10.

(Published under Mary Midgley)

Is Moral a Dirty Word? *Philosophy* 47, no. 181 (1972), 206–28.
The Concept of Beastliness: Philosophy, Ethics, and Animal Behaviour, *Philosophy* 48, no. 184 (1973), 111–35.
The Neutrality of the Moral Philosopher, *Supplementary Volume of the Aristotelian Society for 1974* 74 (1974), 211–29.
The Game Game, *Philosophy* 49, no. 189 (1974), 231–53.
On Trying Out Ones New Sword on a Chance Wayfarer, *The Listener*, 15 December 1977.
The Objection to Systematic Humbug, *Philosophy* 53, no. 204 (1978), 147–69.
More about Reason, Commitment and Social Anthropology, *Philosophy* 53, no. 205 (1978), 401–3.
Freedom and Heredity, *The Listener*, 14 September 1978.
Brutality and Sentimentality, *Philosophy* 54, no. 209 (1979), 385–89.
Gene-Juggling, *Philosophy* 54, no. 210 (1979), 439–58.
The All-Female Number, *Philosophy* 54, no. 210 (1979), 552–54.
Beast and Man, *The Listener*, no. 2624 (1979), 212.
The Notion of Instinct, *Cornell Review* (Fall, 1979)

The Absence of a Gap between Facts and Values, (co-authored with Stephen R. L. Clark), *Supplementary Volume of the Aristotelian Society for* 54 (1980), 207–223.

Reply to Mr. Pratt, *Philosophical Books* 21, no. 1 (1980), 6–9.

Rival Fatalisms: The Hollowness of the Sociobiology Debate, in A. Montagu (ed.), *Sociobiology Examined* (New York, 1980), 15–38.

Why Knowledge Matters, in D. Sperlinger (ed.), *Animals in Research: New Perspectives in Animal Experimentation* (Oxford: John Wiley and Sons, 1981), 319–36.

Moral Melodrama: Mary Midgley Considers How Our View of Darwin's Ideas is More Strongly Influenced by Primitive Economic Theories Than We Often Realise, *The Times Higher Education Supplement,* 16 April 1982, 10.

Viewpoint: Selves and Shadows, *Times Literary Supplement,* 30 July 1982, 821.

Towards a New Understanding of Human Nature: The Limits of Individualism, in Donald J. Ortner (ed.), *How Humans Adapt: A Biocultural Odyssey* (Washington DC: Smithsonian Press, 1983), 517–46.

Deterrence, Provocation and the Martian Temperament, in N. Blake and K. Pole (eds.), *Dangers of Deterrence: Philosophers on Nuclear Strategy* (1983), 19–40.

Human Ideals and Human Needs, *Philosophy* 58, no. 223 (1983), 89–94.

Selfish Genes and Social Darwinism, *Philosophy* 58, no. 225 (1983), 365–77.

Duties Concerning Islands, *Encounter* LX, February 1983, 36–43.

De-Dramatizing Darwin, *The Monist* 67, no. 2 (1984), 200–15.

Sociobiology, *Journal of Medical Ethics* 10 (1984), 158–60.

Sex and Personal Identity: The Western Individualistic Tradition, *Encounter* 63 (1984), 50–55.

On Being Terrestrial, in S. C. Brown (ed.), *Objectivity and Cultural Divergence: Royal Institute of Philosophy Lecture Series* 17 (Cambridge: Cambridge University Press, 1984), 79–91.

Reductivism, Fatalism, and Sociobiology, *Journal of Applied Philosophy* 1, no. 1 (1984), 107–14.

Persons and Non-Persons, in P. Singer (ed.), *In Defence of Animals* (Oxford: Blackwell, 1985), 52–62.

Philosophising Out in the World, *Social Research* 52, no. 3 (1985), 447–70.

How Darwin's Theory of Evolution Has Been Distorted by His 'Disciples', *New Statesman,* 2 November 1985, 23–25.

Correspondence, with Anthony Flew, *Journal of Applied Philosophy* 2, no. 2 (1985), 293–94.

Can Specialisation Damage Your Health? *International Journal of Moral and Social Studies* 2, no. 1 (1987), 3–10.

Freedom, Feminism and War, *African Philosophical Enquiry* 1 (1987).

Keeping Species on Ice, in V. MacKenna, W. Travers and J. Wray (eds.), *Beyond the Bars: The Zoo Dilemma* (Wellingborough: Thorsons, 1987), 55–65.

The Flight from Blame, *Philosophy* 62, no. 241 (1987), 271–91.

Embarrassing Relatives: Changing Perceptions of Animals, *The Trumpeter* 4, no. 4 (1987), 17–19.

Evolution as a Religion, J. Durant (ed), *Darwinism and Divinity (1985): (reprinted in shorter form in Zygon* 22, no. 2 (1987), 179–94.

A Report of the Church & Society meeting in Brazil, in *World Council of Churches Church and Society Newsletter* (1988).

Beasts, Brutes, and Monsters, in T. Ingold (ed.), *What Is An Animal?* (London: Unwin Hyman, 1988), 35–46.

Teleological Theories of Morality, in G. H. R. Parkinson (ed.), *An Encyclopedia of Philosophy* (London: Routledge, 1988), 541–67.

The Ethics of Modern Debt in *Credit Management: Journal of the Institute of Credit Management,* August 1988, 33–35.

Logic of Disaster: The Case for Philosophy, *Times Higher Education Supplement* (8 July 1988)

Open Letter, *Philosophy* 63, no. 243 (1988), 1–2.

On Not Being Afraid of Natural Sex Differences, in M. Griffiths and M. Whitford (eds.), *Feminist Perspectives in Philosophy* (London: Macmillan, 1988), 29–41.

The Reality of Human Wickedness, in David M. Rosenthal and F. Shehadi (eds.), *Applied Ethics and Ethical Theory* (University of Utah Press, 1988), 306–321.

Myths of Intellectual Isolation, *Proceedings of the Aristotelian Society,* LXXXIX, Part 1 (1988–89), 19–32.

Are You An Animal?, in G. Langley (ed.), *Animal Experimentation: The Consensus Changes* (New York: Chapman & Hall, 1989), 1–18.

Practical Solutions, *The Hastings Center Report* 19, no. 6 (1989), 44–5.

Why Smartness Is Not Enough, in Mary E. Clark and Sandra A. Wawritko (eds.), *Rethinking the Curriculum: Towards An Integrated, Interdisciplinary College Education* (New York: Greenwood Press, 1990), 39–52.

Homunculus Trouble, or, What Is Applied Philosophy? *Journal of Social Philosophy* 21, no. 1 (1990), 5–15.

The Use and Uselessness of Learning, *European Journal of Education* 25, no. 3 (1990), 283–94.

Fancies about Human Immortality, in *The Month,* 2nd new series 23, no. 11 (November 1990), 458–466.

Rights Talk Will Not Sort Out Child Abuse: Comment on Archard on Parental Rights, *Journal of Applied Philosophy* 8, no. 1 (1991), 103–14.

The Origin of Ethics, in P. Singer (ed.), *A Companion to Ethics* (Oxford: Blackwell, 1991), 3–13.

Is the Biosphere a Luxury? *The Hastings Center Report* 22, no. 3 (1992), 7–12.

Towards a More Humane View of the Beasts? in David E. Cooper and Joy A. Palmer (eds.), *The Environment in Question* (London: Routledge, 1992), 28–36.

The Significance of Species, in S. Luper-Foy and C. Brown (eds.), *The Moral Life* (Harcourt Brace Jovanovich, 1992).

Philosophical Plumbing, in A. Phillips Griffiths (ed.), *The Impulse to Philosophise: Royal Institute of Philosophy Supplement 33* (Cambridge: Cambridge University Press, 1992), 139–51.

Reply to Marc Bekoff, *Environmental Values* 1, no. 3 (1992), 256.

Strange Contest: Science versus Religion, in H. Montefiore (ed.), *The Gospel and Contemporary Culture* (London: Mowbray, 1992), 40–57.

Beasts versus the Biosphere, *Environmental Values* 1, no. 1 (1992), 113–21.

The Idea of Salvation Through Science, *New Blackfriars* 73, no. 860 (1992), 257–65.

The Four-Leggeds, The Two-Leggeds and the Wingeds, *Society and Animals* 1, no. 1 (1993), 9–15.

Must Good Causes Compete? *Cambridge Quarterly of Healthcare Ethics* 2, no. 2 (1993), 133–42.

Visions, Secular and Sacred, *Milltown Studies* 34 (1994), 74–93.

The End of Anthropocentrism? in R. Attfield and A. Belsey (eds.), *Philosophy and the Natural Environment: Royal Institute of Philosophy Supplement 36* (Cambridge: Cambridge University Press, 1994), 103–12.

Darwinism and Ethics, in K. W. M. Fulford, G. Gillett & J. M. Soskice (eds.), *Medicine and Moral Reasoning* (Cambridge: Cambridge University Press, 1994), 6–18.

Bridge-Building at Last, in A. Manning and J. Serpell (eds.), *Animals and Human Society: Changing Perspectives* (London: Routledge, 1994), 188–94.

Practical Utopianism, in C. Thick (ed.), *The Right to Hope, Global Problems, Global Visions* (1995), 39–44.

Zombies and the Turing Test, *Journal of Consciousness Studies* 2, no. 4 (1995), 351–2.

Reductive Megalomania, in J. Cornwell (ed.), *Natures Imagination: The Frontiers of Scientific Vision* (Oxford: Oxford University Press, 1995), 133–47.

Trouble with Families?, Co-Authored with Judith Hughes, in B. Almond (ed.), *Introducing Applied Ethics* (Oxford: Blackwell, 1995), 17–32.

The Challenge of Science; Limited Knowledge, or a New High Priesthood? in A. Race and R. Williamson (eds.), *True to This Earth: Global Challenges and Transforming Faith* (Oxford: Oneworld Publications, 1995).

The Mixed Community, in James P. Sterba (ed.), *Earth Ethics, Environmental Ethics, Animal Rights and Practical Applications* (New Jersey: Prentice Hall, 1995), 80–90.

Visions, Secular and Sacred, *The Hastings Center Report* 25, no. 5 (1995), 20–7.

Darwin's Central Problems, *Science* 268, no. 5214 (1995), 1196–98.

The Ethical Primate. Anthony Freeman in Discussion with Mary Midgley, *Journal of Consciousness Studies* 2, no. 1 (1995), 67–75.

Sustainability and Moral Pluralism, *Ethics and the Environment* 1, no. 1 (1996), 41–54.

One World—But a Big One, *Journal of Consciousness Studies* 3, no. 5/6 (1996), 500–14.

Earth Matters; Thinking about the Environment, in S. Dunant and R. Porter (eds.), *The Age of Anxiety* (London: Virago, 1996), 59–62.

The View from Britain: What Is Dissolving Families? Co-Authored with Judith Hughes, *American Philosophical Association, Newsletter on Feminism and Philosophy* 96, no. 1 (1996).

Can Education be Moral? *Res Publica* 2, no. 1 (1996), 77–85.

Science in the World, *Science Studies* 9, no. 2 (1996), 49–58.

Pi in the Sky, *Third Way* 19, no. 2 (1996), 11–14.

Visions of Embattled Science, in R. Levinson and J. Thomas (eds.), *Science Today: Problem or Crisis?* (London: Routledge, 1997), 35–50.

The Soul's Successors: Philosophy and the Body, in S. Coakley (ed.), *Religion and the Body* (Cambridge: Cambridge University Press, 1997), 53–70.

Are Families Out of Date? co-authored with Judith Hughes, in H. Lindemann (ed.), *Feminism and Families* (London: Routledge, 1997), 55–68.

Skimpole Unmasked, *History of the Human Sciences* 10, no. 4 (1997), 92–6.

The Morality of Creature Comfort, in *Times Higher Education Supplement*, 11 July 1997.

Putting Ourselves Together Again, in J. Cornwall (ed.), *Consciousness and Human Identity* (Oxford: Oxford University Press, 1998).

The Problem of Humbug, in M. Kieran (ed.), *Media Ethics: A Philosophical Approach* (London: Routledge, 1998), 37–48.

Defend Which Freedom? in *Living Marxism* no.115, November 1998.

The Myths We Live By, in W. Williams (ed.), *The Values of Science: The Oxford Amnesty Lectures* 1997 (New York: Westview Press, 1999).

Being Scientific about Our Selves, *Journal of Consciousness Studies* 6, no. 4 (1999), 85–98.

Mind, Matter and Gaia, in *Gaia Circular*, 2, no. 1, (spring 1999), 9.

Should We Let Them Go? in Francine L. Dolins (ed.), *Attitudes to Animals: Views in Animal Welfare* (Cambridge: Cambridge University Press, 1999), 152–63.

Intelligence, Wisdom and Folly, in Stephen C. Barton (ed.), *Where Shall Wisdom be Found? Wisdom in the Bible, the Church, and the Contemporary World* (Edinburgh, 1999).

Determinism, Omniscience, and the Multiplicity of Explanations, *Behavioral and Brain Sciences* 22, no. 5 (1999), 900–1.

Towards An Ethic of Global Responsibility, in T. Dunne and Nicholas J. Wheeler (eds.), *Human Rights in Global Politics* (Cambridge: Cambridge University Press, 1999), 160–74.

Midgley on Murdoch, *The Philosophers Magazine* 7 (1999), 45–46.

Descartes' Prisoners, *New Statesman*, 24 May 1999.

Brutal Kinship, *Nature* 399, no. 6736 (1999), 537.

Monkey Business. The Origin of Species Changed Man's Conception of Himself for Ever. So Why, Asks Mary Midgley, is Darwinism Used to Reinforce the Arid Individualism of Our Age?, *New Statesman*, 6 September 1999. (Review)

Trouble with the Zeitgeist, in *Journal of the Oxford Society*, 51, no.1 (1999): reprinted as Sorting Out the Zeigeist, Changing English: *Studies in Culture and Education* 7, no. 1 (2000), 89–92.

The Origins of Don Giovanni, *Philosophy Now* 25 (1999–2000), 32.

Alchemy Revived, *The Hastings Center Report* 30, no. 2 (2000), 41–3.

Biotechnology and Monstrosity: Why We Should Pay Attention to the Yuk Factor, *The Hastings Center Report* 30, no. 5 (2000), 7–15.

Both Nice and Nasty, *New Statesman*, 13 March 2000.

Earth Song, *New Statesman*, 2 October 2000.

The Need for Wonder, in R. Stannard (ed.), *God for the 21st Century* (Radnot: Templeton Foundation Press, 2000), 186–88.

Individualism and the Concept of Gaia, *Review of International Studies* 26 (2000), 29–44.

Consciousness, Fatalism and Science, in N. H. Gregerson, Willem B. Drees and U. Gorman (eds.), *The Human Person in Science and Theology* (Edinburgh: T&T Clark, 2000), 21–40.

Human Nature, Human Variety, Human Freedom, N. Roughley (ed.), *Being Humans: Anthropological Universality and Particularity in Transdisciplinary Perspectives* (Berlin: Walter De Gruyter, 2000), 47–63.

Why Memes? in H. Rose and S. Rose (eds.), *Alas, Poor Darwin: Arguments Against Evolutionary Psychology* (London: Jonathan Cape Rosenthal, 2000), 67–84.

Wickedness, in *The Philosophers' Magazine* (spring 2001 and autumn 2001)

Wickedness, in Lawrence C. Becker and Charlotte B. Becker (eds), *Encyclopedia of Ethics* (2nd ed, 2001).

Individualism and the Concept of Gaia, in K. Booth, T. Dunne, and M. Cox (eds.), *How Might We Live? Global Ethics in a New Century* (Cambridge: Cambridge University Press, 2001), 29–44.

Homage to Gaia: The Life of an Independent Scientist, *Environmental Values* 10, no. 1 (2001), 141–42. (Review)

The Problem of Living with Wildness, in Virginia A. Sharpe, B. Norton, and S. Donelley (eds.), *Wolves and Human Communities, Biology, Politics and Ethics* (Washington: Island Press 2001), 179–90.

At War Over Animals, in *The Tablet* (17 February 2001), 233–234.

Walk on the Dark Side, *The Philosophers Magazine* 14 (2001), 23–5.

Being Objective: The Idea of Scientists As Impartial Observers Is Hard To Shake, But Is Complete Detachment Justified? *Nature* 410, no. 753 (2001), 753.

The Refractory: Vision, *The Lancet* 357, no. 9266 (2001), 1455.

(with John Ziman), Pluralism in Science: a statement, in *Interdisciplinary science reviews* 26, no. 3, (autumn 2001), 153.

Heaven and Earth, an Awkward History, *Philosophy Now* 34 (2001–2002), 18.

Does the Earth Concern Us? *Gaia Circular* (2001–2002), 4–9.

Choosing the Selectors, in M. Wheeler, J. Ziman and Margaret A. Boden (eds.), *The Evolution of Cultural Entities: Proceedings of the British Academy* 112 (Oxford: Oxford University Press, 2002), 119–33.

Reply to Target Article: Inventing the Subject; the Renewal of Psychological Psychology, *Journal of Anthropological Psychology* 11 (2002), 44–45. The Works of Mary Midgley 239.

Pluralism: The Many Maps Model, *Philosophy Now* 35 (2002), 10–11.

How Real Are You? *Think* 1, no. 2 (2002), 35–46.

Understanding the War on Terrorism, *OpenDemocracy*, 24 October 2002.

The Problem of Natural Evil, in C. Talliaferro and Paul J. Griffiths (eds.), *Philosophy of Religion: An Anthology* (Oxford: Blackwell, 2003), 361–7.

Science and Poetry, *Situation Analysis* 2 (2003), 29–31.

Great Thinkers—James Lovelock, *New Statesman*, 14 July 2003.

Criticising the Cosmos, in Willem B. Drees (ed.), *Is Nature Ever Evil? Religion, Science and Value* (London: Routledge, 2003), 11–26, with replies by Silvia Volker and Hans Radder.

Mind and Body: The End of Apartheid, in D. Lorimer (ed.), *Science, Consciousness and Ultimate Reality* (Exeter: Imprint Academic, 2004), 173–97.

Science and Poetry, in J. Haldane (ed.), *Values, Education, and the Human World* (Exeter: Imprint Academic, 2004), 219–33.

Atoms, Memes, and Individuals, in J. Haldane (ed.), *Values, Education, and the Human World* (Exeter: Imprint Academic, 2004), 234–49.

Do We Ever Really Act? in Dai A. Rees and S. Rose (eds.), *The New Brain Sciences: Perils and Prospects* (Cambridge: Cambridge University Press, 2004), 17–33.

Why Clones? *Network Review* (The Scientific and Medical Network) 84 (2004).

Zombies Can't Concentrate, *Philosophy Now* 44 (2004), 13–14.

Us and Them, *New Statesman*, 13 September 2004.

Souls, Minds, Bodies, and Planets (part 1), *Philosophy Now* 47 (2004), 33–35.

Souls, Minds, Bodies, and Planets (part 2), *Philosophy Now* 48 (2004), 10–12.

Souls, Minds, Bodies, and Planets, in Anthony O'Hear (ed.), *Philosophy, Biology, and Life: Royal Institute of Philosophy Supplement 56* (Cambridge: Cambridge University Press, 2005), 83–104.

Mixed Antitheses, in James E. Huchingson (ed.), *Religion and the Natural Sciences: The Range of Engagement* (Eugene, OR: Wipf and Stock, 2005), 6–39.

The Many Maps Model: How Scientific Pluralism Works, in K. Almqvist and E. Wallrup (eds.), *Consciousness, Genetics and Society: Perspectives from the Engelsberg Seminar 2002* (Stockholm, 2005), 143–148.

Visions and Values, *Resurgence* 228 (2005), 18.

Mapping Science: In Memory of John Ziman, *Interdisciplinary Science Reviews* 30, no. 3 (2005), 195–7.

What, If Anything, Is Moral Relativism? in *Sea of Faith Network*, no.73, (2005), 8–11.

Rethinking Sex and the Selfish Gene: Why We Do It, *Heredity* 93, no. 3 (2006), 271–2.

Dover Beach Revisited, *Think* 4, no. 12 (2006), 69–74. Also in P. Clayton and Z. Simpson (eds.), *The Oxford Handbook of Religion and Science* (Oxford: Oxford University Press, 2006), 962–78.

Dover Beach: Understanding the Pains of Bereavement, *Philosophy* 81, no. 2 (2006), 209–30.

Editorial Introduction, *Journal of Consciousness Studies* 13, no. 5 (2006), 8–16.

Introduction: The Not-So-Simple Earth, in M. Midgley (ed.), *Earthy Realism: The Meaning of Gaia* (Exeter: Imprint Academic, 2007), 3–9.

What Do We Mean by Security? *Philosophy Now* 61 (2007), 12–15.

A Plague on Both Their Houses, *Philosophy Now* 64 (2007), 26–27.

Mary Midgley on Dawkins, *Interlog: Exploring Buddhist-Christian Christian-Buddhist Themes*, 10 August 2007.

Why Farm Animals Matter, in M. Dawkins and R. Bonney (eds.), *The Future of Animal Farming: Renewing the Ancient Contract* (Oxford: Blackwell, 2008), 21–32.

Does Science Make Belief in God Obsolete? Of Course Not, *John Templeton Foundation* (2008), http://capabilities.templeton.org/2008/overview/question.pdf.

Love and Its Disappointment, *Philosophy Now* 75 (2008), 42.

Heresy at the Royal Society, in *Science & Public Affairs* December 2008, 11.

Mary Midgley, in M. Gordon and C. Wilkinson (eds.), *Conversations on Truth* (London: Continuum, 2009), 142–54.

Sorting out pseudo-Darwinisms, in *The Bible in Transmission* (Bible Society, spring 2009).

The Mistake about Darwin, in *Varsity* 2 October 2009.

Purpose, Meaning and Darwinism, *Philosophy Now* 71 (2009), 16–19.

Darwinism, Purpose and Meaning, in Anthony O'Hear (ed.), *Philosophy and Religion*: Royal Institute of Philosophy Supplement 68 (Cambridge: Cambridge University Press, 2010), 193–201.

The Pseudo-Darwinist conspiracy, in *RSA Journal*, 156, no. 5544 (Winter 2010), 36–39.

Against Humanism, in *New Humanist* 125 no.6, November/December 2010, 35–39.

Why the Idea of Purpose Won't Go Away, *Philosophy* 86 (2011), 545–61.

Developmental Doubts, in C. Jaeger et al (eds.), *European Research on Sustainable Development. Volume 1: Transformative Science Approaches for Sustainability* (Springer, 2011), 9–21.

Darwinism, Purpose and Meaning, in *Royal Institute of Philosophy Supplement* 68, (2011), 193–201.

The Mythology of Selfishness, *The Philosophers Magazine* 53 (2011), 35–45. November 2011.

On Being an Anthrozoon: How Unique Are We? *Minding Nature: A Journal of the Center for Humans and Nature* 5, no. 2 (2012), 11–16.

Death and the Human Animal, *Philosophy Now* 89 (2012), 10–13.

Are You An Illusion? Why Today's Neuroscientists Could Do with a Little More Philosophical Training, in *IAI News*, 11 August 2014.

Does Philosophy Get Out of Date? *Philosophy Now* 103 (2014), 18–21.

Scientism and Free-market Jihad, *Open Democracy*, 19 November 2014, https://www.opendemocracy.net/en/scientism-and-freemarket-jihad/

Devout Disbelief: Claims That We Do Not Exist Are based on a Fundamentally Outdated Conception of the Self, in *IAI News*, 7 May 2015.

INDEX

Note: Page numbers followed by 'n' refer to notes.

For Product Safety Concerns and Information please contact our EU
representative GPSR@taylorandfrancis.com Taylor & Francis Verlag GmbH,
Kaufingerstraße 24, 80331 München, Germany

Printed and bound by CPI Group (UK) Ltd, Croydon, CR0 4YY

10/05/2026

02107033-0009